DATE DUE

APR 18 2008			
1-3-06			
GAYLORD			PRINTED IN U.S.A

Also by Jim Bailey

The God-Kings and the Titans, St. Martin's Press, New York, and Hodder & Stoughton, London

Sailing to Paradise

The Discovery of the Americas by 7000 B.C.

Jim Bailey

Simon & Schuster
NEW YORK LONDON TORONTO SYDNEY TOKYO SINGAPORE

SIMON & SCHUSTER
Rockefeller Center
1230 Avenue of the Americas
New York, New York 10020

Designed by Levavi & Levavi
Manufactured in the United States of America

10 9 8 7 6 5 4 3 2 1

Library of Congress Cataloging-in-Publication Data

Bailey, James, 1919–
Sailing to paradise : the discovery of the Americas by 7000 B.C. / Jim Bailey.
p. cm.
Includes bibliographical references and index.
1. America—Discovery and exploration—Pre-Columbian. I. Title.
E103.B34 1994
970.01—dc20 94-43619
CIP

ISBN: 0-684-81297-5

To the unknown Thomas Edisons
of the far distant past

Acknowledgments

Especial thanks to Maurice Temple-Smith for rewriting much of this book from popular dialogue form into a respectable history and to Susan Smuts-Steyn for so assiduously wrestling with my handwriting and for picking up all the odd jobs for which I haven't thanked anybody else. I'm not sure what they all were, but they got done and I can only assume that she did them.

Editorial material:	Professor Barry Fell
Proofreading:	Stella Gavshon
Photography:	Chester Maharaj Stanli Opperman
Provenance of African Art:	M. Saliou-Mbaye M. Cisse Mamadou M. Birane Thiam
General Advice:	Dr. Graham Baker
Typing:	Barbara Bailey Jessica Bailey
Line drawing:	Nicholas Syfret Barbara Bailey Jessica Bailey
Geology:	Dr. Louis Murray Dr. Fred Cornwall Dr. Francis Thackeray
Reference Books:	Professor Reuben Musiker
Contemporary West Africa:	Dr. David Williams

Goethe's *West-Ostlicher Divan* (collection of poems) quoted from Darmstaedter's *Handbuch:*

Wer nicht von dreitausend Jahren
Sich weiss Rechenschaft zu geben,
Bleib im Dunkeln unerfahren,
Mag von Tag zu Tage leben.

"A river flowed out of Eden to water the garden, and there it divided and became four rivers. The name of the first is Pishon; it is the one which flows around the whole land of Havilah, where there is gold; and the gold of that land is good; bdellium and onyx stone are there. The name of the second river is Gihon; it is the one which flows around the whole land of Cush. And the name of the third river is Tigris, which flows east of Assyria. And the fourth river is the Euphrates." [Bdellium is normally translated as a precious white substance and variously, therefore, as pearls. But pearls are scarcely associated with gold, while in Amazonia tin is white, precious and associated with gold.]

GENESIS 2: 10–14

"Some [Amerindians] say that the Garden of Eden was located somewhere on what is today the Bolivian altiplano, and that this was the cradle of the human race; others believe that the word Andes comes from antis and have detected a link with the lost continent of Atlantis; while others again trace descendence from Shem, the son of Noah, after the biblical deluge."

MARGARET JOAN ANSTEE
Gate of the Sun: A Prospect of Bolivia[1]

Wonders are many on earth, and the greatest of these
Is man, who rides the ocean and takes his way
Through the deeps, through the wind-swept valleys
Of perilous seas that surge and sway.

SOPHOCLES, Antigone

"The host of specialists narrow their field and dig down deeper and deeper until they can't see each other from hole to hole. But the treasure their toil brings to light, they place on the ground above. A different kind of specialist should be sitting there . . . and piece all the different facts together."

THOR HEYERDAHL[2]

"And indeed much of ancient history could be rewritten as a struggle for the domination of quarries and ore-deposits or metal-supplies!"

ROBERT J. FORBES,
Studies in Ancient Technology[3]

Map of the Americas. *This map is much as the rather eccentric Posnansky envisaged the importance of Tiahuanaco on the early American continent. In fact the area from Ohio to Chile, as drawn here, at some time consisted of associated states governed by related kings according to the rules of association set down by the founding fathers of the dynasty in the second half of the second millennium* B.C.*: a sea league of western Europeans and western Semites, running the joint between them. Tiahuanaco produced gold, silver, copper, arsenical and tin bronzes. The Andes are almost as high as the Himalayas. To Middle Eastern metal traders, depending on whether they used the Pacific or Atlantic routes, the incredible mountains were the striking thing.*[1]

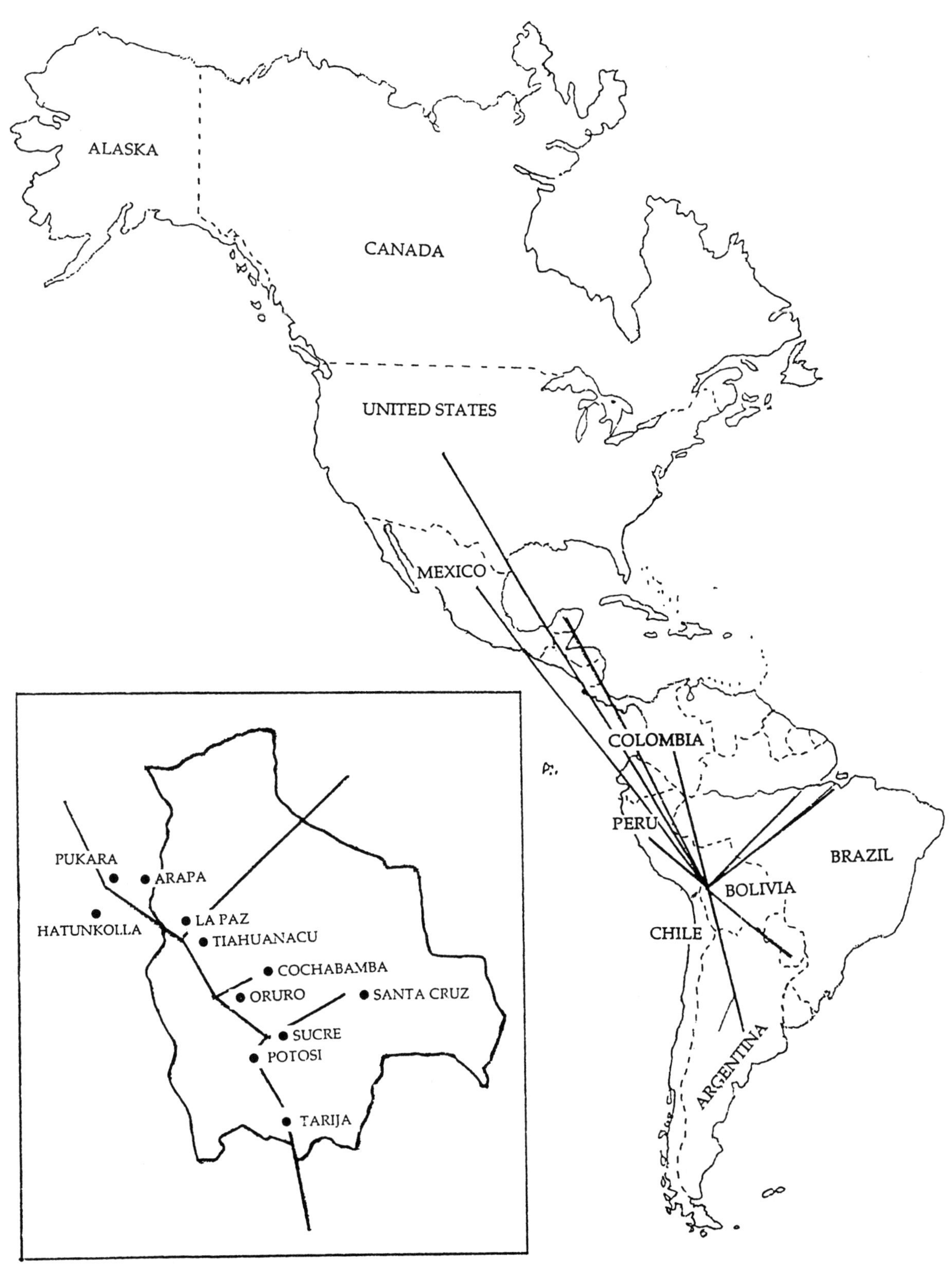

ALASKA
CANADA
UNITED STATES
MEXICO
COLOMBIA
PERU
BRAZIL
BOLIVIA
CHILE
ARGENTINA
PUKARA
ARAPA
HATUNKOLLA
LA PAZ
TIAHUANACU
COCHABAMBA
ORURO
SANTA CRUZ
SUCRE
POTOSI
TARIJA

Contents

Introduction

"Writing need not be the only way of expressing thought."
BARON NORDENSKJÖLD

In history there have been periods when particular materials have been in critical supply. No one will understand the history of the last forty years without appreciating that oil was critical to us. Similarly in the nineteenth century the juxtaposition of coal and iron: this juxtaposition was found in the Ruhr of Germany, in the Midlands of Britain, around the Great Lakes of North America. The history of metallurgy dictates which kind of mineral deposit is exploitable at what date. But since, in the Bronze Age, the skill of the smiths only permitted them to use stream tin and not vein cassiterite, the relatively few sources of alluvial tin juxtaposed to copper, in the enormous quantities that were required—not just for armies but for adornment, for agriculture and for carpentry tools—made the juxtaposition of alluvial tin and copper all important. For the arms race in the Middle East was as formidable then as now: with the same hideous treatment of the conquered. *Vae victis!* So you had to be prepared to pay through the nose for this alloy. The Bronze Age had started with a bronze compound of arsenic and copper, but arsenical bronze proved too dangerous to handle, hence the god of the smiths in Greek mythology was always lame. So they changed to a tin-bronze, ten percent of tin gave you the standard high-quality bronze. But bronze only began to come into general use around 3500 B.C.—a bronze figure in the second city of Troy has been found and another in Non Nok Tha in Thailand from this period. Thus, prior to this, for ordinary affairs, copper was used. As they could not smelt copper in its normal deposits of oxide or sulfide until around 4000 B.C., they were compelled to use pure or native copper and hammer it into shape with stone mauls. The only place in the world where pure copper exists in substantial quantities is in North America, on Isle Royale and the Upper Peninsula of Michigan, although some of the great North American copper boulders had been rolled by the glaciers of the Ice Age further south. And around these copper deposits are literally hundreds of thousands of stone hammers. Small amounts of pure or native copper are also found in Bolivia, at Corocoro, but insufficient to be important.

The radio carbon dates given for the start of this copper extraction go back to 5000 B.C., but these had not been recalibrated by dendrochronology, which will take us back toward the beginnings of the sixth millennium B.C.[1] Copper had begun to be used in the Old World in very small quantities by 7000 B.C. or even earlier. We must allow that run-of-the-mill copper deposits will have had their quota of pure copper associated with them. Here a caution must come in. Most subsequent scholars have argued that the charcoal that had been carbon-dated to 5000 B.C. arose not from fire setting but from forest fires and that the date for the commencement of copper extraction from Lake Superior should come down to 3500 B.C. Since there would seem to be no way by the study of charcoal to distinguish between these two provenances I have kept to the first dates given because they are consistent with all the other related facts.

Subsequently gold began to be handled and it may be that in some quarters copper came eventually to be looked upon as the poor man's gold. This was the period that came ultimately to be admired as "the Golden Age." To sun worshippers, gold was especially prized. The quality of the art of this period was impressive, both in Mesopotamia and Egypt. We must be sensitive to the belief that there had once been, in very fact, an age of excellence, the Age of Gold: not just nostalgia for the past but simple fact. This explains why most of the best brains, over thousands of years, saw human history as a story, not of Progress but of Decay, almost up to the hideous savagery of our own century.

A final point with which this book must start. Metals do not go walkabout. They are in the same positions today as eight thousand years ago. So the absence of metals in the vicinity of the Fertile Crescent and the presence of metals in their specific type of deposit in the various parts of the world where they are today is our fundamental discipline, allowance of course being made for ancient mine workings. So what we will be doing is to return to an understanding of the maritime dimension to early history, the evidence for which becomes, I would suggest, as the book goes on, overwhelming and, viewed as a whole, irrefutable.

Gold became enormously important, not just for adornment but as a metal especially sacred to sun worship, which would seem to begin during the fifth millennium B.C. At periods in the ancient world, silver was more costly than gold. And lapis lazuli came to Mesopotamia and Egypt from Afghanistan and from Quetta, for it was greatly prized. There was also the amber trade from the Baltic to the Mediterranean. And the spice and incense trade.

It is perhaps the absurd university belief in inevitable human progress as you go forward in time, and thus regress as you go backward in time—so what the Classical Greeks could not do their predecessors in history must therefore be incapable of—that has led to the total distortion of our history books. And thus of our own intellects. We must turn to looking at history as one interconnected story, certainly from the start of farming and metallurgy up to the present day. The Classical Greeks themselves admitted that there had been more long-distance sailing prior to their own times.

The deep ocean is today unsusceptible to archaeology: to learn of its past we must listen to its shores. Hence the balance of this book and the consideration given to both sides of the Atlantic and to both sides of the Pacific, although marine archaeology is just beginning.

As I worked on this subject I became increasingly impressed by the skills of the early prospectors; they seem to have little problem in discovering metals anywhere in the world, their limitations were those of the smith and the development of his technology. And then it dawned on me that the beds of streams, after millions of years of soil erosion with heavy metals lodging on the streambed while particles of soil would be washed away, it dawned on me how those first streambeds, bright with gold and silver, must have scintillated to those first prospectors. Add to this the plant indicators, the presence of those very few plants that can survive a heavy burden of metals in the soil.[2] How indicative to early prospectors!

Little wonder that a sage said that perhaps the greatest of men and the greatest of events have not appeared in our history books.

In this book I dwell on the African scene at length: partly because of my personal knowledge of it: chiefly because Africa was as much a part of the Atlantic trade as America. My Ghana friends have told me that almost all the states in Ghana possess prehistoric gold mines; I was offered a place in the Nok polo team, where the ancient tin mines are located in Kano Province, Nigeria; I have been in Kinshasa, where copper and gold greatly fund the country; I have spent time on the copper belt of Zambia, cowboy country, whose towns grew out of the copper trade. My good friend the late Professor Raymond Dart carbon-dated the extraction of kohl—used for eyeshadow in ancient Egypt—from a Zambian antimony mine dating back to 4000 B.C. My friend Cyril Hromnek, writing on Zimbabwe, says that Zimbabwe possesses 1,200 prehistoric gold mines and 150 prehistoric copper mines. Certainly, when the English turned up a century ago, in my father's day, the prospectors came to be called "blanket prospectors" because they did not scour the country with geologist's hammers but rather offered a blanket to any local who would show them a prehistoric mine shaft; then they went down it to find out at the bottom what their predecessors had been mining. You may drive hundreds and hundreds of miles across the bare African savannah and suddenly you encounter a huge city with skyscrapers, Johannesburg, existing only because of gold; you may drive more hundreds of miles further and you encounter Kimberley with its smaller skyscrapers, existing only because of diamonds. I asked a head of Anglo-American—about the largest mining group in the world—if any

The Succession of Ruling Groups Distinguished by Their Religions as Recorded, Not Consistently, in Greek Tradition.

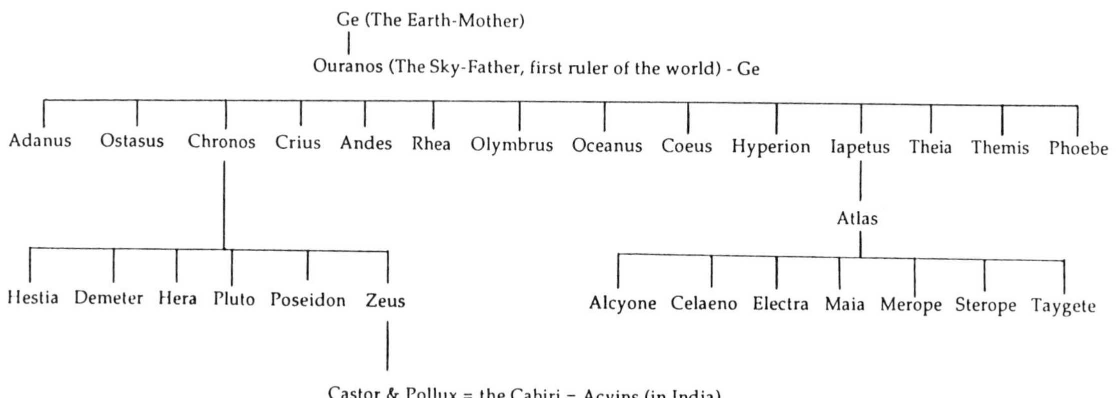

PLATE 1

When tradition says that Poseidon did this or Chronos that, it is not superstitious nonsense but describes what the people who worshipped those gods were doing. When a god begat another god it is a description of colony and mother country. The god-kings were not just objects of worship but also the commercial leaders of their societies. The distinction between sons and daughters is one of patriarchal and matriarchal society. Castor and Pollux, the Dioscuri, the twins, were called the Anakes—anaku *being the Akkadian for bronze: their festival was the Anakeia and their temple the Anakeion, meaning bronze worldwide. Castor is the Greek* cassiteros *for tin, Sanskrit* kastira; *and Polydeuces, perhaps "much coveted," a synonym for copper. They are the same as the Cabiri,* kabar *being Sumerian for bronze and Kochab being the mariners' star in the constellation of Draco. The Bacabs, the culture heroes of the Maya of Guatemala, being a palindrome of* kab. *Greek tradition said that the Dioscuri spent half the year in the underworld and half in Greece on Mount Olympus. The underworld in this context I hold to be America. They were engaged in the bronze trade. In India the twins were called Acvins and, like the Dioscuri, also came ultimately to be associated with cavalry. Chronos was called the brother of Atlas by Philo of Byblos and for millennia the Middle Eastern people and the Atlas people of Western Europe worked the sea routes together. Time was sacred to these Middle Easterners, whose outlook perhaps St. Augustine described in the words:* "Non in tempore sed cum tempore finxit Deus mundum." *Not in time but with time God created the world. This is perhaps why the stone circles of Britain were both the sophisticated calendar clocks and the sacred places that they were: erected by both the Middle Eastern traders and their European associates. Demeter gave birth to Persephone, who, tradition said, was raped by Pluto. This occurred on an island near the west coast of Spain. This resulted in her also spending part of the year in the lower world, part of the year in Greece with Demeter. Ceres and Demeter were the same person. The Sumerian goddess Ereskigal was a goddess of the lower world. Kigal just means Great Mother. May not the Sumerian Eresh and the Italian Ceres, for half of each year associated with the underworld, be two variants of the same name? Hephaestus, god of the smiths, was also named as father of the Cabiri,*[1] *understandably enough. When Christ's disciples are said to have forecast the end of the world in their lifetime they would have meant the end of an era; to the West an era, to the Hindus a yuga, to the Mexicans a sun: and the disciples were totally correct. Diodorus Siculus said that there were eleven Titans based in the neighborhood of Knossos, Crete.*[2]

of his mines had been mined prehistorically, and he replied: "Almost all of them." And the product of these mines today is almost entirely for export. So when I noticed the location of Tiahuanaco, a city twelve thousand feet up in the Andes—while writing this book near Johannesburg—I asked myself whether its extraordinary position is not due to the wonderful silver mines of Potosí, and the gold and bronze trade of the Amazon below it, the metals as in Africa also for export. I append a map of the southern and central African prehistoric mines for gold, silver, tin and copper as recorded by a leading geologist of southern Africa, Percy Wagner. Though he only discovered a relatively small number of the prehistoric mines there, his map reveals at a glance something of the extent of these earlier labors (Plate 3). Then, just as in Africa today, almost all those metals were exported, because we can see that the locals, the San or Khoikhoi or Bantu, had little use for them. And then we discover that the Ngwenya iron mine in Swaziland was mined for red body paint, ocher, hematite, at least forty thousand years ago, the miners using Mesolithic stone tools and leaving them in the shaft: the discovery made by my friends Professor Raymond Dart, Peter Beaumont and the late Adrian Boshier.

This led me to ask whether America had enjoyed, at the time of Christopher Columbus—as the universities teach—an Immaculate Conception?

PLATE 2
The religious trademarks of the early multinationals left engraved on the rocks or as decoration on pottery before sailors were literate. It must be understood that the meaning I have given to each symbol is an abbreviation: each symbol represents a complex, and perhaps profound, philosophy about which we presently know too little. Except for Antarctica, these trademarks are found around the world, each symbolizing a specific Weltanschauung. *At the same time they are company logos belonging to the early multinationals.*

Egyptian hieroglyph for time and the sun.

Simple cross symbol for the stars and the sky god Ouranos in Greece, Ante in Egypt.

Sun symbol, marks the god-king.

The wheel, a sun symbol: with four or eight spokes: to the Dakota Indians of North America the symbol of a unified universe.

Maltese cross composed of two double axes symbolized rule over the four quarters of the earth: particularly sacred with the Incas and Aztecs; in use in Iran from the fourth millennium.

The saltire, earth worshippers' symbol, originally crossed arrows. Formerly Anat's cross, Christianized as St. Andrew's cross.

The spiral, the serpent: the earth worshippers' symbol for infinity, for time being cyclic, for metempsychosis.

Double bronze axe of Sumer and Crete: symbol of power, and also of regeneration.

Swastika, a symbol of the god incarnate on earth who by his suffering is enabled to control the wheeling universe, the above and below, the left and the right.

Egyptian hieroglyph for the sea: trademark for the sea god generally. These meanders appear as early as 5000 B.C.

Concentric arcs, symbol for the sun rising on the first day of Creation, in the sun worshippers' religion.

Ox-eyed Hera, the Mother Goddess, mother of all living things.

Cave painters used iron and manganese oxide for paints and obtained black paint from calcined bones.[3]

1. Economics Underlies History

"The mythology of the Greeks, which their oldest writers do not pretend to have invented, was no more than a light air, which had passed from a more ancient people into the flutes of the Greeks, which they modulated to such descants as best suited their fancies."

FRANCIS BACON, *The New Atlantis*

In the Bronze Age bronze was everything. It was for use, it was for war and it was for glory. If you lost a war your sons and daughters were appropriated by the victors and the surviving males enslaved. For almost two thousand years the richest and most powerful societies on earth based their most important activities on the possession and use of bronze.

When Homer describes the palace of "great-hearted Alcinous" he speaks of whole walls sheathed in bronze, stretching "from the threshold to the innermost chamber." The threshold itself is bronze, and Homer mentions it as a sign of grandeur, just as he notes that the doors are golden and their posts are silver. Many people will dismiss all this as a poet's fantasy, but his hearers must have found it credible.[1] At the least it tells us how the ostentatious use of bronze was accepted as one of the great symbols of wealth and power, and we know from archaeological finds that there really were palaces with doors and walls covered with sheets of bronze: not to mention vast quantities of gold and silver; for a time silver fetched more than gold. Homer describes the Greek army in its attack on Troy: "Even as a consuming fire maketh a boundless forest to blaze on the peak of a mountain, and from afar is the glare thereof to be seen, even so from their innumerable bronze, as they marched forth, went the dazzling gleam up through the sky unto the heavens."[2]

In Solomon's temple at Jerusalem the Bible records that there were two brazen pillars each twenty-three cubits high (about forty feet) and a huge bronze bowl that weighed two hundred tons without its brazen stand.[3] Again, we may take this as a pious exaggeration, but even if we scale the report down considerably it still represents an extraordinarily lavish use of metal for the glorification of a very small country. Josephus says that the Hyksos had a garrison of 240,000 armed men at Avaris and the Egyptians attacked them with an army twice the size.[4] The fact that every man thought that he had to have a dagger prompted the development of metallurgy.

What is beyond dispute—for everywhere their relics make it clear—is how widely the use of this brilliantly versatile alloy had entered into the life of the peoples who could obtain it. Behind the scenes in Alcinous' palace, the cooks were using bronze implements, for if anyone was rich enough to afford any sort of metal knife or ladle at all it would have been made of gold, silver or bronze. The soldiers guarding the palace wore bronze armor and carried bronze weapons. The carpenters who first built and furnished it used bronze tools; a kit of such tools has been unearthed in Crete, strikingly similar to those used by carpenters today, except that they are all made of bronze. From about 3500 B.C., when bronze was first invented, until the coming of iron at the end of the second millennium, bronze was the essential material for every society around the eastern end of the Mediterranean, and especially for the rulers and their armies. Of course, almost nothing is said of the terrible conditions of the slave miners,[5] later described as the great blot on Hellenism, but perhaps at its very foulest when the Christians had finally taken over in America: convict labor, seemingly, throughout much of the period.

To make bronze you need copper and tin, and over the centuries great quantities of these metals were consumed. Much of the bronze used would have been recycled, but even so the demand for new metal would have been immense. Where did it all come from? Tin melts at 232 degrees C and copper at 1084 degrees C.

Copper deposits, right around the world, take the following form: on the top of the deposit is pure or native copper, below that oxidized copper such as malachite, below that an enriched sulfide zone containing impurities like arsenic, below that sulfides alone.

The first copper objects that we know of, such as beads, pins and awls, turn up from around the ninth to the seventh millennium B.C., as at Ali Kosh in western Iran and Cayönü near Ergani in Anatolia. We find copper objects in Egypt from 5000–4000 B.C., and small pieces of azurite in use in Crete by 6000 B.C. Over that period copper was in use from the Adriatic to Japan.

The development of copper smelting begins as early as the sixth millennium in Anatolia and Iran, and had reached Britain and China by the second millennium B.C. Small pieces of vitrified copper have been found at Catal Huyuk in Anatolia from 7000–6000 B.C. In the Balkans the first copper tools have been found from around 4700 B.C. At Anau in Turkmenistan the Copper Age starts from around 5500 B.C.

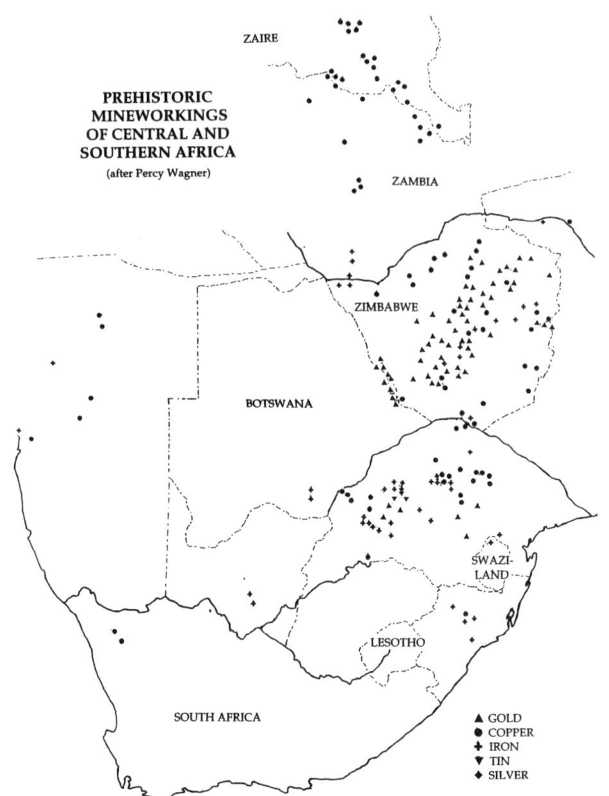

PLATE 3
This map gives a small sample only of the prehistoric mine workings of central and southern Africa. In Zimbabwe alone there are 1,200 prehistoric gold mines and 150 prehistoric copper mines. The bulk of the metal will have been exported then, as now. There is urgent need today for a study, worldwide, of prehistoric mine workings, both as to date and to quantity, to better understand the economies of the ancient world: without which no sensible history of the ancient world can begin to be written. The importance of the metal trade is underscored by the way history was divided in those days by the prevailing metals: the Age of Gold, the Age of Silver, the Age of Bronze, the Age of Iron. When one sees the extent of prehistoric mine workings across the length and breadth of sub-Saharan Africa one sees the foolishness of saying that a Speke or a Burton, a Stanley or a Livingstone discovered the sources of the Nile. A stranger in a bar in Nairobi came up to me and explained that the amount of time white men spent in the last century searching for the sources of the Nile was due to the fact that the Baganda women are the most beautiful in East Africa. The highest mountain peak in East Africa is called Kilimanjaro; in the Andes it is called Klimani. Are we confident that this similarity of names is chance? Pliny the Elder (A.D. 23–79) states that the South Pole is under ice like the North Pole. This presupposes a very real geographical knowledge.[1]

The oldest gold artifacts appear from the end of the fifth millennium B.C., but it may be supposed that gold was used earlier but was at first too precious to be left around in graves.

Arsenical copper then came to be used, derived either from the natural conjunction of the two minerals or, more likely in many cases, purposefully combined. High arsenic alloys could be made by co-smelting copper oxide with an arsenical sulfide such as orpiment.

However, arsenical bronze was too dangerous for the smiths to handle, so we find tin-bronze coming into use; the earliest we know of is from 3500–3200 B.C. at Ur, the Ubaid culture, using axe heads with around 10 percent of tin, which was about the optimum alloy. Conservative Egypt seems to start using bronze by 2600 B.C. A tin bracelet was found in Lesbos of c. 3000 B.C. Bronze started to be smelted in Britain and Spain around 1600 B.C.

Now, the only tin that could then be used was alluvial tin and this exists in substantial quantities in few places in the world: Malaya, China, Bolivia, Cornwall, Saxony-Bohemia and Nigeria. Bronze, therefore, necessitated long-distance trading. At present the sources of ancient Egyptian and Cypriot tin are supposedly unknown.[6]

Bronze and brass alloys in pre-Shang China may go back to 3000 B.C., but Chinese history and the high Bronze Age in China commence about

1500 B.C.[7] and there is little evidence for the use of copper before this.

There are in fact only two places in the world where native copper can be found in abundant quantities: the smaller one is around Corocoro, a Bolivian town near the headwaters of the Amazon, but this is of little consequence; the other, which produces large quantities, is at Lake Superior, on the border of Canada and the United States, specifically on the Upper Peninsula of Michigan and, mined still earlier, on the lake island of Isle Royale. Various mining companies still mine there today. (Plate 8 shows one of the huge pure copper boulders still extant from the region of Lake Superior.)

Mining and the fashioning of copper tools and weapons were carried on there from the sixth millennium B.C. to 1000 B.C. The workings have been carbon-dated and the results show that the earliest of them, recalibrated by dendrochronology, go back to early in the sixth millennium. Literally hundreds of thousands of stone tools left behind by those first miners have been found, some of them associated with the bones of the extinct mastodon. This dating is very significant, for it means that the use of copper began at about the same time in America as around the Black Sea and in the Middle East. If this is just coincidence then it is long odds. If the conventional view is right and America, apart from Siberia, was isolated from the Old World before Columbus, it is strange that both communities should have struck on the use of this particular material within a few hundred years of each other. As this book goes on we shall find ourselves faced with other equally interesting coincidences! The stone mauls used for copper extraction around Lake Superior were of a type used for early mining everywhere.[8]

The use of the earthenware kiln for smelting, sometime in the fifth millennium, made it possible to reach the temperatures needed to smelt copper from ore. This opened up many new sources of copper in the Old World. From then on the sheer quantitity of ore available was not a problem. There were, for example, extensive copper mines in Sinai, to which the Egyptians of the First Dynasty (around 3000 B.C.) mounted expeditions on a considerable scale. Usually about two hundred people would be involved, but there are Egyptian records of as many as eight thousand, with five hundred pack animals.

Despite this, the North American trade in copper with other parts of the world continued. The mines on Isle Royale did not go out of use until 1000 B.C. Just as we cannot account for the supply of native copper (and, later, alluvial tin associated with copper) in the Old World, so we cannot find evidence in the New World that anything like enough metal was used there at this time to absorb the output of the mines. The North American metal was then exported, just as almost all African metals are exported to this day, although a lot of copper came to be used across America later on.

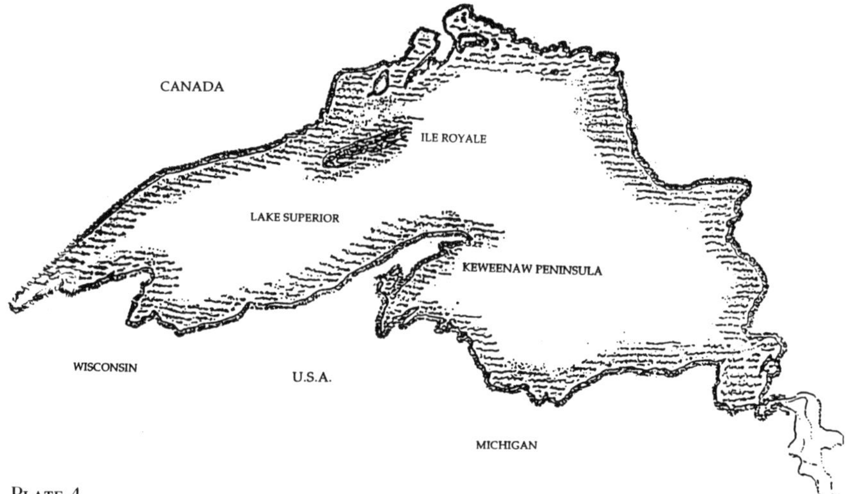

PLATE 4

A map of Lake Superior showing Isle Royale and the Keweenaw Peninsula where the earliest pure copper was extracted in economic quantities from what seems to be around 6000 B.C. *Much of it was in the form of boulders of pure copper. To the Greeks these were the golden apples of the Hesperides, the island in the remote west beyond the Atlantic: to the Welsh these would be the apples of Avalon. Compare the Welsh name Avalon for the Island in the middle of the Ocean to the Hebrews the name Havilah of Genesis, for the land around which the Pishon flows. Notice that the Keweenaw Peninsula and Siskiwit Bay both carry the root* akawa *in their names, a root associated with the matriarchal society. In the Quechua language of Peru and the Aymará language of Bolivia* anta *means copper-colored or copper; perhaps that is how the Andes, known as copper mountains to the Indians, were so called.*[2] *So the island toward the mouth of the St. Lawrence called Anticosti may carry an old word for copper in its name, as indeed may Antilles and Ontario. The origin of the male sky god is placed along the shores of the Atlantic Ocean.*[3] *Homer says: "Ocean from whence the gods are sprung."*[4] *The first sky gods were collectively called by the Greeks Ouranos; they were ordinary kings but because of their benefactions a superstitious people turned them into gods and identified them with the stars.*[5] *Diodorus later says, while discussing the tin trade, that there is an island in the open sea directly opposite Scythia—a name for northern Europe—that is called Nisos Basileia, i.e., the royal island; in French it translates as* ile royale. *The scholiast suggests that this is Heligoland but Hel is the name not of kings but of the Scandinavian earth mother and it seems impossible that one of the turning points in human history should be marked by such a misnomer. Surely when the French called the epoch-making scene of the start of metallurgy Isle Royale, the Bretons at least among them knew what they were doing. Diodorus associates amber with the island but there is amber in North America as well as in the Baltic. Early references hint at, not just the start of the male sky gods but also that their early development happened, not in the Old World but in the New World. America and its metal resources were far more significant to world history than is presently understood.* Mutterrecht, *traces of the matriarchal system, still survives with the Iroquois of North America, as the* akawa *name might lead one to suppose.*[6] *The Francthi cave in southern Greece reveals that by 7500–7000* B.C. *the inhabitants were already involved in deepwater sailing.*[7] *Catal Huyuk, on the Mediterranean coast of Anatolia, had started by 7000* B.C., *making its money from the obsidian trade, the arms trade, perhaps, of that day. Caves were sacred places in the old Greek world: to wit, the Cave of the Nymphs in the* Odyssey *and the Corcyrian Cave on Mount Parnassus. The very name seems to trace back, through the Latin* cavus, *to ak-ava, the mother goddess, whose dwelling place was within the earth. I judge that our word* copper *ultimately derives from the Great Goddess,* akawa, *and that Ouranos, in Egypt Anu, whose spouse was the Great Goddess Antu, provided the later name for copper in Aymará and Quechua. Language thus suggests that the first American copper came from North America, and subsequently from South America. The name Quebec may derive from a palindrome of* akawa. *In later years much copper was smelted in North America.*

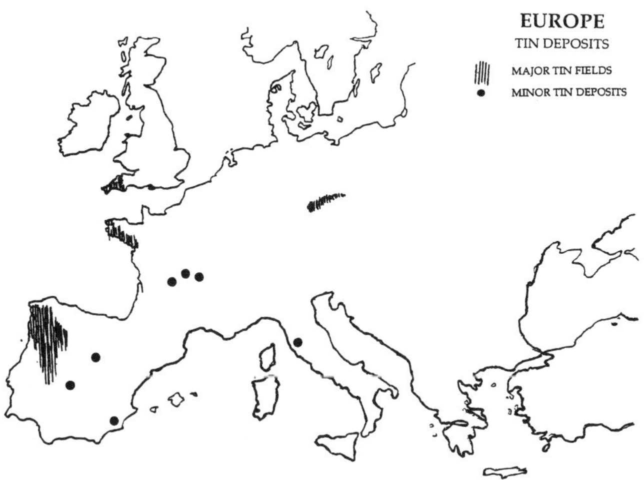

PLATE 5

The Mediterranean was called by the Hebrews of the Bronze Age the Sea of the Philistines, which, in the second half of the second millennium B.C., *indeed it was.*[8] *The Philistines were known as the Anakim, or the Bronze Traders. Their power was destroyed at the beginning of the twelfth century* B.C. *The reputation of the Philistines has come down to us through the Jews, which is like asking Shamir about the Palestinians. Dolmens are found all the way from the shores of the Baltic to Tunis. The Bronze Age tribes of North Africa were reported to be red-haired and blue-eyed; red-haired Typhonians and apt for human sacrifice as such. In the great Roman classic, the* Aeneid, *it has not I think been noticed that Aeneas in Latin means bronze and that the name of his father, Anchises, bears a similar name to that of the Akkadian name for bronze,* anaku, *and that the skills of metallurgy in the Bronze Age would seem to have passed from the Middle East to the Mediterranean and not vice versa. In similar vein Pausanias gives the pedigree of red-haired Rhadamanthus, Cretan king and judge in the underworld: his father was Hephaestus, the lame and famous bronzesmith, and his grandfather was Talus, the bronze man, in tradition, of Crete.*[9] *Cretan ossuaries were placed next to the seashore in the belief that the next world was transmarine:*[10] *you took a skiff to it. To the early matriarchal world the night was scared. The English word fortnight goes back to the period when time was measured by nights not by days. There were clock stars whose rising near the north told you the time of night. When the Greeks attacked Troy it was with 1186 ships, suggesting an army of one hundred thousand men*[11] *and indicating the amount of bronze that would be deployed by the states of that period.*

The Sumerians and Semites came into Mesopotamia around 3500 B.C. The Sumerians, around 3000 B.C., used bronze. In principle, the idea is simple. By alloying copper with as little as 5 percent tin its hardness and strength can be greatly improved. To obtain the best quality bronze, however, with the toughness and cutting edge of a good weapon, 10 percent tin is needed. Hence, when the use of bronze became general, large amounts of alluvial tin were needed and its supply became the limiting factor. With improved technology the copper mines of much of the world could now be worked, and where was the alluvial tin to come from to turn all this copper into bronze? Because of the destruction of the trees around the Mediterranean it became advantageous to have timber for charcoal, copper and tin belts close to each other, and a river to provide access and transport.

The old legends that the Age of Bronze became more aggressive and bellicose than the ages that preceded it are true. The competition for supplies of tin must have been intense, human populations had massively increased, and as this competition began to take the form of resource wars it must have led to dangerous instability. The victors in these wars could enforce their access to the materials that made further victories more likely, for a soldier armed and armored with bronze was at a huge advantage. So the powerful became more powerful still. It was an age of great empires and the struggle intensified as the populations of the Middle Eastern countries grew. As R. J. Forbes remarks, "Much of ancient history could be rewritten as a struggle for the domination of quarries and ore-deposits or metal-supplies!"[9] This is the center of our argument in this book.

Tin is one of the rarest metals used in antiquity. Its average crustal concentration is only 2 parts per million (ppm), compared with 13 for lead, 55 for copper and 50,000 for iron: with the noble metals, silver strands at 0.07 ppm and gold at 0.004 ppm.

In the search for tin there was a further difficulty. Just as the first workers

PLATE 6

THE BOUSTROPHEDON STYLE OF WRITING. *This is a Cretan inscription of 500 B.C., still being written boustrophedon. Boustrophedon writing paid equal honor to the right and left hands. Very many Bronze Age scripts were written boustrophedon—as the ox pulls the plow—so we have to look out for palindromes and for words written from right to left, as well as left to right, since both directions were correct and were used alternately. The left side was sacred to women, the right side to men: left-handed people would prefer writing from right to left, right-handed people the reverse. The first figures that we have of the Great Goddess date from around 30,000 B.C.*[12] *The Indo-European patriarchal society savagely destroyed the matriarchal civilization of Old Europe; but it was often a gradual process across the world. For many years the societies ran parallel.*

Julian the Apostate, at the very end of the matriarchs' period, describes them thus: "Who is the Mother of the Gods? She is the source of the intellectual and creative gods, who in their turn guide the visible gods: she is both the mother and the spouse of the mighty Zeus; she came into being next to and together with the great creator; she is in control of every form of life, and the cause of all generation; she easily brings to perfection all things that are made; without pain she brings to birth, and with the father's aid creates all things that are."[13] *However, the men said: "Father Anu created kingship and kingship civilised mankind."*

Female figurines have been found from France to Russia dating from around 30,000 to 15,000 B.C. This is the "Venus of Willendorf." These figurines may be the source of the worship of the Great Mother. The Paleolithic graves of young children show an early care for the dead. The first religion was possibly ancestor worship, but since the only ancestors known were mothers, this movement may have crystalized into the worship of the Great Mother. Mother Goddess figures appear in India by 16,000 B.C. India has been claimed to be the richest area for prehistoric art.[14]

in copper had to find it in native form, so the first makers of bronze had to find tin in the form of alluvial deposits close to copper.

Singer et al.'s *History of Technology*[10] suggests that it was not until Roman times that vein cassiterite could be used, and if that was so, then the whole Bronze Age depended on finding supplies of alluvial tin.

It is easy to overlook the details of technology when writing history. Great kings like Sargon, emperor of Sumer and Akkad, left monuments and inscriptions to record their deeds. Of the man or group of men who first alloyed copper with tin not a single record of memory remains. Yet it was those smiths who made Bronze Age history possible. You could say with some truth that they invented Sargon and all the other warrior kings whose power helplessly depended on that one stroke of innovative metallurgy.

What little knowledge we have of the smiths is a good illustration of the way in which records and traditions tend to ignore the ordinary facts of everyday life. Who bothers to inscribe a memorial to the commonplace, to a practice, however vital, that has been taken for granted for generations? Only archaeology provides the evidence, and sometimes societies maintain legends in which ordinary events appear in strangely distorted forms. It is with the interplay of these two types of evidence that this book is largely concerned, and the smiths are a good example. Their work is to be seen wherever a Bronze Age site is excavated, and now, with modern methods of dating and chemical analysis, we can begin to learn much more about their craft, in the process discarding a heap of unquestioned assumptions.

As to legends, there are two that may throw some light on the metalworkers of this time. One is the story of Vulcan, the Titan who spent his life laboring at the subterranean forge. He was a cripple, and this can be attributed to his handling of arsenical bronze. For many smiths may have been more or less disabled because the ores they used contained arsenic and so were physically damaging to handle. The word "subterranean" is a translation of the Greek *hyperchthonia*, meaning originally the opposite side of the planet or where the sun was at midnight, in that specific sense the underworld.

The other myth is that of the Cyclops, the race of giants having a single eye in the middle of the forehead, one of whom imprisoned Odysseus and his men in his cave. It was the Cyclops who forged Zeus's lightning. Robert Graves suggested that their single eye was in fact a symbol, a sun circle, stamped on the foreheads of the bronzesmiths to make them permanently recognizable in case they should try to leave the country, taking their all-important trade secrets with them.[11] If Graves's guess is right, it is a further indication that Bronze Age rulers were in no doubt as to where the basis of their power lay. In Greek, Agamemnon was called *anax andron*, or king of men: the word *anak* literally means bronze in Akkadian: compare German *König*. He who possessed bronze ruled. Let us note that it is the very hiding of these trade secrets that has necessitated the writing of this book. Genghis Khan means Genghis the Conqueror.

It was therefore a critical moment when, as early as the middle of the third millennium, sources of tin for the Middle East began to dry up. Sometime around 2300 B.C., in the era of Sargon the Great, unalloyed copper weapons came into use again in Mesopotamia, where first-class bronze weapons had been the rule.[12] No military leader would have accepted that disadvantage if tin had been available. Sargon, having defeated the Sumerians on land, was probably confronted by the opposition of their fleets and worldwide trade associates.

Sargon himself mounted overseas expeditions to secure supplies of tin. Contemporary inscriptions record that he crossed the sea in the west, and in a general review of his empire he is credited with control of two "lands beyond the Upper Sea" (the Mediterranean). The *Cambridge Ancient History* suggests that when the records spoke of the tin land they actually meant lead and were referred to Anatolia, but this is most implausible. Anatolia is not beyond the sea from Mesopotamia: the two regions lie close to each other within the same landmass. Sargon did not make a short coastal trip along the eastern end of the Upper Sea. The records claim that he voyaged to the west beyond the Mediterranean, and they speak the truth.

It is now generally recognized that supplies of tin had to be brought in from somewhere to the west. Despite extensive searches, no adequate sources have been discovered in the lands where bronze was most used. Although bronze was possibly invented in Sumer, the smiths there would, from the very beginning, have had to find their materials elsewhere, for the alluvial soils of Mesopotamia bear no metals. And let us remember that it was notorious at the time that the biggest ships were built at Tartessus, on the Atlantic, not the Mediterranean coast of Spain. Material to my argument is the fact that specialists like James Muhly, who writes an entire book searching for sources of bronze for the Bronze Age, concludes that he doesn't know where their tin came from, but it was probably from the east.[13]

The Classical Greeks thought that the Cassiterides—the tin islands—were Cornwall and the Scillies, but the Classical Greeks were often mistaken in their beliefs about earlier ages. Some experts claim there is evidence that Cornish tin was not traded internationally until the sixth century B.C., others that it began about 2000 B.C. The Bible gives the source of tin as Tarshish, alias Tartessus, a port on the Atlantic coast of Spain. But though there were tin mines in Spain they were worked even later than those in Britain, and in any case their output was too small to supply the enormous demand, and they were not near Tarshish. Tarshish must have been no more than an entrepôt, where tin brought from further afield was stored and transshipped before being taken through the Mediterranean to its final destination.

Homer said that tin came out of the Atlantic to the Mediterranean and, with Britain, Brittany, the Erzgebirge and Spain ruled out, there are only two places beyond the Strait of Gibraltar that could supply tin in anything like the quantities that they used. One is Africa, the other is the Americas.

The African mines were certainly useful—and used—but it was in America that the main sources of tin were to be found. So big are the deposits there that they are still not worked out and U.S. Steel has been dredging placer tin out of the bed of the Amazon and its tributaries to this day. Along with the contemporary gold strike in Amazonia have been found additional sources of tin. A gold nugget weighing 63 kilograms was found in Amazonia in 1983.[14]

These placer deposits consist of particles of metal washed down the river from their origin in hills in Bolivia near Lake Titicaca, but alluvial tin deposits also exist widely in Amazonia on their own account, as do great quantities of gold. And the Andes provide one of the world's greatest supplies of copper. By 4000 B.C. axes in Egypt were being made out of impure native copper.

The Amazon also provided limitless supplies of wood that could be turned into charcoal and used for smelting and casting the metals, while the Middle Eastern countries had exhausted their own timber by the same process at a surprisingly early date in the Bronze Age.

So it was possible for the whole process of bronze making to be completed on site. The finished ingots could then be shipped without any wasted weight, and the long journey down the Amazon, across the Atlantic and through the Mediterranean could well have been more economic than much shorter journeys carrying heavy, clumsy cargoes of ore overland. (We know that Bronze Age peoples generally tried to smelt at the mines for this reason,[15] and there was a phrase in Aristotle describing such desirable places as "well-wooded and having navigable rivers.")

With the coming of bronze, then, the South American mines acquired a unique importance, but even before that, North American finds were being worked for copper. Certainly in the fourth millennium and probably as early as the beginning of the sixth, prospectors were journeying out to find ways of meeting the Fertile Crescent's need for copper. Later we shall be reviewing evidence that several thousand years ago a mining city comparable to Kimberley or Johannesburg in modern Africa existed high up in the Sierra near the border of Bolivia and Peru, where the surrounding peaks of the Andes soar up to twenty-five thousand feet and seem, like Atlas, to hold up the sky. This is how Atlas came to be associated with mountains and how the Egyptian hieroglyph for colony or distant land consisted of a series of mountain peaks.

In the early days of metallurgy the precious minerals were held in some awe. In Egyptian texts of the time, the words for native copper, metal in general and mine are also used for wonder, precious and astonishing.[16] In such a climate it would not be surprising if important sources of wealth like the mines of America gave rise to a whole series of legends, handed down from generation to generation for centuries before writing was invented. Some of them are explored in later chapters, but one must be mentioned here. Heracles eleventh labor was to bring back from across the sea the golden apples from the Garden of the Hesperides. Now it is true that various opulent rulers, including both the Incas in South America

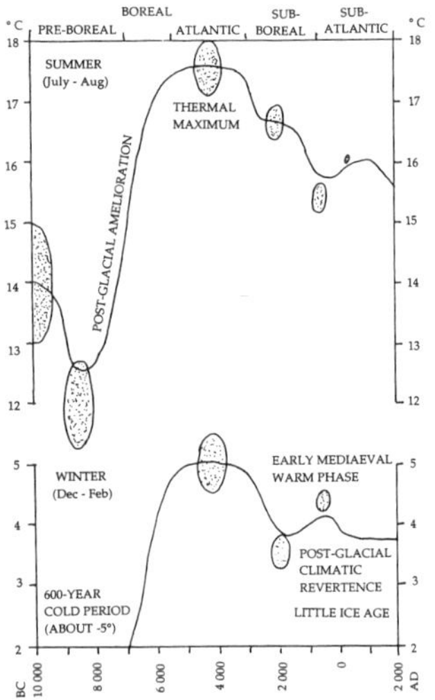

PLATE 7

Air temperatures in the lowlands of central England. Trends of the supposed 1,000 year and 100 year averages since 10,000 B.C. (the latter calculated for the last millennium) (after Lamb, 1966). Shaded ovals indicate the approximate ranges within which the temperature estimates lie and error margins of the radio carbon dates. Note that the preboreal phase begins about 8300 B.C., following the end of the glacial period. There were woods on the Shetland Islands 5000–3500 B.C., where no tree can grow today because of high winds. Pollen analysis shows that the climate in the North Atlantic was much less formidable during the Copper Age, as revealed by this climate graph. The early medieval warm phase explains the 350 years when the Scandinavians colonized North America and the subsequent graph explains why they stopped. When climates change, birds and plants move accordingly, and so do humans and other animals. Pollen analysis is a useful tool. After the ice had withdrawn from Scotland, the first Scots were called Eachans[15]—a name reminiscent of the matriarchal awa-ak*—and they first populated the west side of the Hebrides.*

and, according to Ezekiel and to the Gilgamesh epic, rulers in the Middle East, have made a display of their wealth by hanging imitation fruits made of precious metals from trees around their palaces.[17] This very specific practice was identical in both regions in both the Old World and the New: it is described in Ezekiel, and was known to have been in use in Phoenicia. It is also true that any poor man may well dream of a country where gold hangs from the trees in shining nuggets, as easy to pick as apples and each one worth more than he could hope to earn in a lifetime of labor. But it is worth considering that there is something substantial in such a story, particularly when the myth adds a number of details that do not obviously stem from the simple wish-fulfilling fantasy. That fantasy makes the story gratifying to tell and to remember, and so gives it a long life. It did not necessarily generate it, with its curious surrounding details, in the first place; that congruence must be explained: the Peruvians, the Phoenicians, the Mesopotamians all having this very specialized practice, and even the ancient Japanese knew about it. It should be noted that in those early days gold was mostly found in native form and no smelting was required.

If we are willing for a moment to think of Heracles's labors in that way, the Garden of the Hesperides is not hard to place. In very early days men were voyaging out to find the lumps of native copper that could be worked into the implements essential to their lives. In one place they found them in an abundance they had never seen anywhere else in all their world-quartering journeys. On Isle Royale and the neighboring shore of Lake Superior, the "apples" lay ready for their hands—not truly golden, perhaps, but formed of a substance that on any real assessment was far more important to their lives. This was where the myth was born. It was not in the Mediterranean, or indeed anywhere in the Old World, but on what is now the northern border of the United States that those early voyagers stumbled, with astonishment, on the real Garden of the Hesperides. In Greek tradition the Hesperides were islands far out across the Atlantic. In Welsh tradition the Atlantic Isles were known as Avalon of the Apples or Glas Innes. In Welsh *innes* means island and *glas* is simply Atlas. To Mesopotamians the land in mid-ocean was *Kur;* in Sumerian *En* means lord of: hence, perhaps, Inca. The apple Eve gave to Adam may well have been the military material, copper: the Tree of Knowledge how to secure it for himself—and thus the fuss that was made about it! It is worth considering whether the Mesopotamian *Kur* is not an abbreviation of the matriarchal *akawa.*

Below are the main points made in the set of papers edited by Professor Drier and Octave du Temple and published in 1961.[18] In my judgment they record the real start of the Age of Metals and the island on which, Greek tradition said, kingship began.[19] And remember, in Greek tradition as well as in Middle Eastern tradition, the gods were born out of Ocean.

It has been estimated that the workings on Isle Royale and the Upper Peninsula of Michigan represented the efforts of 10,000 men working for

1,000 years or, therefore, 2,500 men over 4,000 years: and that somewhere between 250,000 and 750,000 tons of copper were removed (p. 30).

The Indians did not know who the miners were. A Chippewa legend says that their forefathers drove out a white race, who might have been the miners (p. 30).

An American elephant, a mastodon, was killed by the miners and found with their remains, indicating that copper mining was carried on when the mastodon lived in America (p. 30).

It is questioned whether the miners and the mound builders are the same people. The mounds on the upper Mississippi have been likened to the barrows in England (p. 39).

Wooden bowls were used for bailing water out of the pits, and wooden levers for levering the copper out. There is the impression of former plowing on a wide scale, but this is disbelieved in some quarters (p. 43).

Copper implements taken from the mounds differ entirely from the Amerindian copper implements (p. 49).

No graves or human remains from the era of the copper workings have been found that can be referred to (p. 51).

There is a copper mine in Munster in Ireland with grooved hammer stones associated with it, which are identical to those used around Lake Superior (p. 51). (Another authority makes the identical comment about a small, prehistoric copper mine in Cheshire. The name Cheshire reads like "the shire of the earth mother.")

Modern Indians were ignorant of everything to do with this mining (p. 63).

Copper chisels, wedges, knives, spear points, rings and bracelets have all been hammered into shape from a mass of native copper, and not smelted (p. 68).

Copper found in the mounds has silver inmixed: the Lake Superior copper, alone in America, is associated with silver (p. 68).

At the central mine forty-six tons of copper were found in one pit (p. 70).

There are no traces of habitations or burial places (p. 72).

These pits out of which copper has been extracted extend over a distance of 150 miles in length and four to seven miles in width (p. 76).

The shores of Lake Superior have the only large-scale deposits of native copper in the world and are still mined (p. 79).

The amazing perfection of their workmanship resulted in the copper tools being the prototype of the tools of our present civilization (p. 79).

There were no crucibles or melting pots: nothing is cast (p. 79).

The mound builders were contemporary with the American mammoth and with the Stone Age of Europe (p. 82).

There were stone tablets found in a Michigan mound (p. 151).

One copper boulder has been discovered weighing eighteen tons; many

PLATE 8
Huge copper boulder found near Lake Superior and placed on a trolley. These were the golden apples of the Hesperides. Here was the start of the Age of Metals on the Isle Royale of Lake Superior, in Greek perhaps the nesos basileia. *Some of the Lake Superior copper boulders were pushed by the glaciers of the Ice Age as far south as Ohio.*[16] *The local Amerindian name for Isle Royale was, interestingly enough, Minong. The early sailors set out to find minerals and came back also with ideas. The first kings, it has been said, were navigators. Let us remember that in Greek tradition Hades reigned, not in a fixed place underground but in an ideal country of which very little, by classical times, was known.*[17]

Bighorn Medicine Wheel (below): a large circular arrangement of stones erected by prehistoric people in Wyoming and believed to be an astronomical device, like the stone circles of Britain. It is said to have been much tampered with subsequently.

PLATE 9

REED BOATS, WICKER BOATS. *The guest house* (mudhif) *of a modern Marsh Arab village (right): a traditional form of reed architecture already seen to be illustrated in carvings of the protoliterate period (from Leacroft, 1974). Such a house, turned the other way up, has the makings of a wash-through reed boat for the people at the mouth of the Tigris-Euphrates. In the Bronze Age, Diodorus Siculus says that an Indian king, Strabobates, made four thousand reed boats to defeat Semiramis. Reed boats are still in use on Lake Titicaca in South America, constructed in the same way as the ancient reed boats of the Middle East.*

The Irish curragh (left), a wood and hide boat that might be built large enough to carry twenty or thirty men and in which, tradition says, St. Brendan voyaged to America. A paddle in Yorkshire has been found dating to 7500 B.C. and a dugout in Holland to 6300 B.C.[18] *From the eleventh millennium B.C. obsidian was being shipped from Melos to mainland Greece.*[19]

The Irish coracle depicted here, a skin and hide boat, was of a type used also on the Tigris and Euphrates in Iraq, in Tibet and in India, as well as by the Celts to this day in the west of Britain. In Iraq the hides are replaced by bitumen from Hit. In Iraq the vessel may be built big enough to ferry horses and heavy cargoes. Coracles were used on the Spey until recent times. Babylonian skin boats were capable of carrying 150 tons.[20]

are around one hundred pounds. One boulder of pure copper was found on Isle Royale weighing 5,720 pounds, too heavy for the ancients to take away (pp. 63, 75, 78).

Copper extraction commenced on Isle Royale, evidence that it was water people who began it, the island giving them protection against attack by the local land people.

The Amerindian name for Isle Royale was Minong (p. 163).

The antiquity of the copper mining is shown by the way native copper artifacts had time to become carbonates (p. 125).

Hesiod wrote a poem on the discovery of metals that was entitled "The Idaean Dactyls" but, like so much else, it is lost.[20] Hence, also, the need for our labors. Diodorus Siculus describes the conditions under which the miners had to work once the arts of mining into the earth had been developed. The miners were slaves and were worked to death. (This is the origin of our contemporary financial term amortization.) They wore no clothes and were permitted next to no rest. The soldiers guarding the slaves spoke other languages so the miners could not prevail upon them. The miners carried lights before them. No pity was taken over sickness, age, or fatigue.

Diodorus sums it up: "In such manner and with such labour and industry is gold prepared in the frontiers of Egypt. And certainly Nature it selfe doth teach and evidently shew, that gold is painfull to find, hard to keep, full of care to make gains of, and the use of it is intermingled with grief and pleasure."[21]

2. Tracks on the World Ocean

"Ocean, from whence the gods are sprung."
Iliad (XIV, 201, 302)

The beginnings lie almost unimaginably far back in time. No one can know when the first boat was built, but there must have been a moment when a man, clinging to a lump of wood to save himself from drowning, first realized that here was a technique that did not have to wait for an emergency. It could be used as a deliberate way of increasing one's range and safety in water. That first step taken, it can only have been a matter of time before men came to see that an even better result could be achieved by binding several logs together to make a raft, or by hollowing a single large log out to make a boat. Other techniques were tried and proved successful. Boats could be made from bundles of reeds or some other buoyant material, lashed together in shapes that cut easily through the water. Bark or hides could be stretched over a light wooden framework. Later, planks were cut and fastened together to make what to us are "ordinary" boats, either clinker- or carvel-built.

None of these inventions can be dated, but it is likely that they were made many thousands of years ago. The earliest rafts or boats were probably used not for travel but for fishing, and as Professor Raymond Dart has pointed out, the need to fish goes back a long way, for thirty thousand years before the agricultural revolution occurred (in round numbers, agriculture begins about 7000–8000 B.C.): "Dependence upon fishing rather than the diminishing hunting available during the last Ice Age had been facing all the peoples inhabiting Europe, the Near East and North Africa."[1] If boats were used for much of that time, then the thousand years that separate the Viking ship from the nuclear submarine account for only a tiny portion of mankind's long experience of building and using boats. There was a whole style of living off the shoreline practiced by people the

Plate 10

Chronologies of Egypt

Not until the fifth Dynasty were the Egyptian Kings believed to be the equal of the gods. The twelfth Dynasty was held to be the high point in Egyptian literature. Diodorus Siculus claims that knowledge of the gods and the stars began in Egypt and that there had been an immense study of astronomy in Egypt since antiquity, and that the Thebans, in particular, claimed to be the first to study philosphy as well as astronomy.

GENERAL CHRONOLOGY OF EGYPT

Period	**Dynasties**	**Dates**
PREDYNASTIC PERIOD		TO 3050 B.C.
ARCHAIC PERIOD	I–II	3050–2685 B.C.
OLD KINGDOM	III–VI	2685–2180 B.C.
FIRST INTERMEDIATE PERIOD	VII–EARLY XI	2180–2040 B.C.
MIDDLE KINGDOM	LATE XI–XII	2040–1782 B.C.
SECOND INTERMEDIATE PERIOD	XIII–XVII	1782–1570 B.C.
NEW KINGDOM	XVIII–XX	1570–1069 B.C.
THIRD INTERMEDIATE PERIOD	XXI–XXV	1069–664 B.C.
LATE PERIOD	XXVI–XXX	664–332 B.C.
PTOLEMAIC PERIOD		332–30 B.C.
ROMAN PERIOD		30 B.C.–A.D. 395
BYZANTINE/COPTIC PERIOD		A.D. 305–641
ARAB CONQUEST		A.D. 641

CHRONOLOGY OF THE THIRD INTERMEDIATE PERIOD

(after K.A. Kitchen, The Third Intermediate Period in Egypt. 2nd Edition, Warminster, 1986)

DYNASTY	**KINGS**	**DATE (B.C.)**	**HIGH PRIESTS AT THEBES**
XX	Rameses XI	1098–1069	Amunhotep
	Renaissance Era	1080–	
	Smendes at Tanis	1080–1069	Herihor
			Piankh
XXI	Smendes	1069–1043	Pinudjem I
	Pinudjem I	1054–1032	Masaharta
	Amenemnisu	1043–1039	
	Psusennes I	1039–991	Menkheperre
	Amenemope	993–884	Smendes
			Pinudjem II
	Osorkon The Elder	984–978	
	Sicmun	978–959	Psusennes
	Psusennes II	959–945	
(It is probable that Psusennes the high priest ascended the throne as Psusennes II)			
XXII	Shoshenq I	945–924	Iuput
	Osorkon I	924–889	Shosenq
	Shoshenq II	Circa 890	Smendes
	(The high priest Shoshenq ascended the throne as Shosenq II)		
	Takeloth I	889–874	Iuwelot
	Osorkon II	874–850	Nimlot
	Harsiese	870–860	(co-regent only)
	Takeloth II	850–825	Osorkon
	Shoshenq III	825–818	

	XXIInd DYNASTY		**XXIIIrd DYNASTY**	**DATE**
	Shoshenq III	818–773	Petubast	818–793
			Iuput I	804–803?
			Shoshenq IV	793–787
	Pimay	773–767	Osorkon III	787–759
	Shoshenq V	767–730	Takeloth III	764–757
			Rudamun	757–754
	Osorkon IV	730–715	Iuput II	754–720/715
Circa 72B	Osorkon IV	Iuput II	Pefjauawybast	Nimlot
	(Tanis)	(Leontopolis)	(Heracleopolis)	(Hermopolis)
	XXIVth DYNASTY		**XXVth DYNASTY**	
	Tefnakht I	727–720	Piankhy	747–716
	Bakenrenef	720–715	Shabako	716–702
			Shebitku	702–690
	XXVIth DYNASTY		Taharqa	690–664
	Necho I	672–664	Tantamani	664–656
	Psammetichus I	664–610		
656	Psammetichus I reunited Egypt.			

Greeks called Ichthyophagae. Old fishtraps have recently been found dating back to 30,000 B.C.

In the nature of things, boats are unlikely to survive for long. They are made of materials that rot and they are kept on or near water. The few ancient boats of which remains have survived were preserved by lucky and unusual conditions, and the fact that we do not have any relics of boats from other times and places does not prove that they were not commonly in use. Compared to a building or even a fragile pot, a boat is ephemeral.

Almost all the evidence of boats that has come down to us is, therefore, comparatively recent, relating to what in this context we may think of as modern history, that is, since the building of the pyramids. But it would be quite wrong to suppose that what we know about is all there was.

It is reasonably certain that the men who set out on the early exploration or trading voyages seven or nine thousand years ago were the heirs of a tradition that already stretched back far longer than the span of centuries that parts their time from ours.

If this seems surprising, it is largely because we are apt to underestimate the ability of early peoples to innovate. We forget that the most primitive skill was once a new technique, developed perhaps in a flash of insight. We should never assume that *Homo sapiens* of the very earliest cultures was any less intelligent than ourselves, and if his actions seem crude and purposeless to us it may simply be that we have failed to understand them. This kind of misunderstanding can distort our view of history, as it did that of the archaeologists who suggested that dugouts would not have been used before the coming of bronze tools because the process of hollowing them out would have been too laborious. In fact you can see dugouts being made in West Africa today by a much cleverer method that is probably almost as old as the dugout itself. A tree trunk of the right size is cut to length, trimmed, and rolled into the river. It is left there until the outer part has soaked up water just far enough to provide the shell of a boat, and then the log is hauled back on land and the dry heart burned away. Tools are needed only for finishing, not for the main task of hollowing out. A similar method of making dugout canoes with only stone axes as well as fire was used by the American Indians, by the Cherokee for example.[2]

The above example illustrates a limitation of mind that we shall constantly have to guard against in our study of early voyaging. It is easy to assume that we know how something must have been done in prehistoric times, or why it must have been impossible, without stopping to ask whether there was not in fact a perfectly effective method that we have missed—perhaps a method that can still be seen in use among preindustrial peoples whom the scholars nevertheless deem quite simpleminded.

The investigators such as Thor Heyerdahl who have managed to avoid this trap have shown that boats do not have to fit our preconceptions to be capable of long voyages. In the hands of people who understand them, the

PLATE 11

Funerary boats were attached to pyramids as early as the First Dynasty.[1] The solar boat of King Cheops, 143 feet long, is shown lying in its stone dock cut out of rock near Cairo. The Egyptians portrayed the sun and moon traveling across the sky in boats. The Third Dynasty of Egypt had ships 170 feet long, Egyptian shipbuilding surpassing that of Rome. The Pharaoh Sneferu, 2900 B.C., *had boats 150 feet long.[2] Strabo says: "The ancients made longer journeys, both by land and by sea, than men of later times."[3] The pharaohs in the early dynasties were buried alongside boats. The relative importance of a particular aspect of life will always be reflected and preserved in ritual and art. For example, the Dutch, during the period of the Dutch East India Company, turned out the best marine painters of all time. In some traditions Oceanos and Tethys, the god and goddess of the ocean, not just the inland waterways, are the creators. This is substantiated by the way the English words governor and government stem through the Latin and the Greek to ship's helmsman and to the steering oar. This is how civilization started, dependent on boating.*

An American, Hugo Vilhen, in his bathtub-sized craft, five foot four inches long, in which he sailed from Canada to Britain in 104 days, taking the record from Briton Tom McNally, who had sailed from Portugal to Florida during the same year, 1993, in a boat half an inch longer than Vilhen's. Probably neither party was aware that this had all been done before! Compare Heracles, Plate 15.

reed boat and the balsa raft can cross the widest oceans, and in one respect these "wash-through" vessels have the advantage over our own types. Because their buoyancy comes from the materials they are built of, rather than from a watertight skin, they can be holed or swamped without being sunk.

Reed boats were developed by the peoples who lived by the mouths of great rivers, where reeds are plentiful and timber is scarce. Some societies used both reed boats and wooden boats, whichever were most suited to the job at the time. This was so in pre-Columbian Peru and also in Egypt, where the first planked boats that we know about were made: the planks were sewn together and the joints caulked with fiber. The advantage of a sewn boat is that for portaging you need only to unsew the planks, then, when you had carried your planks past the rapids, you could sew them up again.

Skin boats may perhaps have originated the other way up—as houses. Thirty thousand years ago the European hunters on the edge of the icecap built themselves shelters of wooden branches and stitched hides: once such a structure has been made watertight it is very like an upturned boat. A little collection of crude shelters has just been found by the shores of the Mediterranean dated to three hundred thousand years ago.

We know very little about the means by which the earliest ships were propelled, but by the time of the predynastic Egyptians a combination of

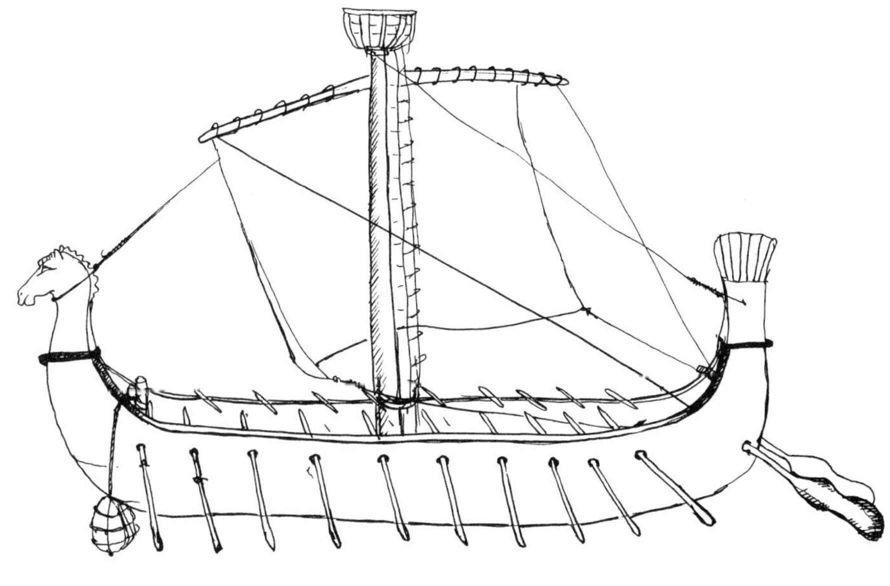

PLATE 12
Bronze Age Phoenician vessel. Incense was one motive for long-distance sailing in the Bronze Age. In Ancient Egypt, incense was presented by the pharaoh himself to the god. It was also used for religious purposes by the Maya of America, the Shang in China, the Harappa civilization of India, Assyrians, Phoenicians, etc. In the second millennium B.C. *the King of Ugarit disposed of ships each capable of carrying five hundred tons. In Egypt each town and village was built on an artificial mound that kept it above the annual inundation; so water transport was an everyday affair.*[4] *The god the Greeks called Chronos, the Romans Saturn, was to Canaanites El, cognate with Allah; as is the Jewish Yahweh.*[5] *One of his symbols was a bull.*

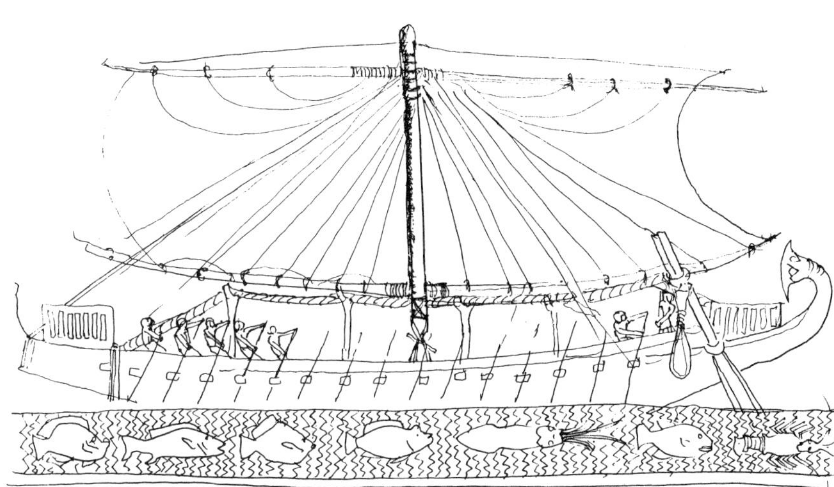

PLATE 13
PREDYNASTIC (GERZEAN) REPRODUCTION OF A SEA ATTACK. *Egypt in its day was described as the mightiest kingdom in the world and the temple of the whole world. Both statements contain much truth. When the Egyptians did their own mining, as in Sinai, Diodorus Siculus describes the miners as slave laborers, chained, with lamps on their foreheads, guarded by soldiers.*[9]

One of the ships belonging to the fleet of Queen Hatshepsut. Indications as to the earliness of sailing skills are in part available. Man reached Australia in 40,000 B.C. *involving a sea crossing of 180 kilometers on the Java-Timor route: 95 kilometers on the Celebes-Moluccas route.*[6] *Tasmans, looked on as the most backward of all human beings—I said to the late Bruce Chatwin "forty thousand years behind" and he at once corrected me by saying "one hundred thousand years behind"—used bark bundles or reed bundles or both as boats.*[7] *Before a sail was used, branches would be fastened to the prow of a boat to catch the wind; one can see them thus portrayed on predynastic Egyptian pottery. There is a tradition of rafts as the first vessels in Oceania.*[8] *An easy living could be made by hooking seagulls as well as fish while drift voyaging. But, little by little, long-distance sea travel became a highly organized and highly lucrative activity.*

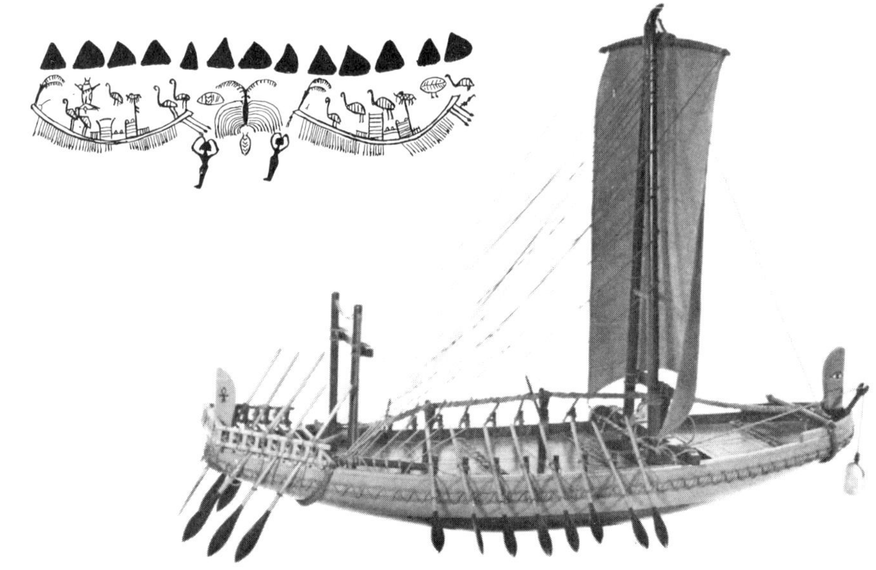

Plate 14
Predynastic (Gerzean) Egyptian boats, approximately penteconters. The design above is the hieroglyph for colony, mountain, distant land. Early boats carried branches of trees on the prow in place of sails. The earliest Egyptian boats were reed boats.

Egyptian ship of about the eighteenth century B.C. *A medium-sized vessel, not a longboat. According to the* Cambridge Ancient History, *some of the Egyptian ships working the Mediterranean even had stowage space for chariots and stalls for horses.*[10] *A large Egyptian vessel might have as many as two hundred warriors on board.*[11] *The Greeks sent 1,186 ships to attack Troy. To show how simple is the Atlantic trip, here is a newspaper report: "Eric Peters, from London, landed on the French Caribbean island of Guadeloupe at the end of a 47-day trip across the Atlantic in a 6-foot plastic barrel with a sail. He left Hierro Island in the Canaries on Christmas Eve and claims his was the first barrel to cross the Atlantic." It is clear, as with the Hyksos, that there were sea leagues from very early times. Egyptian shipbuilding surpassed that of the Romans. Egyptians of the Third Dynasty had ships 170 feet long.*[12]

rowing and sailing was in use. Pictures on pottery show ships with up to sixty oarsmen, who would have had to be at work most of the time. Each ship also had one large square sail, but this was only useful when the wind was blowing from behind, and at other times had to be lowered.

When it comes to the size of early ships, we have to forget a lot of our preconceptions about what can be done with different types of construction. To us, for example, a skin-covered boat means something like the Welsh coracles and Irish curraghs still seen today. These are all quite small—much closer to a dinghy than a ship—but Herodotus records that Babylonian skin boats could carry loads of 150 tons.[3] Reed ships, too, could reach considerable sizes. Heyerdahl describes the use of large oceangoing reed ships and balsa rafts by the Peruvians up to the time of the Spaniards.[4] In the last few years the Atlantic has been crossed by a single man in a rowing boat and another man in only a barrel. And other incongruous craft have been used for making what is a quite simple voyage.

Our best information on early ships relates to the Egyptians. We know that in predynastic times they were using both plank boats and reed boats made from papyrus, and by the fourth millennium they had reached the stage where they were building boats as much as one hundred feet long. Toward the end of the Third Dynasty (c. 2550 B.C.) Pharaoh Sneferu is recorded as building, in the course of one year, one ship 170 feet long and six ships of one hundred feet. In a dock cut out of the rock next to the pyramid of King Cheops is a "solar boat" intended for the use of the king's spirit after death. It is 143 feet long. Around 1500 B.C. an Egyptian barge took the two obelisks of Queen Hatshepsut down the Nile. It was two hundred feet long and eighty feet wide and weighed, with its load, 1,500

Plate 15

Heracles at sea in a coracle. Pots were early attached to rafts as buoyancy tanks, which I believe is what this picture represents. Note the pattern on the rim both of the cross and the squared spiral. This coracle type of boat was known in Babylon as a quffa, *a name, I judge, with* akawa *as its root. Diodorus Siculus says that Heracles' club and lion skin prove his antiquity.*[13] *He brought the inhabited world under cultivation.*[14] *Oral literature is not to be despised and this tradition, recorded by the great Sicilian Diodorus, must count when assessing whether the start of agriculture around the same time in four separate parts of the world, i.e., Southeast Asia, Southwest Asia, Mexico and Peru, all about 7000* B.C., *was a matter of spontaneous invention, polygenesis—as the establishment requires—a common unconscious as Jung requires, or this recorded tale is true. Such evidence as there is, as we shall see, points to the latter. Heracles was a great astronomer, Diodorus records*[15]*—so necessary to navigation. That civilization started with maritime societies is evidenced by the English word government, tracing back to the Greek for a steering oar, and the English word governor, tracing back again through the Latin to the Greek, for a ship's helmsman. That the Heracles people went on their many and diverse adventures in missionary spirit to benefit mankind is stated clearly by Diodorus.*[16] *That the Strait of Gibraltar was known as the Pillars of Heracles suggests their prominence as early sailors. Heracles encompassed the entire world,*[17] *tradition recorded. The Heracles people were part of the eastern Mediterranean Pelasgians, or sea people, so the traditions that the Pelasgians conquered the west and the north of Europe and that Heracles was a god to the Celts of Gaul are, I believe, related. The coracle was used not only on the Tigris and Euphrates in addition to the Celtic coast of Western Europe but also in India and on the Yalong River in Tibet. Coracles were originally made very simply and inexpensively of animal skins and wooden spars, but in ancient Babylon the skins were replaced by bitumen, these coracles having been described as "lidless baskets." Eskimos also use boats made of wood and animal hides. The larger hide boats and wood boats used in Ireland are called curraghs and tradition said that St. Brendan voyaged to America with three curraghs crewed by twenty or thirty men in each. Large ferry coracles on the Tigris-Euphrates could carry horses and also heavy loads.*[18] *Magnetite was known as "the stone of Heracles" because it provided him with his compass, as it does for migrating birds, whales, bees, salmon in a natural form. The earliness of the period in which Heracles flourished is stated by Diodorus: "He was at the beginning of the generation of mankind."*[19] *Sumerian Gilgamesh, who wore a lion skin, wrestled with Enkidu, was king of Uruk, and went on an immensely long sea voyage to Utnapishtim, may have been of the Heracles clan. Gourd rafts, gourds preceding pots, were used in Africa, Southeast Asia and pre-Columbian Mexico.*[20]

tons. This was admittedly a river boat, but there is evidence that the Egyptians had seagoing ships that could carry two hundred men and others that had accommodation both for horses and for chariots. At about the time of Queen Hatshepsut's barge, ships of five hundred tons were being built in the Phoenician city state of Ugarit. Egyptian shipbuilding was ahead of that of Rome.

Plate 14 shows a reconstruction of an Egyptian ship of about the eighteenth century B.C. It is clearly a well-developed design, and a long experience of sailing must have gone into it. This ought not to surprise us for we know that, even before the Egyptians, other cultures had been building impressive ships. The Egyptians were in close contact with the Sumerians, whose early epic of Gilgamesh, King of Uruk, tells of its hero constructing a wooden boat ninety feet long. Gilgamesh dates from about 2600 B.C.: the first surviving text of his exploits from 2000 B.C.

PLATE 16
Archaeological sites of Middle America. In Mexico, it has been worked out, a man could grow enough food to keep a family of three in only 120 days. That allowed him plenty of holidays! Mexico has the largest deposits of silver in the world. The Maya of Guatemala depicted some of their gods as bearded and even with handlebar mustaches, to a beardless people.[21] *The Maya used a sign for zero before Europe.*[22] *Hundreds of thousands of acres in Arizona were irrigated in prehistoric times. The irrigation system of Tezcuco was similar to that described by Plato for Atlantis and provided a similar system for defense.*[23] *The Mayan travelers' god was called Ekehuah,*[24] *which sounds like a variant for Heracles. The Mexican god of water was called Nakawa, which reads like an* akawa *name also. But we must notice that at La Venta bronze and goldwork seem to have been unknown. The Maya supreme God, Itzamná, was represented by an iguana or monitor lizard. Itzamná was a beneficent sky god, father of the arts and sciences. Time was god in Central America as in parts of the Middle East*[25] *with the god Chronos, whose followers were sailing out of the Mediterranean to handle the Atlantic trade. To the far-sailing Greeks, the island of Calypso was in the Far West, of Circe in the Far East.*[26]

It is not sensible to assume that all this building of large and well-designed boats sprang suddenly out of nowhere. We know how slowly and hesitantly European ship design advanced, so that even in the late fifteenth century Columbus's flagship, the *Santa María*, was a small and comparatively clumsy affair of eighty to one hundred tons. What happens with any technique is not generally an unbroken advance, but a series of moves forward interrupted by times when the technique becomes cruder or is wholly lost in some historic upheaval. If ships were being built under the pharaohs larger than any that would be built again until the nineteenth century A.D., it is highly likely that people of still earlier times were able to construct smaller but viable oceangoing boats. After all, their development does not depend on great wealth or extensive political organization, as does, for example, large-scale irrigated agriculture. What is needed is time to experiment and an exploratory spirit. Given those things, boats could have been built very early on that were capable of crossing the Atlantic and the other seas with ease; and from then on the difficulty lay not in shipbuilding but in acquiring the techniques of navigation, including a knowledge of winds and currents.

Landsmen often have unrealistic notions of what sea travel is like. Perhaps the most persistent is the idea that it is inherently easier to journey over land than over water. In a country with good roads and efficient vehicles this may be so, but in early times it was far from the truth. Particularly when it came to moving heavy loads the reverse was true. A large block of stone may need a dozen men with rollers and levers to inch it laboriously forward, even across level ground. Put it on a raft and a single person can quite literally tow it through the water with one finger. Even a wheeled vehicle, until the coming of the railway, was a clumsy substitute for a boat, and as late as the eighteenth century the English crisscrossed their country with canals in recognition of the greater efficiency of water travel. For most of the great prehistoric age of sea travel the wheel had not been invented. Such long-distance tracks as there were across land were likely to lead through hostile territory and over terrain that was difficult going for men and for pack animals. In those early times the rule was simple: the land divided, the water united. It was for that reason that the Mediterranean formed a unit in the way the landmass of Europe did not. Another landsman's fallacy is that a sailor looking for safety rather than adventure will hug the shoreline, staying in sight of land. In reality, if you are in a true seagoing boat it is the land that is the danger. In exceptionally heavy weather ships do get overwhelmed by the wind and waves of the deep oceans, but far more are wrecked on coasts. If you are caught off a lee shore in a ship that cannot sail into the wind, it needs only a moderate wind to blow you to inevitable destruction.

The third fallacy is that the world ocean is a fairly homogeneous body of water, and sailing across it in one direction is much like sailing in another. It is easy for us to believe this as we speed across it in our power-driven ships, but in the long ages of sails and oars no one could have thought so. Winds and currents make some voyages easy for the most primitive craft and make others nearly or quite impossible for all but ships of advanced design. Our marine knowledge was developed over an immense period of time.

Fed on these mistaken ideas, most people suppose that it must have been far easier for early sailors to get from end to end of the Mediterranean than to cross the Atlantic. The fact is that the Mediterranean is a tricky sea to navigate. There are no long-distance currents to carry the sailor where he wants to go, and no constant winds either. Mediterranean winds are unpredictable and can turn suddenly fierce. Particularly at the eastern end, the sea is crowded with islands on whose shores many ships have been wrecked.

By contrast, the Atlantic presents a far more straightforward challenge. For a start, the shortest distance between Africa and South America is less than the length of the Mediterranean, and the distance from West Africa to the mouth of the Amazon is almost exactly equal to it. But by far the most important factor is the pattern of winds and currents. One need only glance at the map on Plate 77 to see how extraordinarily favorable it is. Two great circular currents swirl endlessly around in the North and South Atlantics, the northern one driving almost straight from the bulge of North Africa to the Caribbean. Above this current the trade wind blows in the same direction. A barrel thrown into the sea at the right point will find its way to America with a lot less fuss than Columbus made about his trips! Even without the help of the wind, the current alone, flowing at about one knot, will get it there in two or three months. And some currents flow at two or three knots.

The truth is that for anyone who sailed around the bulge of Africa in a primitive ship it was not hard to get to America. The difficult thing was to avoid going to America! If a crew allowed themselves to drift or be blown just a little too far from the coast, they would be lucky if they were not caught up in the strong combination of current and tradewind and, like it or not, deposited some weeks later in the Caribbean.

This, of course, assumes that early sailors from the Mediterranean voyaged around Africa. We shall be looking at this question below, and here we need only note that there is admirable reason to believe that they did. Homer tells us of voyages beyond the Gates of Heracles (the Strait of Gibraltar) and it would be quite surprising if, out of all the sailors who traversed the Mediterranean, none had tried to explore beyond it. The only dispute lies in settling just how early in prehistory the American voyages began, and we shall soon see that it was very early indeed. And northern Europeans themselves speedily followed suit.

If African voyages are accepted, then there is no point in balking at journeys to America. In our own day various adventurers have made the crossing in craft not much more advanced than a barrel: in 1952, for example, Dr. Alain Bombard sailed and drifted from Morocco to Barbados solo on a rubber and canvas raft. No one could hope to follow a set course around the Mediterranean in so crude a craft, and the converse necessarily follows. As soon as seagoing people had ships that could navigate the Mediterrean with reasonable success, they had ships that were more than capable of making the Atlantic crossing.

There was, of course, still a major difficulty. When you had reached America you had to come back. Once again, a look at the map shows that this is by no means as hard as might be supposed. When it reaches the coast of America, the Atlantic current continues to circle around and, as the Gulf Stream, sweeps eastward toward Europe. One half of it then swings south and returns to North Africa, passing the entrance to the Mediterranean on its way. The winds, too, though less reliable than the west-blowing tradewinds to the south, set predominantly in the right direction. Europeans from the fifteenth to the nineteenth centuries A.D. made use of this pattern: it was there to be used just as much in the fifth millennium B.C. It is these circling currents that led to the ancient description: "the circling river of Ocean."

Of course it is nothing like as easy to find your way around this circular route on the real ocean as it is to run a finger over it on a map, but that does not prove it was never done. All we need suppose is that a number of ships coasting around Africa were blown off course and carried across the Atlantic. Many of them would no doubt have come to grief, wrecked or stranded in an alien land from which they could find no way to return. Still, over the centuries (and it is centuries or rather millennia that we are talking about) it is surely likely that one ship—just one—would have found

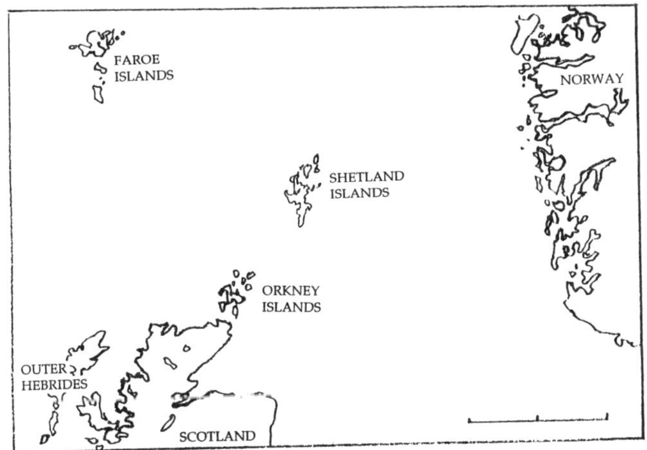

PLATE 17
The Orkney Islands, much like the Shet- or Set-lands, were starting-off points for freighters taking the stepping-stone route to the Americas. As we shall see, the evidence supports the belief that the first kings were navigators. Iberian pottery and stone artifacts resemble those of Skara Brae in the Orkneys because, as we shall see, we are dealing with long-distance Mediterranean traders. The name Orkney (Latin: Orcades) may derive, not from the Latin orca *for a type of whale, but from Akawa and Ana, the sky god who seized the North American trade from the matriarchs, Akawa. Skara Brae had privies with drains. Woven cloth was used by the henge people, not skins. However, Tacitus describes the altars in Anglesey in Roman days as slaked with the blood of prisoners. The Celts were head-hunters. The cult associated with the human head is very ancient in origin, going back, it has been suggested, as early as 500,000* B.C.

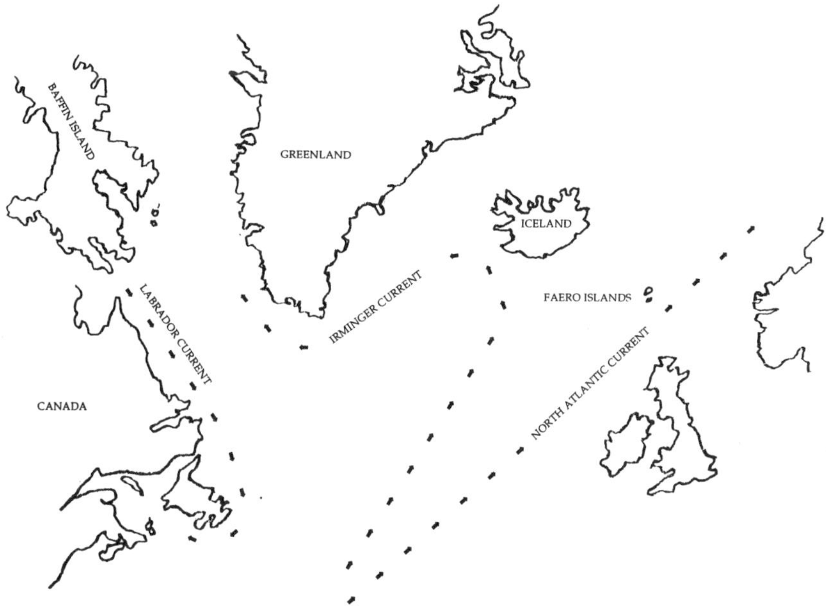

The currents affecting the stepping-stone route to the St. Lawrence. Ireland protected ships from the prevailing southwest wind, so the Irish Sea was important. The North Sea in the far north was called by the Romans the Sea of Chronos.[27] *The ocean currents are the tradewinds of the sea. We know that obsidian was being transported by sea as early as the eleventh millennium, and that in the Balkans ceramics depicted sailing boats by 6000* B.C.[28] *Additional evidence of the cosmopolitan background of the early long-distance traders: let us notice that a peculiar story of a fish eating itself, starting at its tail, is found on Rockall, far west of Scotland in the Atlantic, and also in the Buddhist tradition of how Ananda, king of the fishes, ate his own tail. The meat-drying tower, the Taro, found at St. Kilda, west of Scotland, has parallels all the way to central Africa.*[29] *The Gulf Stream moves at the rate of four or five knots.*

its way through the islands on the north side of the Caribbean into the east-going currents and winds and been carried safely home.

And then the story it brought back of fertile lands a few weeks' sail away would certainly have sent some adventurous crews on what would now be deliberate voyages of exploration. Again, the majority of them might be lost; but some would be likely to survive, and to carry back reports of a vast and sparsely inhabited country with unknown riches in store. That in itself would be enough to ensure a stream of voyagers—as it was when Columbus brought news of the West Indies and those who followed soon afterward began to loot the American mainland on a prodigious scale.

One objection may be raised here. If all this could happen in such early times, why did it not happen again later on? How was it that for three thousand years before our day this voyaging continued but subsequently it happened rather less often?

One answer is that the climate is not constant. The graph on Plate 7 shows how much it has changed over the last twelve thousand years, and in studying that pattern we should remember that a five-degree change in average temperature can have very dramatic effects. (Recent studies of the greenhouse effect have warned us of this.) In the sixth millennium B.C. there was a climatic optimum over the North Atlantic that made sailing easier and safer. This warm period lasted for about three thousand years and then the weather began to worsen, with average temperatures eventually falling almost halfway to what they had been in the last Ice Age. When, for other reasons as well, the great age of seagoing ended in about 1200 B.C., the climate no longer favored a renewal, and it has remained less congenial until our own day.

Another reason why Atlantic voyaging was not taken up on the same scale again after it was interrupted was that subsequent to the invention of steel the economic imperative of bronze no longer existed. Almost every country has deposits of iron. Steel was first made in the Near East around 2000 B.C. but did not come into general use until 1200 B.C.

Once again, we must try to rid ourselves of preconceptions about those "primitive" sea peoples. They were primitive only in the literal sense that they were the forerunners. Far from being ignorant, they were masters of the highly developed skills of a marine naturalist, and once those skills had been lost it might well take thousands of years to rediscover them, as it had taken thousands of years to build them up in the first place.

Finally, it is certain that very many people did in fact cross the Atlantic and very many returned. For a long time no respectable historian would admit that the Viking stories of Vinland, a country beyond the western seas, were anything but stories. Now we know that the Vikings really did found a colony in North America and maintained it for 350 years. The pope even appointed a bishop to Vinland. In the same way, it is quite likely that not all the tales of saints and heroes who crossed the Atlantic to the legendary country on the other side were fabrications. In most cases they had their origins in reality. But no one makes a brouhaha about them, only about Columbus and his Christian thugs.

The rediscovery of America by the Norsemen happened when, having colonized Greenland in A.D. 986, a simple sailor by the name of Bjarni, returning to Greenland from Iceland, missed Greenland—which takes a helluva lot of missing—and reached North America by accident. The second Norse voyage to America, A.D. 1002–3, was conducted by Lief, son of Eric the Red, who found a lot of wild grapevines there—as well as wild corn—and, accordingly, named his part of North America Wineland. Lief's brother, Thorrald, felt that his brother had not sufficiently explored, so he set sail to Wineland, but while exploring in America died of an arrow wound. Thus the Scandinavian colonizing of North America began, continuing until the middle of the fourteenth century.[5] It is impossible that their compatriots, the Norman kings of England, would be in ignorance of these events: a time of extraordinary Scandinavian achievement that saw them conquer Normandy, conquer Britain, conquer Kiev, conquer the two Sicilies, and raid as far afield as the approaches to Byzantium. Nor is it possible for the Norsemen over the whole of that area to be in complete ignorance of what their compatriots and relatives were doing in North America over those 350 years. The work of archaeologists has confirmed the sagas, and Scandinavian runes, carved on the rocks of North America, have been found and translated. It is just worth noting that the Greek god Dionysus was the same as Hades, who ruled on the other side of the Atlantic Ocean and was the same as Osiris, who ruled in the underworld. Dionysus was god of wine and thus may be responsible for the subsequent abundance of wild grapevines there. Anthropologists also say that the religion of the Amerindians all down the Pacific coast of North America is Dionysiac.

What was different between A.D. 1000 and 5000 B.C. was the nature of the societies from which the sailors set out and to which they returned. The exploratory, seagoing orientation of early Mesopotamian and western European cultures contrasts very strongly with the introverted superstition of Europe in post-classical times, where the Vikings were an exceptional people. Someone who returned to Sumer with stories of a land beyond the sea would have had a very different reception among the seamen thronging its ports—where life centered around the quay—than someone returning to early medieval or Dark Age Europe. Not all societies are able to make use of all forms of knowledge. The pre-Columbian inhabitants of Central America did know about the wheel but it is said could find no use for it except in toys. We shall look at this later on. There may be an analogy here with the way different peoples deal with travelers who have deliberately or accidentally discovered a new land. However, the positive evidence that for a time horse and chariot were in use in Central America deserves close

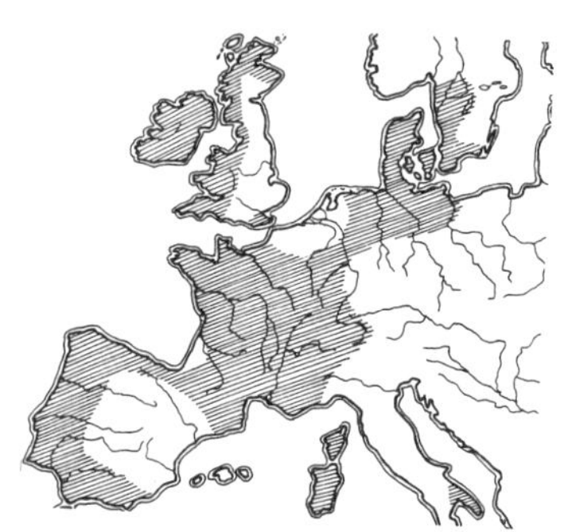

PLATE 18
The areas with these early shaft graves are shaded and are found along the Atlantic shores of Europe. Those in Brittany go back to 4800 B.C. and are among the earliest monumental architecture in the world. Place names bear witness to the degree the Baltic people were involved: atl *names like Baltic, Latvia, Letts, Tallinn and the Dan people in Danzig, Denmark, Brandenburg, Sweden. So the dragon ships and horned helmets of the Vikings only reproduced the gear they had used three thousand years before in their American colonies. The Baltic rock engravings further support this. Passage graves in Britain start after 4200 B.C.: they are found along the Atlantic seaways and are heavily concentrated in the far north of Britain: e.g., the Hebrides, Orkneys, the northern tip of Scotland. Diodorus Siculus records that the Greeks were sent into Greece by the gods. This is paralleled by the way the Aga Khan, believed, I am told by some of his followers, to be a god, prompted his followers to move from Africa to Canada in the last decade or two.*

scrutiny: African horse sickness brought over in a cargo from West Africa could have put paid to horses very quickly.

If the first voyages of exploration were to lead to a widespread and lasting system of trading, it must have been through the development of a large body of knowledge. We have here been considering the Atlantic crossing, but later we shall look at other routes and our thesis is that, for thousands of years, a regular network of trade routes existed, not just across the Atlantic to the east coast of America but down both coasts of Africa, through the Indian Ocean to the countries of the Far East and across the Pacific between Asia and the west coast of America. If this is anywhere near the truth, the sailors must have had accurate and reliable techniques of navigation. They had to possess a considerable knowledge of winds and currents, the seasons and the movements of the stars. What reasons are there to suppose that they did?

Let us begin with an oddity. The Classical Greeks believed that the world was bounded by the circling river of Ocean, and this has been taken ever since as a belief that something like an ordinary river flowed around the known world and divided it from whatever lay beyond. This would be a curiously naive idea. What sort of river is it that flows endlessly around without source or outlet? Since it can have no fall, always ending where it began, what drives it along? And since the universities believe in human progress, people before the Classical Greeks must have been more ignorant still, as universities suppose.

The puzzle is answered if we look at one of the Scandinavian sagas, which declares unambiguously, "There is a river in the sea which has the sea for its bed, the sea for its shore." We have to ask ourselves which is the more likely: that a seagoing tradition preserved the knowledge of ocean currents, or that a belief in a "circling river" persisted over several millennia but that it started as a piece of nonsense and later became a description of the truth. If we accept that the belief was originally based on knowledge, then we must also accept that the only way in which men could have known about those currents was by traveling upon them.

This is certainly a hint, not a proof, that the early sailors had a wide knowledge of the ocean. It is significant because it is only one of a number of indications. To assess them we must first ask what sort of knowledge, what sort of navigational skills those early sailors might have had.

For a start, they must have been much more personal than those we use today. The "haven-finding art" *was* an art, in strong contrast to the routine application of technology that navigators now rely on. It depended on highly developed personal skills, the ability to "read" the ocean in ways that are a mystery to the uninitiated. As an instance of this, Heyerdahl has described the amazing way in which Polynesian canoemen could find their way over long distances by observing variations in the pattern of waves and wavelets on the surface of the sea—variations so subtle that an untrained observer simply could not see them. The New Zealander David Lewis made a study of Polynesian navigation,[6] which was guided by the sun, by the stars, by birds, by the shape and direction of the waves. It is a reasonable rule that the less equipment men possess, the better naturalists they have to be. It is likely that the Stone Age African people, the Khoisan, had a more intimate knowledge of the flora and fauna of their country than any of the peoples who succeeded them. Sailors who travel long distances learn that the ocean has many different faces in its different parts. Those who rode the Gulf Stream on their way back from America would have noticed at once, what is visible to anyone today, that it is a different color from the waters through which it flows. As it runs up the American coast it is a deep indigo blue, clearly distinguishable from the greenish or grayish water inshore of it.

Engraved stones from the Boyne River area, Ireland, portraying the characteristic Aegean spiral of the religion of the earth mother, also used by the Polynesians. The present friction between south and northern Ireland would seem to go all the way back to earth mother versus sky father. The Boyne monuments date from 3700–3200 B.C.

Not only the color but also the taste of the water changes in different parts of the ocean. A hundred miles out from the mouth of the Amazon the differences are marked enough to tell the sailor that he is approaching his goal, and the same thing is true off the mouth of the Nile or any other great river. The sea bottom also changes, and to bring up a sample of the silt all that is needed is a bit of tallow smeared on the lead that sailors from very early times have used to gauge the depth of the water.

Seaweeds, too, vary in different parts of the ocean, and the flights of birds were almost the principal guides. The Celts must have followed the skeins of duck and geese in spring when they migrated to their breeding grounds in Iceland, and the geese could have led them on to Greenland, or helped the Norsemen sail beyond that to the American shore. Even some South African birds nest each year in Greenland. Birds can also be a sure sign of the closeness of land. We know that the Sumerians took their own birds with them to release when they were lost: if they were beyond reach of land the bird would come back to the ship, as in the story of Noah.

The birds were also the first to make use of another navigational aid that may possibly have been used by men in early times. In the heads of some migrating species zoologists have found tiny pieces of magnetic fiber, a naturally magnetized oxide of iron also known as magnetite, which occurs in certain rocks. A workable compass can be made by taking a splinter of

Engraved stones from Knockmany, County Tyrone, showing the face of the earth mother, concentric circles, the zigzag line symbol of the sea god and the other signs characteristic of our period whose significance is presently unknown. With the matriarchs and their breakaway group, the Heracles people, responsible for early trading it is worth asking whether akawa *names, from the Irish "wake" to the "abacus," do not signify this early origin: perhaps including Skara in Skara Brae in the Orkneys, and indeed Orkney from Akawa-Ana, and the Amerindian squaw, the Khabur river, the Keweenaw Peninsula, Siskiwit Bay, coven of witches and so on. There are passage graves that are Irish, Breton, Scots, Welsh, all along the Atlantic seaways.*

magnetite, fixing it to a straw and floating it in a bowl of water. Indications that at least some early people knew about the use of the lodestone have been found in America, where magnetite objects have been unearthed at a number of Olmec sites. Also, Robert H. Fuson[7] has described some Mayan buildings and ceremonial sites that look as if they are meant to be aligned north-south but which just miss the mark. Further, they are not even quite aligned with each other. Now, the Maya were a very exact and mathematical people, and Fuson's explanation is that the buildings were never intended to be aligned with true north but rather with magnetic north. Since the magnetic pole slowly wanders, buildings put up at different times would face in slightly different directions.

In the early sixth century B.C., Thales of Miletus is said to have studied the magnet, and also the electrostatic attractive power of amber. The magnet would have been a piece of lodestone. Once again it must be emphasized that there is no a priori reason to suppose that earlier ages were ignorant of things that the Classical Greeks did not know. The use of the lodestone could quite well have been known many thousands of years before Thales, and the knowledge lost and recovered, perhaps more than once.

Dating from the third millennium, there is a very suggestive passage in the Gilgamesh epic. Urshanabi, the sailor, says to the king: "Gilgamesh, your own hands have prevented you from crossing the ocean; when you

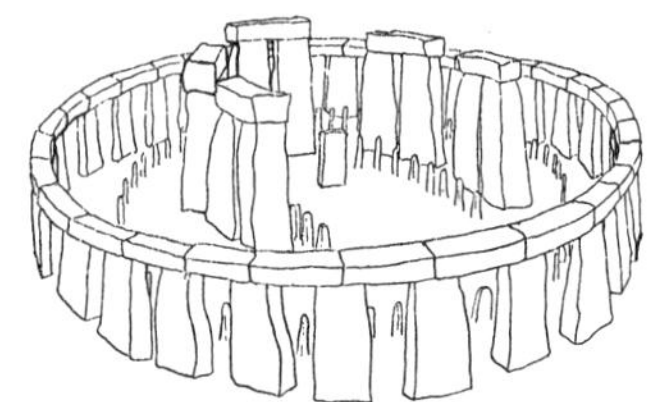

PLATE 19

The megalithic observatory and temple of Stonehenge. Stonehenge was first erected about 2800 B.C. by builders with an understanding of mathematics and astronomy of considerable sophistication, capable of setting out ellipses based on Pythagorean triangles. In my opinion, Stonehenge served as a calendar clock for marine peoples rather than farmers, probably mining the small deposits of gold and copper then found in the western side of the British Isles, but more importantly, concerned with the Atlantic trade as a whole. The neighborhood of Silbury in the west of England is said to possess the greatest quantity of Neolithic monuments in the world. The second largest of these British stone circles is on the island of Lewis at Callanish on the northwestern tip of the Hebrides, a large capital investment, of little use to farmers but convenient for sailors. The North Sea used to be called the Sea of Chronos by the Romans, Chronos meaning the Time People: the people for whom time was sacred. So these circles were also chapels for those people to whom sun and moon were sacred. It would also deter strangers from meddling with the observatory. Alexander Thom notes that an accuracy of 0.1 percent was maintained in the five to ten thousand megaliths across Britain. Megaliths around the world were sea-oriented in their distribution. Two centuries ago there were still four thousand standing stones at Carnac in Brittany.[30] The Stonehenge people were wide-ranging traders and financiers.[31] Nothing much has changed. Here is Homer's Odyssey *on the subject: "Who, pray, of himself, ever seeks out and bids a stranger from abroad, unless it be one of those that are masters of some public craft, a prophet, or a healer of ills, or a builder, aye, or a divine minstrel . . . for these men are bidden all over the boundless earth.[32] I looked at this stone circle as a boy. The last five thousand years have seen a process of miniaturization, so that we can now carry our calendar clock on our wrists. It seems to me that a corresponding miniaturization has happened to the religion itself. Time was then the moving image of eternity and the duty of the sovereign was to take his part in divine Creation. Let us look on Stonehenge as an early theodolite for observing the motions of the heavenly bodies: the fifty-six Aubrey holes a single-purpose computer for forecasting eclipses of moon and sun.*

PLATE 20

Phoenician colonies after 1190 B.C. *Herodotus said that they came from the Red Sea to the Mediterranean and we think we know where that is. But in the same way as Colchis, the supplier of copper, can apply to several places which supply copper, so the name Red Sea can possibly apply to those places where "the Red Men," the Phoenicians, were concentrated. So "the Red Sea" meant the Caribbean, and the Phoenicians returned to the Mediterranean once the bronze trade was over. Many people once supported the notion that Geryon's island, Erythia, was far in the west beyond the Atlantic.*[33] *Erythia in Greek means red. The importance of the Suez Canal to Egypt is emphasized when Herodotus narrates that 120,000 Egyptians perished when it was being redug under Pharaoh Necho. According to Strabo and Pliny, it was first dug under the second millennium pharaoh, Sesostris. Erythie, a place name for one of the Hesperides, thus on the other side of the Atlantic, was also the country of Atlas as well as the Hesperides, so we can be confident it was America.*[34] *Baal, a god of the Phoenicians, cousins of the Hebrews, died each year and was resurrected to restore the fertility of the crops.*[35] *Chronos, the west Semitic divinity, was called "king of a distant wonderland."*[36] *So when tradition tells us that kings came to Egypt from Punt, Punt may designate where the Punic people came from, which, at the date referred to, would be America.*

In the early Irish record, the Book of Invasions, there is easy travel between Greece and Ireland. Given a raw deal in Ireland, you sailed back to Greece and took part in the fighting between the Philistines and the Athenians; given a hangup in Greece, you sailed back to Ireland. For the Irish in their stories show on a small scale what was happening to the world at large, a decline in sailing skills and geographical knowledge as we enter the Iron Age. In the Bronze Age Irish records, we have the account of thirty-four ships with thirty men in each, quite a large fleet, reaching Ireland from the Caspian.[37] *Bronze started to be used in Byblos about 3500* B.C. *The principal supplies of bronze for the Mediterranean came from America: from the Erythian island beyond the great sea.*[38] *It is also worth noticing that south of Aleppo in the ninth millennium* B.C., *goats were herded, einkorn grown and pottery was already in use. The Assyrian supplies of bronze for Anatolia were delivered to Kanesh, hence perhaps its Assyrian root for bronze,* anaku. *Tartessus, on the Atlantic, not the Mediterranean, coast of Spain was fabulously rich in silver. A glance at Plate 168 explains why.*

destroyed the things of stone, you destroyed the safety of the boat." Gilgamesh protests: "Why are you so angry with me, Urshanabi, for you yourself cross the sea by day and night, at all seasons you cross it?" Urshanabi replies: "It was those very stones that brought me safely over." Polynesians today carry stones in their boats that now have no purpose but which in their great days of voyaging may have been magnetic. Gilgamesh was making a very long sea voyage to Utnapishtim, the Faraway: Pishtim bearing the same root as Pishon, "the Gusher," the first river of Paradise.

The Polynesians, as Heyerdahl found out, were able long ago to make voyages of many months and return to the tiny island from which they had set out. Also they have Greek words in their language and employ the spiral symbol of the earth mother. One of their techniques was to use a coconut to tell the latitude. The method was brilliantly simple. Standing at the latitude to which they wanted to return, they took a nut, drilled two holes in it and filled it with water up to the holes. So long as the water just reached both the holes the nut was exactly positioned by the horizontal. Then a third hole was drilled, corresponding to the height of the sun at midday, and if the sun shone through that hole at midday at the same time of year the user knew that he was back on the correct latitude. He then only needed to sail east or west to strike his destination. A Polynesian at Oxford University explained this to me.

To find one small island in the immensity of the Pacific is a far harder task than to cross the Atlantic. If the Polynesians mistook their position by a couple of dozen miles they could sail right past their island without ever seeing it. The Atlantic sailor can hardly do that: he is bound to make landfall somewhere on the right continent. If he doubts his ability to navigate accurately he can always employ the method of deliberate error, setting a course that he knows will take him too far north or south. Then, when he sights land, he knows which way to turn. If he has even a crude method of knowing his latitude he will not have left himself far to sail.

Just how crude a method can be effective is easy to demonstrate. Hold your forefinger horizontally at arm's length. If you can tell the height of the sun with an error no greater than the thickness of your finger then you have it within one and a half degrees. This corresponds to an error of about a hundred miles on the earth's surface, which means that if you are aiming at the center of the Amazon you will arrive somewhere inside its estuary.

There is, of course, a proviso. You must understand enough about the movement of the sun to know its height at noon on a given latitude at any particular time of year, and then you must have an accurate enough calendar to know exactly what time of year it is. Immediately, this gives a reason for the extraordinary accuracy with which some early peoples worked out their calendars. The solar calendar is said to have started at Heliopolis, the city of the sun, in 4241 B.C.[8] By the middle of the first millennium B.C. the Mayan astronomers had computed the length of the year with an

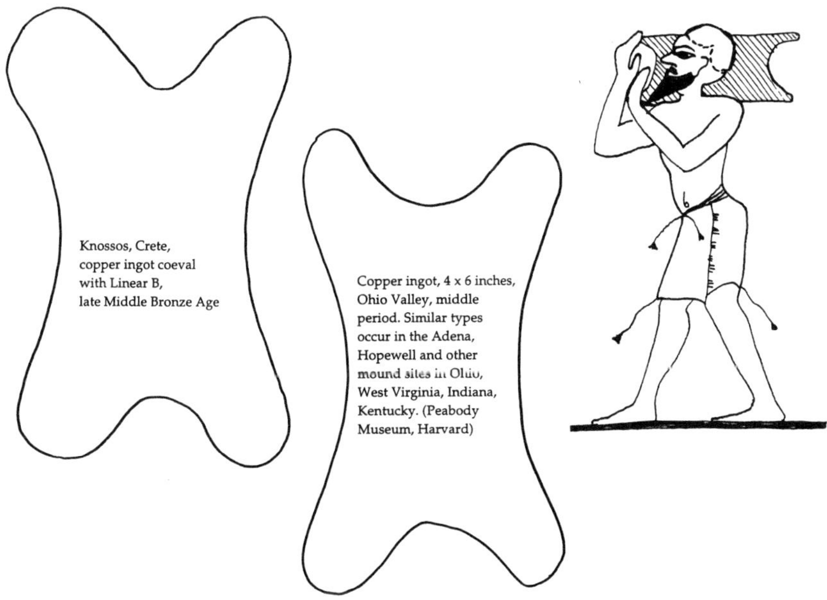

Knossos, Crete,
copper ingot coeval
with Linear B,
late Middle Bronze Age
Copper ingot, 4 x 6 inches,
Ohio Valley, middle
period. Similar types
occur in the Adena,
Hopewell and other
mound sites in Ohio,
West Virginia, Indiana,
Kentucky. (Peabody
Museum, Harvard)

PLATE 21
American mound archaeological sites contained a considerable number of oxhide ingots.

Man carrying oxhide ingot from the Tomb of Huy at Thebes (after Davies, courtesy of the Metropolitan Museum of Art). Oxhides provided one of the earliest forms of currency: so when metal ingots began to be made they were made in the shape of oxhides, they were thus easy to pick up, and were therefore known as oxhide ingots. Catal Huyuk in Anatolia produced the earliest smelting slag c. 5800 B.C. and some of the earliest copper objects from the middle of the seventh millennium B.C. The Toltecs and Aztecs had traditions of coming from Atlan, across the Atlantic. In the Greek dictionary Atlas and Atlan are synonymous. The Welsh for sacred is llan, *as in Llandaff Cathedral. The sacred place in the west of England is Glastonbury. The Irish Sea, partly protected from the southwesterlies, was an important part of the route for the North Atlantic trade pursued by the two multinationals, Mesopotamian Chronos, the Time People, and his brother trader Atlas, originally from Western Europe, both chiefly concerned with the copper and bronze trades. The stone mauls used for early copper extraction were the same everywhere. Copper was to be found in seven or more counties in Ireland.*[39] *In Mesopotamia interest and loans were known from pre-Sargonic times. There was private as well as state business. Rentals were paid in silver, grain and livestock. They had a rich variety of commercial terms by Sargon's day. Ebla to Mesopotamia, Mesopotamia to Indus trade was common at the time. In Sargon's Mesopotamia many standards of weights and measures were used alongside each other.*[40] *Our golden wedding ring is a solar emblem.*[41]

error of only one part in 1.8 million—about seventeen seconds a year—an accuracy not achieved in Europe until the nineteenth century A.D. The chances against this being a lucky guess are enormous, and the only other possibility is that it was based on accurate observations kept up over many centuries—probably millennia.

What reason could there be for such endlessly painstaking precision? Astrology is one explanation, and it is true that some American cultures placed great emphasis on sequences of destiny recurring in elaborate mathematical patterns. Another possibility is that a priestly caste needs reasons to exist and to maintain its privileged position: it helps if it can be seen to be the repository of mysteries (including mathematical and astronomical mysteries) that ordinary people cannot fathom. To my mind, however, explanations of this sort are not fully satisfactory. Sooner or later, if one is dealing with a very long period of time stretching over the rise and fall of a number of cultures, a pattern of behavior is surely likely to break down if it stems merely from irrational superstition and does not also provide solid benefits.

The suggestion that all this refinement of observation was in the service of agriculture is not even superficially plausible. What possible benefit does a farmer get from knowing the length of the year to the nearest minute or even day? He does not want to know on which day he will be planting or harvesting in fifty years' time, and he only needs quite a rough knowledge of the seasons to plan this year's work. Seed time and harvest will always depend more on the weather in any one spring or summer than they do on knowing with certainty that a particular day is, say, the two hundred and

Plate 22
Birdmen, Beam Scale and Oxhide Ingots.

Bead from Crete (after Evans, Scripta Minoa I) showing an oxhide ingot. Cylinder seals, the principle of the rotary printing press, were in use in Mesopotamia from 3500 B.C. *The earliest seals are looked on as being aesthetically the best.*

Seals from Cyprus (after Ward) showing oxhide ingots, birdmen, beam scale, sun and moon symbols.

forty-third day of the year. The European calendar has had to be reformed more than once because it had drifted into obvious error. Despite that, the farmers went on planting corn or setting the ram to the ewes at the right season without help from the astronomers. Farmers' calendars are set by the flowering of certain bushes, natural events around their farm that, over centuries, they had learned to observe and to follow.

Of all the activities in which, as far as we know, early peoples took part, only one demands an accurate knowledge of astronomy and geometry for purely practical reasons, and that is navigation, with its accompanying discipline, cartography. In the Gilbert Islands the same word is used for *navigator* and *astronomer*, and our own word *geometry* comes from the Greek for *earth measurement*—clearly an important science for anyone planning a long voyage. Columbus's ridiculous blunder in thinking—and persisting in thinking—that he had reached India when he had covered less than a third of the real distance arose partly because he was working on a hopelessly faulty measurement of the earth's circumference, picked up from Toscanelli.

What is most interesting about this is that, in emulation of the Egyptians, the Greek Eratosthenes had made a far more accurate measurement. Nothing could show up more clearly the fatuity of the idea that time always brings progress—barring, of course, the hiccups of a few regrettable "dark ages." And once we have disposed of the progressivist fallacy we face the question: if Eratosthenes, seventeen centuries before Columbus, was so much better a geometer, why could not even earlier attempts to measure the earth have been as successful as Eratosthenes'? Or perhaps even more so? The Greek Eratosthenes cross-checked measurements in Egypt. We need to examine the evidence with an open mind, and in doing so we must not be put off by the fact that a great deal of nonsense has been talked about "the wisdom of the ancients." No sensible historian wants to be found in the company of those credulous believers who have persuaded themselves that all sorts of mysterious powers can be wielded by the initiate who has unlocked the Secret of the Pyramids or deciphered some old book on alchemy. Any number of self-deluding fantasies have been spun around this theme, but we must not be so anxious to distance ourselves from them that we fall into the contrary error of refusing to accept that there were ever any important matters on which very early cultures were better informed than people who came later. We do not have to credit them with pseudo-mystical powers. All we need do is remember that knowledge can be lost as well as gained, particularly in the periods of turmoil that have punctuated the histories of all peoples and particularly in times before the invention of writing. When a purely oral tradition was once interrupted it could never be recovered, and any discoveries it embodied had to be laboriously made all over again in a later age. Nor should we forget that each new ruling dynasty "rearranges the truth" after it has taken over—such as has happened in Eastern Europe but latterly. The persisting belief in a flat earth is a good example of the way in which knowledge can be lost or at least ignored. A seaman necessarily accepts that the earth is round: he only needs to look at the bending ocean skyline and to see how boats disappear and reappear as they sail away and sail back. Yet thousands of years after sea voyaging had begun, landsmen still held to the idea that the earth was flat. It is hard to believe that any predominantly seagoing culture, however early, was not in that respect far in advance of much later land-bound peoples: the Dutch South Africans are a case in point, with their president Paul Kruger at the start of this century firmly and irremediably convinced that the earth was flat.

Cylinder roller stamps of fired clay are still used by South American Indians to paint designs on their bodies[42] and are used in Nigeria to paint designs on pots. The beam scale was in use in Peru as in the Old World. Diffusion may be of ideas rather than things.

There is, then, no reason in principle to reject evidence that preliterate societies made accurate measurements of the earth and of the movements of the heavenly bodies. The question is, does such evidence exist? Unquestionably it does. Apart from the abstract evidence of ancient calendrical systems there are numerous significant remains that could not be more solid—the great megalithic monuments of Britain and northwest Europe, of Tiahuanaco and North America, of Algeria, South India, the Caroline Islands. A. Thom has made a detailed study of the stone circles of Britain,[9] notably Stonehenge, from which he concludes that they were essentially built as "calendar clocks"—sophisticated devices for computing date and time. It is now generally agreed that their construction was in some way governed by astronomy, and Thom believes that the builders used them to take sightings not only on the sun but also on the moon and on stars of the first magnitude. Behind the layout of these temple-observatories he sees an understanding of mathematics and astronomy of considerable sophistication, and he maintains that they were set out with an accuracy that today would require surveying equipment of some delicacy. He points out that the unit of measurement used in the layout of these circles varied by only 0.1 percent across the length and breadth of Britain, and he believes that they knew by 2000 B.C. that π was 22/7. He writes:

Bronze stand from Cyprus (after Schaeffer, Encomi-Alasia) with man carrying oxhide ingot and with the religious symbol of the sea god above him.

The oxhide type of metal ingot is shown in these illustrations, associated with the birdman on one seal from Cyprus.

> It is remarkable that 1000 years before the earliest mathematicians of classical Greece, people in these islands [Britain] not only had a practical knowledge of geometry and were capable of setting out elaborate geometrical designs but could also set out ellipses based on Pythagorean triangles. We need not be surprised to find that their calendar was a highly developed arrangement involving an exact knowledge of the length of the year or that they had set up many stations for observing the eighteen-year cycle of the lunar nodes.

According to Thom, the stone-circle calendar clocks of Britain were erected over a period of less than five hundred years, starting about 2800 B.C.;

PLATE 23
MEGALITHIC GROUP AT MESSA IN CYRENAICA (top). *Stone circle at Sillastani, Peru (below left). So-called Tomb of the King at Sine, Senegal (below right), showing the same type of stone circle on the Atlantic shore of Africa as was erected on the western shores of Britain. There are five hundred thousand stone circles in the Canadian province of Alberta alone. While most of them are tiny and may even have held down the edges of tents, aerial photography reveals that some were big, were accompanied by a bank and ditch, had a man-made mound inside them—and we must remember that the Creation Mound was the symbol that underlay both pyramid and ziggurat—and that there was a break in the mound and ditch at precisely the point where the sun's rays would first fall at the summer solstice. These Alberta circles enjoyed a central position at the village site.*[43] *Compare the trilithons of Stonehenge, Plate 19, with the trilithons of Cyrenaica and of Tonga in the Pacific, Plate 80. According to Leley and Roy Adkins, the earliest stone circles date from 3370–2670 B.C. and no stone circles were built after 1200 B.C.,*[44] *the termination of the Bronze Age. The* Dictionary of Archaeology *states that "true stone circles" were found only in Britain,*[45] *but this is to ignore North Africa and Senegal, let alone Tiahuanaco, the taulas, stone circles in Minorca, circles near Güstrow, at Boitrin in eastern Germany and a group of stone circles in Poland. There is also a megalithic alignment on the island of Sylt in eastern Germany.*[46] *Professor Colin Renfrew points out that the Hopi and Cherokee Indians had astronomical practices very similar to those in use at Stonehenge.*[47]

but other megalithic monuments go back much further in time. The dates presently given for the erection of these stone circles are from 3000–1200 B.C., dates that coincide with the beginning and end of the Bronze Age.

There are megaliths in Brittany that go back as far as 4800 B.C. and 5445 B.C.—beyond the earliest monuments of China, Egypt or Mesopotamia. Of course not all the earlier works were involved with astronomy, but we do know that over in Ireland, along the River Boyne, great megalithic mounds were raised in the Copper Age whose entrance passages and skylights were aligned with the sun, the moon and the planet Venus at the solstice or equinox.

One event that some megalithic circles were apparently built to predict was the lunar eclipse. As with early astronomy in general, so in this particular instance we have to ask why anyone should have wanted to know about them. Again, we can put it down to superstition and a wish to overawe the ignorant masses, but a much more practical reason can be given. In a world without mechanical clocks and without any means (such as radio or telephone) of transmitting messages almost simultaneously over a long distance, the lunar eclipse is about the only event that provides a time signal over a large part of the earth. Using that signal, observers can take sightings on identical stars from different places at the same moment, and so develop accurate and mathematical cartography. No one armed with that technique would have made Columbus's blunder.

One strong indication that megalithic calendar clocks were used in the service of navigation lies in their siting. They are ranged along the western and northern edges of Europe, where they enjoy a climate that is conspicuously unsuited to astronomy, but where they are close to the coasts from which sailors would have set out on transatlantic voyages or on which they would have landed after coming up from the Mediterranean. It is also worth noticing that water clocks, clepsydras, were used by the Sumerians in the fourth millennium B.C.[10]

Thom reckons that there are between five thousand and ten thousand megaliths of all kinds in the British Isles. There are a few in the south of Ireland and they become more common as one goes north, up the west of Scotland to the Hebrides, Orkneys and Shetland. (The second largest stone circle, after Stonehenge, is at Callanish at the northwestern end of the Hebrides, on the island of Lewis.) Only a small number of them belong among Thom's calendar clocks, but they are evidence that the culture or cultures that built them looked toward the sea. We also know that the custom of building with huge stones—with megaliths—first began along the Atlantic shore of Europe. Many of the megalithic monuments carry symbols used by Mediterranean sailors: for example, the geometrical patterns on the rock at New Grange, near the River Boyne in Ireland, find their closest parallels in the art of Iberia. It is also notable that the siting of megalithic monuments on the west of the British Isles coincides with the gold of Wicklow and the principal copper deposits, nearly all in the west of Britain, which were worked out during the Bronze Age. Cyclopean stone structures were erected, not only by the Mycenaeans in Greece but also by the citizens of Peru. In Ireland Knowth, erected 3500 B.C., is clearly a calendar structure by the River Boyne.

We can therefore say two things with fair certainty. First, the stone circles and some other megalithic structures, whatever other reasons there may have been for building them, had as one important function the computing of dates and times. Second, they were erected by peoples who were in contact with the sea and with sailors. It is therefore highly likely that they were used to aid cartography and navigation and no equally plausible explanation has been proposed. Given the accuracy with which they were built, it seems probable that the system of navigation they served was itself far more precise than conventional accounts of early peoples ever allow. The earliest date for the erection of a megalith is 5445 B.C. in Brittany. The great alignments there are at Carnac, a name that is a palindrome of *anak*, the Babylonian word for bronze. Brittany possesses small deposits of tin and copper. Glyn Daniel writes: "It is not, therefore, surprising that in South Brittany there should develop a number of non-funerary megalithic monuments—the great stone avenues—which are without parallel in Western Europe."[11] I think we must consider whether they did not mark, because of their date and their place, the scene of the creation, where the Aryans began to take over from the matriarchs: the patriarchal societies that worshipped a male god in heaven, not the Great Goddess under the earth. Before the area was called Carnac, it was called Men; to be compared with the Aryan Manu and the name Menhir.

This chapter has, I hope, shown that—to say the least—it is not foolish to believe that even before the Copper Age long-distance voyaging was possible. The three vital necessities were ships, favorable winds and currents, and a knowledge of the sea and of navigation. The previous chapter showed that Copper and Bronze Age people had a powerful motive for setting out on a very widespread system of trade; but even if they had the means and the motive, the big question still remains: what evidence is there that they actually did voyage out across the world ocean? In looking for the traces they left behind, we shall start with the most important of their destinations: America. For it can scarcely be argued by my critics that the ancients walked from the Mediterranean to America.

Professor Alexander Thom points out that there are thousands of stone circles in Britain, nearly all in the north and west of the island. We know that there is one on the Senegal River, also, perhaps, the New Hampshire medicine wheel, one twelve thousand feet up in the Andes by Tiahuanaco, close to the great silver mines, several in Algeria. At the beginning of our book, then, we repeat: why this pattern, this distribution, why the extraordinary concentration on the west and the north of Britain?

The tiny Orkney Islands in the north of Scotland boast prehistoric monuments unsurpassed in Britain or in continental Europe. Also consider that Mesolithic man would have depended for sustenance on fishing, hunting and plant collecting, of which only fishing could take place on any great scale in the Orkneys. Yet there were on these small islands 150 barrows and cairns and nearly one hundred short cists. Why the capital investment? The question is not asked.

That you could make your fortune out of one voyage is stated in the *Odyssey*. Homer writes: "He showed me all the treasure that Odysseus had gathered, bronze, and gold, and iron, wrought with toil; verily unto the tenth generation would it feed his children after him, so great was the wealth that lay stored for him in the halls of the king."[12] This, seemingly, after philandering for seven years with Calypso!

That this trade continued into Roman times will become steadily clearer as this book proceeds. Plutarch (46–120 A.D.) records that Sertorius had met sailors who had returned from two Atlantic Islands ten thousand stadia from Africa.[13] Theopompus of Chios, born c. 380 B.C., makes Silenus describe the Meropids as dwelling on a continent beyond Africa and the islands of the ocean, in a land with cities, where gold and silver are so common that they have less value than iron. While Plutarch, in his essay "On the Face in the Moon's Orb," refers to Greeks settled on the great continent beyond the Atlantic.[14] Posidonius suggests that the story of Atlantis is possibly not an invention. Socrates says bluntly that the Atlantis story "has the very great advantage of being a fact and not a fiction."[15] Diodorus Siculus refers to "the islands of the Ocean. There is a very great island towards Africk, of sundry days sailing. . . ."[16]

All this, quite simply, corresponds with the discovery of numerous Roman artifacts in America, a Roman galley sunk off the coast of Brazil, Seneca's celebrated reference to land the other side of the Atlantic Ocean and so on. It seems likely that when some of the Phoenicians returned to the Mediterranean after the collapse of the bronze trade, founding Utica and Carthage, some of the Atlas people will have returned to base themselves in Italy, Atalia: hence the similar and hideous gladiatorial games of Aztec and Romans; the decimal system used by both; the eagle, the symbol for the legions in both countries. Under these circumstances, the memory of America could never, to the two trading peoples, have been lost. Amerindians are brown-skinned. The Greeks used the term Phoenician, meaning redmen, for the different clans of Western Semites. So the term Red Indian may have derived from this long period of Phoenician government across large parts of America.

3. The Huge Islands in the Middle of Ocean

"Ocean, whose waters encompass the whole world."
HOMER, *Odyssey*

For thousands of years in prehistoric time events of America and the Old World were interlinked, this book will argue. Without reference to the transatlantic trade in copper and alluvial tin one cannot begin to understand the cultures and events of the Fertile Crescent between 6000 and 1000 B.C.; nor can one make sense of American prehistory. One day it will be possible to write the story of that commerce in greater detail. At present we are looking at the broad outline. Although the evidence available to us today is fragmentary and dispersed, it is conclusive in demonstrating that there was a long and influential relationship between the Old and the New Worlds. There are simply too many facts for which no other explanation is coherent, and in this and the following chapters we shall be reviewing them. It will be useful to start by giving a brief outline of the story into which it seems to me the fragments fit.

Somewhere around 40,000 B.C. it is accepted that the first people began to move into America. The Mongols, the first discoverers of America, came across the land bridge that then joined Alaska to the eastern tip of Siberia, and they moved south down the coast and across the plains until they had spread right across the northern continent. In time they passed through the narrow neck of Panama and occupied the southern continent also. These first people had been in America for the better part of thirty thousand years before they acquired the arts of agriculture: the earliest agriculture has been found both in Peru and on the Pacific coast of Mexico where, about 7000 B.C., red peppers, avocados, squash and gourds were being cultivated. Possibly the people who brought agriculture to America did so by crossing the Pacific from the west. By c.7000 B.C. the bottle gourd, *Lagenaria siceraria*, indigenous to Africa or India, begins to be used on the Pacific coast of America. It was clearly a useful plant and would seem to be one that the agriculturalists took with them. At c.7000 B.C. it was also in use in Thailand, found in the Spirit Cave and in Mexico.[1]

The vital step out of the Stone Age into the first age of metals, the Copper Age, would seem to have been taken at Isle Royale, for the only large-scale source of pure copper was around Lake Superior. The first workings there date, I believe, from nearly 6000 B.C., recalibrated by dendrochronology, and again it seems certain that an outside influence was at work: the copper was for export. Even if the native Americans had begun to make extensive use of copper at a far later date, the full and continued exploitation of the deposits was undertaken by mariners and traders from across the Atlantic. The evidence is that they chiefly used the "stepping-stone" route from the Irish Sea and northwest Europe. This takes the sailor by a series of hops, none more than a few hundred miles long, from the British Isles, past Iceland and Greenland to the North American coast. Like the route further south between the Canary Islands and South America, it could have been followed by quite simple ships, certainly during the period of mild climate in the North Atlantic that prevailed from about 6000 B.C.

The next landmark that we can make out is the appearance of cotton in Peru around 3600 B.C. and in Mexico around 4000 B.C. This is far earlier than its first known use in India, 2400 B.C. The cotton grown in America was a hybrid between a Southeast Asian cotton and a native American cotton, and thus also points to transpacific contacts. By 3000 B.C. the Chinese were farming with an indigenous American plant, the peanut.

Later, copper and alluvial tin from the Andes and Amazonia respectively became so important and continued to be important for so long that the area became the center of attention for trading peoples, and its civilization was the source and inspiration of much that followed in other American cultures, for example from Bolivia crossing the Andes to Peru.

The first prospectors to reach the Americas were earth-worshipping peoples from around the Black Sea and their breakaway masculine group whom the Greeks knew as Heracles, the hero the Celts knew as the God Ogmios and the Phoenicians as the god Moloch. They were followed later by patriarchal sky worshippers whom the Greeks called Ouranos, and the Mesopotamians Anu.

We have record that in the third millennium, when supplies of tin ran out in Sumer, Sargon the Great mounted an expedition to the west to secure overseas supplies. Here, strikingly, the history of America has to be seen as a function of Old World history, with the dominant Old World state controlling the American supplies and deriving much of its power from America. After the fall of the Sumerian city-states in 2003 B.C., control passed to the Babylonians and Assyrians, with their suppliers the Phoenician and Aegean mariners. For a long time the Cretans were also a dominant power in this matter. The relationship of the cities of Syria and

Canaan to the great land power Assyria would seem to resemble today's China and Hong Kong.

During the second millennium the Mycenaeans developed colonies in America. The city of Tiahuanaco, twelve thousand feet up in the Andes, has a name that resembles the Greek Linear B, *teo wanak*, which means in Mycenaean Greek god-king, while the city on top of the wonderful silver mines, Potosí, resembles the Sumerian equivalent for their priest-king, i.e. *patesi*. These Andean silver mines were incredibly productive. In Mexico the chief was called *uinic*.[2] Subsequently, various sea peoples joined as allies in a struggle that was one of the great turning points in world history. The Peoples of the Sea attacked Egypt, the Hittites, Ugarit and other Phoenician ports. In the war that followed, the Mycenaean civilization was destroyed, broken in a last battle in Egypt in 1182 B.C.

Due to the arrival of the steelmaking process, the American trade in copper and bronze was largely ended. It was not merely the disruption caused by war, it was the bankruptcy of the bronze traders, the *anakim* of the Bible, caused by technical progress. During the forty-five years the struggle had lasted, the Bronze Age itself had been coming to an end. This was the first great war partly fought with weapons forged from what was to be the material of the future, steel. The Age of Iron had begun, known at the time as "the terrible coming of iron."

The first evidence of iron being used for weapons and tools—we are not talking of meteoric iron—is in Anatolia around 2000 B.C., and by 1200 it had come into general use among the Mediterranean peoples. The first iron—in fact a primitive form of steel—was not superior to bronze: it was just much more readily available, i.e. cheaper. Iron mines are common in the Old World and as soon as men were able to smelt the ore they had a source of raw material for tools, and above all for weapons, that did not depend on distant voyages. The balance of forces swung decidedly in favor of the great land powers and away from the seagoing peoples who had previously controlled their access to the essential metals on which their civilization depended. It was this that made the Peoples of the Sea, a syndicate of half a dozen multinationals of their day, turn against the land powers, in an attempt to regain by military means the wealth they had previously earned by their command of transoceanic trade. Iron supplied the democratic weapon.

At this point the intimate link between America and the Mediterranean is weakened. Some trading on a far smaller scale did still go on: the inscriptions on the rocks in the Americas prove this; also witnessed by various finds, including Hebrew coins and Celtic, Semitic, Indian rock inscriptions, and the remains of Roman galleys found off the coast. No doubt over the centuries a number of ships also drifted or were blown westward across the Atlantic, as must have happened from time to time in the past. As more sailors learned to read and write more rock inscriptions would appear in America.

It is interesting that the use of iron never became common in America. The American cultures continued to use copper and bronze, perhaps simply because there were such plentiful supplies, but perhaps also because iron is not a good material for a subtropical climate: it rusts too quickly. Furthermore, the Maya did not use any metals, or so archaeology presently suggests.

Columbus sailed into the Caribbean, not the first but the last in a long line of exploratory mariners—perhaps he was the most ignorant as well as the most destructive in his results of all these mariners. Within a few years the Atlantic was again being crossed and recrossed by people from the east, but these latecomers were not peaceful traders who brought an enlightened civilization with them. They came to loot and to enslave, and what they brought were guns, bigotry and epidemic disease. The modern European reign of terror had begun.

When the Spaniards arrived they encountered—and destroyed—three main civilizations, the Aztecs, the Maya and the Incas. The Aztecs, under their emperor Montezuma, were ruling over a large part of Mexico, which they had conquered two centuries previously when they invaded the declining Toltec empire. (The Toltecs were essentially the same people as the Olmecs, Toltec being the name by which they were known in America and Olmec the name given by European archaeologists, meaning "the Rubber People." Toltec culture lasted from 1500 B.C. or a little earlier until it was overthrown in the thirteenth century A.D. by the Aztecs.) The name Atl was that of the creator-god in Ancient Mexico. It also meant water in the Mexican language Nahuatl. Can this similarity to Altas and the Atlantic be chance?

The Aztecs were a notoriously cruel people whose decadent religion demanded the mass sacrifice of many thousands of human victims. Nevertheless, despite this savagery, the Aztecs did still retain many traditions that had originated in far earlier times with the cultured and gentle Toltecs: a people who professed to sacrifice butterflies rather than human beings or animals. The Aztecs liked to trace their origins back to their far more civilized Toltec predecessors.

South of the Aztecs, in Guatemala, were the Maya. The Mayan empire, originating by their own dating in 3113 B.C., August 10, began to break up around A.D. 900 and by the time the Spaniards arrived had splintered into a number of tribes. The Maya dated the commencement of their empire to the day on which four white gods, four white culture heroes, Bacabs, arrived with their shiploads of sailors across the Atlantic "to escape the Flood."

In Peru the Spaniards encountered the Incas. When they arrived the

PLATE 24
EUROPEAN-STYLE HEADS FROM TIAHUANACO. *Stone heads of the first period of Tiahuanaco encased in the walls. They appear more European than Amerindian. In Mycenaean Greek* teo *means god and* wanak *means ruler. The Canary Islands were an important stopping-off point for sailors taking the middle passage to America. In the language of the Canary Islands, Guanch,* guanac *means the state, which, with a soft g, links both Linear B and the Andean city. In Guanch* eheide *denotes the ancient islanders. In the Canary Islands they mummified corpses as in Egypt and Peru; in all three places some of the mummies had blond hair. At Cuzco in Peru was the Coricancha, meaning "town of gold," a temple whose inner and outer walls were covered with plates of pure gold. The temple looked down on a garden whose trees and even the garden implements were made of precious metals, much as described in both Ezekiel and in the Gilgamesh epic.[1] In ancient Mexico mummification was also practiced. In Tiahuanaco they built with cyclopean stone walls of fitted masonry as I have myself seen at Mycenae, and in both places trapezoid doors were used. In ancient times there was mining for tin around Tiahuanaco on a very big scale and agricultural terraces right up the mountains.[2] The Andes rise almost as high as the Himalayas and so the Netherworld was known as the Great Mountain.*

Incan empire was huge: one writer has claimed with excessive exaggeration that the territory conquered by the later Incas was of greater extent than the Roman Empire.[3] It was also immensely rich. When the Spaniards conquered Cuzco they are said to have looted from that one city more gold than the whole of Europe then possessed. The Incas were the last inheritors of a tradition that, despite breaks and disruptions, stretched back many thousand years. The Spanish barbarians wrecked a civilization in which firm, just rule and strict private morality seem to have prevailed, and in my estimation the reason for this was that the Incas had managed to preserve the moral heart of their long tradition. They were, if you like, a fossil society whose manners traced back to the real Golden Age. In Sumerian *En* means "Lord of" and *Kur* was the Sumerian name for the Americas and for mountain, hence perhaps *Enkur*, spelled Inca today.

Like other American cultures, these three that were still in existence when the Spaniards arrived, were all ultimately interconnected. The logic for Tiahuanaco's existence, as we saw in Chapter 1, was the coincidence of silver mines, copper mines, tin, and a virtually inexhaustible supply of timber for the charcoal used to smelt the metals and to form them into ingots. There was also gold, but it was the production and use of bronze that made South America and the Fertile Crescent the twin poles of the ancient world during the Bronze Age. What in scale Brazil is to Portugal, the American colonies of those days became to their mother countries.

The obvious objection to this idea is the sheer distance of these mines from their customers east of the Mediterranean, and in particular the fact that they were separated from the Atlantic coast of South America by almost the entire width of the continent. Once again this objection becomes much less formidable if we remember the comparative ease of water transport. As the map on Plate 26 shows, the headwaters of the Amazon and its tributaries reach within a hundred miles of Lake Titicaca. So, too, do those of the River Paraná, which runs southeastward to empty into the Atlantic at Buenos Aires, from where the traders could make use of the South Atlantic circle of winds and currents shown in the map on Plate 77. The Amazon today is navigable by steamers for most of its length and, owing to the extraordinary flatness of its drainage basin, anyone following the right tributary is within two hundred miles of Lake Titicaca before he has risen six hundred feet. The river passes over a number of rapids and is subject to floods, but it would have provided a perfectly usable route down to the sea from the mines in the Andes. We should also remember that while bronze may be heavy cargo, it is also a compact one; when cast into ingots it is easily handled and stowed. To the north the Amazon system is connected to the Orinoco via the Casiquiare canal. The annual discharge of the Amazon is five times that of the Congo, twelve times that of the Mississippi.

If it seems strange that an important center of a civilization should have been at such a height, more than twelve thousand feet above sea level, the first answer is simply the excellence of the supplies of metal nearby. They are some of the biggest deposits of silver, copper and alluvial tin anywhere in the world. Think of the reason for Johannesburg's existence in South Africa. Another answer is that the place was highly defensible, and however benevolent the relationship between traders and natives, it would be unrealistic to suppose that defense was never important. Despite its height, Tiahuanaco was able to support a productive agriculture. As the map on Plate 41 shows, at one time or another a large area of land was brought under cultivation. A system of ridged fields covered two hundred thousand acres, and in general the lakeside people became expert in terraced agriculture (essential on steeply sloping sites) and in irrigation. The coastal plain of Peru is largely desert, but when it is efficiently irrigated it can produce three crops a year, as can the coastal region of Mexico. This very fertile Peruvian coast could have been an additional source of food for the great mining complex two or three hundred miles away in the mountains. And the sea, because of the cold Antarctic current, is prodigiously rich in fish.

The earliest settlement at Titicaca was probably on an island in the lake, the Island of the Sun, but later the city at the center of it all was Tiahuanaco. The ruins of the city now lie twelve miles from the lake but it is clear that when it was built it was on or near the shore: the remains of a dock or mole have been excavated. On the landward side the place was defended by a large moat, for which the stone was partly taken from an island in the lake. From the ruins that have been found it is also clear that the city must originally have covered a very large area.[4]

An interesting question is how the system of trade worked between the great center of metal production and the consuming countries east of the Mediterranean. What did the traders bring to America in exchange for what they took away? The short answer is: people. Rather than carry boatloads of trade goods for six or eight thousand miles on the westward journey it was far easier to take the craftsmen who could make the necessary things on site. The potter is less fragile than his pots, and weighs very much less than his own output over a lifetime. Still more importantly the incomers brought administration. They organized a new and far more civilized way of life in the places where they settled and formed the ruling class. So long as they provided the native workers with the necessities of life, food security, life to a higher standard than they had enjoyed on their own, who was to stop them shipping the output of the tin and copper mines wherever they wished? It would be surprising if there had never been any attempts at rebellion, but for the most part the American Indians probably knew when they were well off. The sea peoples brought with them what must have

A ceramic figure from Tiahuanaco resembling an Asian Indian. In the island of Lanzerote is a place called Tabayesco, to be compared with the Mayan Tabasco: there is a Gorgano on Tenerife to be compared with the Gorgon Islands off northwest South America: the Canary Island goddess of women is Moheira or Mohebe; compare this with the Greek goddess Hera or the west Semitic goddess Eve. The high god in Peru was Pachacamak, in the Canaries he was called Achahu Canac. Pachacamak was "he who controlled the whole universe." Textiles first appear in Peru about 4500 B.C.[3] In next-door Paraguay, the Amerindians worshipped three male gods called Ursana, perhaps the Greek Ouranos in trinitarian form, and the goddess Quipoli, surely an akawa *name. The god was a solar divinity, trinitarian, and had had a virgin birth.[4] Of the white god in South America Pierre Honoré writes: "To the Chibchas he was Bochicha, to the Aymara Hyustus, and to this day they will tell you that he was fair and had blue eyes."[5]*

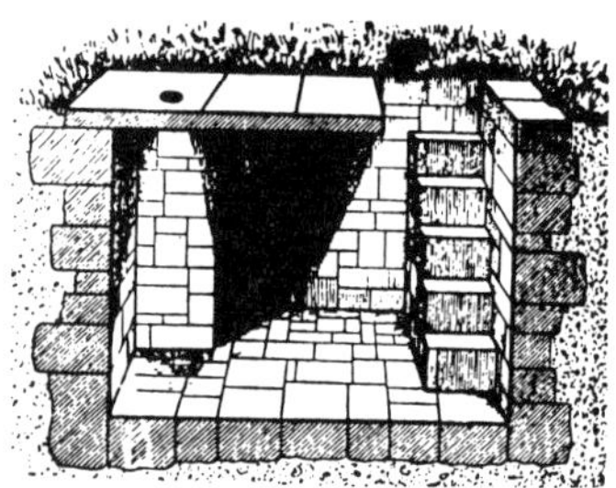

Plate 25

An identical Egyptian-Tiahuanaco custom. *The ceiling of this Tiahuanaco death chamber shows the same small hole for the bird of death present in the burial ritual of the Egyptians. Potosí, near Tiahuanaco, produces silver, tin, copper and lead.*[6] *Harold Osborne, writing on the two Peruvian tribes of the Andes, the Aymarás and the Quechuas, says: "Yet allowing for all distortion one cannot but be profoundly surprised by the many similarities between early Andean and medieval European belief and practice in all aspects of sorcery, divination, demonology, necromancy and other forms of intercourse with the marginal, spiritual forces. It is astonishing indeed that beliefs and practices so similar grew up among branches of the human race out of contact for twenty millennia."*[7] *The silver of the Potosí mines was sufficient to be able to make a bridge one yard wide that would stretch from Potosí to Spain.*[8] *The god of the silver mines was called Tio*[9]*—compare this to the Latin* deus, *Greek* theos, *Mycenaean* teo. *The older Peruvian and Bolivian megaliths were very similar to those in Britain and Brittany.*[10] *In brief, the Incas had traditions of the Creation, the Flood and of a god, Vira Cocha, some of whose acts were very similar to those of Jesus Christ,*[11] *including walking on water. In Greek Linear B* teowanak *means God-king; in Mexico* halach uinic *means warrior chief.*[12]

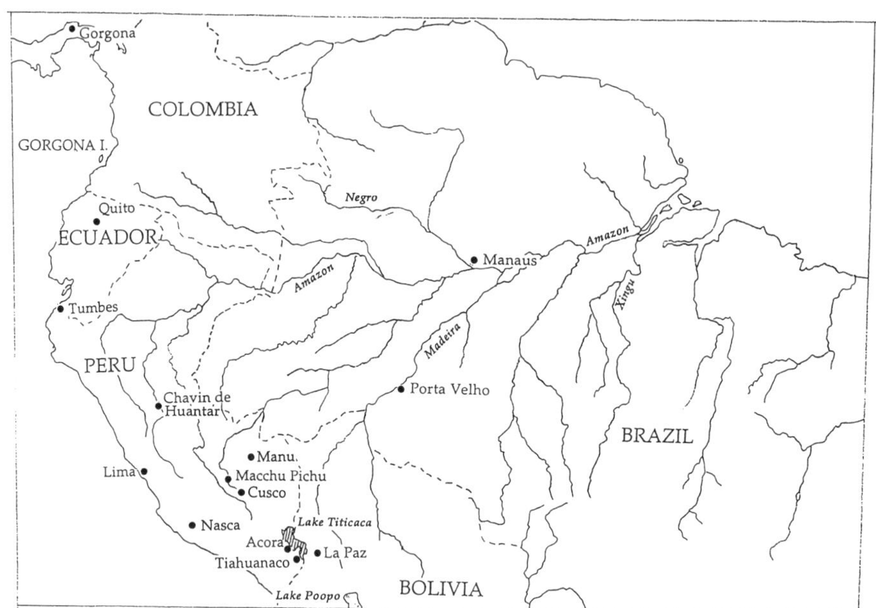

seemed like a magically higher level of technology. It was natural to accept their rule. Through religion the rulers identified with the colonized and formed coherent nations.

Another interesting question concerns the things the traders did not bring. When the idea of contacts between the Old and New Worlds is raised, one of the standard objections is the absence in America of such important inventions as glass and the arch.

That, then, is a broad picture of how the transoceanic trade in metals affected the history of America. We now come to the central question: what evidence is there that any of this actually happened? Are we dealing in realities or just spinning stories? I repeat: we must remember from the very start that the ocean is not yet susceptible to archaeology, we must listen to the shores.

In assessing all this it is useful to start by asking ourselves what kind of evidence we can hope to find. For most of our period there was no written history, and for much of it no writing at all. It was followed by a time of great disruption, "the terrible coming of iron," in which most written records were destroyed and oral traditions were bound to be interrupted. Before we reach a period from which anything like systematic records have survived, more than a thousand turbulent years have passed. It is as if our knowledge of Periclean Athens rested on a study of the anecdotes current among ninth-century friars.

We should also remember what kind of thing popular traditions deal with. They do not cover generalities, but particular events and heroic acts.

PLATE 26

***THE MAP OF AMAZONIA** (opposite), with its gold, silver, copper and tin, along with so many rock inscriptions in a great variety of early Iron Age and Bronze Age scripts. Panama is only forty miles across from the Atlantic to the Pacific, so it was not too burdensome for sailors arriving from one ocean subsequently to set out on the other. The first Spaniards to sail down the Amazon described meeting, living by the river, a tribe of Negroes who were cannibals, and white and martial women with long hair down to their waists, the Amazons, then ruled by their queen, Conori. In the flood season the Amazon, the Orinoco, the La Plata are all interconnectable by boat. Both the Africans and the Amazons had much gold and silver: the Africans using stone knives but living off gold and silver plate.[13] Mrs. Anna Roosevelt has recently discovered pottery by the Amazon going back to around 6000 B.C.[14] There were until recent times African Amazon warriors in Benin state. The Amazon has wonderful supplies of fish and there are ten times as many fish species in the Amazon basin as in the whole of Europe's rivers put together.*

Map of South American archaeological sites with the Amazonian approach route. It is over this area that Bernardo da Silva Ramos, who was born in Manaus, recorded his great variety of Old World scripts carved on the rocks, some of which we reproduce later. On the island at the mouth of the Amazon, ancient Cretan-type pottery has been found. In Ecuador of the third millennium B.C. identical pottery was in use as in Japan of the same date: and Ecuador is at the receiving end of the Pacific countercurrent. Among the Maya uinic *meant chief.[15] Toward the northwest of Amazonia was a subtribe of the Arawak called Kabiyeri: name to be compared with the Mediterranean sailors' gods called the Cabiri.[16] Friar Gaspar de Carvajal described the first trip down the Amazon by Pizarro's men and their meeting with Indians who worship a sun god called Chise.[17] Tradition claimed that Peru was the land where one does not die.[18] Compare this Amerindian tradition with the identical tradition of Ireland, of Mesopotamia, of Japan about the land in the middle of Ocean. At Pacosal, on the Amazon island of Marajo, we find double urns and ex-voto clay ships, as in the Old World.[19] As this book proceeds it will become clearer that down the Amazon were shipped the biggest supplies of bronze for the Bronze Age Mediterranean. In Guiana the medicinemen used the very specialized little instrument, the bull-roarer, to frighten away evil spirits. This peculiar instrument was used in all parts of the world. For the presence on the river of both black people and of Amazons—in addition to the evidence of Friar Carvajal and Orellana—is the later evidence from the German Ulrich Schmidt, traveling between 1535 and 1552, and of Hernando de Ribera, given before a notary under oath.[20]*

The Yurupari of northwest Amazonia—like the Arawaks and Barasana—have a sacred ritual where the men whip each other, as with the Yoruba of western Nigeria. And both use bull-roarers.

The true source of the Amazon is the river Vilcanota, surely an anaku *or bronze root to its name. Diodorus Siculus wrote, with complete accuracy, that the Amazons in his day were living in the remote west on an island called Hesperia.[21] And that they were on the Thermidon River there, he adds.[22] The Sumerian for river is* Buranun, *which has been suggested as the origin of the name Peru.*

We should not be surprised that no general history of prehistoric navigation was handed down. The Norse sagas do not give a general account of Viking invasions and settlements in North America, just as popular culture today contains no information on the tonnages of shipping passing through Liverpool docks but vividly remembers the first man to sail solo around the world. The tradition of long-distance sailing was in fact handed down in folk memory—in oral literature—and stated by maritime peoples around the world.

The first evidence we shall look at consists of the legends that were current on both sides of the Atlantic, those in the Old World concerning a land beyond the ocean, and those in America that told of the coming of strange white peoples from the east. Let me stress that I do not believe that a legend can in itself be a proof of this or any other historical theory. It can only be a pointer, directing our attention to interesting possibilities. A body of legends becomes a significant part of the proof only when it jibes with the concrete finds of archaeology. Archaeology without legend is blind: legend without archaeology is guesswork.

Many of the legends on the eastern side of the Atlantic have come down to us through Classical Greece and Rome—though of course it does not at all follow that they originated there. One that did not reach us through that route is the Jewish account in Genesis of the rivers of paradise, which was mentioned earlier, and which provides the title to this book. We can now see why it was important to list the minerals that were to be found on the first river, Pishon (perhaps alias the Amazon), and why the Americas were so persistently known as the Paradise Land. So important were the metals that the history of the world, as we have seen, was distinguished by them: the Age of Gold, the Age of Silver, the Age of Bronze and the terrible Age of Iron. And perhaps the even more terrible age of uranium is to come!

An earlier record of a visit to America was noted in Chapter 1, the account of Sargon's expedition to the "Tin Land" of the west when supplies of tin ran out in Sumer. What makes the connection between this expedition and the great mining center on Lake Titicaca still more likely is that, as the Verrills write:

> In the innumerable inscriptions dealing with Sumerian history frequent references are made to the "Lake of Manu" sometimes associated with a "cloud lake," and usually designated as being in the "Mountains of the Sunset," a semi-fabulous or traditionary land which, apparently, the Sumerian explorers were seeking on the voyages to the "Sunset Land."[5]

Lake Titicaca is the only lake that fits the description and the most ancient remains of pre-Incan civilization are those on the Island of the Sun at Tiahuanaco.

The Egyptian myth of the defeat of Osiris goes back a thousand years earlier than the final destruction of the Sumerians. Osiris, the god of the Osiris dynasty, was remembered as the great creator-god of Egyptian culture and he was said to have taken civilization around the world. It is interesting to note that the dates of the real Osiris seem to coincide with the first cultivation of cotton in Peru (about 3600 B.C.). Cotton, as we shall see, is a particularly significant crop, and there is little doubt that at the time of Osiris some contact between Egypt and America took place. In fact, Egyptian tradition is explicit that when the Set people booted the Osiris dynasty out of Egypt, the Osiris people established themselves in America and ruled there. That was in the *Tuat*, the place where the sun was at midnight, the Paradise Land. Tradition said that both Isis and Osiris were children of Chronos, which supports the belief that it was Mesopotamians who put together united Egypt.

It was from Egypt, if we are to believe Plato, that the legend of Atlantis came to Greece. In the *Timaeus* Plato describes how Solon, the great Athenian law giver, visited Egypt and was instructed in history:

> One of the priests, who was of a very great age, said: O Solon, Solon, you Hellenes are never anything but children, and there is not an old man among you. Solon in return asked him what he meant. I mean to say, he replied, there is no old opinion handed down among you by ancient tradition, nor any science which is hoary with age.[6]

The reason given for this by the priest was that periodic calamities had overtaken Greece and broken the continuity of its traditions—which indeed they had—though his account of great conflagrations caused by the heavenly bodies cannot be taken literally but perhaps should be looked on as droughts. The more stable society of Egypt had retained far older memories, he claimed, and among them was that of Atlantis, a huge island that lay in an ocean so big that the Mediterranean formed only a kind of harbor to the ocean.

In the *Critias* Plato returns to the subject of Atlantis and gives more detailed descriptions of it. It was, he says, "an island greater in extent than Libya and Asia,"[7] that is, in present-day terms, Africa and Eurasia, and can therefore hardly be identified with the seventy-five acres of little Thera of the Mediterranean, much as the universities enjoy doing so. Quite obviously no one could have supposed that an island of anything remotely like Atlantis was to be found in the Mediterranean, least of all could it be Thera. The entire Mediterranean Sea could not possibly have contained it. Other Greek writers also stress the huge size of this island beyond the sea. In the fourth century B.C., for example, Theopompus wrote of it as "an island of immense extent."[8] There is only one land beyond the Atlantic that qualifies for these descriptions and that is America, the two Americas, both North and South.

Aristotle, too, writes of an island, many days' sail from the Pillars of Heracles, which he describes as fertile and wooded and crossed by navigable rivers, and later various Roman writers also referred to it. Statius Sebosus correctly puts it at forty days' sail from the Canary Islands, and there is a glowing account of it by Diodorus Siculus:

> There lies out in the deep off Libya an island of considerable size and situated as it is in the ocean it is distant from Libya a voyage of a number of days to the west. Its land is fruitful, much of it being mountainous and not a little being a level plain of surpassing beauty. Through it flow navigable

> rivers which are used for irrigation and the island contains many parks planted with trees of every variety and gardens in great multitudes which are traversed by streams of sweet water; on it also are private villas of costly construction, and throughout the gardens banqueting houses have been constructed in a setting of flowers, and in them the inhabitants pass their time during the summer season, since the land supplies in abundance everything which contributes to enjoyment and luxury. . . . And, speaking generally, the climate of this island is so altogether mild that it produces in abundance the fruits of the trees and the other seasonal fruits for the larger part of the year, so that it would appear that the island, because of its exceptional felicity, were a dwelling place of a race of gods and not of men.[9]

South America is in fact only a thousand miles from West Africa, the length of the Mediterranean, as we have seen, so it presents no great hardship to get there. Some ancient writers seem to have been discussing the Sargasso Sea, where the seaweed, growing upon the waves, "holds the ship back like bushes."[10]

Such extravagant praise of America has done much to discredit the idea that Atlantis was a real place. Since no real country is ever quite so perfect, we jump too easily to the conclusion that the whole thing was a fairy story. But this does not follow. To most agriculturalists, a land that is capable of raising three crops a year, as the coastal plains of Peru and Mexico could do, must seem fertile and luxurious beyond any ordinary expectation. It could easily happen that reports of such a country, distant and mysterious but still real, should become confused with that recurring belief in a land of the blessed that is common in many societies, often as a home for the dead. It is best to see descriptions of, say, the Elysian Fields in both these ways. On the one hand they give a mythical account of the perfect land all peoples yearn to believe in; but then, mixed up with that, is a recognition that there was a real America (or Atlantis) that real men had sailed to. The asphodel was a plant associated in tradition with the Elysian Fields. According to the *Encyclopaedia Britannica*, the asphodel is to be found around the Mediterranean and in California.

It would have been particularly easy among sun-worshipping peoples for this distinction between belief and reality to become blurred. Where does the sun go when it sets, and where is it before it rises? Obviously in some far country to the west or east. Since, as we shall see, sun worship coincided with a growth in world trading, the confusion would have been easy. The Egyptians called the home of the midnight sun the *Tuat*, and they placed it in the east during the period when their trading was largely in the east, and in the west when they turned toward the Atlantic. It should not surprise us that Osiris was said to rule over it, nor that the other name for it, *Khenti-Amenti*, means Field of Reeds, a very appropriate name for the shore of Titicaca, where reeds grow in profusion and boats are made from them.

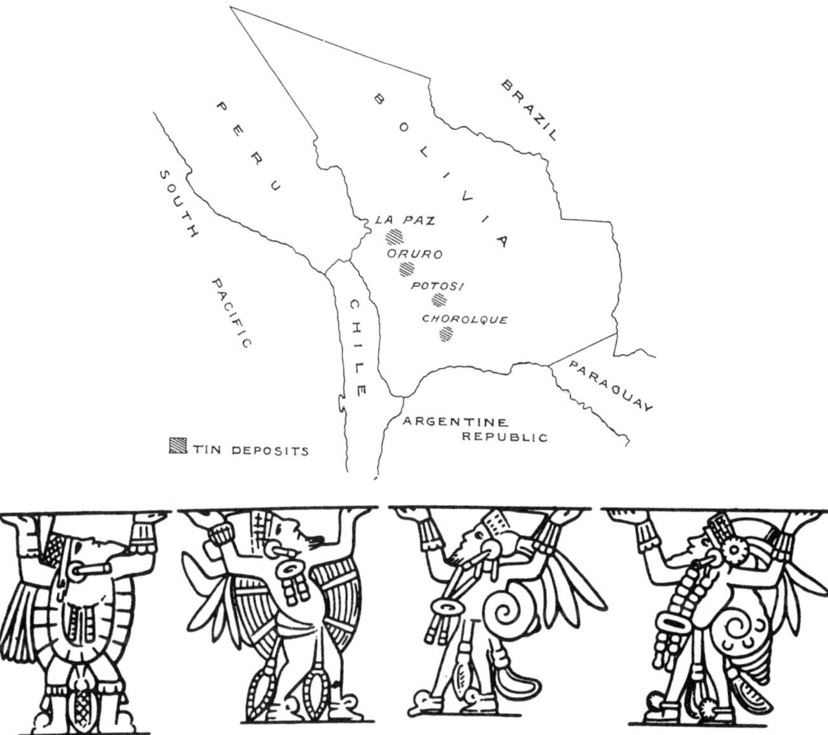

PLATE 27

TIN DEPOSITS OF BOLIVIA. *There is a place called Llallagua in the heart of the Bolivian mining country, a name which would seem to combine* agua, *a Poseidon name, with an Atlas name.*

THE FOUR BACABS, *set at the four sides of the world to hold up the sky. Each wears his insignia—a turtleshell, a spider web and two kinds of shell—seemingly snail shells. The Bacabs wear special loincloths and are usually bearded Atlas figures. These four are from columns in the Castillo at Chichén Itzá. Fray Bernardino de Sahagún wrote in his* Florentine Codex *that in ancient Mexico, on an eclipse, the Aztecs hunted out men with fair hair and white faces to sacrifice to the sun. The ancient Egyptians did the same. Culture heroes, once they lost political control, became vulnerable.*[23] *Sahagún goes on to say that the Toltecs "like the inhabitants of Babylon, were wise, learned, experienced." Some of them had been the inhabitants of Babylon in simple fact. Thrones, litters, scepters, crowns, purple for royalty, were all shared by the Old World and the New. Franciscan missionary Sahagún, in the sixteenth century, recorded the song of Quetzalcóatl, Toltec god of Mexico:*

> *All the glory of the godhead*
> *Had the prophet Quetzalcóatl. . . .*
> *See, his beard is very lengthy;*
> *See, exceeding long his beard is;*
> *Yellow as the straw his beard is!*[24]

The temple walls of the Toltec capital, called Tula, or Tollan, are said to have been covered either with gold plate or silver,[25] *as were the Incan temples. As in Egypt, Mayan pyramids were funerary monuments.*[26] *In ancient tradition, snail shells carried the ingredients of Creation. The Yoruba of southern Nigeria had the Deluge story, believed they came from Canaan at the time of Nimrod and that the materials for existence were kept in a snail shell.*[27]

The Toltec capital, Tula, means simply the Place of Reeds: the two traditions, Egyptian and Mexican, coincide precisely. And Dilmun, which the universities say is Bahrain, also means the Field of Reeds and was also known as the Paradise Land far to the east of Arabia, which scarcely describes Bahrain; any more than the land bigger than Africa and Asia put together describes the seventy-five acres of Thera. *Amenti* is the Coptic for Hades, the land where Hades ruled.

The underworld is another example of two different beliefs becoming elided. Anyone seeing bodies buried beneath the earth might easily think of their spirits inhabiting some subterranean world of the dead. On the other hand, when sailors noticed, as they must, that ships disappeared over the edge of a curving world, where were they to suppose those ships went? If they journeyed far enough around that curve they must surely end up underneath the lands from which they had set out. They would have reached the underworld. Once again, it would have been easy to confuse the real with a mythical land. But for the businessmen, there was nothing mythical about it. Of course, every lunar eclipse one may observe the curvature of the earth.

The belief in a land beyond the western ocean persisted. In Irish legends it was known as Tir na Og, the Land of Eternal Youth, or Mag Mel, the Plain of Joy. Mag was traditionally the son of Set, perhaps equated with

Plate 28

The wash-through Mesopotamian style reed boat used by Thor Heyerdahl on his fifty-seven-day voyage from Morocco to Barbados covering 3,270 miles. The reed boats still used on Lake Chad resemble those still used on Lake Titicaca. It was the primeval waters, Egyptian tradition said, that provided the source of everything in the world.[28] *Dr. Glyn Daniel, general editor of the Thames & Hudson archaeological books, calls Thor Heyerdahl's excellent demonstration "academic rubbish."*

Plate fibula from Thebes (far right) (overall length 13.5 cm; National Museum, Athens), showing a simple sailing boat of the period. The sea people came to be associated both with sailing and with cavalry; in Greek tradition this was especially true of Poseidon. It was the unexpected use of cavalry that helped the sea people called the Hyksos take over Egypt, even as, more than three thousand years later, unexpected cavalry helped the Spaniards take over Mexico and Peru. The Hyksos were expelled from Egypt by the sky-worshipping people in what Greek tradition called the Titanomachia, c. 1570 B.C., and set up in business again as the ruling class in Mexico. An Amerindian prince, Fernando de Alva Ixtilxochitl, says of them: "These Toltecs knew how to write and to reckon, to rule with justice and to build magnificent temples. Toltec soldiers wore copper helmets." Other traditions credited Quetzalcóatl with bringing the art of picture writing . . . and teaching the Toltecs to become master builders. Legend states that their capital was Tula or Tollan.[29]

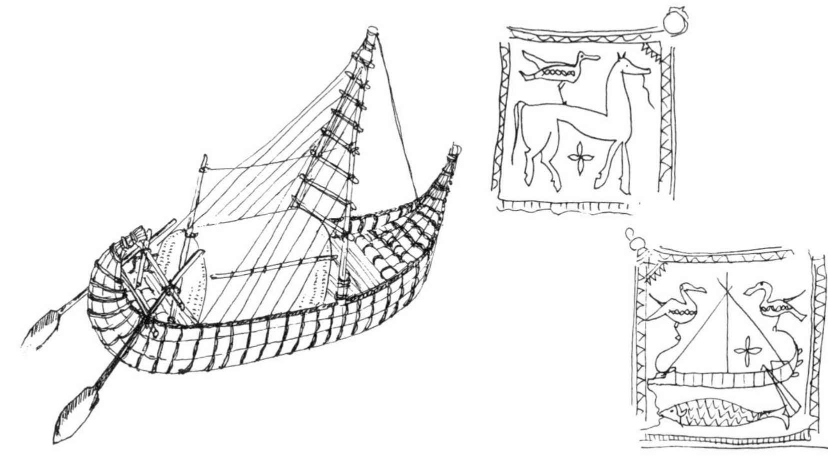

the Scottish Mac. By our era the memory of the real America was fading in the past, even if occasional adventurers did go there and return. To the Welsh, the land in the middle of the ocean was Avalon of the Apples: compare this with the Greek Hesperides of the golden apples. Hence, of course, the names Glastonbury and Glasgow, and the many *llans* in Welsh names, when in Welsh *llan* means sacred. In Greek *atlan* and *atlas* were synonymous. King Madoc of Wales planted his own colony in North America during the period when the Scandinavians were settling Vinland.

There is a tantalizing reference in Plutarch's *Moralia*, in the section entitled "On the Face in the Moon's Orb," written in the first century A.D.[11] He describes how every thirty years a ship leaves Britain on a sort of pilgrimage. The story is far from clear, but it seems as if the ship travels along the stepping-stone route to America, and the impression one receives is that the route had once been economically important and the custom of making the journey lingered on as a religious or commemorative ceremony of what once had been vitally significant to the Celts.

On the western side of the Atlantic the traditions telling of arrivals from across the ocean are widespread and persistent. All the most important civilizations—Aztec, Mayan, Incan and Toltec—look back to their foundation by white culture heroes who arrived mysteriously by sea. The most famous of these legends was that which the Aztec king Montezuma told to Cortés, his Spanish conqueror:

> Long time have we been informed by the writing of our ancestors that neither myself nor any of those who inhabit this land are natives of it, but rather strangers who have come to it from foreign parts. We likewise know that from those parts our nation was led by a certain lord (to whom we were all subject), and who then went back to his native land. . . . And we have always believed that among his descendants one would surely come to subject this land and us as rightful vassals. Now seeing the regions from which you

say you come, which is from where the sun rises, we believe and hold it certain that he [the Spanish king] is our natural lord.[12]

This belief in "the second coming" proved catastrophic for the Aztecs. Because of this belief the Aztecs were halfhearted in their resistance to the Spaniards and paid the price of enslavement. No one seems to have noticed that the Maltese cross, painted on the sails of Spanish galleons, was a sacred symbol kept behind the throne of the Incas of Peru and imprinted on Mexican and Mayan codices and had been adopted by the Christians. Small wonder that the Amerindians were grievously misled. The Maltese cross symbolized rule over the four quarters of the earth and had been in use in Iran from the fourth millennium B.C. It will have been a symbol of some of their early culture heroes.

The culture hero at the center of the Toltec legend was Quetzalcóatl, whose name means the plumed water-serpent. He was a white god who arrived in Mexico from the east, bringing with him the arts of civilization, and his reputation was that of a gentle teacher. He ruled that no living thing was to be harmed unnecessarily. The impression one receives is of a civilization that started with an enlightened morality but which degenerated as its centers were overthrown by barbarous tribes from outside, culminating in rule by the Aztecs, who totally reversed Quetzalcóatl's teaching about human sacrifice.

Like other American culture heroes, Quetzalcóatl was said to be white. Constance Irwin mentions a comment made by Torquemada that "Quetzalcóatl was a white man; *era Hombre blanco;* a large man, broad-browed, with huge eyes, long black hair, and a great rounded beard: *Il a barbe rande y redonda.*"[13] Another Mexican belief was that their capital city, Teotihuacán, was built by white giants. Perhaps northern Europeans qualified for this description.

The Maya gave a similar account of their origins. They even claimed to remember the exact date. On August 10 in 3113 B.C. four Bacabs arrived by ship in Guatemala, with their crews, from across the Atlantic. They brought with them many of the skills of the Old World. The depiction of them on columns in the Castillo of Chichén Itzá shows them bearded and European in appearance (Plates 27 and 52), Atlas-like, holding up the roof. The Mexican Atlas figures were associated with the Toltecs.

The Maya kept memories of other white culture heroes. The most important was Itzamná and he, too, came across the ocean, but from the west in what was known as the Great Arrival. He taught and civilized the people, was the patron of healers and diviners and knew the mysterious properties of plants.[14] There was also a Lesser Arrival, which probably came later. The Japanese high god at this time was Itzanagi and Japanese artifacts of this period have been found in America: the main Japanese goddess was Itzamná, an identical name with that of the Mayan great god.

The natives affirmed—says Fray Bartolomé de Las Casas—that in ancient times there came to that land twenty men, the chief of whom was called "Cocolcan." They wore flowing robes and sandals on their feet, they had long beards, and their heads were bare. They ordered that the people should confess and fast. Kukulcan instructed the people in the arts of peace, and caused various important edifices to be built at Itzá. He also founded the city of Mayapán. Compare this Mayan tradition with the Irish tradition of Cuculhan, also called Setanta—a Set name—who fought in Ireland with his black soldiers. And then remember the great African stone heads erected by the Toltecs in Mexico, obviously of people of power and unarguably African.

To the west of the Maya lived a tribe called the Tzendal whose white culture bringer was named Votan. Compare this name with the early English god called Woden. Votan invented hieroglyphic signs, collected the people into villages and taught them how to cultivate maize and cotton. He is also said to have measured the earth.

In Peru there is an ancient tradition that white men came from the "sunrise across the water" and erected temples and statues on the Island of the Sun and on the mainland near the lake. Also, that a second group of white men arrived, calling themselves the "Stone People," and that their leader was accompanied by his governor, his servants and many men, women and children. According to these same traditions the first of these white strangers transformed men to stone to serve as statues, and as proxies to guard his newly acquired land after he left. As the natives regarded these strange white men as gods, it would have seemed perfectly reasonable that they should be able to do this.

Peruvian tradition recalls that the first Inca arrived at Tiahuanaco after a flood, and the same story was told by the Maya: their great gods arrived from across the Atlantic to escape the flood. In the valley of Mexico there was also a pre-Columbian tradition of a flood and of a Mexican Noah called Tapi. He was a righteous man who, following God's instructions, built a ship and took on board two of every kind of beast. He even released a dove to find dry land. This resemblance to the biblical story can hardly be coincidence, since we have evidence that a lot of the refugees after this man-made flood in Mesopotamia took off, quitting Mesopotamia: we have the story of departure and the story of arrival.

Another Mexican legend that bears a significantly close resemblance to a biblical story is the building of an immense tower so high that it touched the sky. This presumption angered the gods, and they destroyed the kingdom. This echoes Josephus's version of the building of the Tower of Babel. Josephus recounts how, after the collapse of the tower, the inhabitants of the land were scattered, going to all the continents and, taking ship, to many of the islands of the world. The fact that this story is also supported by Yoruba tradition in Africa gives force to the belief that it is, ultimately, based on a real event. Just as—as we have seen—the other event that is described in great and explicit detail is the old Babylonian story of the Flood—a historical man-made flood, not a theological flood—entitled *Atrahasis:* a flood occasioned by the terrorism of the bosses, not, as is taught from every pulpit, by the inherent wickedness of the workers.[15]

We have, then, a substantial body of legends in America recalling the arrival of culture heroes from across the ocean, many of whom are specifically said to be white. In Europe and the Mediterranean and Middle Eastern countries generally there are corresponding legends about journeys to a vast land across the ocean, whose descriptions are surprisingly consistent with one another but match no country and no island nearer than America. What is particularly striking is that all these stories face, as it were, in the right direction. We do not find Old World legends of culture heroes arriving from beyond the western ocean; we do find Oriental legends of a vast and paradisiacal country many years' sail to the east. Now, it is true that any culture could easily make up stories about mighty ancestors arriving out of nowhere; and any people living on the edge of an immense and unexplored ocean would surely speculate about the wonders waiting to be found on the far side by anyone heroic enough to reach it. The trouble is that both these opportunities for storytelling apply equally. Why did each side pick only one kind of story to tell, even when a number of different peoples seem, quite independently, to have told it? If it is a coincidence it is a strikingly improbable one—more improbable, it seems to me, than the idea that, underneath, all the stories were fact.

Even so, whatever the probabilities, they do not amount to proof. For that we must turn to the hard facts of archaeology.

Before we do so, let us notice the problems confronting us with immunity and disease. Once the Spaniards had reached America, the Old World disease of smallpox cut swathes of death through the Amerindians, the New World disease of syphilis cut swathes of death through the Old World. Even a pope, His Holiness Pope Julius II, is said to have caught syphilis then.[16] Diseases are not ordinarily recognizable to archaeologists. Viruses change their nature. In the last decade both malaria and AIDS have changed their natures. And doubtless will do so again. Herbal medicine and antibiotics were in use from ancient times across much of the world. We must notice this very real disease argument against earlier culture contact, while equally noticing it is a subject about which we presently know all too little. But certain it is that other animals—sheep or cattle—rapidly lose their immunity—within one generation—when they are no longer exposed to stock diseases. Hermes was a messenger of the gods to Hades, a description that correctly suggests a fair amount of contact between the Old World and the New.[17] He was also *psychopompos*, conveyor of souls to the next world, as was also the Greek goddess Hectate.

4. The Marks of the Voyagers

"We are sons of Canaan from Sidon, the city of the king. Commerce has cast us on this distant shore, a land of mountains. We set [sacrificed] a youth for the exalted gods and goddesses in the nineteenth year of Hiram, our mighty king. We embarked from Ezion-Geber into the Red Sea and voyaged with ten ships. We were at sea together for two years around the land belonging to Ham but were separated by a storm [literally "from the hand of Baal"] and we were no longer with our companions. So we have come here, twelve men and three women, on a . . . shore which I, the Admiral, control. But auspiciously may the exalted gods and goddesses favour us!"

THE PARAÍBA INSCRIPTION

PLATE 29
CUNNING LITTLE TRICK ON BOTH SIDES OF THE ATLANTIC. *American mixing bowls, which whistled when you filled them with liquid, were in use from Mexico to Peru. This one is Mixtec from Mexico (Museum of the American Indian). Compare this very specialized little trick with the Greek-described mixing bowl below. Two thousand years and more ago there was in the Hellenistic world a special class of man who enacted bogus miracles, for whom there was a special Greek name,* thaumaturgos, *or wonder-worker, miracle-worker.*

This extraordinary inscription was found on the coast of Brazil at a place known as Paraíba. It is written in the Phoenician language and script and this translation of it was published in 1968 by Dr. Cyrus Gordon.[1] If it is genuine it is obviously incontrovertible evidence, but in the nature of things it is hard to prove that any such inscription is genuine. (Sometimes, of course, it is quite easy to expose a fake.) At least one authority believes on stylistic evidence that the Paraíba inscription is a forgery, but Dr. Gordon is satisfied that it is not.

A second inscription was found near Rio. Three thousand feet up, the following words were cut into a vertical wall of rock: "Tyre, Phoenicia, Badezir, Firstborn of Jethbaal. . . ." If it is genuine, the wording dates it to the middle of the ninth century B.C.[2]

In assessing the merits of these inscriptions it is hard to take a balanced view, and just as easy to fall off the tightrope on either side. Those who want to believe in them are tempted to accept them without probing too deeply for possible flaws. Those who oppose the whole idea of a maritime dimension to early history cry "forgery" without much more thought. The very fact is that if the rock inscriptions across the Americas prove to be genuine—and there are very many indeed of them in very many different scripts—then the conventional histories have been wildly mistaken.

We find ourselves on firm ground when we come to deal with all the other inscriptions that are significant not so much for what they say as for the script in which they say it. A large number of these have been found across the Americas and the similarities between the scripts and glyphs of the Old and New Worlds are so many and so striking that in my view we must either declare the whole lot to be forgeries or else admit that they prove precisely what they seem to prove.

In the iron mines of Brazil scores of inscriptions have been found carved on the walls in letters that have been identified as ancient Greek and Phoenician. The first recorded notation seems to be in a book published in Lisbon in 1586, the account of a traveler to Brazil who copied down some of these unknown letters. Some time in the 1860s a mining inspector had his attention called to letters carved on the rock inside another mine in the same area. The inscription was copied and sent for examination to Rio. From there it was sent on to Paris, to the French Academy, which identified the letters as ancient Phoenician, dating from about the time of the Trojan War.

The largest collection of inscriptions was made by a Brazilian rubber tapper who worked in the Amazon jungle in the early years of this century. When he was nearly fifty, Bernardo da Silva Ramos decided to sell his plantation and devote himself to his collection of coins. He toured the Mediterranean to study the countries where they had been minted, and while he was there he noticed examples of ancient scripts similar to letters he remembered seeing scratched on rocks in the Amazon jungle. He spent the rest of his life—more than twenty years—copying these inscriptions and noting their locations, before finally dying of fever. Later, in the 1930s, his book was posthumously published under the title *Inscripcões é Traducões da America Prehistorica.*

The Brazilian government declared the book fraudulent and asserted that the inscriptions were nothing but chance marks worn in the rock by wind and water. This, however, can be dismissed at once. There is no possible way in which the inscriptions recorded in da Silva Ramos's book could be the product of natural erosion. For a start, there are far too many of them—well over a thousand inscriptions, mostly from the Amazon basin. One or two marks closely resembling writing might be produced by chance: but complete inscriptions in one script is inconceivable. There are only two possible explanations. The first is that the inscriptions are genuine, and if they are then I have no doubt that they were cut by people who, during those early days, were employing their own Old World scripts. I leave the reader to judge whether the similarities in Plates 30–32 are likely

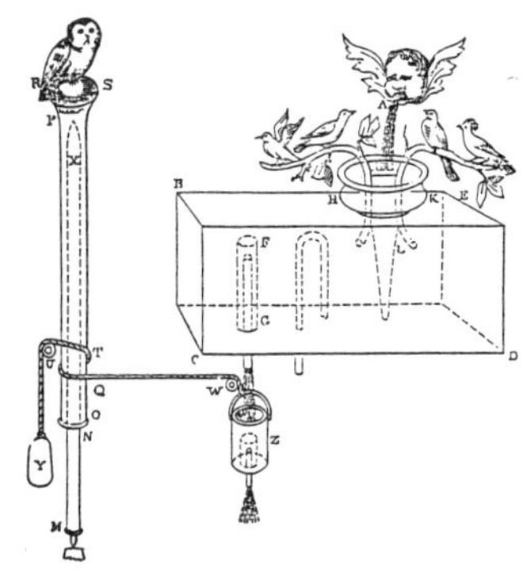

Hero of Alexandria, fl. c. 150 B.C., published a treatise on pneumatics, consisting of material previously published by other authors. He displays here a very, very specialized little trick whereby, by pouring water into a pot, the displaced air causes the artificial birds to whistle.[1] *He elsewhere publishes the principle of the steam engine and how, by the use of siphons, you can turn water into wine.*

Now, the point of this illustration is that in both pre-Columbian Mexico and pre-Columbian Peru the same principle was in use whereby, by pouring water into a pot, the pot was caused to whistle.[2]

to have occurred by chance, or whether so many identical symbols could have been independently invented by two separate peoples.

Did da Silva Ramos fake them? That is the only alternative, and I believe he can be declared innocent. What is reassuring is not his expertise but, paradoxically, his ignorance. In his book he not only recorded the inscriptions but made efforts to translate them, and the results are laughable. He believed everything to be either Classical Greek or Hebrew, including a lot of marks that are clearly nothing more than doodles. It is perfectly obvious that he was a simple rubber tapper without any knowledge of ancient writing, much too ignorant to be a convincing forger. Some of the symbols he copied are Indus Valley, a script first published by Marshall in 1927, a book not very likely to be available to him.

A further collection of rock inscriptions up the Amazon was made by another Brazilian, Alfredo Brandao, whose book *A Escripta Prehistorica do Brazil* was published in 1937. His fieldwork was much less extensive, but he still gave a number of examples of inscriptions he had found, comparing some of them with other ancient scripts. Plate 32 shows some of the results. While Brandao's fieldwork was less extensive than that of da Silva Ramos, he had a far better understanding of what he was about.

A more apparently qualified observer was Professor Marcel Homet, an archaeologist and for fifteen years professor of Classical Arabic at the University of Algiers. He traveled the Amazon basin to view its antiquities and published his discoveries.[3] The tone of his book is not very impressive but his fieldwork is useful. He was particularly struck by the similarity of the megalithic monuments of the Amazon to those of Algeria and also of the inscriptions on them: immediately understandable as soon as one realizes that the merchant marine of North Africa was lodged there to exploit the South American metals trade with the Mediterranean purchasers.

Apart from these and many other parallel inscriptions, various individual objects have been found in different parts of America that are marked with Old World scripts.

Dr. Henriette Mertz discusses the inscription on the American Fletcher Stone, and Plate 30 shows how closely it is matched by an Old World script.

Another important example is a tapestry found at Pachacámac, an ancient city whose remains are about ten miles from Lima. The city once had a population of several hundred thousand people and was the holy city of old Peru. A vast number of objects have been excavated from its graves and rubble and among them is the tapestry whose symbols appear to be substantially the Hittite script.

Hittite scripts also appear, according to Mrs. Verrill, on certain obsidian disks dug up in Utah, which are identical in form with disks found in the valley of the Nile near the Egyptian pyramids. Mrs. Verrill maintains that the symbols are of the type found in Hittite glyphs and in the archaic, so-

Plate 30
***American Fletcher Stone** (right).*

Symbols from standard Old World scripts (right).

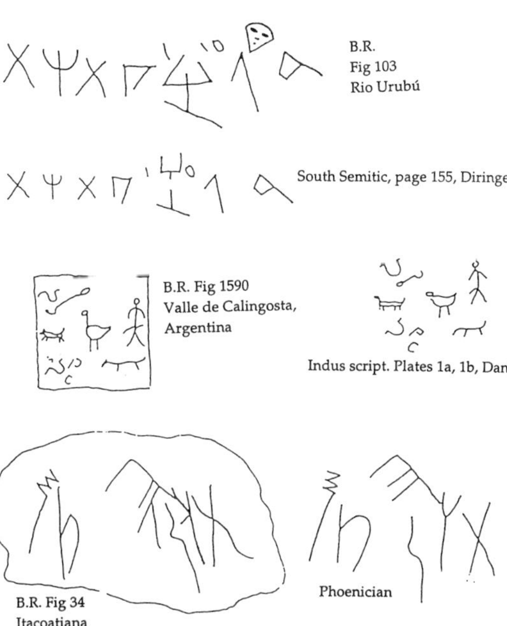

Bernardo da Silva Ramos' rock engravings in Amazonia identified with Old World scripts. The inscriptions copied by da Silva Ramos are marked B.R., accompanied by their number in his book and their geographical position. Next to each of his inscriptions I have placed a series of symbols taken from early Old World scripts from standard works on these scripts, chiefly by Dr. Diringer, for comparison. The reader can judge for himself whether these parallels are likely to have occurred by chance. Da Silva Ramos was the former rubber tapper in Amazonia who copied a multitude of Amazonian rock engravings. There would seem to be no way they could be chance. My wife, Barbara, did most of the identification.

The top group contains inscriptions from the American Fletcher Stone; the bottom group is composed of similar symbols from the standard works on Old World scripts. George Jones, in his History of Ancient America, *lists some of the Hebrew religious practices common also among the Amerindians: the Deluge story, the dove of peace, the Ark of the Covenant in which is deposited some mystery known only to the priests, likewise the Ark is never suffered to touch the earth; Amerindians offer burnt offerings, they have their corn and harvest feasts, a great feast in direct analogy with the Passover, a breastplate worn by the Indian chief priest containing twelve shells or stones of value in direct imitation of the pectoral worn by the Hebrew high priest; they have their cities of refuge or huts of safety; they wear phylacteries; they have one god they call Ye-ho-vah, they rejoice with the word Hal-le-lu-ya; they believe in the immortality of the soul, they practice circumcision.*

B.R. Fig 753
Manãos

Sidon, 5th-12th Century B.C.

B.R. Fig 757
Manãos

Punic. Diringer

B.R. Fig 1495
Rio Madeira
Amazonas

S. Semitic

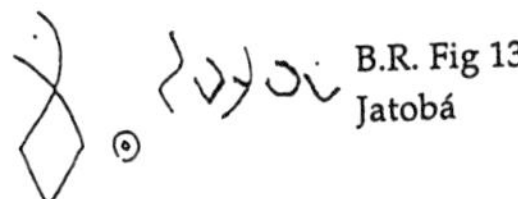

B.R. Fig 137
Jatobá

Kharoshthi script

Indus script

B.R. Fig 752
Manãos

Early Phoenician, Diringer

B.R. Fig 756
Manãos

Semitic, Diringer

B.R. Fig 1012
Valle de Cachoeira
de Matapy

Indus script

B.R. Fig 1712 Columbiana

Telagu-Canarese script
and Brahmi script, Ojha

called Sumerian script. Just recently an engraved stone in North America dubbed the Cherokee Stone—because the establishment said the Cherokees had carved it—has been shown to carry a script that is Hebrew of between the first and eighth centuries A.D. The Hebrews were among the very, very many peoples who were in America long, long before Columbus.

On the other side of the Atlantic, a circular clay disk was found in the Minoan palace at Phaistós in southern Crete. The Phaistós Disk has been

PLATE 31

MORE OF BERNARDO DA SILVA RAMOS' ROCK ENGRAVINGS IN AMAZONIA IDENTIFIED. *The petroglyphs of Amazonia seem to resemble entries in a visitors' book. Strabo describes Indians coming into Libya, a starting point for a trader route to Amazonia: "Certain authors see in the Marousiens the descendants of the Indians who came into Libya in the train of Herakles."*[3]

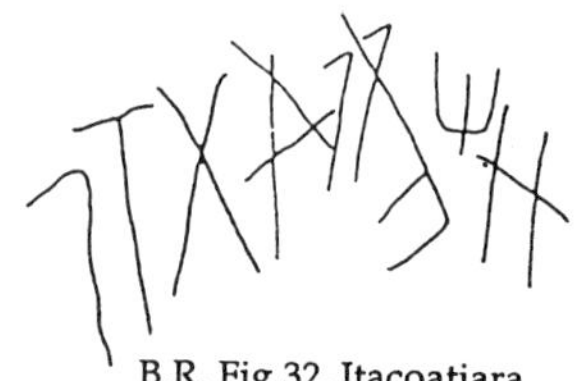

B.R. Fig 32, Itacoatiara

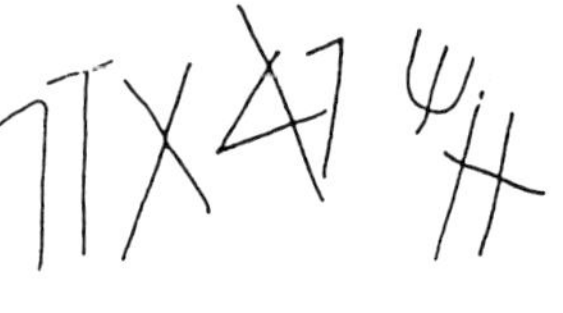

Early Hebrew and Iberian
Most letters are common to both.

B.R. Fig 1350
S. Joãs do Sabugy
Rio Grande do Norte, Brazil

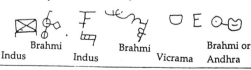

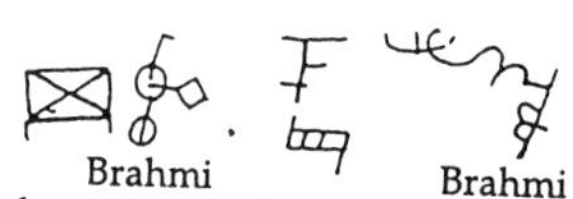

Indus Brahmi Indus Brahmi Vicrama Brahmi or Andhra

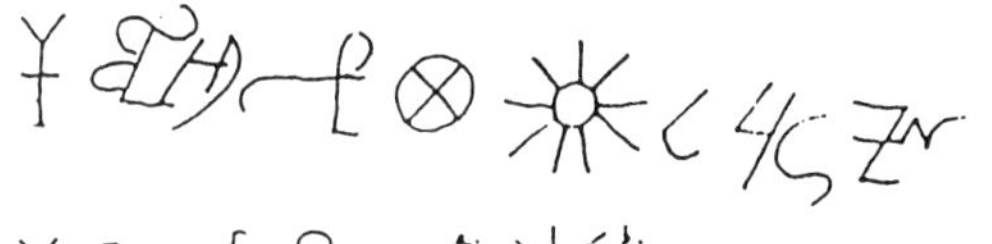

B.R. Fig 1334
S. Joãs do Sabugy
Rio Grande do Norte, Brazil

Kharoshthi script, Ojha a.b. Indus script

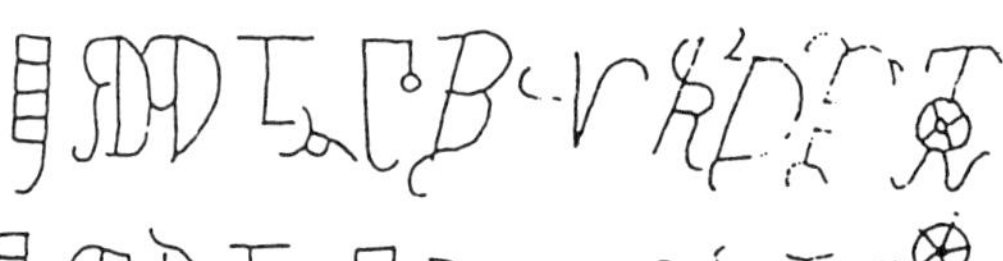

B.R. Fig 1366
S. Joãs do Sabugy
Rio Grande do Norte, Brazil

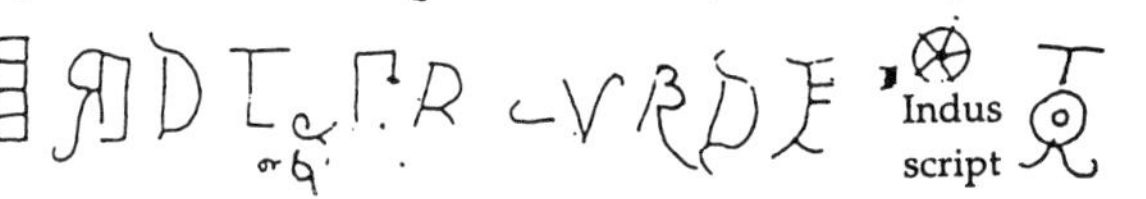

or Brahmi

Indus Brahmi script and other scripts derived from Brahmi. Ojha

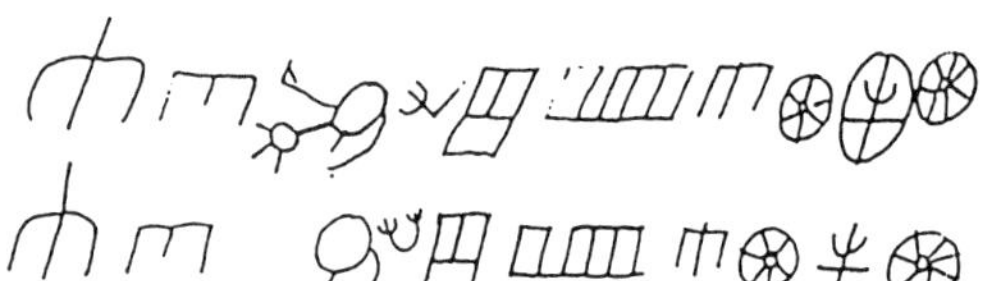

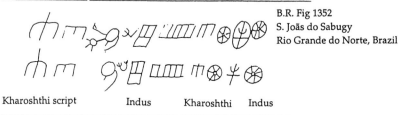

B.R. Fig 1352
S. Joãs do Sabugy
Rio Grande do Norte, Brazil

Kharoshthi script Indus Kharoshthi Indus

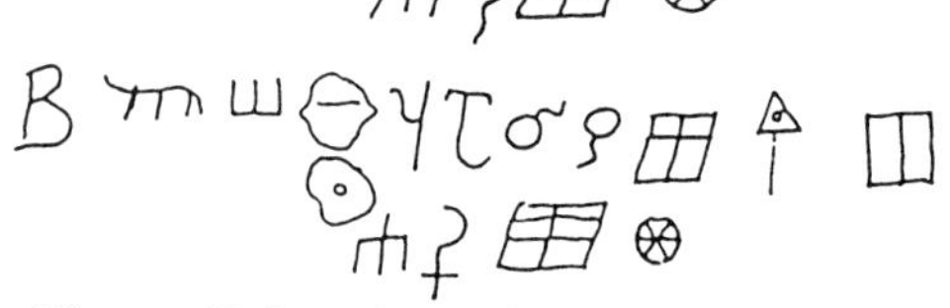

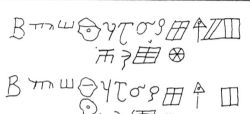

B.R. Fig 1354
S. Joãs do Sabugy
Rio Grande do Norte, Brazil

Mixture of Indus script, Brahmi and Telegu-Canarese

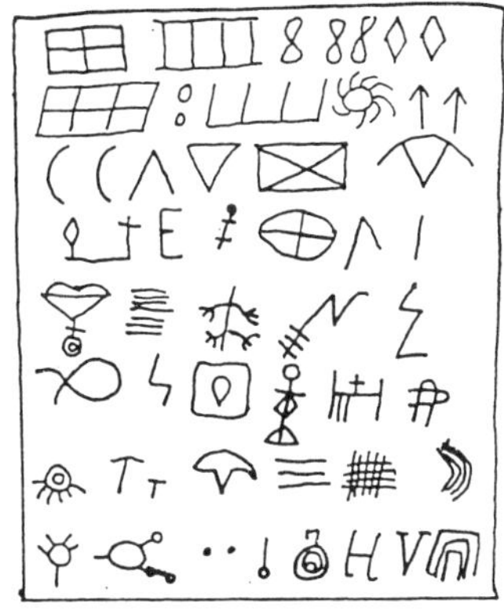

Plate 32

Alfredo Brandao's Rock Inscriptions Identified.

Brandao's Brazilian rock inscriptions (far left).

My selection of corresponding Indus signs (left).

On the left is a Brazilian inscription given by Brandao and on the right is a set of similar symbols taken from the Indus script. Alfredo Brandao worked on the rock inscriptions of Brazil quite independently of da Silva Ramos: he did not do as much fieldwork as da Silva Ramos but he had a better idea of what he was doing.[4] More of Brandao's Brazilian petroglyphs I show below (left).

Brasil pre-historico	Caracteres Sabeanos	Caracteres mepalitnicos	Signos de Creta e affins	Signos da Etruria	Signos do Egypto pre-historico	Signos sumerianos	Signos berberes	Alphabeto Grego primitivo	Alphabeto Phenicio	Alphabeto Hebraico primitivo	Alphabeto Iberico primitivo
ΛVΛ	Λ V	Λ V	1 V	↑ 7	Λ	V V	Λ	Λ	1 7	1 1	V
ΛΛV	ΛΛV	ΛΛV	V Λ	V Λ	X	V		∃	N N	N	∃
⋒∩U	⋒∩U	∩ ⋒		m	∩		U		⋎		∩
⊥IΨ	+ Ψ	⋇ √	ˎ	Ψ	⚓			Ш	Ш	Ш	
‖≡	‖≡	‖≡				≡ =	||||				
+X+	+ X	+X†‡	+X+	+ X	+	+	+ X		Ч+	+ X	+ X
⧗4⧗	⧗	⧗ ⧗	⧗⋈	⧗⋈		⋈⧗	⧗⋈X	4	A 4	9	9 P
TTT	T ⅄	TTI		T T	T			T			T
ΔV	Δ		ΔΔ	◊	ΔΔ	Δ9Δ		ΔΔ	⊿	Δ	D
ZЧ	ЧЧƸ	Ʒ S	7~	7			ϟ	ЧЧ	Z Ч	Ч	Ч
EEШ	E E	E	E	E		⊓		E			E
HH⌶	HHH	H	HBB	BB9	B	H	⌶▭	B		B▭⌶	B H
⊞▭	⌗B	#	#⊞	⊞	⊞#	⊞▦		⊞			⊗

dated between 1700 and 1600 B.C., and is attributed to the Pelasgians, the Peoples of the Sea. It is stamped with pictographs that have also been found on other Cretan objects, and in Plate 121 some of them are compared with symbols used on the Aztec codices surviving in Mexico, and they can be seen to be similar.

The Cretan script also seems to have been the original basis of Mayan writing. Pierre Honoré has made a study of it and in his book *In Quest of the White God*, he writes: "Among the most frequent symbols in Mayan script are those for their days and months. *Chuen, Eb, Akbal, Ben, Manik, Caban, Eznab*—such are some of the names—sound distinctly Semitic."[4]

They are indeed very like the names of the ancient Phoenician and Greek letters; some in fact, are almost identical. Here are a few instances—giving the letters in Greek, Phoenician, and Mayan in that order:

Greek	Phoenician	Mayan
Alpha	aleph	ahau
Beta	bejt	baaz
Gamma	gimel	ghanan
Epsilon	eh	eb
Iota	iud	ik
Kappa	koph	queh
Lamda	lamed	lamat
Tau	tav	tihaz

In many cases the Phoenician and the Mayan have very similar "characters" for the same letters, and also similar meanings for the characters.

Now, the Maya cannot possibly have hit upon not only the names but also the order as in the Phoenician alphabet. So at first sight it looks as if the Mayan script had come from the Phoenicians. But the Phoenician characters are very simple, in contrast to the complicated day symbols of the Maya. It therefore seems probable that both scripts have a common root, older than the Phoenician script, from which they both developed.

This old script must have been pictographic—i.e., it must have been pictorial. For the Mayan symbols are much more like hieroglyphs than they are like the Phoenician letters. They can hardly have come from Egypt, for the Egyptian hieroglyphs were based on very different principles, but they are extremely like the symbols of the ancient Cretan pictographic script. Both scripts have simple symbols in common, like circle, cross, hand, eye, etc.; but both also contain many symbols so abstract you cannot see what picture they were taken from. Almost identical abstract symbols could not have been invented independently in two different parts of the world.

It would be highly significant if the same phonetic values could be proved for both symbols, but this is where research still disappoints us. While such values for Cretan Linear B have largely been worked out, we do not know them for the older script form of Linear A, or for the Mayan symbols. In the few cases, however, where we know the phonetic values of both Cretan and Mayan symbols (e.g. the glottal "p" and the "t") they tally.

It seems safe to say, therefore, that the Mayan legends were right. They learned the art of writing from the White God from across the sea, and the script he taught them was a Cretan script.

The most distant evidence of all comes from a small island far out in the South Pacific, Easter Island. Under the huge stone heads for which the island is famous some wooden tablets were found, and were taken away on a ship in the middle of the nineteenth century. The script carved on

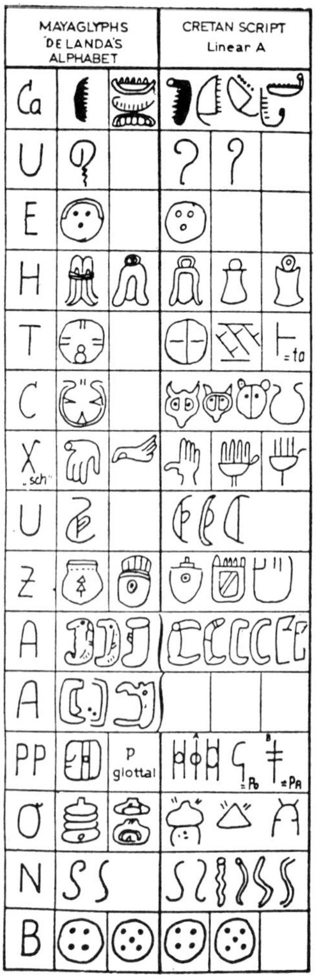

Plate 33
Signs in the Mayan script compared with signs in the Cretan Linear A script. *It is inconceivable that the similarity of Landa's glyphs and the ancient Cretan script is chance. Bishop Landa was the third bishop of Yucatán. Crete would seem to have been a highly cosmopolitan offshore haven where Middle Eastern sailors of many sorts represented by the god Chronos joined with the Aegean peoples of the island represented by the goddess Rhea. An ancient conception of the kingdom of the dead was that it was upside down:*[5] *correct enough if it was America.*

them was unidentifiable and remained so until the 1920s, when the Indus Valley civilization was unearthed and found to have used a related script. Plate 34 shows that the similarities are extraordinarily close. The Amerindian tribe called the Cuna possess in their script three signs that are identical with Chinese both in form and meaning. The name Cuna may relate to *anaku*.

The usual dismissive explanation—that the inscriptions are forgeries—cannot possibly be accepted in this case. The script the forger would have had to copy was completely unknown until many years afterward. This fact also disposes of another objection, for it was later discovered that the tablets had been carved in the eighteenth century A.D., simply as copies of older tablets still, which were by then falling to pieces. Where could the eighteenth-century copiers have got their designs from if they were not faithfully taken from earlier ones based ultimately on the Indus script? The resemblances to that script are too close and too many to be put down to coincidence, and this argument would apply however many recarvings were made over the centuries.

This, of course, shows a connection between the Indus Valley and Easter Island. It does not directly implicate America. Thor Heyerdahl, however, believes that the script was in fact brought to Easter Island by way of America and in a subsequent chapter we shall be investigating links with India that make this very possible. The evidence provided by this great variety of totally identifiable scripts carved on the rocks of America puts paid to Jung's idiotic argument of a collective unconscious. Apply to him Occam's razor: "*Entia non sunt multiplicanda praeter necessitatem:*" i.e. entities are not to be invented when it is not necessary.

This is by no means a complete account of all the inscriptions in America that resemble Old World writings. They have been found all the way from Argentina to Nova Scotia, and while many of them relate to scripts that have not yet been deciphered they clearly derive from origins east of the Atlantic or west of the Pacific. They are not of American Indian provenance. We know beyond any shadow of doubt that for three and a half centuries or so there were Scandinavian settlements in North America between the eleventh and fourteenth centuries A.D., and they left their runes carved on the rocks of North America, precisely in the same manner. If they are forgeries, then the nineteenth century must have witnessed some indefatigable scholars scurrying across the two Americas, busily forging inscriptions in out-of-the-way places and leaving them behind on the off chance that someone else would later discover them and be taken in by the hoax!

There are forgeries among the American inscriptions, but the exposure of "Piltdown Man" as a fake did not make rubbish of the theory of human evolution. There are usually some fakes in any field of work. The point is that every single significant inscription in America has to be a fraud if the anti-diffusionists are to hold their position. If one—just one—is genuine,

EI IV EI IV EI IV EI IV

PLATE 34

COMPARISON OF EASTER ISLAND AND INDUS VALLEY SCRIPTS. *The Easter Island script and the Indus script, comparison made by de Hevesy. From this it is likely that the scripts are related. The script, according to Heyerdahl, was brought to the island from South America. South America was colonized from India both by the Pacific and the Atlantic routes. The Easter Islanders call their island Tepito te Henua, the* omphalos, *the navel of the earth: the same title as was given to Delphi, Cuzco, Nippur, Ile Ife.*

Plate 35
Old World—New World Comparisons.

Mexican Tláloc with bolt of lightning, a rain god similar in appearance to Hadad, the Phoenician rain god. The Mexicans slew many children on the mountaintops on the first day of the year for the gods to bring rain.[6]

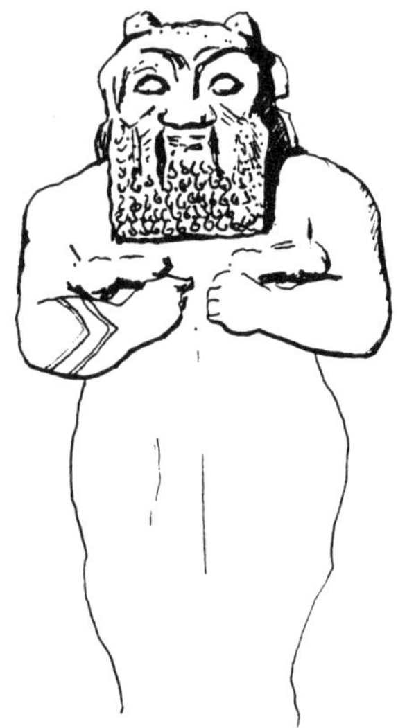

The Colossus of Amathus, the Phoenician statue of Melkarth.

then pre-Columbian contact with the ancient world east of the Atlantic is proved. The cat is out of the bag!

The study of religions cannot, perhaps, offer the same almost conclusive proof of contact as the study of writing. It can, all the same, be very suggestive, and when a number of facts seem to be pointing us in the same direction we should investigate them seriously. The general development of ancient religions is the subject of Chapter 25. Here we look at certain specific symbols and rituals that appear to have been brought to America from the Old World.

First let us take something that is no more than a hint. The four Bacabs who were said to have brought civilization to the Maya were associated in Mayan tradition with bees, and in Guatemala today they are still the patrons of beekeeping. The earliest rulers of the delta in Egypt used the bee as a symbol and a bee goddess was prominent in Crete. In Indian tradition honey was associated with the twin gods of the sailors, the Acvins, and we shall later see substantial reason to associate twin gods with bronze. There was also wide use of the butterfly symbol in both Mexico and Crete, as also among the Masai in East Africa and certain peoples in West Africa.

Bees and butterflies—these, it can be said, are obvious metaphors of sweetness and of airy flight. Different cultures might well have lighted on them independently. This is not so clearly true of the lotus, a common motif in Egyptian and Phoenician art that often reappears in Mexico. It is a still more doubtful explanation of such man-devised symbols as the Maltese cross and the swastika, which were used in the ancient Middle East and also in Peru and in other countries the seagoing peoples visited—but not elsewhere, such as Australia.

One of the most important and distinctive symbols in any culture is that which marks a king. In both Egypt and America this was a serpent on the brow.

In both those places, also, some of the same gods were worshipped. The chief deities of both were the sun god and the moon god, and in each culture there was a bird associated with the sun gods.

The great Phoenician god Melkarth also turns up in Mexico where, at Balsas, a clay head of very distinctive appearance was found. Plate 35 shows how clearly it resembles the head on the Phoenician colossus at Amathus.

The Phoenicians also had a rain god, Hadad, who was similar to the Mexican rain god Tláloc. Both figures carried a thunderbolt in the right hand, both were robed and bearded. (The beard, as we shall see, was very significant.) Two of the three examples of a bearded Tláloc were found on a mountaintop where toy chariots were also found (chariots—in America!) and where tradition said that children were sacrificed. Children usually have toys imitating things that parents use and from the Far East there seem to come allusions to horses and chariots in early Mexico, as we shall discover later on.

The Phoenicians were enthusiatic believers in child sacrifice, which they continued to practice until the destruction of Carthage. The Mexicans also held that, since children were the most precious gift they could surrender to the gods, they were the most acceptable and effective sacrifice.

Another repellent custom common to the two sides of the Atlantic was flaying a man alive. The Aztecs made a frequent practice of this in religious ceremonies, the priest then wearing the skin over his own. In Assyria flaying alive was a common punishment, later taken over by the Persians. The Phrygian god Marsyas was held to have been flayed alive on the orders of Apollo.

Self-laceration by devotees in a state of religious frenzy was another common practice both in Mexico and among Old World peoples including the Phoenicians; and so, too, was the existence of a special class of castrated priests.

Head of baked clay found at Balsas in Mexico, looking like the Phoenician god, Melkarth. When commerce began in Mexico, Quaquauhpitz was ruler. Compare this name with the akawa *root which we find associated with the Heracles people or the matriarchal society with which Old World trading contacts began in America. They began by selling red and blue feathers, colors symbolic of the matriarchal and patriarchal societies,[7] retaining their political significance to this day.*

Burial customs are often very distinctive of a culture and we should give considerable weight to the numerous urn burials found by Professor Homet around the Amazon. He writes:

> A majority of ancient peoples believed that reincarnation was possible only under certain circumstances: the body must keep its shape so that it would be prepared to receive the vanished soul again on its return to a corporeal form. These impulses led to the formation of two burial customs among prehistoric peoples: mummification and double burial. It is the second custom which is well known in earliest America and which has been carried on into our day. We actually met with it during an expedition into the unexplored region of the Northern Amazon, a red-painted skeleton was being laid away in an earthenware urn. The urns were biconical in form and are set in grottoes and rock crypts, the walls of which are decorated with drawings. On the Amazonian rock-crypts one can see swastikas, triple triangles, zigzag lines, spirals, meander fret work, forms which one could call pure Mykenaean or Trojan, which is to say they are so analogous that only a common fountain head can be assumed.
>
> These urns which we were to find for the first time in the North Amazon, are identical with the Etruscan ones in Italy and those found in Lausitz in Germany. They are also very similar to the urns in Brittany which date back to the Celtic epoch in France. And all these urns are the relatives of those of prehistoric Crete.[5]

Back of a slate mirror, southeastern Veracruz, Mexico. It resembles Egyptian bas relief carving of the Semites, certainly not Amerindians.

Beliefs about death can also express themselves in the forms of the tombs used, leaving clear and permanent evidence. One very interesting example of this is the small hole left in the top slab of Egyptian tombs to allow the soul, in the form of a bird, to escape. This highly distinctive feature is also found in graves at Tiahuanaco, and I cannot believe that such a far-fetched idea occurred quite independently to the two peoples (Plate 25).

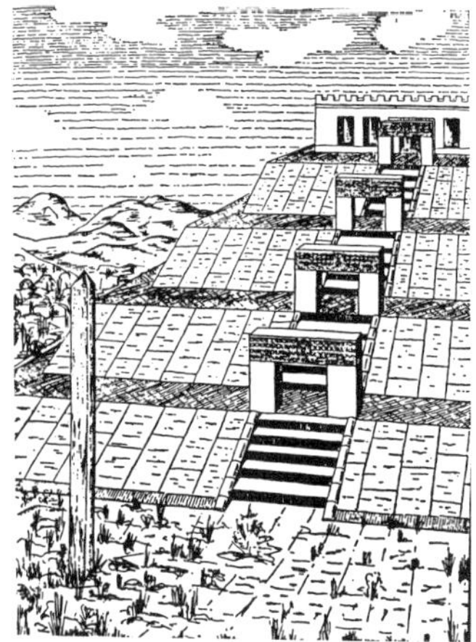

PLATE 36
The obelisk in front of the Temple of the Moon at Puma Punca, Tiahuanaco, virtually identical to obelisks in Egypt. Inca tradition said that the gods began from Lake Titicaca and the Sumerian tradition was of the mountainland, Kur, far to the west of Mesopotamia, where was Dilmun, the Paradise Land, home of the gods and of the dead.[8] *In Egypt the co-Creator god, Set, after being defeated by Horus, slowly became our devil, Satan. Set's symbol was the head of a creature like a jackal or coyote. In central California, the coyote was both co-Creator and evil spirit.*

When grave goods were provided for the dead it was, among other things, to bribe the dead not to return and trouble their associates in this world: haunt them, perhaps kill them.

Religious beliefs in general are embodied on the grandest scale in religious architecture and in America this took a distinctive form: the stepped temple or ziggurat of Mesopotamia, of Denmark, Britain and Southeast Asia. In Central America almost all temples were of this type, and an amazing number were built. One city alone contained some three hundred, some small, some huge, and Mexico has been claimed to be the country of a hundred thousand of such pyramids: tiny, of course, as well as great. In the west of England, Silbury Hill (Plate 122) can be seen to have been originally stepped, as was the temple on the Isle of Man.

Some of the ziggurats are enormous. Among the ruins of Tiahuanaco, by Lake Titicaca, is the Acapana. The Verrills describe it as:

> an immense truncated pyramidal hill one hundred and seventy feet in height and measuring 496 by 650 feet at the base and with each side almost mathematically in line with the respective cardinal points of the compass. Originally the entire surface was faced with huge rectangular stone blocks and smaller stones, but the greater part of these has been carried away by the railway workers and the natives.
>
> An immense stone stairway once led to the summit but only a few of the steps of enormous stones now remain. The greater part of the top of the man-made hill is occupied by a huge artificial lake provided with beautifully cut and fitted and most scientifically designed overflow conduits. Although the original purpose of the Akapana is not definitely known, yet there seems little doubt that it served the combined purposes of a place of worship and a gigantic baptismal font, very similar in its design to such fonts on artificial hills in the Near East and known to the Sumerians as *Apasus* or *E-Abzus*.[6]

Here we touch on the critical point, the similarity of American ziggurats to those of the Middle East. Most obviously there is the general form of the stepped pyramid as such. After the commencement of the third millennium this was virtually the only kind of temple characteristic of Sumer, Akkad, Babylon and Assyria, where ziggurats were built or repaired from 2900 to 800 B.C. But it is not only the general form of these pyramids that is common to the Middle East and to America. In both regions there was a temple on top for the benefit of the god that—again in both regions—was also used by the priests for astronomy. In both regions the sides of the temples were often accurately aligned with the four points of the compass. In both regions a broad flight of steps, a Jacob's ladder, led from the ground to the temple at the summit. Outside at least two of the temples in Peru, at Puma Punca and Tiahuanaco, were obelisks like those of Egypt. In Mexico the stepped temple for the goddess was round, which agrees with the Old World opinion that the square shape belonged to men, the round shape to women. Notice that the magnetic compass had to have been in use millennia before the time of Christ.

One of the vital questions about these American ziggurats is when they were built. The scholarly opinion used to be that they were put up far too late to have been copies of Middle Eastern models, as expressed by Jacquetta Hawkes in her criticism of my earlier book, but we know that was mistaken. The earliest American ziggurats fall well within the period of construction in the Old World. One, near Cuernavaca in Mexico, was excavated by Dr. Byron Cummings. It looked at first like a large overgrown hill that had been covered by streams of lava, but under the lava was a stepped temple of great complexity. It has been dated around 1600 B.C.[7] Others go back even further and Edward Lanning cites research showing that great ceremonial centers, including ziggurats, were being constructed on the coast of Peru between 2500 and 1800 B.C.[8] If this dating is correct, then ziggurats began to be built in America only a few hundred years after they began to be built in the Middle East—a near incredible coincidence if the two sets of people knew nothing of each other, and this was independent invention, as the universities require.

The coincidence becomes still more stretched if Lanning is right in giving the same early dates for some distinctive burial customs shared by Peru and the Old World, such as multiple burials in which servants were sacrificed to accompany their masters into the next world, and the practice of mummifying dead bodies. Mummification was carried out in the more arid parts of America by simply allowing the bodies to dry out, but in the damper regions they were eviscerated and treated with resin and oil, as in Egypt and on the Canary Islands. Artificial tears of various materials were placed on the face coverings of mummy masks in South America as they were in Egypt. Like the Romans, the Incas placed a metal disk or obol in the mouth of a corpse: doubtless to pay Charon and the cabin crew as they traveled to the next world. Food and drink were placed beside the corpse to keep it supplied until it reached the next world.

The Mexicans also made masks for the faces of the noble dead, like the Phoenicians, the Mycenaeans and the Akan on top of the gold mines in Ghana; and the Mexicans indulged in extensive trepanning, again like the Old World. Once more we must ask, what are the chances of these practices being arrived at independently?

This same question recurs constantly when we consider the sheer number of arts, crafts and techniques, the same assemblage that appears both in America and in the lands around the Mediterranean. Some examples are given by Lanning in his study of the early period on the Peruvian coast. They include the development of art in many materials, the use of spindles and spindle whorls, mirrors made of jet, earplugs, slings and other things.

Pre-Columbian America is said not to have known the wheel, but toys found in children's graves all the way from Mexico to Panama prove otherwise. Dogs in pre-Columbian America were similar to dogs in the Old World and were also mummified as in Egypt.

Wheeled toy found at Remojadas, Veracruz. Others have been found in various places in Mexico and Panama. There was a cultural phase in Mexico earlier than the Toltec/Olmec one in the Cuicuilco valley.[9] Cui was the Mexican name for the earth mother, to be compared with Greek Gaea, Babylonian Ki, etc. The Spaniards found so many female idols on an island off Yucatán that they called it the island of Women, Isla Mujeres.

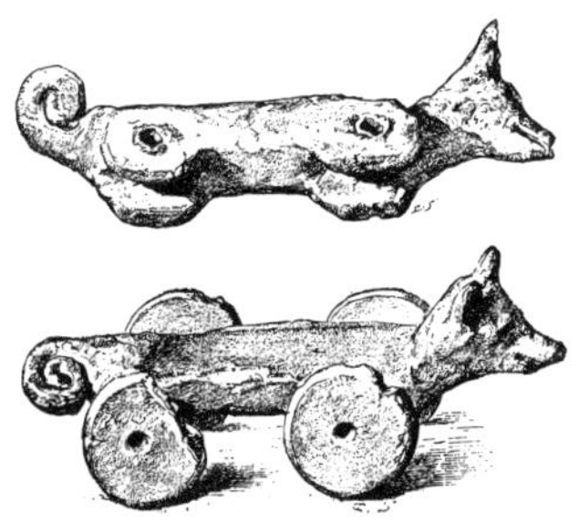

Carts, children's toys found at Popocatépetl by Charnay. Dogs as wheeled toys were also found in Mesopotamia.[10]

PLATE 37

Egyptian pyramid of Saqqâra by the Nile, 2800 B.C., the Egyptians being sun worshippers. Mexican ziggurats are idential with these first Egyptian ziggurats and Marcel Homet states that their mural paintings are identical. Mexico carried the same story of the Great Flood, which they called Catena-ma-Noa, which reconstituted in Semitic, Homet claims, simply means Flood of Noah. As the Central American ruling class were first the Poseidon people and then Hyksos refugees after being booted out of Egypt, all this is quite understandable. The little chapel on top of the ziggurat, missing now in both America and Mesopotamia, was used for astronomy. The Atlas people, known as the Seth people to Mesopotamia, Set to Egypt, were recognized as the real developers of astronomy. Pliny, in his Natural History, *writes: "the firmament explained long before by Atlas."*[11] *"Atlas, son of Libya, invented astronomy."*[12] *Egyptian pyramids and Mexican ziggurats were both aligned to the cardinal points. The pyramid and the ziggurat were ceremonial representations of the primeval hill, which, tradition said, emerged out of the waters and from which Creation began. The name of the Creator God of Heliopolis who did this was Atum. Ionian visitors judged the Egyptian gods to be the same as Greek gods with some differences.*[13] *Several ivory statues, sculptures and bas-reliefs of the First Dynasty were among Egypt's best, Massoulard maintains. Saqqâra is the most ancient Egyptian pyramid.*

Pyramid of the Sun outside Mexico City: note the similarity both of form and function. Virtual identity in ecclesiastical architecture presupposes virtual identity in culture. In the Mexican language Nahuatl, spk *means crocodile, to be compared with Egyptian* sbk; *in Nahuatl* papolotl *means butterfly, compare with the latin* papilio; tlalli *means land, compare with Latin* tellus, teo *means god as in Mycenaean Greek, and so on. The four sides of the Mexican teocallis faced the cardinal points of the compass.*[14] *The altars on the teocalli were crowned with perpetual flame.*[15] *The Tlazcalan tribe in Mexico functioned decimally like the Romans and, like the Romans, used an eagle as the symbol of their army. The Mexican Nahuas and the Hyksos built identical ziggurats and decorated them identically.*[16] *There were between fifty and a hundred major ziggurats in the lower Rimac valley alone, near Lima, Peru.*[17] *Tenochtitlán, site of present-day Mexico City, has been described as being in its day one of the world's largest, most beautiful and sophisticated cities. The Christians destroyed every city of ancient America. The Pythagoreans called the number ten, the decimal, atlas. Doubtless, in the little chapel on the top of this ziggurat (now missing) took place the sacrifice of the one perfect youth to the Supreme Divinity. I have myself seen the Pyramid of the Sun and the Pyramid of the Moon outside Mexico City. It is worth noticing that* nechoseth *was Hebrew for bronze, that Atl and Seth were two names for the same god, that in the Bible Enoch was the son of Seth—may not bronze therefore be the source for the name of the third or fourth largest city in the world at that time, Tenochtitlán? Let us also note that* kalia, *in classical Greek, meant shrine. Seth or Set's hair was red,*[18] *suggesting that his people were Celts.*

The stepped temple or ziggurat of Baksei Chamkrong, Angkor, Cambodia. *It is in the style of the post-Flood architecture of Mesopotamia. To begin to understand this earlier "global village" one must appreciate that in addition to the ziggurats of Mesopotamia, Southeast Asia, the Americas, there was a ziggurat ninety feet high on the island of Boeslinde, Denmark, and the mound, Silbury Hill, in the middle of the great array of ancient structures in the west of England, was originally in stepped form. There was also a simple form of stepped temple used in Polynesia.*

That Southeast Asia was closely in touch with Mesopotamia is evidenced by their ecclesiastic architecture and the name of the site of their early bronzeworking, Non Nok Tha, seems also to support this. That they were in touch with America is evidenced by the fact that the cotton grown in America from 4000 B.C. onward was a hybrid of Southeast Asian cotton and a native American cotton, so from that early date at least the Pacific provided no impassable barrier. The very specific type of cylinder seal that came into use in Mesopotamia around 3500 B.C. was also subsequently in use in Ban Chiang in Thailand—near Non Nok Tha—and was also used across North, South and Central America. Babylonian and Hindu astronomy were clearly similar.[20]

Plate 38
Predynastic (Gerzean) Egyptian cylinder seal.

Thai and Pre-Columbian cylinder seals. *Top row from Ban Chiang in Thailand, second row from Costa Rica. They were used by Amazonian Indians to apply paint to their bodies. They were also used in ancient Mexico,*[19] *in coastal Peru, in the lowlands of Colombia and Ecuador as well as in Mesopotamia and Egypt. There was a primitive alphabet used in Egypt, Crete, Caria and Spain in predynastic times.*

The question recurs with double force when one of these techniques seems to be invented in many places at about the same time. Perhaps the greatest example of this is the occurrence of the agricultural revolution in widely separated parts of the world at roughly the same time. Consider the case of America, which was supposed to be isolated from the rest of the world, except across the Bering Strait. The agricultural revolution happened in the Middle East around 8000 B.C., and the first evidence of it in America is a thousand years later. The gap between the Old and New World is therefore not great. Archaeology is still in the pre–Louis Pasteur, pre–Joseph Lister stage, when doctors believed that diseases developed spontaneously—as did woodworms in waterlogged wood—in place of being carried and infected: remember the Pasteur phrase, "*omne vivum ex ovo.*" People who really are in isolation from one another do not move forward at such similar speeds. Consider the Africans south of the equator, the Australian Aborigines and the Eastern Slavs. How many of the same inventions did they make independently of one another in the two thousand years before the Western Europeans overran the world? On a shorter time scale, consider the Japanese during their centuries of self-imposed isola-

PLATE 39
THE STEPPED TEMPLE OR ZIGGURAT OF TEMPLE 1 AT TIKÁL, GUATEMALA. *Religion and the temple were the core and center of society and each part of a temple was of symbolic importance. As we have noted, similarity in church architecture identifies similarity in religion and culture. It should be further noted that kings were buried within American ziggurats as they were in Egyptian pyramids. In Mexico the stepped temples were called* teocalli. Teo *means god in Greek Linear B, and* kalia *in Greek means shrine. There are Mayan paintings in Guatemala of white men with blond hair engaged in a sea battle.*[21] *The Mayan calendar had its precise counterparts in China, Siam and Java.*[22] *It was also similar to that of the Egyptians and excellent. Mayan numerology was like that of Mesopotamia.*[23] *The ziggurat, which is symbolizing the Mound of Creation, also provided a place of refuge in times of flood. They were essentially post-Deluge architecture.*[24] *Cortés soon discovered that the Aztecs used them to fight from. It is recorded that Sargon of Akkad's conquests had reached lands beyond the Upper Sea (the Mediterranean) including Anaku (the Bronze Land or America).*[25]

tion. During that time, Europe gave birth to modern science and passed through the Industrial Revolution. The Japanese, who have since proved their enormous aptitude for science-based industry, had not begun to cover the same ground. The idea that human cultures will, left to themselves, progress through the same stages at even remotely comparable speeds is quite simply not true.

Another example of the same advance taking place in two places at about the same time was touched on in Chapter 1, namely the beginnings of copper mining in America on Isle Royale and the Upper Peninsula of Michigan and its use around the Black Sea. In both places it would seem to have started around 6000 B.C., although the dates for Lake Superior have subsequently been substantially queried. Furthermore the stone tools used on Isle Royale were essentially the same as those used in subsequent millennia by miners working the copper mines of Cheshire and of Ireland, indeed around much of the world. Tools can be a very good indicator of contact between peoples. R. J. Forbes has written:

> Archaeology affords us definite proof of the continuity of diffusion of metallurgy from a certain centre. Gordon Childe pointed out that the same hammer made of a grooved stone lashed to a forked stick heralds early mining in Sinai, Caucasia, the Alps, Spain and Cornwall and that the oldest metal tools and weapons are very similar both in Mesopotamia and Egypt and tend to differentiate from protodynastic times only. Still, certain common tools remain identical for a very long time over vast areas.[9]

It has recently been argued that developments in metallurgy in the New World more or less kept pace with the Old. If so, then this is very strong evidence of contact. Again Forbes makes very good sense on the subject:

> Simple primary discoveries such as plasticity and malleability may be repeated but every artefact that consists of a series of discoveries is more likely to have been diffused than reinvented. We must not forget that not need but prosperity is the true mother of invention and that the early metal-worker was not pushed along the path of progress because he had no idea that it was a path at all. Such an achievement as the production of bronze is already sufficiently marvellous and if we would be led to suppose that it evolved independently in the New and the Old Worlds our wonderment would be simply doubled![10]

Weaving was another technique that appeared at suspiciously close times in the Old and New World, about 4000 B.C. in Peru.

Both the horizontal and the vertical types of loom used in Peru were the same as those in the Old World and one of the looms used in early Peru was identical to a loom used in early India in all its eleven working parts.

PLATE 40

REED BOATS AND BIRDMEN IN PERU PORTRAYED ON MOCHICHA POTTERY. *Fishermen in* tortora *reed boats on the coast of Peru with birdmen in attendance: scene painted on Mochicha pottery, Pacific coast of Peru. As in Egypt, the Incas' sister was queen in her own right.*[26] *Like a custom of today, no shoes were to be worn in the Incas' temples.*[27] *The coastal valleys of Peru were a natural paradise.*

A Mochicha pot, on the Pacific coast of Peru, carries the picture of a reed boat with men wearing bird masks alongside. The Incas had cairns in the countryside to which, as in today's Scotland, every passerby was expected to add a stone;[28] *as in Scotland I have added mine. Cuzco, the capital of the Incas' Peru, was known as "the navel" of the earth,*[29] *as was Delphi, Easter Island, Nippur, Mexico's Tenochtitlán, etc., as we have already seen. Spanish chronicler Cieza de Léon records the presence of a white man with a beard by Lake Titicaca from a time before the Incas. He was a mighty man who taught the people everything to do with law and civilization. He was creator of all things and commanded men to be good to one another and live without violence.*[30]

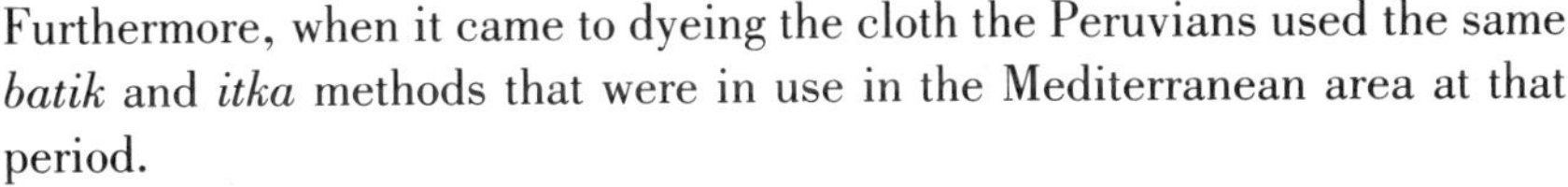

Furthermore, when it came to dyeing the cloth the Peruvians used the same *batik* and *itka* methods that were in use in the Mediterranean area at that period.

As with textiles, so with bronze: it was not just the general discovery but the particular techniques that were common to both sides of the Atlantic. Both the *cire perdue* and the *mise en couleur* methods of casting were used in Mexico and South America as they were around the Mediterranean.

In building, too, apart from the fact that similar kinds of ecclesiastical buildings were erected on both sides of the Atlantic, similar techniques were used. The huge blocks of stone at Tiahuanaco were held together by copper rivets (sometimes even by gold rivets), a method of construction found also in Assyria and Etruria. It seems likely that the blocks were sawn out of the rock face by a method used by the Cretans, who cut the rock into *ashlars* with bronze saws. It should be noticed that the system of government used in Peru, government by god-kings—as we have seen in Greek Linear B the word for god-king is *teo wanak*—was a form of political control that used to be almost worldwide and that still continues to this day: in Japan, with the Ismailis, in Africa, in Southeast Asia.

Another technique used in Crete and at Tiahuanaco was that of building a wall by putting up two outer faces of large stones and filling the gap between them with soil. And in the temple at Chavin, known as the Castillo, there was an ingenious system of air conduits carrying fresh air to every room, similar to the system in the Cretan palace at Knossos.

The ancient Peruvians also shared an architectural subtlety with the Athenians, the trick known as *entasis* by which all apparently straight lines are very slightly curved, so as to give an impression of strength and even straightness. This device was also used on the first ziggurat at Ur, two thousand years before it was employed on the Parthenon.

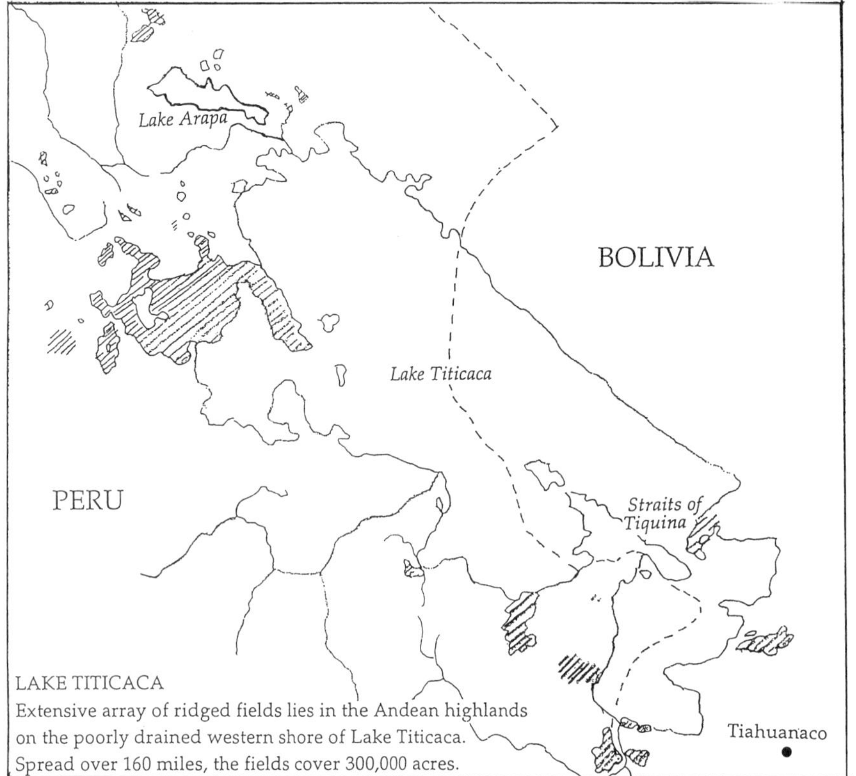
Lake Arapa
BOLIVIA
Lake Titicaca
PERU
Straits of Tiquina
LAKE TITICACA
Extensive array of ridged fields lies in the Andean highlands on the poorly drained western shore of Lake Titicaca. Spread over 160 miles, the fields cover 300,000 acres.
Tiahuanaco

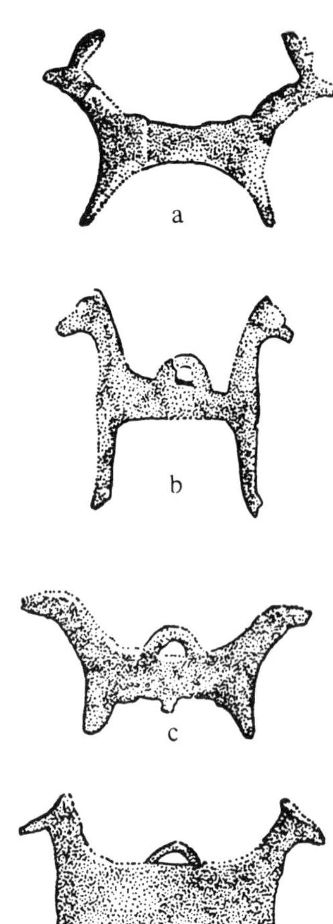
a
b
c
d

Plate 41

Lake Titicaca. *Extensive array of ridged fields lies in the Andean highlands on the poorly drained western shore of Lake Titicaca. Spread over 160 miles, the fields cover 200,000 acres. Amerindian tradition said that Tiahuanaco was built by white and bearded men, and that it was the principal site of a foreign white race.*[31] *In the Incas' Peru the blond women met by Pizarro were called by the Amerindians, as in Plato, "the children of the gods."*[32] Patesi *means political boss in Sumerian: compare this to Potosí, the nearby Andean city next to the silver mines. Lake Titicaca is 12,508 feet above sea level. Binding reeds and placing earth upon them was a means of farming in a swamp.*[33] *I believe this method of farming lies behind the Mesopotamian description of the Americas as "the Field of Reeds." In South America it was certainly employed in eastern Bolivia, western Ecuador, northern Colombia and coastal Surinam.*[34] *The Incas did have some writing, according to Montesinos, on processed leaves of the plantain, but the priests forbade the use of it. The ridged-field irrigation farming of South America was like that of Melanesia and tropical Africa.*[35]

Heine-Geldern drew attention to the almost identical figures of double animals from (a) Kedabeg, Kulakent, Georgia; (b) Luristan, Persia; and (c) and (d) Tiahuanaco. Other interesting similarities are that the Incan name for the earth mother was Pachamama and the Sumerian name was Mama: princesses were called pallas *and we must think of Pallas Athena, and the inheritance of the nation of Peru passed to the daughter, the Inca having to marry his sister. In the Peruvian language of Quechua, gold is* coro; *in Mycenaean Greek it is* kuruso, *in Bolivian Aymará it is* qori. *Carpenters' tools in bronze closely resembled the carpenters' tools of today and furnish an interesting linkage.*

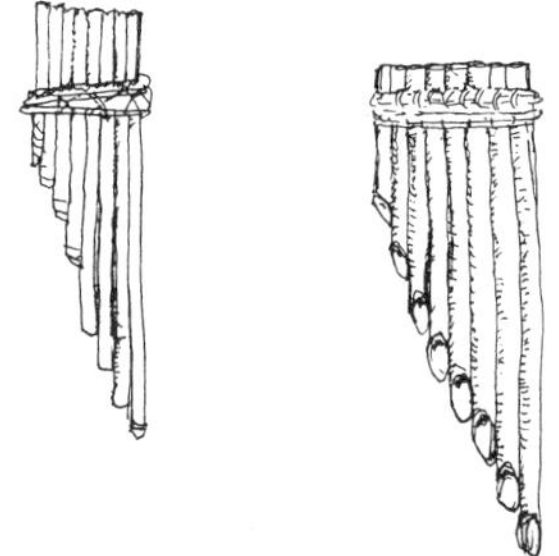

Panpipes from the Solomon islands (left) and Bolivia (right).

To round off this list of shared techniques and inventions, let us consider five very different items: irrigation, boats, seals, mosaics and wheels.

Like the people of the Middle East, the Peruvians were much concerned with irrigation, especially on the dry coastal belt where watering made all the difference between highly fertile agricultural land and a barren desert. By cutting irrigation canals they drew off the water from the rivers running westward out of the Andes, but they also tapped underground sources by digging into the sloping ground horizontal wells called *guanats*, long tunnels with vertical shafts for ventilation. This very specialized system of collecting water is used in the Middle East to this day.[11]

It is also worth noting that the water code of Hammurabi, king of Babylon around 1800 B.C., closely resembled Incan practices.

Two peoples who lived on the shores of lakes might well hit on the idea of using reeds to make boats. What is striking about the boats on Lake Titicaca and those on the Nile is their similarity in construction as well as material.

The use of seals to impress a stamp on wax or some other plastic substance is, of course, common among a number of peoples. Mostly these seals are simply flat pieces of stone or some other material with designs engraved in them. The idea of making the impression by rolling a cylinder over the soft material is much less obvious, but it was used by the Maya, on whose territory a large number of cylinder seals have been excavated, and also, characteristically, by the Egyptians, by the Sumerians, the Akkadians and later the Phoenicians: the earliest Mesopotamian (3500 B.C.) cylinder seals are, in fact, said to be esthetically the best they ever produced.

An interesting mosaic floor was dug up on the Mexican site of La Venta. The pieces of mosaic were found to be laid on asphalt, the same technique as was used in ancient Crete.[12]

Finally wheels. The wheeled toys that have been discovered in America have already been mentioned, and they prove beyond question that the principle of the wheel was known. It is impossible to realize that a toy can move on small wheels and not know that a cart could move on big ones. In fact big wheels have been found, solid stone wheels that may have been used to help move the huge blocks of stone used in the cyclopean walls at Tiahuanaco, some of which weighed as much as a hundred or even two hundred tons. The usual explanation of the fact that wheels did not go into general use in America is the absence of a draft animal, and this seems a perfectly adequate reason. At any rate it is certain that the principle had either been (less probably) discovered by the early American people or (more probably) imported from across the sea. It is significant that wheeled toys, like those found in America, were popular in Sumer and the Indus Valley from around 3000 B.C. And we shall encounter some interesting evidence later on that perhaps, for a limited period, horses and chariots

PLATE 42
Mayan sarcophagus at Palenque, with base broadened, although with the Maya there was no practice of standing the sarcophagus up, while the Egyptians, who employed the same style of sarcophagus, stood it on end. It has to be noted at the same time that the Maya of Guatemala for most of their history did not use metals.[36] *Digging stick weights, such as were shown in Egyptian hieroglyphs and were also used on the Aegean islands and across Neolithic Africa—I possess a large number of the latter—are also found in the Early Classic period of the Guatemala highlands. As in Mesopotamia, the Maya were preoccupied with the mystery of time. Their calendar was capable of dealing in times of more than ninety million years.*[37]

had been used in Mexico, which led to these children's toy chariots being in their graves.

We have already noticed the extraordinary accuracy of the mathematics and astronomy practiced by various early peoples. The Maya, for example, computed the length of the year as 365.2420 days, compared with the modern calculation of 365.2422. This precision of measurement seems to have appeared suddenly among a supposedly primitive people somewhere around 600 B.C. Since it is quite obvious that a measurement like that could not have been made over anything but a very long period of time, the Maya may have been in contact with outsiders with comparable interests and skills.

This calendar required a sophisticated mathematical system able to cope with very large numbers. The Maya had such a system, which included a symbol for zero, something which at that time was shared only by the Babylonians and the Assyrians.

In Peru, too, mathematical astronomy reached a high level of precision. The obvious way to divide the year into two halves is to take the periods between the spring and autumn equinoxes, but in fact this does not give a perfectly accurate result. A small correction needs to be made, and the figure taken by the Tiahuanaco people was the same as the one taken by megalithic astronomers in structures on the east side of the Atlantic apparently used for calculating the calendar.[13] A meeting in America of archaeoastronomers a few years ago allowed that Mayan astronomy was virtually identical with the astronomy of the builders of the stone circles in Britain, a vitally important comparison.

The large stone ring at Tiahuanaco is strikingly similar to European constructions.

A good deal of weight can be placed on similarities of this kind. Neugebauer has emphasized the value of mathematics and astronomy in identifying relations between different cultures. Astronomy, he points out, requires precise numerical constants and scientific treatises and "will often give very accurate information about the time and circumstances of contact."[14]

Before leaving the question of techniques shared between the Old and New World it is only honest to point out that there were a few they did not share. We have dealt with the wheel and, in Chapter 3, with some unused inventions such as glass and the arch. But there are some omissions that seem genuinely paradoxical. One is that no American civilization used the potter's wheel, although it was certainly in use in the Middle East during the period of contact. The answer may simply be that while cultures in contact with each other tend to adopt each other's inventions they do not invariably adopt all of them. The Chinese continue to use an "alphabet" containing tens of thousands of characters although they have now had centuries of intercourse with Europeans who have found out how to do the job with twenty-six. We know, too, that the Maya did not use bronze, although one or two American cultures did. The Chinese have their reasons and so, no doubt, did the Maya. The difference is simply that our knowledge of early American history is too slight to tell us what those reasons were. But the absence of alluvial tin with copper in their own country may well explain the Mayan non-use of bronze. These disturbing discrepancies must be noted, however.

In details of art and design, as in basic techniques, telling similarities with transatlantic models often turn up. Plate 35 shows the back of a slate mirror from Veracruz that dates from the Totonac period. The carving is in characteristic Egyptian style, and the head has a decidedly Semitic look.

A very distinctive ceremonial bronze axe was made in Egypt, pierced so as to leave a figure, modeled in relief, framed by the edges of the blade. The Olmecs used an identical design, as can be seen in Plate 120. Also from the Senufo tribe of the Ivory Coast of West Africa we find the pick of an axe that closely resembles a figure used both in the Mexican and the Cretan pictographic scripts.

Among the relics of the Incas many figures of ducks have been found resembling weights used in Babylon, where the standard talent was in the form of a duck.

Also in Peru, the Chimus produced a very curious kind of double jug in which two containers were connected to a single spout. Similar jugs are found among Cretan and Etruscan ruins.[15]

At Tiahuanaco some figures of double animals were found. This is perhaps an idea two peoples might have conceived independently, but Plate 41 shows that the designs are more similar than one would expect of chance.

Panpipes just like those of the Old World were found in use in Peru, Panama and Colombia. The same panpipes also turned up on the Solomon Islands, tuned to the same pitch (Plate 41).[16]

A particularly interesting stone sarcophagus was dug up at Palenque in Mexico. As can be seen in Plate 42, the base is curiously broadened out. This is a Phoenician style, copied in turn from a wooden type used by the Egyptians.[17] Now the point is that the original Egyptian design was made to be stood on end, while the Mayan sarcophagus was laid flat, so that its distinctive broad base had no functional reason to exist. This disposes of the argument, often raised, that similar objects found in different cultures are simply examples of two peoples striking on the same answer to the same practical problem. With the Mayan sarcophagus there was no practical problem involved. The distortion of its shape has no purpose that one can see. One might use the shape of a coffin to call attention to the head of the deceased, but why would anyone want to lay emphasis on a corpse's feet? There are only two real possibilities: either this was a caprice of design that, by yet another unlikely coincidence, happened to mimic Phoe-

PLATE 43
COMPARISON MADE BETWEEN NEW WORLD AND OLD WORLD ARTIFACTS.

The pattern on this Eighteenth Dynasty Egyptian cup resembles the popcorn variety of maize. In Mesopotamia the calendar was recorded on knotted strings called guhsu, *in Peru they were called* quipu. *With the Sumerians private property and temple communism functioned side by side as with the Incas of Peru.*[38] *When the Inca died he had to be accompanied into the next world by his retainers. On a tablet Gilgamesh, Sumerian king of Uruk, refers to those murdered to accompany him into the next world as "those who lay with me . . . in the purified palace."*[39]

Gorgon from Athens.

nician work, or the Maya were quite simply copying a Phoenician model.

In this section, some of the objects we have dealt with were made in a later period of history, after the great era of voyaging was over. This, all the same, does not invalidate our belief that they indicate a continued contact between the Old and the New World. They could have been based on traditions going back to earlier times, or some of them could have resulted from the later contacts that continued sporadically after regular commerce had ended. The alternative leaves us with a whole series of coincidences, which I myself find hard to accept. It may well be that the collapse of Mayan civilization around A.D. 900 may have been occasioned by diseases brought to Guatemala by Old World sailors in the days when long-distance sailing of the Atlantic had almost, but not entirely, stopped, and immunity had been lost. For with humans, as with stock rearing, immunity can be lost in a generation or two.

Later contact seems to be the only plausible explanation of the other archaeological finds. In Chichén Itzá, as we have seen, there is a Mayan "Well of Sacrifice" into which human victims and votive offerings used to be thrown to appease the gods. Amongst the Mayan work excavators have found a wood and wax doll marked with Roman script that has been dated to the thirteenth century A.D. And near the shore in Venezuela, a hoard of several hundred Roman coins was dug up, the latest of them from about A.D. 350.[18] Could these objects have been accidentally or deliberately planted at some time after the European invasion? In principle it is possible, but who would have taken a doll at least two centuries old across the Atlantic and thrown it down a well? What was a collection of Roman coins, all of them well over a thousand years old, doing in Venezuela? The only plausible reason for doubting the value of these bits of evidence would be that the excavators were "doing a Piltdown"; and there is absolutely no reason to suspect them of that. On any reasonable balance of probability these Roman objects show clearly enough that some contact across the Atlantic in that period still existed. And what the men of the fourth and thirteenth centuries A.D. could do, with their limited knowledge of the world and of astronomy, the men of the third and fourth millennia B.C. could have done far more easily with their well-organized cartography, geometry and astronomy. At this point we will do well to record Seneca's lines in his play *Medea:*

For at a distant date this ancient world
Will westwards stretch its bounds and then disclose
Beyond the main a vast new continent
With realms of wealth and might.

This, surely, is not just the invention of a great writer and philosopher but some sort of awareness of what had been going on in the not-so-distant past and, in fact, had not totally stopped. Christopher Columbus made his own translation of these lines before setting out.

Some of the strongest evidence of contact comes from plants. If a species known to have originated on one side of the ocean can be clearly shown to have reached the other before Columbus, then only two things are possible: either it came over by "natural" means, such as seeds floating across the sea, or else it was brought by human visitors. The certainty with which this can be decided varies between different plants. Let us begin at the uncertain, tentative end of the scale.

There is a certain blue-eyed grass, *Sysirinchium Bermudiana*, which from prehistoric times has grown only in Bermuda and in Ireland.

The silk-cotton tree, the bombax, an excellent timber for dugouts, is found on both sides of the Atlantic. It is not known to which side it is native.

A botanist, Galletly Wilson, working in the Karamajong area of Uganda, argues that tobacco, a native American plant, was used across Africa as snuff long before the arrival of the Portuguese. And that the indigenous American sweet potato was also in use in Uganda before the days of Columbus. The pre-Columbian name for the sweet potato in parts of America is *kumari*, a Sanskrit name, not an Amerindian name.

Another indigenous-to-America plant, the peanut, is said to have been cultivated in China by 3000 B.C.[19]

In the ruins of Pompeii murals have been examined by a botanist and found to contain accurate portrayals of two plants that are both thought to originate in tropical America, the pineapple and the soursop (*Annona squamosa*).[20]

Another plant native to America is embodied in two gold pots from Egypt, whose design seems to reproduce the form of a cob of popcorn maize (see Plate 43).

When we turn to cotton, we move from the realm of hints to that of near-certainty. All domestic American cottons are what are known as tetraploids; that is, they contain two sets of recognizably distinct genes. One set resembles the genes of American wild cottons, the other the genes of all Asiatic cottons, domestic and wild. There is no possible way this could have come about except by the interbreeding of the two stocks.

We know that cotton was being used in Peru in the fourth millennium B.C. using fibers from the cross-bred Asian-American plant. The conclusion seems to follow without doubt: at some time before that the seeds of Asian cotton had been brought into America, and they did not come by natural means. Even if a few seeds had managed to drift all the way across the Pacific they could never have remained fertile after months of immersion in salt water. Some anti-diffusionists have produced theories about land bridges across which men could have carried them at around the time the hybrid appears in America, but these are fantasies, quite unacceptable to the geophysicist.

Godhead from San Augustia, Columbia.

Gorgon from Syracuse.

Lenzon from Chavin de Huantar, Peru.

Above is a comparison that has been made between Greek and South American Indian Gorgon-type masks. In Homer the Gorgon is described as a "portent of Zeus that beareth the aegis."[40] M. L. West, writing about Hesiod's Theogony, *says that the Gorgons were sea nymphs. The sea nymphs were not exactly toothsome! Hesiod refers to the Gorgons "who dwell beyond the glorious Ocean . . . where are the clear-voiced Hesperides."[41] They seemingly came from the Americas to Greece, and not vice versa.*

PLATE 44

INDIAN SCULPTURE AT PRE-COLUMBIAN COPÁN. *This carving depicts elephants and mahouts on Stela B at Copán. Opponents of the theory of cultural diffusion argue that these are not elephants but macaws with turbaned mahouts on their heads! As these pages proceed we must begin to consider whether the Indus Valley civilization was not conducted, in its patriarchal period, by the same Seth-Atlas peoples as were running the Middle East and, in due course, much of the rest of the world. For a period Seth was also ruling Upper Egypt. It was only after being thrown out of the Old World that they set up in business in the New.*

PLATE 45

The human plumed serpent depicted in ancient Egypt. Compare this with the Mayan god Cucumatz, who was depicted as a serpent with feathers. Cucumatz was the androgynous Creator, the Maker.[42] *This drawing comes from the tomb of the Egyptian pharaoh Seti I. The Christian historian Eusebius wrote that the first and most divine being was the serpent in the form of a hawk. In Mayan tradition the Creator God Cucumatz moved across the face of the waters. In Mexico the Creator was called Quetzalcóatl, the human, plumed water serpent: just as the Greek Typhoen was depicted in Greece. The Aztecs' female plumed water serpent was called Cihuacóatl,*[43] *Cihua to be compared with Greek Gaea, Babylonian Ki, etc. Quetzalcóatl also wore a mitre like the kings of Upper Egypt and like Christian bishops. His title was Lord of the Wind, like Enlil, high god of Sumer. He was a sun god, in Mexico revered for his gifts of science and the arts. The Egyptian Creation Mound, the primeval hill, was called Benben, which emerged from the waters of Chaos to become Atum, the Lord of Creation. In Scots, mountain is called Ben, hence Ben Nevis, etc. Texts tell us the Egyptians were not seamen, they had a great fear of dying abroad, because they did not wish to miss the funeral ritual. In Egypt the province or nome was called* snwr, *compare this with the Ivory Coast tribe called Senufo. Ptah, god of Memphis, was the divine artificer who created the sun god. He was worshipped as the patron of all arts and crafts, and his high priest accordingly bore the title Chief of the Masterworkmen.*

PLATE 46

THE TITAN CHRONOS OR SATURN REPRESENTED BY DRAGONS. *The Titans' dragons being the source of the Vikings' dragonships at one end of the world and the Chinese dragons at the other: not to mention Quetzalcóatl, the Mexican Creator God in person, nearly always depicted as a dragon. The Titans as such were symbolized by the dragon. When the Titans, the Hyksos, were thrown out of Egypt, Greek tradition said that they were imprisoned in Tartarus (alias America). In the Middle East the power and wealth of the dragon Kur was proverbial.*[44]

Strong as the case is for cotton, there are three plants for which in George Carter's estimation it is even stronger. He classes them as "proven cultural transfers," that is, "plants that even the bitterest opponent of transpacific diffusion admits were carried by man to or from Asia and America." They are the sweet potato (*Ipomoaea batatas*), the coconut (*Cocos nucifera*) and bottle gourd (*Lagenaria siceraria*).

The sweet potato is an American plant, but it is clear that it had been introduced into Polynesia a long time before the Europeans arrived, long enough for variations in its form to have appeared, and also variations in its name, and for it to have taken an established place in mythology and ritual. The name given to it in Polynesia, *kumar*, is the same as in one part of America. It is also very close to two Sanskrit names, *kumari*, the lotus (another edible rhizome) and *Kumara*, the earth mother. It is now generally recognized that the sweet potato was carried across the Pacific in pre-Columbian days from America.

The coconut is an ancient and important plant in Southeast Asia. For a long time there was a controversy over when it reached America but it is now generally reckoned that it was present when the Spaniards arrived, and there is good evidence for this in Spanish documents. Despite what has sometimes been said, the coconut cannot remain viable after floating for a long time in seawater. The longest time for which a coconut is known to have kept its fertility in these conditions is not nearly long enough to have let it cross the Pacific on the weak equatorial countercurrent, as it would have had to do to reach America. George Carter concludes: "Man carried the coconut either to or from America. In view of its great importance in Asia and its apparent unimportance in America I think it probable that man carried it to America, probably relatively late in pre-contact times."

This figure comes from a Greek pot portraying Typhoen, who, in Greek poetry, stood for the latter Peoples of the Sea. He is depicted as a human, plumed serpent, as was Quetzalcóatl, the god-king of Mexico, whose very name in Nahuatl means quetzal for the sacred quetzal bird, with cóatl *meaning water serpent: the Mexican plumed human serpent. In Jewish tradition there was enmity between Jahweh and Tehom, the sea people: their version of St. George and the Dragon. The Arabs called Tehom Al-Tinnin, a suggestive name.*[45] *The dragon is located on islands in the western part of Ocean.*[46] *The importance of a mountain to western Semites in the far west of Ocean and the far east of Ocean, should be noticed. Typhon means Foam of the Sea as does Vira Cocha, the divine culture hero of the Incas. The fighting between Typhoen and Zeus, Greek tradition said, was literally worldwide. Such historical evidence as we have of the end of the Bronze Age supports this. Having been defeated in battle, the Typhoenians were the principal cause of Seth hatred in ancient Egypt.*[47]

The bottle gourd is one of the most widespread plants in the world, grown not as food but as a container. It is quite literally used as a bottle. It was one of the earliest plants to be cultivated in America, probably even before maize and beans, around 7000 B.C., as archaeologists have recently found. It is not, however, a native American plant but originally comes either from India or, more probably, from Africa. Once again the suggestion has been made that seeds or fruits could have floated across the sea, but no one has been able to keep one viable in saltwater for the necessary time. George Carter makes the strong point that in general the only plants whose seeds can successfully cross large stretches of seawater are those that naturally grow on the shore and produce buoyant seeds or fruits. There is a known pattern of dispersal for such plants, and it does not include the crossing from Asia to America, or from Africa to America.

The naming of plants can give a clue to their origin. The sweet potato is one example; another is maize. It is a native American plant and if it had been brought to Europe after Columbus's voyage one would expect it to be called "American corn" or perhaps "Spanish corn." It was not. In England around 1600 it was known as "Turkie" or "Sarazen" corn (that is, Turkish or Saracen) and the same Turkish origin is given to its Italian, Dutch, Swedish, German and even Spanish names.[21] In at least one old report maize is said to have been brought into Spain by the Arabs in the thirteenth century. Just how much earlier than that it was carried into the Middle East from its American home we do not know, but we can be reasonably sure that it was.

The Thanksgiving bird, the turkey, presents us with a similar paradox. It, too, is a native of America, but you would not guess that from the names given to it by different peoples. In French it is called *dinde* or *dindon* ("from India"); in Dutch and Afrikaans it is *kalkoen* ("hen of Calicut"); in Turkey itself it is *hindi;* and in India one name for it is *peru.* All this strongly suggests that it was brought to Europe from America by way of India and the Middle East. Professor Colin Renfrew says that India is a confusion with the West Indies, but, search how he will, he will not find Calicut in the West Indies. Try again, Professor Renfrew!

Lastly, a curiosity. In the *Critias* Plato says that in Atlantis there were

Plate 47

Mexican human sacrifice. *Scene of Itzá sacrifice to the sun god, who emerges from the jaws of a rattlesnake. The victim is held by four youthful* chacs. *They, the high priest and attendants (some omitted in this drawing) wear Toltec costume. Almost surely a sacrifice of the orders of Jaguars and Eagles, from a gold disk recovered from the sacred* cenote. *Pulling out the heart at the earliest part of the ceremony was also an especial feature of some Greek sacrifices.*[48] *The purpose of some forms of human sacrifice was to restore harmony to the universe. Michael Dames, writing of the Avebury Circle, comments: "Whatever the religion, when someone embraces freely the symbols of death, or death itself, then it is consistent with everything that we have seen so far that a great release of power for good should be expected to follow. The community can live on as a rational order because of the unafraid self-sacrifice of its priest."*[49] *Dames suspects foundation sacrifices under the henges in Britain and the sacrifice of a young man to Baal in Perthshire. Human sacrifice had an obvious transactional quality. Foundation sacrifices, humans immured under new buildings, were practiced widely among western Semites, West Africans and by Amerindians across America. The sacrifice was a redistribution of life force. Among the Dogon of Mali, a volunteer, buried standing, was the foundation sacrifice of a village. Human sacrifice was the propitiation of the powers that control the universe. From the Bible see: 2 Kings 23:10; Jeremiah 19:5; Psalms 106:37; and the Druids, the Celtic priests, who packed their victims into huge wicker images for burning. Similarly, in the* Popol Vuh, *the Maya kidnap strangers and sacrifice them to increase their own strength and vigor.*[50] *At Heliopolis the Egyptians used to sacrifice three men each day to Hera.*[51] *However, the Carthaginian practice of sacrificing children was only a religious twist to the common antique practice of exposure, of population control. Menelaus sacrificed two Egyptian children to improve the weather.*[52] *Epimenides of Crete sacrificed two human victims at Athens.*[53] *Sacramental cannibalism was part of the Greek Orphic rites,*[54] *which themselves originated in Egypt. This sacramental cannibalism is sublimated in the Christian Eucharist. The human victim was scourged before being sacrificed, as was Christ. Is this psychologically unrelated to the twentieth-century practice of sending millions of young men—the noblest and the best—to run on each other's machine guns? The Canaanite religions, like the Aztecs, sacrificed people on a vast scale. Cyrus Gordon writes: "The Moabite King Mesha tell us on his stela how he sacrificed thousands of captives to his god, Chemesh. Even the Hebrews practiced this grim rite at Jericho."*[55]

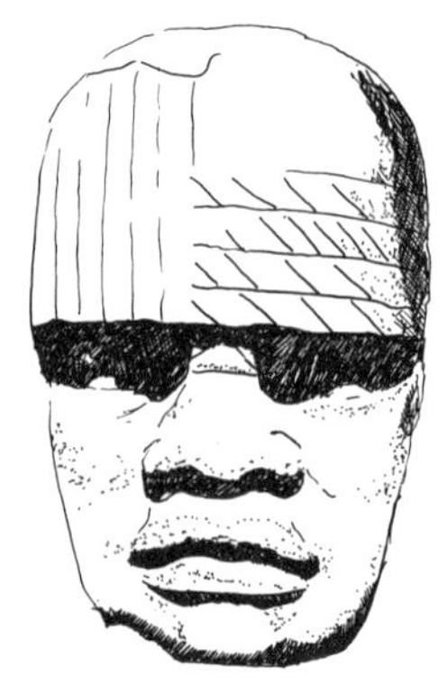

Plate 48

The Pre-Columbian African Presence in America. *Here is one of the indisputably African stone heads of the Toltec/Olmec culture of Mexico, 1550* B.C. *onward, though perhaps initiated a lot earlier. In addition to these sculptures of Africans, let us place the well-attested tribe of Africans living along the Amazon River and the Malian tradition of dispatching a large fleet of canoes westward across the Atlantic. That Quetzalcoatl, the high god of Mexico, was often painted black seems to tell us something. Occasional Amerindian traditions, seemingly referring to very early days, describe African soldiers, blacks, fighting in various parts of America. It is all part of the cosmopolitan nature of the early world. Cortes, when he pitched up in Mexico, had some black soldiers with him.*[56]

a number of elephants. On the face of it that seems to rule out America, where it used to be thought that the native American mammoth had died out by 5000 B.C. Victor Von Hagen, however, believes that it survived until 2000 B.C., which would put it well within the time range for the origin of Plato's legend. Though this in no way proves that Atlantis was America, it does remove an anomaly that had seemed to show that it was not America.

There is, incidentally, our Mayan carving (Plate 44) which clearly shows an elephant head. It is a measure of the extremes to which the opponents of early long-range sailing will go that, despite the turbaned mahout shown above the elephant's head, they argue that it is not really an elephant at all but a macaw, a parrot with a turbaned rider on its head!

If commercially valuable plants provide evidence of contact, the evidence from human beings is even more direct. Nothing could do more to validate the legends of transoceanic visitors than finding people descended from them, both black and white.

There are persistent reports from the European conquerors that they

Plate 49
Some of the Totally Foreign Portraits in Pre-Columbian America.

African boy's head from Chichen Itza. The Mayan god of war was black.[57]

Phoenician grotesque mask from Sardinia, similar to a Mexican Toltec/Olmec style positioned here next to it.

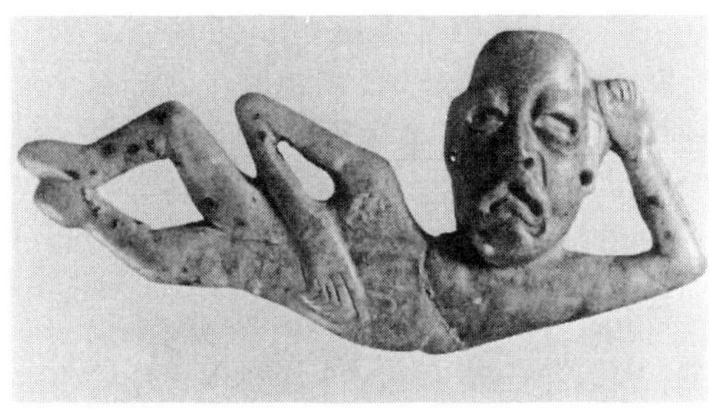

Small jade "dancing figures" from Mexico: San Geró, Guerrero (left), Tepatlaxco (left).

encountered white people. Columbus himself came across white Indians in Guanahim, today's San Salvador, "as white as any Spaniard," and Pizarro saw white-skinned Indians in the Amazon basin whom he described as corn-blond. He also reported that the Incas were white, and this is confirmed in the writings of Garcilaso de la Vega. De la Vega was himself the son of an Incan princess and a Spanish soldier, and, to record the history of his mother's people before it should be obliterated by the newcomers of his father's race, he wrote *The Royal Commentaries of the Incas*, a great historical narrative that covers a period of five hundred years before the arrival of the Spaniards. He not only records that the Incas were white: he mentions a relative of his own, who was "as white as an egg."

Perhaps the most striking of all the white people encountered by the Spaniards were the Amazons, the female warriors who apparently dominated

PLATE 50
A European head carved in stone, from the Toltec/Olmec culture of Mexico. Other Toltec/Olmec figures were Chinese or part-Chinese in appearance, which supports the statement in Plato that the Atlantians also had colonies on the other side of the Pacific. This Toltec/Olmec carving has been described as looking like "Uncle Sam" in person.

the men of their region. Fray Carvajal was the padre to the first Spanish expedition down the Amazon and his report of their first brush with these fierce fighters is detailed and specific:

> It must be explained that [the Indians] are the subjects of, and tributaries to, the Amazons, and, our coming having been made known to them, they went to them to ask help, and there came as many as ten or twelve of them, for we ourselves saw these women, who were there fighting in front of all the Indian men as women captains, and these latter fought so courageously that the Indian men did not dare to turn their backs, and anyone who did turn his back they killed with clubs right there before us, and this is the reason why the Indians kept up their defence for so long. These women are very white and tall, and have hair very long and braided and wound upon the head, and they are very robust and go about naked, [but] with their privy parts covered, with their bows and arrows in their hands, doing as much fighting as ten Indian men, and indeed there was one woman among these who shot an arrow a span deep into one of the brigantines, and others less deep, so that our brigantines looked like porcupines.[22]

"These women are very white." The statement could not be more definite, and since they fought virtually naked it cannot have been a matter of face paint mistaken for real skin in the heat of battle. Here, surely, were real descendants of those Amazon warriors against whom, Herodotus records, the Greeks fought at the River Thermodon (the "hot river"—a very reasonable description of the Amazon). There are similar reports from Orellana and a totally independent German visitor to Amazonia very many years later. Christopher Columbus himself also reported finding Amazons on the Caribbean island of Martinique.

Fray Carvajal, furthermore, reported that the Spaniards were repeatedly attacked by very tall men who stained themselves black and kept their hair clipped short. These seeming Negroes seem to have been matched by other Africans in various places. Peter Martyr, an acquaintance of Columbus, wrote: "The Spaniards found Negro slaves in this province [Darién]. They only live in regions one day's march from Quarequa, and they are fierce and cruel."

Gomora remarks that in crossing the Darién isthmus "Balboa found some negroes. He asked them whence they got there, but they could not tell, nor did they know more than this that men of colour were living near by, and they were constantly waging war with them."

Quatrefages sums up like this: "Black populations have been found in America in very small numbers only, as isolated tribes among very different populations. Such are the Charruas of Brazil, the Black Caribees of St. Vincent in the Gulf of Mexico, the Jamassi of Florida . . . such again is the tribe of which Balboa saw some representatives in his passage of the

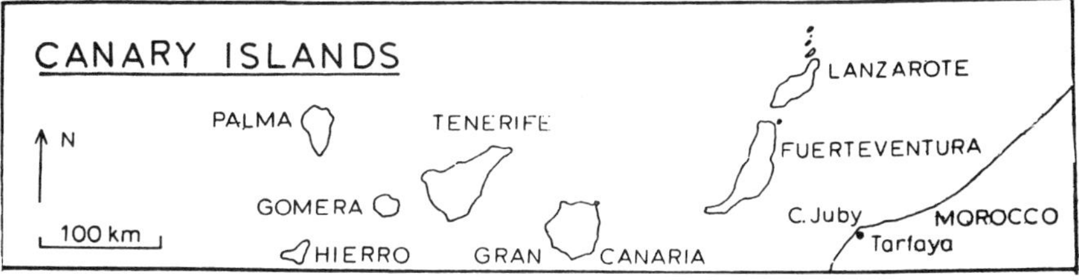

PLATE 51
The Canary Islands provided the starting-off point for ships taking the middle passage to America or trading down West Africa. The citizens of Tenerife spoke Guanch. They were called Guans like a tribe along the Volta River for whom I used to publish. Schliemann's last and greatest archaeological dream was to excavate the Canaries and Mexico. Bride fattening was practiced on the Canary Islands as at Calabar, at the mouth of the Cross River, one of the great trading rivers of West Africa. All Guanch mummies had red or fair hair. The Spaniard who conquered the Canary Islands first sold his two sons to an Arab moneylender to finance his expedition. Sculptured stones have been found on the Canary Islands with symbols similar to those found on the shores of Lake Superior. Mummies found on Las Palmas were associated with red ocher.

Isthmus of Darien in 1513."[23] We have reports of the Malian king Mousa sending a fleet of canoes across the Atlantic well prior to Columbus; this may explain some of the evidence.

The evidence of racial outsiders surviving in America from pre-Columbian times is both more immediate and more tricky. Even if we can rely on the reporter, we need to be sure that the people concerned were not introduced since the conquest.

Professor Homet says that he found an Indian tribe who were white and looked like Arabs. They were known as the Syriana, which in Semitic means "our Syrians."[24] Then, in June 1985, the discovery was announced of an ancient city of the Chachas in the eastern Andes, where some people still survive to this day with blond hair and blue eyes.

Any report of that kind must obviously be treated with great care: half a millennium of total isolation is a hard thing to prove. We are on much firmer ground when we come to consider the evidence of actual pre-Columbian people whose bodies have been preserved ever since.

There is a tradition that the Incas had red or brown hair, and red hair is totally foreign to all Amerindian peoples. In *American Indians in the Pacific*, Thor Heyerdahl has color plates (xxxiv–xxxvi) showing the varying shades of hair on certain Peruvian mummies. They ranged from brown to carrot.

If we had no other evidence of contact, the ancient sculptures of America would, to my mind, be enough to justify the unhesitating assertion that over a period of many centuries the Old and New World were in touch with each other. Time and again we find figures portrayed in American art that are clearly modeled on originals from across the ocean, and the more we see of them the more unconvincing we find the argument that the resemblance could be accidental.

Take, for example, the head shown in Plate 48. It is unmistakably African, the portrayal of a type completely unknown among Amerindians. Furthermore it is a realistic and self-consistent portrayal—not a fantasy that happens to look like an African in some ways. If it had been carved in Africa one would be completely unsurprised, but in fact it is one of seventeen colossal African heads made by the Toltec/Olmecs after 1500 B.C. I spoke to the professor of history at the University of Mexico City

A Maya with artificial beard receiving homage, as depicted on a stela at Tepatlaxco, Veracruz. The great achievements of the Maya—graphology, calendar and mathematics—were fully mature when they appeared.[58] The very specialized method of making Mayan screen-fold books was also used for a book found down a well at Nimrod.[59] An artificial beard was the usual attribute of divinity in ancient Egypt.[60]

Plate 52
Bearded priest of the Maya, from a Mayan carving. *The Mayan priests were also astronomers. Maya was the daughter of Atlas in Greek tradition and Atlas was celebrated as an astronomer. Maya was one of the seven daughters, the Pleiades, which means in Greek the navigators' stars. I used to navigate by them myself.*

A carving of a bearded Atlas figure holding up the ceilng at Chichén Itza, *very similar to the carving found at Tula. For the Maya the world had been created five times and destroyed four times.*[61] *Their tradition was one of having come across the sea to Guatemala from the east in twelve paths*[62] *to avoid the Flood. They kidnapped strangers and sacrificed them, as in West Africa today, to increase their own strength and vigor.*[63]

and he advised me that the commencing date for the Olmecs would be a little earlier than 1500 B.C., in his view.

Another of these huge heads was flattened at the top to form an altar, and it had a speaking tube going in at the ear and out at the mouth for working oracles, very much in the style known from Babylon.

A different sort of Toltec/Olmec head, found at Tres Zapotes, is shown in Plate 84. It is a clearly Semitic face, and the earplugs and distinctive style of hat link it with the Phoenicians. Very importantly, it displays a mustache and beard, and American Indians do not produce beards. Their facial hair simply does not grow to such length.

If this one portrait head were the only example of a bearded face in American art one could no doubt find reasons to explain it away; but the truth is very far from that. It would be closer to the mark to say that the American artists were obsessed with beards. Among the portraits with which we shall now be concerned there is a surprising proportion of bearded heads, some of them showing that the Indians went so far as to equip their priests and other notables with false beards. They are also sometimes shown wearing false noses of a large, hooked type. The impression is unavoidable that they are continuing, over a long period of time, to mimic an eastern Mediterranean physiognomy that was established as the archetype of the lord and leader. This consistency argues against the idea that their concern with beards derives from an Amerindian original who, by some genetic sport, did grow a full beard and was admiringly imitated as someone unique and therefore marvelous. If that were so, why would beards be associated with Semitic noses—and even Phoenician hats?

Another bearded European face appears on a stela excavated at the great Toltec/Olmec site of La Venta. The people from the United States who conducted the dig thought it looked remarkably like Uncle Sam (see Plate 50). Both it and a companion figure whose face was lost were wearing pointed, upturned shoes of a style associated with the Hittites and also worn by the Etruscans.

Also at La Venta, there is an altar decorated with a twisted rope design (a typical north Syrian pattern) beneath which is a seated figure that resembles a curious ceramic piece, now in the Louvre, that was found in Cyprus and is thought to have been consecrated to the Phoenician goddess Astarte. Altogether, a Phoenician connection with the Toltec/Olmecs appears to be overwhelmingly supported by the evidence.

Other cultures in Mexico also portrayed bearded and evidently foreign faces. The slate mirror found at Veracruz has already been mentioned and also the bearded rain god Tláloc.

At Monte Albán, a great temple site in inland Mexico, there are carvings that portray distinctively African features and African dancing. There is also a bearded Semitic face, carvings that resemble an Egyptian sphinx as well as the Egyptian sun god Ra, and others in Assyrian style.[25]

Two of the most striking finds are described by the Verrills:

> At Lake Tizcoco, at a depth of fifteen feet below the surface of the mud, a ceremonial stone mace head was dug up and is now in the Chicago Natural History museum. This is unique and unlike any other carved stone object ever found in America but is almost identical in shape with stone mace heads found in the Near East known to have belonged to Naram Sin and his grandfather, King Sargon of Agade, and with existing portraits of identical [sic] features and helmet or headdress. Anyone comparing the Mexican specimen with those shown [the Old World heads] will instantly see the striking similarity between the Mexican portrait mace head and Near Eastern portraits in bas-relief that are known to represent Naram Sin. The beard and features are the same. The helmets with the chin covers are identical, even to the links under the chin, as are the segmented or quilted top of the helmet and the twisted rope-like decoration encircling the lower edge. It is utterly inconceivable and beyond reason to believe that any ancient Aztec, Toltec or other Mexican artisan could have conceived such a human being as is so obviously accurately carved on the mace head. Even admitting the bearded men were common and frequently are depicted in sculptures and paintings of the ancient Mexicans, the beards were never of the type shown on the mace head.[26]

PLATE 53
***HEAD OF AN AZTEC NOBLE* WARRIOR.** *This Nordic-looking face somewhat resembles T. E. Lawrence. Pedro Pizarro wrote of the Incas of Peru: "The ruling class in the kingdom of Peru was fair-skinned with fair hair about the colour of ripe wheat. Most of the great lords and ladies looked white like Spaniards." Columbus himself mentions that he had often seen Indians who were nearly as white as Spaniards.*[64] *In Mexico the most ancient city was said to be Teotihuacán, which, Mexican tradition alleged, was built by white giants.*[65] *Prescott tells us that the most prized stone in ancient Mexico was green and was called* chalchiritl. *Of course copper oxide is green and the Greek for copper or bronze is* calchos. *Tenochtitlán was designated the "navel of the earth" by Mexicans, as was Cuzco by Peruvians, Delphi by Greeks, Nippur by Sumerians, etc. The Aztecs claimed their standing and authority by descent from the Toltecs.*[66] *Nahuatl was the lingua franca of the Aztec empire. It had Mycenaean words in it. The Hebrew* nechoseth *for bronze should be compared with Enoch and Atl in the name for Mexico's largest city, Tenochtitlán.*

Even more convincing is the remarkable stone pendant found in August 1936 in Gallo Canyon, near an ancient Pueblo ruin in New Mexico, by Dr. Charles F. Elvers. The pendant or amulet is of very hard dark gray stone of pear shape, about three inches in length, with a perforation at the upper or narrow end and has incised carvings on both sides. On one side there is the figure of a man holding a crooked or serpentlike staff in his right hand and apparently climbing up a slope while looking over his right shoulder. There is a crown on his head but no garments are indicated. On the other side of the pendant is an inscription composed of an elephant head, a triangle, a cross, a circle and two six-pointed stars. These are all symbols or glyphs used in the archaic Sumerian Linear Script.

As corroboratory evidence of the Old World origin of this amulet is the stela preserved in the Louvre in Paris. This famous stone carving commemorates one of Naram-Sin's conquests and shows him standing on a mountain slope, holding a staff or spear in his right hand, wearing a horned headdress and looking somewhat to the right. In short the design on the amulet from New Mexico is a somewhat crude, yet exact miniature replica of the famous stela, even to the general shape of the two stones. While I was admiring this carving an American guide passed, enjoining his clients only to admire the hairstyle!

Moving south, we find portraits of strangely bearded men on Salvadoran pottery and at the megalithic culture site at Cocle. In Guatemala the Maya also produced numbers of bearded figures. The four Bacabs who were their founding gods are usually shown bearded, as in Plate 27, and the other gods are portrayed with precisely modeled beards—some even with handlebar mustaches. The Maya also carved the lotus symbol alongside their bearded gods, who were held to be white, except for the god of war, who was black and had protruding lips after the African model.

In the curious Mayan sarcophagus that has the broadened base, there was a tiny figure carved out of jade. It has been identified by the archaeologists as Kinich Ahan Itzamná, worshipped by the Maya as the first of all their priests, the patron of medicine, learning, writing and books. Constance Irwin[27] compares it with the sort of face you might expect to find at the helm of a Phoenician ship, bearded and hook-nosed. The priest in the Mayan carving shown in Plate 52 is also bearded and has a prominently hooked nose.

At the Mayan Temple of the Warriors at Chichén Itzá there are frescoes that, from our point of view, have the great advantage of being in color. They depict conspicuously blond prisoners.

Finally in this brief survey of portraits of outsiders, we come to a series that must be about the most remarkable that one could ever hope to find. In various American countries, but particularly in Mexico, terra-cotta portrait heads were produced in vast numbers. It seems as if anyone important had to have one made and Zelia Nuttall has suggested that they were used rather like identity cards or passport photographs. Unless they are disturbed, these figurines do not noticeably deteriorate and they were dug out of the graves looking as fresh as if they had come straight from the kiln. One can rely completely on their authenticity, right down to the smallest detail, so that they provide remarkable evidence about the population living in Central America during the time when they were being produced, whenever that was, since I have not seen any thermoluminescent dates for them.

One more very interesting observation emerges from von Wuthenau's work. He looks around the world to see where other pottery portraits have been found, similar in fabrication and appearance to those in Mexico. The first place he turns to is the Mediterranean, and he points out that such portraits can be found wherever the Phoenicians went, in Tyre, Carthage, Cyprus, Ibiza and Cádiz. They are also found on Cretan, Mycenaean and Etruscan sites. Outside the Mediterranean similar works were produced by the West African peoples of Senegal and Chad and by the Nok culture of Nigeria; also in Ghana, but in Ghana the terra-cotta heads from graves that I puchased date from the last couple of centuries. Traveling eastward, von Wuthenau finds them in the Middle East, in Iran and Baluchistan. He notes interesting similarities in the old ceramics of India, and finds the type again in Java, Siam and Japan. In other words, these portraits appear in the Mediterranean homelands of the seagoing peoples and, worldwide, in the countries they visited.

The evidence of contact between America and the Old World is, then, of many kinds, some of which will bear more weight than others. Some lines of evidence, in my estimation, are mere hints, to be treated as useful pointers but nothing more. Others seem to me to be so clear, so unlikely to have occurred by chance, and so hard to explain in any other plausible

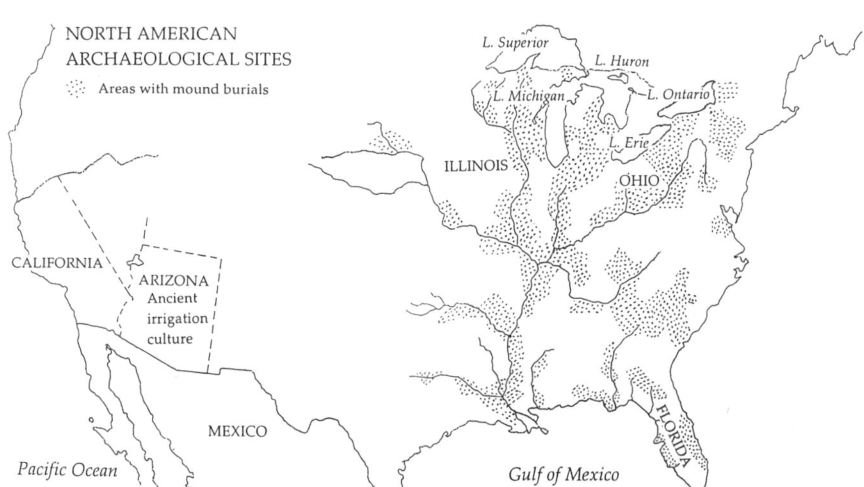

Plate 54
Map of North American archaeological sites and mound burials. *Tenochtitlán was one of the largest cities in the world at the time of the conquest, near Mexico City, when Mexico possessed a population of around 25 million people.*[67] *The irrigation system developed there reads to have been as great and as defensive as the one we are told about in Plato's description of the capital city of Atlantis. In Greek tradition the Titan Hades ruled in the remote west beyond the Atlantic. His other name was Pluto. Pluto was the giver of wealth to mankind because he was the supplier of metals, those precious metals that he had concealed in the bowels of the earth.*[68] *Hesiod says categorically that the Hesperides, where Hades ruled, lay "beyond glorious Ocean."*[69] *Pluto, therefore, stood for an earlier version of a Yankee millionaire. To the Mesopotamians Kur was where the Paradise Land of Dilmun was situated,*[70] *where the gods developed;*[71] *it was the abode both of the gods and the dead;*[72] *it was marked by high mountains. Dilmun and the Toltec capital, Tollan, are not dissimilar,* d *and* t *being interchangeable. Kur was the scene of the rising sun and of the birth of the gods.*[73] *It stood for the term* nether world.[74] *Kur carried off the goddess Ereshkigal to the netherworld. Kigal in Mesopotamia meant the Great Mother, and Eresh is suggestive of the goddess Ceres, also associated with the netherworld,*[75] *written boustrophedon.*

PLATE 55
Surgery, in very early times, included the trepanning of skulls, particularly where warriors had received serious skull injuries in battle. More than a thousand trepanned skulls have been found in Peru. This very specialized surgical practice was used across ancient Europe, where 80 percent of the patients survived this surgery.

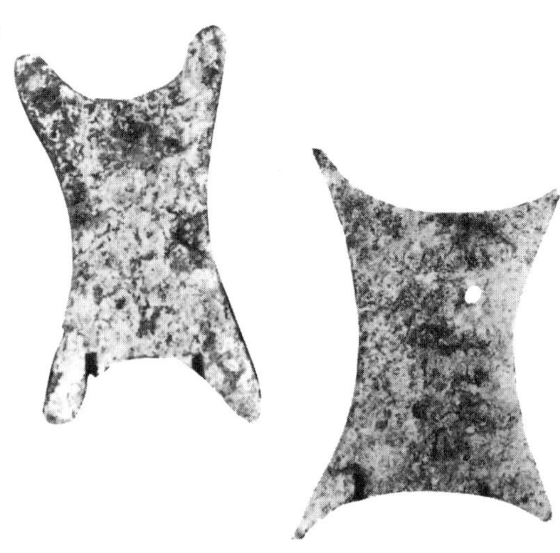

Ingots in the shape of oxhides from Egypt. *Two other types of metal ingot were found in the wreck at Cape Gelidonya, the slab ingot and the bun ingot. Similar oxhide ingots were in use in America. We should notice that the mummification of deceased nobles was practiced in ancient Peru, in ancient Mexico, anciently on the Canary Islands and in ancient Egypt: the practice seems to follow a trade route. In Mesoamerica, as in Mesopotamia, time, called by the Greeks Chronos, was a god. Time was the moving image of eternity.*

way that, even if they stood on their own, they ought to convince anyone who is not determined never to be convinced. Here the mathematics of probability come in.

But what is most impressive is that they do not stand on their own. It is the coherence of different types of evidence that is ultimately the most convincing thing of all. We have, for instance, the Toltec/Olmec culture suddenly springing into existence, and among their remains we find unmistakable sculptures of outsiders, Africans, Europeans and Chinese, as well as the Amerindians. At Tres Zapotes there is the combination of wheeled toys, including a toy chariot, an African face and a Semitic face. We have the great sources of tin, silver, gold and copper high in the Andes: the place matches descriptions in European legends and we can trace a navigable route from there to the Mediterranean down a river now named after the white female warriors who also appear in European legends and whose white descendants were on the riverbank and encountered by the Spanish invaders, and by later and quite independent explorers, not to mention being found on the Caribbean islands by Columbus himself.

In place after place we find not just one piece or type of evidence but several different types appearing together—sometimes appearing for the first time in quick succession, as with the arts, crafts and tools listed by Lanning for the early period on the Peruvian coast. It is, I am convinced, only the belief in inevitable human progress and the resulting difficulty of accepting early transoceanic voyaging that prevents archaeologists from treating all this evidence as convincing. If an obvious land route had existed between the Old and New World in ancient times it would long ago have been agreed that intercourse between them was proved beyond reasonable doubt. For if you believe in inevitable human progress as you go forward in time, which became fashionable two centuries ago, you have to believe in in-

Roman	Iberian	
	Massachusetts (Bourne)	Southern Spain
b	[illegible]	[illegible]
g	V	V
d	X	X
ḍ	[illegible]	[illegible]
h	ǀǀǀ	ǂ
w	Y	Y
ḥ	H	H
ṭ (th)	[illegible]	◇
q	[illegible]	[illegible]
l	Λ	Λ
n	[illegible]	[illegible]
ṣ (sy)	ǀ	)
c (i)	O	O
r	[illegible]	♀
š (sh)	M	M
t	[illegible]	Y

Sound	Style of Syria and Lebanon (Phoenicia) 800–600 B.C.	Style of Punic settlers of Iowa 800–600 B.C.	Style of Punic settlers of Spain 800–600 B.C.
b	9	9, 9	9, 9
g	[illegible]	>	>
d	◁	Δ	Δ
h	[illegible]	Π	Π
w	Կ	↑,	↑, Y
z	I	N, H	N
ḥ	目	ǀǀǀ	ǀǀǀ, 目
ṭ	⊕	[illegible]	[illegible]
k	[illegible]	⊣	⊣, K
l	L	Λ	Λ
m	[illegible]	W	W, Y
š	W	[illegible]	[illegible]
', i	O	O, :	O, :
s	ǂ	S	S
t	†	Ψ	Ψ

Plate 56

Alphabets of the Bourne Stone, *Massachusetts, and of southern Spain (far left), compared by Barry Fell, Professor Emeritus at Harvard University.*

Professor Fell has shown that Bronze Age Europeans—for that matter like many other peoples of that time—were literate and educated, leaving rock inscriptions in Teutonic and Celtic tongues.

Professor Alexander Thom showed that they employed Pythagorean geometry and used basic lengths of megalithic inches, from cup and ring marks to stone circles, demonstrating an educated craftsmanship and precision throughout.

The Phoenician (Punic) colonists of Iowa used an alphabet (left) that shows clearly that their homeland was in the Iberian Peninsula. The Iowa inscription was found at Davenport in 1874, and is written in the Iberian alphabet, whose sound values were determined in Spain sixty years later. Failure to identify the Iowan alphabet led archaeologists until now to suppose that the Davenport finds were fraudulent. (Comparison made by Professor Fell.) Fell dwells at length on the Celtic Ogham script found in Wales and Ireland and which he finds was used widely in North America. I have myself looked at the Kiltera Ogham stone in southern Ireland, which reads, the notice says: "Collabot son of Lug son of Lobchu." A second stone with the word Ritturas *on it has been removed to the National Museum in Dublin. When the so-called Pilgrim Fathers arrived in North America there were 15 million Amerindians, by 1843 their numbers were down to 2.5 million. The Greek word* graphein *for writing, Dr. Diringer says, is related to the German* kerben, *to notch, and we must expect early records to have been kept on tally sticks.*

evitable human regress as you go backward in time so what the Classical Greeks could not do, no one before them could encompass. Stands to reason!

As a postscript to this chapter, let us look at a single extraordinary piece of evidence. This one has the advantage that the probability of its being a chance coincidence can be at least roughly quantified.

There is an ancient Indian game known as *pachisi* played on a board shaped like a cross, each arm of which is ruled into spaces to make a kind of ladder. The pieces are moved after throwing dice. The same game was played in pre-Columbian Mexico, where it was called *patolli.* It is a complex game and in 1962 a student working in consultation with members of the Department of Psychology at Johns Hopkins University calculated the odds against it being duplicated by chance. He found the figure to be 7×10^{22}, that is 7 followed by 22 zeros. If you want to visualize what that figure means, look at it this way. The sun is about 150 million kilometers from the earth. 7×10^{22} is the number of kilometers you would cover if you traveled to the sun and back just over 233 million times!

PLATE 57

FURTHER COMPARISON OF IBERIAN AND PRE-COLUMBIAN AMERICAN SCRIPTS. *Examples of Iberian-Punic alphabets from Iberian and American sites, circa 800–200* B.C. *Adena 1, central West Virgina, Wilson-Braxton tablet; Adena 2, Grave Creek, West Virginia; Adena 3, Susquhanna, Pennsylvania. Aptucxet 1, Komasamkumkanit, Bourne, Massachusetts; Aptucxet 2, North Salem, New Hampshire; Aptucxet 3, central Vermont, temple dedications on bilingual Goidelic-Punic steles.*[76] *Books made of deerhide were in use in pre-Columbian Nicaragua, with painted figures.*[77] *The manufacture of expensive textiles, artistically designed, provided exports from Tyre.*

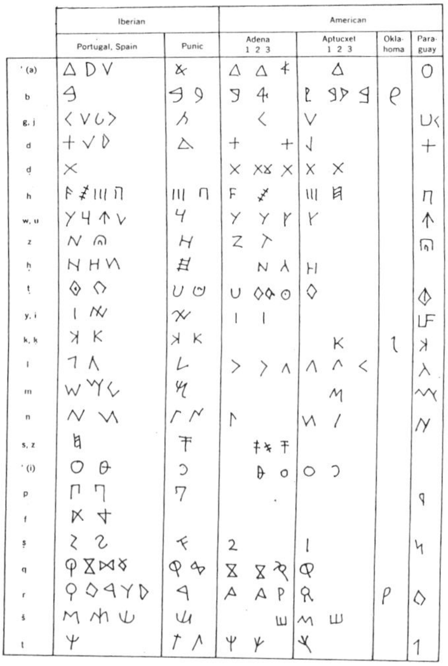

	Iberian		American			
	Portugal, Spain	Punic	Adena 1 2 3	Aptucxet 1 2 3	Oklahoma	Paraguay
' (a)						
b						
g, j						
d						
ḍ						
h						
w, u						
z						
ḥ						
ṭ						
y, i						
k, ḳ						
l						
m						
n						
s, z						
' (i)						
p						
f						
ṣ						
q						
r						
š						
t						

The Amerindian tribe called Tewa used the word *gia* for mother, as with the Ancient Greeks.[28] The pulling out of the heart was a special feature of some Greek rituals, as with the Aztecs in Plate 47. Neither the Aborigines of Australia nor the San peoples of Africa indulged in human sacrifice. I think we shall find these hideous practices were taken from the Fertile Crescent around the world, in Homer's words "along the highway of the fish." Pluto, alias Hades, was looked on by the Romans as a god of riches by way of precious metals. Most West Indian chiefs claimed that the entrance to the underworld lay in their territory.[29] The Caribs originally lived on herbs until a white sky god brought them the arts of agriculture.[30] They hollowed out their wooden canoes by fire as in Africa from West Africa to the Okavango delta, then finished them off with stone tools. They practiced the very odd and specific trick of couvade, in common with many places in the Old World, where, when the wife falls pregnant, the husband goes to bed and feigns pregnancy.[31]

Barry Fell, a New Zealander, formerly professor of Marine Biology at Harvard University, in his excellent book *America B.C.*,[32] makes a study of the old Celtic trade with America by means of the study of the ogham script in the Celtic world and its widespread occurrence in North America near the eastern seaboard of the United States. The author, himself a New Zealander, first learned Gaelic through his mother and her fellow Scots before taking formal training at Edinburgh University. As we can see from our modern world, emigrants tend to choose the areas in the New World

Meaning	Basque		Algonquian		
sun	guzki	ᑯᐢᑭ	gisis gischuch	ᑭᓯᐢ ᑭᐢᒍ–	Ojibwa Delaware
star	šita	ᓯᑕ	skwita	ᐢᐠᐃᐧᑕ	Natick
mist	alphorra	ᐊᓪᐳᕋ	awan	ᐊᐋᐧᐣ	Ojibwa
dew or fine rain	babanda	ᐸᐸᑕ	papad-	ᐸᐸᑕ	Natick
cloudy weather	gohin	ᑯ"ᐃᐣ	guhn	ᑯᐣ	Natick
wind	aize aitse ulauza	ᐊᐃᓭ ᐊᐃᒉ ᐅᓚᐅᓴ	aiowastin outsou lutin	ᐊᐃᐊᐧᐢᑎᐣ ᐅ'ᒍ ᓗᑎᐣ	Cree Abenaki Old Algonquian
water to wash to wash	uds kusi babi	ᐅ– ᑯᓯ ᐸᐱ	utan (-quench) kusit (-flow) papen (-drip)	ᐅᑕᐣ ᑯᓯᐟ ᐸᐯᐣ	Natick Natick Natick
drink river	ziba sipa	ᓯᐸ ᓯᐸ	sipe (-water) sipu (river, etc.)	ᓯᐯ ᓯᐳ	universal universal
flood lake river water	ibai ibaiak	ᐃᐸᐃ ᐃᐸᔭᐠ	(n)ipe ipog	ᐃᐯ ᐃᐳᐠ	universal
ocean (confluence of waters)	ur-keta	ᐅ³ᑫᑕ	kehta	ᑫᑕ	universal
land	uts	ᐅ–	uto wuto	ᐅᑐ ᐅᐧᑐ	Natick Natick

PLATE 58
Similar Basque and Algonquin Symbols. *Professor Barry Fell writes: "This comparative table, taken from my 1979 paper on the decipherment of ancient Basque, shows that the language of the Algonquian Indians contains words of Basque origin. The last two columns compare the related pairs of words as written in the Cree-Basque syllabary."*[78]

Notice that the sun god is called Gisis in Algonquian, Chise among some tribes in the Amazon—spelling is optional—and that to Christians the sacred day of the week is not Christ's day but Sunday, the day of the sun: while to the Jews it is Saturday, the day of Saturn. The game of pelota, played in ancient times by the Basques of Spain, is similar to the pelota played not only at El Tajín in Mexico but also across the Mayan country and Central America generally.[79] *Notice that the name* pelota *would seem to be an* atl *word, as, indeed, would appear to be the word* metal. *Let us notice also that methods of quarrying were similar both sides of the Atlantic.*[80] *Writing on the Amerindians of North America, George Jones states that they knew of the Deluge, the dove of peace, they had their own Ark of the Covenant, which was never permitted to touch the ground, it was kept surrounded by twelve stones, they went in for burnt offerings, a feast in direct analogy with the Hebrew Passover, a pectoral worn by the priests with twelve stones, they have huts of safety (or cities of refuge), phylacteries, knowledge of the One God called Ya-ho-vah. In hymns of rejoicing they used Hal-le-lu-ya, they practice circumcision and believe in the immortality of the soul.*[81]

where the climate is similar to the climate they are accustomed to: so northern Europeans migrate to North America, southern Europeans migrate further south and Africans are disproportionately common in the hottest regions of all. Barry Fell chiefly finds the Celtic ogham script in New England, particularly in Vermont and New Hampshire, just as he finds the same grooved script in Ireland. With some of his correspondence in tables of oghams a certain skepticism would seem to be required; this can be accepted, for there is much that remains convincing.

The period Barry Fell believes this wave of emigration to cover is the first millennium B.C. Fell uses the correct techniques for re-creating a period of history that became lost to us, lost perhaps due to the destruction of the records when the Christians took over: the sort of vandalism that took place worldwide and compelled the writing of this book. He reproduces the rock engravings in his part of America and attempts their translation: he compares similar words in Celtic and certain Amerindian languages and he quotes the Algonquian tradition that their ruling class—histories are histories of ruling classes—came to their country by sea. In addition to the Celtic script on the rocks of North America and Celtic words in the various Amerindian languages, he finds Phoenician, Egyptian, Basque and Libyan words inscribed widely in North America, and as for the Libyan language he follows it as far afield as Polynesia. He correctly finds this Celtic voyaging to America continuing into Roman times. No one seems to have noticed that one of the fourteen Titans listed by Stephanus of

PLATE 59
OLD WORLD AND NEW WORLD USE OF THE LABYRINTH.

Knowledge of the ancient labyrinth of Knossos, Crete, was brought to America by voyagers who carved the Arizona examples (2) and (4) (drawn from photographs made by the late William Coxon). Matching examples from the Old World are given on the left, (1) an ancient coin from Knossos, and (3) an engraving from India. What significance these engravings originally had is now unknown (David Oedel). The labyrinth was depicted in ancient Egypt a thousand years before we know of it in Crete. We must also point out that the comparison of toponyms we also make in this book are auxiliary to the study of protohistory: archaeology, rock inscriptions, language, plant transfers, etc., provide the more solid facts. The king of Texcoco had a vast palace of three hundred rooms, the palace measuring 3,300 by 2,600 feet. Within his palace grounds were numerous mazes.[82]

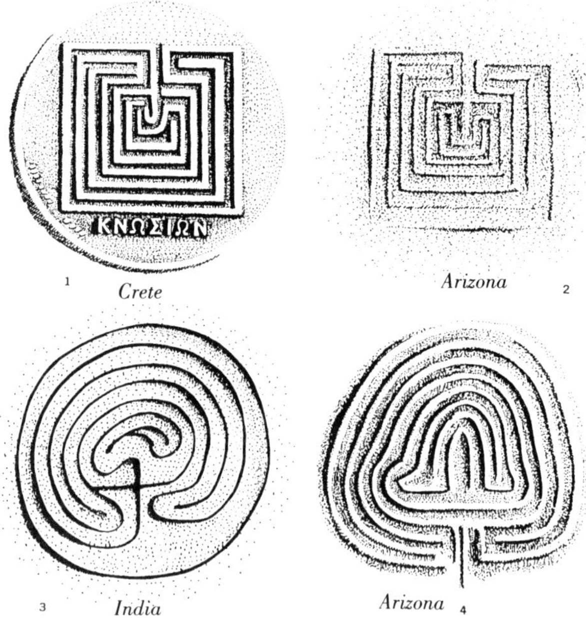

Byzantium is called Andes. That we hear nothing about him in any Greek record is natural enough. The present president of Kenya is called arap Moi: in Kalenjin and Nandi, *arap* means "son of," as *ap* does in Welsh. There are Hamitic words in Celtic.

Barry Fell does not notice that there is a description of this trip—a last, symbolic, thirty-year voyage going on certainly into almost Roman times—contained in Plutarch's "On the Face in the Moon's Orb." Fell suggests that the Celts used the middle passage via the Canary Islands—which likely enough they did—but Plutarch's description is of the alternate stepping-stone route, via Iceland and Newfoundland, and certainly this would be more convenient for Celts from Ireland and the British Isles; seeing that migrating birds were used for navigation right up to the *seculo maravilhoso* of Henry the Navigator and his Portuguese mariners—for birds migrate in spring not just from Britain to Iceland and Greenland to nest within the Arctic Circle, but also as far away as from South Africa. The Vikings found Irish monks already present in Iceland when they in their turn occupied it and the narrative of St. Brendan's voyage described the latter end of this Celtic trip, at one time of such commercial importance. And the Welsh voyages to America of King Madoc in A.D. 1107 merely continued the national custom, at a time when the Scandinavians to the north were into it on a great scale. That there was no hullabaloo about Madoc's two trips is simply because it was a fairly ordinary thing to do: relatives of the Norman kings of England must have been into transatlantic voyaging up to their necks.

Two labyrinths, anciently carved on the rocks of Cornwall, perhaps point out one route these travelers were taking. It is a very specialized trick, little likely to be independently invented.

PLATE 60

CRETAN OFFICER LEADING AFRICAN TROOPS, FROM A CRETAN FRESCO. *Crete was held to be the ideal spot for launching ships to every corner of the world. It was an island of ninety cities and as many nations, because of its geographical position and not because it grew olives, as the* Cambridge Ancient History *supposes. The capital of Crete is named after Heracles and is called Heraklion (Iráklion). Heracles is supposed to have brought under cultivation the entire inhabited world.*[83] *The Heracles people cleared the Amazons out of North Africa. The Amazons then went to Thermodon, which means the "hot river," a fair synonym for the Amazon River, which was where Pizarro's men discovered these ladies. Strabo finds the Solyimi near Libya. The Amazons were said to be associated in Libya with the Solyimi, and the upper reaches of the Amazon are accordingly the Solimoes. The Cretan officer in this picture—not visible here—is known as "the Captain of the Blacks."*

Odysseus claims to have brought nine ships to Crete to take part in the attack on Egypt, which ended in total disaster. Thereafter, he took a holiday, sailing westward out of the Strait of Gibraltar, the Pillars of Heracles, to cross the Atlantic and spend seven years in the arms of Calypso. Homer describes Hermes going on the same trip to Calypso and as needing to cross "so great a space of salt sea-water great past telling."[84] *Homer also places Odysseus's trip outside the Mediterranean in the Atlantic.*[85] *When Odysseus manages to tear himself away from Calypso to return to the Mediterranean, he returns on a wooden raft with a sail, going before the breeze,*[86] *and takes seventeen days to reach the coast of Spain again. He was said to have spent his time on Atlas's island.*

Professor Fell finds not just rock engravings, scripts, words and tradition confirming this North Atlantic traffic, but the stone circle of Mystery Hill in New Hampshire not altogether dissimilar to the stone circles in Britain: dolmens as in Western Europe and oxhide ingots, the earliest form of ingot we know of in the Old World, also in use in the New World; and the very specific labyrinths associated with Crete are to be found carved on the rocks of America (see Plate 59).

Fell finishes up by concluding that the great rivers of America provided the highways into the continent, perhaps a point with which he might have begun. For, as Africa tilts from east to west, America tilts from west to east, so that the Atlantic trade in the Copper and Bronze Ages was the important trade—much contact through there was via the Pacific between the Old World and the New throughout long millennia, the Andes and the Rocky Mountains largely prevented access to the hinterland. In the Middle Ages, of course, we do find the Chinese trading down the east coast of Africa while, as we shall see subsequently, they were also trading down the Pacific coast of America.

Because of the destruction of the records, the establishment believes these perfectly ordinary transatlantic voyages never to have existed. In fact they had been going on at least since 7000 B.C. The earliest reports of America to come down to us are of two huge islands in the middle of Ocean, a description that exactly describes the North and South American continents and their disposition between the Atlantic and Pacific parts of Ocean. The geography of our planet was known from the time of the matriarchal society. Without such accurate knowledge this description of America could not, of course, have been supplied: from very early on indeed they knew it all!

The great economic importance of America was in the Copper and Bronze Ages, but although the North Atlantic climate had deteriorated over this period, commerce nevertheless continued. What Barry Fell has accomplished for North America, Bernardo da Silva Ramos and Alfredo Brandao accomplished for Amazonia and South America. And the nature of the inscriptions Bernardo copied—among them relatively late Indian scripts, Phoenician and other western Semitic scripts of a late date—prove conclusively that trade was being conducted simultaneously with both North and South America from the Old World during the course of the first millennium B.C., dwindling though it must have been by then.

The Irish called America Mag Mel—Mag was the son of Set and Barry Fell likens that name to the Scottish Mac—or they called it Tir na Og, the land of eternal youth—as much a plug to encourage emigrants as calling that lump of ice "Greenland." A top geologist friend of mine who helped me with this book, Louis Murray, was prospecting in Greenland in midsummer. It was snowing and sleeting. He said to his Eskimo companion: "I don't think much of your summer," and the Eskimo replied: "Don't worry, it won't last long."

Bronze Age Irish tradition stated that their most gifted and graceful immigrants were the Tuatha de Danaan, who came to western Ireland from across the Atlantic and eventually returned, tradition says, whence they had come. America was known to Egypt as Tuat, while the Greeks and one tribe of Israel were known as Dan.

The Natick Indians of Boston use the identical name for the constellation, known to us as the Great Bear. Since bears are uncommon in Egypt, Mesopotamia, the Mediterranean and the Atlantic shores of Europe, it would seem more probable that the name came from America to the Old World rather than vice versa. American scholars might do well to peer into the darkness of the past to see whether other inventions ascribed to the Old World might not in fact have originated in the New. For those early empires in the New World became even richer than those in the Old, even as they have done today. There is one most interesting point there. The whistling jar appears in America at something like the sort of time it appears in the Old World. The author who mentions this very specialized device in America was seemingly unaware of its existence in the Old World. Hero of Alexandria published his book *The Pneumatics* at the end of the second century B.C. and describes how an artificial bird can be made to whistle by flowing water. He also publishes the details of Christ's first miracle—how to turn water into wine with the aid of siphons—and the principle of the steam engine, which was only used for producing bogus miracles in temples until some two thousand years later (Plate 29).[33]

5. *Birdmen in Africa*

"Set . . . his skin was white and his hair was red."
LAROUSSE *Encyclopaedia of Mythology*

To Europeans before the last two centuries, Africa was always a land of mystery, the "dark continent" whose vast, unexplored interior stretched away behind the narrow strip of known world along the Mediterranean shore. To reach any part of sub-Saharan Africa meant traveling thousands of miles by sea or else facing the terrors of the desert. Behind the Roman saying that there was always something new coming out of Africa was the sense that almost everything in Africa was unknown, and by Shakespeare's time it was still the country where you might expect to find "men whose heads do grow beneath their shoulders."

The Greeks seem to have had rather clearer ideas, though still within limits. Herodotus writes: "Where the south declines towards the setting sun lies the country called Ethiopia, the last inhabited land in that direction. There gold is obtained in great plenty, huge elephants abound, with wild trees of all sorts, and ebony: and the men are taller, handsomer and longer lived than anywhere else."[1]

By now we should not be too surprised to find that what was fantasy land in our own tradition was far more familiar ground to people living thousands of years earlier, or to people living relatively recently but east of Africa. Just as the Muslim invaders, whose trail of conquest took them right across the continent to Nigeria, knew far more of Africa than did the Europeans of Shakespeare's day—compare the travels of Ibn Battuta—so the sea peoples of the Mediterranean in the third and fourth millennia B.C. regularly sailed to parts of Africa that were unknown to the Classical Greeks and Romans. When after the Flood the world was divided between Shem, Ham and Japheth, it is clear that Shem stood for Sumer, the land of Shinar—the Sumerians did not pronounce their last syllable; Ham was the Sumerian word *amuru* for the west: the Canaanites were never African but the Sumerians and Phoenicians had immense colonies and associated countries across Africa; Japheth remains the Yavans, the Aegean peoples, who in the Indian epic *the Mahabharata* were fighting north of Delhi before the Trojan War.

The Egyptians left records of voyages to a distant "Land of Punt," very many miles away. During the Sixth Dynasty (2400–2300 B.C.) a sailor named Knemhotep visited it no fewer than eleven times. Where was this mysterious Land of Punt? It seems likely that the name was applied by the Egyptians to different parts of East Africa at different times, but one of them, which is of interest to us, was identified by a German professor of chemistry. He examined the cosmetics used by an Egyptian princess of the Sixth Dynasty and found that among them was an eye shadow made from antimony. There is no source of antimony in Egypt, and the mines in Persia and Turkey were not discovered until much later. According to Zvi Herman,[2] the only place it could have come from was southern Africa and the connection is reinforced by an Egyptian bas relief of the Queen of Punt, showing her with the large steatopygic buttocks characteristic of the people of southern Africa at that time.

Zvi Herman also holds that: "According to reputable sources, Rameses III maintained a large colony of Egyptians there (around 1100 B.C.) to work some of the mines and send the gold to Egypt."[3]

Some five hundred years later, Pharaoh Necho (609–593 B.C.) is said to have sent Phoenicians to sail around Africa for him, perhaps to test whether he could move his ships from the Red Sea to the Mediterranean. The report of this voyage is mentioned by Herodotus,[4] who, like later historians, was skeptical. Now, however, it is more generally accepted, and viewed as the first circumnavigation of Africa that we know of. It seems to me that in fact it was by no means the first circumnavigation. More likely Necho was confident that Africa could be rounded because it had already been done, perhaps on various occasions over a very long period of time. The Phoenician inscription at Paraíba, if it is genuine, suggests something of this kind. And with the Indus civilization involved in the Ashanti gold fields—as indeed at one time was my father—India must surely have used the Cape route as well as the Mediterranean.

The so-called Phoenicians, of course, came quite late in the history of world voyaging, and quite late, too, in the history of African mining. We know from carbon dating that mines in southern Africa were being worked by 4000 B.C.,[5] not to mention 40,000 B.C. at the Ngwenya mine in Swaziland; and this suggests that by then a large part of the African continent had been prospected, for how else would antimony have been discovered? There are no special features to direct the prospector to that part of Africa in particular.

To find the beginnings of mining in Africa we have to go back further still, far beyond even the flint mines of the Stone Age. Astonishingly, the earliest African mines we know of go back to about 40,000 B.C. They were not for gold or any other metal. They were for hematite and specularite, two minerals used to provide color in body decoration. By the time the Copper Age started, therefore, mining of some sort had been going on in Africa for almost forty thousand years—ahead, it appears, of the rest of the world.

It is interesting that the gold mines of Zimbabwe are associated with the agricultural terraces of Inyanga nearby. Many of the trees and plants found in this area are indigenous not to southeast Africa but to India and Arabia. This is what we would expect if we remember that in early times the oceans united—including the Indian Ocean. The east side of Africa was visited very early on, and it seems that its mines—not only gold mines but also copper and tin—were heavily worked. It has been estimated that thirty thousand tons of bronze was manufactured and removed from the neighborhood of the Rooiberg tin mine in the Transvaal alone; and Professor Dart has written:

> From a portion of the old Messina workings it has been cautiously estimated by Trevor that tens of thousands of tons of copper were recovered there by the ancients. When we add to these workings at Messina those of the Palabora area north of the junction of the Selati and Oliphants Rivers, which cover many acres and in the aggregate, as in the individual workings, are far larger than those at Messina, those scattered throughout Rhodesia, those of the Tebedzi River region in the Kalahari, those of Macanga territory and Pandamacua on the Zambesi in the east, it will be recognised that the Rhodesian gold centre was ringed on all sides by the enterprise in copper and that a quantity of copper was forthcoming which was more than adequate to meet the demands of the Rooibert-Weynek-Leeuwport tin, and also that of Broken Hill and probably other areas of tin as yet unknown.[6]

However, it was the west coast of Africa that appears to have been chiefly influenced by the sea peoples. For most of the Bronze Age their center of activity was the Mediterranean. For them the natural outward route lay past the Pillars of Heracles, after which they could turn north for Britain, for the stepping-stone route to America or for the Baltic, or south round the bulge of Africa. Often they turned south. We are discussing an Atlantic trade. I emphasize: America tilts from west to east, so the rivers of access are on the east. Africa tilts from east to west, so the rivers of access are on the west: hence the fact that West African culture is incomparably richer than East African: thus the early Atlantic trade, and ultimately the reason why Western Europe is so much richer than Eastern. Napoleon said: "Every country has the politics of its geography."

Once again the Phoenicians have left behind them evidence of how things stood toward the end of the seagoing age. They founded colonies outside the Mediterranean during the late second millennium—for example Gadeira (Cádiz) in Spain about 1104 B.C.—and some time between 520 and 470 B.C. Hanno is supposed to have taken thirty thousand people from Carthage to found seven colonies on the coast of West Africa, the furthest of them 2,600 miles beyond the Pillars of Heracles. As late as the fifth century A.D., St. Augustine recorded that in his day Phoenician was still spoken on the west coast of Africa, as far as Cape Noun. And, of course, Syrians and Lebanese trade all down the coast of West Africa to this day.

The Hyksos, expelled from Egypt, were accompanied to America by their African allies whose portraits have survived in the Toltec sculpture. We can be sure, however, that the connection between Africa and America goes back very much further than that. For anyone returning from the mouth of the Paraná River, the easiest way is to follow the southern part of the circular pattern of currents and winds, which carries one to the African coast near where Angola is today (see the map on Plate 77). It is likely that this route would have been well used, for the Paraná gives access to the southern tin mines of Bolivia and the silver of Peru, and it would also have been a useful alternative route for any group whose rivals had closed the Amazon by military means.

We can say that throughout much of the long period of prehistoric voyaging, the coastal areas of West Africa took part in a common culture that linked them with America on the one hand and with the Fertile Crescent on the other. West Africa is the most sophisticated part of sub-Saharan Africa, and this sophistication derives from the same source as the relative sophistication of Western Europe—the waves of the Atlantic that beat on both their shores.

When we look at the evidence for all this we find, not surprisingly, that much of it takes the same forms as the evidence linking America with the Mediterranean. There are in Africa the same persistent traditions of culture-bringers arriving from abroad. Customs and religious ceremonies echo those of the Mesopotamian, Indian and Mediterranean area, and symbols common to the seagoing peoples around the world are used. Works of art show unmistakable signs of influence, including the fact that some of them portray people who are clearly foreigners.

One of the most significant legends is that of the birdmen. The statuettes in Plates 91 and 93 are of two bronze birdmen from north of the village of Man in the Ivory Coast in the Senufo tribal area. These figures are of unknown date (they were possibly taken from an old grave). Bronze cannot be dated. But they are based on an ancient tradition, which is that in the days of the tribe's first ancestors a race of attractive human birds appeared, possessing all the sciences, which they handed on to mankind in the Ivory Coast. Pictures of birdmen occur in various parts of Africa, even on the east side. In the ruins of Zimbabwe (the great fortified complex after which the state as a whole was named) there are a number of carvings of "birds." In fact a good half of the genuine ones have, seemingly, five toes and so are not birds but birdmen. On their bases they carry symbols (circles and water signs), which we shall find are associated with the seagoing peoples; in this case the symbols of the sun or time, and of the sea.

The connection is made quite explicitly in three Senufo statuettes (Plates 95, 96 and 97). These birdmen have had their masks removed but they are recognizably akin to the men in Plates 91 and 93. In particular they wear the same distinctive skirt or kilt made out of strips of cloth. This in itself gives us a clue. It is the same odd form of dress that is shown on Plate 94, which is Sumerian work from the first half of the third millennium B.C. The second clue is that the curious thing carried on top of the head of the man like a misshapen hat is in fact a reed boat. Here is an immediate connection, for Thor Heyerdahl records that bird masks were worn by the captains of the ancient oceangoing reed boats of which his own boat, *Ra*, was a copy (see Plate 92). They are depicted on rock engravings in his book, *The Ra Expeditions*. Surely, both kilt and Celt are *atl* names.

The connection is emphatically confirmed by evidence from the other side of the Atlantic. Here, unmistakably, on a Mochicha pot from the Pacific coast of Peru, are the birdmen and their reed boats (see Plate 40). For double confirmation, there is the fact that other Mochicha pottery depicts people who are clearly Africans. With the Indus Valley civilization there are many portraits of gods with their upper parts human and their lower parts avian.[7] In the Museum of Man in London there is a wooden birdman from pre-Hispanic Jamaica.

A number of African peoples have a tradition that their cultures originated in Egypt or the Sudan. The Akan tribes of Ghana and the Ivory Coast believe that their ancestors were white and crossed the Sahara to reach West Africa. The Yoruba, who live around western Nigeria, have a particularly interesting tradition that they originated in Canaan and left at the time of Nimrod, of the building of the Tower of Babel (about 2200 B.C.). This ties in with the statement by Josephus in *The Antiquities of the Jews* that a political upheaval at that time forced most of the population of Babylon to emigrate and that they went to all the continents and to many of the islands of the world. The Yoruba tradition confirms the arrival of some of them in Nigeria at just that time. The whole tribe descends, the Yoruba agree, from one common ancestor, Oduduwa, who was both white and a woman. Match this to the Amerindian tradition of the building of the Tower of Babel.

The real importance of studying African religions was well understood by a French team led by Marcel Griaule and Germaine Dieterlen that went out to investigate the Dogon tribe of Mali. With the help of Dogon elders they pieced together the tribe's philosophy, which is partly shared by other

Plate 61

Attic of the Great Hall at Karnak, Thebes (restored by Charles Chipiez). *The temple of Karnak extended over so great an area, sixty-one acres, that you can fit within it St. Peter's, Milan Cathedral and Notre Dame, and still have room to spare. It was earlier called Waset, a Set or Atlas name. Homer, in the* Iliad, *suggests the wealth of Thebes, where Achilles replies to Odysseus, rejecting an offer of bribery from Agamemnon:*

Nay, not for all the wealth
Of Thebes, in Egypt, where
in every hall
There lieth treasure vast; a hundred are
Her gates, and warriors issue forth
Two hundred, each of them with car and steeds.[1]

This says that Thebes possessed twenty thousand chariots, and Diodorus Siculus points out that there had once been one hundred post stations between Memphis and Thebes, each possessing two hundred horses. The oldest of the four temples at Thebes had a circuit of thirteen stadia, a height of forty-five cubits and walls twenty-four feet thick. This would be the Temple of Ammon.[2] *Diodorus Siculus records: "In the days of Osiris priests made golden chapels for the worship of the gods."*[3] *And Diodorus records the claim by the Thebans that they were the first to study philosophy and astronomy.*[4] *Pharaoh Sesostris claimed to be king of the entire world and, much like Alexander the Great, conquered from Thrace to the Ganges.*[5] *Lurker maintains that Sed was a popular god in ancient Egypt whose name meant savior.*[6] *Christianity derives from the Set, sun-worshipping religion, and Christ was Salvator Mundi, or Savior of the World.*

tribes in West Africa. Griaule and Dieterlen argue that their study illuminates not only African culture generally but also the civilized world as a whole. For many centuries the Dogon were cut off from outside influences by the rain forest to the south and by the ever harder conditions of the Sahara to the north, so that they have preserved much of what used once to be a world religion. We shall be looking more fully at that religion in Chapter 14, but it is worth noting here some beliefs held by the Dogon, which indicate that they did not invent their own religion but learned it from others who had access to the world community of seagoing peoples. They are a good example of the important rule that colonies can preserve the customs of the metropolitan country long after that country has itself been destroyed and its records eradicated. So Mesopotamian scholars should go to the former colonies to learn from them and Africanists should also study the previously associated countries of the Fertile Crescent. For example, the Dogon hold that the, as it were, atomic particle, out of which the whole universe is created, is an acacia seed called *po:* while the Epicureans called the minute atomic particles forming the universe *poiotes.* The similarity in name may derive, not from direct contact, but from a common ancestry.[8]

Another African Creation myth is that of the creation mound. Traditional Senufo woodcarvings show the creator standing on a mound with a pot on his back representing the world (Plates 108–110). The similarity with the Greek figure of Atlas is not accidental, nor is the similarity with the Mesopotamian and Egyptian myth that the primordial mound was where the creation began. In reality a mound, or alternatively, an island, had to be the place from which to commence the huge work of creation, if creation meant, as I believe it did, the start of the male civilizing process. The mound was the base camp from which to begin draining the marshes, leveling the fields, digging irrigation canals, making the world ready for agricultural, city-founding man. In Greek the word *ktisis* means both creation and the founding of a city. The Adanse, on the Ashanti gold fields, similarly have one word with this identical double meaning, and the Greeks were known as the Danae. The idea then held of Creation seems to have been thoroughly down-to-earth and practical.

There are other interesting aspects of that Senufo wood carving. It depicts a donkey, and the donkey was sacred to the Egyptian god Set. Fire and water were also sacred to Set and the mask that is shown on the pot has to do with both fire and water. It is in fact a type of mask used by the Tyeli section of the Poro society in a ritual that involves the adepts entering a river up to their necks and spitting fire through the mask. The figure at the top of the carving with its hands between the cheeks of its buttocks is, I believe, a representation of Horus in what is known as the Homosexual Episode during the battle of Horus and Set, as described in the Egyptian Kahun Papyrus and other ancient papyri.[9] The Ivory Coast tribal name Senufo breaks down, I believe, into the Egyptian nefer, meaning beautiful or marine, and the sea people called Set, i.e., Set nefer. A remnant of the Set people, called Peleset or Philistine, gave their name to Palestine and subsequently occupied Sodom and the Cities of the Plain, with the *atl* name Lot coming onto the scene.

It seems to me that the correspondences between the African carving and the Mediterranean myths are too close to be mere coincindence. The carving is a modern one, but that does not disprove the connection. If we agree that its details derive, sooner or later, from ancient Egyptian beliefs, then we must ask when those beliefs, or the symbolic figures based on them were conveyed to an African tribe. If it happened while the myths were part of a living religion, it is easy to understand. If it happened not then but during more recent times, who made it his business to give Senufo wood carvers a course of instruction in Egyptian mythology?

Rituals connected with kingship in Africa are also very suggestive. Akan rituals, for example, have been described as almost identical with those of Egypt of the pharaohs, particularly in the importance given to the throne as the medium through which the king's divinity was transmitted to him. The Ashanti, in Ghana, had a golden stool that symbolized the king's power and in a sense the soul of the nation; for the king was not only the ruler but the personification of his whole people, as were the god-kings of the Near and Middle East.

The Ashanti also made gold masks for the faces of their dead kings, like the Mexicans and the Mycenaeans. Many of the Ghanaian tribes had

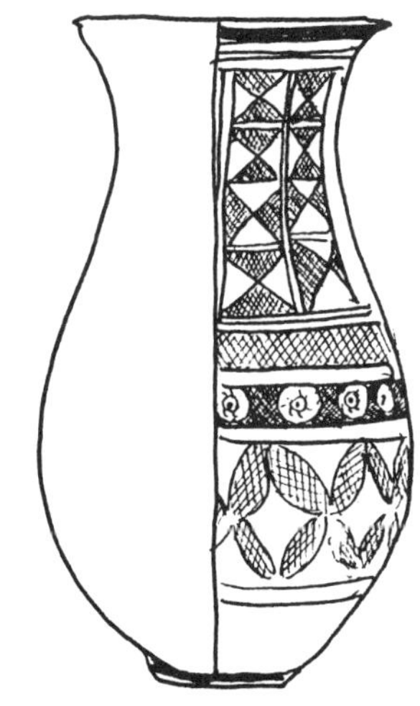

PLATE 62
INDUS VALLEY POT WITH POPULAR VISUAL PUN. *This pot from Lothal shows in its upper half a type of visual punning: this time with the double axe or butterfly normally associated with Crete but found across much of the world: the eye sometimes sees it as a white double axe, sometimes as a black one.*[7] *This punning was used widely in traditional Africa. Lothal is toward the mouth of the Indus River. There is evidence of a great deal of contact between the Indus Valley, Mesopotamia and Egypt. India carried the story of the Mesopotamian Deluge and the Ark.*[8] *In all, the Indus civilization covered 1.25 million square miles, with identical weights, measures, town planning, ceramics, architecture.*[9] *Indus Valley signs are found among Arab and African symbols.*[10]

PLATE 63
THE GREAT PYRAMID OF CHEOPS, *so large that if its stones were to be cut into one-foot cubes and placed alongside each other, they would extend to two thirds of the earth's periphery at the equator. The Sphinx, when I looked at it, seemed to bear African features. The Egyptian pyramids were built to endure for the course of eternity.[11] The Incan Huayna Capac, doubtless about Inca ziggurats, remarked that to keep the people of those kingdoms well in hand it was a good thing, when they had nothing else to do or busy themselves with, to make them move a mountain from one spot to another![12] Diodorus Siculus records "that Orpheus, Musaeus, Melampus, the poet Homer and Lycurgus of Sparta were the first of the Greek sages that passed into Egypt."[13] The stone age in Egypt finished about 5000 B.C. and the Bronze Age started about 2000 B.C. The matriarchal system remained so persistent in Egypt that Richard Briffault could write of an Egyptian woman clerk who later became a governor and then the military commander of an army. Trinitarianism, inherent in the worship of the god Time, Chronos, also entered Egypt. Ancient Egyptians are quoted as saying: "God hath made the Universe, and He hath created all that therein is: He is the Creator of what is in this world, of what was, of what is and what shall be."*

Pottery from Susa (left), fourth millennium, displaying the Maltese cross, symbolic of "king of the four quarters of the world." This was a title adopted by Vira Cocha, the culture hero of Peru, as well as by Old World monarchs: e.g., Naram-Sin claimed to be "king of the four regions," a claim to universal dominion over the whole earth.[14] The Hittite king adopts the title Sar Kissati, king of the world.[15] In Egypt, Osiris claims to civilize the entire world.[16] The First Dynasty kings of Egypt were pious and unbellicose.[17]

a system of double chieftainship, with two royal houses taking turns to rule: so too did the Spartans. Even the litters in which Ashanti chiefs were carried and their great ceremonial umbrellas can be matched in India. Above all, not just in Ghana but right across non-Muslim West Africa, most tribes shared with the Fertile Crescent cultures the custom of killing the chief's attendants, wives, guards, so that they would accompany him into the next world. This practice continues to this day. We find this holocaust also in the royal tombs of Mesopotamia. And among the Incas of Peru. It also served to protect the boss from assassination. Thousands of retainers had to die with the Chimu kings of Peru. When King Sobhusa of Swaziland recently died, the same customs were observed, or so it was whispered to me.

If that custom seems to us a cruel one, we must remember that not everything the "culture heroes" brought with them was good. Sometimes they might be better seen as culture villains. For the society around the eastern Mediterranean during the Bronze Age was, for all its glories, one which came to contain great superstitious cruelty, and as it spread its influence around the world it brought to the innocence of Neolithic hunters the fearful aberrations that had grown up in the early stages of agriculture. The practice of sacrifice was widespread and was essentially human sacrifice. It is not unreasonable to see a link between the Greek myth in which the god Dionysus is torn apart by his ecstatic followers and the Aztec offering of human hearts to their god, who, like Dionysus, was a sun god. Behind the mass sacrifice of Aztec war prisoners and the gladiatorial games fought to the death in the Roman arena, we can see a common origin. Both originally symbolized the cosmic conflict before they became brutalized and vulgar on both sides of the world. Their common origin is represented in their *atl* names, Toltec and Atalia, the use of decimal numbers by both of them, common words in their lexicons, and so on, as we have already seen.

PLATE 64
PARTIAL RESTORATION OF A PALACE AT TELL-EL-AMARNA (BY CHARLES CHIPIEZ). *The scale of the buildings during the thirty dynasties of pharaohs bears witness to the wealth and power of ancient Egypt. The* Cambridge Ancient History *supposes that the population of ancient Egypt had reached 5 million under Ramses III, a fair proportion of the world's population at that time. As a clue to Egypt's wealth, a certain Kamose was sent to plunder the fleeing Hyksos, and he records: "I did not leave a single plank belonging to the hundreds of ships of new cedar, filled with gold, lapis lazuli, silver, turquoise, and innumerable bronze battle-axes. . . ."*[18] *Of the Nordic origin of the sky gods, Diodorus writes: "The chiefest of the gods, demi-gods and valiant men, the Egyptians say, the Greeks used to maintain were of their nation and that they themselves were colonials sent into Greece by the gods."*[19] *Almost all the Egyptian temples possessed libraries.*[20]

Between Ibadan and Lagos lies the city of Abeokuta, whose name, in Yoruba, means "in the shadow of the rock." Not so long ago the then chief of Abeokuta was accustomed to sacrifice children by hurling them off the top of a rock in baskets, just as the Phoenicians sacrificed children to Moloch by throwing them off the top of a temple in a leather bag, and the Syrians, even in Roman times, put children in sacks and threw them off the top of the sanctuary of their goddess Atargatis. The Mexicans, too, as we saw in the previous chapter, made a common practice of child sacrifice. Among other things it was a system of population control.

In the Babylonian story of the creation, a member of the ruling family of the gods, called Kingu, volunteered to sacrifice himself, so that his flesh could be eaten and his blood drunk by the nations being incorporated into the ruling tribe. In other accounts he did not volunteer but was executed. In Africa children are still kidnapped so that parts of them can be removed while they are still alive and eaten by "Big Men" who can afford to pay for this horror. It is in some sense sacramental cannibalism. The Bantu word *muti* for these magical practices has a Coptic origin.

In the Greek legend of the Trojan War, Agamemnon sacrifices his own daughter Iphigenia to obtain a fair wind from Aulis and sacrifices Polyxena, the daughter of King Priam of Troy, to obtain a fair wind back. The Ewe fishermen of Ghana used to sacrifice girls to the sea to improve the fishing. David sacrifices the seven offspring of Saul to improve the barley harvest.[10] Menelaus does the same sort of thing. Caesar, when he entered Gaul, described the Celts as up to the same hideous tricks.

The ancient form of American sacrifice in which each year a single youth voluntarily elected to die for the good of the people was echoed by the sun-

Plate 65
Reconstruction of three temples at Tepe Gawra, Mesopotamia, fourth millennium b.c. *The middle of the fourth millennium* b.c. *seems to have been looked upon as the commencement of "the Golden Age." The Sumerian city-states seem to have started as bicameral oligarchies. Then, "kingship came down from heaven" and the same city-states were then governed by big men, Lugal, carrying a divine burden. These kings addressed their people from the top of the ziggurats as black-headed people.*[21] *carrying the assumption that the rulers themselves were blonds. Sumerian influence spread for thousands of miles in all directions.*

The "Sublime Porte" in the Red Temple complex at Erech, Mesopotamia, fourth millennium b.c. *The colonade stands on a raised terrace at the approach to a sanctuary. It is composed of four pairs of cylindrical brick columns each about 1.5 meters in diameter. The side walls are relieved by projecting half columns. All these features, including the face of the terrace, are completely encrusted in cone mosaics, their painted heads forming a rich variety of patterns. The earliest phase of occupation in Mesopotamia is currently called the Eridu phase, dated c. 6000* b.c., *although Eridu then bore its earlier name of Ku'ara, surely the matriarchal* akawa *name. Capital for trading in Mesopotamia or Egypt often came from the temple, as with the Warri ju-ju in south-central Nigeria. Pigeon post was used in ancient Egypt.*[22]

worshipping Ibos of eastern Nigeria, who, each year, used to sacrifice one of their number as a scapegoat to cleanse the whole tribe. The horrible "foundation sacrifice" described in the Old Testament found its counterpart both among the Amerindians and in West Africa. One can dimly discern that at first the king had to be humiliated and then had to sacrifice himself for his people, after which came his resurrection; but, quite understandably, the kings invented substitutes. At first the sovereign died for the people, now the people die for the sovereign.

Because we are used to the idea of sacrifice it does not seem to us surprising that it should occur in many apparently unrelated cultures. Yet, if we stand back for a moment and try to see it freshly, is it not in fact curious that so many different peoples should independently come to believe—what after all has no possible basis in real experience—that there is an invisible power ordering their lives that will treat them more favorably if they take one or more people to a particular place and kill them? To

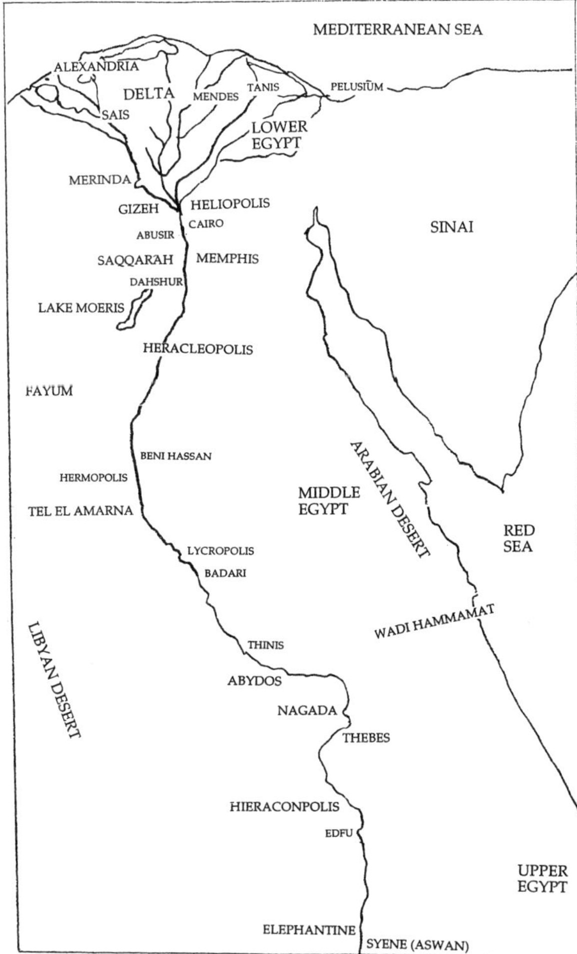

PLATE 66

NILE VALLEY. *Here is the first of the maps of the three metropolitan areas that provided the impetus for the seaborne metal trade: Egypt, the Indus Valley and Mesopotamia in the Old World. The gods started life as men, tradition tells us, and the kings whose rule was beneficent were deified subsequently by the peasantry. The followers of some of these gods set up in business in Egypt and named their towns after their deities: hence Heliopolis, Hawara, Heracleopolis, etc. But "the gods were born out of Ocean," so one must suppose that these new political movements were financed out of long-distance trade. At the birth of Osiris, son of Geb and Nut, a loud, mysterious voice proclaimed the coming of the "Universal Lord";*[23]*—as with Christ. Hundreds of literary compositions were available both in Egypt and Mesopotamia by the end of the third millennium.*[24] *The first canal between the Red Sea and the Mediterranean was cut by Sesostris before the Trojan War.*[25] *At the northeastern tip of the Red Sea is the port of Eilat, named after a Semitic Venus goddess: at the northwestern tip is Suez, which is, of course, Zeus written in reverse: this need by no means be fortuitous. The Nile is four thousand miles long. All Sudanese people along the bend in the Nile possess two kinds of knowledge: esoteric for the elect, common knowledge or moral codes for the profane.*[26] *Egypt came to be known as the mightiest kingdom of its day and the religious center of its day:* "Mundi totius templum." *The Romans levied a 25 percent tax on Red Sea goods.*[27]

explain the worldwide prevalence of this very specific delusion we must resort to one of two possible explanations. The first is some variant on the Jungian idea of a collective unconscious: built into man's mind are a number of patterns of thought that emerge as common rituals and myths. If we do not accept that, then there is only one other possibility: the delusion and its accompanying practices are widespread because religious beliefs were carried through the world by early travelers, missionaries, traders, colonists. For us that presents no difficulty. The travelers were those of whose activities we have already found overwhelming evidence. The Christian and Islamic missionaries of the last centuries are not the only waves of proselytizing but perhaps the fifth wave.

While studying long-distance sea travel, let us pause to take a glance at ancient Egypt, one of the principal consumers of precious and base metals. By 5000 B.C. the first villages began to appear in Egypt, that is,

PLATE 67

INDUS VALLEY. *The Indus civilization, whose script is not yet broken, is said to have controlled an area of India, either simultaneously or with a shifting administration, one thousand miles long and four hundred miles wide. The name of the harbor, Lothal, is like the palindrome* t-l-t, *in Ugaritic the word for bronze. Pliny, in his* Natural History, *reports that the inhabitants of Ceylon, which was a stopover on the tin run from Southeast Asia, were flaxen-haired, blue-eyed and used reed boats in his day.*[28] *Note that the sailing log raft was called* jangada *in India; and* ikada *in Japan; the* balsa *of northwest South America was called* palso *in Korea and Middle Chinese; the small craft was called the* chamban *in Colombia and was called* sampan *in China.*[29] *The Indus civilization was destroyed by earthquake at the end of the third millennium B.C. The Sumerian city-states were destroyed at the same time by "a storm." May not this be in both cases the shifting of the tectonic plates? At the same date, Ireland was flooded by a tidal wave. These cataclysms should be noted, they may recur. The Old World story of the four ages, each destroyed by cataclysms, was known both to Peru and across America. The Indus, Mesopotamian and Egyptian civilizations were interconnected. The Hittites start in Anatolia just after this date, worshipping gods with Indian names and with a pictographic script related to that of the Indus. B. Hrozny says that they had a similar ruling class.*[30] *Paleolithic man has been found in India from 500,000–50,000 B.C.*[31]

well after the erection of the first megalith in Brittany. The Archaic Period sees the gradual development of Egypt and its irrigation systems over two thousand years with the appearance of a number of city-states: Flinders Petrie divides this two-thousand-year predynastic period into the Badarian, Amratian and Gerzean cultures. Around 3100 B.C. Egypt is united and the First Dynasty, forming the Old Kingdom, uses Sumerian architecture. Some of the first pharaohs were almost certainly of Sumerian origin. And the date for the start of the Old Kingdom is the date of the Mesopotamian flood, when the Sumerian political bosses, the kings, sometimes called the god-kings, destroyed their own working class and their own irrigation systems because their political situation had got so badly out of hand. It is reasonable to conjecture that the unification of the Egyptian nation was put through by Sumerians, who brought their latest technology with them, having loused up their own country first. Many Sumerian refugees went off to America and founded colonies there, especially the sea people from Eridu, variously known as Ea, Enki, or Poseidon: but some took over and formed the kingdom of Egypt. United Egypt had forty-two rulers of provinces, nomarchs, so we have an idea of the number of different groups that were thus amalgamated, who had migrated to the country where they could enjoy the good life. The decline of the Poseidon people in the Americas may perhaps be associated with the extinction of the Sumerians in the Old World. But for a thousand

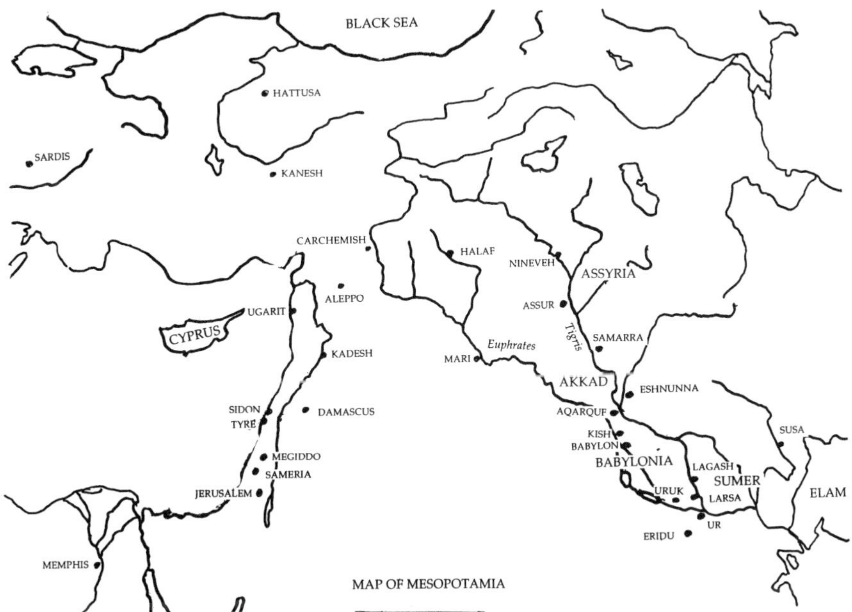

PLATE 68

MESOPOTAMIA. *By 7500 B.C. there was a defensive stone wall around a city in Jordan. At Ur in the Early Dynastic period, royal tombs have been found with the bodies of sacrificed soldiers, female attendants, wheeled vehicles with their draft animals and privileged persons sacrificed and placed in the royal chamber along with the king. These holocausts were also practiced by a number of Amerindian tribes. It is stated that between twenty and eighty thousand people were sacrificed to dedicate the ancient Mexican city of Tenochtitlán: one of the largest and most powerful cities in the world at the time of the conquest.*[32]

Mesopotamia, first with Sumer, then Akkad, then Babylon, then Assyria, controlled much of the world's metal trade. Eridu *in Sumerian means copper, and the river, now called the Euphrates, was formerly called the Eridu River. Enki, the sea god of Eridu, was looked on by Mesopotamians as being the initiator of all civilized life.*[33] *The Sumerian god Enlil was known to the Greeks as Chronos. Chronos was a god of agriculture, ruler of the Golden Age, lord of the Islands of the Blessed, dwelling at the uttermost end of land and sea, a ruler of the gods below.*[34] *The Sumerian university college was called Edubba. The Sumerian farmers' almanac was called* Nariga Ninurta. *Syria was a patchwork of city-states by the third millennium B.C., of which Ebla alone had a population of 260,000 people. Jericho begins as a fortified settlement about 9000–8000 B.C. Mesopotamia was said to be first colonized from the Iranian highlands. Towns began to be built in Mesopotamia around 5000 B.C. The Ubaidians preceded the Sumerians there. The city names are pre-Sumerian.*

The city-states of Sumer built up large populations, perhaps of people attracted by the food security they could provide. Leonard Cotrell estimates half a million people each at Ur, Lagash, Nippur, Kish and Eridu: in fact, a substantial percentage of the world's population at that time.[35] *These irrigation cities produced "the spontaneous harvests of the Age of Gold." The great canal system linked the Sumerian cities. The tradition was passed on that their every day was a heyday. Ebla alone had a population of more than a quarter million by the third millennium B.C.*[36] *Sumer was polyglot and scribes in ancient Mesopotamia were turning out bilingual and trilingual dictionaries.*[37] *Only about six thousand cuneiform literary texts survive.*[38] *Even when the Akkadians had taken over Mesopotamia, they still used Sumerian for theology and law.*[39] *Sumerian city-states began as primitive democracies, kingship came later.*[40]

PLATE 69
CHALDEAN ZIGGURAT. *Temple with square-on plan and double ramp (restored by Charles Chipiez). Sir John Marshall writes: "What was not recognised and what has only been revealed by the discoveries at Mohenjo-daro and Harappa, is that in the Chalcolithic Age India and Western Asia were clearly united by common bonds of civilisation. In the light of this knowledge, it is time to ask ourselves whether these countries may not have been as much influenced by one another in the matter of their religions as in their material culture."*[41] *In the walls of Babylon were a hundred gates built of bronze, with bronze posts and lintels.*[42] *In Babylonia palace and temple worked closely together, as with chief and ju-ju man in West Africa, queen and archbishop in Britain. As late as the Roman Empire cities without waterways were limited in size by the availability of food supplies.*[43]

years Enki, Poseidon, was the ruler of much of the netherworld, the Americas.

Egypt became a lighthouse of civilization to the whole world for three thousand years. It was African. It was not just in Africa, but its language was African, Hamitic, with a large admixture of Semitic, Sumerian, Bantu and European words. As Classical Greece provided the foundation of European culture so ancient Egypt should provide the foundation for higher African education. The universities teach that all the sciences started with Greece, but chemistry, for example, is a science that was itself named after Egypt, *Qemt*, the black land, to be compared with *trst*, origin of our word desert. Our chauvinistic dictionaries do not, of course, go back to non-European languages. The early Christians said, quite correctly, that the Greek philosophers were simply thieves of other people's ideas. That is true. Egyptian civilization was also cosmopolitan and a thief of other people's ideas. That's what ideas are for. It would be curious indeed if some of the inventions and ideas that are attributed to the Old World did not in fact emanate from the New. We call our ignorance of the early Americans their ignorance of the world. But the immense wealth attributed to these early Americans, which provides us with our English word plutocrat, supposes that they were, as today, behind no one in skills and inventiveness. Classical Greece was the place, in time and space, where the Bronze Age and the modern world met and joined hands.

The first god-kings, pharaohs, of united Egypt were clearly mariners. As we have seen, the early pharaohs and their worthies were buried with boats, either real boats or model boats. The tradition that the gods were born out of Ocean[11] is supported by these burial practices: it is a tradition found in Greece, in Egypt and in the Middle East. The word for ocean is *nun* both in Mesopotamia and in Egypt. The sun and moon in contemporary art were painted as crossing the sky in boats. Just as the Dutch East India Company, when it was making its fortune from long-distance sailing, inspired the finest school of sea painters the world has ever seen, so the concentration on boats of the first dynasties of Egypt hints to us where their money was coming from.

The first dynasties of Egypt were associated with stars, the religion of sky worship called by the Greeks *Ouranos*, by the Sumerians *An*. By the Fourth Dynasty they had moved to sun worship, when the pharaoh was associated with sunrise and enjoyed the splendid title of the Golden Horus, which suggests the importance that was by then placed upon that precious metal, gold.

The Egyptians came to look back to the Copper Age as their Golden Age, a Golden Age presided over by either the sun god Re or by Chronos: and they associated that age with sumptuous materials brought from distant lands by arduous toil. This toil is what this book is about.

PLATE 70

COMPARISON OF INDUS VALLEY AND GOLD COAST SYMBOLS. *The gold weights of the Ashanti, placed alongside each other, can be photographed to look like the skyline at Memphis. A fairly similar system of weights was in use at Baoulé in the Ivory Coast. I purchased part of a set from a Hausa trader who had spent two months collecting them in the bush in Ashanti. I pushed in front of him a small brass cube of three-quarter-inch dimension tapering in three steps or stages and asked him what it represented. "It is where Big Man climbed up to the top to speak to the people." In this one sentence, he summoned up the political function of this building as it most affected the crowd and passed on, after some four or five thousand years, its impact on the popular imagination. In Babylon, as in Ashanti, the king's weights were made heavier than the commoners' weights! The standard carat weight used in our contemporary Western world is a truncated pyramid—still! In Ghana the chiefs are carried in litters; among the Maya of Guatemala, the notables were carried in litters.[44] Only a thousand miles or so of sea divided them.*

Ashanti gold weights of the early geometric design. When the Indians were mining the Ashanti gold fields they must, from time to time at least, have used the Cape route as well as the Mediterranean route. The name of the village on top of the Ashanti gold fields is Bekway, which is also the ancient Egyptian name for gold weight, and Egyptian gold weights are possibly related to the Indus weights.[45] A number of different systems of weights ran concurrently to meet the requirements of different trade partners, eight different standards of weights were used in Egypt, obviously depending on the clients; Bequa was the oldest standard. Indus signs are found across not only Sumer, but also African and Arab tribes, including at Selima in the Libyan desert. Bequa was a term used by the Indus civilization for gold as well as by Egypt and Aegineta. There was also a busy trans-Saharan gold trade as well as by sea.

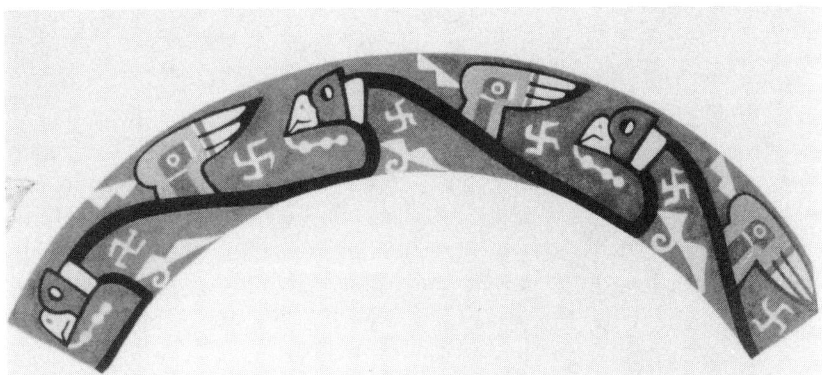

The swastika, a regular symbol on certain Ashanti gold weights, was used on Tiahuanaco pottery as one of their symbols, as in this decoration. Pachacamac was the high god of old Peru. It has been noticed that the Pachacamac cult resembles many African regional cults in its emphasis on oracles, in its multi-ethnic character and its maintenance of a formal and hierarchical organization.[46]

If we examine the distinctive symbols used by the Africans whose countries lie to the south of Egypt we might expect to find them based on Egyptian models. In reality they are not. Instead they are based on the symbols of the sea peoples who traded with Egypt but kept their own separate culture. The Egyptians themselves remained essentially landsmen, and though they did send expeditions down the East African coast, and some perhaps right around the continent, they never had the same impact as the sea peoples. They were as stay-at-home as communists. On West Africa their influence was negligible; that of the sea peoples was all-pervasive, as we see from the way their symbols entered the whole vocabulary of West African art and can still be found to this day. These symbols will be dealt with more fully, but it is worth considering some of them here as evidence of contact between Africa and the Mediterranean.

At Redan in the Transvaal there are a number of rock inscriptions. Among them are a number of sets of concentric circles, the standard sun symbol of the sea peoples, and another of their common designs, the cross within a cross.

The same symbols continue to appear on many African works of art and craft right down to the present day. In Ghana, for example, the tribes of the Ashanti region produce a particular kind of cloth known as Adinkra. The textile itself is a fairly recent invention but the symbols stamped on it are traditional. Plate 140 shows some of them, all identical with those used by the sea peoples.

Another distinctive Ashanti product is the gold weight. The form of currency in Ashanti, and also at Baoulé in the Ivory Coast, used to be gold dust, which was measured out on a beam scale against an elaborate series of weights. These weights were marked with a whole series of symbols including the swastika, the spiral or coiled serpent, the sun's rays, the torque, the cross and the saltire—all symbols of the sea peoples, as was the number notation used on these weights. Plate 70 shows some of these weights, and Plate 71–72 picks out symbols used on them and compares them with similar symbols used in the Indus Valley and Sumerian cultures. Any open-minded scrutiny of these comparisons must surely lead to the conclusion that the similarities go beyond coincidence. We cannot say precisely when communication between the West African and Indo-Sumerian cultures took place, but we can be reasonably sure that at some time, and for a long time, it did, because of the gold mines with some of the richest pennyweight deposits in the world. The use of these symbols in their Mediterranean homeland died out many centuries ago, so that contact cannot have been a recent one. The most plausible explanation is that the communication was made when the symbols were still a living tradition among their original users and when, as we shall see, they were starting to appear in many countries throughout the world.

Another interesting comparison with some of these Ashanti gold weights

Ashanti	***Indo-Sumerian***

Plates 71–72

Ashanti Gold Weights

Indo-Sumerian Comparison. *Sir John Marshall was the author of the great three-volume work on the excavation at Mohenjo-Daro (3200–1800* B.C.*) J. Kinnair Wilson, lecturer at Cambridge in Assyriology, published a small book entitled* Indo-Sumerian *in which he compares similar symbols in use in the Indus Valley and by the Sumerians in Mesopotamia (3700–1950* B.C.*) Here we have drawn in the left column the symbols on the Ashanti gold weights, in the next column symbols taken from one of these two books. Reference is given to Sir John Marshall's work as "J.M.," J. Kinnair Wilson's as "J.K.W.," with the page, plate or figure numbers added.*

The Ashanti gold fields have been described as the richest square mile on earth, which is surely why so many Ghanaian place names resemble those of the peoples of the Fertile Crescent, not to mention a great many other similarities. So the river Tana in northern Ghana is just the Phoenician goddess Anat written boustrophedon: Accra resembles Acre, the harbour of Tema resembles the Greek sea goddess Themis, Assinie and Half Assinie resemble the Mycenaean stronghold of that name; Keta is the name the Hittites applied to themselves; Takoradi would seem to have an akawa *root, while the Ashanti expression for dying or "going west" is going to Alata, an* atl *or Atlas root, as with Atlantis. The Adanse tribe of the Ashanti share the name Dan with the ancient Greeks and, like the ancient Greeks, use the same word for Creation and for founding a city. The Greek word for that is* ktisis, *and outside the capital, Accra, is the village of Kitassi. The indigenous name for Cape Coast is Ogowa, a name we associate with the Poseidon people. The town Elmina does not get its name from the Portuguese mistakenly believing that there was a gold mine there, as the scribes tell us. Anciently there was a town, Elmina, on the Orontes, while inland of it was the town of Tarkwa. Inland of Ghana's Elmina, en route to the gold fields, is also the town of Tarkwa. The conjunction of the two names on that route is little likely to be accidental.*

Ashanti Chief's Property and cobra on Pharaoh's brow

pl. ciii, no 3 J.M.

page 24, no 34 J.K.W.

pl. cxxv, no 175 J.M.

pl. cxxxiii, no 8 J.M.

page 6 J.K.W.

page 24, no 34 J.K.W.

page 6 J.K.W.

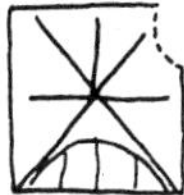

page 36, no 80 J.K.W.

page 17, no 46 J.K.W.

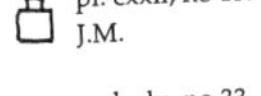

pl. cxxii, no 139 J.M.

pl. clv, no 33 J.M.

Pl. cxviii, no 4 J.M.

pl. cxxiii, H93 J.M.

Ashanti	***Indo-Sumerian***

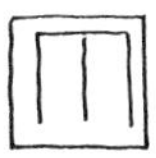

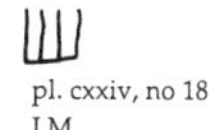

pl. cxxiv, no 18 J.M.

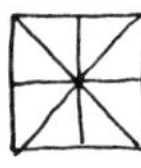

page 20 J.K.W.

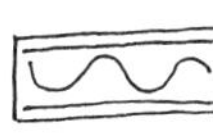

pl. cxxiv, no 253 J.M.

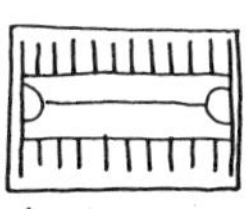

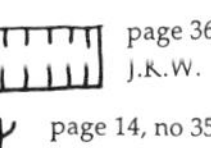

page 36 J.K.W.

page 14, no 35 J.K.W.

pl. cxxiv, no 337 J.M.

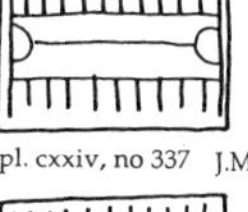

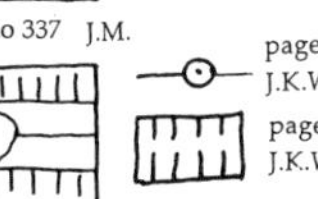

page 25 J.K.W.

page 36 J.K.W.

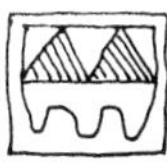

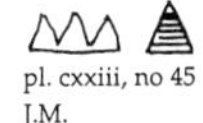

pl. cxxiii, no 45 J.M.

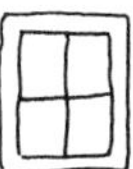

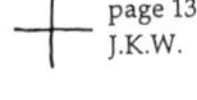

page 13 J.K.W.

page 13 J.K.W.

pl. cxiv, no 503 J.M.

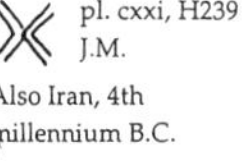

pl. cxxi, H239 J.M.

Also Iran, 4th millennium B.C. Louvre

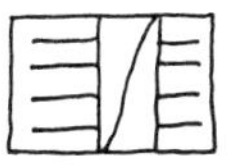

page 36, no 85 J.K.W.

pl. cxxiii, H41 J.M.

can be made by viewing them in profile, as in Plate 70. They look remarkably like a series of ziggurats. This comparison is strengthened by a remark made to me by a Hausa trader. He had spent two months in the Ashanti bush collecting gold weights and I bought some of them from him. I asked him what one of them represented, a small brass, inch-high weight that tapered to the top in three steps, and he answered: "It is where Big Man climbed up to the top to speak to the people." There, thousands of years later, was a clear statement of the political function of the ziggurat. And there have never been ziggurats in West Africa, so far as we know.

These little brass weights are themselves check-weighed against the red and black seeds of a particular acacia, *Abrus precatorius*, the sub-species used of this acacia is indigenous not to Africa but to India. Henri Abel, a French administrator, noted that a system of weights based on the abrus seed is also used in India, and proposed that the system had diffused from the Indus Valley culture to the Ashanti—because of those wonderful gold mines, doubtless producing the richest square mile on earth.

It is significant that these weights, and also the Adinkra cloth, are the products of a culture centered around a series of gold mines that we would expect to have been visited and exploited by the sea peoples. Herodotus tells us that the Carthaginians obtained their supplies of gold from black people, who brought it across the desert from the western shores of the continent. In those days, too, there were land routes across the Sahara, though it is reasonable to suppose that most ores, because of their weight and bulk, would have been shipped by water. Why do more work and take more risks than you need?

The Akan tribe have a tradition that their ancestors were white and came from across the Sahara. Originally the queen was dominant in their society, but over the centuries the king became steadily more powerful and the queen was pushed into the background. Subsequently, we shall see this as part of a gradual, worldwide transition from matriarchy to patriarchy: a most important movement that has been inadequately noticed.

Another sign of contact between Africa and the sea peoples is the earplug. This very curious form of personal decoration had, I believe, a single point of origin from which it spread out to countries in various parts of the world. Some good examples of earplugs worn by Tanzanian tribes, particularly the Wagogo, are in the museum at Dar es Salaam (see Plate 140). Once again the well-known symbols reappear on them.

They appear again in Congolese and Yoruba art, along with the trefoil decoration that was found on an ancient Indus Valley figure at Mohenjo-Daro. In South Africa the sun symbols and the double axe are incorporated in Mapoko house decoration in the Transvaal, and also appear on the earplugs worn by the Zulus and the Swazis.

In Africa, as in America, we find weapons, works of art and other man-made objects whose style connects them with the ancient countries east of the Mediterranean. The number of these different objects is very much smaller than it is in America, but for that there are two reasons. The first is that Africa was never as important to the sea peoples. Using the navigable rivers of South America, they were able to penetrate right across that continent and to exploit the huge resources of copper and tin on the far side, the critical materials then as oil is today. The gold of Africa was an elegant luxury but it was not, like bronze, a necessity: bronze, as plutonium, was the doomsday weapon of its period. The west of Africa, the side to which the sea peoples most easily voyaged, was rich in copper but not in alluvial tin. The impact of the sea peoples was therefore more localized and less intensive than it was in America: remember, also, malaria, the tsetse fly, yellow fever. I suspect, too, that the American Indians proved more docile and responsive than the Africans, better servants, better craftsmen, so that civilizations were more likely to arise in America and to stay in existence when the sea peoples were no longer visiting them. This, I believe, is why the Aborigines of Australia were visited—so the rock engravings would suggest—and abandoned!

The second reason why there seem to be fewer telltale objects in Africa than in America to mark the passage of the sea peoples is that much less work has been done on uncovering them. The ruins of American cities have been dug over by many archaeologists. With very few exceptions, West Africa does not offer such rich sites for exacavation, or the jungle has overgrown them, and the sort of fieldwork that could reveal the traces we are looking for has not attracted many professional investigators. After all, the universities tell us the Bronze Age in Africa did not exist. The reason why this chapter refers to a number of objects that I myself have obtained is not merely that I have had the privilege to pass much of my life in West Africa, it is also that anyone studying foreign contact with ancient Africa must do much of the searching for himself.

All the same, we find enough significant artifacts in Africa to lend considerable support to the other kinds of evidence that we have been looking at. At the largest end of the scale there are the stone circles, megaliths laid out on a plan that reminds one of Stonehenge. Plate 23 depicts one in Senegal. Others have been found along the Gambia River and several in North Africa. One is reminded of a tradition on the island of Lewis that the mighty Hebridean stone monuments were raised in the distant past by white priests and black men who then sailed away, though many of the black men had died and been buried within the circles.

Among smaller objects, weapons can be very indicative of the culture that produces them. The curious sickle-shaped weapon in Plate 123 comes from the Senufo territory in the Ivory Coast and was known to the Fertile Crescent as a harpé. The distinctive thing about it is that it has the cutting edge on the outer, convex side, and weapons of this type were the standard military weapon in the Middle East during the Bronze Age. It seems that originally they had been made of wood with flint or obsidian fastened to the outer curve, but when bronze became available they were cast in one piece, like this Senufo example. It would have been with a "sickle" of this sort that Chronos emasculated his father, Ouranos, in the Greek myth, not with an ordinary sickle as it is customary to translate the Greek text.

One of the American objects mentioned in Chapter 4 was a ceremonial axe with a fenestrated blade, very similar to Egyptian work. The same design turns up again in a Senufo axe (Plate 120) which I bought from a Senegalese trader in West Africa. Another Senufo ceremonial object is the chief's staff in Plate 189. The horned head at the end of the handle is identical with the Mesopotamian representations of the sea dragon Tiamat, while the human figure below it resembles the Senufo sea captains of reed boats, whose heads had been shaped by head deformation.

One of the obvious entry points into Africa for anyone arriving by sea is the Cross River in Nigeria. In previous centuries this was the main supply route to the port of Calabar. Along the Cross River curious monoliths have been found, thickly covered with the symbols of the Mediterranean Bronze Age peoples, the sun circles, the spiral, the Maltese cross and so on (Plates 155 and 156). Altogether 295 carved stones have been found at thirty-nine sites. They are known locally as Atl or Akwanshi figures,[12] and there are several reasons why they are unlikely to have been produced by African carvers working without stimulus from outside. First, they are a rarity in being carved from hard stone (basalt). Other Nigerian carvings are nearly always in wood or soft stone. Second, some of the figures are bearded and wear pointed caps, which make them look much more like Phoenicians than Africans. Third, a number of them are obviously phalluses, and the carving of phalluses was an American and Phoenician custom that the Greeks adopted in their own hermae. Finally, many of them have rows of dots under the eyes, a strange piece of symbolism also found on an American carving, the "Weeping God" of Peru (Plate 162), and on Easter Island. It also occurs on a terra-cotta from Mali (Plate 163). In the ancient tradition God, at the Creation, wept, and his tears became men and women.

The appearance of later figures changes and it looks as if, as Phoenician influence declined, the trading station was gradually absorbed by Africa, the figures became Afro-Phoenician and then African, and in the end the art of creating them was lost. Philip Allison points out that others have described similar shaped stones and laterite blocks from Gambia, Senegal, the Niger Bend and the Southern Sahara. A cylindrical column with rounded top and two raised bosses occurs among groups of worked stones at Tondidaro on the Niger Bend, and is reminiscent of some of the Ogoja stones. A domed stone, carved with a shield-shaped fan, from Tabelbalet in the southern Sahara, which has features in common with some of the Akwanshi, is illustrated in the same work.

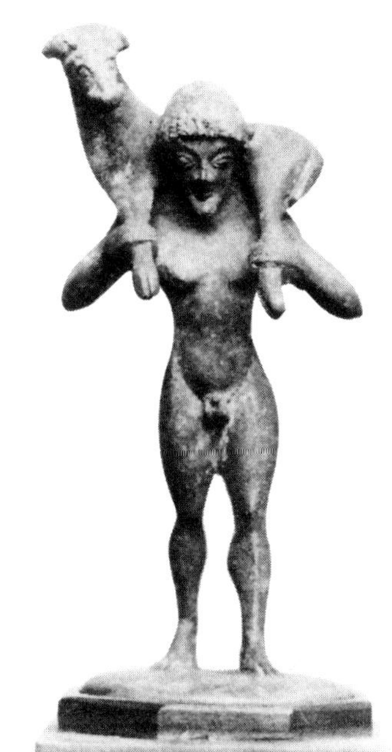

PLATE 73
THE GOOD SHEPHERD. *Man with a ram on his shoulders. The figure is believed to be Pelasgian. Compare this Pelasgian face with the standard Cameroons face from Foumban, in the area of the prehistoric tin mines. The Pelasgians are said by Diodorus in the early days to have conquered the west and the north of Europe and to have intermarried widely with the natives. One must ask oneself why some of the most sophisticated people of their day chose the west and north of Europe. Both in Greece and the Middle East kingship was equated with shepherdship, so the parable of the good shepherd held references to the god-kings of the Mediterranean, a significance subsequently lost by Christians. "The exalted scepter, staffs, the exalted shrine, shepherdship, kingship." This is a line given to the Mesopotamian sea god Enki.*[47] *The Sumerian god Enlil, god of Nippur, was called "the shepherd,"*[48] *and so on. The Hebrew King David was also a shepherd of his people. Attis, consort of Cybele, was also the good shepherd, the* "pastor bonus." *For India, Krishna was the shepherd god, son of Vishnu, whose symbol, like Christ's, was a fish. He was also a savior god.*[49] *In Egypt the shepherd's crook was the scepter, symbol of kingship. It was pronounced* hks,[50] *hence the name Hyksos, so important to our story. Even as late as Plato, Thrasymachus equates shepherdship with kingship. The Hittite monarch was called Chief Shepherd. In Ugarit the chief priest was known as the chief herdsman,*[51] *hence also the Christian crozier. The Hyksos worshipped Seth, the controller of the seas.*[52] *Hammurabi was referred to as "the Shepherd."*

Allison compares the Akwanshi figures to numerous phallic columns in Ethiopia but says that they resemble certain figures in Corsica, the Caribbean and the Pacific more closely than any others. We can no longer be susprised at that. It is also worth noting that the only true script developed in sub-Saharan Africa, Nsibidi, an ideographic script, was used by the Uguakima, a sub-tribe of the Ibo, living on the Cross River, an important trading river that leads to the prehistoric tin mines of the Cameroons.

In Africa, as in America, we find a number of sculptures that clearly represent people or divinities from other lands. Take, for example, the figure from Burkina Faso shown in Plate 151. It is almost identical with the Phoenician god Resheph and/or Baal alongside shown in the inset. Another figure from Burkina Faso (Plate 106) wears a war mask with a crested helmet that makes him look as if he might have fought at Troy. A third carries on his head a sun disk with the pair of horns that was a symbol of the sun-worshipping king when the sea peoples carried the sky god's religion around the world (Plate 149).

Another example is the head shown in Plate 132. It comes from the Cameroons but nothing could be less like an African head. It has, however, very obvious resemblances to Pelasgian work.

Or there is the dancing man from the Ivory Coast (Plate 175) who is clearly Semitic, not African, in both his appearance and his style of dancing. Or the six pendant heads may be questioned from Baoulé in Plate 169, probably originally in gold but now copied in brass. The strange pot in Plate 114 also comes from the Baoulé area. The figures holding it up are bearded and handlebar-mustached in a way that looks most un-African but could well be Semitic.

There is an obvious objection to using some of the figures as evidence. They are recent work, not archaeological finds sculpted at the time of contact with the sea peoples. Against that is the fact that they are all traditional work, and African traditions go back a long, long way and change only slowly. For myself I find it quite believable that modern African and ancient Phoenician sculpture should both derive from an unbroken tradition going back to the days when the Phoenicians were traveling the world. I find it harder to believe that artists in various parts of Africa learned to carve in the ancient styles many centuries after they had become dead forms, familiar only to scholars and the curators of museums in our day. Tell that to the Marines!

6. Lands to the East

For Atlas had worked out the science of astronomy to a degree surpassing others and had ingeniously discovered the spherical nature of the stars.

DIODORUS SICULUS, Book IV

The huge double continent of America cuts the world ocean in two. To the east of it lies the Atlantic. To the west, the Pacific and Indian Oceans form effectively a single vast sea, partially separated by the chain of islands stretching down from Asia to Australia. It is difficult but not impossible for a seaman in a simple craft to navigate through that chain and so to travel anywhere between the east coast of Africa and the west coast of America. But when he reaches America he is up against an impassible barrier. The northern passage through the Arctic ice fields is obviously out of the question, and so for practical purposes is the southern route round Cape Horn, where winds and seas have overwhelmed many ships of far more advanced design than any the early sea peoples commanded.

It is a proof of the extent of the sea peoples' geographical knowledge that they knew from very early on that America was an island, or rather, two huge islands in the middle of one ocean. A number of the accounts of Atlantis, including Plato's, agree on that, and the only way they could have known it was by sailing the oceans on both sides. It is true that anyone arriving on the Atlantic coast of America and crossing the forty-mile-wide isthmus of Panama would have found the sea on the far side, but that would not have proved he was on an island, without much, much further sailing: i.e., exploring the Americas from top to bottom.

So far in this book we have been chiefly concerned with the Atlantic, and indeed for most of the period of world voyaging that was the more important crossing, linking the rich resources of America (and to a lesser extent Africa) to the restless, innovative cultures east of the Mediterranean. But if the Atlantic provided the busiest routes it did not provide the only ones, or even necessarily the earliest. The first contacts between Old and New World might have taken place across the Pacific, and despite the relative difficulty of navigating that far larger ocean, those contacts continued throughout much of the Copper and Bronze Ages and indeed, beyond. It should be noticed that in the Atlantic, sea currents and winds tend to move in the same direction, while in the Pacific they tend to move in opposite directions, so the waves would be higher.

Once again we must remember that until quite recent times the land divided and the seas united. The northern littoral of the Indian Ocean, stretching from the horn of Africa (today's Somalia) around Arabia to India and Southeast Asia was important. The ocean offered clear passage between all these lands, and from the main body of that ocean two long and vitally important inlets, the Red Sea and the Persian Gulf, reached up to the heartlands of ancient civilization in Mesopotamia and Egypt.

Throughout this area north of the Indian Ocean various cultures arose, various peoples moved around, conquering, migrating, settling, mixing with others. There is still no general agreement among historians about who all these people were, where they came from and where they went. For our purposes, fortunately, this does not matter. If we can establish that there was contact between India or China and America, our primary point is made. Just who the people were who made the contact is of secondary importance. In any case we must bear in mind that among the seagoing peoples their racial origin was always less important than the maritime culture in which they took part. I said in the Introduction that the best modern analogy to their organization is not the tribe but the multinational company, groups distinguished by their culture, by their religion, not by race or language as we distinguish today. What we must think of, then, is a broad region within which people—and to an even greater extent information—passed from place to place. Cultural influences spread in both directions, eastward and westward, and it is often impossible to know where the origin of a particular skill or custom lay. Archaeological dating is still not perfectly accurate and what turns up in digs must always depend partly on chance. It is possible, indeed probable, that at any time some object may be discovered that predates similar objects found elsewhere and deemed until then to be the earliest examples.

The limitations of archaeology are tantalizingly evident at the great site of Mohenjo-Daro, toward the mouth of the Indus. This has been excavated as far as the remains of the middle of the third millennium but there work has had to stop. Since the days when "the City of the Dead," Mohenjo-Daro, was a living city, the water table has risen and all earlier levels are now permanently under water. Borings have established that there are remains from far more ancient times but, with present techniques, they

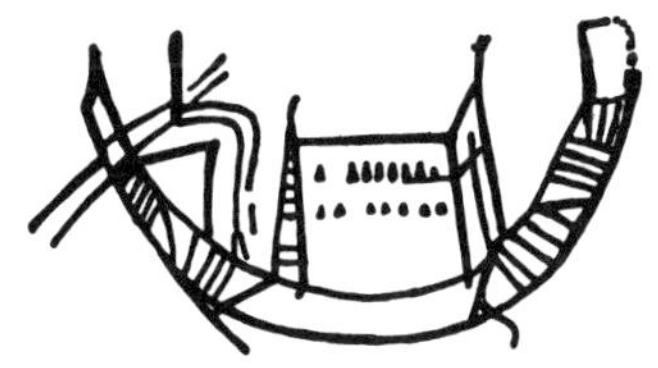

PLATE 74
Reed craft on a seal of the early Indus civilization.

Sir John Marshall, the great excavator of Mohenjo-Daro, claims that the city had no temples, only keeps; perhaps not realizing that, as in ancient America, ziggurats also served as keeps.[1] *The Mexican ziggurats were used as such by the Aztecs when they were fighting Cortés. The monsoon winds of the Indian Ocean provided a unique convenience for travelers.*

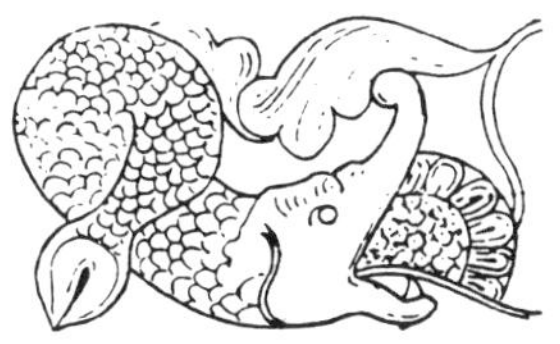

India ***Central America***

The water lily motif in India (left) and at Chichén Itzá, Yucatan (right).

Bronze figure of a dancing girl from Mohenjo-Daro.

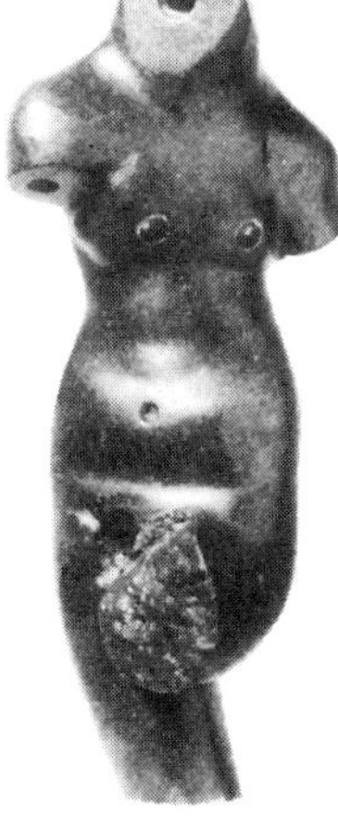

Stone figurines from Harappa reminiscent of Classical Greek carving. Sir Mortimer Wheeler writes: "In 1967 experienced Dutch consultants drilled for UNESCO a series of 24 widely-distributed 'observation wells' at charted spots on the map of Mohenjo-Daro. . . . These wells revealed . . . the astonishing fact . . . that they show occupation debris . . . three times as deep as any archaeological digging is known to have penetrated." So we may in good time discover that the commencement of Mohenjo-Daro dates from the same period as the first cities of Egypt and Sumer, i.e., the fifth millennium B.C. *and earlier: not 2500* B.C. *as the expert Sir Mortimer Wheeler puts it. In fact the floodplain of the Indus Valley has risen by thirty-three feet in the last five thousand years.*[2]

PLATE 75

LOTHAL DOCK. *Its sides are made out of baked brick and it has a well-made sluice gate. Lothal is a palindrome, similar to Ugaritic, meaning bronze: the root* atl *meaning water in Mexican Nahuatl, in Berber and in Greek* thalassa *or* thalatta. *Lothal would seem to have been one of the suppliers of bronze for the Harappa civilization. It is claimed to be the largest dry dock in that early world. There were fire altars at Lothal, fire being sacred to Atlas or Set. The unique nature of the monsoons in the Indian Ocean helps to explain the Indian influence on Africa.*

An Indian tradition was one of almost worldwide travel on the part of India's Aryans.[3] *The archaeological evidence proves this claim to be true. We find the Indus script on Easter Island; the Indian game of patolli played in pre-Columbian Mexico, which, statistically, cannot be an independent invention; we find the indigenous American plant, the sweet potato, bearing a Sanskrit name among some Amerindians; we find Indians mining gold and copper across Zimbabwe; we find the Indus Valley people mining gold in Ashanti; we find a great variety of later Indian scripts among the rock inscriptions of Amazonia and South America generally; we find a loom used in Peru identical with a loom in India; we find in South America the carving of an Indian mahout riding on the neck of an elephant; we find at Tiahuanaco the sculpture of a young Indian: the evidence is sufficient to totally prove the accuracy of this Indian claim. While the sailing log-raft is of rather special construction and is identical on both sides of the Atlantic. It is also called* paisa *in Korea,* pae pae *in Polynesia and* balsa *in Ecuador. While another type of raft used on the coast of Brazil is identical with a raft used on the Tamil coast of India and in both countries bears the same name,* jangada.[4] *From early times in West Bengal the tropical cactus has been growing, indigenous to America, and with it the plant lice cochineal, also indigenous to America, which yields a beautiful red dye.*[5] *The Acropolis of Lothal was trapezoid.*[6]

It is worth noting here that in Southeast Asia and America the same very specialized hunting weapon, the blowpipe, was in use. Among the Japanese and Siamese the same screenfold book was in use as in Mexico. Phallus worship was practiced in Mohenjo-Daro and Harappa.[7] *They also used game pieces like chessmen.*

In India the megalith builders were Dravidian.[8] *With the Indian god Vishnu, his symbols were the pig, the crocodile and the fish. These were the symbols of Set. Vishnu loses his solar attributes to reincarnate as the savior Krishna: Set, the Philistines' sun god, loses his solar attributes to reincarnate as Christ.*

cannot be explored. Even so, we know enough to realize that Mohenjo-Daro, first excavated by Sir John Marshall between 1922 and 1927, was an astonishing place.

It had not been imagined that five thousand years earlier, before ever the Aryans had been heard of, the Punjab and Sind, if not other parts of India, had been enjoying an advanced and singularly uniform civilization of their own, closely akin but in some respects even superior to that of contemporary Mesopotamia and Egypt. The discoveries at Harappa, another city further up the Indus after which the Indus civilization is named, and Mohenjo-Daro placed this beyond question. They exhibited the Indus peoples of the fourth and third millennia B.C. in possession of a highly developed culture. Like the rest of western Asia, the Indus country was still in the Chalcolithic Age—using arms and utensils of stone, side by side with those of copper or bronze. Their society was organized in cities; their wealth derived mainly from agriculture and trade, which appeared to have extended far and wide in all directions. They cultivated crops and domesticated zebu, buffalo, short-horned bull, sheep, pig, dog, elephant and camel; but the cat and probably the horse were unknown to them. They had wheeled vehicles, to which oxen doubtless were yoked. They were skillful metalworkers, with a plentiful supply of gold, silver and copper. Lead, too, and tin were in use, but the latter only as an alloy in the making of bronze. With spinning and weaving they were thoroughly conversant. They fought and hunted with bow and arrow, spear, axe, dagger and mace, but they had not yet evolved the sword or body armor. Hatchets, sickles, saws, chisels and razors were made of both copper and bronze, although knives and celts were sometimes of stone. For the crushing of grain they had the muller and saddle-quern but not the circular grindstone. Their domestic vessels were commonly of earthenware turned on the wheel and frequently painted with encaustic designs; more rarely they were of copper, bronze or silver. The ornaments of the rich were made of precious metals or of copper, sometimes overlaid with gold, of faience, ivory, carnelian and other stones; for the poor they were usually of shell or terra-cotta. Figurines and toys were of terra-cotta, and shell and faience were freely used, as they were in Sumer and the West generally, not only for personal use or ornaments but for inlay work and other purposes.

Their script, though peculiar to India, was evidently analogous to other contemporary scripts of western Asia and the Near East.

The Indus culture would seem to have corresponded in its general features with the Chalcolithic cultures of western Asia and Egypt, but some aspects were peculiar to Sind and the Punjab.

There was nothing in western Asia to compare with the well-built baths and comfortable houses of the citizens of Mohenjo-Daro. In Egypt and Mesopotamia much money and thought had been lavished on the building of magnificent temples, palaces and tombs, but the people seemingly had to put up with insignificant dwellings of mud. In the Indus Valley, however, temples, palaces and tombs were not readily distinguishable from other edifices. Admittedly, at Ur, a group of moderate-sized houses of burnt brick were found, but they constituted a notable exception to the general rule; these disclosed such a striking similarity to the small and rather loosely built structures at Mohenjo-Daro that Sir John Marshall expressed no doubt as to the influence under which they had been erected. He felt justified in

> seeing in the Great Bath of Mohenjo-Daro and in its roomy and serviceable houses, with their bathrooms and elaborate systems of drainage, evidence that the ordinary townspeople enjoyed here a degree of comfort and luxury unexampled in other parts of the then civilised world.

One thing on which Sir John was quite adamant was that the civilization both at Mohenjo-Daro and Harappa was not an incipient civilization, but one already age-old and stereotyped on Indian soil, with many millennia of human endeavor behind it, and that India should be recognized, along with Persia, Mesopotamia and Egypt, as one of the most important areas where the civilizing processes of society were initiated and developed.

> I do not mean to imply by this that India can claim to be regarded as the cradle of civilisation; nor do I think on the evidence at present available that the claim can be made on behalf of any country in particular. In my view, the civilisation of the Chalcolithic and succeeding ages resulted from the combined efforts of many countries, each contributing a certain quota towards the common stock of knowledge.[1]

Although written almost seventy years ago, that last sentence admirably sums up what must be the verdict today. We are looking not for any unique "cradle of civilisation" but for a network of mutual influence, mutual stimulation, between peoples linked by constant travel, most of it travel by sea; globetrotters in—and it is not altogether stretching the phrase too far—the earlier global village.

As far as we can now make out, the first culture to have pervaded the region north of the Indian Ocean was an earth-worshipping, matriarchal society that practiced agriculture and used stone tools. The period falls sometime before the fifth millennium and therefore more than a thousand years earlier than the earliest remains unearthed so far at Mohenjo-Daro. This culture seems to have originated around the Black Sea and to have spread through the eastern Mediterranean and the Middle East to India and China and eventually to the Americas. It took with it the arts of agriculture, while the cult of the Mother Goddess extended eventually around the world. The next great wave was a movement of northern European peoples, which started from the west coast of Europe. It was this Atlantic

Plate 76

Indian and Mexican Figurines.

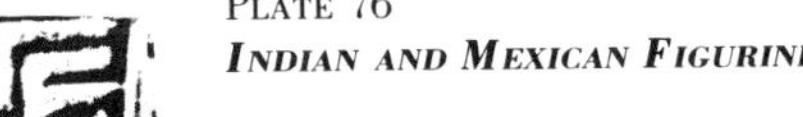

Stamp seals of various designs are found widely in the Indus ruins. The swastika and the cross within a cross are two of the designs used, the swastika still being significant in contemporary history, the cross in contemporary religion.

Malwa pot from Navdatoli, India, decorated with the characteristic Cretan double-axe style.

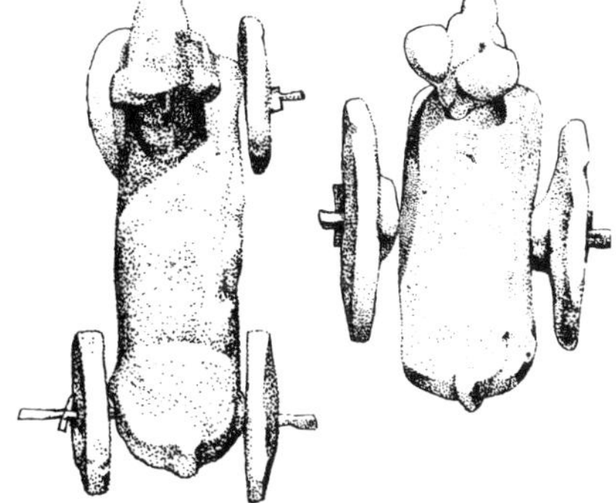

Terra-cotta wheeled toys from Chanhu-Daro, down river from Mohenjo-Daro; compare with the terra-cotta wheeled toys from Mexico (Plate 36).

Terra-cotta wheeled toy carts from Chanhu-Daro. Ancient Indian gold mining took place at Kanara, in Mysore: compare the name Kanara with the Sanskrit for gold, kanikam, *and the Akkadian for bronze.*

Terra-cotta figurines from Mohenjo-Daro, to be compared with the archaic terra-cotta figurines of Mexico.

Three "Archaic" figurines from central Mexico. The sinologist Carl Hentze and the Austrian ethnologist Robert von Heine-Geldern point to numerous common features in the art and religion of early Mesoamerican and Andean cultures, and those of India and the Far East.[9] Let us also remember that fire-walking was practiced at Chamula in pre-Columbian Mexico as in India.

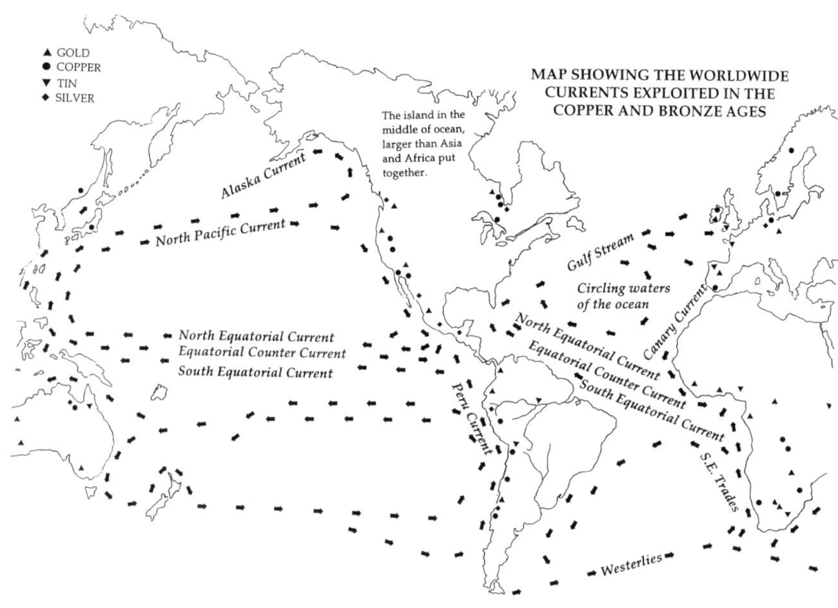

PLATE 77
Map showing the worldwide currents and how much of worldwide sailing in the Copper and Bronze Ages was handled. Homer instructs: "Thou shouldst go to the nethermost bounds of earth and sea where abide Japetus and Chronos."[10] *Notice the word nethermost, or where the sun was at midnight. This nicely points to the contemporary government of Mexico and the Americas by the Atlas people and the Phoenicians. And notice that Strabo twice says that Odysseus went out into the Atlantic to Calypso.*[11] *The quest for metals was the root of foreign trade. Hence also the fact that the pineapple, an admittedly American plant, was found growing in the wild in Hawaii and Polynesia.*[12] *Three species of canavalia bean were found in old graves in Peru dated from 3000–1000* B.C., *an Old World plant,*[13] *and the phaseolus bean, another Old World plant, was being grown in America before Columbus.*[14] *Quetzalcóatl, god of Toltec Mexico, was entitled "Lord of the Air." Enlil, god of the Sumerian cultural center of Nippur, means in Sumerian "Lord of the Air," and his wife, Ninlil, means simply "Lady of the Air." Homer says that the gods were born from Oceanos and Tethys: Tethys sister and wife of the male Ocean.*[15] *In the* Odyssey *the island of Circe has been removed to the far west, and the scene of the descent to the underworld translated to crossing the Atlantic Ocean.*[16] *Since Mediterranean sailors knew both the Pacific as well as the Atlantic routes to America, the sun was reported to sleep at night either on a western or an eastern couch.*[17] *The origin of everything was held to be in the primeval waters. Homer, surely referring to these currents, writes of "softly-gliding, deep-flowing, Ocean."*[18] *He refers also to "the violet-hued deep."*

group of people that built the first megalithic structures in Brittany and they were patriarchal worshippers of the sky god: they took over the copper trade from the matriarchs and financed their own expeditions with it. They mightily developed the irrigation societies and brought them kingship and nationhood. They provided the Aryans of India, and a ruling class eventually for much of the world.

Large works of irrigation can be created and maintained only under a large political unit, while kingship on the scale on which it was practiced in Mesopotamia, the Indus Valley and Egypt demands a large and highly productive agriculture to support its extravagant, hierarchical demands.

It was this culture that flourished in Mohenjo-Daro and Harappa from the time of the earliest excavations until the collapse of the Indus Valley civilization as a result of major earthquakes about 2003 B.C., and it exemplifies the way in which different regions cross-fertilized one another during an age of sea travel. The Sumerians, for example, had a tradition that all the arts of civilization were brought to them by six creatures, half human and half fish, who came up the Persian Gulf in the fourth millennium, after which no important inventions were made in the Middle East.[2] In the other direction, there is some evidence that at one time the ruling class in Mohenjo-Daro was Sumerian or at least cosmopolitan. K. N. Sastri, excavation assistant to Sir John Marshall and later curator of the Archaeological Museum, cites Indus seals showing bull fighting as in Crete, and mentions also the similarity of the "tree of knowledge" legend, found not only in Genesis but also in Sumer and India.[3] Mesopotamia and India strongly influenced East Africa. The Makonde at the mouth of the Zambezi spend their time carving the Tree of Life while the Kikuyu Dedan Kimathi, Kenyan war hero, was ambushed in the Aberdare Forest as he worshipped at a *Ficus religiosa* growing there. Archaeologists have found Sumerian influence in the Indus and Indus influence in Mesopotamia. There is no doubt about the Sumerian influence on Egyptian architecture during the first dynasties (that is, after the two kingdoms of Upper and Lower Egypt combined about 3100 B.C.). The buildings of that time have Sumerian or Mesopotamian influences. From Sumer, too, was probably disseminated the knowledge of how to make bronze: it has been found in northeast Thailand dating from around 3500 B.C.[4] It is worth remembering Forbes's argument that the independent invention of bronze in two unconnected cultures is highly unlikely. And with the name Nok in the site where this Thai bronze was discovered, Non Nok Tha, we recall the Babylonian *anaku*. Indeed, the name *anaku* is associated with almost all the tin mines in the world. We must, however, notice that the Arab name for bronze is much the same as the Akkadian. Early Thailand bronze was found at both Non Nok Tha and Ban Chiang. Cain in Hebrew means smith.

It seems to me well worth investigating whether the collapse of the Indus Valley civilization was not directly or indirectly responsible for some unexplained migrations such as that of Mycenaeans into Greece, the Hittites (who worshipped gods with Indian names) into Anatolia, or of the Jews into Mesopotamia: who by their own account came into Sumer from the east. The names Abraham and Brahmin can be compared. The Brahmin script

PLATE 78

POTTER'S MARKS ON SHANG CHINESE POTS. *When the Hyksos sea people were expelled from Egypt 1570 B.C. a part of them went to Mexico via the Atlantic and set up business on the Caribbean coast. A part, clearly a west Semitic part, first stopped in the Anyang area of China where there is copper and tin, and began the Shang Dynasty and were responsible for the start of the high Bronze Age in China. After a long delay in China, many of them proceeded to Mexico by the Pacific route. As in West Africa, cowrie shells provided the currency for Shang China. Chinese figures and faces appear quite commonly in the Toltec/Olmec culture of Mexico.*

(a) Potter's marks of the Shang Dynasty from Anyang, China. We are talking of a later period now, but it is worth noting that Zeno's very, very specific Greek paradoxes were available in China at the same period as Zeno's lifetime.

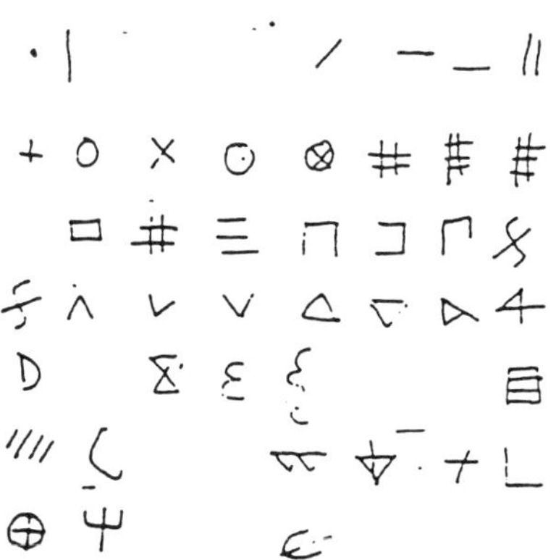

(b) Libyan and Iberian descendants of Phoenician and south Semitic scripts: compare these west Semitic signs with the Shang potter's marks.[20]

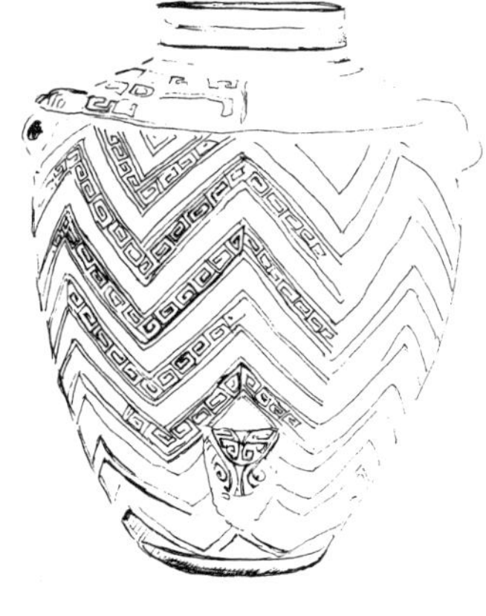

Here is a kaolin pot from Shang China with the chevrons and meanders on it characteristic of the eastern Mediterranean. Human sacrifices by the hundred were made to the king's ancestors in Shang China,[19] *very much as in the rest of the world.*

PLATE 79
Painted pottery, *with spiral, water symbol and sun circle of the Chinese Ma-chia-yao phase from Kansu.*

A type of stepped temple erected in Polynesia. *In Polynesia,* waka *means canoe, clearly an* akawa *name, referring probably to the original matriarchy or its breakaway group, Heracles. The Eskimo name for canoe,* kayak, *might well be an* akawa *name, but a palindrome. Rafts were once used widely in Oceania.*

David Lewis, a New Zealander, made a study of Pacific navigation, pointing out that the aborigines entered Australia fifty thousand years ago, having first to cross forty miles of sea at the Wallace Gap.[21] *He says that there has been an identity of navigational methods across Oceania for something like the last four thousand years:*[22] *he says that expansion across the Pacific began about 5000 B.C., that Polynesian star navigation was so good they felt they did not need compasses, that birds and the behavior of waves also helped with their navigation, that only some Polynesian families specialized in navigation, and that the Pacific system of navigation possibly developed elsewhere than in the Pacific, in fact in common with the whole ancient world.*[23]

He points out that the Polynesian canoemen took a cage of shore-sighting birds with them when they voyaged because birds, by climbing into the air, overcame the curvature of the earth, vastly extending the range of vision. And he adds how the Spaniards totally exterminated the population of one Pacific island in the name of Christ: the Chamarros of Saipan.[24] *There are both Indo-European and Semitic roots to the Polynesian language.*[25] *Let us note the rites of Malekula island in the Pacific, where islanders seeking to improve their social rank raised stone circles and avenues and sacrificed wild boars*[26] *(sacred to Set or Atlas).*

PLATE 80
A POLYNESIAN BOX. *Spirals were important symbols, representing, as we have seen, the religion of the earth mother. Greek tradition refers to mariners sailing to the land in the middle of Ocean both by the Pacific and Atlantic routes. The many Greek words in the Polynesian languages seem to confirm this tradition.[27] The spiral was an important symbol to the Maori. Contemporary work by biochemists on DNA has proved the physical relationship of certain Amerindians, Polynesians, Melanesians and certain peoples of Southeast Asia.[28] It proves their inbreeding.*

TRILITHON IN TONGA. *The Ha'amonga-a-Maui, a massive trilithon in Tonga—unique in Polynesia (Janet M. Davidson). In the Marquesas Islands and throughout Polynesia the sun god, as in Egypt, was called Ra.[29] The Polynesians cultivated the sweet potato, which is indigenous to America. Since the Polynesians were inveterate long-distance sailors and wonderful navigators across the Pacific it is not unreasonable to suppose that they might even have acquired the sweet potato from America themselves.* Te waka *was their name for the canoe, surely an* akawa *name.*

On Easter Island it is recorded: "It is accordingly worthy of note that the small Andean element in the wild flora of Easter Island is entirely restricted to useful plants. These outnumber locally the useful wild plants of Polynesian origin. They also include the economically more important species: the only two phanerogams, the only 'wild' local shrub, and, possibly, the only 'wild' local tree." There was a tradition of rafts as being the first vessels in Oceania.

Ra was the name of the sun throughout the hundreds of Polynesian islands and in ancient Egypt, it was the name of the sun god as well as the sun.[30] It is widely and, in my judgment, correctly maintained, that despite their spread in time and space, all megalithic monuments have a common seed.[31] The use of reed and bark-bundle floats and the simplest rafts in Polynesia could go back to at least 20,000 B.C.[32]

is related to Semitic scripts, not the Indus script.[5] Genesis says that the Jews came from the east and 1800 is about the date of their founding patriarch, Abraham. One thing, however, is certain. This was a period of communication over long distances, when civilizations as far apart as Egypt and India were sufficiently in touch to form a single cultural region right around the northern perimeter of the Indian Ocean. And across the waters of that ocean moved the traders who were not only bringers of goods but also the great communicators of ideas. The Indus Valley civilization collapsed as a result of two huge floods, one around 2003 B.C., one around 1900 B.C., caused, it is suggested, by earthquake, by the shifting of the tectonic plates. Hints from oral literature about a major climatic disaster should be of interest to contemporary meteorologists. Caveat! The fact that the Sumerians perished at the same time, their tradition said "from a storm," may refer to the same earthquakes. The Four Ages were the four different sets of people who succeeded each other as the thalassocrats, and these changes seem to have been brought about not by the new dynasties defeating the old in battle, but by their moving into a power vacuum caused by climatic disaster. At precisely the same period a large part of Ireland was covered by a tidal wave.[6]

From the Indian Ocean the sea peoples reached out still further to the east. The stepped temples of Java, Sumatra and Cambodia show the influence of the ziggurat builders of Mesopotamia. The Bronze Age religious symbols of the Mediterranean are found not only as far west as Spain and the British Isles and America, but as far east as China, Japan and the Pacific Islands. In China it is certain that the irrigation society on the Yellow River in the Anyang area was started by western Semites, as the potters' marks of the Shang Dynasty, 1700–1200 B.C., clearly prove. These immigrants brought the latest technology of the high Bronze Age with them to China: the numbers of immigrants to the Anyang area being reinforced by parties of the Hyksos when they were expelled from Egypt. A standard Shang Dynasty pot decorated with the chevron and meander of the east Mediterranean sea people is shown here (Plate 78). It is worth noticing that the earliest pottery found so far comes from Japan and dates from 9000 B.C.[7] The Chinese emperor ruled by the mandate of heaven as an organ of the cosmos.

In Southeast Asia the traders could have found plentiful sources of tin on two islands, Bangka and Billiton, near Sumatra, and plentiful supplies also in Malaysia, Thailand and Vietnam as well as China.

R. J. Forbes believes, however, that Southeast Asian tin was not much used and that even India procured its tin from the west.[8] This may have been because there are no large deposits of copper close to the Southeast Asian tin mines, so that it was impossible to make bronze on the spot and ship it home in ingots, as could be done from America. That it was traded, however, can be shown by such place names as Kandy, Sri Lanka, Non Nok Tha, Bangka, Kinta River, all seemingly containing the Babylonian-Akkadian word for tin, *anaku*.

The llama of Peru, Bolivia and the Andes, a member of the camel family, was domesticated around the seventh or the sixth millennium B.C.[9] In a language of Peru, Tarma Quechua, the llama's name is *waka*. This is clearly an *akawa* name. We have emphasized that *akawa* is a name associated with the Heracles people or the matriarchal society from which they had broken away: so here is evidence of the truth of the Greek tradition that the Heracles people took the arts of agriculture around the inhabited world in missionary spirit; and when the Greeks in this context used the word *oekumenos* for the inhabited world, they meant just that. Hence also our reason for supposing that when agriculture commenced at about the same time in Mexico, in Southeast Asia, in Peru and in Southwest Asia, it was not Jung's collective unconscious at work, or some other contemporary nonsense, but that the oral literature was accurate: the Heracles people or the matriarchy were traveling worldwide and had got it all started. In Quechua, too, *anta* means copper-colored or copper, so we must repeat the question whether the Atlantic had once meant the copper sea, the Antilles had meant the copper islands, the Andes the copper mountains and the island at the mouth of the St. Lawrence, Anticosti, not to mention Lake Ontario, owed their names to this early copper culture? It is a long shot, but much of Peru's culture crossed the Andes from Bolivia, so it is worth examining. And there is a district on the slopes of the Andes called Anti. In Aymará, the chief language of Bolivia, *anti* means copper also.

In the other direction we should notice that the Great Mother in Ceylon—on the bronze route to Southeast Asia—was called *Kuveni*, and the so-called primitive forest people of whom she was goddess were called Yakkies,[10] both of which read to me like *ak-awa* or *awa-ak* names.

The tradition was that Horus ruled Egypt but that the Set or Atlas people ruled in the second millennium much of the rest of the world. So we ought again to look in Tibet not just at the yak but the possibility that Lhasa is an Atlas name, the Dalai Lama also, and his palace, the Potala Palace, of similar origin: also Mihintale, Matale, etc. After all, Lothal was both a principal port for the Indus Valley civilization and could be a name for bronze. The Telchinese were the inhabitants of Crete before Minos; they were both sea people and ingenious metalworkers. The Cretan capital is of course Heraklion (Iráklion). When the east Mediterranean people brought the high Bronze Age to the Anyang area of China, did they originate the name Chinese, and from the early name for Crete, Telchinia, the name China? It is just worth asking, in view of the engravings on the pots of Anyang during the Shang Dynasty (1600–1200 B.C.) (Plate 78). Let us look further: an area in central Tibet still practices polyandry and the river flowing through it is called Cui. This all speaks for the early global village.

The map on Plate 77 shows the two main routes across the Pacific created by the circling currents of the ocean. The more direct follows the equatorial countercurrent from the Caroline Islands to Central America. This is the shorter route but it has serious disadvantages. It is a narrow band of water, and by sailing slightly off course a ship can find itself being carried backward on one of the west-flowing currents that run on either side. It is also quite a weak, slow-moving current and the prevailing winds blow against it, raising a higher swell than when they accompany each other as in the Atlantic. The longer northerly route is therefore easier to use, and I believe it was more often used by the early sailors. This takes one up the Pacific side of Southeast Asia, along the coast of China and past Japan. It then swings around to cross the ocean north of Hawaii until it approaches the western side of America, where it divides in two, one half running north to Alaska, the other south past California and Mexico to Ecuador. On this route, as on the middle passage across the Atlantic, wind and current are strong enough to carry ships over even against their will, and Japanese fishermen, half-wrecked in storms, have been washed up on the coast of America even in our own days.

Along this route, perhaps accidentally at first but later with deliberate purpose, the sailors from the Indian Ocean came to America. The first maritime visitors of whom we have any traces were those who brought agriculture to the Pacific coast of Mexico around 7000 B.C. It was a thousand years or more later that prospectors from the Mediterranean, using one of the Atlantic routes, began to exploit the copper deposits of Lake Superior. From then on the main route to America for the peoples of the Near and Middle East lay through the Mediterranean and across the Atlantic but, as we said, the Pacific crossing continued to be used to some extent. In practice it can be difficult or impossible to say whether a particular innovation reached America by the eastern or the western route. Take, for example, the bottle gourd, discussed in Chapter 4. Thousands of fragments of this gourd, and some intact fruits, were found at Hueca Prieta on the coast of Peru at a level carbon-dated to 2700 B.C. It must have come originally from either tropical Africa or Southeast Asia, to one of which it is native, but it could have reached Peru by being brought up the Amazon and across the Andes or directly by sea across the Pacific. The earliest date for the use of this bottle gourd in America, which, as we have seen, is indigenous to Africa or India, is 7000 B.C.: contemporary with the commencement of agriculture in the Americas and in Asia, where this African bottle gourd was used at the same date in Thailand.

On the other hand we know of some contacts that were almost certainly made across the Pacific. For example, the formative period in Ecuador began with the first use of pottery on the coast. This has been carbon-dated to 2700 B.C. and the earliest type of pottery is very similar to the pottery produced by the Jomon culture of south Japan at the same period. The two pottery complexes and datings are so strikingly similar that the only explanation would seem to be a trans-Pacific introduction of pottery at around 2500 B.C. I personally checked this pottery out in the museum in Tokyo. Recently, pottery dated 6000 B.C. was found near the Amazon.

There seem also to have been further trans-Pacific visits to Ecuador more than two thousand years later. A. V. Kidder writes:

> During this period the coast of Ecuador seems again to have been visited by voyagers from Asia. At about 200 B.C. a complex of unique and non-American objects appears in the Bahia area and on the Esmeraldas coast farther north (Estrada and Meggers, 1961). The evidence consists of pottery neck-rests; pottery models of houses with columns and deep, saddle roofs; figurines with legs folded one above the other; pottery ear-plugs that resemble golf tees; pottery net weights; and stone and pottery pendants in the form of tusks. This complex, appearing generally to be eastern Asiatic in origin, may also include the coolie yoke, depicted on a spindle whorl from Manabi

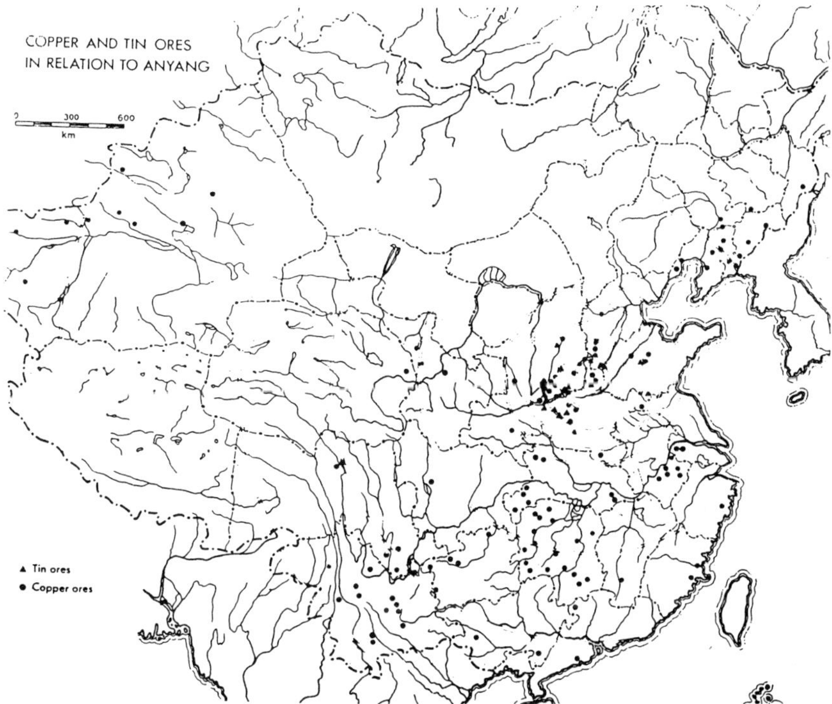

PLATE 81

The Olmec portraits of Chinese in Mexico Joseph Needham, the great Cambridge sinologist, does not seem to refer to; nor the presence in the Cuna Indian script of three signs identical in form and meaning to Chinese; but Needham described his experience of a two-month visit to Mexico in 1947: "I was deeply impressed during my stay with the palpable similarities between many features of the high Central American civilizations and those of East and Southwest Asia." He lists the items they have in common:

Predominance of horizontal in architecture. Sky dragon motifs paralleling Minaga *and* Lung. Amphisbaenas. *Correspondences in Maya and Chinese in the worship of dragon rain gods and in complicated rain-making ceremonies down to minute detail. Cenote sacrifice at Chichén Itzá identical to the brides of the river gods in fifth century* B.C. *China. Split-face designs resembling thao-thieh. Teponatzli drums like mu yii. Tripod pottery like li. Terra-cotta figures and groups and even paintings "so similar to those of Chhu and Han." Dresses of feathers. Double permutation calendars. Ideographic script. Far-reaching parallels in symbolic correlations of colors, animals, compass points, e.g., rabbit-in-the-moon, Aztec and China. Games (patolli). Scapuliamancy. Computing devices. (e.g., quipu in China) Art forms. Jade with all the complex beliefs of China; the Maya placed jade in the mouth of the dead as do the Chinese. Hematology. Ethnobotany. Hookworm. Ethnohelminthology. Metallurgy. Papermaking. Religious art. Great Walls and roads. Musicology: more than 50 percent of Amerindian musical instruments occur in the Burmese hinterland. Folklore. Pottery house models as in Han tombs. Neck-rest pillows. Seated statuettes in the Buddhist rajrapariyaka position. Pan pipes with ceremonial complex. Chinese carrying pole. Sailing rafts. The Chinese emperor ruled by the mandate of heaven as an organ of the cosmos: just like the early Western monarchs.*[33] *Joseph Needham says that the first bronze art in China was the most beautiful.*[34]

and, less certainly, symmetrically graduated pan pipes, which were also widely used in Peru at about the same time. Most of these elements have a very restricted distribution in Ecuador (none of them appear, for example, in the regional culture immediately south of the Bahia region). There is no evidence for continuing contacts with Asia, and, as noted by Estrada and Evans, it is not likely that the arrival of an Asiatic vessel fundamentally changed the culture of the Ecuadorian Indians, already much exposed to foreign influence from Meso-America.[11]

It was colonization rather than chance visits that radically altered cultures. Notice that the indigenous American plant the peanut has been found in use in Zhejiang Province, China, from between 2100 B.C. and 1800 B.C. and was cultivated elsewhere in China from 3000 B.C.

Pierre Honoré believes that between 500 and 400 B.C. people from China reached Peru, and that contact was also made in the fourth century B.C. by people of the Dongson culture of Tongking and Annam, this contact extending as far south as Chile and Argentina.[12] The Verrills also cite a record of a Chinese traveler visiting America in the first millennium A.D.[13] In British Columbia a hoard of Chinese brass coins has been found.[14]

In general, we can take it as certain that contacts with Far Eastern cultures such as China and Japan were made across the Pacific. As we have seen, the Cuna Indians of South America use three Chinese symbols in their script identical both in form and meaning to those of China. The Cuna Amerindians call themselves Tule, surely an Atlas name.[15] This would account for some interesting resemblances noted by Gordon Ekholm between mirrors used in Mesoamerica and the bronze mirrors of China, and between the thin copper axes used as currency in Ecuador and in Aztec Mexico and the knife and axe money of China, and the stone axe hoards in Ghana. Ekholm, incidentally, provides a convincing answer to those ignorant critics of diffusion who emphasize that no Asiatic objects have been found in the New World. He points out that there is abundant evidence of contact between Mesoamerica and Peru, but that objects indisputably belonging to the one have not been found in the other. The same is true, he says, of the United States southeast, where there is plenty of evidence of Mexican influence but no single object of clearly Mexican manufacture had been found. The annual visit of the Manila galleon—so much later—has left no trace in America. Spaniards on an exploration voyage to the Gulf of California in 1544 found large Chinese junks at anchor, whose crews said they had been trading there for many centuries.[16]

Of Nan Matol on Ponapee, Enock has written:

"Ambiguity pervades the huge megalithic remains found on some of the Caroline Islands, Yap, Kusaie and Ponapee. Nan Matol on Ponapee is described as an ancient native fortress, terraces and a pyramid with a great

Standard symbols in Brazil of the matriarchal society (above) and of sun worship (below).[38] *The principal religious symbols of the Bronze and Geometric period of the Mediterranean are found everywhere in the art and on the temples of Central and South America, with, seemingly, the same meanings: swastika, Maltese cross, the simple cross, the saltire, spiral meander, lozenge, sacred mound, duplicate spiral—left- and right-handed—double-axe, crosses within crosses, etc.*

Plate 82

The Shang period ended in 1200 B.C. when the Toltec maritime empire also collapsed. Joseph Needham refers to the Chin period when the Chinese were convinced that drug plants giving longevity or immortality were to be found on islands in their eastern ocean. Needham seems not to be aware of Gilgamesh's voyage across what reads like the Pacific in the Gilgamesh epic to Utnapishtim the Faraway—surely America—in search of "the plant of life." Obviously he could not have known of a Ghana tradition about "the plant of life" and therefore could not have known that the famous Egyptian knife of the two snakes with a plant between them might very well refer to this same belief. There are Chinese records, too, of the Emperor Chhi Shih Huang Ti between 400 and 300 B.C. sending out an expedition with young boys and girls to these islands in the ocean to colonize them. Chinese records narrate that a Chinese mariner, Hsu Fu, was sent to the island on the other side of the Pacific Ocean with three thousand young men and girls to colonize it. There is Chinese literary evidence to back up and support the archaeological finds on the Mariana Islands in the mid-Pacific by 1500 B.C.[35] *And Asian pottery is also found in America of between 3000 and 4000 B.C.*[36] *There is a Chinese report of grapevines and horses being found in Fu Sang, which is by some believed to be Mexico.*[37] *We know the profusion of grapevines in early North America and the indication from children's toy chariots that for a time their parents may even have had the chariots (of which their children possessed toys) with the accompanying horses. White jade, a stone peculiar to China, was also found in the second city of Troy c. 3000 B.C.*

Flint knife of the predynastic age, Egypt. It is worth remembering that the serpent represented the Great Goddess and that she was in charge of herbal medicine.

lodge on its summit platform very much like one of the Mexican teocalli or truncated pyramids. The patterns on the textile fabrics are similar to some of Mexico and Peru. Among the articles excavated were tiny rose-pink beads, made of polished shell, identical to the wampum or shell-bead money of the North American Indians. Similar beads were also discovered in the ruins of Mitla, in Central America. There is a trilithon megalithic monument on the Carolines resembling those of Stonehenge."

Heyerdahl argues that this shows movements of people from east to west across the Pacific and it could well be that the truncated pyramid, originating in Mesopotamia, reached America by the Pacific route, because the oldest American ziggurat so far dated is on the coast of Peru. The Carolines stand at the beginning of the countercurrent that flows toward Ecuador. Heyerdahl might nevertheless be right in believing that the Indus Valley script found on Easter Island (as described in Chapter 4) came to Easter Island by way of America, carried over from Peru.

For the most part, however, it is impossible to say for certain by which route any particular influence traveled, though it is clear that those influences did exist. Compare, for example, the wheeled toys from Chanhu-Daro (downriver from Mohenjo-Daro) with those found in Mexico at Veracruz (Plates 76 and 36). Or the water-lily motif in India and Yucatán shown in Plate 74. Or the metal pins from South America and Asia shown in Plate 202.

A number of the influences exerted on America and mentioned in Chapter 4 originated in India, one of the most striking being the Peruvian loom. G. F. Carter's studies of plants also seem to me to show beyond doubt that there was contact between America and the East. In addition to the plants discussed in Chapter 4 he cites the grain amaranths, native to Mexico and Peru, which were used over a vast area of the Old World stretching from Manchuria through China and Afghanistan to Iran, and which are prepared and used in similar ways there and in America. He also mentions a curious breed of chicken that lays blue eggs, found both in Peru and in pre-Columbian Japan, while he fails to notice that they are also found on the small Scottish island of St. Kilda as well as in Norway; and he believes that the lotus, *Nelumbium Nelumbo*, must have been carried across the ocean by human beings since otherwise a much larger difference would have appeared between the Old and New World varieties during the long geological ages by which the continents have been separated.

Hastings points out the Japanese tradition of an island paradise, ten years' sailing from Japan, called Horaisan,[17] where there is a herb bestowing immortality, a garden composed of precious stones,[18] a mountain called Fusan, in fact more or less a description of the land they called Kur. There is a goddess in Horaisan called Izanami whose husband was called Izanagi:[19] compare these names with the Mayan supreme god and culture hero, Itzamná, who arrived in Guatemala from across the Pacific.

By the fourth millennium B.C. seashell lamps were in use by the Ainu of Japan and in Scotland, Wales and Cornwall.[20] Open floating wick lamps of a similar make came at an early date to be used in Egypt, India and Nigeria.[21] There was, moreover, an interesting similarity between Egyptian and Chinese practices.[22]

A curious piece of evidence turned up about twenty years ago, and was reported in the *Times* of London (July 8, 1970):

> Asians Found America
>
> Two Leningrad specialists in Oriental Antiquity have produced the theory that ancient Asian geographers knew of the existence of the Americas in at least 1500 B.C. The specialists, Lev Gumilev and Bronislav Kuznetsov, based their hypothesis on the deciphering of ancient maps of the world in old Tibetan books, Tass said today. The arrangement of countries and continents on the maps conforms with the knowledge of the world by the ancient Sumerians and Chaldeans, the earliest geographers.
>
> The Soviet specialists concluded that the data contained in the map was known in Asia in the second millennium B.C. "The honour of discovery of the Americas probably belongs to ancient Asian travellers," Tass said.
>
> The agency said the ancient Tibetan maps were known to Orientalists before but were believed to be charts of imaginary lands of fantasy or mystical Buddhist fables. The views changed after a laborious analysis.
>
> The two scholars believe the deciphering of the maps opens the way for interpreting many ancient Indian and Tibetan geographic texts which so far have been regarded as mysterious.

Tibetan names, we have already pointed out, suggest the Atlas-Set contacts of that period.

That, then, is a brief summary of some of the evidence of contact between Asian, European and American cultures by the Pacific route. If it seems scattered and fragmentary, that is, after all, what we ought to expect. For a start, we must remember the scale of our subject, both in time and in space. America stretches for ten thousand miles north and south, and we are concerned with a span of eight thousand years and more before Columbus's "discovery" of it. We must remember, too, that not every contact left traces that would still be visible thousands of years later. It takes more than one ship's arrival to transform a culture.

Well, here is some of the evidence exhibited in this book, but a whole lot more is available, simply a question of space and time. But I judge that I have included sufficient to prove my point.

In conclusion it is worth repeating the opinion of Sir Joseph Needham, the great Cambridge sinologist, that the Amerindian cultures of Central America could not conceivably have developed as they did without contact with China. And from what has been said in this chapter, it is clear that

PLATE 83
SCULPTURE OF AFRICANS IN PRE-COLUMBIAN MEXICO. *Huge stone heads of unmistakable African appearance, found as part of the Olmec culture in Mexico, in Tres Zapotes and elsewhere. In Colombia the sacred artificial mounds were called* tolas, *to the Arabs* tells, *to the Celts of Ireland* tulach, *probably all Atlas words.*

Not relevant to my story, but yet worthy of remark, is the following statement made by Diodorus Siculus (fl. 60–30 B.C.): "The Ethiopians, as historians relate, were the first of all men and the proofs of this statement, they say, are manifest. For that they did not come into their land as immigrants from abroad but were natives of it. . . ."[39] This astonishing statement, made two thousand years ago, archaeology has but recently substantiated.

Statue found in Mexico City depicting a priest or god clad in skin of a sacrificed human. Remember how Apollo flayed Marsyas alive, his musical competitor. Among the Aztecs a man would be sacrificed and his flesh eaten so that the eater should receive the power of the god.[40] *The practice is widespread across Africa and is sublimate in the Christian Eucharist. Note that trepanning was practiced both anciently in the Old World and in the New in Mexico City.*

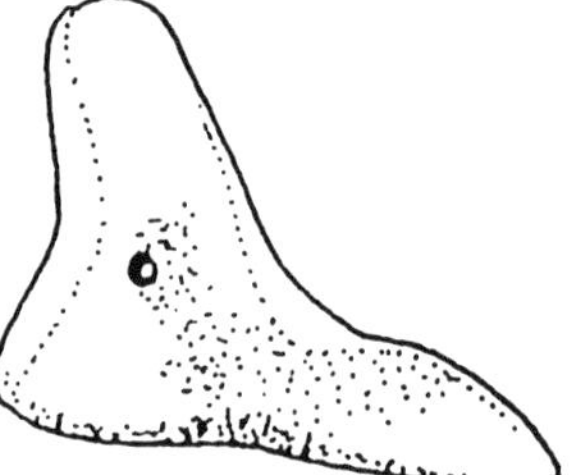

PLATE 84
SCULPTURES FOUND IN ANCIENT AMERICA, WEST AFRICA AND GREECE

This foot is from Thessaly, dating back to 6500–6300 B.C.[41]

Clay head found at Tres Zapotes, Mexico. Note the Phoenician style of hat, the earplugs, mustache and beard.

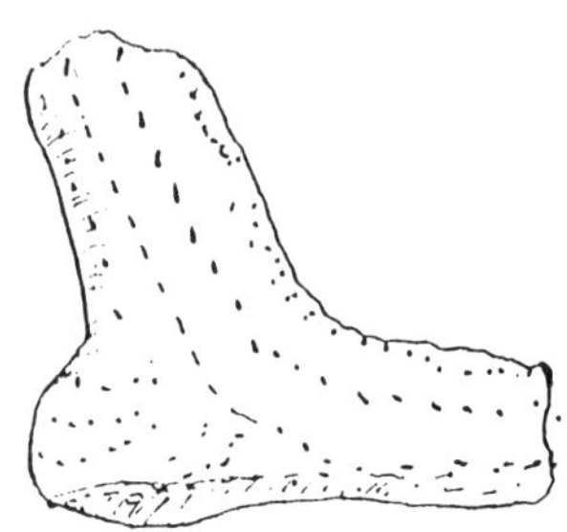

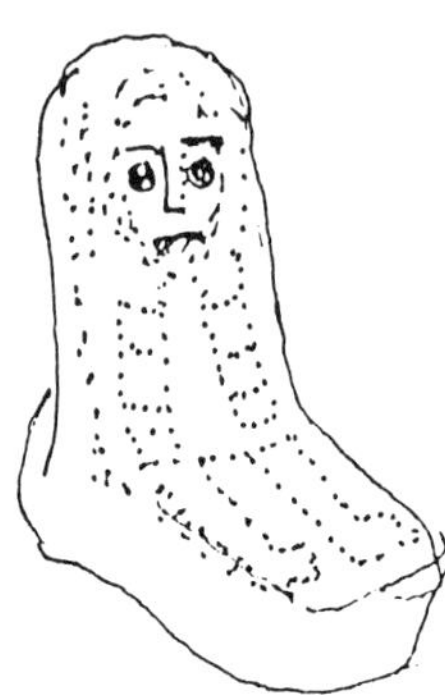

This foot is from the southern Ivory Coast, so the Abidjan vendor told me. The possibility of very early contact indeed between the eastern Mediterranean and West Africa should be considered.

this must mean direct and indirect contact of America with the whole network of civilizations spread around the Indian Ocean.

Chinese classics refer to a country called Fu Sang, which is twenty thousand Chinese miles east of China across the Pacific. It is said to have grapevines and the horse. Some sinologists have said that the country was Mexico and of course we find in Mexico portraits of Chinese faces, in North America grapevines aplenty and in Central America children buried with toy wheeled chariots alongside them, and children's toys tend to copy their parents' kit,[23] as we have already noticed. This is all rather relevant.

7. Negligible Written Sources for the History of Ancient Africa

"In the genesis of any scientific doctrine, there is no absolute commencement; to the extent that when one traces back the line of thought which has prepared, suggested and then announced the doctrine one always comes to opinions which, in their turn, have themselves been prepared, suggested and then announced; and if one ceases to pursue this chain of ideas which have followed one after the other it is not that one has put one's hand on the initial link, rather is it that the chain itself sinks and disappears into the depths of an unfathomable past."

PIERRE DUHEM

Most of the books tell us that Africa south of the Sahara was uniformly illiterate until the Arabs and subsequently the Portuguese arrived. However, there is some evidence that this is not wholly true: certainly there is one exception to prove the rule. For Dr. Diringer reproduces in his standard work *The Alphabet* one script from the Ogoja province of eastern Nigeria called *Nsibidi*. It is a province where is also found beside the Cross River some 295 monoliths, many of which carry the ancient religious symbols of the people of the Fertile Crescent: the spiral, the concentric circles, the lozenge, the double axe, the Maltese cross; above all, the phallus portrait (Plates 155 and 156). A second script, indigenous to Africa, but recently invented, Dr. Diringer maintains, comes from Foumban.

In addition to this one old-established script there is some further evidence for a measure of ancient writing in Africa south of the Sahara. This is to be found on the Ashanti and Baoulé gold weights. This very elaborate system of weights was in use in Ashanti and Baoulé until the turn of the century. They were placed on one pan of the beam scale and gold dust, the currency of the Akan, was placed upon the second. There are two very distinct types of weight: the abstract or geometric signs on the one hand

PLATE 85

THIS BRONZE OF A MERMAID, *a mammy-water,* une sirène, *comes from the upper regions of the Volta River, from a people called Peulh. It depicts one of the earliest sailors and traders holding a serpent, symbol of the earth mother, but with her lower half fish, symbol of a marine clan. Her scales seem to represent the sun rising on the first day of Creation and therefore probably derive from a relatively late period of matriarchy. The Mexican earth mother was associated with a serpent, she was known as "the mother of gods and men": the snake woman whose name was Cihuacóatl;*[1] cóatl *in Nahuatl means water serpent and Ci resembles the name for the earth mother: in Greek Ge, in Babylonian Ki.*

On the Hebridean island of Lewis, where one finds the magnificent stone circle of Callanish, there is again the story of local men marrying mermaids and the marriages easily coming unstuck.[2] *On the island of Lewis, tradition says, priests and black men set up the great megalithic monument.*[3] *The nearby island of St. Kilda, tradition says, was named after an Amazon queen called Kilder.*[4] *The Luo tribe on the shores of Lake Victoria have much the same mermaid tradition. The Bambara of Mali call their mermaid Faro.*

PLATE 86

THE SEATED GODDESS MOTIF. *In addition to the names of the Great Goddess being virtually identical on both sides of the Ocean, the squatting figure motif "recurs distinctly and plentifully in northwest America, Mexico, Guatemala, Costa Rica, Columbia, and Venezuela"*[5] *as well as in the Old World. The ancient Egyptian Creator Goddess Neith is quoted: "I am all that has been, that is, and that will be. Nor mortal has yet been able to lift the veil which covers me." The title* virgin *describes her perennial nubility, not her chastity. The making of terra-cotta figurines goes back to 23,000* B.C.

PLATE 87

The name left by the early matriarchal sea traders, whether as matriarchs or as their male breakaway group known to us as Heracles, is akawa. *So the principal rivers of West Africa, the Niger, the Congo, the Orange, bear indigenous names like Kwa or Kware. In the same way the so-called Bushman Stone used by the San peoples to weight their digging sticks are identical with those used in the matriarchal Aegean, and the San peoples call them* Kwe. *Subsequent names for the earth mother, Ge, Ki, Cui, Coya, etc., would seem to be merely abbreviations of the original* akawa. *The first name for the sacred city of Eridu, "by the sand of the seashore," the oldest and most sacred city of Sumer, was Ku-ara. The earth mother was essentially maritime. To the Phoenicians she was called Asherat-of-the-Sea, Mother of the Gods, Creator of the Gods and in wisdom the mistress of the gods.*[6] *The Chinese made her patroness of sailors.*

When the Greek shipping heiress Christina Onassis gifted her landlocked Russian friend Sergei with a brace of oil tankers it was the old story of mammy-water endowing her landsman husband whom she had loved.

This mermaid has four plaits and eight forelocks, the numbers sacred to the matriarchy. No West African could grow such plaits. The use of sailing boats in old Europe is attested by incised depictions on ceramics from the sixth millennium B.C.[7] *To the Mawayans and Wai-Wai of the Upper Amazon, the ancestress of their race was the daughter of an anaconda snake who had been fished out of a deep pool.*[8] *In ancient times it was females who were associated with water.*[9] *For the matriarchs were the first organized long-distance sailors.*

and the African pictorial figures on the second. It is the abstract form of the weights that we have considered here (Plates 71 and 72).

In sum then, while there had been some knowledge of writing in ancient sub-Saharan Africa, illiteracy had been almost universal. As a result of the general destruction of historical records as well as of almost universal illiteracy, there is scant African written record for the present-day student to work with prior to the recent period of the Islamic states of the Sudan and the Islamic ports along the coast of East Africa (c. A.D. 900–1600).

Before this, in the popular view, all in ancient Africa south of the Sahara was darkness, emasculate and nonexistent.

This almost universal prejudice as to the nullity of ancient Africa was eloquently expressed by Professor Hugh Trevor-Roper, regius professor of history at the University of Oxford, who described African history as a meaningless dervish dance in a picturesque but unimportant corner of the world. I trust that this book will show that Professor Trevor-Roper, with whom at one time I was acquainted, was expressing only his own opinion. For despite the lack of written record I am confident that it will be possible one day to reconstruct an outline of the societies that flourished in West Africa during the Copper and Bronze Ages. It will show that Africa and especially West Africa was an important part of that great and partially interconnected world, that earlier global village, which raised the megalithic monuments along the Atlantic shores of Europe (5400–1200 B.C.); the temples and ziggurats of Mesopotamia (c. 4000–500 B.C.); the pyramids and temples of Egypt (2800–500 B.C.); and the elaboration of Mexican civilization with the so-called Olmec culture (c. 1550 B.C.), which is better

Plate 88

Chinese mermen *(right). The Telchinese of the Mediterranean also had the lower parts of their bodies represented as serpents or fish.*[10] *Sir Joseph Needham, in his* Science and Civilisation in China, *quotes a paper by Przyluski on divine beings with mermaids' tails found in ancient France and in China. We show a pair of them here.*[11] *Needham concerns himself with the way inventions and artifacts come into use virtually simultaneously at both ends of the Old World and offers as an example the way the well-known paradoxes of Zeno of Elea were expressed at almost the same date by Hui Shih in China.*[12] *Needham spends much time considering this simultaneity. It is not impossible that the Telchinese of Crete, whose symbol was a merman, brought both the techniques of the high Bronze Age and their own name to China, as I have pointed out earlier.*

Earth Mother, Athena and Poseidon *(left). A terra-cotta, found at Athens, probably dating from the fifth century* B.C., *portrays Poseidon with fishtail; also the bulky earth mother presenting Ericthonius, a future king of Athens, to the goddess Athena. The Telchinese of Crete were portrayed as mermen, not mermaids—and thus they were later in time—and they also brought civilization to the Aegean island of Rhodes, tradition said. They were famous for their metallurgical skills. The Syrian mermaid was called Derceta.*[13] *Yam was the Phoenician god with a fish's tail.*[14] *Athena was addressed as Pallas Athena and in Ancient Peru* palla *was a title bestowed upon noble women.*[15] *Along the Amazon Amerindians believed that there is a* m'boto *which at night can turn from a merman into a handsome young man who then courts the ladies until daybreak.*[16]

Plate 89

Mermaid from Haiti *(left). This is a contemporary reproduction of a mammy-water or mermaid or La Maîtresse Sirène from Haiti—a cult brought there by Africans. She is reported to be blowing the trumpet for her consort Agwé: Ogawa or Ogava being the name by which the later long-distance sailors, the worshippers of Poseidon, had called themselves. They had kings not queens. The worshippers of Poseidon, Plato's* Critias *states, developed one of the greatest sea empires of all time and became all-powerful in America. This is consistent with the Sumerian tradition that Enki, the Sumerian name for Poseidon, ruled the netherworld.*[17]

Agoue, in the tradition of Haiti, is Master of the Oceans—Oceans in plural. He connects continent with continent and has expensive tastes, Haiti tradition says. While Poseidon was the sea god of the Ionian Greeks and was identified with the gods Ea or Enki of Mesopotamia, Poseidon was also specifically associated with North Africa. He was dark-haired, "god of the sable locks."

It is relevant that the pope is referred to as "The Fisherman," that many of Christ's disciples were fishermen, and that an important Christian symbol in the first centuries was the fish. Of course there is a Christian rationale for all this as for many other pagan customs that they incorporated into their reformed version of the old religions. The symbol of the Bronze Age sea god, Set or Atlas, was a fish. They were sun worshippers, hence the sacred day of the week to Christians is not Christ's day but Sunday. The pope's ring is called the "seal of the fisherman."

A dancer portrays Nang-Ma-Tcha, goddess of the Menam River. Hands in pataka mudra *represent fish fins; from Thailand. We have noticed that this first name for the Great Goddess, essentially a maritime lady, was Akawa in one form or another; Kwannon was the name for the goddess of mercy in China, Korea, and Japan. In China she was often portrayed as a Madonna and Child.*

Another Mesopotamian depiction of a man wearing a fish skin.

PLATE 90

THE MESOPOTAMIAN OANNES. *Mesopotamian culture hero who was half man and half fish, in the Akkadian language called NUN-AMELU. Seven fishermen came up the Red Sea bringing with them the arts of civilization.*

The sea people subsequently acquired kings. The first to make their enormously important appearance in written history were collectively called Oan or Oannes. The word Nun *in both Egypt and Mesopotamia meant ocean.*

I believe the root of the name An to stand for the sky-worshipping people and provided a root for the name of those culture heroes who came to Mesopotamia out of the Persian Gulf allegedly as monsters, half man and half fish. They were both sky worshippers and sea worshippers who had specialized in sea trade. They brought all the arts of civilization to Mesopotamia with them, the Middle Eastern historian Berosus recorded. In the fourth millennium B.C. *there were no vehicles, wheels or transport animals and so water transport was the only means of communication: the merchant marine conveyed minerals and conveyed knowhow. The worshippers of Poseidon came subsequently on the maritime scene. Berosus went on to say that thereafter the Mesopotamians invented nothing for themselves. It is a comment that should be remembered. To support this, notice that it was their sea god, Ea or Enki, who was looked on as the source of all Mesopotamian wisdom. Berosus was priest of Bel in Babylon and flourished c. 250* B.C. *It is worth noticing that in* A.D. *1508 a French ship picked up near the English coast a small boat made of bark and osiers containing seven men—in fishskins. They were considered to be Eskimos.*[18]

called Toltec. This last, progenitive of many magnificent Mexican-Indian cultures, contains mighty stone heads of indubitable African aspect. The whole of that world, I am confident, was across long periods spasmodically conjoined. West Africa, in some real measure, formed a portion of this maritime brotherhood.

The march of armies, the *jihads* of the new religions, both lay and cleric, have obliterated the societies that raised these antique monuments. But somehow or another in West Africa, concealed beneath the luxuriant foliage of the rain forest, many of their beliefs and customs have secretly survived. So that the illustrations on the following pages exhibit not only examples

PLATE 91

BIRDMAN FROM THE SENUFO AREA (22.1 CM). *The birdmen shown in these illustrations are flat castings that, I believe, are of great antiquity. The bird mask represents the black hornbill,* le calao, *which is the sacred bird of the southern Ivory Coast.*

The museum in Abidjan, the capital of the Ivory Coast, says that men wearing bird masks were their first ancestors. The bird masks represent the celestial powers of God in heaven. The bird served as intermediary between sky god and man.

These birdmen, tradition says, according to the national museum, brought with them all the arts of civilization to the Ivory Coast. This claim was partly propaganda, since it is pretty clear that in West Africa, as in most parts of the world, the women led the men in civilization for millennia before the sex switch occurred.

Thor Heyerdahl, who crossed the Atlantic in his reed boat, Ra, *said that the captains of these ancient reed boats were associated with the wearing of bird masks: in his book on Easter Island, Heyerdahl shows rock engravings that allegedly portray these people (Plate 92).*

What the Horus was to Pharaoh's Egypt, the quetzal bird to Ancient Mexico, the black hornbill is to the Ivory Coast.

The district from which these following models all come is that of the Senufo tribe, of the Kafiledjo branch. I would guess that they were found originally by tomb robbers. On seal cylinders of the Second Early Dynastic period of Sumer, the bird shape is shown with the legs and lower body parts of a human body, dressed in a kilt:[19] *i.e., identical with the figures here. Nobody yet realizes how close was formerly the connection between the Fertile Crescent and West Africa. In Mesopotamia the storm bird Zu was represented as half man and half bird. He stole the all-important tablets of destiny from Enlil, while the Sumerian goddess Inanna was represented with the wings and feet of a bird.*[20]

of a profound and little-known art but they also preserve value as documents of history. This history contains, I shall argue, the core and kernel of African and Negro culture: it also contains wonderful philosophies once shared with many other parts of the Bronze Age world, elsewhere erased. It permits us to raise a corner of the curtain that presently hides that ancient world: a world that produced the Golden Age, an age of justice and high creativity, debunked by the universities as mere sentimentality.

Thus I shall be using the word "history" in a very special way. For the proper sources of history are written records and in Africa, as in ancient Peru, there are virtually none. Yet a narrative of the past is not altogether beyond our reach and unobtainable—nor, when it is obtained, will it be unworthy of the word "history." To argue so is either to place too little credence on related disciplines or too great credence upon the written word of history itself.

This world that our flickering rushlight momentarily illumines is patently deeply flawed. It possesses an imagination as brilliant as an arc of lightning, yet it is blind to cruelty: nay rather, cruelty was an ingredient that was essential to its religious life and religion permeated everything and everyone. Perhaps only pain can break through the crusts of insensitivity to let in light, pain as the plowshare: human sacrifice as early theater and as the true origin of staged tragedy: human sacrifice as the actual origin of Aristotle's definition of catharsis, Pity and Terror, as all his contemporaries knew well. The last record of human sacrifice in Greece was in Arcadia

PLATE 92

"Reed boats and bird-headed men seemed to go together, for some inexplicable reason. For we had found them far out in the Pacific Ocean too, on Easter Island, where the sun-god's mask, the reed boats with sails, and men with bird heads formed an inseparable trio among the wall-paintings and reliefs in the ancient ceremonial village of Orongo, with its solar observatory. Easter Island, Peru, Egypt, these strange parallels could hardly have been found farther apart." (*Thor Heyerdahl,* The Ra Expeditions.[21])

Engravings on the rocks of birdmen, who, Heyerdahl says, were the captains of reed boats. The museum in Abidjan is full of examples of the Ivory Coast tradition that culture heroes, men wearing bird masks, brought all the arts of civilization to their country.

Reed boats would seem to have originated with Mesopotamia, because reeds were the only raw material for boat building that they possessed. Time was all-important in that religion so the Greeks called their god Kronos or Chronos. Chronos was identified with the Jewish El. So we find in Ezekiel: "I am El. I sit in the seat of the gods in the heart of the seas."[22] Chronos lives in the Isles of the Blessed. Chronos lives in the underworld.[23] This all adds up to America. Hence the thousand stone circles on the north and west of Britain, bases for the stepping-stone route to the Americas. We tend to be taught that because there is no written record of the early period of so many countries, a vitally important portion of human history did not occur. It is a non sequitur.

PLATE 93

THE SECOND BIRDMAN (17.4 CM). *The reed culture to this day lies at the southern end of Mesopotamia, Sumer, the sea land as it was called in the old texts. Living below an irrigation dam is always dangerous anyway. So in an emergency your reed house can be demolished and quickly converted into a reed boat, a process actually described in the Sumerian flood story called Atra-hasis.[24] Some early sailing seems to have been on log rafts as Heyerdahl put into practice in* Kon-Tiki. *But, first for fishing, then for long-distance voyaging, a reed raft or floating haystack, as it has been described, makes a most adequate water vehicle, an efficient wash-through boat.*

A sail was in use from very early times. An engraving of a boat with a sail from the Balkans of 6000 B.C. is reported by Marija Gimbutas. The Egyptian hieroglyph for air was a sail. Sumerian pictographs showed a ship moved not by oars but by a sail. The waterproof boat and the waterproof house tended to be made of identical materials, merely used the other way up.

The first long-distance sailing was by reed boat or drift voyaging by raft: a sophisticated knowledge of nature has to compensate for an unsophisticated technology. But there is evidence that around much of the world there were ichthyophagae, fish eaters, tribes who lived off the seashores. A fish trap dating from 30,000 B.C. has just been discovered. Such people, over millennia, would learn the ways of the sea with very great precision.

Plate 94
Sumerian figures. *Tell Asmar statues from the Favissa of the Temple of Abu, first half, third millennium. Their type of woolen kilt is made out of separate strips of cloth. Compare their dress with the kilts worn by the birdmen. They would seem to have gone to the same tailor at the same sort of time.*

Sumerian tradition states unequivocally that "man was created to free the gods from laboring for their sustenance": i.e., the god-kings, the royal families, incorporated the colonials—called man—into their societies for very practical reasons.

The netherworld was called by the Sumerians Kur: i.e., where the sun was at midnight—or America. It provided a base for Tiamat, the sea goddess. Kur was famous even then for its power and its wealth.[25]

The cartouche, the oblong rule around the Egyptian pharaoh's name, signified his rule over everywhere the sun circled. The Egyptians employed others to fetch and carry for them, while claiming their own rule over the armies that their minions commanded for them. This claim therefore included where the sun was at midnight or rule over the Americas: a claim that had some, if limited, substance.

around A.D. 200, although as recently as the last century, in their war of liberation against the Ottoman Turks, another human sacrifice was reported from the Greek island of Thera. The Romans, when they built the Forum, buried alive two Gauls and two Greeks as foundation sacrifices. Think what these victims will have gone through.

Eratosthenes was reputed to be the first Greek of the Classical Age to measure the circumference of the earth. He was head of the library of Alexandria (c. 250 B.C.).

I think it is likely that he would have made use of the sun dials, obelisks or shadow clocks, the giant *gnomons* that the Egyptians had already set up to obtain the greatest possible accuracy in this important affair, as well as the *scaphe*, or traveling sun dial, Eratosthenes is described as using. The obelisk might well be also a phallic symbol—season and fertility are interconnected. For by the First Dynasty, c. 3100 B.C., the Egyptians had measured the circumference of the earth,[1] knew the value of π and had established their own measures of the remen and cubit as functions of this circumference.

The source of my West African works of art is somewhat puzzling for there is neither one source nor one kind of source. I believe that the best of these pieces are the treasure trove of tomb robbers. In the first epic to come down to us, the Gilgamesh epic, a story woven around the doings of Gilgamesh, a king of Uruk (c. 2600 B.C.), the eponymous hero goes on an immensely long journey in search of life after death. In the old earth-

PLATE 95
AMERINDIAN LADY RESHAPING HER INFANT'S SKULL. *This style was for aristocrats. It may be that to fit on a bird mask you had to have a re-shaped skull.*

IVORY COAST SEA CAPTAIN WITH ARTIFICIALLY RESHAPED SKULL. *(First of three sea captains: No. 1, 30.6 cm.) The following three pieces are of these birdmen with their masks removed. I believe them to be actual portraits of sea captains, with large noses and receding foreheads. The earlobes have been pierced, one must suppose for earrings. I purchased these figures at the market in Abidjan.*

They carry their own reed boats symbolically on their heads. I judge this to be the correct interpretation. However, the lunate is a standard Senufo fetish still today.

The kilts that all these figures wear seem to be made of unstitched strips of leather or cloth, forming the lower portion of their clothes. It is a peculiar style that marks them very distinctly. Both the words Celt and kilt may be atl *words.*

It is again flat-casting, the metal is good, the pieces are in fair condition. If correctly interpreted these are perhaps the only portraits in existence of the actual captains of reed boats. Their foreheads are heavily receding, perhaps due to a custom among certain sea peoples of head deformation. Beside this Senufo figure from the Ivory coast I have placed a drawing of a Chinook woman, an Amerindian from North America, whose own skull has been artificially remolded in the same way and who is represented following Chinook custom and doing the same to her child. This practice of skull remolding was common along the northwest coast of North America and on the interior plateau, it was found with the Canari tribe of Peru,[26] in Ohio,[27] and with the Maya of Guatemala and the Toltecs of Mexico. With the Maya, head deformation was confined to the upper classes. However, Juan de Santa Cruz reports that the Inca Lloque Ypanqui ordered that all the people in his dominions should flatten the heads of their children so that they might be long and sloping from the front.[28] The Amerindians of the Antilles also went in for this skull deformation.[29] The practice continued in southern France, in Languedoc, until the middle of this last century. The poet Boileau had undergone it.

worshipper's civilization, the civilization of old Europe (7000–3500 B.C.), the serpent represented eternal life, for death is but the sloughing off of a serpent's skin. Each time life was recycled just as the seasons came again: death was just the exchange of one uterus for another: hence burial in the fetal position.

Already in this matriarchal civilization grave goods began to be buried with the dead, not just to display the superfluity of the family wealth but for personal use after death. So great kings still sleep beside great treasure, for their use on their journey to the abodes of the blessed and, additionally, to bribe them to prevent their returning to haunt the living.

Plate 96

Three sea captains, No. 2 (34.4 cm). *Prow and stern of the reed boats are birds, I believe kingfishers, which are still today the sacred bird of the Akan Ashanti tribe. Sacred birds are also widely associated with the Senufo tribe. The emblems on prow and stern of ancient Egyptian boats told you which traders owned which boats. The Akan own the Ashanti gold fields and the Sanskrit for gold is* kanaka.

The late J. B. Danquah, the Grand Old Man of Ghana culture, himself an Akan, pointed out to me that Halcyon was one of the seven daughters (or colonies in which the female religious principle is predominant) of Atlas. Of course another daughter of Atlas is called Maia: a name to be compared with the Maya of Guatemala, whose own tradition states that they came over the Atlantic from the east, where the sun rises, arriving on August 10, 3113 B.C. *and expecting the world to end in—in our nomenclature—*A.D. *2011—a fair prognosis in view of the arms trade. Danquah was a very dear friend, dying in Nkrumah's jails without trial, as a result of legislation that made this possible in Ghana put in by Geoffrey Bing, former Socialist M.P. for Hornchurch.*

The human heads that replace the kingfisher on the third boat have the same rough look as those of the sea captains. It can only be guesswork as to what they represent; whether Heracles or the Cabiri or some other. The receding forehead may have been artificially achieved by head deformation.

Reed boats are still in use today on Lake Titicaca in South America and in West Africa on Lake Chad. We know from the paintings that they were also used, alongside plank boats, in ancient Egypt, and were widely used on the Nile in predynastic Egypt, fourth millennium B.C. *We have further, and this time written, evidence for their use deep into Africa from the prophet Isaiah,[30] although it is not possible to distinguish from this reference from which precise countries the reed boats were coming, which African countries sent ambassadors to the eastern Mediterranean. For Ethiopia in Greek meant "burnt faces" and so could refer to any part of black Africa.*

But contemporary with the burial of the first king with his wealth came the first tomb robber: known in South America as *tomboli*; specifically in Peru as *huageros*. So we have a situation that we would find morbid in animal societies, wherein one part of the group is burying its wealth while another part is digging it up again: on the face of it as bizarre an activity as today's mining of gold in Africa and burying it again in Fort Knox.

Once the West African cultivator has planted his yam or his cassava, or perhaps while his wife is farming, there is time to go over the sacred places that are ancient graveyards in pursuit of gold. Perhaps the keeper of the place is venal and the chief is negligent. Once the gold is discovered pieces of incalculable beauty and historical importance are then melted down and sold to the goldsmiths for so much a fine ounce. In this way the peasant is sure of an unsteady income and the politicians will not detect that he is making money—they might if he were to enter the art trade and there was gossip. They might then step in, the peasant fears, and take over the trade to their own profit. So much has been at stake with these golden objects that murder and mayhem have occurred. One heavyweight boxer was murdered in the old Bristol Hotel in Lagos as a result, our reporter had it, of rivalry around this trade in tomb-robbers' gold.

In the old days Hausa or Senegalese traders crisscrossed West Africa on foot; you could talk to a passing stranger to find he was walking to a

PLATE 97

PAINTED SHERD: NINEVEH. *The semicircles are here associated with the Maltese cross and the double axe. The concentric arcs represent the sun rising on the first day of Creation. Seen differently there is the quadrefoil. This is a common form of visual pun among the traditional designs in West Africa, ancient America, Egypt, etc.*

THREE SEA CAPTAINS, NO. 3 (34 CM). *A high proportion of West African bronzes carry a device made out of concentric arcs: it is, in fact, evidence for genuinely early West African pieces. It is a very distinctive sign and one found widely around the world as well as widely in West Africa, upon pieces of the Bronze Age and early Iron Age. For example: the device is to be found on a few pieces of pre-Columbian art in America, on certain Mesopotamian pieces, and on certain pieces of a style called geometric found in the eastern Mediterranean; employed by Phoenicians, Cypriots and Greeks in the early Iron Age; and with the matriarchal society of the fifth millennium* B.C. *There were nine concentric arcs on the tomb of King Tutankhamen, celebrated young pharaoh of Egypt.*

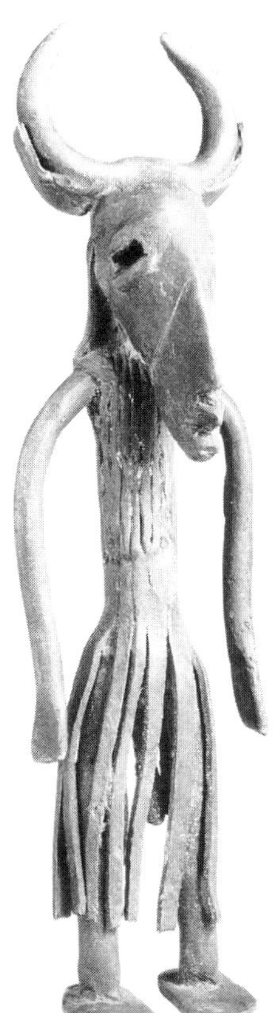

PLATE 98

TWO PIECES OF THE COW GODDESS NO. 1 (24.5, CM). *These two pieces also come from the Senufo tribal area in the Ivory Coast; they wear the same clothes as the earlier pieces and are cast similarly. The metal of which they are composed seems not to be as good as that of the first pieces shown on the earlier pages.*

As a general rule the more ancient and more authentic the pieces the better the metal used for casting.

Nearly all the brasses and bronzes shown here are made originally by the cire perdue *method. This portion of Senufo culture, however, is an exception, the pieces all appearing to have been flat-cast.*

PLATE 99

***Two Senufo pieces of the cow goddess "with buffalo mask," No. 2 (33 cm).** Hathor was an Egyptian and Libyan goddess depicted, somewhat as shown here, wearing the mask of a cow's head. This mask is that of a buffalo. The first piece has horns, this piece bears a characteristic Egyptian head gear associated with Hathor. Mesopotamian goddesses are also portrayed with cow horns. Hathor was associated with love, beauty and music; she was the earth mother.*

Hathor was a cow goddess, a sky goddess, a tree goddess. She was a mighty goddess in Egypt from the earliest times. She can also be warlike and fierce. Bleeker writes of her: "In short she is a majestic personage. The dynamism of her divine vitality commands respect. She has an inflammable temperament. Her wrath is much to be feared, but can be allayed."[31] Essentially the cow goddess represents the earth mother. It is generally held that the buffalo is the most dangerous animal on the African savannah except for an American with a gun. In Greece, the goddess Athena was described as goddess of war and wisdom, in that order. Ishtar was goddess of war and love, in that order. The goddesses were thoroughly bellicose, perhaps due to the expansion of the male-dominated religions at their expense. Among the Senufo, women more than men associated with the spirits. All powers, with the Senufo, derive from the supernatural.

town a thousand miles away. Now traders travel by air. Relatives may well be the carriers and art is smuggled from one country to another until it finishes in a country with hard currency. Often now the dealer with beautiful pieces flies off to Germany, Italy or America to sell direct to collectors. Times have been changing fast.

The bronzes are not worth melting down and so for a long time they passed into French-speaking Africa where trade is realistic, currencies are strong and restrictions are few. The museum keeper provided you with a permit to export, since the art was not from his own country and, anyway, the savants neither knew nor believed in a West African Bronze Age. Good pieces were occasionally to be found in the middle of acres of tourist rubbish. Or maybe the vendor had recognized the value of a particular object and was sequestering it in a backstreet cabin. Dingy rooms around dark backyards occasionally yielded pieces of great significance. I have found the emotional excitement upon discovering what I was seeking so powerful that I could not buy and spiritually digest more than a few works at a time.

Then there are the manufacturers of replicas active everywhere but perhaps the most active with the bronzes of Benin and the Cameroons. Provided that they are accurate imitations, little for the historian is lost because it is the precise form of the piece, not its brass content, which matters the most and must tell the story.

There are also pieces that have been kept in shrines; either there is theft, or the chief and fetish priest are corrupt and so a number of these come onto the market; for with the passing of the old religion passes the authority of the spirits.

I am confident that in many cases copies have been made of important works of art by members of the tribe itself. Let us say the tribe divides; it would be likely that both moieties would wish to house these sacred relics

PLATE 100
THE SENUFO VEILED MAN (30 CM). *The final piece of this type is a particularly strange one; the face is concealed behind a thick veil while his weapon, which resembles lengths of bronze wire twisted together, is equally unusual. Such a veil is used to this day by Yoruba kings. He comes from the same Senufo tribal area, wears the same peculiar kilt, and seems to be cast similarly to the previous pieces, all belonging to the one culture in the territory of the Dan people. On his head is the kingfisher, sacred to the Akan.*

and so copies would be struck. Again, if a piece were to be damaged, or if the original were molded in gold for the chief, bronze replicas might be available for the lesser gentry. In the course of a lifetime of a very old piece, copies may well have been made on a number of occasions. I think they would be cast with great accuracy.

There are certain wood carvings made in the last few years that are, I contend, exact replicas of very ancient and sacred originals. Specific pieces are made within specific tribes and only certain families within that tribe are capable of making them. It may be that in certain cases the first originals were not made in wood but magnificently in gold. For gold was the metal peculiar to the sun god.

Terra-cotta pieces are clearly made for a number of different purposes. Portrait heads in terra-cotta are buried with the dead so that the soul may be recognized in the next world: such practices were used in Ancient Egypt, and the national museum in Cairo exhibits, I have noticed, such heads, two of which were found in tombs associated with the great Pyramid of Cheops. Similar practices are found in ancient Mexico and in old Phoenicia. Today in Ghana, bowls for food offerings for the dead are placed above the newly buried, and their terra-cotta portraits are placed by the bowls. Also there are fetish figures and terra-cottas made for a variety of other reasons.

Carvings in hard stone are rare in Africa. The 295 or so pieces found in the Cross River State of Nigeria bear resemblance, Philip Allison says, to certain pieces found on the Upper Niger and in southern Ethiopia; but the greatest similarity, he states, is found in Corsica, the Caribbean and the Pacific. The author writes the standard work published and sold by the national museum in Lagos.

The museum itself was started out of a collection put together in colonial days by the great K. C. Murray. We used to frequent the same Nigerian fishing village. I asked him one day whether, because of the Bronze Age symbols on these pieces and their anomalous appearance, he did not believe that the monoliths were made in ancient times by a foreign people trading up and down the river. He declared himself satisfied that they were carved by local Africans, and at that, relatively recently. This comment hints at the difference between the establishment opinion and the argument of this book. However, Murray did, in his writings, actually admit that nothing, even as to their age, was really known about these Cross River monoliths.

8. Scientific or Magical Societies

". . . the cult of the gods, the wisdom of the destinies, the basic duties of man in his belonging to his family, group, town, chiefdom, his activity as a farmer, warrior, artist, merchant or in any other profession. In brief, to exist for the Mesoamericans one had to observe the sky. Without skywatchers the ethos of this people, its distinguishing spirit, its own genius would not have developed."

MIGUEL LÉON PORTILLA

The broad distinction commonly made in art is between the Classical and the Romantic. If one should look at the whole field of art on the broadest scale by far the most important division, it seems to me, is not between the Classical and the Romantic but between the Scientific and the Magical. Let us look at it this way.

At its best the Catholic Church is more subtle and profound than the Protestant; it possesses a greater depth of Christian tradition by virtue of its greater maturity, for the Catholics enjoy an inheritance of two thousand years, the Protestants of four hundred.

At some sort of point in time, let us say around seven thousand years ago, many societies began to adopt a mathematical and scientific rationality, at first qualifying and then erasing the great tradition of magic that had obtained previously for, let us say, some one hundred thousand years. This was the road Europe took while Africa remained substantially of the old faith. Before God made the universe, Egyptian record states, his name was Magic.[1]

The mathematical and scientific bent in Europe purged the mind of many of its dark corners but it achieved its spectacular success at great expense, excessively developing one segment of the mind by shutting the door upon others, atrophying sections of the brain as unused limbs atrophy. So while

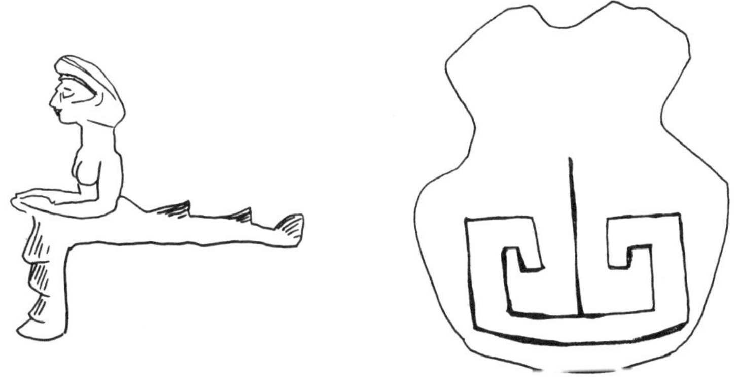

PLATE 101

The Caribbean engraving of a reed boat. *This is the rock engraving from the Caribbean believed by a contributor to* Scientific American *to represent an ancient reed boat. Boats can rapidly pick up the great Atlantic current, which swings westward from northwest Africa, carrying you in the same direction as the prevailing wind, which is the southeasterly tradewind. The same boats were trading both sides of the Atlantic in the Bronze Age so that this Caribbean engraving represents no particular puzzle.*

Further versions of the marine goddess or Selchie: carried under a misericord in Exeter Cathedral, England. And a third-millennium Elamite mermaid: a tradition shared from Scotland, to China, to the Amazon[1] *(top left).*

there are, admittedly, a few illuminati in that rational European world, there is also a great mass of people devoid of depth, devoid of genuine feeling, trivial; while being also the greatest know-alls of all time.

I had this artistic division, between the magical and the mathematical, brought home to me first in the museum in Accra. The museum possesses two beautiful bronze heads made by Jacob Epstein, donated to the museum, if I remember aright, by my acquaintance Kwame Nkrumah; one of a child, one of Paul Robeson. Beside them is the head of a priestess from Haiti, hacked out of the gnarled stump of a tree, also donated I think, by Kwame Nkrumah. The head from Haiti, after I first saw it, haunted me for days: wherever I traveled on publishing business her simulacrum followed me. There are few human beings I have met that have more influenced my life than that wooden carving. She is replete with references, many of which I cannot get at, but the vast psychological complexities that she expresses cast into the shadow those exquisite—but oh so simple—heads of Epstein. The conjunction of the three pieces was a whole lesson in itself.

Now Haiti, as we all know, was liberated from the French by Toussaint-Louverture and Dessalines, liberated for a future of grinding poverty and the gruesome cruelties of Papa Duvalier. Liberty permitted the freedom of the old Dahomey religions to run rife on that rich Caribbean soil. Art was

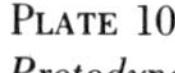

PLATE 102

Protodynastic Egyptian depiction of the Horus falcon symbolizing the sky god and the serpent associated, symbolizing Isis, the earth mother.

The bird, the attribute of the sky god "the Very High, holds and confers immortality in the form of a serpent which he holds in his beak."[2] Dubuisson writes this about religion in Phoenicia. Here is one of my bronzes that exactly reproduces this Phoenician practice, from Burkina Faso.

THE LOBI BIRDMEN (25 CM). *This birdman comes from the Lobi tribe of the southern portion of Burkina Faso. It is crudely executed and, compared with the previous birdmen in this series of pictures, probably of a much later date and now simply a tourist replica but, nevertheless, replicating an ancient piece. It carries a serpent in its mouth, affectionately I feel rather than with hostility: for the serpent and the bird together can symbolize the alliance of these two contrasted religions, the woman-dominated religion of the earth mother in conjunction with the sky religion of the sky father. There are gold fields in the Falémé Valley of Burkina Faso in Lobi territory. By sloughing its skin, to the matriarchy, the serpent symbolized infinity, eternity, immortality. The combination of the two religions, the style of the Bronze Age, led to the Greek word* metropater, *the mother-father.*

essentially tied to religion. As the old African gods depart from the stage of history so the old African artists disappear into the gloom and one of the greatest artistic traditions the world has known (whose influence has not yet reached its zenith because of the general ignorance of the world, in which ignorance Africa itself is as deeply plunged as Europe) is dying. Islam and Christianity have ringed the tree, they have cut around the bark and they are now waiting for that giant of the tropical forest to fall.

Now this art has specific emblems decorative upon it. It should not be taken that they are for ornament, the very word ornament does not seem to exist in that African atelier; every emblem serves a purpose, carrying with it the profoundest meaning. It is a mistake, one I long made myself, to believe that the different symbols are cashable into something quite simple: the spiral as the earth-worshippers' serpent; the Maltese cross as the symbol for rule over the four corners of the earth; the lozenge, a simple symbol for god returning to look at his creation.

Plate 103

The Lobi birdman, 26 cm *(right). The Lobi are a small tribe of Burkina Faso near the border of Ghana. Their culture is one of the simplest in West Africa. This rather inane-looking Lobi birdman has a spiral for an eye and a spiral on its head for a wattle. A chameleon has been placed under the chin, whose long tongue will protect him, if it should be needed, from evil spirits. This piece would seem to combine the patriarchal and matriarchal religions.*

Birdman from Easter Island *(left). Thor Heyerdahl points out that the first people to colonize Easter Island were whites who had emigrated to the island from America.*

Plate 104

The Senufo armlet (11 cm height). *This Senufo armlet carries two pairs of male and female figures, with the frog, crocodile, the tortoise, the scorpion and the chameleon separating them. They again, I judge, represent the Creation. The metal is excellent. The concept of the Creation—the Bronze Age creation that must stretch almost endlessly into the future—because of its misrepresentàtion in Genesis, has been forgotten by us but originally underlay sun worship. The belief in God's Creation through the sovereign represents for democrats, the new sovereigns, a challenge of incalculable dimension, where what you fail to do with your talents has, surely, more influence on history than what you do with them. In Africa, man establishes a mystical relationship with animals, plants and natural phenomena: a philosophy that will have commenced in substantial form with matriarchy.*

PLATE 105

THE SENUFO PENDANT MONKEY *(right). This rather mysterious figure is of the magical tradition of African art, also carrying the semicircles. The lunate shape is a standard Senufo fetish or gris-gris. The Egyptian god Thoth, in Greek Hermes, was portrayed either as an ibis or cynocephalus, as an ape wearing the lunate crescent upon his head. Analogous to the Greek Hermes and the Roman Mercury, Thoth was the messenger of the gods and the god of unexpected wealth, both consistent with long-distance sailings. For Africans, religion starts before birth and continues after death; life itself is part of a religious drama.*

Concentric arcs and the sun symbol with its beneficent rays carved on a rock, Klickitat County, Columbia River, Washington (right). In megalithic art the sun was depicted on the right and the moon on the left.[3]

PLATE 106

(Right): Predynastic Egyptian portrayal of what seems to me to be "the Master of the Animals." (Compare Plate 153.)

The Man in the crested war mask (left) from the Lobi tribe of Burkina Faso (19 cm). This beautifully balanced figure, cast in bronze, wears a mask with a high crest not unlike the helmets with their face pieces under which the Bronze Age heroes fought at Troy. It comes from the Lobi country of Burkina Faso. In its right hand it appears to carry a ceremonial knife, the left hand appears to be gloved. Certainly the recently excavated murals from the island of Santoríni off Crete show boys wearing gloves like the one portrayed here. I looked at them in the museum at Athens. Santoríni covers only seventy-five acres, was previously called Thera and before that "most beautiful" or Calliste.

A closeup of the figure suggests it is almost a boy's head behind the mask. The semicircular religious symbols are strapped to the figure. There are famous ruins with dressed stones in the Lobi area of Burkina Faso. When one takes into account these West African bronzes as a whole, and also takes into account the immense quantity of prehistoric mine workings across Africa, one has to laugh at the university piffle that Africa is the only continent on which the Iron Age preceded the Bronze Age. The bronze traders, the gold traders, the copper traders, the antimony traders were all hard at work before anyone had found a use for iron. And a few of the West African Bronze Age bronzes are exhibited here, which tombs have yielded.

Plate 107
Detail of previous figure. *In African tribal society, much as elsewhere, the history of a tribe is the history of its rulers. Broadly speaking, bronze art tended to be court art, wooden art tended to be popular. Because I am endeavoring to make use of art forms for the raw material of history, most of the pieces shown are in brass or bronze. This is a closeup of the figure with such a crested helmet as could have fought at Troy. As another example of what appears to be wide diffusion, let us notice that the Bambara of Mali use an anvil as an altar,[4] such as is also used in Scotland at Gretna Green. Little of ancient traveling is recorded but we do have notice that the Greek Euthydemes coasted down West Africa.[5]*

Let us take a modern analogy. It is possible to regard the cross as a simple symbol for Christianity: failing to comprehend that this cross embraces the theology of St. Thomas Aquinas, the art of Giotto, the life of St. Francis, the military exploits of the Knights Templars and the Hospitallers of Rhodes. The crescent stands for Islam, but this embraces not just the Koran and the teachings of the desert but the whole spectacular growth of Islamic civilization in Spain, the great architecture, the poets and the Persian Sufis. Similarly the hammer and sickle includes not just the economic revolution proposed by Karl Marx but the whole radical teaching that lay behind him: Turgot and Comte, Saint-Simon and Condorcet, Fourier and Proudhon, Helvétius, Voltaire and Rousseau and the English regicides.

Not one whit less charged with meaning are the religious symbols of the Bronze Age, at once religious symbols and commercial trademarks: for in the Bronze Age the two were inextricably part of each other. God's creation was also a thoroughly practical, down-to-earth affair: a fact which has been lost sight of in today's world.

9. Divine Kingship Worldwide

"There is nothing new under the sun."

Solomon

"The Greeks assumed that the gods spoke their own individual languages."

M. L. West

The god-king, the king who is perceived as the living god, is a form of government widespread in Africa and is especially common in West Africa. In addition, the Egyptian pharaohs were god-kings, as remain the Japanese emperors; one can add to this the monarchs in Southeast Asia; also the former Chinese emperor who was held to be the son of heaven; while the Incan and Aztec monarchs, among the Amerindian rulers, were god-kings, sons of the sun. In Egypt the same symbol in hieroglyphs stood both for god and king and for goddess and queen; divine kingship was thus enshrined in the very script itself. The purposeful confusion of god-king, the political boss, with god-king, the Creator of the Universe, has permitted a great deal of religious sleight-of-hand, on account of which so many have been burned alive. It is a system of government that the Bronze Age maritime peoples took across the world, but then in a rather more honest form, it would appear.

The Greek historian Diodorus of Sicily[1] described how this political and theological system commenced almost fortuitiously, in northwest Europe; after which, crowned with success, it spread he says to the greater part of the inhabited earth. The one reference to an earlier period again is in Aristotle, who finds the sky worshippers functioning in Iran around 6000 B.C. The highlands of Iran may well have been their homeland.

The Christian historian Eusebius puts together, on the basis of the work of eminent predecessors, especially Julius Africanus, the chronology of

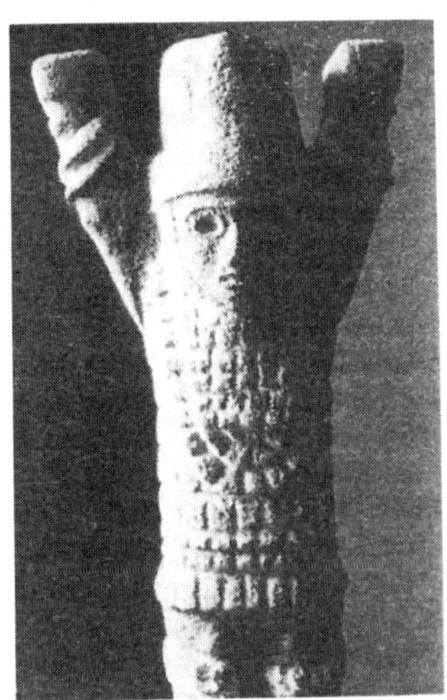

PLATE 108

***ATLAS FIGURE FROM TULA IN MEXICO** (left). These figures were widely used by the Toltecs to ceremonially hold up beams, etc. The immortal, all-powerful Creator of the universe was too remote for humans to identify with. "No one has seen God," Africans say. But he was identified with intermediary divinities. "There are some burdens too heavy for man to bear, they must be placed on the shoulders of God." So there have to be manifestations, hypostases, of the Creator with which the individual can in fact associate: thus Christianity, Islam, Judaism, the various African religions.*

***THE MONROVIA ATLAS** (right). Representing "African power and authority for the world" (55 cm). When I purchased this wooden figure in Monrovia I asked the African vendor what it signified. He replied, "It stands for African power and authority for the world." It is a Senufo carving of modest quality. Yet the tradition accompanying it—that it represents African power and authority for the world—is of vital importance. The unicorn's horn is said to be a second sexual organ.[1] Atlas, wearing a Senufo-type mask, stands on a rather inadequate sacred mound, carries the earth with the world serpent around it on his back, while the bird, representing the sky god, has been domesticated into a sort of hen. It stands on the sacred mount and the set of squares on its cheek represents the irrigated fields, as Egyptian hieroglyphs might suggest.*

Scholars have long argued whether, from the evidence of Greek writers, the mythological Atlas carried the heavens only or both the earth and the heavens. These West African pieces confirm that Atlas claimed to carry both—a double toil. The great African portrait heads from ancient Mexico seem to support the notion that this figure symbolized not just "the white man's burden" but, for a time, "the black man's burden" as well.

ancient times and gives two separate dates for the Creation, one of about 5500 B.C., one of 3900 B.C., which compares with 3760 B.C., which is the start of the Hebrew calendar.

From internal evidence it can be seen that the upper date refers to the Creation of man in northern Europe, the lower date refers to the Creation of Adam or man in Mesopotamia, not the creation of the cosmos. Now, in Akkadian Adam meant red, in Hebrew, earth, and essentially stood for the working class; those whose practice it had been to worship the earth mother, the Great Goddess, the *Magna Mater* whose symbol was hematite or red ocher, the blood menstruated by the earth with which the faithful of that matriarchal religion had been in life raddled and in death buried. *Haemos*, in Ancient Egypt, meant woman as well as copper: just as *akawa* is the root of our word copper and also stood for woman anciently. The insult, "You old cow!" is indirectly relevant.

The higher date for the Creation marks, therefore, the commencement of this new political system, the New Order, which was male-dominated;

PLATE 109

THE PRINCIPAL ATLAS EXHIBIT (102 CM). *This superb woodcarving, neotraditional, reproduces a traditional Senufo figure whose original, I opine, was made in gold. It can have been carved not only by one tribe but by only a few people, from traditional carving families, within that tribe. In the Ivory Coast the Atlas figure is called Bela. In the eastern Mediterranean Atlas and Baal were held to be related divinities, said to be brothers by Philo of Byblos. Bel and Baal were Middle Eastern names for gods. Chronos or Zurvan were bisexual. Atlas is also.*

Atlas is bisexual, possessing both breasts and male genitals, as was the Creator himself in the Titan, Bronze Age tradition. He stands on a sacred mound. Atlas we have already seen is the Greek name for the Egyptian god Set to whom the donkey was sacred. The donkey is carved on the pot, which symbolizes the world. Next to the donkey is a fierce mask. This mask is a fire mask. Each year there is a Senufo festival when certain dancers go down into the river up to their necks and spit fire through the mouth of the mask: both water and fire were sacred to Atlas, fire being looked upon as the sun's rays on earth. In the Bronze Age creativity and bisexuality went together: the political need to keep the two conflicting religions as one.

The little pattern of squares on Atlas is a symbol that meant "sacredness" to the Indus Valley civilization. It represents the irrigated fields which result from the Creation. The unicorn's horn may be an extra sexual symbol.

For a long time the bizarre figure on the lid of the pot puzzled me, in fact until I stumbled across a Middle Kingdom Egyptian text taken from a papyrus from Kahun, on the subject of the Battle of Horus and Set, a battle that is generally believed to have taken place in Egypt in the fourth millennium B.C. *This passage is known as the Homosexual Episode. The papyrus from Kahun runs:*

"The Majesty of Seth said to the Majesty of Horus, How beautiful are thy buttocks! . . . Then, when he shall have given thee strength, do thou place thy fingers between thy buttocks. Lo, it will give. . . . Lo, he will enjoy it exceedingly. . . . Come thou!" There is a similar reference in a text from the pyramid of Pepi II.[2] *It was the Seth people, alias Atlas, who lived in the biblical Sodom. The sodomizing after a battle was to humiliate and to dominate. The name Lot in the Bible may well be an Atlas name. It was Lot's wife, not his boyfriend, who was turned into a pillar of salt! In the Egyptian tradition, as portrayed here, Horus was the pathic.*

it had transcended in its political grouping the provincialism of tribes; it had developed technology and especially metallurgy. It can be compared, though not pejoratively, with the New Order of Adolf Hitler or Pol Pot or with the starting dates for Christian and Mohammedan. It is only the crass ignorance of later scholars to have supposed this idiotic date to apply to the creation of the physical universe itself, misled by the conflation in Genesis of anthropogeny with cosmogeny, doubtless for some political profit or another.

Christians commence their dates from the birth of Christ as speciously as did the heralds of these earlier religions: destroying the records in order to present Christianity as ahistorical, possessing no history, having its own virgin birth as did Christ himself. Perhaps this dishonesty was their prime motive in extirpating the library of Alexandria: and how many other libraries with it; one can positively see them doing it.

The notion of the Creation became that of the dominant, earth-spanning sky god working through human history to bring progress to man. The divine king was the medium through whom the divine cosmic power radiated: his first responsibility was to be the conductor carrying the celestial

PLATE 110

Important detail of the previous figure. The dramatic Ramasseum Papyrus and the frequent references in other ancient Egyptian traditions to the carrying of Osiris by Seth refer to Osiris being carried by boat, Seth being sometimes represented in Egyptian records by a ship. It was a matter of a merchant marine forced to transport the land power on whose support its anchorage and trade depended. The donkey, as portrayed here, was sacred to Set. Christ riding into Jerusalem on his last ride on a donkey may have had symbolic meaning: known to the public then but subsequently lost. On Seth was founded the world—Seth's name means foundation.[3] To Seth the pig was also sacred. Seth was also associated with homosexuality generally,[4] perhaps as befits long-distance sailors. So when Set was ultimately defeated in battle by Horus (by the Pharaohs Amosis, Merneptah and Ramesses), pork became taboo to Semites, homosexuality to Christians, and Set, the god (Lucifer, the light-bearer), became Satan, the devil, the Adversary, the personification of evil. Stands to reason! The Christ child was born between a bull and a donkey: the bull was sacred to El or Chronos, the donkey to Set or Atlas. In Mexico a version of the supreme god called Titla Cauan is referred to as "Thou Sodomite."[5] The name Titla would seem to bear an Atlas root and Cauan an akawa *root. Seth was the chief god during the Hyksos period, his alias Atlas being the chief god during the Toltec period in America.*

PLATE 111

THE THIRD SENUFO ATLAS. *This wooden figure of Atlas holding up the world is clearly of a rather different tradition from the former examples. It also has beard and breasts, the bisexualism of the Bronze Age Creator, and again stands on the Creative Mound. But it has a human hooked nose and a lip-plug. It is not being fanciful to suppose that the pot is the world, the central line around the pot is the equator, the different direction in which the Creation is facing north and south of the equator representing the way currents and whirlwinds rotate in opposed directions if north or south. The Egyptians represented the wise moon god Thoth as a seated baboon. Thoth brought to Egypt letters, science, astronomy and the game of checkers.*

To Atlas fire was sacred. I have pointed out that the Atlas people, principals in the syndicate of sea people called Shepherd Kings who ruled Egypt for 150 years under the dynastic title of the Hyksos, were subsequently thrown out of the eastern Mediterranean, some of the refugees landing in Mexico to become the Toltecs. So it is pertinent to reproduce the figure of the Mexican god of fire (Plate 112), which reposes in the National Museum in Mexico City, drawing attention to a very similar face, the breasts and beard, the pot, there held to be a brazier, carried on his back. The points of resemblance are not fortuitous. They include bracelets, on both arms. The Hyksos principally worshipped Seth, often represented in the form of a ship.

In the language of ancient Egypt, whose script had no vowels, snwr *meant ocean, the province of the sea people. The unusual lip-plug on this Senufo figure was in use in pre-Columbian Mexico.[6] The lower lip-plug was also used by the South American Indians of the village called Artaneses,[7] and Montezuma was supplying his men with lip-plugs.[8]*

The Senufo are a large tribe that inhabits the northern region of the Ivory Coast with some members of the tribe spreading out into neighboring countries of Mali and Burkina Faso. A subtribe, the Nafana, border on northwest Ashanti.

PLATE 112
The Mexican god of fire, Huehuetotl, as portrayed in the National Museum in Mexico City. The design of the cross on his pot I have seen also on similar Senufo pieces in Abidjan. In the Mexican language called Nahuatl, teo *means god as in Mycenaean Greek,* atl *means water as in Berber or in Greek* thalatta, papilio *means butterfly as in Latin. Set or Seth was the Egyptian god of sun, fire and water, so the Indian* suttee *may well derive from it. In the language of the Canary Islands, Guanch,* hu *means great. Fire was looked upon as the instrument for transformation; whether in metallurgy or in cooking. Fire was also looked upon as the divine spark within man. Pliny, in his* Natural History, *writes: "We cannot but marvel at the fact that fire is necessary for almost every operation. By fire minerals are disintegrated and copper produced, in fire iron is born and by fire it is subdued, by fire gold is purified."[9] Both Greek and Latin words replicated in Nahuatl need not surprise us, since Latinus and Graecus were looked on as brothers.[10]*

powers to his people and to their crops. The notion of the Creation was one of a continuing process operating over such vast periods of time the pyramids had to enjoy their degree of durability if they were to survive to its end, perhaps millions of years ahead. Frankfort, writing about the pharaoh, says: "Thus in a series of moves and countermoves, visits to shrines, and demonstrations of loyalty before the throne are woven all the varied bonds which unite the realm and the ruler, the ruler and the gods. While the ritual unfolds, the king moves like a shuttle in a great loom to recreate the fabric in which people, country and nature are irrevocably comprised."[2] The king contained the soul of the nation. He was the instrument of the Creator. For example, the Oba of Benin is believed to wear the robes of the Creator (Plates 203 and 204). With those Benin robes must go a form of coral originating in the Mediterranean, while they used for currency a type of cowrie originating in the Indian Ocean. This surely requires a maritime people to be closely associated with the Bini.

The system of divine kingship provided a blueprint for the life of man that dictated to him down to the smallest detail how his every day should be spent.

God in heaven, and in particular the sun god, was represented by a bird: the eagle to the Romans, the horus falcon in Egypt, the black hornbill in the Ivory Coast, the quetzal in Mexico, the syena in India; for the bird was the intermediary between the sky god and man. The function of Indian kings paralleled that of the gods.

Creation became associated with the primordial hill, the mound of dry earth on which the pioneers lived when they commenced the long heartbreaking job of draining the vast marshes. In Egypt, tradition said, the sacred mount was, among other places, upstream at Karnak and the gods worked their way downriver from there, bringing order and cultivation to what, at first, was morass and chaos. The ancient burial mounds that are scattered across large parts of the earth imitate this sacred start. The mounds within the stone circles of North America are surely of this tradition. Thus time ceased to be cyclical but became directional.

PLATE 113

SETAN, THE SENUFO BIRD OF CREATION (95 CM). *This Senufo bird represents the creative spirit. Its name is Setan, which is the origin, through the Arabic, Greek and Hebrew of our Satan, the Adversary, who fought against Horus, and was scorned after defeat in battle. It is a neotraditional carving and is an example of the way Set, the name of a god, becomes the name of a devil when his people have been defeated in battle by an army with a rival religion: in this case the people of Horus. The very word devil comes from the Indian name for God, Deva, rather than Greek* diabolos, *a divinity whose role was reversed by the Zoroastrians. Hell was first the Scandinavian name for the earth mother, the benign goddess, not for the place of torture: even demon is simply a corruption of the Greek* daemon; *a spirit certainly, but by no means malevolent until the Christians gave it a bad press; in fact a beneficial spirit intermediate between gods and men. Hades was the name of a perfectly respectable Titan ruling in a land beyond the Atlantic in the remote west: in the language of the Canary Islands, Guanch,* eihede *means the islanders in the Land of the Dead, later called Inferno.*

This is the black hornbill of Boundiali symbolizing the Creator himself, whose native name is Setan.

For from the early days the rivers running through irrigable deserts—which necessarily were free of weeds—became the places where capital accumulation could be achieved and where a skilled and leisured class might be sustained.

Now, the museum in Abidjan describes how the great Ivory Coast dance masks acted, as it were, as forms of radio aerials, to attract, to receive and to concentrate the inspiration of the Creator god under whose influence the sacred dancer danced out to the public the whole story of the Creation: the ongoing Creation of the entire civilized world. This was the original purpose of the African masks, experts assert; although they may have even deeper roots than that in the matriarchal world, as I myself have learned.

As we have seen, the Sumerian text *Atra-hasis* which gives both the old Babylonian version of the Flood as well as details of the Creation, makes it quite clear that the technologically advanced families who posed as god-kings became sick to death of digging the irrigation ditches across the vast floodplains of Mesopotamia and so decided to take the uninstructed tribes from outside, train them to a limited extent only and incorporate them into their society as a skilled working class to skivvy for them.[3] It thus permitted the royal families to live at ease. But this act of political convenience was also conceived as a profoundly religious act. A god, one of the royal family, had to be sacrificed so that his blood and flesh could be mixed with that of man, I think by being eaten and consumed. In most texts a god is executed—here he is named Kingu—in some it is left to one to suppose that the god, whose life was to be taken, volunteered to sacrifice himself for the good of thc people. The Mass, the Christian Eucharist, goes back at least six or seven thousand years to this sacred act of Creation: the practice of god eating or ritual murder being now endemic in many parts of Africa; while it is today symbolic only and sublimate in Europe. Ritual murder is the harder to root out because it was originally associated with that which was, in some sense, supposedly great and good.

Atlantean figure,
Chichen Itza.

Atlantean figures,
Sanchi, India.

PLATE 114

THE BAOULÉ ATLAS *(left). This bronze pot comes from the Baoulé district of the southern Ivory Coast, where there survives not only a very rich culture in brass or bronze but also many prehistoric mine workings for gold. It is perhaps a jewelry box.*

There are six figures holding up the world, six being the sacred number to the Semites of old and has thus come down to us in the number of seconds, minutes, hours and degrees to a circle, all being functions of six: such as would have been used by the Chronos people of old and by them brought to Europe: the Chronos people, the great world-spanning Middle Eastern sailors.

The figures themselves, identical to one another, are bald but possess handlebar mustaches and imperial beards. They look very much like Semites, not at all like Africans. We shall meet these people later in other pieces that come from Baoulé. The Baoulé are a branch of the Akan. The figures are part of the cosmopolitan nature of the early world.

I take the two faces on the pot to be the human creation, symbolized as Adam and Eve; the animals around the pot to represent the animal creation, the birds on the bronze lid are black hornbills, representing birds, the sky, the sky gods.

The interesting detail is that the six Atlas figures, or rather the six aspects of the one Atlas, are standing on their toes with their heels raised, thus proving that originally the base for the pot was also curved. The base or Sacred Mound or Primordial Hill was missing when I purchased this piece. Artificial mounds were called tells *in Mesopotamia,* telos *in parts of South America and the Irish for hill is* tulach.

Let me give a curious instance of ancient traditions. I had been drinking in Accra with two Ghanaian friends until late into the night. They said, "You won't know this but we have a plant in Ghana which certain ju-ju men use to bring the dead back to life. If a man dies intestate and people want to know whom he wishes to leave his property to, they place this plant on his lips and he comes back to life to tell them. You want to know how we found out about this plant? There was a hunter in the bush who watched two snakes fighting, the one killing the other. The live snake went off into the grass and returned with a plant between his lips. He placed it on the lips of the dead snake and brought him back to life again."[4]

A few months later I read a somewhat similar narrative as part of the Gilgamesh epic: the narrative existed also in ancient Crete and in ancient Japan and may well be the origin of the two snakes and the flower portrayed on a famous predynastic Egyptian knife handle (see Plate 82). The Gilgamesh epic tells how the snake stole this plant in the first place: the plant that would Make-Old-Man-Young-Again. It is, perhaps, the origin of the

PLATE 115
THE SYMBOLISM OF CONCENTRIC ARCS.

Winged serpent of the Mound Area, Alabama, with concentric arcs.

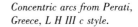

Concentric arcs from Perati, Greece, L H III c style.

A ceramic with concentric arcs from Toltec/Olmec Mexico.

Late Mycenaean bowl (right) painted in Metope style, thirteenth century B.C., *found in a granary in the citadel at Mycenae behind the Lion Gate. Note the standard Bronze Age symbols as part of the pattern, the concentric arcs of the sunrise and the water symbol of the sea god adjoining them, very much as found in West African art. The scale of the bronze trade through the Mediterranean can be appreciated when one remembers that the single island of Pylos is estimated to have carried four hundred bronzesmiths. Top left is the plumed serpent from Alabama decorated in the same concentric arcs*[11] *that are such a feature of West African bronzework. Let us recollect that the Mycenaean age was as brilliant in its way as the Periclean age in historic times.*[12] *All the evidence points to the fact that the Mycenaeans were financed out of their American colonies and American trade, and this on a huge scale.*

medical caduceus, which Apollodorus of Athens[5] attributed to Ancient Crete. Gilgamesh, king of the Sumerian city of Uruk around 2600 B.C., sailed in search of the plant to Utnapishtim, who lived in a remote corner of the world.[6] Ziusudra, the Babylonian Noah, joined Utnapishtim in his Paradise Land where they both lived it up, living like gods. The Cretan rendition of the snake story runs thus: "Polydos kills a snake, then a second snake appeared and, when it saw the first one dead, went away, but returned with a herb which it placed over the body of the dead snake, which was therefore restored to life."[7]

The office of the god-king in India follows the pattern of divine kingship around the world. Indian kings were always believed to be divine. The king is the receptacle for God. The wealth and prosperity of his people depend on harmony with the invisible powers. The king is also an inter-

Plate 116

The Bronze Senufo Atlas and two caryatids; seven pots, Plates 116 and 117 (six small: 18 cm; one large: 35.5 cm). *The tradition behind these bronze Senufo Atlas or Seth figures is again different. Here there are three of them to each pot, two females or caryatids to one male. Atlas was a Titan, which means that the Atlas people had a religion that was a synthesis of the worship of the earth mother, Gaea or Ci, joined to that of the sky father, Ouranos: the worship of the earth mother being at this time, it seems, preponderant. Ouranos lived in his starry palace in the sky.*

The pots carry the semicircle device, the most common of all devices on West African bronzes. I believe the figures on the lid to represent various aspects of the divinity: the earth mother being perhaps portrayed on the lid of the largest pot with the thunderbolt, similar to Jove's thunderbolt.

The very special Senufo mask, found widely on Senufo art in wood, seems to be that of a composite animal with a curiously snub nose.

Egypt, a lighthouse of civilization to the whole world for three thousand years, was African and the main part of its language was Hamitic. But the union of the two Egypts, north and south, was effected by the Sumerians after the Flood, who had destroyed their own economic infrastructure and moved across to take over Egypt. Tradition said that Chronos was the father of both Isis and Osiris. The architecture of the brilliant Old Kingdom of Egypt affirms this. Greek philosophy, the universities tell us, was Greek: but the Greek Sophists sold their schooling to the public on the amount of time they had spent studying in Egypt, studying in Mesopotamia, studying in Iran, studying in India. In the argument that went on in Alexandria between Christian and pagan in the early centuries of our era, Christians said, quite correctly, that there was nothing original to Greek philosophy, they were simply thieves who had pinched the ideas of the peoples around them; the Greek philosophers replied that there was nothing new to Christianity. Both were correct. Ancient Egypt and ancient Greece were an amalgam of many different elements: the Egyptian god Horus was fair-haired, Set was red-haired and there are Hamitic words in Celtic. Osiris was dark. There are Bantu words in Egyptian, the face of the Sphinx, as of many pharaohs, is unarguably African. In Welsh ap *means son of, in Nandi and Kalenjin* arap *has the same meaning; so the present president of Kenya's name means simply "son of Moi." There is no call to believe this similarity to be chance.*

Notice the concentric arcs of the sunrise; the ancient herringbone pattern whose symbolism I do not know; the two caryatids and the one Atlas holding up the world, the androgynous Bronze Age Creator; the earth mother on the lid sitting on the Creation Mound, having modified her philosophy of history to keep abreast of the new fashions (the brass pot of Plates 117 and 119).

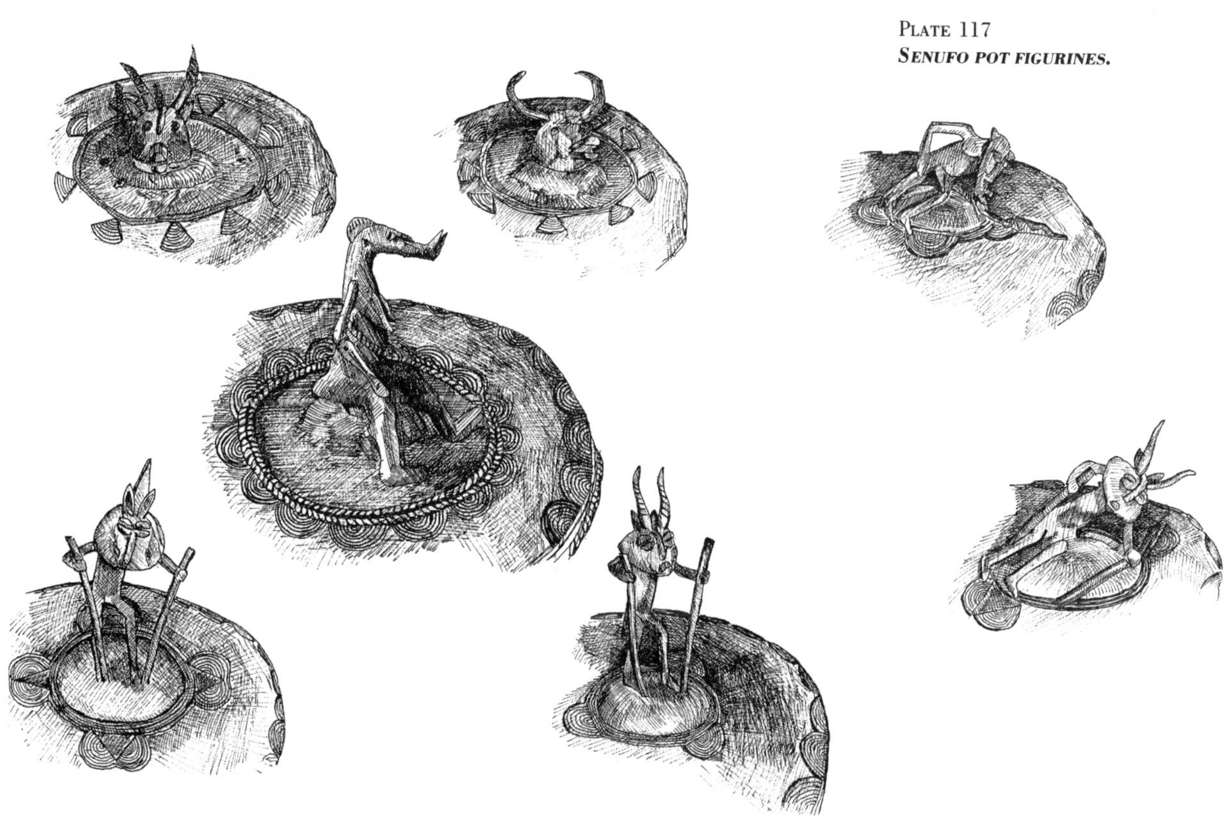

Plate 117
Senufo pot figurines.

mediary between the powers of nature and of society. The king is the bodily existence of an epitome or personification of his community. The king is great by virtue of his station but as an individual he is just a mortal among mortals. Kings were responsible for a bad harvest as much as for a military defeat. Indian kings, rajahs, are therefore identical with their African counterparts, except that in West Africa I have been told that divinity rises up through the stool or throne so that it is chthonic forces that render the ordinary man divine. The sins of the king will bring on his people drought, hunger, disease, wars. In the Rig Veda the king is described as "herdsman of his people," which is an exact translation of Homer's title given to Agamemnon: *Poimena laos,* Shepherd of the Host,[8] a title shared by the Indian god Krishna, interestingly enough. Once we have noticed a close relationship between trinitarian Hinduism and trinitarian Christianity, and located it in the sun worship and sea worship of the Set or Atlas people, our past falls excitingly into shape.

Plate 118

Atlantes from Chichén Itzá. *The Greek word* telos *is also an Atlas word and means burden, while* teleo *means an obligation to pay up, for they were worldwide traders and sailors. Hence the English tally sticks on which tax records were kept and the word tally meaning to reconcile accounts. The Atlas figures holding up the world are not a mere rhetorical claim for world responsibility. Under the name of Seth, Atlas was indeed running Mesopotamia; under the name Set, he was running Egypt; under the name Atl he provided the Creator God in Mexico, provided the name Lothal at the southern end of the Indus Valley, and Dalai Lama, Potala, Minitale at the northern; Senufo in the Ivory Coast, Llan, Somerset, Dorset, Glastonbury, Glasgow in the west of Britain; Latvia, Talinn, Lithuania, Baltic; the Atlantic both north and south. Atl forms part of the name of every second pre-Columbian town in Mexico. Consider also Anatolia, Catalonia, Atalia, Latin, Melitta, Valetta, Mount Atlas, Gibralter in the Mediterranean: with all these we begin to appreciate that the Atlas claim for world control outside later Egypt was, quite simply, not rhetoric but, equally simply, the truth. The Greek word* katholikos, *meaning our word catholic or universal, is very probably rooted in* thalassa *and Atlas: for Atlas was universal in the way thalassocracy provided. This is to understand the Bronze Age and the way, when the price of bronze collapsed and world war followed, their name changed from Set to Satan.*

Altar from Potrero Nuevo. *In Mexico Atlantean figures are associated with the Toltecs,*[13] *while the Greek word,* tele, *in addition to the above, means taxes. Plato says plainly they accumulated their enormous wealth firstly out of mining. Once that is noticed, much of this book falls naturally into place.*[14]

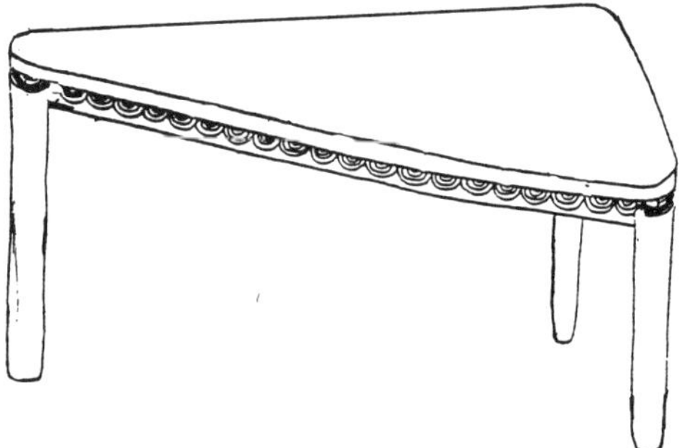

The same decoration of concentric arcs from Transylvania, late fifth millennium B.C., *perhaps portraying the underworld, where the sun was at midnight: this table comes from the matriarchal society. There were nine sets of concentric arcs around King Tutankhamen's tomb, perhaps representing the nine Creator Gods of Egypt, the Ennead.*

PLATE 119

THE BOUND ATLAS (26 CM). *This pot comes from the Baoulé country. It is supported by six very African figures seated, their arms bound together perhaps to display their inseparableness. It would seem to be in the tradition of the Atlas figures holding up the world, already Africanized; physically beautiful but modifying its original, metaphysical meaning.*

The zigzag line for water runs top and bottom of the pot. There is a rather charming and not very fierce lion on the lid between serpents, a matriarchal motif, the woman still on top! Concentric arcs are on the lid.

Metal casting in prehistoric West Africa employed the lost-wax process: the same specialized process as was used across America and the Mediterranean.

10. The Sea Peoples of the Copper and Bronze Ages

"The Pleiades [the seven daughters of Atlas] were prominent in myth and legend throughout tropical America."

ANTHONY AVENI[1]

"With the Navajo the Pleiades were the constellation of the fire-god."

ANTHONY AVENI[2]

We must suppose that rumors of the wealth, the military prowess, the science, the paintings, the literacy, the mathematics, the artificial lakes, the thousands of miles of canals and the astonishing architecture of palaces and pyramids that was Egypt of the Old Kingdom will have been broadcast throughout the world that the sea peoples traveled: not only the facts known but even exaggerated and magnified by travelers. Gorgeous and romantic dreams of Africa to fill the imagination of half the globe!

But the Egyptians for the most part preferred not to leave this sumptuous home and largely left the carrying trade to others. That they were not taken with the sea is evidenced, Herodotus said, by the absence of a sea god as such. They had, after all, gods for just about everything else. When Herodotus denied that the ancient Egyptians had a sea god he completely overlooked the function of the defeated god called Set.

For in predynastic times, in the fourth millennium, the rulers of Upper Egypt were the people who were called Set, and were known to the Jews as Seth, with their offspring Enoch: to the Greeks known as Atlas and, finally, Typhon. These people would seem to have been pushed out of Egypt on the first occasion by the people who worshipped Osiris and Horus, who themselves would seem to have started life as sea people from Byblos in the Levant, although they subsequently became as home loving as the rest of the Egyptian nation. The Greek name Typhon meant "foam of the sea." The white culture heroes who brought the arts of civilization by sea to Peru were called by the Peruvians Vira Cocha, and this means "foam of the sea" also, as we have already seen.

So the Titans flourished, of whom Poseidon and Atlas were prominent members: the Atlas people leaving behind them place names connected with Atlas or Set, especially in Mexico; the Poseidon-worshipping people leaving behind them the name Ogua, or its variants Ogawa and Ogava. They worked out of various ports depending upon whom their customers were as well as the little matter of harbor dues or their equivalents. The matriarchs and the Heracles people, as we have already seen, left behind them the name Akawa, which is, I believe, the origin of our word copper. It also gave us, once it was domesticated, the English word cow; and in Peru the llama, once it was domesticated, the name wak, something like cow in reverse, which became yak in Tibet. And, maybe, the Amerindian squaw and Locmariaquer of Brittany. The oldest and most sacred city of Sumer, Eridu, was originally called Kuara.[3]

But of course there were a great number of other people in sea trading at one time or another. The Greeks remembered the *fourteen Titans* or early multinationals. In the last few centuries West African trade from Europe has been in the hands of Portuguese, Dutch, British, French, Syrians, Lebanese and Danish groups, among others, and they have left behind them their names on the towns and suburbs they occupied: such as Jamestown, Lagos and Christiansborg. Similarly, we can expect to find place names that record these earlier and far longer trading periods dotted along the coastline of West Africa.

And so we find Assinie and Half Assinie as coastal towns in the Ivory Coast and Ghana respectively; these can be compared to the Mycenaean stronghold of Assine. Takoradi would seem to carry the root *akawa*. The Fanti name for Cape Coast, the harbor for the Ashanti gold fields, is Ogua. Elmina is supposed to be the Portuguese for the mine but of course there is no mine there. It may be far-fetched but we know that Al Mina was the name of a port on the Orontes. And, in both Assine and Al Mina, pottery most commonly carried the concentric arcs that are symbols found on so many West African pieces, symbolizing the sun rising on the first day of Creation. Behind Al Mina on the Orontes lies the town of Tarkwa, behind El Mina in Ghana lies the town of Tarkwa. Accra is similar to Acre, Dena carries a name reminiscent of the Dan people or early Greeks. Tema was the name of a district in the old Middle East and Themis the name of a sea goddess in Greek mythology, *Thm* is Ugaritic and *tamtiu* is Akkadian for sea, Ghana's *Keta* was the old name for the Hittites, while the Accra suburb of Kaneshie, near where I had my flat, is reminiscent of Kanesh, the trading town on the upper Euphrates where the Assyrians used their own sort of checks. Kisi in Guinea, whence curious artworks come, is the

Sumerian spelling for Kish. There is also a town in Upper Egypt spelled Kusae, the hieroglyph for which is a figure between two animals (Plate 153). There is also the Ogowe River in Gabon where there is gold, and Gabon itself may be an Ogawa name, such as is the present Chinese name for Canton: Guangzhou.

Again, one group of aboriginal people in Ghana were known as Guans and in the Ivory Coast, Aguans: the same name goes for the original citizens of Tenerife in the Canary Islands, and the worshippers of Poseidon generally. The capital of Burkina Faso, where the trans-Sahara caravans arrived, is called Ouagadougou. Dougou is the local name for town and since names were mostly reversible, it was the town of the Agua people who in the early days traded across the desert. Malik, the Phoenician word for Lord or God, appears as a place name in the Spanish Malaga, perhaps also giving a name to the Cameroons tribe next to the tin mines called the Bamalike. The tribe next to the Bamalike is the Bamoun and one sea people of which we lack almost any record is called Moun. Tigot is the Guanch or Canary Island word for heaven: the principal, secret, religious society in Ghana is called Tigari and the god Tigari's wife is called Hawa, the Semitic version of the Old Testament Eve. But I run on.

In the Bronze Age there was—the evidence suggests—a considerable amount of sailing between the Mediterranean and South America. The Atlantic countercurrent is the narrow strip of ocean that moves eastward where so much of the rest of the tropical Atlantic ocean travels westward. Commencing north of the Amazon mouth, the countercurrent finishes up against the coast of Ghana. This may be an additional factor when we consider the many foreign place names, reminiscent of the Bronze Age, along those welcoming and relatively salubrious shores, where there is a break in the formidable barrier of rain forest, today generally called the Dahomey Gap.

But we must confront an African tradition that tells a contrary story. Most of the tribes carry histories that tell of a relatively recent arrival at the coast, say in the last thousand years. There is also a tradition of the forest being inhabited by little people or pygmies, used in the chiefs' retinues. This shows that the coast could not have carried a heavy African population previously or the pygmies would have been killed off or absorbed, as happened subsequently. Histories, anyway, are histories of upper classes: the African masses, the evidence suggests, having been resident on the West African coast from the third millennium B.C. onward.

We must suppose that the tribes newly arrived from the Sudan absorbed the not very populous remnants of earlier peoples and were in turn greatly influenced by them. For we can expect that each district would have retained its local fetish and would have recruited its fetish priest from among the older people; the appeasing of the local fetish would have been thought essential to a successful future for the immigrants in the new land. So the

PLATE 120
The ceremonial Burkina Faso axe (48 cm) *(bottom).*

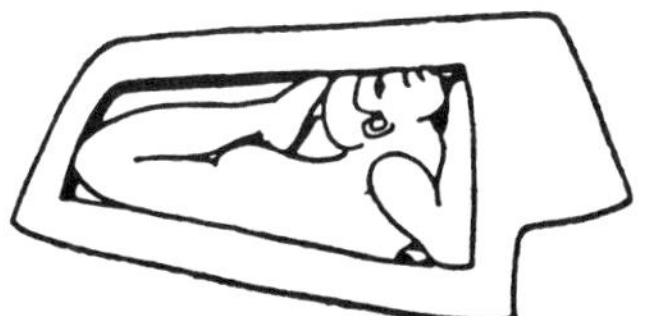

Ceremonial axes, fenstrated: from Egypt *(upper)*: ***from the Olmecs*** *(lower). When I had finished the preceding volume to this book entitled* The God-Kings and the Titans, *my general theory persuaded me that the works of art I had found similar both in the Fertile Crescent of the Bronze Age and also of Ancient America should also be available on the West Coast of Africa. Stands to reason, I argued, that an ancient people who were mining and trading on the western shores of the Atlantic would be doing the same on the eastern.*

In my chapter on ancient Mexico I had reproduced—the idea was not original to me—the ceremonial axe blade from ancient Egypt with a lion fretted into it and compared it to a similarly fretted axe blade from ancient Mexico, with an acrobat depicted within it; I had also placed—again not my idea—certain Mexican pictographic signs alongside certain Cretan pictographic signs to show that the similarity could not be by chance; imagine my pleasure, therefore, when I discovered this ancient Bobo axe whose blade was similar to the Mexican blade and whose pick was virtually identical to the Mexican glyph (compare with Plate 121). The originals from The God-Kings and the Titans *are reproduced here. After all, the proof of a theory is that it actually works. Toads were earth symbols among the Aztecs as in the Old World and they are represented below the blade and pick of the axe.*[1] *In Yoruba tradition the Yoruba sea god, Olokun, destroyed most of the inhabitants of the world in a great flood.*[2]

military power of the newcomers would have been matched by the spiritual powers of the older people and thus a merger on reasonable terms for all may have been obtained. The all-powerful divinities of lagoon and forest would be what the Romans called *magni dei majorum gentium*, the great gods of the older peoples. In this way the ancient traditions of the country would continue undisturbed.

For this reason we need not believe that the traditions of immigration belie the claim for a far, far earlier culture. And part of this culture, it is reasonable to suppose, had originally been tied up with the Atlantic trade.

Only the great German anthropologist Leo Frobenius seems to have recognized the existence of some of this early international trade. He appreciated the unique qualities of the southern tribes in West Africa and called the coastal strip Atlantis. This is a misnomer. Atlantis was simply a name for America at a time when it was controlled by the Atlas people, say 1570–1000 B.C. It is of course true, as later pages will show, that West Africa was an integral part of that great Atlantic community of long ago, intermittently linked by sea to America in the west and to the Fertile Crescent and Indonesia in the east, as African music evidences. This is how, in one sense, the great spiritual and artistic adventure of Africa commenced, but of course it commenced far earlier than Frobenius conceived. One way or another, sub-Saharan Africa contributed mightily to the great spiritual adventure of the Fertile Crescent itself.

The name Europe, they tell us, is derived from the West Semitic languages and means "where the sun sets," or western. One must therefore propose

Plate 121
Dolmens in Massachusetts (Westport), above, and Carrezeda, Portugal, below. Dolmens were megalithic tombs of simple form.

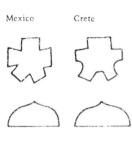

Painting (above) of the circular ziggurat on the Isle of Man before it was destroyed and built over. These goddess temples marked the early stepping-stone route to Mexico.

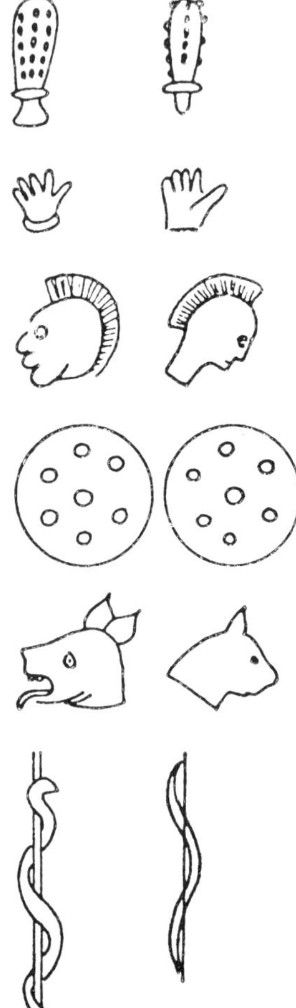

Comparison (left) of Aztec glyphs from Mexico with Cretan glyphs on the Phaistós disk by Svein-Magnus Crodys. Notice the pick of the ceremonial Burkina Faso axe and the clearly similar reproductions of the same head in Cretan and Mexican glyphs to that in Plate 120. There was one god behind the many gods of Africa,[3]—who was never represented—even as there was one god behind the sun god of Peru and of other parts of America, the sun having been a necessary symbol for the plebs but not believed in by the cognoscenti. It was the sky god in various languages called Ouranos, Anu, An, etc. One Mexican form of human sacrifice was virtually identical with the Roman gladiatorial games: with the Mexican god Atl and the Roman Atalia this is not fortuitous. Aztec and Inca knowledge of the calendar was unsurpassed.[4] The vast majority of Mexican archaeological sites have still to be explored. The Toltec long count for their calendar commences 3113 B.C.

Plate 122

Silbury Hill, in Wiltshire, is near Avebury and Stonehenge. *It is 130 feet high, requiring the moving of 670,000 tons of chalk, which has been estimated to require 18 million hours of work with antler picks.*[5] *It is stepped at the top. The name Sil possibly derives from the Great Goddess in her own right,*[6] *and the Ave in Avebury surely refers to the west Semitic name for the Great Goddess, Eve in Genesis, Hava or Hawa elsewhere in west Semitic. Compare this circular monument to the earth mother, with the circular ziggurat of Mexico devoted to the earth mother: both sides of the Atlantic monuments to the male or the androgynous god had a square base, to the earth mother a round base. Silbury was erected about 2600* B.C. *For modern man Nature is an It, for ancient man it was a Thou. Silbury is the largest man-made mound in Europe. Let us notice that the goddess Lissa is found in Dahomey as mother of Sun and Moon, and also in East Africa.*[7] *The Silbury Hill mother was conceived in water. In Britain's folk tradition, the mermaid was a Silkie, derivation from this divine lady, Sil.*

The Celts came to Britain after the megalith builders and it has been suggested that the Celtic priests, the Druids, would have been descendants of these earlier folk. In pre-Celtic times in Britain, women were paramount as they had once been around the entire world. Silbury Hill is the tallest neolithic structure in Europe.

The builders of the stone circles had clock stars, whose rising near the north told you the time of night, and warning stars which foreboded sunrise. Even small communities had their own small observatories.

Michael Dames suggests that the hill was supposed to participate in the fattening of the moon, the transformation of corn from green to gold, and the stirrings of an unborn child.

Cuicuilco: the pyramid in Mexico devoted to the earth mother, Cui; therefore its base is circular and not square. Compare it with its English equivalent above at Silbury. As befits matriarchy it is said to be the oldest stepped temple in Mexico. The Aztec mother of gods and men was called Coatlicue, the water serpent earth mother.[8] *Another Mexican Great Goddess was Teteo Innan:*[9] *notice that Teo was God in Greek Linear B and Innana was a Great Goddess in Mesopotamia.*

PLATE 123

Reproduction of a cylinder seal from Béthel (left) representing the god Ashtar holding both a harpé and a lance, and his spouse, Ashtart, with the head of a lion, holding both a lance and the Egyptian cross of life.

The Senufo harpé (above) with the double axe or butterfly of Crete in two places on it. This weapon is identical with the Sumerian harpé, in Crete called harpeion. *The butterfly motif in Crete represents the soul, or the soul of fallen warriors. It is found also on Masai shields and on a Bronze Age lunate from the Orkneys.*

This is an important piece. It carries both on the handle and the haft the double axe—or butterfly, different authors use different descriptions—usually associated with Minoan Crete. This much is certain.

It looks to me as if this standard weapon had originally been made of wood, carefully strapped for strength, with a leather handle and a flint or obsidian blade. Once metallurgy had started, the wooden piece simply provided the mold and the whole was subsequently cast as one piece in bronze. It is thus identical with the Sumerian harpé.

It is composed of good metal; it is in excellent condition except that a piece is missing off the end. The Greek harpeion *means sickle. When, in Greek tradition, Chronos removes his father, Ouranus's, testicles with a flint sickle it refers to the Sumerians defeating the sky worshippers using the Sumerian standard military weapon, the harpé, originally edged with obsidian.*

In its day this weapon was used right across the Middle East to Anatolia where the Hittites were equipped with it. With early metallurgy the straight blade of a bronze sword was weaker and the outside of a curve possessed additional strength.

This is what Georges Contenau, in his book Everyday Life in Babylon and Assyria, *has to say: "A second badge of kingship was a pole ending in a metal crescent, with a serrated outer edge. This was purely a stylised version of the 'harpé,' which was the name given to the weapon by the Greeks when they first encountered it. It was widely used by the Sumerians and we know all the stages of its development. It began like a shallow sickle and consisted of a bit of wood in which sharp flints were fixed with bitumen. Later, after the discovery of metals, the blade was made of bronze. Finally the whole weapon was made of metal in the shape of the oriental sabre called the yatagan, the cutting edge of the 'harpé' was the outer side of the blade."[10] In the Sumerian tradition heaven and earth were split apart with a copper sickle: i.e., in the Copper Age the patriarchs dominated the matriarchs with the aid of this weapon.[11]*

a similar origin for Iberia, Hibernia, Yoruba, Maghreb, Rabat, Eboricum or York, Berwick and so on: thus emphasizing the early influence of the east Mediterranean on the Atlantic shores; the high importance of the Chronos people.

In the August 28, 1992, issue of the journal *Science* it is stated that the earliest evidence for metallurgy in America appears in the central Andean region at about 1500 B.C. The authors, of course, overlook the primitive metallurgy around Lake Superior dating back to far, far earlier days. Else-

PLATE 124
THE SHEPHERD'S CROOK. *Atlas, according to Greek tradition, was also a shepherd. The reader must not believe, like the naive authors of the* Cambridge Ancient History, *that this means that he played a pipe to the summer bleating of the ewes. It means the contrary. It means that the Set or Atlas sea kings looked upon themselves as so far superior to the natives, the colonials whom they governed, that they were a different order of creation, like a shepherd to the sheep. This equation of kingship to shepherdship comes out frequently in the old Mesopotamian texts, it comes out in Homer's* Iliad *where the kings of both Greece and Troy are styled* poimena laos, *shepherds of the host, and above all it comes out in the Egyptian pharaoh's regalia where, by virtue of his kingship over Upper Egypt, which had been the realm of Set, he carries the shepherd's crook. So when the shepherd kings invaded Egypt again and ruled the land again for 150 years, it was the same sea people returning, the Hyksos perhaps driven from their homelands by drought. And when Egypt was attacked by the Peoples of the Sea (1235–1190 B.C.) part of the alliance was very much the Hyksos returning for a repeat performance. After the domestication of plants and animals, in the last analysis, the title shepherd king referred to the domestication of men themselves. It was certainly an Aegean title.*

The people to whom Christ spoke the Parable of the Good Shepherd will have understood its political content, an understanding subsequently lost to us.

The survival of a custom going back to the fourth millennium B.C. is found in the Christian bishop's pastoral staff, which is this same shepherd's crook, symbol of monarchy in Upper Egypt.

Montezuma, the Mexican king, was wearing the mitre when Cortés invaded Mexico. And we have already seen that it was the Atlas or Set people, in a culture known to the academics as Olmec, who laid most of the foundations for the ancient Mexican nations and their political system of divine kingship. Socrates, as recorded in Xenophon's Memorabilia, *commented on this royal symbol at some length.*

where it is stated that the Aztecs were not using bronze when the Spaniards arrived because, perhaps, of a shortage of tin in Mexico.

In sub-Saharan Africa, as we have seen, there is evidence enough for early mine working but so little evidence of the use of metals by the local folk that the experts can argue that Africa is the one continent where the Iron Age preceded the Bronze Age. So the lack of evidence for the use of metals by the Amerindians before 1500 B.C. does not preclude the Americas from being the scene of mining and of the flourishing export trade in minerals to the Mediterranean and the Far East in much earlier times. For we know from the Greek story of Prometheus's theft of fire that the secrets of the art of smelting were confined to the ruling class and were forbidden to the colonized: hence the position in Africa.

The Poseidon worshippers, the great sea people who for a long time, tradition said, ruled the land the other side of the ocean from the Old World, were associated with horses. This somewhat surprising combination of sailor and cavalry also comes through with the Celts, part of the Atlas people as their name implies. In fact, the Celts would largely supply the Roman cavalry in the Roman armies, and the old horse brasses, I have noticed, carry symbols of the sea peoples.

The earliest horse keeping we have knowledge of is in the Ukraine, with the Svedni Stog culture of the Ukrainian copper age, going back to 4300 B.C. This area is 155 miles south of Kiev and by this time horses were

PLATE 125
This figure is the Egyptian hieroglyph meaning sceptre and rule.

The Fulani chief's symbol of office (right). The bronze crook, made of excellent metal, is covered with spirals. It is the shepherd's crook, and like the pharaoh's staff of office portrays the king as a shepherd king. In the old days the Fulani may have provided pharaohs for the throne of Egypt. The shepherd's crook and the corn grower's flail were the two symbols of royalty for the thirty dynasties of pharaohs. I purchased this piece in Abidjan. The Christian bishop's crosier or pastoral or shepherd's staff confirms this ancient tradition.

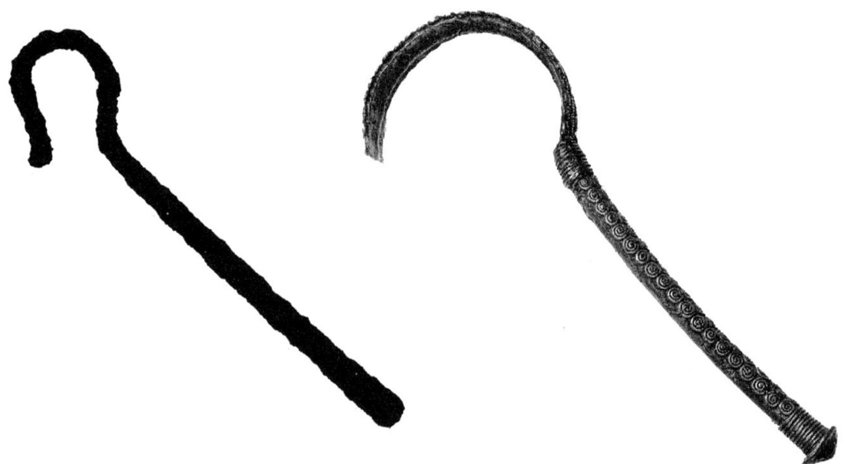

being used as mounts. This area is joined to the Caspian Sea by the Dnieper. It is reasonable to suppose that the sea traders of that illustrious early area of civilization around the Black Sea would cross over to the Caspian and trade up and down the Dnieper. The traditions of wisdom, of skills, of craftiness attributed in those early days to the sea peoples derived from their ability to appropriate other people's ideas as well as their trade goods. From this early horseback riding developed the chariot, the horse cart, when the steed replaced the ass and the ass onager, and, with it, tremendous military advantage accrued to these sea people. It is with chariots, some of them guarding the ships on the rivers, that the horse trots onto the pages of history.[4]

11. The Mermaid, a Tradition Across the Atlantic Trade Routes

"The Yoruba descended from Nimrod."

OKOI ARIKPO

The best authorities maintain that the English mermaid was a tall story carried back from West Africa by sailors; whilst her seductive wiles were derived, given sufficient rum, from a sighting of the strange mammal, the manatee or dugong. May Nelson rest! For it seems to me that this explanation is improbable.

All down the coast of West Africa: the Ivory Coast, the Gold Coast, the Slave Coast, the Bight of Biafra, the African fishermen have the clearest ideas about the mermaid or, in their own parlance, *mami wata*, mammy-water, such clear and distinct ideas as Descartes would have found acceptable (see Plate 86).

The water-mammy or mammy-water, *La Sirène*, is a lady from the waist up, a fish from the waist down and perennially young. In that ebony world she is nevertheless white. She has long hair. She combs her hair. Some mammy-waters have fair hair, tradition says, some dark hair. Her significant attribute is that if you should marry her and remain faithful to her she will provide whatever you may need. How important this tradition is was brought home to me when there was money missing from my office till in Lagos. The miscreant was laid off and I spoke to him subsequently about it. He was a delightful person, a friend, and I was sorry to see this happen. A chance acquaintance had arranged his marriage to a mammy-water. He had gone, he said, to Bar Beach in the early hours of the morning; the mermaid had risen up out of the sea and the wedding had been arranged by this go-between. The miscreant was told that he had to find £250 to pay for the cocks and sheep that must be sacrificed to the lady. So he used his own savings, then his wife's savings, and then he had dipped into my till.

THE GAGGED TRAITOR OR SLAVE. *This painful, striking and arresting piece coming out of southern Nigeria portrays a traitor or a slave; gagged, hands tied together, head tied back to the hands and feet attached to a stake in the ground. To me it has always symbolized the plight of the editor in Africa! The gag is to prevent vengeance magic.*

The style would seem to be both African and European; this latter composite style belongs to the magnificent school of Afro-Portuguese art. It need not be more than a century or two old. Such history as it carries is plain to see. I give it as a modern example of how art can retain history. It is also a relatively modern example of hybrid art, African and Mediterranean. To the African practice of eating parts of a live human being to acquire their power—my friend J. B. Danquah called it among the Akan tribe "god-eating"—I add a picture of a similar practice in pre-Columbian Mexico.[1]

PLATE 126

HUMAN SACRIFICE AND GOD EATING IN PRE-COLUMBIAN MEXICO *(after Paso y Troncoso). Note also that Mexicans used kettledrums and horns, as in the Old World, to beat a retreat.*

Julius Caesar described the practice of human sacrifice flourishing in his day among the Celts of Western Europe: the taking of auspices from a study of human entrails; the construction of a huge wickerwork cage in which the human victims were placed, after which the whole thing was set alight; other Celtic victims were drowned or hanged.

At first, like everybody else, I found it difficult to make head or tail of this narrative. But after enquiry among my rougher friends I heard that there was a Ghanaian ex-serviceman who had been to India with the Gold Coast Regiment and that he was operating this confidence trick in town. He employed a Lebanese prostitute and covered her with luminous paint, giving her, I suppose, some sort of artificial fish's tail and letting her rise up out of the breaking waves, then sitting her upon a chair: all this in the early hours of the morning when we are all at our most credulous.

"You have not asked me why I stole the money," the miscreant said to me. "No," I replied, dry-mouthed, "why did you steal it?" "You see," he said, "if you should marry a mermaid, and are faithful to her, she will obtain for you anything you want. We needed more transport for the circulation department and this was my way of getting it."

After this revelation I became increasingly aware of the vividness of this superstition along the coast. Now, clearly, the object of the fisherman's love was no manatee. It referred, it seemed to me, to the girls of the white traders who had come in to trade from the sea, but there would seem to be no reason to believe that the first European traders, the Portuguese, the Dutch and the English, would give rise to a story of people who were half fish, and feminine to boot.

But there had been, in far remoter times, a cultured sea people who were called half fish, whom Berosus—the first Middle Eastern historian, who wrote around 300 B.C., a priest of Marduk—described as having come to Mesopotamia in antediluvian times. In Greek they were called Oannes (Plate 90). (It should be noted that early sea peoples used fish skins for clothing.)

Berosus stated that in Mesopotamia in antediluvian times, by inference

PLATE 127
This is a sculpture of Zeus Hypsistos or "Most High" from near Byblos. He was also known as Baal Shamim in an eleventh century B.C. *inscription, or Elioun. Note the symbol of the monitor lizard beside him, the Creator's vicar on earth. The symbol might also be the origin of the cross of Lorraine. This is where the English name comes from, monitor lizard.*

DOGON STATUE (16 CM). *This little bronze figure comes from the Dogon of Mali, from Bandiagara. On its head it carries the schematic symbol of the monitor lizard, the Creator's vicar on earth, hence its name. Its apron is composed of concentric semicircles. Something like the headdress can be found in ancient Egypt. It is the Dogon tribe of Mali that has proved to be a people possessing a profound metaphysical system and also, I judge, to be a repository of one of the lost philosophies of the Fertile Crescent, much as Dieterlen and Griaule believed.*

The Dogon of Mali inhabit the upper Niger near Timbuktu, which was of course one of the great centers of learning for the West in the Middle Ages, and a repository of ancient texts. The Dogon have maintained their far more ancient culture in their rocky fastness with great tenacity.

Vital to our understanding of their profound philosophical background is the name of the peoples who preceded the Dogon in that country, who were called the Tellem. The root t-l, *which means water in Berber, gives us the Atlas Mountains in Morocco and in the Nahuatl language of Mexico where it also means water. The depth of thought and sophistication of the highest African religions are greatly undervalued by the rest of the world. They can help us better to understand related cultures, both among the Amerindians and across the Fertile Crescent.*

PLATE 128
THE YOUNG GENTLEMAN FROM THE CAMEROONS. *This slim young man stands with his face and the palms of his hands facing skyward, doubtless a religious gesture but yet suggestive of the Cretan paintings of the young athlete behind the bull in Crete waiting to catch the tumbler somersaulting over the bull's back. He came from Foumban in the Cameroons. On his body are imprinted concentric arcs and cowrie shells.*

Plate 129

Portraits of Ancient Sailing and Sailors. *Two pictures of Greek boats on early Iron Age Greek pottery. Notice the bird symbol on the prow of the left boat and the butterfly symbols above the right boat.*

The vessels depicted on Greek pottery of the Geometric Period, c. 750 B.C.*, the center illustration showing the cut-in style of shield that succeeded the figure-eight shield in the Aegean.*

in the fourth millennium B.C., there came to the Mesopotamians out of the Red Sea a series of six creatures who were half man and half fish, ichthymorphic, called individually and collectively *Oan*, in Greek *Oannes* or John. These creatures brought all the arts of civilization with them: letters, towns, temples, laws; in brief, whatever makes for human well-being; and from that time on nothing worthwhile in Mesopotamia has ever been invented.[1]

These amphibians are so described because they were sea people; half woman or man and half fish, because they made their living on and by the sea. Until the invention of the airplane, the radio, the Telstar, the undersea cable, the maritime peoples benefitted not only by their ready access to minerals but also by their unique access to the ideas and inventions of

Plate 130

The long-distance sailors of the Copper and Bronze Ages were also prospectors, traders and miners. The miners were often slaves. Our present accounting term, amortization, derives from working a slave to death in order to make a margin on his original cost. Lucretius describes: "When men following up the veins of gold and silver, probing with the pick deep into the hidden parts of the earth, what stenches the mine breathes out underground? And what poison goldmines may exhale! How strange they make men's faces, how they change their colour! Have you not seen or heard how they are wont to die in a short time and how the powers of life fail those whom the strong force of necessity imprisons in such work?"[2]

Galley with ram, oars and sail: from a silver Roman denarius, 44–28 B.C.

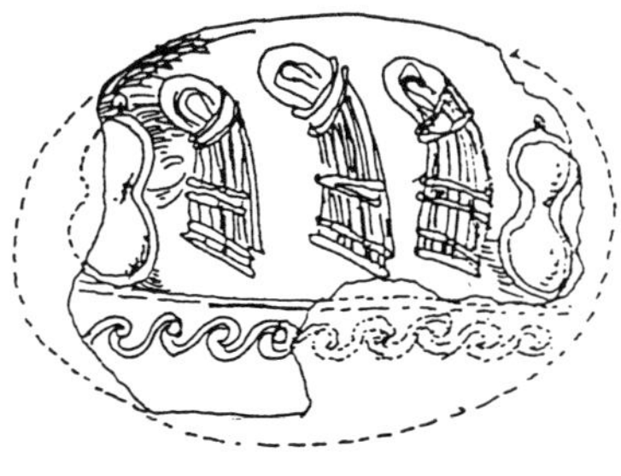

The figure-eight Cretan shield, left and right of a clay sealing from Knossos.

Phoenician bronze coin of around 500 B.C.*, carrying the design of a boat, a coin recently found in the Bahamas.*

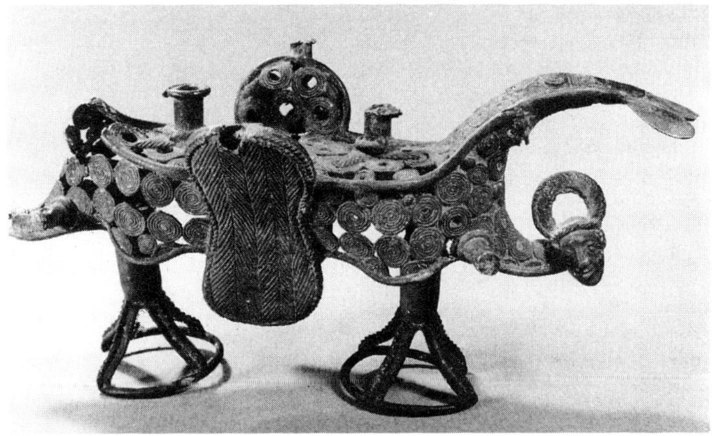

PLATE 131

This sixty-four-foot oceangoing canoe, carved by Haida Indians from a single log, is now at the Museum of Natural History, in New York. It would seem to have its own peculiar figure as a stabilizer on the stern. James Hornell, who wrote a classic book on early ships and navigation, states that the big canoes used on Lake Victoria Nyanza are totally Indonesian in their structure, not African.

A Bronze model of a Bronze Age Mediterranean boat from the grasslands of the Cameroons (16 cm). The art from there suggests a Cretan origin to this boat. This model boat was sold to me as a siren or mermaid, la sirène, *but it is clearly a two-masted boat with a ram (broken off) a prow of a sort (broken off) and a fishlike tail that was broken but that was also mendable. I glued it back on. Interestingly, it is an outrigger on one side. The face on the stern may be an adaptation of Tiamat, goddess of the deep waters. The hull is composed of spirals, the Mediterranean religious symbol for the earth mother, a divinity to whom water was even more important than land.*

Shipbuilding for fifteen hundred years changed little. This vessel is recognizable from Cretan pictures of boats, also early Iron Age pictures of boats up to the boats reproduced upon Greek and Roman coins. However the figure-eight shield on the sides of the model is distinctly Cretan in style so that the earlier date for this piece might be the correct one.

It would then be one of the only bronze models of a Bronze Age boat in the world. It appears to have been hit by a pick when it was excavated. There are ancient tin mines near Foumban. I judge it to be an original. The human head acts as a stabilizer on the stern and should be compared with the masked human with the same function used by American Indians (above). Let us note that the early population of Mexico used paper to write on, following the same procedure used by the ancient Egyptians and Phoenicians for papyrus manufacture.[3]

others. They were the sole purveyors not only of minerals but of gadgets and know-how. For this reason Enki, the Mesopotamian sea god, was a god of wisdom, crafty, all-knowing.

The second people whom Berosus records as having come to Mesopotamia in antediluvian times, bringing their skills, were called Odacon. Here the "O" is again the prefix. The name Dacon is suggestive of Dagon, whom we know of from the Bible as the grain god of Sidon. The name is also suggestive of the Dogon of Mali, whose principal deity is a god of water. Dagon was also represented as a fertility god.

I was talking one night to Nigerian fishermen friends. They were de-

Plate 132

Large Cameroons mask (far right) from Foumban (38 cm). *Cameroons art is widely copied. This magnificent mask may be an original but it is more likely, in my opinion, to be a very high-class replica; for our historical purposes no worse for that. It comes from the Bamun tribal area, who are a branch of the Tikar tribe whose capital is Foumban.*

The face itself is continuously repeated in the art of the Cameroons. To my eye it looks more Pelasgian—the pre-Hellenic sailors of the eastern Mediterranean—than African.

However, the figure on the top of the mask (left) has a quite different cast of countenance, he might have come from anywhere between Cairo and Pakistan. He is caught, like Laocoön, in the coils of a snake while he is held by the arms by two black hornbills: the vipers representing the worship of the earth mother and water; the black hornbills representing the sky father. Specifically, vipers represented an ancient sea people called Echidnae.

The Titans combined the two religions, so that his situation may not be quite as perilous as it looks. Alongside is a closeup of this smaller face. Masked dancers are held to be dancing out the Creation or the progress of the world and the world order,[4] hence the importance of masks.

Plate 133

For comparison: Ericthonius, Bronze Age king of Athens, represented with the lower half of his body a snake. The serpent people, the Ophiones, were early sea people sailing out of Egypt and Greece to distant places in pre-Hellenic times.

Another view of the Cameroons mask (above right), with birds and vipers, echidnae. *Compare this with the face of the Pelasgian figure being the "Good Shepherd" (Plate 73.)*

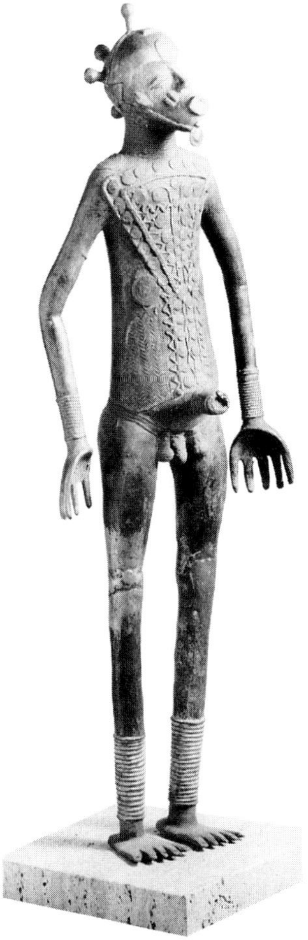

Plate 134

Statue from the Cameroons (68 cm). *This wild and magnificent figure from the Cameroons, whether king or commoner I do not know, shows that powerful imagination that informs some of these pieces that are, in my opinion, of mixed descent; hybrid styles, products of the Africa and the Fertile Crescent of long ago. The herniated umbilicus is a feature of this culture. It may be that this hybrid art is greater than either society would have achieved by itself. A slightly herniated umbilicus was much coveted by Senufo young people.*[5]

His dress consists largely of spirals or the zigzag lines of the sea symbol. His navel is artificially extended, the navel is the point through which the mother brings life to the child. His hair is clustered and his testicles appear to have been artificially divided. To adequately catch and describe his symbolism would, I suspect, require a book in itself. He is from the Bamoum. The culture appears to be mixed African and Aegean. In the ancient Aegean the umbilical cord symbolized healing, even life itself.

scribing to me how they use the sounds that fish make to help them with their catch. They paddle twenty miles or so out to sea before dawn in their dugout canoes, they told me, and then sleep in the bottom of the boat after the sun rises, except for one fisherman who puts the handle of the paddle to his ear while the blade is in the sea. By this means he can pick up the vibrations made by a school of fish. Once he hears a shoal the rest of the crew wake up to start fishing.

But a fisherman may also climb out of the canoe to put his head under the water, they continued, to listen to the fish in order to tell which ones are about. It is "like telephone," they said. Some "make noise like bird," some "like cow." And then they swore that if you go a full forty miles out to sea you might hear mammy-water. If I remember aright, she was said

Plate 135

Bronze or brass pipe of the Cameroons (40 cm). *Pipes are a great feature of the Cameroons. In general, the bigger the chief the bigger the pipe. They are used in much the same way as the pipes of peace in America. The pipe is carried by a retainer behind the chief. Should he find two of his people quarreling, they must first of all settle down and smoke for ten minutes before he can take up their case and decide between them.*

The style of the man on the pipe stem is like the Greek god Pan or that of some of the Luristan bronzes. Luristan is a westerly district in southern Iran from which came the Kassites, who ruled Mesopotamia for a period.

The figures and emblems on these bronze tobacco pipes make it most doubtful in my mind that the originals post-date Columbus. This is again from the Bamoum area of prehistoric tin mines.

PLATE 137
THE HOOKED NOSED PIPEBOWL FROM THE CAMEROONS. *This terra-cotta clay pipe portrays a man with a nose so beaked it appears to be deformed or artificial. He has what appears to be a crudely portrayed bird on his head. It is just worth noting that in ancient Mexico a carving portrayed a noble personage wearing a false beard and what appeared to be a false, hooked nose: in imitation, it has been suggested, of the original culture heroes who brought to them the arts of civilization.*

PLATE 136
TERRA-COTTA PIPES FROM THE CAMEROONS (SEE NEXT PLATE). *The figure has a short beard with a bird in flight above his head. It could be a seabird, skua or petrel.*

to "make noise like cow." The Irish tell of a woman of divine loveliness coming ashore in a spirit curragh and leading men away to the land of the gods.[2]

Now, the legend of marrying a mermaid, a creature that is half woman and half fish, is also found in the Hebrides: where, additionally, if this composite creature is half seal, she is called a *silchie*. And a similar story is told by the Amerindian tribes at the mouth of the Amazon. On the island at the mouth of the Amazon has been found Cretan pottery.

The word *mammy*, so common in West Africa, is not the most obvious word for a young girl or a woman but *mama* is Sumerian for the Mother Goddess herself. It bears the identical meaning in Peru, the Pacific Ocean being called *Mama Cocha*, Mother Ocean. However, it is also claimed that mama is the first sound that every child makes naturally.

12. Why the Sea Trade Ended, Bringing Isolation and Backwardness to America and West Africa

"There is more to be feared from the passions of men than from all the convulsions of Nature."

EDWARD GIBBON

"Wild beasts are said to have occasioned the Invention of Arms, which Men afterwards turned against one another to gratify their Ambition and Thirst of Dominion."

THE REVEREND MR. KENNEDY

The picture of the ancient Atlantic trade that can be drawn from such traditional material as was recorded, joined to the more recent findings of archaeology and kindred disciplines—archaeology now rendered more accurate by virtue of the techniques of radiometric dating—is far different from the accepted opinion of the academics.

Let us recall that at the start of the Copper Age, approaching 6000 B.C., the techniques of metallurgy generally did not exist, so that the only copper that could be exploited was pure or native copper, although a little copper smelting would seem to have started early in Anatolia at Catal Huyuk. The only place where we know pure copper to have ever existed in abundance is on Lake Superior in the middle of North America, to be precise on Isle Royale and the Upper Peninsula of Michigan. From there, carbon dating would seem to tell us that large quantities of native copper were removed between 6000 B.C. and 1000 B.C., approximately the start of the true Copper Age in the Old World and the end of the Bronze Age. To the best of our knowledge little copper was being used in North America for the early part of this period, almost none on the Isle Royale or its environs, so that we can be confident that most of it was exported. It is tempting to suggest that the only peoples who are known to have been using quantities of copper at this early date, the earth-worshipping inhabitants of the Balkans and the Near East, were obtaining it from the only place from which quantities of copper are known to have been available. However, some quantity of pure copper was available at the top of almost every copper deposit. Of course, the American market would have gradually developed. We also learn from the experts on climate that the prevailing conditions in the North Atlantic were far warmer and less stormy than those that exist today. The pill that the reader must therefore swallow is the acceptance that, first, the earth-worshipping and the Heracles people, secondly the Ouranos and Poseidon people, thirdly the Chronos people, fourthly the Atlas or Atlantic people by origin living along the western shores of Europe, were better and wider ranging clans of sailors than many of the peoples who succeeded them. It is quite a big pill to swallow but must, I emphasize, be swallowed. The evidence admits of nothing less.

But, of course, to allow them to have been grand sailors is to permit them to have traded down the west coast of Africa as well as of Europe. Indigenous names for the West African rivers, the Niger, the Congo, the Vaal, follow the *kwa, kware* pattern, the matriarchal pattern.

Now, there was alluvial tin to be had on the Jos plateau of Nigeria, in the grasslands of the Cameroons, in Gabon, in Zaire at Kolwezi, in Ruanda and Burundi, in the Transvaal north of Pretoria and in Swaziland near Nokwane. But none of this, although it was almost all mined in prehistoric times, is on a large enough scale for the vast demands of the ancient world.

While very small quantities of alluvial tin might be hauled from Brittany, Bohemia, Spain, Iran, Cornwall, the greatest quantities of alluvial or eluvial tin that were available required long-distance sailing. Some deposits were in Southeast Asia and China, some in western Brazil and Bolivia. Access to these South American deposits was provided by the Amazon and we must suppose the great circular currents to have been employed for this vital part of the carrying trade. Doubtless Southeast Asia provided bronze for clients that lay nearer to them, but the tin deposits were not close to copper. The Canary Islands would provide a starting point for the Mediterranean sailors taking the middle passage across the Atlantic, and the name Canary, I suggest, refers to *kan*, the Akkadian for bronze, read boustrophedon, not for big dogs, as one classical writer supposes.

Greek tradition suggests that in the Copper Age nations were relatively peaceful, differences being settled by agreement or by casting lots. This was thought to permit God to decide. Hesiod records that the Bronze Age became increasingly bloodthirsty and warlike, I think perhaps due to the pressure of mounting populations on limited resources—in addition to the temptation presented by the terrible excellence of the weapons; both may have brought about this demoralization.

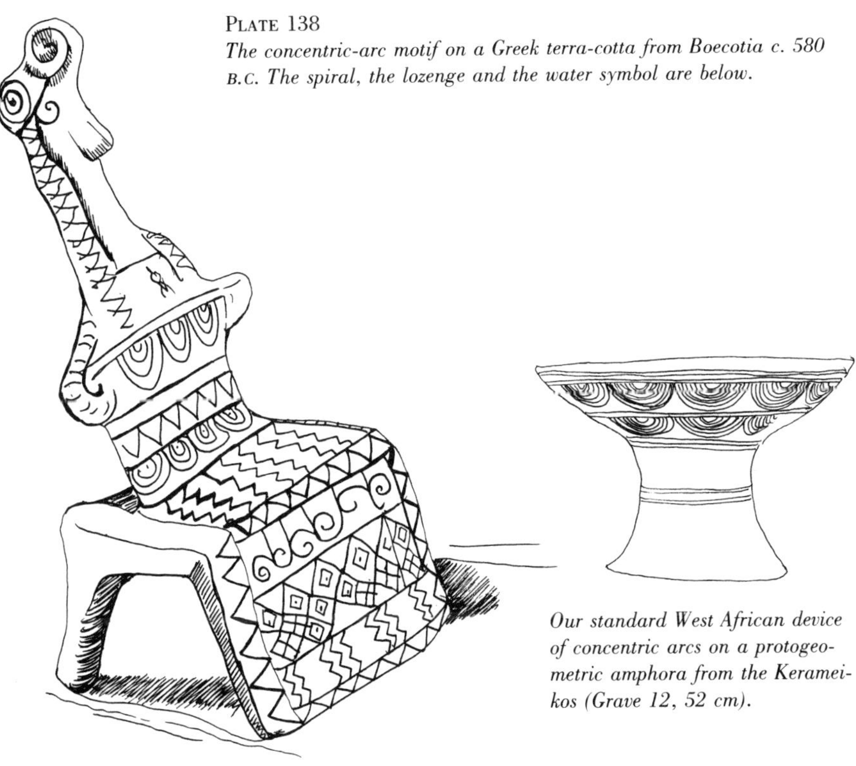

PLATE 138
The concentric-arc motif on a Greek terra-cotta from Boecotia c. 580 B.C. The spiral, the lozenge and the water symbol are below.

Our standard West African device of concentric arcs on a protogeometric amphora from the Kerameikos (Grave 12, 52 cm).

THE DOGON SCHEMATIC PORTRAIT. *This is a bronze piece from the Dogon with a schematic portrait: this piece of ultramodern schematic portraiture resembles an art tradition of the earth worshippers of Eastern Europe and western Russia that can be between five and ten thousand years old.*[1] *Notice the concentric arcs. The Dogon divide their people into those few who have deep knowledge of their immensely rich and complex culture and those who have simple knowledge. In Dogon tradition the sons of God were albinos or extreme blonds. This coincides with the Amerindian tradition that in the first or second sun things were run by the white-haired giants: after them came the red-haired and finally the black-haired.*

Disaster struck in 1219 B.C.—the Egyptian records say—when Egypt under the Pharaoh Merneptah was attacked by the Peoples of the Sea. The attack was repulsed. They came again in 1182 B.C. by land as well as by sea and were again defeated. Homer's tale of the destruction of Troy was a small episode in that period of anarchy. The subsequent attack on Egypt launched from Crete was briefly described by Odysseus as a cover story. It could only serve as a plausible cover for him if the circumstances described were known to his audience to be true. He said that within months of the fall of Troy an invasion fleet assembled and an attack was launched from Crete against Egypt, an attack that was hopelessly mismanaged, permitting the Egyptian chariots and bowmen to cut to pieces the invaders, killing most of them and selling off the survivors into slavery.[1] The mention in the *Odyssey* of a solar eclipse visible from the neighborhood of Ithaca confirms that the Greek and Egyptian dates agree.[2]

It looks very much as if the trade with Africa and America fell away after the end of the Bronze Age substantially because the need for bronze diminished and the price of bronze will have collapsed. The sea peoples were defeated in their long campaign, and of course many of the countries of the Old World who would have been purchasers also lay in ruins. Then,

Plate 139

This stone carving of the king of the Dogon portrays an aging man with heavy beard, something between two and three feet in length. Such a beard is not possible to Africans. To Iamblichus as to Plotinus, much as in Africa, the ideal world was a hierarchy of gods, from the ineffable, unsearchable One, down, tier below tier, through successive emanations, to the gods that are immanent in the world. The Dogon believed, not unlike certain tribes of the upper Amazon, that each man had an animal twin.[2] The Baluba and Bakongo of Zaire carry a story very similar to the Tower of Babel story.[3] Head deformation was practiced by the Nakere.[4] In early Africa as in early America, the long beard portrays the newcomer from abroad; it cannot be grown by the indigenous peoples.

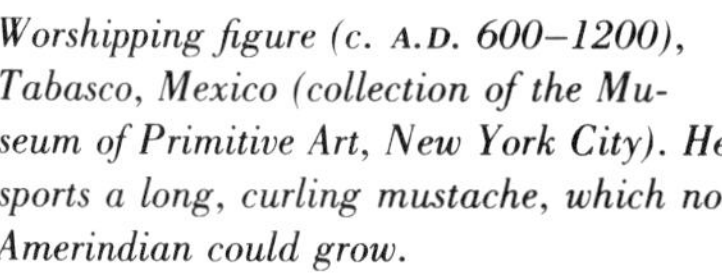

Worshipping figure (c. A.D. 600–1200), Tabasco, Mexico (collection of the Museum of Primitive Art, New York City). He sports a long, curling mustache, which no Amerindian could grow.

some say, there was a curious pluvial period followed by a period of prolonged drought in the east Mediterranean that must also have hit their economies. More confidently, the experts on climate point out that conditions in the North Atlantic were deteriorating at this time, so that by the middle of the first millennium B.C. the North Atlantic was even colder than it is today. Rock engravings show it did not halt the sea trade with America, it merely diminished it.

In sum, the great days of Atlantic sailing were over until the Celts, the Norsemen, and then the Spaniards and the Portuguese started it up again. But although the great days were over, some contact with America was maintained by the Phoenicians and by other peoples, including Hebrews; by Chinese and by Indians, by Irishmen, Polynesians, Scots and Welshmen. The discovery of Roman coins, the ogham script, Hebrew coins and scripts, a Roman pottery head in America and a sunken Roman galley or two, suggest that there remained some slender and covert contact between the

Old World and America across the Atlantic. There was, however, much more solid contact across the Pacific between America and the Indians, the Chinese and the Polynesians after that, or so the evidence would seem to suggest.

If the West African trade was a part of this general Atlantic decline, we can draw a picture, if only by reflection, of when it most widely flourished and over what period it gradually disappeared. It was the gradual failure in the Iron Age of the sea link with the Mediterranean that explains the technological backwardness of Africa. It was the presence of the sea link with the Mediterranean in very ancient times that also explains, in my opinion, the remarkable quality of West African art and thought. The later contact with Indonesia and South India across the Indian Ocean especially influenced African music, the musicologists assert. The ultimate failure of this Atlantic sea link will have contributed to the impoverishment—and thus the weakening—of the Mediterranean nations; the decline of both partners after the arteries of trade had been severed. There will be wise heads who would argue that this isolation held some spiritual compensation for Africa, which is exemplified in their art.

13. West African Customs That Are Similar to Those of the Ancient Fertile Crescent

"Into this background of Nigeria's negro life there has been woven many elements from other culture patterns, mainly Hamitic, Semitic, Egyptian, Cretan, Phoenician and in more recent decades Western European."

OKOI ARIKPO

"They take them to the place of burial and there give these Indians much maize wine, so much that they become drunk. And, seeing them without feeling, they put these people into the tomb to keep the dead man company."

PEDRO DE LÉON (on the Quillacingas, 1554)

Let us look now more deeply into the old custom of retainer burial. Whenever Sumerian monarchs or early Egyptian monarchs were buried, their retainers, their wives or some of their wives were killed to accompany their lord into the next world and there they were all supposed to continue to look after him as they had previously done upon earth. By this means they earned their own immortality. Likewise food and drink were left with the king so that he should want for nothing on his last journey before he reached Paradise Land, while his jewels and his golden things were buried with him. In many instances wives and retainers were closed up living in the burial chamber with the corpse: they had a harp with them on which they played the song of death, while they sat around in that ghostly atmosphere awaiting their extinction. Something of the sort was exhibited until recently in the national museum in Kampala, Uganda: having been the practice in Uganda with the burial of their kings. The Inca monarchs of Peru died similarly.[1]

Chief Nii Bonne in Accra, Ghana, led the boycott against the British colonial administration. As befits Ghana they were very civilized demonstrations, largely eschewing violence but involving the boycotting of shops and a few other things. Chief Nii Bonne was a warm and kindly character but he somehow or other managed subsequently to fall foul of the reigning political party. Thus when his new American car was taken off the ship standing off Accra the CPP had arranged—so he alleged—for it to be tumbled into the sea in place of being brought ashore by the surfboats. He was clearly a colorful character, so we wrote up his life story for *Drum*. I thus came to know him, shaking his hand on greeting him with that two-handed shake deemed in Ghana to be proper for chiefs, even minor chiefs of Sierra Leone creole origin. In the course of nature he died. His steward died on the same day. The family told me it was quite a coincidence.

A small chief must have only a few retainers killed to accompany him into the next world, a big chief, as befits his lordly pride and power, must have many. Ancient custom in Ghana requires us to pour libations: the ancestors are always thirsty!

When the late chief of the Ashanti, the Asantehene died, we sent a reporter and a photographer to Kumasi to cover the brilliant ceremony. The Ashanti are the great, warlike tribe of Ghana, with the saying: "Though a thousand fall, a thousand come tomorrow." I shall always regret that newspaper business prevented me from taking the opportunity to go to the funeral.

Anyone who was not an Ashanti quit Kumasi, the Ashanti state capital. The *abrafo*, the Ashanti execution squads were out, looking for victims. The nightwatchmen, known as the watchnights, left their buildings and huddled together for protection under a street lamp. No one dared take a taxi for they did not know if the driver had been paid to deliver him to the executioners: likewise no taxi driver dared take a fare lest his passenger delivered him to his death. The Asantehene's body lay in state for a week while people filed past to pay their last respects: the corpse had been rubbed in gold dust or specularite so that it glistened. Gold is the metal of the sun: it is the metal that runs through all the ceremonies of the Ashanti tribe. When the Asantehene takes his last drink upon earth it should be water heavily impregnated with gold dust so that the gold should run through his corpse.

It was rumored that over a hundred people had been killed by the tribal executioners to accompany the Asantehene into the next world. Furthermore the lesser chiefs of Ghana attended the celebration, many of them bringing human heads to roll into the grave of the Asantehene as their customary funeral gift, or so one chief told me. The head represents the whole man, an attitude in Latin called *pars pro toto:* it also represents the soul.

The power of the chief comes up to him through the stool: it is the stool that conducts these magical powers from the earth, endowing a formerly ordinary man who sits upon the stool with his divinity. Before he became chief this Asantehene had been a warehouseman. When we wrote up his life story we carried a photograph of him playing golf with the English commissioner of police, Collins.

In the fishing village near Lagos which I frequented—the village where I had been given the story of the cries made by fish—there were fishermen of three tribal groups: Yoruba, Togo-Ewe and Ga. Each group had its own ju-ju and its own chief. A chief had died, I think it was the Togo chief. I was invited to attend his funeral obsequies. Fortunately or unfortunately I was too busy in Lagos and could not attend the celebration, but my friends informed me that an old man who had been sent to Lagos to fetch supplies for the village ceremony—doubtless special supplies of food and drink—had been killed to start the function in a fitting manner, while four days later two strangers were killed to round off the ceremony. It was well I was not there.

But there are other ancient rites still flourishing in West Africa from that sanguinary but brilliant period of the Bronze Age: the presence of which among so many other witnesses assures us of the close connection between the West Africa of today and the Fertile Crescent of the Bronze Age of long ago.

The town next to Lagos and inland from it is called Abeokuta, which means in Yoruba "in the shadow of the rock." The chief of the town, and chief of all Egbaland, the old *Alake*—he is now dead—was accustomed to throw live children off the top of the huge diabase rock, the Olumo rock, that overtowers the city, in order to propitiate the local gods. The live children were put into baskets before being thrown down. The Phoenicians had the same practice, their live children being first placed in leather bags before being cast from the top of the temple. I was flying from Lagos to London in the colonial days and found myself sitting next to an English subaltern of the Nigeria Regiment. I asked him where he was stationed. He replied Abeokuta. I asked him if he had heard of this bestial practice. He said yes: in fact, on the Friday of the previous week they had given a tattoo in town: rumor had it, he said, that on the Tuesday two children had been hurled from the top of the rock to ensure that they had fine weather. At one time one of the Alake's granddaughters had designs on marrying me. O Hermes, god of the crossroads!

Next to the Cameroons on the eastern border of Nigeria is a tribe called the Jukun. Their king is permitted, or, at least, used to be permitted, to reign for seven years only, much like the old European and Egyptian kings described by Sir James Frazer in *The Golden Bough*. He accepts the honor knowing that he will in this way shorten his life. A few years ago the Jukun king, who had been a schoolteacher, hit world headlines by refusing to be killed, arming and barricading himself within his house. It was noticeable that he died of "natural causes" shortly afterward. This should be compared

PLATE 140
Some stamps made out of gourd skins for Ashanti Adinkra cloth: they include the butterfly or double axe; the concentric circles of the time, or sun symbol; the eight-pointed rosette and the water symbol, all found in the Americas. In Ghana people are named after the day they were born: Kwame Nkrumah, Kojo Botsio, etc. In a number of American Indian tribes, people were also given their day names: not only in Mexico but elsewhere in Central America.[1] The double axe was an instrument of slaughter and, at the same time, a symbol of renewal from sacrificial death: Good Friday and Easter.

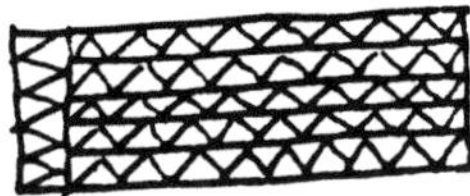

The butterfly or double axe and the water sign from the painted cave on Grand Canary. Bride fattening was practiced on the Canary Islands as at Calabar, in Nigeria, at the mouth of the great trading river, the Cross River. The Canary Islanders were trusting and humane when the Christian thugs turned up and wiped them out.[2]

Designs on the Wagogo earplugs exhibited in the museum of Dar es Salaam carry the religious symbols of the Mediterranean in the Copper and Bronze Ages. The custom of wearing earplugs may have had a single point of origin and been carried wherever the paragons established colonies in the New World and the Old.

Plate 141

Ekuaba figure, Ghana. *This wooden Ashanti doll is one of the common Ekuaba figures, carried by women for the sake of fertility. The ancient earth worshippers' sculptural tradition, referred to on the previous pages, produced Cycladic idols, fertility dolls on the Cyclades Islands of the Aegean that are not dissimilar in form and are similar in function with these in Ghana. The very name Ekuaba suggests the great goddess, the water people and the Latin name for water,* aqua, *which comes through in the English aquatic and aquarium. The spherical bored stone, used widely by the San peoples, and known popularly as the Bushman Stone, was also in use on the Cyclades and in ancient Egypt of the third millennium* B.C. *as well as in South Africa. The San people call it Kwe. I possess a number of these stones. I think Kwe is merely a version of* akawa. *The great J. B. Danquah, my old friend, writes that the original name of the Akan tribe was Okwi:*[3] *surely an* akawa *name, for they were originally matriarchal. The Sumerian Enlil and Ninlil begat the Sumerian moon god Nanna, which is the title used for Akan chiefs.*

to the nine seasons allotted the divine Minos, perpetual King of Crete. In the earliest days of monarchy, the king himself had to die, to be sacrificed, in order to maintain the vigor of the ruler: and, before he was killed, he had to be humiliated and scourged.

Nkrumah caused to be erected outside the Legislative Assembly in Accra a fine statue of himself, bought off an Italian sculptor, which described him as "the Founder of the Nation." The ascription caused a good deal of offense at the time so that when the army coup under Colonel Kotoka and Major Afrifa relieved Ghana of a dictatorship that had become burdensome in the extreme, the statue outside the assembly was overturned and broken. Now, the interesting point is that the ground was then excavated under the statue to find out if a human being had been killed as a foundation sacrifice to be buried under the monument. In fact there was no skeleton but the search showed that belief in this ancient custom, which pre-Columbian America used to practice, was in West Africa still alive and well.

Among the Yoruba there is a masquerade called an *Egungun.* It comes out at night; the members of its cult live near the palace of the Oba of Lagos. The word in Akkadian for the great gods is *igigi.* The chief of the Egungun cult is called the *Bali,* whom I at one time knew. *Bali* is also the old Akkadian name for king. The Akkadian word for high priest is *Sangu mah;* the Bantu word for the medicine man, the ju-ju man or woman is *sangomah.* The same word is used by blacks in New Guinea. If you as a non-cult member touch the *Egungun* or reveal its secrets you must die; as Uzzah had to die in the Old Testament for touching the Ark of the Covenant. Quite recently the *Egungun* was dancing at a festival. One of the priests was sitting out with friends watching it. He left his friends casually saying that he must go and dance. This remark was overheard by another cult member. The speaker was arraigned before the chief of the sect for imparting its secrets and he then denied what he had said. A few days later he was dead. I made the chairman of the *Egungun* society a director of my Nigerian publishing company!

PLATE 142
A Cyladic idol for comparison with the previous figure. In Ghana, as with certain North American Indians,[4] there is a belief that man lived within the earth before he lived on the earth: surely part of the matriarchal religion. With certain tribes in Ghana, they claim that they emerged from a hole in the earth. When important buildings were erected—as with the Forum in Rome—it used to be the practice for humans to be buried alive underneath as foundation sacrifices. The Muisca Amerindians of Colombia had a "custom of driving the main supporting piers of their palaces into the earth through the living bodies of young girls. The use of human flesh and blood was thought to ensure the solidity and safety of the structure."[5]

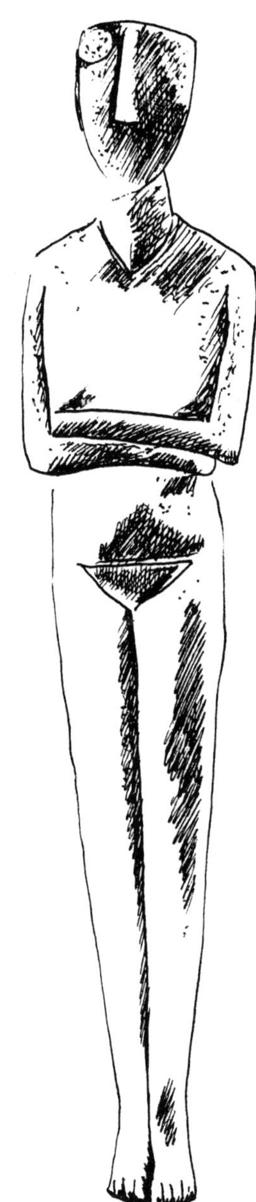

The Ewe tribe worship the God Yehve, a name not unlike the Hebrew Jahweh. Recently there was a court case when some fishermen from Keta were put on trial for sacrificing a man to the sea god in order to improve the fishing. The Ewe also follow the Semitic practice of sending their daughters out as prostitutes working for their god. The Phoenicians also used to charm the sea with human sacrifice. The Efik of Calabar claim an Oriental origin, from Palestine or Egypt. They claim monotheism; like the Jews they carry with them the Ark of God; they have a secret society called *Ekpe,* which was originally a woman's society.[2]

The practice of god eating, which we have already discussed and which we find in Mesopotamia at least as early as the time of the Creation, has led to one of the most widespread forms of human sacrifice in Africa, the trapping of a victim and then eating the parts that are cut from him while he is alive. This is to bring success and power, to acquire his life force. This practice is widespread in West Africa and is also found as far south in Africa as Lesotho. In the early days of my publishing in Nigeria, a singer, Nzimanje, was found murdered in Lagos. Our reporter wrote a story about the murder, recording the gossip in town that his tongue—for he was the most popular singer—had been sold to a leading politician who coveted the singer's mass following. Whatever the truth of the rumor—it was never proved in court—the rumor itself suggested belief in the efficacy of these practices.

The scale on which these ancient forms of human sacrifice still occur in Africa can be seen when the chief in the eastern town of Abakaliki, who was also head of the secret *Odozi Obodo* society, was brought to court and hanged for the ritual murder of some 450 people.

For a happy relic of the past let us move to the island of Lamu off the Kenya coast. It bears the same name as the Babylonian goddess of the sea, which may be fortuitous but certainly the island customs would not look out of place beside the temple of Ashtarte. The Masai name for God is *Enki,* the same as the name of the sea god of Sumerian Eridu; while the Kikuyu and other tribes use *Ngei,* merely a corruption of *Enki.*

In the *War Against Jugurtha*[3] Sallust describes how in a boundary dispute between the Greek citizens of Cyrene and the Carthaginians it was agreed that the boundary should be affixed at the point demanded by the Carthaginians provided two citizens of Carthage, the brothers Philarni, consented to be buried alive there. This they volunteered to do out of patriotism and the Carthaginians erected an altar at the spot where they were so buried.

Almost all these so-called African customs will have been based on foreign customs introduced by white men from abroad a long, long time ago: i.e. during the periods of sea travel that we are discussing. For in the ancient world the idea of Creation and the idea of Sacrifice seem to have been, for many peoples, inseparable.

14. The Philosophy of the Dogon Tribe of Mali; Its Connection with the Fertile Crescent

"Is there anything whereof it may be said, See, this is new? It hath been already of old time, which was before us."

ECCLESIASTES I:9

Professor Marcel Griaule, assisted by Germaine Dieterlen and a team of collaborators, undertook an intensive study of the philosophy and religion of the Dogon tribe, a group living around the Upper Niger, which had previously been considered as somewhat backward. The team investigation has taken place over a period of some thirty years with the active assistance of the Dogon tribal elders. Professor Griaule looks on this philosophy as one of the roots of African civilization. He also appreciates—and in this he is almost alone—that the Dogon have retained one of the cosmologies of the ancient world of the Fertile Crescent: he understands the profound significance of this fact, while despairing of his ability to persuade others of its truth.

Amma, he says, is the name of the Dogon supreme sky deity. In time Amma married Earth. He spoiled his first creation but made a success of the second. He gave birth to a twin god called Nummo, who was the god of water, and who was half human and half serpent. Nummo's symbol is an undulating line, which represents Nummo in motion. Professor Griaule does not mention that this is also the Egyptian hieroglyph for water and that the twin Greek gods, the Dioscuri, were also represented as half human and half serpent. One was a son of the Greek sky god. The name for the Dogon sky god Amma should be compared with the Mesopotamian sky god Ana: the Dogon Nummo with the Mesopotamian Nammu.

Nummo in his turn gave birth to eight spirits, or rather four twin spirits, each of whom is bisexual. It is to be noticed that tradition says that the civilization of ancient Egypt was started by eight creative spirits operating in the marshes of the Nile who were symbolized by four frogs, and four serpents. The number eight represents the waters from which the light of Creation dawned. The life force of the earth is water, the Dogon believe. Water also produces copper. The Dogon knew that gold is the younger brother of copper (an awareness that the use of copper came before the working of gold takes us back to 4000 and 5000 B.C.). Nummo gave copper to man.[1] The supreme deity first thought and then designed Creation. But it was necessary first to speak the Word for Amma's Creation to occur. Thus the Word and water were all-important to Creation. The Dogon believe,

PLATE 143
HORNED HELMET FROM BURKINA FASO, THE MOSSI TRIBAL AREA. *This bronze mask carries horns on the helmet. Horned helmets were a sign of divinity*[1] *in early Anatolia, Mesopotamia and the Levant. For the rest he carries the semicircles, religious symbols widely carried on West African bronzes, symbolic of the sunrise. The pharaoh used to be addressed as the sunrise. The sun god in Mesopotamia never achieved the importance that he held in Egypt.*[2]

PLATE 144
THE BRONZE HORSEMEN OF BURKINA FASO. *Burkina Faso is one of the few parts of Africa to produce bronze horsemen—along with Benin, Chad and the northern Cameroons—whose horsemen appear to belong to a brave but later period. These pieces go back to a time when there were no stirrups. It was the invention of stirrups in the fifth century A.D. that permitted the development of the heavily armed knight. So we find the rider has leather strips sewn onto his cloth jacket for protection, quilted armor; otherwise he uses a bronze shield and a bronze helmet. The helmet has horns but it is hard to say whether they were intended to be the horns of an animal, the symbol of divinity or the curve of a ship. The rider has a small, spade beard. The weapon in his right hand, perhaps it was a javelin, has been broken off and lost. The horse is a magnificent specimen, the thickness of the reins suggests that he had a hard mouth or an indifferent bit! All these horsemen are probably Mossi. The horns of cattle were associated generally with the moon goddess.*[3]

PLATE 145
MOSSI HORSEMAN, BURKINA FASO. *This Mossi horseman wears a Phrygian or Phoenician type cap. He is small, with short beard and a flat face. The nag he is riding did not belong to him, I bought him separately. The shield carries the water or sea symbol at the top and this mysterious face lower down. He carries a short sword in his right hand whose scabbard is strapped to his left thigh. The pommel on the saddle or saddlecloth is high, front and back, like the traditional saddles used in northern Nigeria today, on which I have ridden.*

as with all people of an oral tradition, in the creative power of the Word. In all this one is reminded of the first lines of the Gospel according to St. John and the way a confidence in the power of water and the Word runs throughout Christianity. From some of the earliest records of Egypt comes the tradition of Creation by the Word, including the tradition of Ptah, god of Memphis. The name Ptah resembles the Latin *pater*, meaning father.

The commencement of things is the greatest secret of Amma. But the universe began—the Dogon maintain—as an egg: this figure of speech means that the physical universe commenced as a giant nucleus and expanded from there. In modern parlance the Dogon favor—it is not too extravagant to say—the Big Bang Theory. Amma is himself this nucleus. The universe is infinite yet measurable. At this point one must consider the Orphic theogony—which came from Egypt—that the universe started with an egg; a later act of creation giving rise to the Ophiones, who were half man and half serpent, the symbol of the matriarchs.

The spiral is at the center of all created things: our galaxy, the Milky Way, is a spiral, as is the whirlwind. Indeed the spiral is at the center of all life, the Dogon say. We must now remember Crick and Watson's discovery of the nature of DNA and the shape of the double helix.

PLATE 146

ANOTHER BRONZE HORSEMAN OF BURKINA FASO. *While ingots would be moved, where possible, by water (land routes as ever being comparatively uneconomic), there is evident sign that a land route across the Sahara was being used by horsemen. The Sahara may have then been a little less forbidding, and in any case Boville, in his classic study* The Golden Trade of the Moors, *shows how the Sahara was crossed in the Middle Ages even as it is occasionally crossed by camel caravans today, which I have watched coming into Kano. I discussed this subject with Professor A. W. Lawrence, brother of T. E. Lawrence, working at Ghana's university.*

This horseman of the Mossi tribe has no stirrups; he is armed with a double spear, symbol of the duality of the earth worshippers; he has a cap or helmet in the shape of a crocodile tail, the crocodile being sacred to the sun, and his shield is in the militarily improbable shape of a diamond, symbol in some religions—I believe that of Poseidon—of divinity. On the shield is a face but whether it represents Heracles or Poseidon or some other totem I have as yet no certain evidence.

The diamond shape in some West African religions signifies the path God took when he came back to look at his Creation.

The capital of Burkina Faso is called Ouagadougou, which, as we have already remarked, means simply the town of the Wagga or Agawa people. It should be noticed that there is a village in northern Ghana called Paga that has sacred crocodiles. Paga is an acceptable variation of Wagga. Shortly after we carried a photographic coverage of the sacred crocodiles of Paga in the Ghana edition of Drum *magazine the crocodiles ate their own priest. The double spear remains a symbol of the emirate of Kano to this day. Double spears were the armament of Homeric warriors.*

The *po*, the Dogon word for the grain of millet, is that particle from which the whole universe is composed; it is, as it were, the atomic particle. Life placed within this tiny grain is in a kind of fermentation; in the interior of Amma (i.e. the universe), many things ferment. Amma's material is limited and thus matter must disintegrate as well as be created: a balance must be maintained between the two. The end of man is implicit in his beginnings: the end of the universe was implanted in it from the start, all events are linked together in the unfolding of universal history. Compare the atomic particle of Epicurus, *poites*, with the Dogon atomic particle, *po*.

This is the universe in which man must operate. The Dogon lines up the bed in his bedroom north and south because this is the way the earth lies as it were, the points on which the earth pivots. When the Dogon are buried their bodies are laid with the head to the north, as were bodies in predynastic Egypt. The bodies of women are laid on the left side, those of men lie on their right. Of course, almost worldwide the left side is sacred to women, the right side to men; this little matter alone is evidence of almost universal contact.

Houses are normally square but those set aside for menstruating women

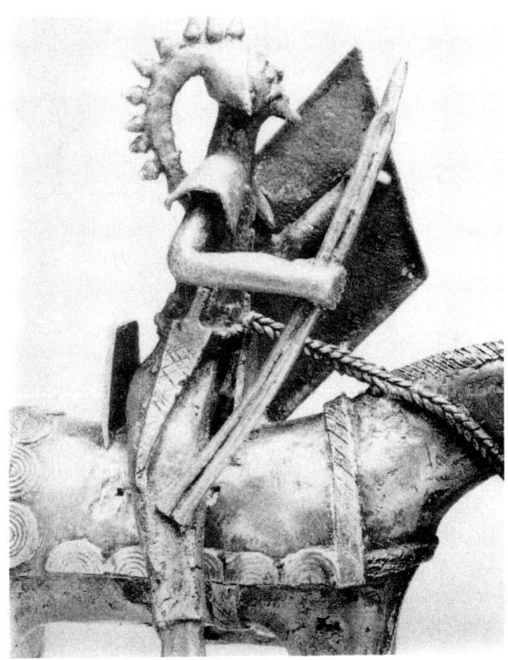

PLATE 147
Closeup of the double spear of the previous figure. Notice the concentric arcs on the saddlecloth and the lozenge-shaped shield. That lozenge shape, according to the Dogon, is the shape of God's path when he returned to inspect his Creation.

are round to resemble the womb. A village should be built in the form of a square running from north to south like a man lying on his back, with the streets going either from north to south or from east to west. At the north is the council house, built on the chief square, which is the symbol of the primal field. It is worth noticing that in Mexico the stepped temples or ziggurats sacred to the sun god are nearly all on a square base, but that of Cuicuilco, sacred to the earth mother, Cui, is circular.

Death was brought into the world by a serpent. The serpent was actually an old man who had turned into a serpent. Having become a spirit he should have spoken the spirit language, the Dogon insist, but he broke the prohibition, speaking to the Dogon in their own tongue: so the serpent had to die and after it all men had to die. This is not altogether unlike the narrative of how the serpent brought death into the world contained in the book of Genesis.

A skirt of red fibers is properly for women. The sun is female, as it is in Japan, Germany and Ugarit. The sun is molten copper, which is why solar rays are called *menndi* (copper water). *Mendi* is also the place to which the souls of dead Dogon travel: on foot, on horseback, on pack oxen and nowadays in packed trucks. It should be noted that in ancient Egypt heaven was called *Khenti Amenti* and that *Amenti* lay to the remote west of Egypt, where the sun went at night. The Mende tribe of Guinea perhaps received its name from this place. Kwame Nkrumah's mother was of that tribe and the Mende are matrilineal: which is why he could become joint

PLATE 148

FOUR MASKED FIGURES WITH SKI STICKS. *These four little figures are from Burkina Faso, probably Gussi. They are not so very different from the figures of the Pueblo Indians of Arizona, where in the irrigated desert old copper mines exist. In both countries men, thus masked, danced the sun around.*[4]

There is nothing whatever extraordinary or unusual about such a connection—if such a connection did once exist—for the early sailors ransacked the globe for metals, always limited, however, by the state of metallurgy in their day, which decided, along with the geographical locations, whether deposits were to be commercially viable or not.

University scholars who smell of the lamp look upon the sea as a barrier without appreciating that for the experienced sailor, capable of living off both sea and shoreline, in the manner of the ichthyophagae, the sea unites, it is the great means of communication, the ocean is one the world over, the skills that command one part of the ocean can command all oceans. Ichthyophagae means, in Greek, fish eater, and describes the peoples who lived on the shoreline, with fish traps, once almost worldwide. Fish traps have recently been discovered going back to 30,000 B.C., as we have noted earlier.

Before the wheel and before the domestication of draft animals, water transport provided the only unarduous means of travel and of carrying goods. Porters go sick, go on strike, above all are scared to leave their traditional tribal areas. Drift voyages on rafts, with supplementary buoyancy provided by gourds, carried the early adventurers across the seas, pioneering, over a long period of time, routes for the more sophisticated watercraft that were to follow. The relative ease of sea travel explains why modern Europe discovered the sources of the Amazon three centuries before discovering the sources of the Nile.

PLATE 149

THE HEAD OF THE SUN WORSHIPPERS' PROCESSION (29 CM). *This is a cheap tourist replica of a neotraditional piece from Burkina Faso of the Mossi tribe. Nevertheless, I believe, it reproduces its original faithfully enough for our purpose. Just as the leader of a Catholic procession carries the cross, so do the leaders of the sun worshippers' procession carry the sun disk, the horns symbolizing the divine sun king. The cowries were early currency. It has also been suggested that cowries resemble vulvas and would represent fertility. West African cowries came from the Indian Ocean and so, necessarily, imply sea contacts across long distances.*

Sun worship was monotheist yet trinitarian. God was present in three forms: in the form of the Father, whose symbol was the sun disk, in the form of the Son, which was the king, the political boss; as the Holy Ghost, which was the real god who ran through the universe like honey through the honeycomb—to use the Stoic simile. Yet there was with sun worship only one God as in Christianity. In some sects the trinity was interpreted with the Mother Goddess, Santa Sophia, as the Holy Spirit. This is to be compared with the Egyptian family trinity of Osiris, Isis and Horus and the various Canaanite family trinities of father, mother and son in other city-states.

So widely in Africa was sun worship carried that in the Bantu group of languages that now covers three parts of Africa south of the Sahara, the word for the sun and the word for God is sometimes either related or identical. Heracleitus of Ephesus said, "This ordered universe [cosmos] which is the same for all, was not created by any one of the gods or of mankind, but was ever, and is, and shall be Ever-Living Fire."[5] The sun was the great marker of time and the god time, Chronos, was inevitably trinitarian: past, present, and future, but yet one God.

president of Guinea. *Amenti* is the Coptic for Hades. Can this be chance?

Now the seventh Nummo, according to Dogon tradition, was the Master of Speech, the Master of the Word. He sacrificed himself—the Word is the most important thing there is—for mankind. He might have expressed it, the Dogon priest said, in the words: "My head is fallen for man's salvation." He permitted himself to be eaten for man's salvation. So the present-day practice in Africa of ritual murder is endemic just because it is looked upon as the divine act. The man who dies lying down does not see much suffering. But the seventh Nummo died standing up. To die standing up, the suffering is greater. That is why Nummo, in order to organize the world, died standing up. For if you wish to reorganize the world, you are obliged to witness great suffering. Let us emphasize that at the start of kingship the king had to die for his people: subsequently the people have had to die for their king.

The Great Nummo are heaven's smiths, although it is the forging of iron, not the working of bronze, to which the Dogon tradition refers. The fire of the Dogon smithy was stolen from heaven, as in the Greek tale of Prometheus. Now, in the days of the working of metals, especially of iron, it is nonsense to suggest that Prometheus or the smith stole fire and gave it to man, for man had used fire already for one million years. Clearly, the fire that was stolen was the industrial technique of working with fire at such high temperatures that metals could be made serviceable: copper was made useful in the form of a bronze alloy, iron could be tempered into steel. It was the god-kings who had developed this technique: the other

PLATE 150

***The King in Reed Armor* (41 cm).** *This royal figure with its sophisticated worldly-wise expression gives every appearance of being equipped with reed armor and a reed helmet. Now, Herodotus, in depicting the long files of the enormous Persian army that crossed into Greece, describes a Persian detachment as being protected in this sort of way with reeds and that the detachment was of Indian origin.*[6] *But it is also worth remembering that Sumer, in lower Mesopotamia, had a reed culture with reed boats and reed houses: it was, after all, almost the only raw material that the Sumerians possessed in their sea-land and they had to make the most of it, along that is with the mud out of which it grew. When the Classical Greeks burned the royal Persian town of Sardis they recorded that the ordinary houses were built with reeds.*

This is yet another figure from yet another Mossi culture in Burkina Faso, the totality of which shows, without a shadow of doubt, how cosmopolitan Burkina Faso once had been.

This figure bears a resemblance to the Yoruba spirit, the Egungun.

The core of this model's spear is made of iron, so these specimens were clearly made later, perhaps much later than the Bronze Age, although the original statue might itself have been made of gold and long since been melted down. Homer refers to the use of a long pike for sea fighting, jointed with rings[7]*—like this figure.*

societies needed to acquire this vital technology and they stole the trade secrets from the bosses. The smithy came down from heaven and revolutionized the world.[2] Because the arts of metallurgy were withheld from the colonized by those early colonists it allows the universities to claim that Africa was the only place in the world where iron preceded bronze.

Aeschylus refers to Prometheus stealing *panteknou pyros*, the fire of technology.[3]

The zodiac of the Mediterranean, Professor Griaule says, can be fully explained from the point of view of Dogon cosmology and metaphysics, and he explains it, house by house, over several pages. Professor Griaule then continues about himself:

> But the European had no illusions about how such an argument was likely to be received by recognised specialists in academic circles. . . . Has it not been established once and for all that the African has nothing to give, no contribution to make, that he cannot even reflect ancient forms of the world's thought? Has he not always been relegated to the level of a slave? Consider the carvings of the great civilisations of antiquity! Where do the Negroes figure in these? Why, in their proper place, among the lesser races! What influence do you attribute to them?

To which Professor Griaule himself makes answer: "It is not a question for the moment of influence exercised, but of influence received and preserved. . . .

"But the discussion is futile," he goes on. "One is lucky to meet nothing worse than sovereign contempt embracing alike the investigator and the object of his study. Unconscious hatred is a common phenomenon."[4]

MAN WITH JAVELIN. *This bronze piece from the Mossi tribe in Burkina Faso of a warrior armed with a javelin, a round shield with the spiral engraved on it throughout, and the pointed Phoenician or Phyrgian cap, should be compared with a Phoenician bronze shown by Donald Harden in his standard work on the Phoenicians, as also shown here.*

Both figures equally resemble the standard Phoenician god Baal. In Hausa, the language of northern Nigeria, a white man is called Baturi or a Tyrian, which was often used for me personally.

PLATE 151
A similar Phoenician bronze figurine of the god Reseph from Antaradus, end of second millennium B.C. Reseph was looked on in Canaan as the god of plague or of war, his name means "flame."[8] *Ugarit, Byblos, Sidon, Tyre, Shechem and Jerusalem had a common language and culture.*[9] *The name Canaan would seem to be associated with the Babylonian name for bronze. For Canaanites the mountain at the entrance to the underworld was called Kankaniya.*[10] *Compare this with the Greek tradition that the foundations of Tartarus, the underworld, were of bronze.*

Examples of the way the customs of West Africa can throw light upon the history of the ancient world are numerous, especially among the pre-Christian, pre-Islamic masonries of the coast. The secret society within a secret society, the Oro cult of the Ogboni, uses a very specific instrument indeed, a bullroarer, to terrify the public in the early hours of the morning, especially in order to make women obey their husbands. In America, the centre of this identical practice is eastern Brazil, opposite the coast of Africa, but it stretches all the way down to the tribes of Tierra del Fuego. The Amerindian Bororo use bullroarers that have been supposed to be the voices of the dead, while the Bacairi use the same word for bullroarers as they use for thunder and lightning.[5] In Lagos, Nigeria, I have heard the patter of bare feet in the early hours of the morning as the Oro cult, with their bullroarer, passed my flat. It took me time to discover in Lagos that the bullroarer had first been used by the women to terrify the men. And that the plague god of Lagos, the Oro, resembled the plague god of Babylon, the Ora.

15. Biblical Creation and the Flood

"The other gods, we are told, were ordinary men who attained to immortal honour and fame because of their benefactions to mankind."

Diodorus Siculus, Book IV

The works of art I have shown here—some very ancient, the majority modern replicas, and others between these two extremes—almost all reveal forms that are of great antiquity: thus you may have a replica either struck or carved yesterday whose shape was first conceived five or six thousand years before; even as a traditional story may pass from father to son across millennia. It sounds very extravagant but that really does seem to be the case. My authentic pieces, such as the harpé, Plate 123, prove that, in parts of Africa, bronze preceded iron as elsewhere in the world.

The reader must disabuse himself of the historical errors, superstitions and pious frauds that his education will probably have saddled him with. The Creation story of Genesis is the conflation of two different stories about two totally different subjects: the first story, the one of lesser importance, is a conjecture about the creation of the cosmos, cosmogeny; the second story is a historical story and it is the story of the creation of Adam or man, anthropogeny. The two were conflated because sky and earth had to be in union for fundamental religious purposes. The state at first was supposed to be the microcosm of the universe, functioning with the precision of the stars—and with their lack of originality!

The story about the creation of Adam is the narrative about the creation of man by God. Now, the Hebrew word used here for god is *Elohim*, a plural, meaning gods. The plural "gods" was written originally in the Hebrew and the plural "gods" was originally intended by the Hebrews; gods, not god: plural not singular, and like much of the Old Testament it is good history, twisted for political purposes like so much of history everywhere.

Now, the gods were not the mysterious divinities of a polytheistic society, they were a group of ordinary men with an advanced technology who had come to be worshipped as gods on account of their benefactions and skills. Originally, Diodorus suggests,[1] this was not of their intention but it developed out of ancestor worship into the system of divine kingship that we know today: monarchs of Africa, monarchs of Southeast Asia, the emperor of Japan still share this common inheritance.

The Yoruba had a story of the Creation at which their founder, *Oduduwa*, was present. The Egyptians had at least four Creation stories; all finish up—if they do not begin with—the name of the one, male, sky god worshipped by the ruling class of that society at a specific date. In every case they are political and historical stories, which become theological by reason of the king or pharaoh being the channel through which the supreme divinity acts and is manifest in human history. So the Jewish story in the Old Testament, the Sumerian story, the Babylonian story, the stories of Heliopolis, Memphis, Hermopolis and Thebes, along with the many Creation stories of Africa; of the Yoruba, the Bambara and the Dogon, indeed of half the peoples of the world, all are different species of the same genus.

The date of the Creation is not a foolish date for the creation of the universe, but a historical date accurately defined to mark the start of the new religious and political order for a specific group of people. This ultimately meant control by a fairly small group of people, who worshipped God in heaven, not a goddess under the earth; who passed property through the male, not the female; whose symbol was a bird for the sky, not a serpent for the earth; who traditionally favored the right hand, not the left hand; who believed in odd numbers, not even numbers and duality; who believed in squares and not circles; whose favored color was blue for the sky, not red for the blood of the menstruating earth mother. The conflation of the two different stories of Creation with different subject matters—the creation of the universe and the creation of man—was due to pious fraud, prompted by the then theological belief that the macrocosm of the universe and the microcosm of the state had to be congruent and one. Each group of people has different dates, necessarily, for when they were incorporated into the patriarchal society. "Thy will be done on earth as it is in heaven." The initial philosophy was one of time as cyclic, like the seasons or the stars. "As it was in the beginning, is now and ever shall be, world without end, Amen."

The Christian historian Eusebius, who relied heavily on the work of Julius Africanus (in five books subsequently lost), gives a date of 5200 B.C. for this major ideological upheaval, and doubtless the calendars of many peoples once began their dating from this particular year. The Ethiopian date given for the Creation is 5492 B.C. Jewish calendars to this day all date from the Creation but set a more recent date to this—a date that of course applies to the creation of man not the cosmos—the equivalent of 3760 B.C. I believe myself that this Jewish date exactly records when the Mesopotamian ruling clans incorporated those particular Semites into the society controlling the four great irrigation rivers—the four rivers of Paradise; namely the Tigris, Euphrates, Nile and, perhaps, Amazon: for Pishon, the gusher, was associated with *bedil*, sometimes translated as tin; but certainly America was known almost universally as the Paradise Land and Bolivia believed itself to have been the scene of the Creation.

It is generally accepted that the name Adam is merely the Akkadian word for red, *Adamu*, a name which symbolizes the uninstructed, earth-worshipping working classes of those days. In Hebrew *Adama* means earth.

The Sumerian text *Atra-hasis*, only recently translated into English, states explicitly why Adam, symbol for the working class of the area, was incorporated into their society by the god-kings. It describes how this working class came to be taught to do manual and semiskilled labor. For the junior branches of the royal family were sick of digging the endless irrigation ditches of Mesopotamia; they had literally gone on strike, threatening to overturn their rulers unless something was done about their excessive toil. Thus local natives came to be brought down from the hills and recruited from foreign countries so that they should do manual work for the aristocracy, who might then live a life of leisure.[2] This is not to be sneered at, for only a leisured class, free of the manual labor involved in digging canals, could have nourished the technical inventions and the intellectual expertise that would lead to further progress: a technological progress eventually shared by all mankind. One of the primary functions of the early priesthood was to be custodian of the calendar. The traditions everywhere point to the fact that the god-kings were blond: Atlanteans, from the Atlantic shores of Europe.[3] The Classical Greeks carried the tradition that some of their forebears had been ordered down into Greece from the Atlantic shores of Europe. With the earliest records of Egypt comes the tradition of Creation by the Word, including the tradition of Ptah, god of Memphis.

The system worked almost too well. The native population that flocked into Sumer, which means lower Mesopotamia only, increased by leaps and bounds. To add to the troubles of the ruling classes, the secrets behind their higher technology had been passed on to the lower classes by rebellious members of the royal family: Prometheus's theft of fire, in the fourth millennium B.C., as we have seen, was not the theft of fire itself, which had been in widespread use for a million years and more, but it was the theft of the technological skills behind obtaining high temperatures for working the various metals, especially bronze. It was the secret of military technology.

Worse still, the caste system broke down when certain members of the upper classes, the Brahmins of their day, bucked the system and began to doodle good-looking, working-class girls. The Brahminical language was Semitic, not Indo-European.

Thus, according to the Sumerian text *Atra-hasis*, the Flood was not a natural disaster brought about by the celestial creator of the universe to punish mankind for its sins by means of an excessive rainfall; it was a flood deliberately created by the Sumerian ruling class. After first trying to thin out the working class by disease and by drought, which led to cannibalism, they resorted to the Flood—in Sumerian called *Abubu*—which indeed it was[4]—and breached the dikes at a time of flooded rivers in order to drown the masses and put a summary end to their increasing trade union problems. They pulled the plug on them. The Sethites drowned the Cainites. The gods themselves first congregated in Nippur, storing their written records securely with them upstream to be out of harm's way. If I have used the vulgar speech in these last two paragraphs it is because it best conveys the meaning of this ancient tale. The terrorism of the bosses has subsequently, from every pulpit, been described as the natural wickedness of the workers. "*Et fuit diluvium.*" "The Flood overwhelmed them."

Now the traditional names: Cain, Abel, Seth, Enoch, Atlas, Heracles, Poseidon, Horus, etc., etc., do not normally represent either gods or even individual men; they generally represent the societies whose gods or totems these were.

After the Flood, when the economic infrastructure of lower Mesopotamia had been destroyed and it could no longer sustain a large population, survivors quit in large numbers taking their technological skills with them and scattered across half the world. According to Josephus there was a second exodus when political trouble flared up again during the construction of the ziggurat of Babylon, upstream from Sumer. Josephus says specifically: "From that hour, therefore, they were dispersed through their diversity of languages and founded colonies everywhere, each group occupying the country that they lit upon and to which God led them, so that every continent was peopled by them, the interior and the seaboard alike; while some crossed the sea on shipboard and settled in the islands. Of the nations some still preserve the names which were given them by their founders, some have changed them, while yet others have modified them to make them more intelligible to their neighbours."[5] Because the present-day fashion is for historians to be specialists, no one has appreciated that Josephus's description of the second exodus from Mesopotamia, peopling all the continents—which therefore includes Africa—is precisely matched by the African and Amerindian tradition of the white and bearded culture heroes who arrived bringing with them the Mesopotamian bag of technological tricks.[6] The story of the Flood of Noah, of birds sent out from the ark, is widespread across America, taken there by Mesopotamian refugees, a process that is totally understandable. Moreover the word angel in the texts

PLATE 152

STONE FIGURE FROM KISI IN GUINEA (21 CM). *I have met nothing else in Africa to resemble this. The main figure is male and it is, I suppose, God with his Creation, the as yet unborn souls. The ancient goddess of nature in Greece had her body festooned with unattached souls.*[1]

Holes in the figure is a Kisi style. It was a style of the early matriarchal Balkans, end of the sixth millennium B.C., and Marija Gimbutas hazards that the holes were for collecting rain-water, so sacred to the Mother Creator.[2]

It has been the anomalies that I have ultimately found most fruitful. To my eye this piece rather better resembles Mayan art out of Guatemala than African art. But of course we should remember, as J. B. Danquah pointed out in this sort of context, Maia was a daughter of Atlas, and Atlas, part of the time anyway, was African. Maia was sister of Alcyone, the Halcyon, the kingfisher, a symbol of Danquah's own tribe, the Akan. Today, much of Africa's gold is transported to Fort Knox in America; may not something similar have been happening previously in some manner?

did not at first represent a spiritual being, somewhere between god and man, it represented merely a minor scion of the royal and divine family, whether legitimate or cross-bred.

Now that the reader is awake to the religious and political reality of the period, he will understand that the God who delivered to Moses the ten commandments on Mount Sinai was merely the territorial boss giving to Moses the laws he must observe while passing through his territory. Similarly, the God who decided to settle a vagrant Jewish tribe in that area was the local political leader, the god-king. But your title deed to your land is more impressive if you can misrepresent that it was signed, not by the local god-king, but by the creator of the universe. Who wouldn't?

The stepped temple, or ziggurat, of Mesopotamia, is functional, post-Flood architecture. Josephus specifically says so: "Nebrodus, son of Noah, built a tower higher than the water could reach";[7] so that there should be places of safety for the people across the plains of Mesopotamia in the event of flooding due either to natural causes or to acts of terrorism (on whosoever's part). Before the Great Flood c. 3116 B.C. Mesopotamian architecture had resembled much more closely our present-day ecclesiastical or commercial architecture (for example, Eridu and Erech Temples, Plate 232). So while the religion itself reconciled the worship of the sky father and the earth mother, specifically in the annual festival of the hierogamy, the architectural style was also a response to the immense cultural shock occasioned by the flood and the fear arising from vulnerability to purposeful flooding, the flooding possibly being repeated by disgruntled elements in the nation.[8]

So where the ziggurat was taken by Mesopotamian refugees around the world, to Egypt, to Zeeland in Denmark, to Southeast Asia, to certain Pacific Islands but, above all, to Peru and Mexico, there the story of the Flood, of the Temptation and the Fall was carried, and the Paradise Land—to the Polynesians the land of *Matang*, from which some of their ancestors had fled—remained to haunt them. In this study Adam, in historical fact,

PLATE 153
Part of a complicated pot stand from Tell Agrab, Early Dynastic II in Mesopotamia. I think it represents the "Master of the Animals."[3] In America, the same "Lord of Beasts" is found among certain Guianese tribes[4] and with the Tupian Korupira.

From Torslunda, Öland Island, Sweden: a sixth century A.D. *design, seemingly of this traditional subject.*

The Egyptian hieroglyph for the town in Upper Egypt called Kusae.

Soft-stone carving form Kisi. I bought this crudely executed stone figure from Kisi in Guinea because it seemed to represent the earth mother between two heraldic lions: sometimes the earth mother was so represented, sometimes her consort and son—the Master of the Animals. I include examples from ancient times for comparison of both.

The animals appear to be swallowing her arms up to the shoulders. Guinea is the home of the important African religious shrine of Kankan of which both Dr. Kwame Nkrumah and the second premier of Sierra Leone, Albert Margai, were devotees.

Its customs may be sanguinary. Kisi was the Sumerian name for the town known to the Bible as Kish. Next to it is the Egyptian hieroglyph for the town in Upper Egypt called Kusae. J. B. Danquah wrote about god eating in Ghana: it was also practiced in the Americas.

Plate 154
The Cretan goddess, mistress of the animals, depicted between two lions. Cretan belief was that everyone possesses two souls, one human and one animal. I believe this matriarchal belief, shared with a tribe of the upper Amazon, underlay the Egyptian belief in gods with human figures and animal heads. I think perhaps that the Neolithic practice of hunters and their shamans dressing up as animals underlay this matriarchal belief. The Disana, a small Amerindian subtribe of the Tukano Indians who live in the Colombian northwest Amazon, use the bullroarer, like the Oro cult of the Yoruba of West Nigeria, believing it to be the voice of the power of the sun; use feathered headdresses that they liken to the sun's rays; employ a Master of the Animals whom they call Vai-Mahse, who negotiates with the shamans of the surrounding tribes as to who shall have to die in order to maintain a balance between the human and animal populations.[5] *They also believe art to be the highest form of communication.*[6] *The Master of the Animals is an insatiable satyr. As in the Old World, the color of the earth is red, the color of fecundity and the blood of living beings.*[7] *The jaguar represents male energy; the serpent, the anaconda, represents female energy as in the Old World. The Aztecs also believed in the Lord of the Beasts, and that every human had an animal alter ego. This belief, originally preceding the civilization of Egypt, may explain the Egyptian gods with animal heads. The Master or Mistress of the Animals was found in ancient America, Asia, the Middle East and Europe.*

From Sutton Hoo, East Anglia, Britain (top right): a design that seems to portray the traditional Master of the Animals, though of a much later date.

Cretan goddess

Sutton Hoo

was actually expelled from Eden. Both sides of the ocean carried stories of a Paradise, of there being an Eden, of there being the land of eternal youth, of there being the abode of the blessed. As often as not, it refers to the Americas. The phraseology of the Far East and of Ireland in this matter is identical. For, throughout the irrigated areas, once the land was leveled and the canals dug, you could indeed refer to "the spontaneous harvests of the Age of Gold."

There is a curious story recorded by Garcilaso de la Vega. Archaeologists have recorded from the Far East bones of an extinct species of human being, *Homo giganticus*, fourteen feet tall. De la Vega passes on to us a Peruvian story of the arrival on the shores of Peru in ages past, in huge reed rafts as large as big ships, men so big that an ordinary Peruvian reached only up to their knees and the giants' eyes were as big as small plates.[9] It is a story of maritime contact that possesses a peculiar interest of its own, and should, I think, be followed up.

Identity of musical instruments and musical forms in very different parts of the world provide additional arguments for diffusion. The late Hugh Tracey, whom I knew, points out that the Chopi on the southeast coast of Africa use a xylophone and a seven-note scale with it in which there are no semitones. He points out that this equitonal scale is highly artificial and is an astonishing one for anyone to use: yet the identical scale is also used in Siam and by the West African Malinke tribe north of the Ivory Coast. The musicologist Curt Sachs wrote: "To those who, during many years of work, have observed time and again how the rarest cultural forms . . . occur in widely scattered parts of the world" with both the symbolic and the functional aspects preserved, it presents a great picture of world-circling cultural kinship, created over thousands of years by man himself.

16. The Mesopotamian Tradition About Atlas, Alias Seth and Set

Atlas "knew the sea in all its depths."

Atlas "perfected the science of astronomy and was the first to publish to mankind the doctrine of the sphere."
DIODORUS SICULUS, Book III

The Egyptian dossier on Seth or Atlas is sketchy, like all Egyptian records. For the destroyers of records have made good havoc. The Mesopotamian tradition comes to us not only through Genesis but through a variety of other Middle Eastern sources, fragmentary and difficult of interpretation, yet they help to bulk out the story. I shall use in this chapter Jewish, Christian and Gnostic literature, supported by the *Nag Hammadi* texts.

Adam and Eve—Eve stands for the earth mother, the mother of all living things, the original working class of Mesopotamia after the sky worshipper's revolution—begat three children as we all know: Cain, Abel and Seth. Cain and Abel, the record says, were twins. These so-called children represent different peoples. The Cain people killed off the Abel people, the farmers killing off or driving away the bedouin. But the Cain people were rebellious and it was therefore they, the texts say, who were drowned in the Flood.

The Seth people were thus the survivors. Mankind was descended from Seth. This means in effect not from the blood of Seth, for amongst other good reasons the Seth people were few in number. Rather the Seth people carried the civilization of Mesopotamia and Egypt around the world: in this cultural sense mankind was descended from Seth. The Seth people first appear in history as Libyans; but we can trace these red-headed Libyans to Celts and Nordic forebears from the Atlantic shores of Europe, who had taken over North Africa to cash in on the carrying trade.

PLATE 155
THE AKWANSHI AND ATL STONES OF THE CROSS RIVER. *In the Ogoja province of eastern Nigeria near the Cross River were to be found some 295 standing stones, some in phallic form with human portraits and geometric shapes carved onto them. They stand variously from two to six feet high.*

The peoples inhabiting this area, the Ekoi, were the users of the Nsibidi script, the only indigenous script in use in Africa south of Ethiopia.

These portrait phalluses and standing stones resemble the figures erected to the Greek god Hermes and to the Egyptian Thoth, as tradition has described them for us.

The spiral, the sun circle, the double axe and the Maltese cross carved upon some of these stones were also the symbols of Bronze Age religions. The apparent tears below the eyes resemble similar cicatrices upon statues in Peru, known popularly as the weeping gods of Peru. The ancient tradition said that the Creator wept as he was creating and his tears were turned into men and women.

The names Akawa and Atl resemble the names of Copper and Bronze Age sea people: to wit, the Heracles or matriarchs and the Atlas sea peoples. The figures themselves are clearly related to the terra-cotta idols from the upper Niger in Mali. The notion of Creation was that of the male god-king turning human savages into full human beings, depicted thuswise in America, in Greece and in West Africa. In Calabar, at the mouth of the Cross River, the Efik tribe carried with them the Ark of God, like the Jews; they believed that every human being had a soul in an animal, as in Crete and along the Amazon; they believed that witches could travel around at incredible speed, as in Europe; and that wives and servants should be killed to accompany dead kings, as in America, Africa, and the Fertile Crescent.

Seth's character is divine: this means that the kings of the Seth people were god-kings; Seth himself—the story goes—was a god. To the Seth people, alias Atlas—fire was divine and symbolized Seth's worldwide rule. Fire was a fragment or aspect of the sun, fire was divine because to the Seth people the sun was divine. The crocodile symbolized the ancient solar deity and was called in Egypt *Sebek* and in the ancient language of Mexico, Nahuatl, *Sepek*, as we have already seen.

Seth gave birth to Enoch, according to the Egyptian historian Manetho, 1,282 years after the Creation. This means that the Enoch people, an offshoot from Seth, began an independent existence at this date: around 2480 B.C. if the latest of the dates for Creation is intended, and if year here means a solar cycle not a lunar cycle.

Seth is associated with the idea of the Resurrection. The Greek word for resurrection, *anastasis*, is said to contain the root *Set: anasetasis.* Seth is also called Shath, which symbolizes the reincarnation of the spirit.

Cain invented weights and measures. His offspring Tubal-cain invented metallurgy, the traditional books tell us.

According to Jewish chronology, Adam was 130 years old when he begat Seth; according to Greek chronology he was 230 years old. So that if we take the approximate Mesopotamian date for the creation of Adam of 3760

PLATE 156
WEEPING FIGURES FROM NORTH AMERICA. *Weeping figures are a common feature in the art of the south of North America and in ancient Peru as, also, in some of the art of West Africa.*[1]

A phallus portrait (right) made in terra-cotta from Pacoval, Brazil (Bernardo da Silva Ramos, Fig. 377). It should be compared to Plate 158.

PLATE 157
Another Akwanshi or Atl stone. A protuberant navel is a feature of much African carving, it emphasizes the point at which the mother feeds her powers into the child. Human sacrifices used to be made to these Akwanshi stones.[2] *Notice what appear to be tears below the eyes. I have looked at some of these figures in the Lagos museum.*

The Egyptian tradition was that the Creator wept at the Creation, and from his tears were formed men and women. This was associated both with the Egyptian god Khepera[3] *and from the tears of the sun god Ra.*[4]

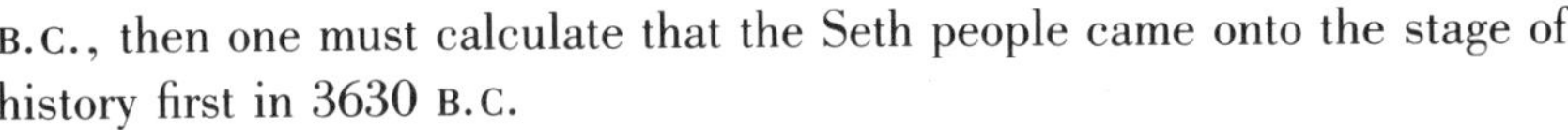

B.C., then one must calculate that the Seth people came onto the stage of history first in 3630 B.C.

Seth means one who drinks water, the Greek word is *potismos*, but by water is meant the fluid of wisdom. For water was sacred to Seth and was looked upon as that which brings the earth to life. This etymology must be compared with that of the Sumerian, Libyan and Greek god Poseidon, in the next chapter.

Seth built the city of Damascus.

On Seth was founded the world, in fact Seth's name means foundation. Other names given to Seth in addition to foundation were cup, plant, seed and resurrection.

Seth can also mean strong and powerful.

Seth's son Enoch is called both scribe and astronomer. The usual translation of the Greek word *astrologia* as astrology represents the prejudices of the translator: the word can mean either astronomy or its decadent form astrology, and astronomy is the correct translation here.

The attributes of scribe and astronomer are also given to Seth. These two attributes may have rubbed off onto Seth from his own offspring Enoch, but I do not think so; they were good for both communities.

This phallus portrait comes from Kisidougou in Guinea. Dougou means town of; Kisi is the Sumerian for the town we known as Kish. Sumerians, they tell us, did not pronounce the final syllable of words. Compare this with the phallus portrait from Peru. I purchased this piece in Abidjan.

PLATE 158
This portrait phallus comes from Chavin de Huantar in Peru. It closely resembles portrait phalluses from West Africa as well as early sculptured figures found at Tiahuanaco. The god Dionysus was associated with the phallus and was also god of the underworld and America.[5] The coastal valleys of Peru were a natural Paradise.

For Seth wrote down the names of the stars and the movements of the stars: without records, eclipse prediction would not be possible. The astronomical teachings of the Watchers—I think this name "Watchers" only means the astronomers—were engraved on rock. In Britain they may well have been recorded on tally sticks, which would not survive, even if kept under cover, for that length of time. Oghams are only tally sticks carved on rocks; for obvious reasons tally sticks will be likely to be the more ancient in time: the name suggesting their use by Atlas, one of the two principal communities to build the stone circles of Britain. Hence other words like tell, toll, tallyman, etc. The Chronos people of Canaan would seem to have been the initiators of these megalithic calendar clocks. The English word "Catholic" comes from the Greek, meaning universal, and has for its root the sea people: *atl*, *thalassa*.

Adam, too, tradition says, possessed books; they were named: *The Book of Wars*, *The Book of Astronomy* and *The Book of Signs*.

The Sethites in antediluvian times inscribed their scientific teaching on two pillars, one of brick and one of rock: if there was to be a flood, then the rock would survive it, even if the brick dissolved in the waters.

It should be noted that the Egyptians also had a tradition that Thoth—whom the Greeks called Hermes—wrote upon pillars before the flood.

Plate 159
The megalithic alignments at Ménac, near Carnac, Brittany. *Brittany held a fair amount of alluvial tin but little copper. Before this area was called Carnac it was called Men,*[6] *perhaps to be compared with the Aryan Manu. The earliest megaliths known are here, going as far back as 5435* B.C.,[7] *approximately the date of the Creation as given by Julius Africanus. I believe this is the reason for the huge investment in stonework, for ceremonial purposes, not as an observatory. Carnac has a greater quantity of megaliths than in any part of Europe. The patriarchal societies spread out from here, financed out of the Atlantic trade, which they had purloined from the women. Perhaps Brittany should look on itself as having been the scene of the Creation. The earliest shaft graves are in Brittany, 4800* B.C., *and start not much later in Britain. Carnac has been described as the Mecca of the megalithic world. I don't believe anyone understands their historical importance. Perhaps the word* dolmen *derives from* men *as here, and* atl. *This celebrates one of the great turning points in history. Diodorus Siculus recorded that the birth of the gods was among the Atlantians,*[8] *and I believe this massive and contemporaneous investment marks the European site. The first male gods were called Uranus or Ouranos by the Greeks. Diodorus Siculus said Uranus was the first king of the Atlantes, a just and pious race living on the shores of the Atlantic. Uranus produced a calendar from observing the movements of the stars and was an able astronomer,*[9] *as he was required to be for navigation.*

Before Adam died, tradition says, he built himself a mausoleum beyond Mount Moriah, which, some say, is the site of present-day Jerusalem.

Eve and Seth came to Adam's deathbed and brought fragrant spices for his food: to wit crocus, nard, calamus, cinnamon and other spices. The plain food of those days will have been much improved by spices so that the spice trade, like the incense trade, will have promoted early sailing: down the Red Sea or the Persian Gulf, eastward toward Indonesia.

Adam was buried in the cave of Macpelah, a double cave on Mount Moriah where he was born, and eight people, in sum, were eventually buried there: Adam and Eve, Abraham and wife, Isaac and wife, Jacob and wife: four pairs like the four pairs of creative gods who began the civilization of Egypt.

Seth had to write down the details of Adam and Eve's life to prevent their being lost subsequently.

The Sethites studied astronomy and geometry. The conjunction of these two disciplines in this Seth tradition is highly important. It shows that the correct translation of the Greek word *astrologia* is astronomy because the discipline of geometry is less likely to be developed for the sake of astrology. Furthermore, it throws light upon the origin of the word geometry. Literally it means earth measurement, and the accepted opinion, as we have seen, is that the discipline and its name began with the need in Egypt to resurvey the farms after each annual inundation: that is, geometry, earth measurement, farm surveying. Yet the association of geometry with astronomy at this most early date is susceptible of another explanation that in my judgment is the true one: that geometry and astronomy were studied and developed together, certainly for the measurement of time and date but also for simple astronavigation and to make out the geography of the earth itself,

PLATE 160
North American phallic menhir photographed at the time of its discovery on the top of what was then named Phallus Hill, South Woodstock, Vermont. This, with others, has since been transported to the Castleton Museum, Castleton, Vermont (Peter J. Garfall). These phallic symbols are not, I believe, for titillation but symbolize the creative power of the male sky god. With it follows the creation of the common people because they then received their souls from the sky god, or so the bosses taught. There were phallic Etruscan and Indian gravestones.

PLATE 161
Phallic claystone talisman from Algeria (after Rossello-Bordoy, 1969). The engraved strokes appear to be North African ogham script, spelling the Punic word Q-F, *presumably matching the modern Arabic* qaf, *and meaning "stand erect." Although phallic stones occur in the Iberian region, this inscribed form from northwest Africa seems most closely to parallel the oghamic Celtic phalli of Vermont. Uninscribed phalli have been considered Neolithic, but this example should probably be referred to the late Bronze Age or early Iron Age. Numerous table knives with phallic handles have been found in the ruins of houses and military barracks of Romano-Celtic sites.*

PLATE 162
EUROPEAN-TYPE PORTRAITS FROM PRE-COLUMBIAN TIAHUANACO ON THE BORDER OF BOLIVIA AND PERU. *Two sculptures of human faces that were encased in some interior wall of the Sun Temple. The faces show the coca* mascajo, *which enlarges the cheek. Circumcision, ritually removing an infant's foreskin, was practiced by certain peoples in Peru, Africa, Egypt, as well as by Jews and Muslims.*

The so-called Weeping God of Tiahuanaco. Compare this with the symbolic dots under the eyes of the Cross River monoliths of Ogaja province, Nigeria. The Egyptian tradition ran: after the Creation of the world, Ra wept and his tears gave birth to man and woman. Harold Osborne, in his book Indians of the Andes, *notices an almost total similarity between the Amerindian and European approaches to sorcery and demonology.*[10] *Huira-cocha, the supreme Incan Creator god, has solar attributes and, also, like Christ, walked on water.*

Carved head from the Third Period of Tiahuanaco, which was formerly encased in the interior walls of the Sun Temple. Allowing for its primitive technique this is similar to those that are found in the semi-subterranean building of the First Period of Tiahuanaco.

so necessary for long-distance trading. When, in the nineteenth century A.D., Japan was opened up to the West, the Japanese concentrated first upon acquiring the Western skills of astronomy, mathematics and navigation. Josephus said: God gave Noah and some other ancients long lives in return for their contributions to geometry and astronomy.[1] And, certainly, farm surveying has no need whatever for a study of circles and spheres.

PLATE 163
THE IDOL OF MALI. *This magnificent terra-cotta figure, suggestive of a phallus portrait, comes from the upper Niger in Mali. Stylistically it relates to the Cross River monoliths on the lower Niger studied by Philip Allison, who published for the Nigerian National Museum in Lagos on this subject. The Niger would have supplied one of the great access routes to the hinterland of Africa.*

Allison states, as we have already seen, that there are 295 carved stones at thirty-nine sites, called Akwanshi Stones or Atl Stones, beside the Cross River in the Ogoja Province of Nigeria, now part of the Cross River State, the only district in Africa, as we have mentioned, that possesses an ancient script of its own. Such hard stone carvings are rare, he says, but fairly similar ones exist on the upper Niger and in southern Ethiopia. The most similar, he says, are to be found on islands in the Caribbean.

When Seth himself came to die he was buried in the Cave of Treasures and there were left in his tomb books containing certain secrets. The term, the Cave of Treasures, suggests the amount of luxurious grave goods buried with him and with his people.

Seth also invented the Hebrew letters. Diodorus Siculus said it was the Pelasgians, not the Phoenicians, who invented the alphabet, but they may be related peoples.

There was a general deterioration in standards after the Flood. Seth himself came to be looked upon as the *semen mundi*, the intellectual not the genetic seed of all mankind.

There came to be two conflicting ideas about Seth: first, that he represented the righteous throughout the ages; second, that he brought on the Flood and the steady moral deterioration that followed it. The conflicting opinions depended upon which religious group the writer belonged to.

This is an example of how the reputation of a man depends upon who writes his obituary.

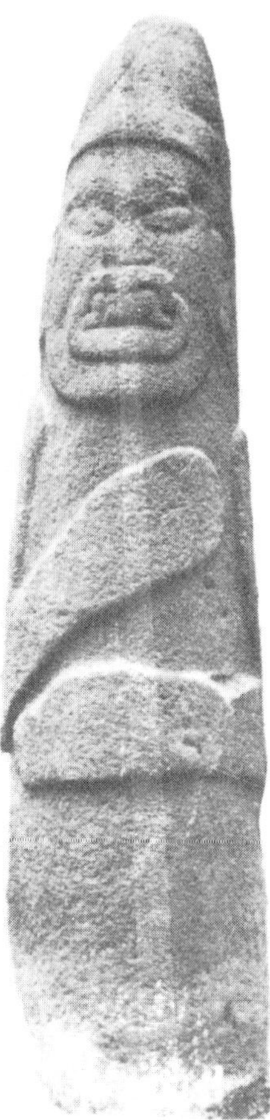

PLATE 164
MEXICAN PHALLUS PORTRAIT *(left), from Huamelulpan in Toltec/Olmec Mexico; compare with Zaire phallus portrait.*

Zaire phallus portrait (right). A crudely executed phallus portrait from Zaire, widely copied and sold to the tourist trade. The circles upon it probably symbolize the male sun god.

The languages of Zaire are Bantu languages, where, as we have already noticed, commonly the word for god and the word for sun are related. These figures should be compared to the rude and ithyphallic Hermae of ancient Greek cults.

PLATE 165

ANOTHER VIEW OF THE ZAIRE PHALLUS PORTRAIT. *The god Thoth was held by the Egyptians to have been their culture hero, one who in predynastic times brought to them the art of writing, the use of the law, the practices of medicine and astronomy, and the use of weights and measures. He was patron of doctors. Above all, he was believed to possess deep wisdom and profound insight. He was associated with phallus portraits.*

The Greek god Hermes was largely a Greek version of the Egyptian Thoth; indeed Melampus argued that all the Greek gods originally came from Egypt.

The images of Hermes, the Hermae, were erected widely in Greece in streets and on squares. They were marble or bronze pillars surmounted by a bust and given further human semblance in the case of the male by the addition of genitals. Pausanias observed that at Cyllene "the image of Hermes, which the people of the place revere exceedingly, is nothing but the male organ of generation erected on a pedestal."[11]

To the Greeks Hermes was the son of Zeus and Maia, the daugther of Atlas. He was also called Atlantiades, i.e. of the strain of Atlas. To the Egyptians, Thoth made peace in the fighting between Seth and Horus, to the Greeks he was the herald of Zeus, and also of the gods of the lower world. He was the god of commerce and of unexpected riches.

This is among the reasons for believing that the phallus portraits of the Cross River, which we know were called Atl as well as Akwanshi Stones, derive from the ancient sea traders of the Bronze Age Atlantic trade and portray and commemorate their dead kings. Related, too, are the phallus portraits of Guinea, of the upper Niger, of Zaire, as well as of ancient America.

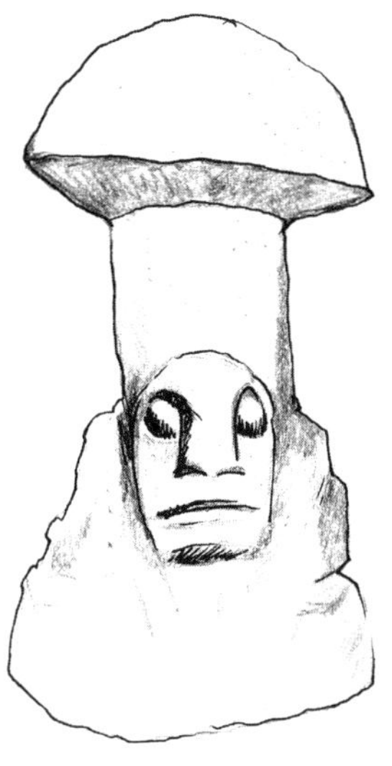

Mushroom or penis stone (left), Guatemala City, said to represent male ancestor worship, as in China.[12]

On the first judgment of Seth, because of the evil seed scattered around the world, the *semen malitiae*, there was needed the return of Seth, resurrecting, coming again, reincarnating in the person of Christ. In fact, Epiphanius stated that Christ was a descendant of Seth. The Gospel of the Egyptians and the work of the Pseudo-Tertullian go further and identify Seth with Jesus himself.

In fact, the *Pseudo-Tertullian* says that Christ is *tantummodo* Seth: i.e. quite simply Seth or Atlas. Seth's symbol was a fish, as was that of the Indian god Vishnu, father of Krishna, the shepherd; not to mention Christ, the good shepherd, symbolized, for the born-again Christians, by a fish.

17. Of West Africa and America

"Okeanos and Tethys [the god and goddess of the ocean] were the parents of Creation."

ARISTOTLE

It behooves us—having followed the developing fortunes of the sea people who worshipped the sun but for whom fire and water were also sacred, people whom we have said were widely based across Africa—now to concern ourselves with their fortunes in the New World. For a fortune in the New World they assuredly made, as well as in Africa.

At the same time as the Hyksos were bundled out of Egypt and their own mother countries in their turn were taken over and controlled by the Egyptians, so that the pharaoh ruled from Ethiopia and the Sudan to northern Syria (as we have seen), colonies of refugees were planted on the Gulf coast of Mexico, in coastal towns now called Tres Zapotes, San Lorenzo and Veracruz. These colonies (as one may suppose from their carvings) included black Africans, whites, Semites, and people who give the appearance of coming from China. In the old Mexican language called Nahuatl the word *atl* means water as it does in the North African language Berber; the word *tepe* in Nahuatl means hill, mound or mountains as it does in northern Iraq, and the word *teo* means god both in Nahuatl and in the Mycenaean language called Linear B. The frequency with which the word *atl* has been combined with so many old Mexican place names, the similarity of Mexican sun worship to that of Egyptian sun worship, Mexican ziggurats being virtually identical with their counterparts in Mesopotamia, conjoined to a host of other similar features conspire to tell us that these are our sea people, in my judgment certainly a detachment of the very syndicate of sea peoples hurled out of Egypt and the eastern Mediterranean by Pharaoh Tethmosis, sometimes called Amosis.[1] In Greek mythology the widespread fighting is called the Titanomachia, the war in which the sky-worshipping patriarchal people, symbolized by Zeus, defeated the sea peoples, which included the Hyksos, known as the Titans: peoples who balanced the male and the female religions, and who were the seafaring multinationals of the Bronze Age.

Now, the Gulf coast of Mexico is tropical, the vegetation is tropical rain forest, the land is swamp broken by lagoons and rivers. It is natural for colonists to select that part of a new world in which to live that most resembles their former home. In our own days, the British and northern Europeans have preferred North America, the Spaniards and Portuguese the warmer parts of America, while Africans now predominate in the tropics. So that while the impetus for much of this Mexican colonization will have come from the eastern Mediterranean, I think we must expect tropical West Africa to have provided some part of the leadership, or they would not have selected an area so climatically unlike Egypt and the Mediterranean yet so similar to the rain forest of the Guinea coast. Thus we find the rainfall in Alvarado is 91 inches, in San Andŕes Tuxtla 83 inches, in Coatzacoalcos the rainfall is 100 inches and in Minatitlán 122 inches: they had preferred a very special environment indeed, closely similar to that of West Africa.

This culture provided the all important foundations for the future Mexican civilization and for subsequent societies in Central America, especially the Toltec.

Our sun-worshipping Set or Atlas people, as we shall see in the bronzes and woodcarvings of West Africa, carry the world on their shoulders (Plates 108–111, 114, 116–119). This is the way they depict themselves. And we have noted how in Mesopotamia the same Atlas people have an alternate name, that means foundation. A certain Catholic friar, who was in Mexico shortly after the conquistadors, recorded his studies of the Aztec Indians in the *Florentine Codex* entitled *General History of the Things of New Spain by Fray Bernardino de Sahagún.* At the start of the third book, in which he deals with the commencement of the Mexican gods, he records this fragment: "How the gods had their beginning . . . there at Teotihuacan . . . when yet there was darkness . . . there all the gods . . . debated who would bear the burden, who would carry on his back—would become—the Sun." It was an earlier rendition of "the white man's burden": I suppose this is what these early Atlas figures were about.

We should note too that white, light-colored people, according to Sahagún, were especially selected by the Aztecs to be sacrificed as a particularly dainty dish for the sun,[2] while at a solar eclipse the Aztecs hunted down men of fair hair and white faces[3] to be an extraordinary sacrifice. This was also the standard practice in ancient Egypt. Neither custom would have obtained if there were not surviving in those societies whites with red or fair hair. Of course, with the Efik at Parrot Island downriver from Calabar, it was albino girls who were especially selected for sacrifice.

I have described earlier the numerous similarities in plants, symbols, customs, scripts that will help to identify fundamental connections between the Old World and the New, so I would rather turn back now to an Egyptian description of these brilliant developments on the American continent at this time, a description passed on to us by an Athenian traveler before the last of the Egyptian archives—the nation that was the muniment room not only for her own archives but for half the world—was destroyed by foreign invaders.

Plato, in his own book entitled the *Critias*, preserved Solon's narrative, which Solon had been given in his turn by a priest from Sais, in the delta of Egypt. This tale said that the followers of Poseidon over very many centuries had built up an empire across Atlantis, or South and North America, based on irrigation agriculture that had eventually become unequaled for its wealth, such wealth as had never been before and it was unlikely would ever be again. They had erected great temples and palaces. In course of time Poseidon had fathered five pairs of male twins, of whom the eldest or principal son was called Atlas. Notice the emphasis on divine twins. In these tales the word "son" refers to a people whose branch of religion was predominately that of the sky father rather than the earth mother, and the society had grown up and developed in the territory of the parent, the colonial power. There may be, but there does not require to be, either consanguinity or a common language for the cultural relationship to obtain, which is expressed as father and son or mother and daughter in the theogonies of this period; sufficient for the societies to be that of metropolitan power and of colony. It is worth noting that the Akkadian word for twins is *Talim*, of the same root as Atlas. The sea god whom the Greeks called Poseidon, the Sumerians and East Africans called Enki and the Akkadians Ea, as we have already seen. It was essentially a Middle East achievement.

I am confident—but it is partly surmise—that the name *agua* in all its forms marks the territory of this Bronze Age imperial power. I am confident that the Poseidon worshippers were partly Sumerian, although they had subsequently had North African bases and bases around the Mediterranean. Indeed Poseidon had also been an important divinity both in Crete and among the Ionians, and in parts of Greece as well as in Mesopotamia. Place names define both the countries and the single ports that the worshippers of Poseidon formerly occupied. But sea people move around in order to cash in where they can make most money.

The name Poseidon is believed to be cognate with the Greek words, *Potamos*, river, and *posis*, drink.[4] Poseidon was god of water, as was Seth. He was also associated with earthquakes, for he ruled on the earthquake belt, and with horses, for the sea people had brought cavalry to the west, with the Hyksos to Egypt and subsequently across Europe.

Both the Poseidon people and the Atlas people had been great sea traders, especially traders in metals. The names of metals suggest that the Atlas people had been some of the principal carriers of copper and bronze. The stem *t-l* is also found in the Greek pre-Hellenic word for sea, *thalassa.* The Ugaritic word for bronze is a palindrome, the letters *t-l-t,* while the Hebrew word is *nechoseth,* the anagram of Enoch attached to the name Seth. The Akkadian word for tin, or tin-bronze, is *anaku,* closely similar to the Hebrew Enoch, while Hebrew itself is a related language to Akkadian. In Greek mythology the bronze man defends Crete and he is called Talus, an Atl name. The Greek name for metal has an *atl* root, *metalleia.* The seaport near the Indus civilization was Lothal, another palindrome of *atl,* as we have already seen, and as far afield as Tibet the *Atl* name predominates.

Also in Greek mythology Atlas is called in one place the son of Libya or Africa; in another place the Son of Asia; and he is in a third place also called the son of neat-ankled Clymene, a lass whose mother and father, respectively Tethys and Oceanus, were sea divinities, and associated with Hades, who ruled in America, the remote west. So tradition places these as sea people, almost worldwide in their range. One Egyptian tradition said that the pharaoh ruled Egypt while Set ruled the rest of the world. At that time it was very nearly a global village, as today—because the Egyptian description was the truth of the matter, simple as that.

In the *Critias* the Atlas people are quite independently stated to control bases in the island continents of America, the western Mediterranean and North Africa; also certain colonies in the Far East. That in the second half of the second millennium they had outposts on the Balearic Islands is suggested by the name of the Balearic Bronze Age watch towers, *talaia* or *talayot.* And that it was a sea people who built these watchtowers is confirmed by the accompanying graves, which are naviform, i.e. their graves were styled to resemble an upturned boat. Let it be noted that this culture resembles the contemporary Sirtes culture of Tunis, as indeed it should if tradition was correct. For the *Critias* expressly states that their power stretched as far as Tunis. It logically precedes the song of the United States Marines: "From the halls of Montezuma to the shores of Tripoli." We must look at the root *atl* in the place names of the Basque country, Catalan, Italy as Atalia and the northeast of the Mediterranean, Anatolia: a combination of Ana the sky god and his offspring Atlas, rather than the Greek for "where the sun rises" as is sometimes erroneously suggested.

In Greek tradition Hades was a person, not a place, a Titan who ruled in the remote west, somewhere far out in the Atlantic. We have already noticed that the Canary Islands provided bases for ships using the currents to voyage to South America and in Guanch, the language of the Canary Islanders, *eheide* means "the ancient islanders in Hell or Hades," i.e. to the remote west of the Canary Islands.[5]

Long-distance sailing largely, but not entirely, ceased at the end of the

Bronze Age so that as geographical knowledge deteriorated, Hades, who had been a perfectly decent ruler down under, where at midnight the sun shone, was therefore converted into a place. Hades, no longer down under, became the place of punishment, the underworld beneath one's feet at the supposed igneous center of the earth, not that rather gladsome stone-rich world that was bathed in sun when the Old World lay in darkness. The Christians could raise money by hellfire sermons using this propaganda.

The Roman name for Hades was Pluto, "Lord of the world beneath." From the unprecedented wealth that accrued to Poseidon or Hades or Pluto—have it as you will—comes the English word plutocrat, someone stone-rich. But as the Bronze Age knowledge of America was lost, Pluto, the American millionaire, came rather to be looked upon as Lord of Hell, the demon who presided over the furnaces in the place of punishment inside the earth, not the rich lord of a country the obverse side of the globe. So from the same name Pluto we derive plutocrat upon the one hand, plutonic or volcanic rocks upon the other: a bizarre combination brought about by the decline in civilization, and thus in general knowledge, after the end of the Bronze Age. Farmers' pitchforks are two-pronged. In hell the devils' are three-pronged to ape Neptune's trident, who had for so long been the lord of America or the underworld.

I do not believe that we should look upon it as unlikely that some of the gold then accruing to these millionaires of America was mined and carried there from West Africa even as happens to the same gold today. And that the magnificent palaces of Crete—island, Homer said, of ninety cities and as many nations—the vast wealth of Egypt, the gold of Mycenae, much was derived from long-distance, ocean-crossing trade. And that the poverty of these areas subsequently was due to the loss of that trade—both American and African trade—not to mention the war that was intended to preempt that economic decline.

To show what the reopening of the oceans meant to the Renaissance, I will quote the economist John Maynard Keynes as reported by the journal the *Economist.* According to Keynes, "the origin and fountain" of all British foreign investment and the British Empire occurred four hundred years ago:

> On September 28, 1580, the news reached London of the return of the Golden Hind. Francis Drake was the first modern British sea captain to circumnavigate the globe. More important, he brought home a heavy cargo of gold, silver, diamonds, emeralds and spices, plundered from Spanish colonies and treasure ships.
>
> His sponsors were the most successful investment syndicate in British financial history. They received a return of 4,700 per cent—after the main shareholder, Queen Elizabeth, had taken her share. Drake's booty enabled

> Elizabeth to pay off all her debts and to invest £42,000 of the balance in the Levant Company.

From this evolved the East India Company, which created, in time, British India and South Africa.

In his *Treatise on Money*, Keynes argued that Drake's huge injection of capital revitalized the economy of Elizabethan England, and the royal investment in Drake's journey was the root of all subsequent British foreign investment.

He estimated that by the late 1920s the £42,000 invested abroad by Elizabeth had accumulated by compound interest to "the actual Aggregate of our foreign investments, or, say, 100,000 times greater."

Characteristically, Keynes argued that it was not just the absolute value of Drake's treasure (2m or 3m sterling) that mattered but "the indirect effect on profit and enterprise; the increment of the country's wealth in buildings and improvements being multiplied well beyond it."

With such a large and sudden increase in the volume of bullion, rises in prices soon outstripped those in wages. But merchant London of September 1580 was jubilant, and England's sailors were moved to seek their fortunes in the Americas, an inspiration that grew into the West Indian and the North American British Empire.

Don Bernadino de Mendoza, the Spanish ambassador, demanded that Drake's treasure be returned. Elizabeth offered him no compensation. Her profits were more than her entire annual tax receipts. As Drake had killed nobody in Spain, she argued, who was to be recompensed?

The infusion of capital into England percolated throughout the entire economy of the country, altering relative prices everywhere. Yet, as important as the effect of the piles of gold and silver was the audacity of the venture itself. The voyage raised the horizon of British capitalism.

The Spaniards called Drake the master thief of the unknown world but the news of his great act of international burglary spread across the face of England like an enormous smile. It is not unreasonable to suppose that financial successes of this sort of order had already been made at our early date, motivating the Copper and Bronze Ages and their worldwide sea trade. Witness the fruits of Odysseus's one trip.

18. The Sculptor and the Unwritten Tradition

Thus men forget
That all Deities reside in the Human breast.
William Blake, *The Marriage of Heaven and Hell*

The area broadly named West Africa, whence most of the African art in this book comes, stretches from Senegal in the north to northern Angola in the south. It extends from the mouth of the Congo to the vast stretches of the western Sudan, the upper reaches and watersheds of the Niger, one of the great rivers of the world. West Africa's importance to this book is that much of its culture is ultimately derived from the early Atlantic traders in copper, gold and bronze.

Camara Laye suggests that, after a few decades of independence, the western Sudan might in the future become the nodal point of a new civilization. The whole area he discusses is somewhat comparable in scale to that of Europe and western Russia.

Along the coast runs a broad belt of tropical rain forest with a rainfall that reaches in part two hundred inches a year; further inland is scrub and thornveldt, tailing off to the east in desert sand.

Across this desert, in the palmy days of Rome, Carthage and Cyrene, traveled caravans carrying ivory, gold and slaves. In the north, Africans have mixed their blood with Moor, Tuareg, Phoenician, European and Arab. William Fagg suggests that the Hausa word for white man, *Baturi*, by which I was always greeted in my Kano office, in origin means Tyrian or Phoenician; literally, the Tyrian people. While in Yoruba territory the white man was called Oimbo, short for hymnbook!

The earliest of these Nigerian sculptural traditions so far to be carbon-dated is that of Nok, whose terra-cotta figures come from around the tin mine in Kano Province and date from 500 B.C. It has been pointed out that it is from the start a polished art and its roots, therefore, must have grown far earlier. The empire of Ghana, founded by the Berbers, stretched from Senegal to the Upper Niger and was powerful from the fourth to the thirteenth centuries A.D. The empire of Mali was at its height under Mansa Musa, who dispatched a thousand war canoes across the Atlantic to seek land beyond the ocean—they never returned—and himself went on a fabulous pilgrimage to Egypt around A.D. 1324, where he distributed so much gold to the poor he depreciated the value of that noble metal. It is not impossible to suppose that he had sufficient knowledge of the destination of both expeditions—i.e. to Cairo and to America—for both to be planned carefully.

On the ruins of Mali the Bambara erected in 1660 their empire of Segou and Kaarta. In Burkina Faso a Mossi-Degomba empire was founded in the eleventh century A.D. Ashanti, Dahomey, Ife and Benin were not without indirect contact with the Mediterranean and the Orient. In Nigeria, there developed a series of important empires: Yoruba, Benin, Nupe, Jukun and Bornu. The king of Benin, the Oba, wore as part of his regalia as Creator a type of coral that comes only from the Mediterranean.

The plastic arts in West Africa, Elsy Levzinger suggests, best flourish in those specific areas where the earliest religion of matriarchy had formerly been rooted.

The status of the sculptors themselves in West Africa was of the highest nobility in the king's court, working at the king's command and risking death if they were to deviate from this royal monopoly. They looked upon their work as sacred, fasting and separating themselves from their people before they commenced a piece, expressing in it not only their own personality but that of their collective, the tribe and its devotions. In this disciplined way traditional pieces may be reproduced faithfully across immense stretches of time. Behind every genuine African work of art there flashes the Miltonic glint of celestial armor.

The approach to the metalworker was different, if ambivalent. In many societies he was as honored as the sculptor in wood, in others the smiths had to live as a caste apart, marrying only within their own groups.

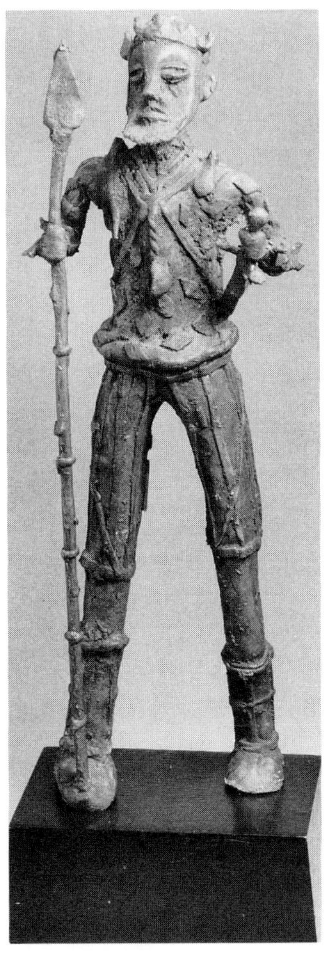

PLATE 166

THE VANDAL KING FROM THE MOSSI TRIBAL AREA OF BURKINA FASO. *This monarch, with the extraordinary length of leg, looks much more like one of the barbaric hordes that passed from Europe into North Africa in the Dark Ages than a local African—suggested by the face, by the spade beard and his general make and shape.*

The half gourd for a drinking cup on his back, the spear, the sword clinging to his side, the clothing fortified with strips of leather, the mattock, while perhaps being standard equipment for the troops, are also, I believe, symbolic with him.

The shoes, which are symmetrical, will not readily tell you by the footprint which way the person is traveling. They are also easier for walking on desert sand, and shoes of this unusual design are so used in sub-Saharan Africa to this day. As to the spear in his hand, we may point to Homer's reference to a spear as "pipes jointed with rings" (Iliad, *xv, 678).*

Historical tradition for illiterate peoples is necessarily stored in the memory, to be handed on by word of mouth. The whole of the tribe's tradition is not memorized by one man; certain families and groups specialize so that the chair in different kinds of history is held by members of different clans. In ancient Mali laws were proclaimed verbally and the bards of the west Sahara were veritable talking documents, the *griots*. Thus to illiterate societies where there were no visual records in the form of written history, the visual record of history in the form of art is doubly significant. This is what this African art is partly about; and its record goes a long way back in time indeed. The *griots* were the guardians of the tribe's history.

The whole concept of the Word, as we have seen already, was as fundamental to the theology of the Dogon as to the writer of the Fourth Gospel, St. John, or to the priest of the god of Memphis, Ptah. The masters of the Word, the theologian-bards, in the Sahel called by my friend Camara Laye "*les griots*," are of the greatest importance to their societies. A chancellery of these theologian-bards carries the highest influence. In fact, in some circles the start of literacy was resisted because reading and writing damaged the memory and destroyed the power of concentration of the people. The *griots* were talking muniment rooms.

To the theologians of the Sahel there are degrees of knowledge: there is the superficial knowledge of their tradition that the ordinary man may possess, there is a deep knowledge that is given only to the select. Confronted by the encroachment of Islam from the north and Christianity from the south, African tradition has very much gone into hiding, gone to ground as it were. If one is permitted, like the research party of Griaule and Dieterlen, access to this deep knowledge one is fortunate indeed.

In sharp contrast to the art of Europe, African art—with a few exceptions as at Ife—is the antipodes of realism. Furthermore, I am confident that little is present for decoration alone. Each symbol and each portion of a good work is capable of deep meaning and of a deep explanation: as often as not in the profoundest religious terms. Thus, because of my own inevitable limitations as well as in pursuit of brevity, the captions to these pieces are occasionally overly tight-lipped. African art has been called profoundly sculptural and has also been compared to music. The world knows no greater sculptural tradition—even if the world does not know it.

What is the religion that has inspired this majestic art, the wonder and beauty of it all?

While there are a multitude of West African religions, the broad principles of Bantu beliefs have been described by Elsy Levzinger in the following way. There is an all-powerful Supreme Creator who delegates portions of his power to lesser gods. Works of art do not depict the Supreme Creator but only the lesser gods. God also injects his power into the first ancestors of the tribe, who may or may not be twins. Heroes in tribal history

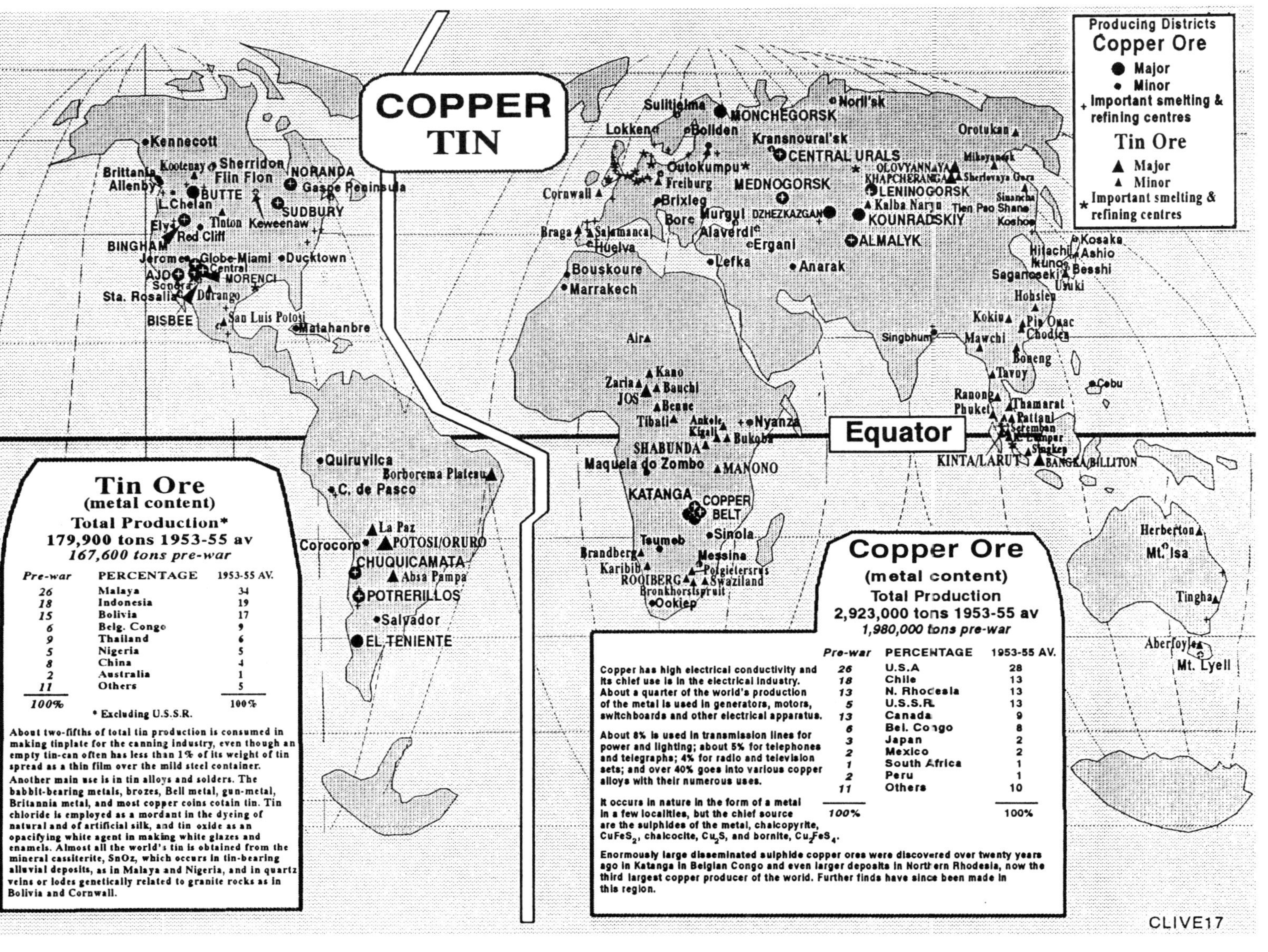

PLATE 167
MAP OF THE WORLD'S COPPER AND TIN DEPOSITS.

may be deified and in many—but far from all tribes—the king will be a god-king, transmuted by his office and his throne and regalia into divinity. The attire of the Oba of Benin is supposed by the Bini to be that of the Creator himself. It should be noted that the Egyptian word for the seed of Creation was BNN and that the Egyptian language did not reproduce vowels but left the reader to add them.

Not only do each of these gods possess their own fields of force, but animals, plants and things also have lesser fields of force. The office of the priest, the king, the ju-ju man is to keep all these fields of force in proper harmony with one another. If ill will or misfortune brings disharmony, then human sacrifice is a way of cleansing the sin and restoring the balance of forces. What Europeans call magic is really just this attempt to restore a cosmic balance by means of human sacrifice.

Sculpture provides support for gods and for the ancestors. In portraying an ancestor, the weight of sculptural tradition prevents realism. Whole villages may be devoted to sculpture as a sort of family industry but among the sculptors a few will stand out for their individual excellence.

In the same way as the individual's force has to be harmoniously integrated into all the fields of force in the cosmos, so the tribe itself must be looked upon as a tight, coherent whole: a unity from the first ancestors to the last children in the distant future; in this unity sculpture also has its domain in quality of a symbol.

In teaching the plastic arts the master has to teach his pupil not only the craft itself but the religious belief behind the craft: in fact the metalworker may double as both smith and priest. In African society, children's games are often a catechism for their religion.

Among the Basongue, human sacrifice was formerly considered necessary to reinforce the power of a ritual mask; this was also true in northeast Liberia and in many other parts of West Africa. Today this human sacrifice is sometimes substituted by the sacrifice of a cow in place of a kidnapped individual. There have been people who specialize in stealing children, imprisoning them on a small farm in the bush and selling them off to such as require a human sacrifice. Today clients may be driving up in expensive Mercedes-Benzes to obtain their human victims.

Elsy Levzinger repeats the academic view that Africa was the one place in the world where the Iron Age preceded the Bronze Age. This cloistered opinion is part of the absurd European belief that in Africa all was darkness virtually until the arrival of Dr. Livingstone and the carpetbaggers of Europe. In West Africa archaeology is in its infancy—it is mostly conducted by tomb robbers—and therefore not too much attention should be paid to the negative evidence that so far no bronzes have been found in association with carbon dates for the Bronze Age. Ninety-nine percent of excavations have been done by these tomb robbers—in their search for gold they are unaccompanied by learned professors.

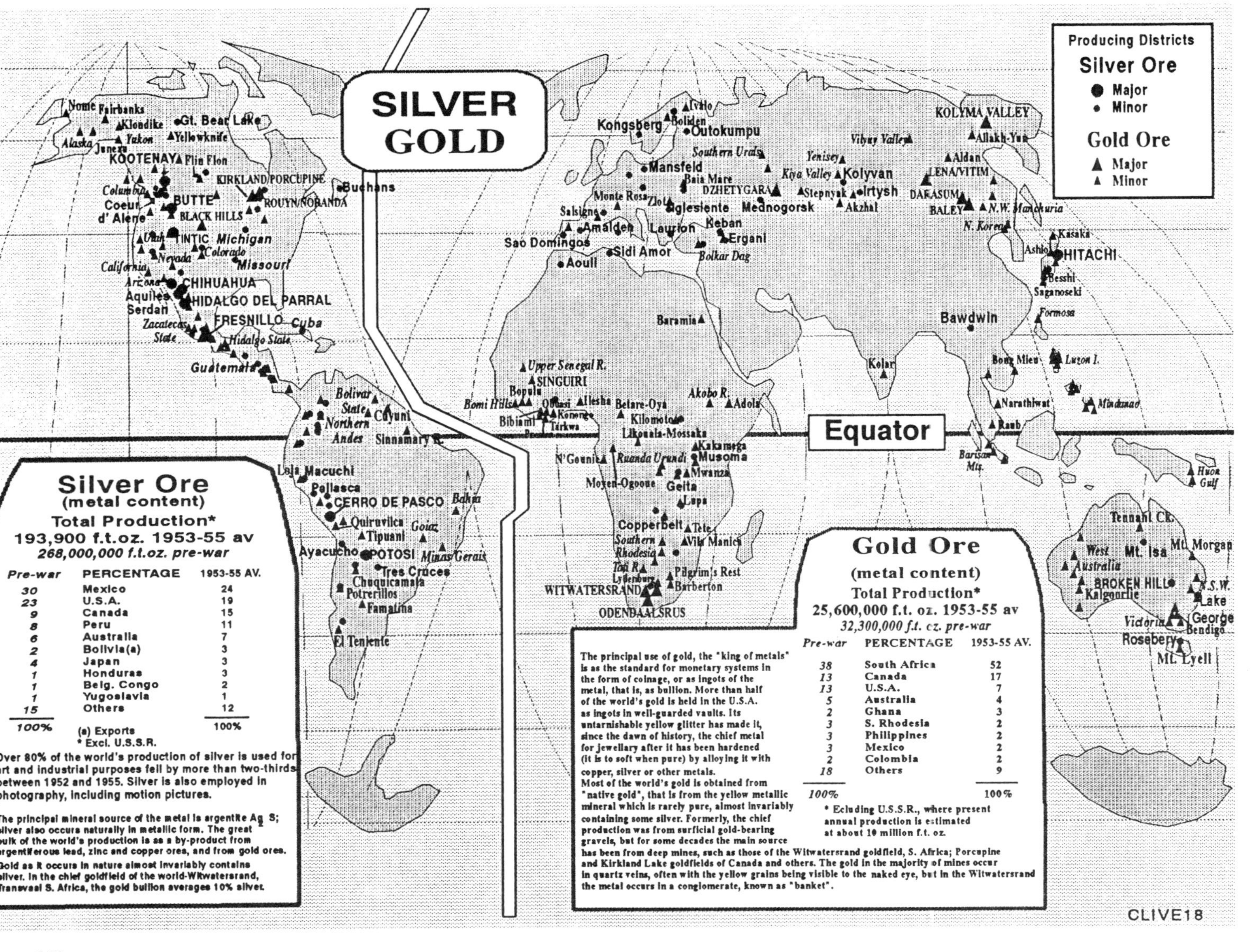

PLATE 168
Map of the World's Gold and Silver Deposits.

PLATE 169
SIX LITTLE BRONZE MASKS OF WOMEN (9 CM). *These masks are singularly beautiful. They come from the Senufo country of the Ivory Coast. They are pendants, made of nice quality metal. The concentric semicircles mark these bronzes as they do so many others in West Africa. The appearance of the pharaoh was identified with that of the rising sun.*[1]

The concentric arcs or semicircles used on a large vase from Kruto-borodintsi, western Ukraine. Late Cucuteni period.[2]

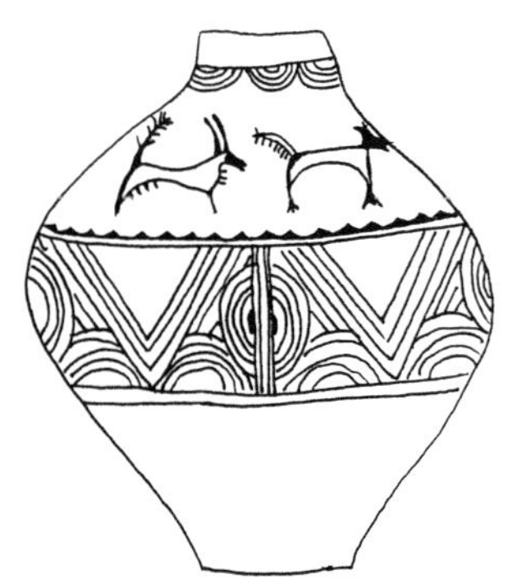

Ceramic from the island of Sacrifices (Mexico) with concentric arcs.

Art provides the incunabula of illiterate societies.

So we have seen that African religions are frequently surviving portions of what were once world religions, that the whole world was partially interconnected in the Copper and Bronze Ages, and that our present religions possess long histories that their proponents have done everything possible to conceal or rewrite. There was an earlier global village, in some partial but real sense. That is why we find Greek words in Polynesian, Hamitic words in Celtic—and so on. A study of the societies on the eastern shores of the Atlantic is not uninformative about the societies on the western. That the Spanish port of Tartessus, on the Atlantic coast of Spain, was celebrated for its wealth in silver[1] should be attributed not to local silver mines—of which there are none—but to the immense wealth in silver of the Americas.

19. The Ashanti Gold Weights; Their Connection with the Indus Valley

"They say the Lion and the Lizard keep the courts where Jamshid gloried and drank deep."

OMAR KHAYYÁM

The English golden guinea, the coin that typifies gold for the English, acquired its name from West Africa. The richest deposits of gold in West Africa are in central-southern Ghana, but there were also small deposits, now mostly worked out, nearby in the Ivory Coast.

The tribe that controls both extensive gold-bearing areas is called the Akan. They possess a number of subdivisions. Winning gold was their principal industry, selling it was their principal commerce, while the gold dust served as their means of exchange. From their trade in gold and slaves they were enabled in this modern age to equip themselves with more and better firearms than their neighbors, and so they latterly increased their power and territory; in addition, they were ruled by a series of remarkable men who built up the Ashanti Confederacy in central Ghana, notable for its complex religious, military and economic organization.

Their means of exchange was gold dust. The gold dust had to be measured. For this they used a small beam scale and a large variety of brass or bronze weights, marked by distinctive shapes and symbols. A certain French administrator in the Ivory Coast, a M. Henri Abel, devoted time over a number of years to their study. He says that there are seven families or classifications to these weights; with each weight divided into a male and female form, and then the king's weights, which are a series that is something like 30 percent heavier than the others. Indeed some of the king's weights are so big as to be terrifying, for they can designate the amount of gold that a whole people must pay as a war indemnity. When M. Abel inquired how people felt about these royal weights, he received the Ghanaian answer: "You do not rub against a porcupine." But of course the difference between the king's and the commoner's weights and also the so-called male and female weights perhaps represents the interest to be paid on the capital when the borrower returns it.

The unit against which the weights themselves are tested is the seed of a particular acacia, the carob tree, so that fourteen-carat gold is fourteen seeds of the carob tree. The Greek word, *keration,* from which the English word, carat, is derived, is itself named after the carob tree. Why, it is asked, do the skillful jewelers of Ashanti and Baoulé bother with these trinkets made of brass when they could weigh their gold directly against acacia seeds? The answer given is that these Akan weights convey a message, they provide information, they lay down rules for each negotiation, they are part of the infinitely complex culture of the tribe, whose imagination and whose life have been dominated by gold.

The weights themselves can be divided into the geometric and the pictorial. It is only with the symbolic and the geometric form of weights that I concern myself here; the narrative and the pictorial weights, while beautiful and charming, are irrelevant to my story.

The first thing to notice is that some of the symbols on these weights are clearly numbers. The Akan were uniformly illiterate, which suggests that the geometric weights cannot be an Akan invention.

Then M. Abel records the tradition associated with certain of the symbols, which reveals that some of these symbols anyway possess identical meanings to the same symbols used in the Mediterranean of the Bronze Age. He also says that the mathematical system distinguishing these different weights is the same as that used in the ancient Indus Valley civilization of India. Later students have suggested that there is more than one outside influence: octagonal weights, for example, being associated with Byzantium. Running concurrently were a number of different systems of weights depending on whom you were trading with.

Many of the symbols are similar to Sumerian or ancient Indus Valley signs; indeed from the sign list drawn up by Marshall, the excavator of Mohenjo-Daro, the similarities are suggestive. The stepped temple, the Egyptian pyramid and the Mastaba certainly appear to be reproduced in miniature among these weights.

It is also worth noting that while *bekwa* is the old Egyptian word and Aeginetan word for gold, it is also the name for the village on top of the Ashanti gold fields; and that the Sanskrit word for gold is *kanikam,* which may well be the source of the tribal name Akan, meaning the Gold People, not to mention the Indian mining tribe, the Canarese of Mysore. Indus names and Mesopotamian and Egyptian names could be related, and the name bekway was also used by the Indus Valley people.

In short, I am arguing that the geometric Ashanti gold weights—in strict contrast to the more beautiful narrative weights—were once not confined to the Baoulé and Ashanti tribes or to the Akan in general, but were used

PLATE 170
A clay figurine of the late fourth millennium from Cernovada, Romania.

Woman's head from Grotte du Pape, Brassempouy, Landes, France, Gravettian, c. 20,000 B.C. Saint-Germain-en-Laye, Musée des Antiquités Nationales.

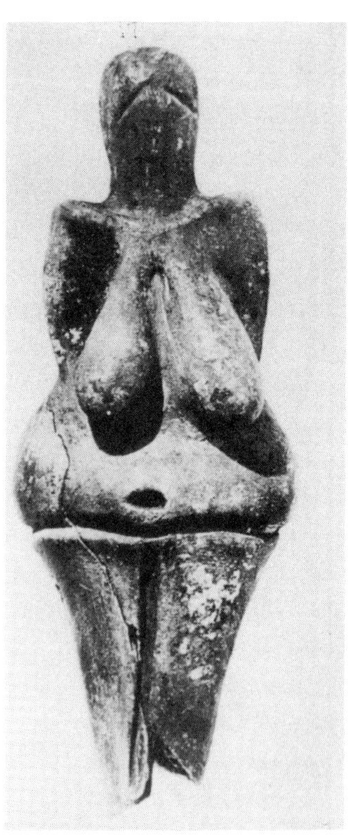

Woman from Dolni Vestonice, Czechoslovakia. Gravettian, c. 21,000 B.C. Baked clay. Brno, Moravian Museum.

THE RELIGION OF THE EARTH MOTHER. *The first civilized religion that we know of—and its carvings go back to 30,000 B.C.—was the worship of the earth mother. If the earliest religion was ancestor worship and there was no system of marriage, you knew who your mother was but you could not know who your father was: which is, I believe, much how the religion of the Great Mother commenced. There is overwhelming evidence that it spread around the world before the patriarchal religion edged its way in. The patriarchs rubbished their predecessors so as to conceal these simple facts. Michael Dames, writing on Silbury, points out that "the squatting [female] figure recurs distinctly and plentifully in North West America, Mexico, Guatemala, Costa Rica, Colombia and Venezuela, and is undoubtedly the dominant motif in Pacific art."*[1] *He points out that matriarchy was the religion of pre-Celtic Britain. Archaeology leads one to suppose that much of matriarchy's early development took place around the Black Sea and then it subsequently girdled the earth. Diodorus Siculus stated that the queen in Egypt had more power than the king, and husbands made obeisance to their wives.*[2] *Isis was adored by all the world as inventress of herbal cures.*[3] *Erech, in Mesopotamia, was described as "the city of hierodules, courtesans and sacred prostitutes to whom Ishtar was mistress."*[4] *In the Stone Age the identity of the child's father was purposely repressed and the wife's brother was dominant in the family. This led to the pretense of parthenogenesis.*[5]

PLATE 171
The city of Ashur on the Tigris, in the Middle Assyrian period, as seen from the northwest. A drawing by Walter Andrae himself, toward the end of his ten-year excavation. These would seem to have been the controllers of the world's metal trade: the New York of its day. Marduk, the sky god of Babylon, was believed to have control over the totality of the universe.[6]

throughout a wide trading empire that had been in business with the Fertile Crescent during the Copper and Bronze Ages. All this is consistent with the overwhelming evidence for international contact revealed in other Akan works of art, such evidence as is exhibited in these pages; with the books of Eva Meyerowitz demonstrating the parallels between the ancient Egyptians and the Akan societies in addition to my parallels.

Sir John Marshall, who published in 1931 the results of the first systematic excavation of the ancient cities of the Indus Valley, while presumably in total ignorance of our West African scene, was not, nevertheless, unaware of the possible connection. He wrote:

> An open-minded consideration of the evidence led, in 1924, to the conclusion that the similarity of some of these [Indus Valley] signs in form [not in use or meaning] to Sumerian signs showed an early connection between Sumer and the Indus Valley. That connection has since been conclusively proved to have existed. An open mind may equally find very close and remarkable similarities between some of these signs and the marks of Arab and African tribes; such signs have also been found at Selima in the Libyan desert. Some will certainly hold that the resemblances are accidental. They may equally be due to a traditional use of certain trading marks which has lasted until a comparatively recent period.[1]

So that the whole of these resemblances may not be judged to be accidental and the resulting inference that sub-Saharan Africa had been linked with the Fertile Crescent during the Copper and Bronze Ages cavalierly dismissed, let us look deeper into the balances and weights used in ancient times.

The small beam scale held in the hand, such as the Ashanti employ, was in use in Babylon for thousands of years. The hand-held beam scale began life, it has been suggested, in emulation of a man carrying two pails from a yoke. It was in use by the fourth millennium B.C. if not even earlier. It was used in ancient Peru also, where the beams were made of bone and they used buckets in place of pans.

Stone and glass, it has been suggested, make the best weights because they do not oxidize. The carob seed was widely used around the world as a measure of these weights. The standard Greek weights, which were kept in temples, were made of bronze. Imperial Rome and Byzantium used brass for weights.

PLATE 172
THE BAOULÉ MASK FOR THE HARVEST FESTIVAL. *This giant mask—its scale is shown by the relative size of the two people holding it—is brought out once a year in the Baoulé district for a great ceremony that is a harvest festival. The eyelids are formed out of concentric arcs, representing that momentous sunrise of the first day of Creation. When I bought the piece, the two characters holding up the mask were described as slaves. Perhaps this has been the fate of many culture heroes once their tricks have been learned and their culture absorbed. The cross is on the right side of the face, the saltire on the left.*

PLATE 173
THE BLACK HORNBILL WITH A HUGE SPIRAL FOR WINGS *(right). This model of a black hornbill, the divine bird of the southern Ivory Coast, carries an elaborate spiral for wings, symbol perhaps of the ideas of matriarchy and eternity. It comes from the Banafara tribe of Burkina Faso.*

BELL, BRAZIL *(left)* ***(3 CM HEIGHT).*** *Gilt tumbago; lost-wax casting, with the incised decoration added at the wax stage. The bell contains a metal pellet. This was made first and was then incorporated into the core material over which wax was laid to form the bell itself. Probably Quimbaya zone, Brazil.*

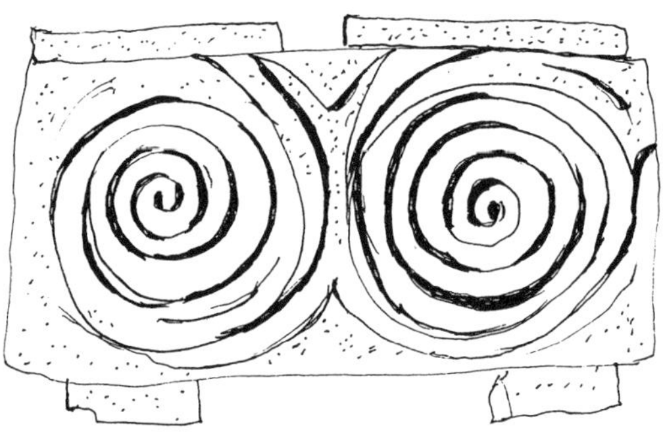

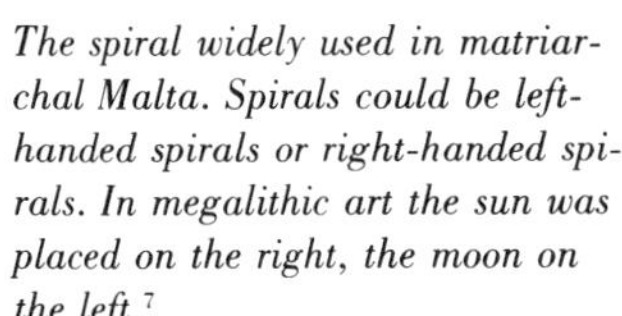

The spiral widely used in matriarchal Malta. Spirals could be left-handed spirals or right-handed spirals. In megalithic art the sun was placed on the right, the moon on the left.[7]

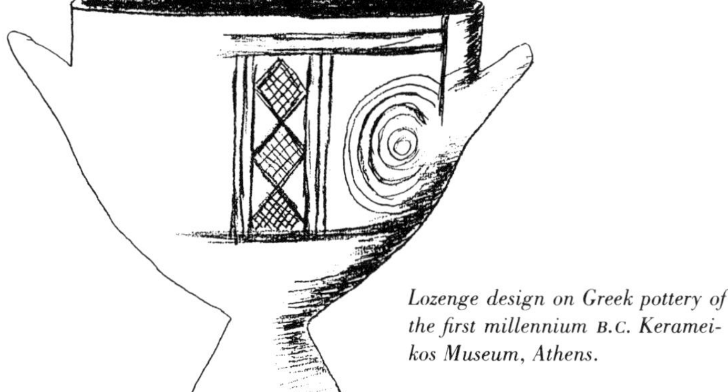

Lozenge design on Greek pottery of the first millennium B.C. Kerameikos Museum, Athens.

PLATE 174

The spiral, along with the diamond shape or lozenge, used as a design motif on ceramics in Bolivia, department of Potosí.

***BANGLE FROM THE BANAFARA TRIBE, BURKINA FASO.** This little bangle carries a double spiral, a common enough Bronze Age motif in the Mediterranean, Polynesia, Ireland and elsewhere for the matriarchal society.*

Here is the same symbol from Amazonia, copied by Alfredo Brandao. The spiral stood for a coiled snake, infinity in time with the matriarchal society in general: with the Dogon tribe of Mali it also represented the fundamental structure of the universe, instanced in the shape of the stellar galaxies. This was before Crick and Watson had discovered the double helix as the shape of DNA!

Now not only do the symbols on the Ashanti weights bear resemblance to the symbols found in the ancient Indus Valley and Mesopotamia, and not only is the mathematical scale similar, but the form of the weights also is sometimes similar to the forms used in the Fertile Crescent. Indian weights included snakes and pyramids; Jewish weights used turtles. Even today the carat weight used by jewelers is in the form of a truncated pyramid. Objects believed to be weights were excavated at Chanhu-Daro in India. They weighed the same as the standard pound of ancient Italy called the Oscan pound. The type of acacia whose red seeds are used is the *Abrus precatorius*, a subspecies of acacia tree native to India, not Africa. The stem of the *Abrus precatorius* also served in India to provide adhesive when soldering jewelry.[2]

It is important to standardize weights throughout a trading empire and also to have standard weights preserved in one place to ensure that the public is not cheated. In Greece and Rome, perhaps also in India, the standard weights were kept in temples. In Imperial Rome they were kept in the temple of Jupiter Capitolinus or the Temple of Castor, which was also a fiscal depot and a sealer's office for adjusting weights.

Octagonal weights were used in Byzantium and by the Arabs; one or other of these trading empires may be responsible for the small number of octagonal weights used in Ashanti.

PLATE 175
THE DANCING SEMITE WITH CASTANETS (14 CM). *This figure looks like a Jew dancing, complete with castanets as if he were a character from the film* Fiddler on the Roof. *It comes from the Baoulé district. The dancer appears to wear a headcloth. His stand has the shape of an oxhide ingot.*

It would be a surprising figure to come from the African rain forest of the Ivory Coast if it was not clearly part of a coherent bronze culture there, admittedly only one of a number of contrasting cultures.

The beard has acquired this unusual shape because the side whiskers are purposely formed as a trompe l'oeil: as you turn the figure to the right, the head visibly turns to the right in the dance; similarly as you turn the figure to the left, it seems to switch leftward. It has the trick of a good portrait painter when the eyes of the portrait follow you wherever you are in the room. This is not an accident. It is a cunning optical illusion on the part of a capable craftsman.

Bronze statue of the Ingot God from Enkomi, standing on a base in the form of an oxhide ingot. Twelfth century B.C. *Enkomi is in Cyprus. Horns were a symbol of divinity.*[8]

PLATE 176
A closeup of the dancing Semite giving a better idea how the tromp l'oeil works.

PLATE 177
THE CHILD'S HEAD CUT OFF WITH SICKLE OR HARPÉ FROM THE IVORY COAST. *This inscrutable figure with a severed child's head in the left hand and sickle in the right bears close similarity to the "Semites" of Baoulé on the previous pages. He has a long beard and handlebar mustache, improbable in an African, and sits upon an African chief's stool. The piece is vaguely suggestive of the Greek tradition in which the Middle Eastern god Chronos cuts off his sky father's testicles with a flint sickle. At that point the divine expression may have been similarly inscrutable.*

PLATE 178
THE HIEROGAMY OR SACRED MARRIAGE. *These small bronzes are sold today to amuse or titillate tourists. Originally, I believe, they represented the annual ceremony of the sacred marriage, the hierogamy, when in the small chapel at the top of the ziggurat the sky god came down and fertilized the virgin. Herodotus describes in detail how the ceremony was still being enacted in his day. This was the main ceremony in the small chapel on the ziggurat.*

The male figure here is clearly of the same Semitic culture as the one group of Atlas figures holding up the world; as the dancer with castanets; as the priests holding the Baoulé Mask. I judge him therefore in some sense to be both royal and divine; hence my belief that this annual copulation originally was for religious rather than for secular reasons and underlies our contemporary belief in the Virgin Birth, the Parthenos.

This is but one example of what this book is about, the cosmopolitan nature of the early world.

PLATE 179

In North America these circular designs (right) are found on a granite boulder near Etowah Mounds in Georgia. The boulder is now on the campus of Reinhardt College, Waleska, Georgia (Margaret Perryman Smith, photo, courtesy Campbell Grant). They are standard cup-and-ring stones such as are found on every continent.

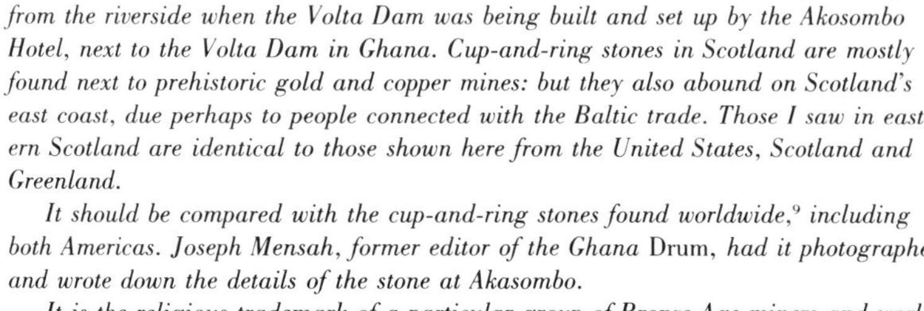

CUP-AND-RING STONE *(left)* **FROM THE VOLTA RIVER, GHANA.** *This was picked up from the riverside when the Volta Dam was being built and set up by the Akosombo Hotel, next to the Volta Dam in Ghana. Cup-and-ring stones in Scotland are mostly found next to prehistoric gold and copper mines: but they also abound on Scotland's east coast, due perhaps to people connected with the Baltic trade. Those I saw in eastern Scotland are identical to those shown here from the United States, Scotland and Greenland.*

It should be compared with the cup-and-ring stones found worldwide,[9] *including both Americas. Joseph Mensah, former editor of the Ghana* Drum, *had it photographed and wrote down the details of the stone at Akasombo.*

It is the religious trademark of a particular group of Bronze Age miners and worldwide navigators. I think it is the religious symbol of the Chronos people with a gnomon wedged into the cup and time recorded by the gnomon's shadow in the ring. The Chronos people were the time-worshipping people, originally from the Middle East. To each individual it would therefore have religious significance.

Cup-and-ring stones (below) from Greenland.

Cup-and-ring stones from southern Scotland (right), where I have seen them in abundance.

PLATE 180
ETHIOPIAN PHALLUS PORTRAITS. *In the Sidamo district of Ethiopia alone there are 1669 stone phallic figures counted by Azais and Chamgord personally with, they estimated from reports, up to ten thousand in total over an area stretching across Ethiopia and almost as far south as Lake Turkana.*[10] *Philip Allison doubts that the carvers of these Ethiopian stones bear any relation to the carvers of the Akwanshi figures of Nigeria. The evidence advanced in this book points not only to the same Bronze Age multinationals operating down West Africa as well as down East Africa but, like the multinationals of today, trading and mining across the world: leaving their records carved in stone or deposited in place names or trapped forever in the amber of language. European archaeologists have sought a megalithic society to suit their monuments. This book endeavors to make a solid contribution to that end. The male-dominated societies expressed their part in God's creation thus. They claimed that gynecologically children were born only from the sperm of their fathers and that the mother's womb was merely the receptacle of that sperm. But that the divinity should be endowed with a gender suggests that the divinity is often a reflection of society rather than vice versa.*

The carob tree, which as we have seen supplied the seeds that provided the fundamental weights for the ancient world, is popularly called St. John's bread. The English name John in Greek is Ioannes, and it was the sea people symbolized by the name Oannes, who, tradition said, originally brought all the arts of civilization to Mesopotamia itself. The plot thickens.

20. The Biological Evidence for this Early Contact

"Those who forget history are condemned to relive it."
GEORGE SANTAYANA

The Sudan is a country of 950,000 square miles, nearly the size of India. The first two motor cars to arrive in the Anglo-Egyptian Sudan, so the story goes, suffered a head-on collision. We must allow that a few of the parallels drawn in this book may likewise be fortuitous but this cannot be so, for statistical reasons, with the great and coherent assemblage of all the evidence. Also, whereas it may plausibly be argued that some few of these works of art may have been independently reinvented, no one is ever going to reinvent a plant or an animal. So let us now turn to the biological witness: for botany can drive home the point that there has to have been worldwide ocean sailing for long, long millennia before Columbus.

J. Galletly Wilson, now retired in Kitale, Kenya, is a botanist who lived in Karamoja Province of Uganda for twenty-two years, first arriving in 1952 to take up his duties as plant ecologist and then as agricultural officer. There he found botanical evidence sufficient to persuade him that maize, tobacco and the allegedly native American plant, the sweet potato, had been in use in Africa for a long time, reaching back to an age far anterior to Columbus.

Wilson finds a similarity between the ancient Egyptian culture and that of the Turkana and Karamajong, which is, after all, somewhat to be expected. But, proceeding further, he finds similarity between Cretan or south European names and those in use among the Karamajong, mistakenly explaining all this with a common Ice Age culture. Wilson does not realize that languages that are unwritten change too fast to be relied upon to retain such resemblances over a span of eight to ten thousand years. He cites *halos* in Greek and *alos* in Karamoja for a dung-smeared floor on which grain was threshed; *ekeria* in Karamoja designates *posho*, or flour, which he compares to *Keria*, the grain god of Crete, perhaps we should have said the goddess *Ceres*, and the English word *cereal; amilot* in Karamoja means chaff, which he compares to English milling, and he notices the Karamoja word for grindstone as *emyelet*. In fact he claims three hundred clearly accorded words between Karamoja and various Celtic languages. Since the evidence for culture contact is more widespread in South America than East Africa we may not invoke an Ice Age or a land bridge for explanation; merely the long-distance trading, mining and colonization that was such a feature of the Age of Metals, in which a number of different peoples who sailed across the Atlantic also traded right down Africa.

The vast Karamoja region is semi-arid. J. G. Wilson was surprised therefore to find wild sugarcane growing there *(Saccharum officinale)*, a plant that thrives on high humidity. He found in a seasonal pan near Amudat, in Pokot country, wild rice and wild *simsim*, and he found wild bananas *(Ensete ventricisum)* in forests on Moroto and other mountains. The wild banana was not grown by the Tepes tribe for food but they used its seeds for beads. He also found the wild date palm *(Phoenix reclinota)* growing in a very atypical habitat—as high as nine thousand feet up a mountain—whose seeds were also used as beads. He found, too, the climbing bean *(Dolichos Lablab)* in a further remote habitat on Moroto mountain. He points out that on the north side of Moroto mountain are the remains of ancient terraced fields that had once been irrigated from a permanent stream. He says that much the same evidence is found in the Marakwet area of Kenya, with numerous stone circles and old roads associated with them.

Wilson believes that tobacco *(Nicotiana rustica)*, a quite different species from the smoking tobacco used by the Portuguese and Dutch *(Nicotiana Tabacum)*, was being grown by Africans all the way from the Sudan to the Karamajong and South Africa. When the Europeans came, they failed to notice it, he suggests, because it was not used for smoking but for snuff. As evidence that the use of this snuff is far more ancient than Bartholemew Díaz, he cites the identical name for a snuff-horn as used by the ancient Egyptians and the Karamajong, *abwi*.

One Amerindian name for the sweet potato is *chaco*. The Teso people of Uganda call it *achok*, and the Karamajong, *achokit*. Another Amerindian name for the sweet potato—Wilson says—is *yete* and the isolated Labwor tribe of Uganda call it *ayeta*. While in Malaya it is called *kemarung* and by the Karamajong, *arunget*.

The Polynesian language itself shows similarities with Karamajong, he says: the first uses *lei* for a sharp tooth and *akule* as dried fish, while the Karamajong call a large tooth, or tusk, *ekelai*, and fish in general *ekolia*. In Polynesia, *etak* means a promontory reference point, in Karamajong the word is *atakanu*. Wilson then lists a series of similar words in Karamajong and the Indian Naga language for simple objects as evidence that crops and cultivation in ancient Africa were from the very beginning not developed in isolation upon one continent only.

KARAMAJONG WORDS	NAGA WORDS
edula: a large granary basket	*duli:* a large granary basket
ekai: a house	*aki:* a house
akikup: to dig	*akuphu:* a hoe
akiru: rain	*atikru:* a rain clock
aiyong: I, personal pronoun	*iye:* I, personal pronoun
akujuk: V-shaped hoe handle	*keju:* V-shaped hoe
aramet: a stone axe	*methie:* a stone axe
apar: flattened metal object	*pharua:* metal hoe
apusit: urine	*ipuzu:* urine

The Indian writer on Indian prehistory, Sankarananda, argues that the Vedic records clearly state that the Vedic Aryans who migrated into India were a marine people who sailed both east and west from India, reaching America. He writes:

> the *Rigveda* has been found to be the book of a marine people. The people traded with lands beyond the seas, amassed great wealth by maritime trade. . . . They crossed and recrossed the oceans, they carried on trade with foreign lands. . . . The Indian mariners who went out of India, never to return again, are traced in the Nile and the Euphrates Valleys in North Africa and Crete in the west, in the east they are traced in the Easter and Caroline Islands and Peru, and in north China.[1]

Other botanists have considered the common bean, the grain amaranths, the silk cotton tree, out of which dugout canoes are made in West Africa, as vegetation that had been carried from one continent to another in pre-Columbian times.

I, myself, would like to draw attention to the asphodel, the plant par excellence of the Elysian Fields, which is to be found around the Mediterranean and also, anciently, in Oregon and California. Truth is, work on the migration of plants has barely begun.

In my earlier book, *The God-Kings and the Titans,* I brought together as much of such evidence for this early contact as was available in 1970. I did not wish at that time to go beyond what the specialists had already published. Since then several important books have seen the light of day; especially useful has been the work of Lithuanian-born Marija Gimbutas, professor of European archaeology at the University of California, who collected the results of three thousand excavations in the Balkans and Eastern Europe; and the work of D. P. Agrawal, the leading Indian archaeologist. They now permit me to state my case rather more precisely.

Their findings have enabled me to chart with greater accuracy the peoples who commanded the seas. I give here only the simplest outlines. The first wave of long-distance sailing was undertaken by the matriarchal peoples whose symbol was a serpent. Of these, the Heracles people were a heroic but not uniformly popular breakaway group, not popular with the ladies anyway.

The second wave of long-distance sailors were Aryans, who moved from Iran into Western Europe, Mesopotamia and the Indus Valley. Although patriarchal people, they subsequently combined forces with the matriarchal tribes. Then Mesopotamians, i.e. Sumerians, Akkadians and other Semites, largely took over the sea routes of their predecessors, along with the Mycenaeans and Cretans and other Mediterranean sea peoples; including the Phoenicians—when the name is restricted to its narrowest sense—who continued to the tail end of the great days of sailing.

All of these peoples, at one time or another, were acquainted with all the seas of the world. To these must be added specifically Pacific sailings, especially by the inhabitants of Japan around the first half of the third millennium B.C. and by Indian and Chinese mariners. The world is large enough for the activities of the various thalassocrats to greatly overlap, female- as well as male-dominated societies.

We are, I emphasize, unambiguously talking about a great deal of systematic sailing, not just an occasional, chance voyage: we are talking about a merchant marine, not a single fishing boat cast up on a foreign shore by a remarkable storm. For it has been correctly pointed out that societies are conservative, building up resistance to adopting new ideas or new cultivars, so that we ought to associate culture transference, and plant transference specifically, with a deep and prolonged association, rather than with an occasional and chance shipwreck.

The collectors of Greek tradition, especially Hesiod and Diodorus Siculus, have really hinted at much of this story already. For Hesiod's theogony gives us the succession of divinities—it is effectively the succession of thalassocrats distinguished by their religions—who preponderated in the Fertile Crescent. Diodorus tells us that the sky-worshipping, patriarchal peoples of the northwest of Europe had joined forces with a group of Pelasgians, presumably from the eastern Mediterranean, who had extensively intermarried with the locals, probably Celts and Germanic peoples, and went on to conquer the inhabited world, the *oecumene*. And when Diodorus used the phrase, the inhabited world, that is literally what he means. It is an expression that we can now confirm included both Africa and America. The evidence supports the statement that each of these waves of cultural expansion slowly spread across the *oecumene*, not one wave only; that there were exchanges of skills and that the metropolitan countries grew fat and greatly benefited by this long-distance trade, particularly in metals.

When this Atlantic trade largely, but not entirely, stopped at the end of the Bronze Age, time almost stood still for 2,500 years—so important are communications to us all. The Dark Ages of Europe and the Dark Ages of Africa and the Dark Ages of the Aztecs have a common origin. And the resistance of the various peoples of the world to the violent expansion of Europeans at the end of the fifteenth century A.D. was proportionate to their previous isolation. Africa was never wholly isolated—before the Portuguese had come the Arabs; before the Arabs, the Indians; before the Indians, the Carthaginians; and before Carthage, the great press of sea peoples such as we have outlined here. Amerindian contact with the Old World largely stopped at the end of the Bronze Age; while the Australoids of Australia were nearly, but not quite, isolated for fifty thousand years and the Tasmanians the most isolated—and ultimately therefore the most vulnerable—of them all. But despite the ever increasing power of the male-dominated societies, in a few parts of the world the matriarchal values lingered on.

In the Bronze Age, during which there was equal honor to the male and female, the king was likened to the shuttle in a great loom, which wove together his people, Nature and the Creator in one tapestry. The pollution by the societies of communist Russia is surely an example of contemporary devastation, alongside the annihilation of the Amerindians of the Americas, of course. Gunnar Thompson writes that "over 75 million Amerindians died during the march of European civilisation across the continents."[2]

21. The Scandal of the Classical Greeks

"Antiquity is full of the praises of another Antiquity still more remote."

VOLTAIRE

It is understandable that when Europe woke up again with the Catholic illumination of the thirteenth century and with the Renaissance, recovering her Greek inheritance from Byzantium, from the Muslims in Spain and from old manuscripts in monasteries, the Greek thinkers appeared to be a marvelous and miraculous race. Similarly, when the Hebrew Old Testament was the only book surviving out of the extensive literature of the Middle East, it was looked upon as sacred. When Greek science and philosophy stood alone, it is understandable that they appeared to be miraculous.[1] In just such style, when a few books first reached the Yoruba at their sacred city of Ile Ife, although the Yoruba were uniformly illiterate and had no idea of their content, the books were placed on the altar and worshipped.

But since Champollion, taught by the great de Sacey, translated Egyptian hieroglyphs, a system of writing that had been formerly available to the West up to the time of the Romans; and since Assyriologists obtained a reasonable mastery of Sumerian in this century; and since successive teams of archaeologists have unearthed some of the ancient cities of the Fertile Crescent, it is now impossible to look on the Greek scientists and philosophers as existing in isolation. So to teach, as remains the contemporary fashion, that the ancient Greeks invented almost everything from geometry and the atomic theory to the ballet is a scandal. It is the systematic indoctrination of the young with falsehoods, the more attractive for their appeal to European conceit. Without the wholesale destruction of the records, the European academics could not have passed off these damaging and misleading deceptions.

Let us take a look at how the ancient Greek writers themselves viewed these matters. They made no bones about the fact that they looked upon Egypt, not Greece, as the home of immemorial wisdom. They traveled to Egypt as young men in order to learn, and there have survived some details of their visits. Plutarch says: "The wisest of the Greeks . . . [were] travelling into Egypt and conversing with the priests. Eudoxus, for example, they say, received lessons from Chonupheus of Memphis; Solon from Sonchis of Sais; Pythagoras from Oenuphis of Heliopolis."[2]

Plutarch himself traveled to Egypt to acquire knowledge; his treatise on Isis and Osiris results from that visit. In his life of Solon he narrated that Solon studied under Psenophis of Heliopolis as well as under Sonchis the Saite, the most learned of all the Egyptian priests at that time.

Thales (fl. 587 B.C.) of Miletus, a Greek harbor on the Near East mainland, is known as the father of Greek philosophy. It is noteworthy that the earliest savants lived in the Greek cities in Asia, or on the Aegean islands, and only later is the torch of learning taken up by the Greeks of mainland Greece. Thales is said to have introduced generalized Egyptian methods of mensuration and thus "founded" geometry. His central scientific theory seems to have been that all things start from water and return to water. It may be that he was descended from the sea people called Atlas, to whom water was sacred, and that his name shared a common root with the ancient Greek name for sea, *thalassa.*

Pythagoras (fl. 570 B.C.) from Samos stands in a dominant and commanding position at the start of Greek philosophy. The Egyptians are said by the Greeks themselves to have taught Pythagoras geometry and other sciences during his stay in Egypt of twenty-two years: the Phoenicians arithmetic, the Chaldeans astronomy, the Magians the formulae of religion and practical maxims for the conduct of life.

Since Pythagoras himself wrote nothing and later traditions about his life were associated with miracles natural to illiterates, such that he possessed a golden thigh, we must rely upon Iamblichus, who wrote his biography. But what is clear and irrefutable is that these were the intellectual influences available in the eastern Mediterranean of the period and which Greek scholars of the period expected other Greek scholars to imbibe. Other important influences are hinted at with the tradition that Pythagoras was said to be descended from the Tyrrhenian Pelasgians, the Pelasgians having been highly accomplished citizens of Greece and Crete in the Bronze Age, while the sage himself is said to have identified with the Hyperborean sun god, Apollo; the Hyperboreans having developed considerable sophistication in mathematics and astronomy, as the stone circles of Britain demonstrate.

Whatever the truth of these assertions by his fellow Greeks, they clearly show up additional and important potential influences on the intellectual life of this period. Aristotle wrote a separate work on the life of the Pythagoreans but this is lost. It was the current belief in antiquity that Pythagoras had taken extensive travels, not only to Egypt for twenty-two years but also to Arabia, Phoenicia, Judea, Babylon and even India, and we have no reason to disbelieve this. Pythagoras traveled in order to acquire the scientific knowledge available in his day and to speak with the fountainheads of religious as well as of scientific wisdom.

Plato (c. 429–347 B.C.), greatest of the Greek philosophers, is said to have traveled to Egypt, among other places, to study. Eusebius says of him:

> This same Plato, too, after having attended the teaching of the Pythagoreans in Italy, was not contented with his studying with them only but is said to have sailed to Egypt and devoted a very long time to their philosophy. This testimony indeed he himself bears to the Barbarians in many passages of his own discourses, and therein, I think, does well, and candidly confesses that the noblest doctrines are imported into philosophy from the Barbarians. Accordingly in many places, and especially in the *Epinomis*, you may hear him mentioning both Syrians and Egyptians in the following manner:
>
> The cause of this is that he who first observed these phenomena was a Barbarian; for it was a very ancient region which bred those who first took notice of these things because of the beauty of the summer season, which both Egypt and Syria fully enjoy. . . . Whence the knowledge has reached to all countries including our own, after having been tested by thousands of years and time without end.

Eusebius goes on to add: "Let us take it then that, whatever Greeks may have received from Barbarians, they work out and finish it with greater beauty. So says Plato."

Pythagoras had taught that number underlay all nature and that this number could be expressed in dots, of which the number ten, the sum of the first four numbers, was sacred and was called the *tetractys*. Now, Leucippus and Democritus are supposed to have developed this further and to have jointly invented the "Greek" atomic theory wherein the Pythagorean numbers, represented as dots, became the indissoluble atoms of which various combinations and patterns formed the elements. Of Leucippus we know almost nothing. It is likely that Pythagoras's extensive travels, he was born in Samos not Greece, to the intellectual centres of the world from a country that had only just relearned to write, had given him much or all of his fundamental teachings. Similarly we must notice that Democritus had for his tutors Magi, Persian philosophers whom Xerxes had shed during his ill-fated expedition into Greece. Democritus later spent his patrimony as a young man on extensive travels to Egypt and the East to acquire knowledge. Is it not reasonable to suppose that he later taught what he had then learned? If not, why go? In addition, there is a solid Greek tradition that the atomic theory had originally been brought to Greece by

Mochus, who was himself a Phoenician philosopher living at the time of the Trojan War (c. 1190 B.C.).

The crystalization of the Greek intellect, as we are informed, lies in the geometry of Euclid (fl. 300 B.C.). Euclid is believed to have been born of Greek parents settled at Tyre, the former Phoenician center. He lived at one time in Damascus. He was invited by the first Ptolemy to leave Syria and to come to Alexandria either to join or to create the mathematical school there. Proclus has written about the history of geometry prior to Euclid. The Egyptians, he said, invented geometry for land surveying, with especial interest in defining the boundaries of farms after their boundary marks had been lost in the annual inundation. The Phoenicians, he said, developed arithmetic to benefit their commerce. Euclid at that time had access to many records that are now lost, including the work of earlier Greek mathematicians like Eudoxus. We must notice carefully Euclid's position in time and space. It was accepted in Classical Greece that Egypt had been the home of geometry. Euclid worked in Alexandria shortly after the Macedonian conquest of Egypt and of the Middle East and northern India. We must appreciate that Alexander (356–323 B.C.) took his scientists on campaign with him so as to loot as much learning as possible from the countries he conquered. For the first time in the history of Classical Greece, the sciences of Egypt, northern India and the Middle East had become freely available. Not to single visitors now, but to the Greek schools outside Greece placed in the centers of that world that the Greeks themselves always recognized to be the world of learning. Is it not then reasonable to suppose that Euclid had compiled and organized the geometrical work of others, much of which had only just become available to the Greeks themselves? All this is resoundingly stated in Greek by later Greek and foreign writers, not once but on many occasions. Let us glance at what they say.

Josephus, the eminent Jewish historian, writes about Greek learning generally:

> For you will find all things among the Greeks to be recent, having come into existence, as one might say, yesterday or the day before; I mean the foundation of their cities, and their invention of the arts, and the registration of their laws; and the writing of their histories is almost the latest object of their attention.
>
> Doubtless, however, they themselves admit that the most ancient and most constant traditional record is that of the events which have occurred among the Egyptians, and Chaldeans, and Phoenicians (for at present I omit to include ourselves with these).
>
> For they all inhabit regions which are least subject to destruction from the surrounding atmosphere, and have taken much care to leave none of the facts of their history unrecorded, but to have all continually enshrined by their wisest men in public registers.

> But the region about Greece has been invaded by thousands of destructive plagues, which blotted out the memory of past events: and as they were always setting up new modes of life, they each of them supposed that their own was the beginning of all.
>
> Moreover all with one voice acknowledge, that the first among the Greeks who philosophized about things celestial and divine, as Pherecydes the Syrian, and Pythagoras, and Thales, got their learning from Egyptians and Chaldeans, and wrote but little.[3]

Diodorus Siculus (fl. 30 B.C.), the eminent Greek historian, puts it thus:

> After having thoroughly explained these points, I must state how many of those who have been famed among the Greeks for intelligence and culture made a voyage to Egypt in ancient times, in order that they might gain some knowledge of its customs and culture.
>
> For the priests of the Egyptians report from the records in their sacred books that they were visited by Orpheus, and Musaeus, and Melampus, and Daedalus, and besides these by the poet Homer, and Lycurgus the Spartan; also by Solon the Athenian, and Plato the philosopher; and that there came also Pythagoras of Samos, and Eudoxus the mathematician, Democritus of Abdera also, and Oenipides of Chios.
>
> And as evidence of all these they point to the images of some, and the names of places or buildings called after others. Also from the branch of learning studied by each, the priests bring proofs of the fact that they had brought over from Egypt everything whereby they gained admiration among the Greeks.
>
> Thus Orpheus, they say, brought away from the Egyptians most of the mystic rites, and the orgiastic celebration of his own wandering, and the fable concerning those in Hades. For the rite of *Osiris* is the same as that of *Dionysus:* and that of *Isis* is very similar to that of *Demeter*, with only the change of names.[4]

Eusebius (fl. 300 B.C.), the Greek-speaking Christian historian who wrote in Greek, again puts it thus:

> we shall show that the Greeks and even their renowned philosophers had plagiarised all their philosophic lore and all that was otherwise of common benefit and profitable for their social needs from barbarians. . . .
>
> I shall show then almost immediately how, from various sources, one and another of these wonderful Greeks, by going about among the Barbarians, collected the other branches of learning, geometry, arithmetic, music, astronomy, medicine, and the very first elements of grammar, and numberless other artistic and profitable studies. . . .
>
> But you must not be surprised if we say that possibly the doctrines of the Hebrews have been plagiarised by them, since they are not only proved to have stolen the other branches of learning from Egyptians and Chaldeans

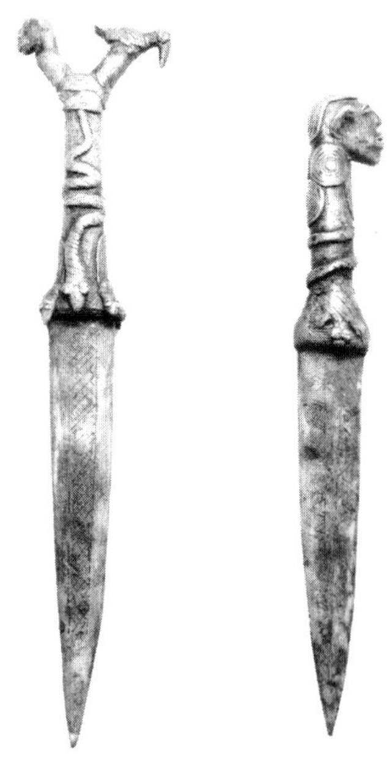

Plate 181
Senufo bronze daggers. *These two bronze daggers might have fought at Troy. You cannot cut with them, they are thrusting weapons, hard as steel, what Homer called "pitiless bronze." The antennae style of hilt of the one on the left was a standard style of dagger hilt in the Bronze Age, all the way from Britain to China. The right-hand dagger has a head to its handle resembling the heads of the sea captains who wore bird masks, and who had their heads artificially deformed when young. I purchased these African bronze daggers in Abidjan. The worship of the ancestors, to whom libations are poured, goes on across much of Africa. The ancestors are looked upon as super-elders.*

and the rest of the barbarous nations, but even to the present day are detected in robbing one another of the honours gained in their own writings. . . .

First among these Pythagoras, the pupil of Pherecydes, who invented the name "philosophy," was a native, as some say, of Samos, but according to others, of Tyrrhenia; while some say that he was a Syrian or Tyrian, so that you must admit that the first of the philosophers, celebrated in the mouth of all Greeks, was not a Greek but a Barbarian.

Pherecydes also is recorded to have been a Syrian, and Pythagoras they say was his disciple. He is not, however, the only teacher with whom, as it is said, Pythagoras was associated, but he spent some time also with the Persian Magi, and became a disciple of the Egyptian prophets, at the time when some of the Hebrews appear to have made their settlement in Egypt, and some in Babylon.

In fact the said Pythagoras, while busily studying the wisdom of each nation, visited Babylon, and Egypt, and all Persia, being instructed by the Magi and the priests: and in addition to these he is related to have studied under the Brahmans [these are Indian philosophers]; and from some he gathered astrology, from others geometry, and arithmetic and music from others, and different things from different nations, and only from the wise men of Greece did he get nothing, wedded as they were to poverty and dearth of wisdom: so on the contrary he himself became the author of instruction to the Greeks in the learning which he had procured from abroad.

Such then was Pythagoras.[5]

In the *Chronicorum,* Eusebius says:

Pythagoras was not as wise as the seven Greek sages but wished to be called a lover of wisdom, that is a philosopher.[6]

Eusebius quotes Democritus boasting about himself and his own far-flung travels in pursuit of learning:

But of the men of my time I have wandered over the most land, investigating the most distant parts, and have seen the most climates and soils, and listened to the greatest number of learned men, nor did any one ever yet surpass me in the construction of lines accompanied by demonstration [geometry], nor yet those Egyptians who are called *Arpedonaptae,* for all which purpose I passed as much as five years in foreign lands.[7]

Clement of Alexandria (c. A.D. 150–215) writes:

The healing art is said to have been invented by Apis the Egyptian . . . and afterwards improved by Aesculapius. Atlas the Libyan was the first who built a ship, and sailed the sea. . . . Astrology also was first made known among men by the Egyptians and Chaldeans. . . .

PLATE 182
Three dogs with human faces: Baoulé weights. These three little figures come from Baoulé or Ashanti with the body of a dog and the face of a man. The three faces are all different and look much more like English club bores than they resemble the present-day citizens of Ashanti. Compare them with the Assyrian composite animals.

Human headed dog, cast in tumbago, from Quimbaya, Colombia.

Assyrian composite animal.

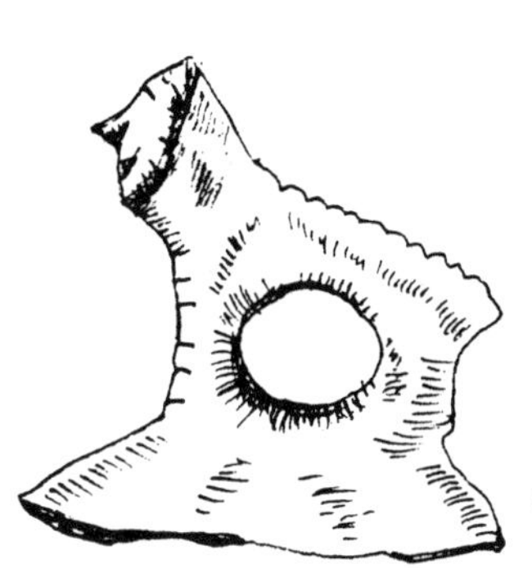

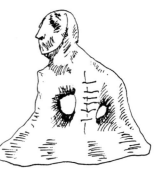

Lid handle in the form of a dog with a human mask from Gorni Pasarel, central Bulgaria, east Balkan civilization.

The dog, a double of the moon goddess.

Dog, the howler by night, was the goddess's principal animal. How important a role it played in the mythology of old Europe is emphasized in figurines of marble, rock crystal and terracotta, portraying the animal as a whole or its head alone in the form of cult vases shaped like a dog, or dog figurines attached to vessels or forming the handles of vases or cups. The handle of a graphite-painted vase from Gorni Pasarel in central Bulgaria shows a dog wearing a human mask. Its body is notched on the back and front possibly to emphasize the dog's aggressive characteristics. A large vase discovered at the Cucuteni site of Podei has a handle of a dog with forelegs stretched out and the hind part of the body raised up.[1]

PLATE 183
MASK WITH CANOES FOR HORNS. *This superb Burkina Faso mask of the Banafara people is a replica. The ears of the mask are dugout canoes. The chameleon on the forehead is a common design, the tongue of the chameleon being placed to prevent evil entering into the man by the nose. The flaps on either side of the face carry the water symbol. The chameleon is also a symbol for transmutation. The device below the eyes, which looks a little like tears, should be compared to the very similar trick quite commonly used on the Weeping God of ancient Peru (Plate 162). There are two thousand different tribal groups in sub-Saharan Africa.*

> The Egyptians again first taught men to burn lamps, and divided the year into twelve months. . . .
>
> The same people again were the inventors of geometry. . . . Kelmis and Damnameneus, the Idaean Dactyls, first discovered iron in Cyprus. And the tempering of bronze was invented by Delas, another Idean, or as Hesiod says, a Scythian.
>
> We have heard too that the Persians were the first who made a carriage, and couch, and footstool, and the Sidonians first built a trireme. The Sicilians who are close to Italy were the first to invent a lyre, not far inferior to the harp, and devised castanets.
>
> Robes of fine linen are said to have been invented in the time of Semiramis, queen of the Assyrians: and Atossa who reigned over the Persians is said by Hellanicus to have been the first to use folded letters.[8]

It must be acknowledged that Clement of Alexandria and Eusebius of Caesarea were Christians taking part in a controversy with their pagan contemporaries, but it is most unlikely that they would have expressed these views so boldly and unambiguously within the Greek world if these views did not hold water, not only because they would have been objects of ridicule in a society that at that time very much knew the facts of the case, but also because they were very learned men.

Finally, let us examine the surviving records to see what Greek inventions existed before their Greek so-called inventors.

Pythagoras's theorem, his most celebrated invention, is represented by Needham to have been used in China around 2200 B.C. Thom has recognized its use in the construction of numerous stone circles of Britain (3000–1200 B.C.). It is found expressed on a Babylonian clay tablet and was in use in Babylon a thousand years before Pythagoras.

Professor W. G. Lambert of Birmingham University writes that, in fact, the whole of the Elements of Euclid were available in Babylon around 2000 B.C. The purport of this must be appreciated, for the Elements of Euclid were looked on as the quintessence of Greek intellectualism, but they certainly are not Greek. I discussed with Professor Lambert his enormously important cuneiform translations and am most grateful to him.

The best-known practical invention of the brilliant mathematician Archimedes (c. 287–212 B.C.) is the water pump known as the Archimedes screw. This type of pump was in use earlier to water the hanging gardens of Babylon. It was also known to the Greeks as the Egyptian screw.

Philip of Macedon is said to have invented the military formation of the phalanx but we can now see from their art that Sumerians were using this formation two thousand years earlier.

The alphabet itself was brought to Greece by Cadmus the Phoenician. The very name "chemistry" simply means Egypt, the country which gave that science to Greece. Forbes, who writes on ancient technology, says that twenty names for metals in Greek, and six for rocks, are of Assyrian

PLATE 184
TWO BRONZE MASKS FROM BAOULÉ. *These masks from the Baoulé Beoumi district are made out of good metal and may be originals. Both have crosses on the cheeks. The hair, or what appears to be hair, is looped as if it were straight hair rather than African hair. The two faces look to me to be Eurafrican rather than African. The two birds on top of the masks are again black hornbills signalizing people who worship a male god in heaven, the sky god, rather than ancestor worship or the worship of the earth mother. They symbolize the stars, Ouranos. I believe these to be death masks that have perhaps come from old graves. The mask was the receptacle of invisible divine forces.*

origin, thus pointing out the route by which metallurgy had reached the Classical Greeks.[9]

The architecture of the Parthenon is in a style fairly similar to that of the temple of Karnak in Upper Egypt, erected more than a thousand years earlier.

The standard Greek measure of distance was the stadium. The Egyptian royal cubit was 0.525 meters in length. There were 300 such cubits to the stadium, or 157.5 meters. Seven hundred such stadia form 1 degree of the perimeter of the earth. The Egyptian royal cubit was in use long before the Classical Greeks existed. It is highly unlikely that the stadium and the cubit would be so neatly related if they belonged to two different and unrelated systems of mensuration: the stadium is therefore most probably Egyptian in origin. The Egyptian royal cubit is a unit equally neatly related to the length of the circumference of the earth; its earliest use, therefore, supplies some indication as to when the size of the earth had been accurately measured. It was in use from the first dynasty (3100 B.C.).

The Greek-Sicilian geographer, Eratosthenes, is credited with having first measured the earth. He traveled to Egypt and took the distance of Alexandria from Syene, which lay on the north-south meridian. This distance is five thousand stadia. Working on the basis that the sun's rays that strike the earth are parallel, Eratosthenes at the summer solstice took the difference in angle subtended by these rays at the two stations and from this calculated the curvature of the sphere of the earth and thus the length of its circumference to be 252,000 stadia or 39,690 kilometers, a figure that is almost precisely correct.[10]

And indeed we have the tradition that the size of the earth had been calculated long before by the Atlas people or Atlantians, who were known to the Egyptians as Set and who had ruled in Upper Egypt in predynastic times. Pausanias calls them: "Atlantes, and those who profess to know the measurements of the earth."[11]

In sum, we have been sold the equation that what was new to the Classical Greeks was new to the world. The equation is fallacious. Of course there is no need to go to the other extreme and say that the Classical Greeks

The second male mask. The cross carried on the cheeks of these two masks is a pre-Christian symbol of the greatest importance. It symbolizes the start of the first worship of God in heaven, which came at the time of the so-called Creation, c. 5500 B.C. In the Vedic literature of India the primordial man is hanged upon the cosmic cross. He sacrifices himself in order to recreate the universe, as did Odin on the tree Yggdrassil. The cross then also symbolizes the axis of the rotating universe joining the upper with the lower position of the universe, the left with the right,[2] although this is more properly portrayed by the swastika. Odin also had a spear thrust in his side, while he was dying, in order to save the universe. The cross was anciently an important religious symbol, from India to Scandinavia. Patriarchy may well have commenced in northwest Europe where matriarchy still persists today with Notre Dame etc. French cathedrals were mostly built on sites previously occupied by temples to the earth mother.

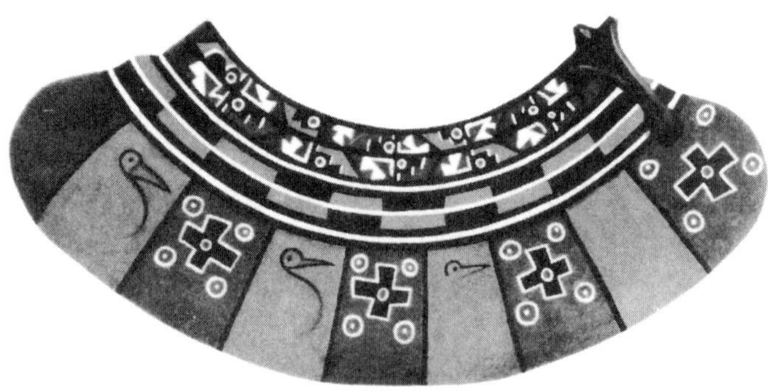

PLATE 185
The cross and sun circles on pottery from Tiahuanaco.

invented nothing. They were an ingenious people and it may be that in addition to rendering more elegant the ideas that they had so aptly purloined, they subsequently added ideas and developments of their own. The Greeks naturally enough took over the scientific and intellectual accomplishments of their neighbors as soon as they had again learned to read and write. Once Alexander had conquered Egypt, Mesopotamia, Iran and northern India, the Greeks were in an even better position to pillage their ideas.

It is clear that the Classical Greeks themselves made little attempt to hide whence they acquired their knowledge, while the Hellenistic Greeks of the Macedonian empire organized libraries and scholars to be able to exploit the marvelous intellectual inheritance that was the booty of these conquered nations.

The central teaching of classical scholarship is that the scholar must not depend upon commentators and cribs for his information but must go back to the source. So whoever repairs to the Classical Greeks for the historical origins of Western science runs counter and contrary to that scholarship, for the Classical Greeks provided the cribs and the commentators.

Until this is appreciated, it is not likely either that adequate money will be directed to the preservation and publication of Egyptian papyri and Middle East clay tablets or to the relevant archaeology.

Standard works on Greek thinkers express their indebtedness to other Greek thinkers, as if Greeks had been insulated from the outside world or as if Greeks alone had concerned themselves in the past with questions of science, mathematics and philosophy. However, it is clear that the intellectual paramountcy of Greeks in Europe was primarily due to their geographical position; being the nearest European neighbors to the scholars

PLATE 186

BABOON MASK FROM THE SENUFO, A REPLICA (23.8 CM). *This mask, part human, part baboon with the horns of a small antelope, is artistically powerful. The figure standing on the forehead seems to be stylistically halfway between the lowbrows of the Dan pieces and the more common and far more beautiful African figures that so often adorn more recent Senufo art. The baboon was a symbol for the Egyptian culture hero Thoth. In Africa even today, which would seem earlier to have been true of much of the rest of the world, the supernatural is all part of the workaday world: deities, familiar spirits, ancestral spirits and human beings are conjoined.*

in Egypt and the Middle East they were quite simply in the best position to pick their brains.

Our dictionaries, which trace the origin of our words only as far back as Greek and Latin, provide a subtle form of brainwashing. The Bronze Age reached an intellectual level in certain quarters that we did not recover until the last century or two. Hence the widespread belief in human degeneration and decay expressed by some of the best brains throughout much of the past. They were correct. For the story of the Golden Age is not simply nostalgia for the past but a true story of a thousand years of peace, justice, and prosperity. Until we realize this, and grow sensitive to the wonderful achievements of our forebears, we will not understand the present day or be able to plan for the future.

PLATE 187

BAOULÉ MASK THAT LOOKS AMERINDIAN. *This neotraditional mask is a replica cast for the tourist trade, made from indifferent metal. Nevertheless this mask, which comes from Baoulé, is interesting because of its form. The face looks Amerindian, with its slit eyes and wild expression. It is backed by the sun's rays, fair enough if it is the portrait of a god-king who worshipped the sun, who, in a sense, was the sun himself, as were the Amerindian monarchs as well as many African monarchs. The black hornbills are again carried on top of the mask. He has a lip-plug, as has the Atlas figure from the Senufo country, which resembles the Mexican god of fire.*

African portraits are found on Mexican stone carvings, on Mexican terra-cotta figures excavated from pre-Columbian graves and from Mochicha pottery on the coastline of Peru. It need not be altogether surprising, therefore, if one should find Amerindian portraits in West Africa and Amerindian-style artifacts in West Africa. Tradition said that black troops fought for Cuchulain in Ireland and black men worked with white priests on the stone circle of Callanish on the Hebridean island of Lewis.

Many African tribes tell us that the mask was not formerly the exclusive property of men: the women at first used the masks to terrify men and get them to toe the line.[3]

PLATE 188
El Sayed's hieroglyph for Neith. Alan Gardiner, writing earlier, gives a rather different version of Neith's symbol. The temple of Neith at Sais, Plutarch tells us, carried the following inscription: "I am all that has been, that is and that will be. No mortal has yet been able to lift the veil which covers me."[4]

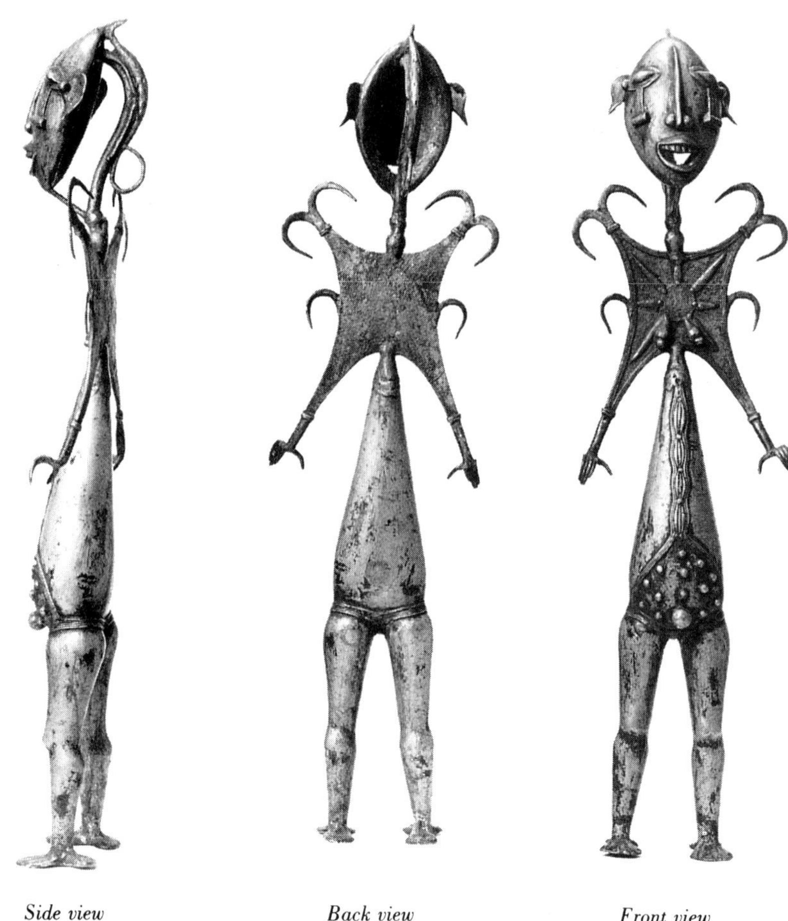

Side view *Back view* *Front view*

BRONZE FIGURES FROM THE CAMEROONS, MODELED LIKE A BEE. *Such figures, female and male with masks for heads and what appears to be an oxhide for a chest and the ever-present chameleon lying along the skeletal attachment to the skull are from the Bamalike tribe. These are the wildest castings that I have yet found from the Cameroons. The last time I talked to a visitor to the small town of Fumban, I was informed that there were then fourteen European sellers of antiquities waiting for the tombs to be robbed and the trove to come in. Also, the faking by duplication of Cameroons art is now a major industry. These are replicas.*

Hides formed one of the earliest currencies. Perhaps for that reason metal ingots were commonly made in the form of hides, and these Bronze Age ingots were in fact called oxhide ingots. Fumban is next to the prehistoric tin mines of the Cameroons, around which are towns beginning with the letters NK.

These figures have an insectlike appearance, I think the bee is intended. It is worth thinking back to the bee goddess of ancient Crete and of the delta of Egypt, and remembering that to the Roman poet Virgil, bees were semi-divine. A hive of bees is the archetypal matriarchal society. Melissa, Didymus recorded, was the first of the Cretan priestesses to be known as a bee.[5] *The Mayan culture heroes called Bacabs were associated with bees and were patrons of beekeeping. The designation for the Egyptian king of the Northern Kingdom was a bee. These hooks exactly replicate the symbol for Egypt's Great Goddess of wisdom, Neith,*[6] *who rose up out of the sea, created everything and gave birth to the male gods. The Melissae were priestesses of Rhea.*

22. The Source of the Bronze for the Bronze Age

"Prometheus stole the mechanical arts—and fire with them (they could neither have been acquired nor used without fire)—and gave them to man."

"Prometheus . . . carried off Hephaestus' art of working by fire, and also the art of Athene, and gave them to man."

PLATO, *Protagoras*

In the last decade a number of books have been published on this subject, as well as a long article in the learned journal *Scientific American*, that leave the reader, having worked through their accurate and scholarly pages for illumination, almost as much in the dark as before he started on them.

In 1978 Michael Heltzer published an excellent monograph from Haifa, with the help, among others, of Haifa University, in which he used principally tablets from Ugarit to show price fluctuations and trade connections in western Asia during the Bronze Age. After an extensive analysis of clay tablets he shows that tin was at its cheapest in the center of the Assyrian empire; specifically, he states, in the towns of Nuzi and Arrapha, which are not far from Nineveh and Ashur. This, he says, is where future archaeologists should look for the ancient tin mines. But northern Iraq is not terra incognita; it would be impossible to extract tin on the scale on which it was used without leaving the appalling mess inevitably associated with very large-scale open-cast mining. And, of course, alluvial tin is washed out of lodes: no such lodes anywhere in this area are known. Heltzer writes: "Tin was cheapest in Nuzi of all the societies of the ancient Near East. Our only explanation for these facts is that tin-mines existed not far from this region."[1] On page 108 he had already written: "The question of where the tin came from, during the period under discussion, has never been answered. No traces of ancient tin-mines have yet been found in Asia Minor, Syria, Cyprus, Transcaucasia and Iran dating from the second millennium B.C. The mining of tin in Europe (Bohemia) began in later times." He coyly does not include Iraq in this list but he admits elsewhere in his pages to the nonexistence of tin in that country.

James D. Muhly, who was co-author of an article in *Scientific American* of the same name as this chapter heading, published the results of his researches in a separate volume.[2]

On page 169 he says that alluvial tin was the only kind of tin available to the Bronze Age smiths. On page 170 he says that alluvial or stream tin must be close to a tin lode.

On page 255 he says that there is no tin in the Mediterranean and that the great Bronze Age civilizations of Greece and Crete were left without any obvious source of tin. There is some tin, he says, in Sardinia but there is no evidence that it was ever used in antiquity. On page 292 he says that large quantities of tin were sold by Assur to Anatolia. On page 306 he says that the tin must have come from northwest Iran but in the same breath he admits that tin is not known there. Kanesh in Anatolia was the recipient of Assyrian tin—hence perhaps its name.

Muhly thinks a lot of the tin came from the Far East but entertains the possibility of sources in northern Syria and northwest Iran. He is aware[3] of the overwhelming importance of water transport but this still does not open his eyes to the answer to his question. So he concludes his lengthy book agnostically: "The present study makes no definite claims. The material covered is enormous in range and in extent and the available evidence is frequently quite unsatisfactory. Often it has been possible only to outline the necessary course of future research. This study does not represent the conclusion of my research; hopefully, it is only the beginning."[4]

Let us go immediately to the first point. What Michael Heltzer found was not the geological source of Bronze Age tin but the center from which the tin trade was controlled: where the tin was refined and where it was doled out to other heads of state at varying costs but with tight political strings attached. Ashur, Nineveh and related towns provided the metal exchange of the day, the futures market and the pivotal point of power politics. It was not the Assyrians who were the great miners or seamen. Their power derived from the political manipulation of the seaports and their city-states. The next part of the description of this Bronze Age trade covers the relationship of the great land power to the relatively competent city states of the coast. It surprisingly resembles our contemporary story of mainland China and Hong Kong. Akkadian became very close to being the *lingua franca* of the world. The Bible says that the whole world was of one language and of one speech.

In 1979 the Akademisk Forlag of Copenhagen published, under the general editorship of Mogens Trolle Larsen, a series of papers from various contributors under the general title: *Mesopotamia: Power and Propaganda.* This described the economic and political relations between the giant Assyrian power of the mainland and the seaports of the coast in a way that is valuable for our story. It is necessary to appreciate the economic and power structure of the period before going on to answer the question that this chapter has set itself.

Empires, this volume stated, are initially financed out of the loot of the conquered. Pandit Nehru argued that the Industrial Revolution in Britain was financed out of the loot of Bengal. The imperial power then takes in both tribute and the income from exports that pay for the military structure that maintains control. This leads to an imbalance—the industrial development of the conquering power and a lack of development in the subjugated. The author fails to notice that trading without colonialism can lead to an even greater imbalance, hence contemporary Japan.

Mesopotamia imported minerals and timber and exported manufactured goods, food and textiles. It was a dense trading area, connected with Egypt and the Mediterranean to the west, Iran and India to the east. It was intensely competitive. It was also inventive; allegedly producing bronze, abstract writing, advanced weaponry and commercial techniques. In order to produce more food to pay for more imports the nations of the Middle East were continuously under pressure to expand. There was a great development of private capital but state capital remained the greater.

Assyrian traders were already important in 2000 B.C.—the Akkadian traders had been enormously important four centuries earlier—and the movement of Assyrian conquest westward was prompted by a need to control her trade routes. She imported raw materials from the periphery of the empire and exported manufactured goods in return, or technicians.

Now, this was the scenario when Assyria came to deal with the seaports of the eastern Mediterranean. These ports Assyria deliberately left alone. In fact one author describes Assyria as being very much in the hands of the gnomes of Byblos: Assyria controlling their relationship by treaty and, maybe, inserting her own political officers, but leaving these coastal cities otherwise to go about their own business within parameters. The Phoenician cities are described as being parasitic on the mainland and as being interstitial: in other words, as being the middlemen between the consumer and the producer of the raw materials. On page 274 the author emphasizes the value to these seaports of monopolizing the sources of production of these various commodities, and on page 229 the author emphasizes the importance of every Middle Eastern power keeping open his routes to the Upper and Lower Seas, the Mediterranean and the Persian Gulf so that monopoly prices could not be raised against it. By 1600 B.C. the Levantine cities, Michael Heltzer says, were pivotal in the power structure of the Middle East.

To sum up the argument so far:

1. Where our authors say minerals did not exist they did not exist.

2. Where Michael Heltzer found the cheapest tin, he did not find the geological source but the economic and political centre of the trade, which lay in the capital of Assyria in the second millennium B.C.

3. In the second millennium B.C. Assyria imported many of her raw materials from beyond the borders of her empire.

4. Her trading stretched around the world.

The question is if, as these authors seem to show, Assyria controlled the bronze trade not by directly fetching it so much as by a series of sophisticated commercial arrangements with the shipping fleets with contracts enforceable, in the last analysis, by the matchless Assyrian infantry, where did the various shipping companies themselves fetch it from? For guidance, let us return to our slightly bemused authors.

Muhly, on page 243 of his book, points out that the oldest and most sacred city of the Sumerians is called Eridu, while the Sumerian name for copper is *uradu*. On page 243 he also points out the *Siparru* is the Sumerian name for bronze and is similar to the upstream Sumerian town of Sippar. He points out, on page 209, that the district Chalkis derives its name from its chief industry, copper- or bronzeworking. He points out that the word *t-l-t* in Ugaritic means both copper and bronze and that there was then a Syrian port called Atlag. We know that copper and Cyprus share the same name. We know from the Gospel according to St. John that the Greek for frankincense is *libanon* and for myrrh is *smyrnon* and we may wonder whether country and town were named after the incense trade. We know that the Phoenician port Arad means copper and that the Egyptian name for the Sudan, *Nwb*, means gold; that Hattus, the capital of the Hittite empire, was written with the ideograph for silver, the same name for silver being used in Ugaritic.

We have learned from our authors that the Assyrians controlled the Middle Eastern bronze trade at the height of the Bronze Age and that in those early days it was not altogether uncommon to name a town after its chief import or industry, even as happens today. So it will be interesting to look at the Assyrian word for tin, which both Heltzer and Muhly correctly give as *anaku:* a name found at almost all the sites of the tin deposits of the world.

We know that the majority of places are not named after their chief product.

That the university authors failed to see the direction in which their own work pointed stems from the prejudice that our Copper and Bronze Age ancestors were incapable of ocean sailing.

University iconoclasts knock down only those gods that are no longer worshipped.

For the sake of ease of reading, I have presented only a relatively small amount of the evidence I have available for worldwide sailing in general and sailing from the so-called Old World to the so-called New World, in particular from 7000 B.C. onward. Gunnar Thompson, in his recent book *American Discovery*,[5] gives a whole heap more of this American evidence. It is clear from my evidence as well as his that Columbus could not conceivably discover America, for it had never been lost in any relevant sense whatever.

23. Right-handedness and Left-handedness, a Worldwide Tradition—Also the Origin of Our Terms the Political Right and Left

Oh, ye mistook! Ye should have snatch'd his wand
And bound him fast. Without the rod revers'd,
And backward mutters of dissevering power,
We cannot free the lady that sits here
Bound in strong fetters fix'd and motionless.

JOHN MILTON

I shall endeavor to show in this chapter that the terms the political right and political left with their associated colors and rosettes of blue and red respectively and their contrasted policies of hierarchy and egalitarianism, can be traced back nine thousand years. I shall make this endeavor in the full knowledge that there are no historical references to these phrases more than a century or two old and that beyond this point the argument must depend upon the thread of inference.

Let us dive headfirst into the middle of the topic and take a look at the table of opposites attributed to Pythagoras. It is given in Aristotle.

limit	unlimited
odd	even
unity	plurality
right	left
male	female
resting	moving
straight	crooked
light	darkness
good	bad
square	oblong

To make sense of this table, and neither Aristotle nor Cornford make much attempt to do this, we must appreciate that the pre-Socratic Greek philosophers, including Pythagoras, were not miracle men who invented well nigh everything—a ridiculous academic opinion—but for the most part were deeply serious men intent to recover the knowledge that had been lost at the end of the Bronze Age. They can be compared to Adelard of Bath, Roger Bacon, Michael Scotus, Poggio and all those early European savants who from the twelfth century A.D. onward struggled to recover the knowledge that had been lost with the collapse of the Roman Empire. Only in our case the Classical Greek philosophers were seeking to retrieve the sciences lost at the end of the Bronze Age, when the civilizations of Crete and Mycenae, the Phoenician cities of the coast and the Hittite empire inland, all sank down and disappeared from off the face of the earth in a common destruction. As we have already seen, the pre-Socratic philosophers were not the brilliant innovators the universities believe, but somewhat unoriginal men who correctly conceived that their first duty was to recover and reestablish the ancient widsom. So we find Thom arguing that the principle of the right-angled triangle (Pythagoras's theorem) was known to the builders of the stone circles in Britain, from 2800 B.C. onward. Elsewhere it is argued that it was known to the Chinese of the same period, while Professor Lambert, Professor of Assyriology at the University of Birmingham, states that the whole of Euclidean geometry was available in Babylon at the start of the second millennium B.C.

Once we become aware of the degree to which these early Greek philosophers were merely repeating the learning of the Bronze Age, then it is easier to put this table of opposites into proper perspective. For the early history of the West, attested both by archaeology and Greek tradition, states that the first civilizing religion was the worship of the earth mother, the *Magna Mater*, that brought into being the civilization of old Europe. This flourished from about 7000 to 3500 B.C. according to Marija Gimbutas, and stretched from southern Poland to the Black Sea, the western Ukraine and Greece. It also extended as far as Africa, India, China and across both Americas, I must here add.

Some of the qualities of this nature religion were that the spirit at death went into caves under the earth, that its adherents were buried with a piece of red ocher representing the blood of mother earth—a practice that became worldwide—that you believed in immortality, for death was the sloughing of a skin as the serpent sloughs its skin, that offices of power in society went to women, and that property descended through women, not through men. This society seems also to have put emphasis upon the left side, perhaps because that is the seat of the heart and the side on which a mother will hold a young child. Red ocher, iron oxide, is called by us hematite, and *hemet*, as we have seen, is the Egyptian word both for woman and copper. Hence comes the phrase "the red-light district."

Around the middle of the sixth millennium, soon after the date Eusebius gives for the Creation, Gimbutas describes, along with Greek mythology, that a different society of people who worshipped a male god in heaven, not a goddess under the earth, pushed across Europe and in the course of the next millenium or two broke up this old religion, with its early form of writing, its small towns, its sailing boats and its temples. The worshippers of God in heaven, whether as a sky god or a sun god, formed small aristocratic groups, essentially monotheistic; in some but not all cases believing in a strictly finite future for human history; in government by the few, not by the many; in property passing through the male, not the female; and higher education being confined to the ruling clique. The worshippers of God in heaven specialized in irrigation agriculture and in metallurgy. The tension and conflict between these contrasting lifestyles is a key to

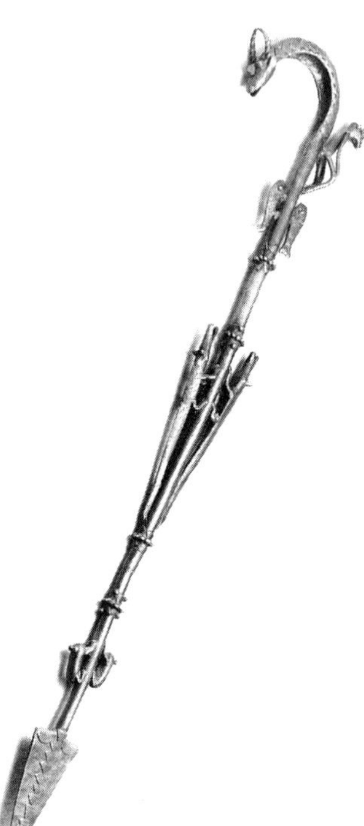

PLATE 189

SENUFO CHIEF'S STICK (94 CM). *This is a Senufo chief's stick made in bronze in two parts that were then welded together. It is a replica, if such a word can be applied to a part of the regalia still in use today.*

The serpentine creature on the handle, with horns and a semihuman face, in my judgment represents Tiamat, shown on Plate 190, the watery abyss, the original Mesopotamian goddess of the deep waters and the sailors and sea raiders who commanded them. Thus it became the head of the dragon, a creature associated with water and which traditionally breathed fire. For comparison I have reproduced an actual Mesopotamian bronze of Tiamat (Plate 190). The sea captain on the staff—if such it is—has the same appearance of head deformation as the kilted sea captains known previously. Tiamat was the Great Goddess and thus mother of all the gods. In Middle Eastern records Tiamat appears sometimes to be based on the other side of the Atlantic, raiding, Viking-like, the Old World.

Below it down the staff appear to be two fish, two crocodiles and two frogs, eight creatures in all. The crocodile was sacred to Atlas or Set, the frog was worshipped by the Egyptians as a symbol of immortality and symbolized half the original eight creative spirits in the delta.

Another Senufo chief's stick, this time in wood, exactly reproduces the staff of office associated with the kingship of Upper Egypt, with the head of the Set animal on the top and the double tail at the bottom, the same double tail shown by the Egyptian hieroglyph for Set, representing the female influence. At Hermopolis in Egypt it was believed that the Creation began with eight spirits: four male with the heads of frogs and four female with the heads of serpents.[1]

Tiamat (right), the dragon mother of the Babylonian pantheon, pursued by Marduk.

PLATE 190

MESOPOTAMIAN TIAMAT: CREATOR GODDESS. *This sculpture is to be compared with the handle of the Senufo chief's staff. Mesopotamian influence was widespread across Africa: the fig was sacred in Mesopotamia: it was while praying at a fig tree in the Aberdares, the* Ficus religiosa, *that the Mau Mau leader, Dedan Kimathi, was trapped: equally the fig was sacred to the Maya of Guatemala.*[2] *So many very, very specific customs were almost worldwide in their spread. The peculiar practice that when the wife is in labor the husband goes through labor pains, the couvade, is still practiced by many tribes of North and South America, in southern India, in China, in Borneo, Greenland and Kamchatka, but we know of it practiced formerly in many other places as well. Couvade means hatching,*[3] *a most curious and specific custom. Tiamat was mother of Kingu. Kingu was executed for his rebellion against the male gods. Another Senufo chief's staff copies the Set animal, as portrayed in Egyptian hieroglyphs. I believe the Set animal may prove to be associated with the American coyote. Set became the trickster god in Egypt. To Mexicans the trickster god was called Coyotl. Atlas was another name for Set. Tiamat, goddess of the sea raiders of that early period, may have been partly based in the Americas.*

In the Osirian belief the dead pharaoh descends with Osiris across the western horizon to the underworld, the island where is the Tree of Life, which is the domain of Poseidon to the Mesopotamians, the island of Utnapishtim in the Gilgamesh Epic, and to the Phoenicians the abode of El.[4] *Tiamat was the primordial Mesopotamian Creator goddess and represents the power of the ocean waters. She uses the minor god Kingu to lead her forces, who is defeated and sacrificed. Tiamat had the power to appoint rulers.*[5] *Toward the end of the Bronze Age only Marduk could defeat Tiamat.*[6]

understanding the Copper and Bronze Ages. The mythical animals symbolize the two religions when, probably for political convenience, they were made compatible; the eagle represented God in heaven; the serpent, the lion and the cow represented Mother Earth, with her dominion over animals both wild and tame. Hence the dragon is the synthesis of the serpent of the sea and earth worshippers, with the feathers of the eagle and the face of the lion. The gryphon and the winged bull of Assyria would seem to have had similar functions. And emphasis upon the right-hand side might well refer to the hand most used for weapons and for the sword arm.

Now, the Greek historian Diodorus Siculus records that the sky worshippers conquered the greater part of the inhabited world, the *oecumene*. This statement I believe to be fairly literally true. And because they became top-dog, writing up the records, a pejorative sense was given to the qualities of the nature religion, which they now tried to suppress: the left is sinister, darkness or evil, while correct is right: the left is gauche, the right is adroit. The witch is evil, the wizard is wizard. Eve is born out of Adam's rib, not Adam out of Eve's rib, and so the rubbish goes on.

The tension between these two lifestyles, the old matriarchal, maritime religion and the new worship of God in heaven, spread wherever these two religions spread, across the *oecumene*. Where they spread the table of opposites has spread, although, with its vast extension in time and space, variation has crept in.

PLATE 191
These two figures are of ancient Mexican art, exhibited at the Hayward Gallery, London, 1992. Figurine (a) carries a cross on her right cheek, symbolizing, I believe, the sky god; a saltire on her left cheek symbolizing the goddess: Anat to the Phoenicians, Neith to the Egyptians, one of their Creator goddesses. On her breast are the simple hieroglyph for the sun or time and also the symbol for the sun and its rays. Below that again is the meander, a design widely employed in the Old World and below it the Egyptian symbol for colony and distant land.

Figure (b), part of the same exhibition of ancient Mexican art, has for me an overwhelmingly ancient Egyptian appearance.

The Phoenicians, the sea traders of the Middle East, used the saltire, Anat's cross, as on the left cheek of this Mexican figure. Philo of Byblos, quoting Sanchuniathon, said that their god, Chronos, sacrificed his only-begotten son, Ieoud, dressed before sacrifice as a king. Obviously it was a rite of substitution for the king. The Carthaginian practice, however, of sacrificing children was only giving a religious twist to the common antique practice of child exposure for the sake of population control. The Tophet was an essential part of family planning. These practices Phoenicians shared with their colonies.

In modern times the subject had been taken up again by Robert Hertz, a French sociologist killed in the obscene slaughter of the First World War, and continued by a series of contributors to a volume entitled *Left and Right*. In ignorance of the historical ramifications of the subject, the contributors have concentrated upon the customs associated with right- and left-handedness, pointing out that there is no physiological reason for the status and predominance of the right. They do not seem to suspect, in these tables of opposites appearing in almost all parts of the world, their deep historical roots.

From the customs and traditions of the Meru of Kenya they derive the following table:[1]

right	left
north	south
white clans	black clans
day	night
first wife	co-wife
dominant age division	subordinate age division
man	woman/child
superior	inferior
east	west
sunrise	sunset
sun	moon
light	darkness
sight	blindness

political power	religious authority
successors	predecessors
older	younger
white man	black man
cultivation	honey collecting[2]

Among the Amboyna of Indonesia the following:

right	left
male	female
land or mountainside	coast or seaside
above	below
heaven or sky	earth
worldly	spiritual
upward	downward
interior	exterior
in front	behind
east	west
old	new[3]

PLATE 192
The circles on top of this gourd are probably sun symbols. On a number of designs worldwide there is an optical illusion between a black and a white symbol. Here the effect is achieved with the black Maltese cross and the white four-leafed clover, or quadrefoil, the eye tending to slide from one to the other. It is a sort of visual pun. The Maltese cross was a sacred symbol to ancient Mexico and ancient Peru and is carried additionally on the English crown. Visual punning was very much an Egyptian trick.

THE GOURD THAT MAY BE A HEMISPHERE (13 CM DIAMETER). *I think the shortage of ancient pottery in West Africa is explained by the profusion of gourds: the bottle gourd* (Lagenaria siceraria), *for example, being native to Africa. In this sense, it was a gourd culture, the gourd skins being decorated with precisely the same designs as would have been placed upon the pots. The African bottle gourd was in use both in America and in Thailand from 7000 B.C.*

According to the Greek historian and prehistorian Diodorus Siculus, the Atlas people were famous for teaching the doctrine of the sphere. This means the cosmic sphere even more than the fact that the earth itself was spherical—which they also knew. The movements of the sun, the moon, the stars and even the planets were taken to be spherical. God was defined as a perfect figure that had neither beginning nor end; which definition is met by the surface of the sphere. The squares created by these lines are in sets of eight (compare Plate 197).

This gourd carries the chief Adinkra design, which, I believe, will one day prove to be a half globe of the northern hemisphere, with longitude and latitude marked on it. There is also the Maltese cross and the so-called St. Andrew's cross placed on the temperate zone where our Set people were mostly living. The Set or Atlas people were long-distance sailors who knew the earth was round and from very early days indeed had measured its circumference. The Adinkra design is Ashanti and is found on top of the Ashanti gold fields. The Ghanaian tribe called the Adansi controlled the gold mines before the Ashanti drove them off. The Greeks used the one word, ktisis, *both for the Creation and for founding a city: the Adansi word for Creation carried the same double meaning, founding a city as well as creating the world. They were practical guys, as indeed were the peoples of the Bronze Age generally. The pharaoh claimed not only to be king of Egypt but divine king of the entire world. Sargon of Akkad had been called Sar Kissati or king of the world. This claim for catholicism was based on fact.*

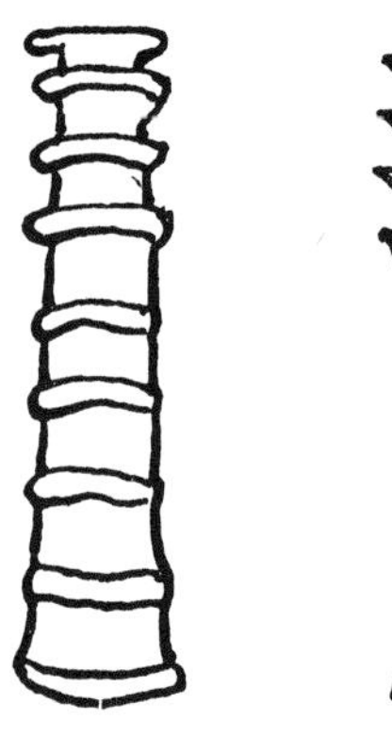

PLATE 193
The Egyptian symbol of the spinal column of the maritime god Osiris. Osiris was also known as Dionysus and Hades. This is the Egyptian Djed symbol, representing stability.

Among the Maori of New Zealand the following:

male	female
virility	weakness
descent of the paternal line	descent of the maternal line
east	west
offensive magic	sorcery
right	left
white figure of a guardian angel	demons and devils
good and beautiful	bad and ugly
life	death
sky	earth
high	underworld[4]

Among the Chinese, they also note the following. While the opposition and tension between these two worldwide religions were alleviated in Mesopotamia by a synthesis of the two sets of belief, a mixture symbolized by composite animals and where the hierogamy, the marriage of the sky god to the virginal earth mother, was the principal ceremony on top of the ziggurat, in China the two religions were compounded into one coherent philosophy of life called yin and yang, in which both religions were treated equally and were equally essential, rotating with a rhythmic and cyclic alternation:

male	female
sky	earth
yang	yin
breath	blood
father	mother
face east	face west
chief, a rising sun	vassals
square	circular

A minute and detailed etiquette ensured that each allegiance, and thus in a sense each class of society, was accorded similar honors.[5]

Of all societies the Chinese is popularly believed to have had the

BOBO MALTESE CROSS. *The Bobo tribe live in the west of Burkina Faso, with much of the art coming from the Bobo-Diylasso area. They are a larger tribe with a somewhat richer culture than their neighbor, the Lobi. This piece makes use of the Maltese cross for a headdress and has an unidentifiable bird on the headdress. The eyes are formed out of spirals. The arms arch much like the Egyptian portrayal of the sky goddess. It is difficult to make sense of the tutu unless it be the Egyptian Djed figure. The Maltese cross was the sacred symbol behind the Incas' throne, was reproduced on Central American codices, is on the crown of Queen Elizabeth of England and symbolized rule over the four quarters of the earth. It was also on the Spanish conquistadors' sails, and perhaps explains how they cakewalked the Americas, because it had represented, for something like five millennia, that which was gentle, civilized and good.*

greatest continuity with its own past. It comes as no surprise, therefore, to find the Chinese emperor, until this century, described as the Son of Heaven, for it was from the heaven-worshipping peoples that the system of monarchy came. Equally telling is that the opposition to the monarchy was rooted among the peasants, finding its expression into this century in the secret societies with mellifluous names. These centers of opposition to the emperor worshipped an eternal mother, known as Mother without End, and wore a red garment as a symbol of their allegiance. Our contemporary communists took over the symbols of the earth mother and debauched them.

Christianity is a religion influenced by this dual tradition. Psalm 118, verse 16, says: "The right hand of the Lord hath the preeminence." The good thief is crucified to the right of Christ, the position of honor. And in pictures of the Last Judgment, the Lord's raised right hand signifies the place of abode for the blessed, his lowered left hand points to the jaws of hell for the damned. With death both traditions are offered, although they

PLATE 194

DOGON CHIEF'S STOOL *(right). This is a chief's wooden stool of the Dogon tribe of Mali. It would seem to represent the eight creative spirits that, among other things, began the creative process in the delta of Egypt. The shape of the supports of the stool is egg-shaped, which the Dogon believed to have been the shape of the nuclear universe before the Creator inserted the spiral of life within it and set it in motion. The religion of Orpheus, which Orpheus brought to the Greeks from Egypt, also maintained that the original nucleus of the universe should be compared to an egg. The seat is not circular but elliptical, like the path of the planets. Above the figures is the matriarchal saltire, originally formed of crossed arrows.*

STOOL FROM COSTA RICA *(left). The design on this pottery stool from Costa Rica is not unlike the design on this wooden Dogon stool from Mali but, admittedly, there are other African stools virtually identical in design with these Atlas type figures holding up this Costa Rica seat.*[7]

Atlas figures holding up a Polynesian drum.

are mutually inconsistent and contradictory: in one tradition the body is to be buried in the earth to rise corporeally upon the last day, and in the other the soul goes off to heaven to be on the right hand of God while the body returns to earth and is of no account. The sun is sometimes a symbol for Christ in religious art and thought.

The worship of God in heaven, which may have originated in Iran but which, according to Diodorus, later spread out from the Atlantic coasts of Europe conquering the greater part of the inhabited world, provided a small ruling class to each society it took over. But it seems only slowly to have converted the masses who had been won to the earth-worshipping religion in previous millennia. As we have already seen, in the Creation story of Genesis, Adam in Akkadian quite simply means the color red, while his consort, Eve, *Hawah* in Arabic, was the earth mother, mother of all living things. Together they represented the working class of Mesopotamia.

So the left side, with red for red-ocher, represented the masses, while the right, with blue for the blue of the sky, represented the forces of order, discipline and hierarchy. The extension of this table of opposites to societies around the world bears witness to its great antiquity even if we did not possess, in the Greek tradition of the Birth of the Gods, the ancient records. It also bears witness to the degree these societies, from China to Africa, had formerly been interconnected.

The communist dialectic traces its origins from Marx and Hegel, from Hegel through the Neoplatonists to Plato. The academics find its origins in the question-and-answer of the Socratic method. The origin of our present political controversy lies in the overwhelming politico-religious experience of the Copper and Bronze Ages; when the thesis was earth worship, its antithesis was sky worship, and the ensuing synthesis of the two, of which Christianity derives from one among many differing examples, predominated in many parts of the world. Associated with this is the world-sailing god, Chronos or Time, which is essentially trinitarian, divisible into past, present and future, yet one god.

These, then, are the ancient roots of our present conflicts.

Both religions in their day had great successes and it serves no good purpose to describe the differing factions not just as different but as evil. Perhaps the present-day partisans of either side will be more relaxed if they notice that in the Bronze Age the greatest exponents of private enterprise, the sea peoples, were reds, while the blue-blooded monarchs, who also claimed to be God on earth such as did the Incas in South America, ran systems of government akin to totalitarian communism! Our present-day antipathies can also be looked on as those who worship God the Past, the conservatives; those who worship God the Future, the radicals; and those who worship God the Present, the youth and the artists. To Chronos-worshippers these are just three aspects of one God, three aspects that deserve equal veneration.

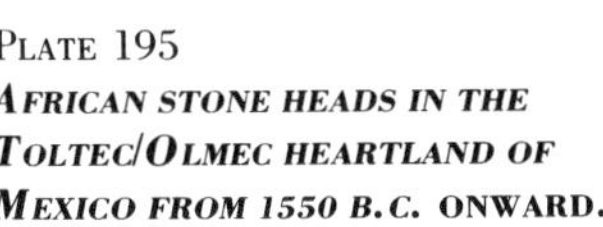
PLATE 195
AFRICAN STONE HEADS IN THE TOLTEC/OLMEC HEARTLAND OF MEXICO FROM 1550 B.C. ONWARD.

Tres Zapotes I.

San Lorenzo VI.

San Lorenzo IV.

La Venta I. There were oracles at La Venta like those of Phoenicia.[8]

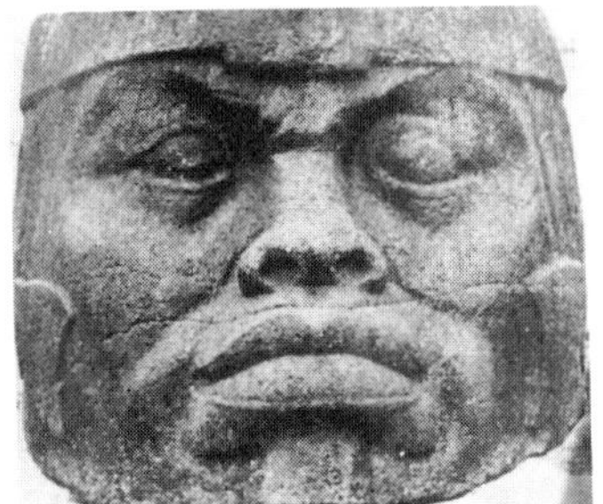
Tres Zapotes II.

PLATE 196

OLD WORLD ARTIFACTS IN PRE-COLUMBIAN AMERICA. *Bronze sword blade dating from the Bronze Age, of European origin, discovered among some Mayan ruins near Mérida, Yucatán.*[9] *Claudius Aelianus (A.D. 170–230) reported that knowledge of the existence of a huge island out in the Atlantic was a continuing tradition among the Phoenicians or Carthaginians of Cádiz. Pausanias (fl. A.D. 150), Greek geographer, states that far west of the ocean there lies a group of islands whose inhabitants are red-skinned and whose hair is like that of the horse. This knowledge was common property, obviously enough since the Phoenicians, who had returned from America to the Mediterranean with the collapse of the bronze trade, nevertheless continued with the Atlantic trade.*

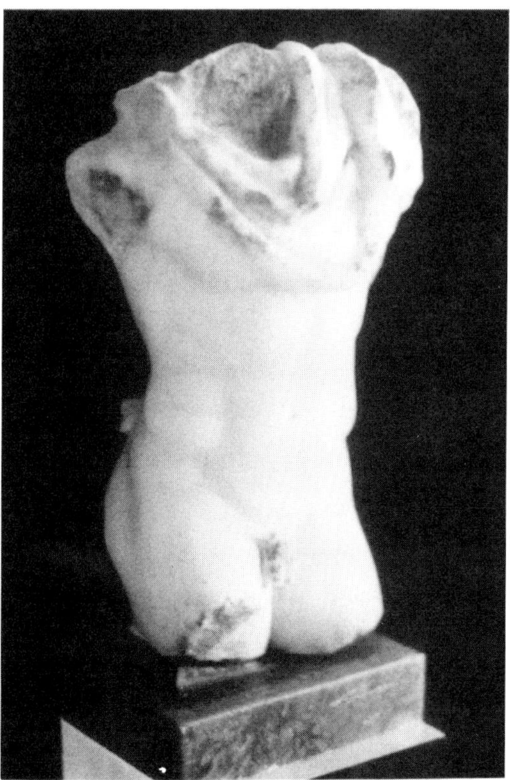

Roman torso of Venus, made of marble, discovered in the Gulf of Mexico in a fisherman's net during the past century. Plutarch (A.D. 46–120), in his dialogue "On the Face in the Moon's Orb" records that far west in the ocean, in the latitude of Britain, lie certain islands beyond which stretches a great continent. There, during a period of thirty days, they have almost unbroken sunshine and light. During the night the sun disappears only for an hour but it never really becomes dark.[10] *We must be totally clear that the knowledge of America was never lost.*

PLATE 197

THE SACRED NATURE OF THE SPHERE. *Giant basalt ball, one of hundreds in Costa Rica. It is 7.03 feet in diameter and weighs about sixteen tons. It is within a quarter of an inch of being a true sphere. A few of these giant stone balls are found in Honduras, Belize and Mexico. The surface of the sphere was believed by the ancients to be the divine shape, at once boundless and finite. One Greek word for astronomy is* sphaera *or* sphere. *Because of the perfect nature of the sphere, a Roman writer announced:* "Deus est ballum," *or God is a ball. Professor Thom, whom I spoke to on the telephone in his last years, wrote that the builders of the stone circles before 2000 B.C. used π as $^{25}/_{8}$ not as $^{22}/_{7}$. The English mile is that dimension which gives the circumference of the earth as approximately twenty-five thousand miles and the diameter of the earth as approximately eight thousand miles. The dimensions of the mile are functions of eight—the number sacred to the matriarchs—thus suggesting that the earth had been measured from the very earliest times. When the Gauls told Julius Caesar that they knew the measurements of the earth and its geography this was not only true but they had known it for a very long time indeed.*

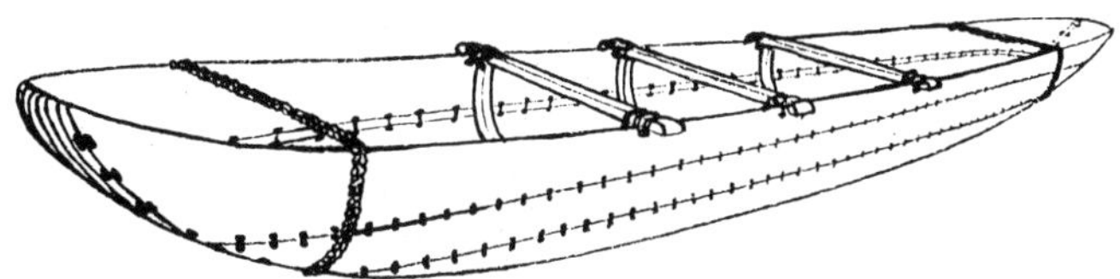

The North Ferriby boat, dated around 1600 B.C., was found in the Humber by E. V. Wright and his brother, with whom I was at one time acquainted. It is a sewn boat, which permits it, confronted by waterfalls or rapids, to be unsewn, carried around the obstacle, and then sewn up again. Ocean sailing does not in fact require large boats. Robert Marx writes that over the last century there have been more than 120 solo or two-man ocean voyages, including a ninety-three-day crossing from Japan to San Francisco in a nineteen-foot sloop.[11] We may add here that "Gaelic tales abound in allusions to a beautiful country situated under the sea. . . . Belief in it is found in the mythology of almost every race."[12] This, of course, refers to "God's own country," the earthquakes around 1190 B.C. and the subsidence of small portions in the Caribbean and perhaps off Peru.

Plate 198

The Trapezoid Doors in Mycenae and Peru: This is Mycenae, Treasury of Atreus. *Throughout Peru and throughout the vast Incan Empire, the trapezoid door—not to mention trapezoid windows and niches and even plazas—was the preferred design. It is also worth noting that ancient Peru and Mexico used a decimal system—as did the Romans—and in Pythagorean mathematics the number ten was called Atlas. Mycenae had no mines and no natural sources of wealth. In Mexico Atl was the name of the supreme god.*

It is also worth noting that Si was the name for the moon in Peru and Sin in Mesopotamia. Note that the Toltec culture of Mexico and the Chavin of Peru show signs of being closely interconnected.

The same trapezoidal door, set in the same cyclopean stone walls at Tiahuanaco. Until we understand that Mycenaean colonies and Cretan colonies in America were as much larger as the United States is to Britain and Brazil is to Portugal, we understand nothing of this ancient world. When tradition says that Minos and red-haired Rhadamanthus were both kings of Crete and kings and judges of the underworld, the underworld refers to their huge American colonies, not to a nonsensical religious concept for raising money, the place of eternal punishment. There is a possibility that a Greek name, Hypachaioi, is not to be translated as "lesser Achaeans" but as American Achaeans, Achaeans from the underworld, where the sun was at midnight. Hyperchthonia, "down under." In Crete blocks of stone masonry were fitted with metal rivets,[13] much as in Peru.

PLATE 199
AXE MONEY FROM AMERICA, CHINA AND GHANA. *Too soft for practical use, the large axes at left were made of serpentine for rituals. Some weigh as much as twenty pounds. Harder, finely polished jade axes at right were buried years later as a second offering; this collection (left) is from America.*

A small Chinese soft stone axe useful only as a token.[14] *Dr. Joseph Needham specifically links the third century* B.C. *to the second century* A.D. *as a period when many Chinese fleets set sail searching for "the Isles of the Immortals," in the eastern ocean. The Aztecs and Maya treasured jade as dearly as the Chinese and all three placed jade beads or jade carvings of cicadas in the mouths of the dead.*[15] *He notes as well that slat armor, characteristic of China and Japan, is also found in America and all three used conch shell trumpets. Needham also points out that Tyrian purple was made from the mollusk purpura and that this was the basis of the Incan dye industry. Dr. Needham writes: "The outstanding originality of the pre-Columbian metalworkers in Central and South America will not be disputed by anyone but many of their subtlest techniques do inescapably show a close connection with similar ones in the Old World."*

This small stone axe head is one of a hoard found, and one sample given to me, by a mining engineer from the Ashanti gold fields of Ghana. William Fagg told me that it would be the butt end of a worn-down hand axe. But the stone is soft, a type of soapstone, and the axe head could never have performed any practical function for that very reason. The axe symbolized power.

Now, we know that in the Bronze Age symbolic tools were employed for currency. But more specifically ceremonial stone axes were used in the pre-Columbian southeast of North America[16] *and in China as Chinese axe money.*[17] *Polished stone axe heads were traded the length and breadth of Neolithic Britain.*

Thin copper axes were used as currency in Aztec Mexico; they were also found in Ecuador and Peru.[18] *There were similar soft-stone ceremonial axes used by the Toltec/Olmec culture of Mexico (1500* B.C.*). Another of the many similarities in culture between West Africa and ancient America is the way that in Ghana chiefs speak through linguists, a practice Christopher Columbus encountered on arrival in Cuba.*[19] *Ghana is at the receiving end of the Atlantic countercurrent.*

Plate 200
The golden stool of the Ashanti. *"We shall meet, but we shall miss him." On the left stands the gold-plated, now vacant, personal stool—"the Nyansopo"—of Otumfuo Sir Osei Agyeman Prempeh II, waiting to accompany his departure to Bremang, the place of the dead kings. The Nyansopo buries the black stool next to it to be preserved in the Asantehene's grave.*

The Egyptian goddess Isis, among other things, was the pharaoh's throne.[20] *The mysterious chthonic powers of the soil, derived from the goddess, were conducted by the stool or throne to the king, rendering a formerly ordinary man divine: the divine king of his mighty tribe. The king personified the soul of his entire nation and, like a shuttle in a great loom, wove together the forces of nature, the divine Creator and the soul of his people.*

In ancient Mexico also the chair was the symbol of authority.[21] *The Amerindian Mixtec king was, like the Asantehene, given a death mask and his retainers were also killed and buried with him.*

It is an Ashanti belief that all men are immortal as children of the sky god Nyame, possessing a soul that at death returns to God.[22] *The foundation of all the Greco-Roman mysteries is that of death followed by resurrection.*[23]

Plate 201
Baoulé bronze box for gold dust. *This bronze box, with the crocodile on the lid, is for holding gold dust. It comes from Baoulé. The crocodile was sacred. The water symbol is embossed on both sides of the lid. There are ten stripes on either end. In Guinea the crocodile is the symbol of all metalworkers, as it was the symbol of the Set and Atlas metalworkers called Hephaestus.*[24] *"Gold is as plentiful as dust" a king wrote Pharaoh Amenhotep III in a plea for gifts. The Ivory Coast is one of the places it will have come from. The Baoulé are Akan who emigrated there under Queen Poukou. Akan chiefs will only speak through linguists, as was the practice in pre-Columbian Cuba.*[25]

The King of Cambodia on a golden throne, under a golden parasol, being carried to his houseboat for the Fête des Eaux. Both litter and parasol are part of the royal regalia of the Akan tribe of Ghana—a practice not found in other parts of Africa.

PLATE 202
This bronze pin from Burkina Faso, the front and obverse of which are shown above, resembles the left-hand pair of bronze pins from Peru and Asia. The comparison between the pins of pre-Columbian Peru and of Asia was originally made by Heine-Geldern. The motif of this pin is the spiral, a shape that the Dogon tribe believes to be at once the heart of all microscopic life as well, of course, as it being the shape of the great star galaxies. The Dogon tribe inhabit Mali and Burkina Faso.

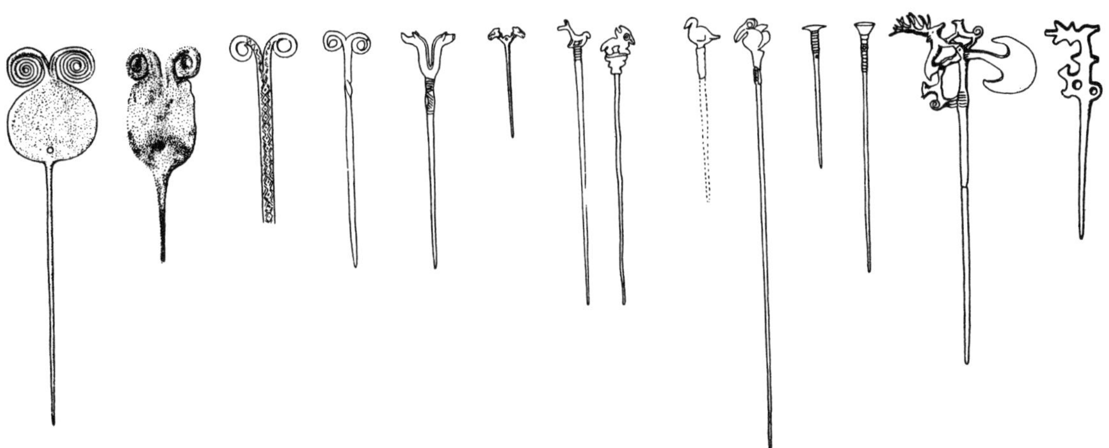

Metal pins from South America and Asia. These pins, found on both sides of the Pacific Ocean, are only a few of the many objects from these areas that exhibit an extremely close resemblance in form and function. Such pins are about the length of old-fashioned hat pins, and were used to fasten clothing. With each pair, the South American is on the left, the Asian is on the right. While we are on the subject of South America let us note that the Amerindians of Paraguay anciently believed in the Virgin, the Virgin Birth, the marvelous boy who became the sun; also in the immutability of the soul and of heaven.[26] *Pachacamac, the high god of Peru, provided oracular predictions, favorable intervention with the elements, protection against disease, specialized knowledge as to the favorable times for planting and harvesting,*[27] *just like an African god.*

PLATE 203

BENIN OBA. *This Benin figure, in my opinion an excellent example of magical art, is replete with references. Christianity was brought to West Africa by the Portuguese as early as the end of the fifteenth century, hence the symbol of the cross. I think the little figure holding the cross in one hand and the Ogboni sword in the other is probably the chief's praise singer. The Ogboni are the Yoruba secret society to which I was once offered to be made a member.*

But what is of particular interest is the set of bogus pigtails attached to the Oba's cap. In the same way as their famed culture heroes are believed to be mimicked by the Mexican notables who sported false beards and even false beak noses in pre-Columbian times, so the Oba wears false pigtails. Few Europeans and no African can achieve this adornment. But Minoan Cretans or Indians and Indonesians could be represented thus. On some plaques, Benin Obas are also represented with serpent tails for feet. It should be remembered that the pre-Hellenic inhabitants of ancient Greece, (i.e. before 1900 B.C.) were sea people called Ophiones, portrayed as the top half human and the bottom half serpent. The Oba of Benin, like Aaron, carries a serpent staff. The Yoruba next door to the Bini worship the supreme god called Malokun, a name suspiciously like the Phoenician Moloch. Malokun brings wealth and comes from the sea. The innumerable minor Yoruba deities are simply his intermediaries, manifesting him to the Yoruba.

PLATE 204

OBA OF BENIN (DETAIL OF PREVIOUS FIGURE). *The Yoruba, to whom the Bini are related, place the Creation of the World at Igbo Idio, in the center of Ife. Oduduwa, their founding ancestor, who was white and a woman, was present at the Creation. Benin art is held to have been influenced by the earlier and very beautiful art of Ife. However, to my eyes, Benin art is the superior, possessing far greater imaginative power. There are beliefs at Ife, according to William Fagg, similar to those of pre-Classical Greece. The ancient Egyptian name for the seed that started the Creation is Bnn. In Egyptian vowels were not written but supplied by the reader.*

The imperial city of Benin is close to the creeks of the Niger Delta, the mouth of one of the great communication rivers of West Africa. The King or Oba of Benin kept all brass casting as the royal prerogative: popular art was in wood, court art in bronze. Brass casters in Benin were prohibited, under pain of death, to work for anyone but the Oba.

At times, this Edo-speaking people called the Bini ruled an empire that stretched from Dahomey to the east of the Niger River. The power and wealth of the empire is reflected in their great sculptural tradition, one of the outstanding art traditions of the world. Let us note that the cire perdue method of casting bronze—the lost-wax process—was anciently used not only across the Fertile Crescent and Africa but also across the Americas.

PLATE 205.
A MEXICAN STONE HEAD *(right)* **FROM THE TOLTEC/OLMEC PERIOD, 1550 B.C.** *Colossal head. Monument 1 from San Lorenzo, height nine feet four inches, Museum of Anthropology, University of Veracruz, Jalapa. The distance between West Africa and South America is only the length of the Mediterranean, so there should be no surprise in finding Africans in east America. The scale and magnificence of these portraits assure that they must have been persons of power. These belong to the Toltec culture, by the universities called Olmec, commencing about 1500 B.C. With the name Toltec, we should notice that* tol *is simply an Atlas name and in Greek* Tekton *can be translated as either carpenter or master craftsman, meaning the Creator. That the church uses the first translation gives Christianity a nice democratic touch. When you want a builder in Mexico you still ask for a toltec, so in the New Testament it is likely that there is a purposeful mistranslation, not a contradiction. In a recent archaeological report in London's* Daily Telegraph, *the archaeologists said that the Philistines were Mycenaeans—which in part they were—and great builders of course. In their colonial base of Mexico they were in simple fact called Toltecs, or master builders. It is worth remembering that with the undoubted physical diffusion by the sea lanes of peoples and artifacts comes also stimulus diffusion, immigrants carrying ideas and technology, like cire perdue casting, not just artifacts.*

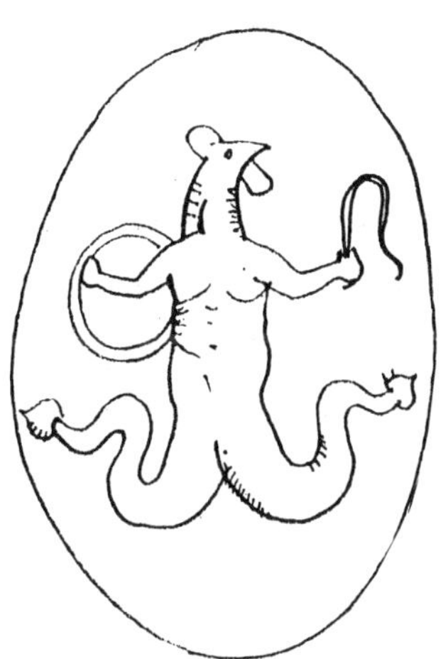

CERAMIC BENIN PLAQUES *(left). There are a number of Benin plaques where the Oba is portrayed with the bottom part of his body a fish or a serpent. I believe this practice may hark back to the days when mammy-waters traded up the Niger, for Benin stands close to its mouth. Traditionally the Benin people swear either by the king or the sea. There were also sea people known in pre-Hellenic Greece as the Ophiones or Serpent People, dating to around 2000 B.C., whose symbol was a man for the upper portion of his body, a serpent for the lower part. There is also a Scottish tradition of such a one living on the Stack Rock, an island northwest of Scotland.*

PLATE 206
This represents the supreme Gnostic deity with bird's head and serpent legs, given for comparison with the Benin figures above.

Benin art. These two figures are off plaques of the Benin fetish king and his attendants. The king, isolated here, has catfish legs. The Phoenicians had the mermaid, Derketo.

Gnostic seals

It has been suggested that the Phoenicians used a rooster to symbolize the god Thoth.

In addition to the two Benin plaques are Gnostic seals. The Gnostics were part of the Middle Eastern religious traditions, including that of Ioannes or John the Baptizer. The human body has a bird for a head and a double serpent for the lower part of the body, symbolizing the synthesis of the worship of the god in heaven and the goddess under the earth whose friend and familiar was the serpent and whose symbolic numbers were even. There may be a common ancestry to the two traditions.

Plate 207
The Worldwide Lozenge Symbol.

Zingu digging sticks from the upper Amazon employing the lozenge motif.

The Inca in his litter. Drawing by Guaman Poma from an Incan chronicle. Compare the lozenge symbol on the Incas' palanquin with the same symbol on the brow of the Oba of Benin. The high god of Peru, Vira Cocha, walked on the water as did Jesus Christ.[28] The lozenge was also a sacred symbol to the early matriarchal society.[29] Ghanaian chiefs also have to be carried in litters as I have watched on innumerable occasions. Theology is frequently political.

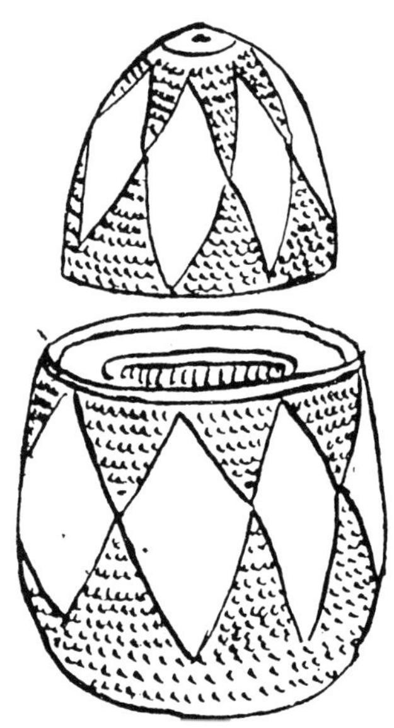

Predynastic Egyptian pottery using the lozenge device.

Polychrome tripod jar, Chupicuaro culture, Guanajuato. Late Formative Period (14 cm height).

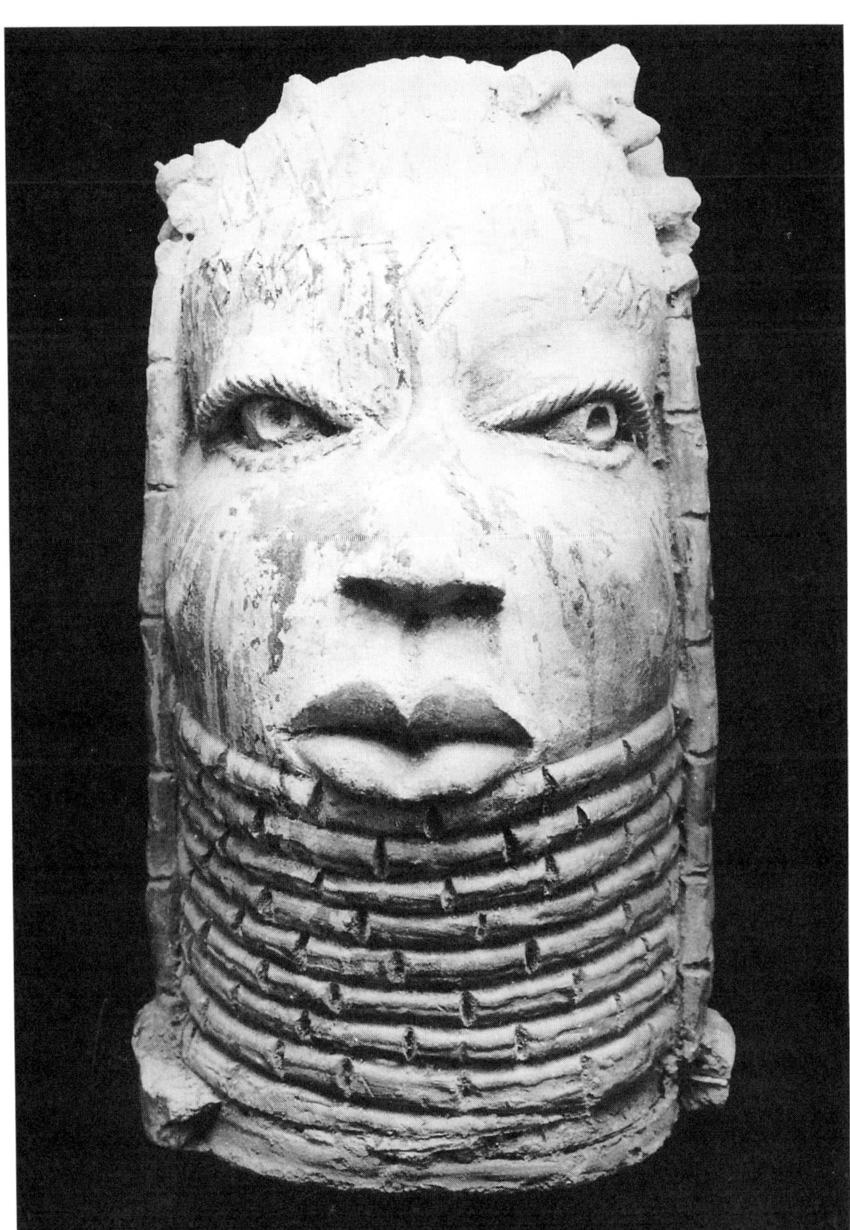

PLATE 208
TERRA-COTTA OBA OF BENIN.
This superb piece of comparatively modern Benin art, unsurpassed in sensitivity and power, will stand comparison with any sculpture. The diamond-shaped mark on the forehead is an ancient symbol of divinity. It is found engraved on some of the Boyne graves of Ireland; it is described by the National Museum in Mexico City as symbolizing divinity in the Mexican tradition; it is a symbol used in the civilization of old Europe (7000–3500 B.C.); it is the shape of the shields used by the sea people visiting Burkina Faso, as we showed on previous pages. The Dogon believe that God, having created the Cosmos, traveled in a diamond pattern across the universe when he came back again to look at his creation. The Inca had this lozenge design on his litter. Crampton points out that, like the ancient king of Stonehenge, the ancient king of Dorset (near Maiden Castle) also wore a finely designed breastplate, lozenge-shaped, measuring six inches by four and a half inches, suggesting that the adornment was a symbol of monarchy.[30]

This Cretan figure is closely similar to many Benin figures.

PLATE 209

NOTES ON THE ANCIENT CULTURE OF NIGERIA. *William Fagg finds it curious that the Bini of Benin, although positioned as the city is near the mouth of the Niger River—one of the great trading rivers of Africa—should share certain myths with the Ancient Greeks.*

The Bini are related to the Yoruba. The great German anthropologist Leo Frobenius, in his book The Voice of Africa,[31] *makes a study of the Yoruba, concluding that the tribe possesses a culture of great subtlety, depth and antiquity, much of which is shared with cultures of the ancient world of the eastern Mediterranean. Of course, the Yoruba tradition states unequivocally that their ruling class came from Canaan at the time of Nimrod: the name Canaan associates with bronze. Frobenius correctly concludes that the people of the coastal areas of West Africa widely came under influences that arose out of Atlantic contacts and that some of this contact was also shared anciently with America, Frobenius noticing similarities between the customs of the Yoruba and those of the Maya in Guatemala.*[32]

Frobenius also noticed that in the Yoruba system of government by god-kings the life of the king was terminated by the priesthood: with the Jukun of Eastern Nigeria after seven years, with the Alafin of Oyo after seven or fourteen years, as in the European studies by Sir James Frazer. Frobenius noticed as well the very large quantity of mound burials that had formerly occurred; also that there was retainer burial along with the king; and that much jewelery was buried with the nobility and was being unearthed by tomb robbers fossicking among ancient graves. He shows that the Yoruba, and the Yoruba alone among West Africans, share the custom of making burnt sacrifices, along with the Jews and the ancient races of the Mediterranean, and that most of these common cultural practices were confined to the littoral tribes. The Yoruba, we should note, also use divination boards like the early inhabitants of Mesopotamia.

Frobenius had evidence in his hand to go further but failed to do so. He noticed the widespread use of the titles Balé and Baloma across West Africa, from the Yoruba to Lake Chad and the Niger bend, without noticing that Balé is the Akkadian word for king. He noticed that the earth mother from whom the sixteen gods were born was called Yemaya (page 204), without noticing that Maia was one of the seven daughters of Atlas after whom the Atlantic itself was named, and that the number eight in ancient Europe had especial importance for the earth mother; and the Maya are the inhabitants of Guatemala, whose white and bearded culture heroes had crossed the Atlantic to avoid the Flood, or so the Maya recorded.

Oloron was the name of the supreme Yoruba sky divinity: the name would seem to be a compound of El, the Semitic sky divinity known to the Greeks as Chronos, joined to the Greek sky divinity Ouranos, Chronos's father. The name of the Yoruba sea god Olokun, whom Frobenius fairly accurately likens to Poseidon, would seem probably to be a compound of El and Okeanos. Shango, the thunder god whom Frobenius compares with Jupiter Tonans, sacrificed himself by hanging on the tree Amjo. Frobenius should have compared him to the Germanic god Odin, who sacrificed himself by hanging on the tree of knowledge Yggdrasill. In Greek the double g has the effect of ng *as in evangel, so even the names of the sacred trees may be related.*

The sacred city of Ile-Ife was known to the Yoruba as the navel of the world and Cuzco had also the same title and function for ancient Peru, as did Easter Island for the Pacific, Delphi for Greece, Nippur for Sumer, etc.

As in Africa, the worship of God in Egypt and Assyria, in Mexico and Crete, demanded the creation of artistic beauty for his service.

PLATE 210

MIDDLE EASTERN PEOPLES COLONIZING BOTH SIDES OF THE ATLANTIC: MEXICO'S JAGUAR-HEADED DIVINITY. *In Nigeria's Ondo state is Idanre, one of the oldest sovereign communities in Yorubaland, although a small one. The inhabitants claim that this is where Noah's ark landed and they in fact still possess the never-rotten ark. In addition, they claim to possess Oduduwa's crowns, Agboogu's footmark, the "ever black" sea and 464 steps, a multiple of four, which lead to the old palace of former Idanre Obas, and an unreadable letter engraved on a rock in some ancient script.*

This may be just another of those curious and agreeable tales in which West Africa abounds and no more than that. However, the root of Idanre is Dan and we have already found the Dan tribe of the southern Ivory Coast associated with birdmen and with reed boats. That there was a Dan tribe of Israel, and that the Greeks were known as the Danae should also be noted. Israel had three maritime tribes, according to my friend Dr. Cyrus Gordon.

The most persistent myth to be found among the Amerindians of South and Central America is a story of their leaders, their white culture heroes, arriving in America having sailed there to avoid the Flood—across the Atlantic. The story of the Flood was widespread among Amerindians: the Incan empire abounded in it. Similarly, the Yoruba of southwest Nigeria possessed the Flood story. This being the case, it is not impossible that some skippers of boats decided not to cross the Atlantic but to stay on in West Africa instead; hence, maybe, the curious legend of Idanre. It is a possibility that should not altogether be discounted.

We repeat that the deep oceans are not yet susceptible to archaeology; for evidence of the enormously important maritime dimension to our history we must therefore listen to the shores. We have fully documented records of the Flood refugees from Eridu, the Poseidon/Enki worshippers escaping from Eridu just in time; we have the fully documented tradition of the refugees having arrived in America to escape the Flood. The Middle Eastern god Ishtar and his spouse Ashtarte were represented in the Old World with lion or lioness heads. It would seem that when they colonized Central America, the Chronos people, Zurvan—since there are uncommonly few lions in the Americas—were symbolized with jaguar heads,[33] the American equivalent of the lion. Here they are. With the Maya the jaguar is called Balam. They merely exchanged the African lion for its American equivalent.

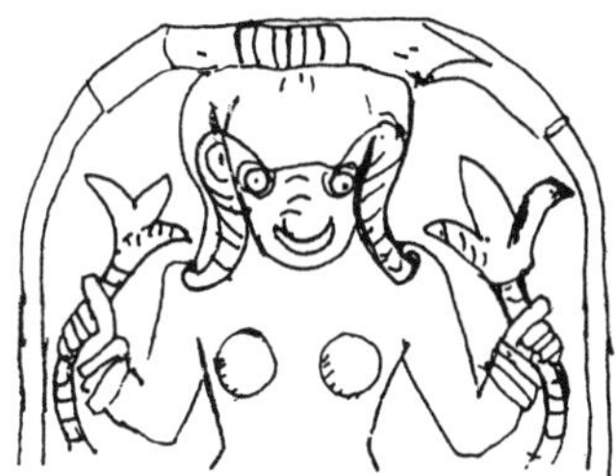

The lioness-headed Ashtarte carved on an axe, a figure now in the Louvre. She is holding a lotus, her customary style. Ptah, god of Memphis, equated by the Greeks with Hephaestus, by the Romans with Vulcan, had a lioness-headed consort called Sekhment.[34]

The goddess Ashtarte standing on her symbolic lioness with Anat's cross on its tummy. She holds in her hands two serpents and two lotuses.

A "jaguar-child" from Oaxaca, Mexico, Toltec/Olmec culture.

PLATE 211

THE INCENSE BURNER FROM THE ISLAND OF LAMU. *This replica brass pot comes from the island of Lamu off the north coast of Kenya in the Indian Ocean. Unlike the West African pots it is for incense; accordingly it has apertures in the sides. Lamu or Lahamu is the name for the ancient Babylonian goddess of the sea, a name perhaps also retained in the Maldive Islands.*

The incense trade was ancient in the Indian Ocean. According to the Greek historian Diodorus of Sicily, all temples to the sky god burned incense that came from one special island in the Indian Ocean, which he called Panchaea.

The top of the pot is modeled in the form of the lotus bud, the lotus symbolizing the divinity in Upper Egypt, and in India symbolizing the rising sun. Around it are eight crocodiles, perhaps symbolizing the eight creative spirits who, tradition said, began civilization in the delta of Egypt. The Buddha was born out of a lotus. The crocodile was sacred to the sun and sea god Set. The Egyptian sun god Ra was wrapped in the bud of a lotus.[35]

The east coast of Kenya in general, and the island of Lamu in particular, were regularly visited by Chinese trading vessels in the Middle Ages, hence perhaps the four Chinese dragons on the sides of the pot, the four dragon feet on which the pot rests, and the four dragons that form handles for the pot. The Chinese at the same time were trading with the Pacific coast of America.

The dragon, of course, was more anciently the symbol of the Bronze Age sea people. Beside the prehistoric tin mines of Rwanda is the Ankole tribe and anaku *is the Babylonian for tin. The Rwanda capital is Kigali and* kigal *in Sumerian meant the Great Mother, the predecessor of Lamu: the two main tribes in Rwanda are sun worshippers, the Tutsi and the Bahutu. Utu was the Sumerian name for the sun god. The influence of ancient Mesopotamia on East Africa is greater than is realized. How much we should respect their mutual labors!*

PLATE 212

DETAIL TO PREVIOUS FIGURE. *An Egyptian text dating from the time of the fourth Ptolemy locates the birth of the Ogdoad, the eight creative gods, in Egyptian Thebes. The text begins with a reference to "eight great and mighty ones of the beginning, the venerable gods who came into being at the beginning of all things . . . conceived in the ocean, born in the flood, a lotus came forth in which was a beautiful child who illumines this land with his rays. . . ."*[36] *Here are the eight creation spirits in the form of crocodiles, sacred to Set, around the bud of the lotus. The sun god appeared in Hermopolis in a lotus flower. At the headwaters of the Nile bark cloth was made anciently in Uganda: it was made anciently in pre-Columbian America.*[37] *I possess some of the Uganda bark cloth. In Egypt it was written: "a lotus bud floated on the primeval waters on which was the infant sun, Horus."*[38] *The lotus was the primeval cosmic flower.*

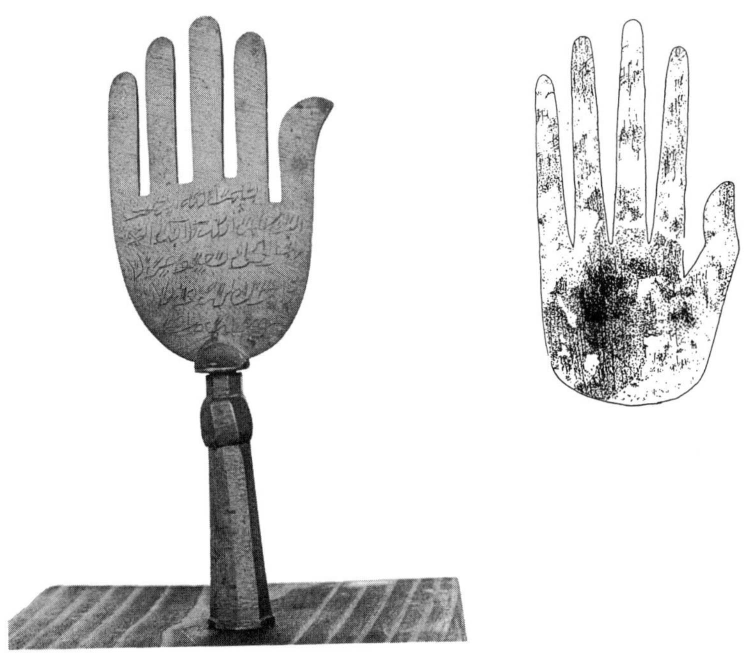

PLATE 213

HAND FROM THE COURTROOM IN ZANZIBAR *(far left). This metal hand comes from the courthouse on the island of Zanzibar. Witnesses used to hold it and swear by it. After the revolution the hand was no longer used and the Koran was substituted for it. So I bought it from a Dar es Salaam curio shop.*

It should be noted that the ancient Egyptian goddess Isis was accompanied in her processions by one holding the model of a left hand, which symbolized justice.[39]

This mica grave offering (left), in the form of a hand, was made by the Hopewellian people of Ohio (original in the Field Museum of Natural History, Chicago).

PLATE 214

Greek tradition recorded that the earth mother Athena was born out of the head of Zeus: this pretends that the earth mother had started life as a colony of the sky father. But our archaeological and traditional records agree in asserting the opposite. We have already noted how each new ruling group rewrites history to suit itself. We have also noted that colonies are wonderfully conservative and preserve the original traditions most faithfully, even if they have been corrupted in the mother country. So here are two Senufo (Plates 214 and 215) traditional carvings that show how the male sky god, symbolized by the bird, was a colony of the earth mother and not vice versa as patriarchal propaganda pretended. Likewise, we may suppose that in Genesis, originally Adam was born out of Eve's rib—both gynecologically as well as archaeologically true—but when the men took over the story was reversed for political convenience in a very contemporary manner.

PLATE 215

This Senufo traditional wooden carving portrays, I believe, Zeus being born out of the head of the earth mother, Hera: not the opposite as Greek tradition tells us, the story having been rewritten for political purposes!

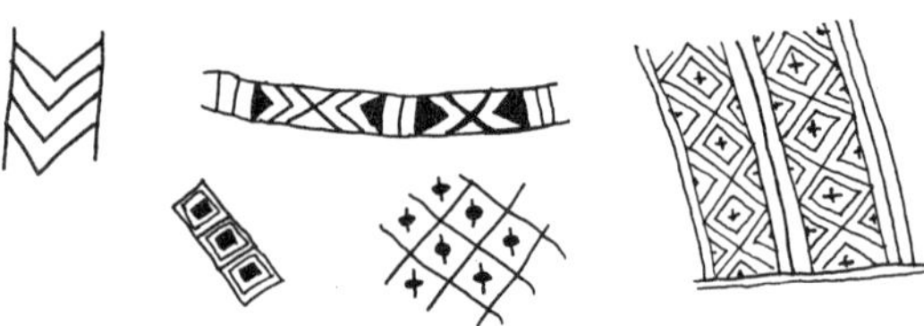

Tierradentro. Designs from the interior of an underground tomb with painted walls and pillars. The standard Old World symbols of the lozenge and of the Phoenician goddess Anat's cross appear on this tomb in Colombia.

PLATE 216

THE ETHIOPIAN INTERMEDIATE DRAGON. *This scene of St. George and the Dragon comes off an Ethiopian cross. It is an intermediate dragon: one of the dragon ships of the raiding Bronze Age sea people to which paws have been added. It should be compared with the reed boats associated with birdmen reproduced on Mochicha pottery from the coastline of Peru. The dragon ships of the Bronze Age sea people had encircled the world five thousand years and more before Magellan. George is the Greek for farmer: the legend represents not just Horus versus Set but the underlying tension of land people versus the contemporary Vikings, i.e. at one time, much of the world against ancient Egypt. The Egyptian word Tuat for the underworld is clearly the underside of the earth, not the center of the earth.*[40] *In Canaan a name for sea, in addition to Dragon, is Lotan:*[41] *compare the Biblical Lot, the Greek Atlas. The damage the sea peoples effected continued not just with the Vikings but also with the Algerian corsairs.*

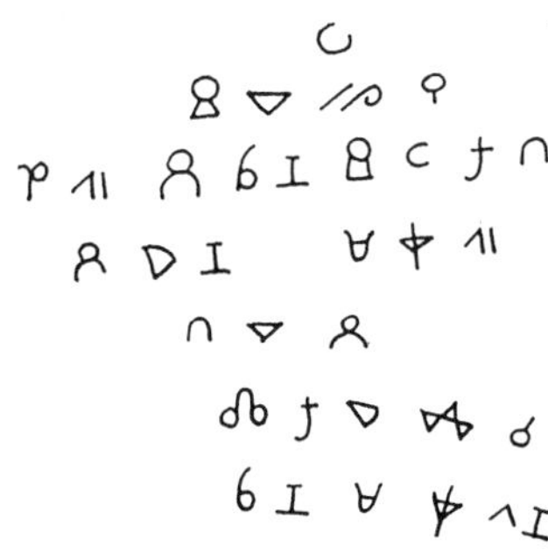

Plate 217

Zimbabwe petroglyphs. *These signs found in Zimbabwe matched to ancient scripts of the Fertile Crescent both come from Dr. Diringer's standard work on* The Alphabet.[42] *If the reader now refers to Plate 3 of the prehistoric mine workings of Zimbabwe this will all fall into place. The most recent figures are of about one thousand prehistoric gold mines and about 150 prehistoric copper mines in that country. Notice that these Semitic scripts appear similarly in Amazonia (Plates 30 and 31).*

Ugarit North Semitic script

Cretan hieroglyph

Semitic

South Semitic Early Ethiopic

Libyan script

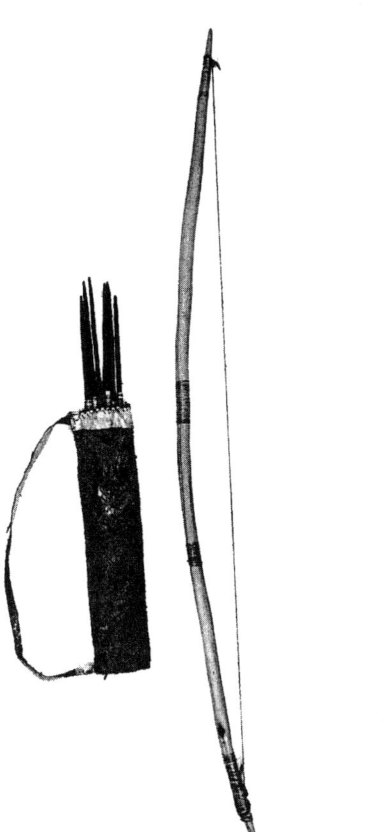

Tiny love bow. The diminutive San (Bushmen) use a tiny bow—about fifteen inches long and arrows with soft points with which they shoot, Cupidwise, the girl of their choice on the backside to signal their affection, during the love dance.

This likeness to the amorous behavior of the tiny Greek love god Cupid should be noted. The Bantu word muti, *meaning magic and medicine, should be compared with the similar Coptic word of a similar meaning; compare the Bantu* kaya *for house with the Greek* aikia, *and so on. Long-distance miners and traders will be responsible for the parallels. The Okavango Bushmen were using reed boats until recently, as are still used on Lake Titicaca and Lake Chad.*

With the southern African San peoples, the hare was a moon animal, as with the goddess worshippers of Greece.[43]

PLATE 218

THE HILL OF THE JACKALS AND LONG-DISTANCE TRADE. *Fifty miles east of Messina in the northern Transvaal, where the ancients mined and smelted copper, is a giant sandstone rock called Mapungubwe, or the Hill of the Jackals. It was held to be sacred by the local Africans, and to point at it, they believed, was to court death. It can be climbed only with difficulty.*

After a particularly heavy storm, gold was noticed shining in the ground and altogether something like a hundred ounces of gold artifacts were then dug up.

Professor van Riet Lowe estimated that about ten thousand tons of earth had been carried to the summit of the hill so that in times of siege its gardens could support quite a large population.

It is likely that the peoples using this mountaintop near the Limpopo River were of a later period than the period we are chiefly concerned with; they were Iron Age people, but other artifacts conclusively prove that they were in touch with extensive trade routes beyond Africa. Red beads were found that came from India, yellow ones probably from Mesopotamia or Egypt, pink ones thought to be of Abyssinian or even of Roman origin, and several fragments of Chinese pottery, including one piece clearly identified as late Sung (A.D. 1127–1279) were found.

Burial of chiefs or kings had been performed with ceremony. Later excavation brought to light a chiefly or royal burial where the skeleton was associated with 130 gold bangles. Below the skeleton's arm lay an exquisitely made black polished bowl. Excavated near the skeleton was a gold circlet and a gold sheath, symbols of office, and also pieces of gold plate that had once been part of a wooden headrest.

Plate 219

Isis nursing Horus, after his virgin birth. Ptolemaic bronze. Isis would seem to be a name associated with Ci, the Babylonian earth mother, merely written from right to left. In Egypt you wrote either way, it was Ci-Ci backward. It is just worth inquiring whether the Babylonian Ci, the Greek Ge, the Dutch Zee, the English sea, are not variants of the same name, because the earth mother was, of sheer necessity, a maritime lady: even as the ocean in Peru was called Mama Cocha or Mother Ocean. Isis was connected with the demi-monde. Temple prostitutes were a foretaste of Paradise, understandably enough! Isis was also the patroness of sailors. Little has changed. Nevertheless, the majority of Egyptian customs, Diodorus Siculus said, were Ethiopian,[44] *i.e. African. Isis was looked on by the Egyptians as mistress of all land and sea, dispenser of justice (note my reproduction of the left hand of Isis from the courtroom of Zanzibar, Plate 213), and possessor of magical power.*

Principal facade of the temple of Luxor (restored by Charles Chipiez). The eight creative spirits that began, tradition said, the civilization of Egypt started in the delta: subsequently the capital first moved to Memphis and then to Thebes. In the same way that in Egypt power moved from the seacoast further and further inland, so, in Mesopotamia Eridu was known by the Sumerians as their oldest city, and uradu *in Sumerian means copper. Further upstream is the town of Sippar, which in Akkadian means bronze, while the Sumerian capital had moved to Nippur. In course of time power moved inland again to Babylon, Ashur and Nineveh. This is the way the wheel, the draft animal, the building of roads slowly altered the balance of power. It is also worth noticing that the corbeled arch was in use in ancient Egypt, in ancient Peru and Central America.*[45]

PLATE 220

THE ZIMBABWE BIRDMEN AND BIRDS NEXT TO FIGURES FROM ANCIENT AMERICA. *About half the so-called Zimbabwe birds have five toes, about half three toes: hence some represent birdmen and some birds. Carbon dating of the various ruins and their rebuilding has thrown up dates from around* A.D. *500 to 1500.*

The tradition of the sacred bird and the sacred birdman is, however, Bronze Age and Copper Age in origin. The symbols on the base of the stone avians, the circle and the sharp zigzag lines, represent the sun and either water or fire. I used to think that the latter was the water symbol but looking at it again the angles seem rather acute. Other religious symbols of the earliest periods of metallurgy appear on local pottery and on excavated artifacts, suggesting that the gold mining in Zimbabwe may have started at a most early date, long before the famous buildings were erected.

The so-called Renders Ruin revealed widespread Indian Ocean trade with Zimbabwe in the late Iron Age. To quote the official pamphlet on this later, Iron Age period: "The Renders Ruin was named after Adam Renders, the man who guided Carl Mauch to Zimbabwe. Part of a large hoard of trade goods was found in this area which included a glazed Persian bowl with Naskhi writing, Chinese celadon and stoneware, a Persian tin-glazed bowl with blue designs, engraved and painted near-East glass, an iron spoon, an iron lamp-stand with copper chain, a copper box, two copper finger rings, two bronze bell-shaped objects, several hundred thousand glass beads, several kilograms of wire, cowrie shells and coral."

Yet again it reveals extensive trade outside Africa, trade continuing into relatively recent times. It is worth remembering both for the symbols on the Zapotero Island figures and on the Zimbabwe birds, Pindar's description of the Aegean island of Rhodes as "bride of the sun and daughter of the sea."[46]

A view of the Zimbabwe birdmen or birds.

Symbols of sun and sea worship, like the Zimbabwe symbols, on figures on Zapotero Island.

24. The First Great Periods of International Trade

"Who knows whether the best of men be known, or whether there be not more remarkable persons forgot, than any that stand remembered in the known account of time?"

SIR THOMAS BROWNE

The colonialism of the last four centuries of Western Europe had religious roots as well as the motive of trade. Very often the small missionary party preceded the posse by quite a number of years. Apostle means literally one who was sent out—"Go you and preach the gospel in all lands"—and the apostles went out two by two, ahead of the troops. The English word Catholic derives from the Greek *katholikos*, meaning universal, and so its roots may be Atlas or the sea, *thalassa*, as we have already seen.

The drift of this book, as the argument so far has shown, is that Christianity owes much less than is commonly thought to Judaism, much more to sky worship and to its subspecies, sun worship, that was the religion of the Philistines, the sea people called Set or Atlas, who worshipped the sun and earth, for whom also fire, earth and water were sacred. This particularly comes through in the Fourth Gospel, the Gospel of St. John. The Greek for John is Ioannes. The precursor of Christ is John the Baptist, Ioannes Baptizon. His menu of locusts and wild honey is a typical Neolithic diet. John baptised with water but announced one who would come after who would baptise with the Holy Spirit and with fire. Jesus is the Greek form of the Hebrew Joshua, and Joshua was the son of Nun, or Ocean. While Jesus was the son of Mary, a name like the Latin for sea, giving us marine, maritime, etc. This ties in with the widespread tradition that the gods were born out of ocean.

The seacraft of the peoples based, among other places, in Libya, visited most parts of the world; colonizing, mining and trading. They had linked up our whole globe by sea. Communication has been of greater importance than is generally appreciated: while the oceans were being crossed and recrossed and the world was partially interlinked there was wonderful progress; when at the end of the Bronze Age ocean travel largely ceased, half the world, including parts of Africa south of the Sahara, for three thousand years made small progress or even decayed; as a limb from which the circulation had been withdrawn atrophies.

The Set or Atlas people, from the Atlantic shores of Europe, and subsequently also from Libya, colonized with a profoundly religious drive behind them. The story that the Incas of Peru had retained of their own dynastic start described how the Incan apostles of the sun god—recent though all this is—went forth two by two to convert, reform, civilize, discipline, enrich the naked savages, still living in small groups in holes in the ground across Peru; or so the Incas pretended.

When the Christian missionaries came back to the old Atlas territory in America and West Africa after a lapse of nearly three thousand years, for the most part the old faith had slid to such an extent that the Christian fathers did not even recognize that they were actually taking part in a repeat performance, in a second, perhaps even a fifth vast wave of conversion; although it was this realization that led to the cruel deception of the Amerindians. Father Junod of South Africa, who wrote the standard work on the Mashona tribe, and was accustomed to accompany convicts upon their last walk to the scaffold, was sensitive to his secondary role and commented upon it to me, but he seems to have been virtually alone in this all-important awareness. Much of Christianity was largely the old Set religion modernized and reformed, and the Christian missionary urge to convert in the service of God was in fact paralleled by their earlier predecessors, who shared a part of their theology with them. But on the first occasion many of the missionaries were African, white and black Africans working together.

From all this we can reasonably deduce that when Christ pronounced the Parable of the Good Shepherd it may well have contained for his listeners some political reference to the shepherd kings; when he rode upon an ass on his way to Jerusalem it was because the donkey was sacred to Set, as we can see on our carving of the Senufo Atlas; that when he gave the Parable of the Gadarene Swine he referred to the historical attack by that offshoot of the Atlas people to whom the pig was sacred—led by the dynasty of Gadeirus (giving their name to Cádiz, Gadeira (Gadara), and also the Moroccan ports of Agadir and Mogador). The attack was launched against the powers of the eastern Mediterranean and it terminated in the rout of the attackers (1219–1182 B.C.); fighting on such a global scale that its memory would still be grim twelve centuries later. Eusebius, among the greatest of Christian historians, said that Christianity was ancient, from even before the time of Moses, only the church was new.[1]

So when, at the center of Christianity, Christ sacrificed himself as a voluntary gift for mankind to take away the sins of the world, and suffered much before He died upright, He reproduced the central act of the Set

PLATE 221
Temple of Kukulcan, Chichén Itzá; the ziggurat is twenty-four meters high. Mayan children used to be sacrificed, as in Phoenicia and Abeokuta, Nigeria, by being thrown down from the top of the temple steps to the bottom.[1] *In America as in Egypt, burials took place within the ziggurat or pyramid. We must face up to the fact that no metal was in use with the Maya when the Spaniards arrived. The god of travelers whom the Maya worshipped was called Ekchuah, reminiscent of the name left by the Heracles people and the matriarchal society generally from very early times. This style of architecture was developed in Mesopotamia to provide a place of refuge in case of another Great Flood. I. E. S. Edwards describes the principal ceremony in the temple on the top of the Mesopotamian ziggurat: "On the top-most tower there is a spacious temple and inside the temple stands a great bed covered with fine bedclothes, with a golden table by its side. There is no statue of any kind . . . a single native woman who, as the Chaldeans, the priests of this god, affirm, is chosen for himself by the deity. . . . They also declare . . . that the god comes down in person and sleeps upon the couch."*[2] *When a new set of thalassocrats took over in the Old World the losers fell back on the Americas, so when the male sky god Zeus took over, the Titans were confined to Tartarus, or the Americas, i.e. where the Mongols or Tartars were.*

religion, knowing that anyone who wishes to change the world must first suffer. It is this central concept of self-sacrifice that distinguishes this one Indo-European religious tradition: distinguishes and sweetens. Christ was merely the one self-sacrificer—in a long line of self-sacrificers—on whom the camera of history has focused.

Christianity brought a reform of the old Set religion, purifying it both of its essential abuses and of the meaningless superstitions into which it had declined. More important, where the Set religion had been elitist, the Christian version was democratic and universal.

For after the breakdown of civilization at the end of the Bronze Age, the old religion had lost its dynamism as the old ruling classes were absorbed: in Europe the system of god-kings ceased—the *Götterdämmerung;* while the intellectual and moral contents of the old religion were increasingly lost sight of, human sacrifice flourished; but it was no longer self-sacrifice but only the crudest and most cruel form of human exploitation practiced by the powerful upon the weak, even if the sacrificed were often strangely persuaded themselves to take part in the ceremony of the sacrifice.

In this book we have shown, at the least, examples of African art that are not normally displayed either in books on art or in museums. But I hope I have also been able to give evidence for this powerful linkage between West Africa, America and the Fertile Crescent during the Copper and Bronze Ages, for this early Atlantic trading.

It can be seen from all this that African societies, protected on the one side by the Sahara desert—growing ever more formidable as a barrier over these last six thousand years—and the tropical rain forest on the other, have retained philosophies shared with the Fertile Crescent that had become extinct and consigned to oblivion everywhere else. The West African rain forest became a great fossil bed for societies that the power politics of the ancient world had otherwise exterminated. There is so much to learn.

To readers who might object that I have brought certain West African philosophies into the light only to imply that they are largely foreign, I shall have two answers: first, that when societies are interconnected it is by no means easy to know where and by whom new ideas and new techniques were first invented; second, I must point out that much of the religion of Mecca came from Jerusalem, much of the religion of Jerusalem came from Egypt and Mesopotamia, and many of the diverse religions of Egypt and Mesopotamia came from far distant cradle lands. There is hardly a nation today that can lay claim to have invented either its philosophies or its religion, so closely have we all been intermingled in that distant global village that we have been studying here.

25. Earth Mother: Sky Father

"The Trident of Neptune is the Sceptre of the World."
LEMIERRE, 1755

"Atlas and Saturn, noblest Sons of Ouranos."
DIODORUS SICULUS

"Atl, Aztec Creator—God, whose Fourth Age terminated in cataclysm."
MICHAEL RORDAN, *Encyclopaedia of Gods*

Very early in its history, humankind began to understand that all things come from the earth. However separate we each feel ourselves to be, we are in reality all parts of a living whole, which shaped us as the child is shaped in the mother's womb and which continues to nourish and sustain us until the moment of our death. This metaphor of the womb lies at the center of the earliest religions: it was the great earth mother who was the early object of man's worship; and the earth was not to be polluted, since the earth was sacred.

This is confirmed by Greek tradition, which held that the first religion was that of the Great Goddess and that all the arts of civilization were developed by the early cultures over which she ruled. (The nine Muses, who represented all the highest arts, in Greek tradition, were feminine.) It certainly seems likely that it was the women, in an earth-worshipping society, who first began to practice agriculture by domesticating plants, and that it was not for another thousand years that men, the hunters, domesticated animals. Isis, the Egyptian earth mother, was credited by the Egyptians with domesticating wheat and barley and being the goddess of medicine and healing; patroness of navigation and sailing. The earth mother was called *Mami* in Sumer, *Mama* in Peru.

The name of the earth goddess to the Greeks, as we have seen, was *Ge* or *Gaea*, and when we speak of her religion being an early one we mean very early indeed. A carved figure depicting a characteristic earth mother effigy has been found in central Europe and dated to around 30,000 B.C. Also, the custom of burying a piece of red hematite with the dead, symbolizing the blood of the earth, was practiced in ancient Europe, in ancient South Africa and among the aborigines of Australia, and, as we noted in Chapter 5, one hematite mine, the Ngwenya mine in Swaziland, was being worked before 40,000 B.C. for the sake of its red body paint, Professor Dart stated. In the language of ancient Egypt, *hemet* means woman. From the earliest times there was an association of the feminine principle with the primal waters,[1] and with the color red. It is where the name Mary, mother of God, comes from. For the god-kings were born out of Ocean; just as Joshua, the alternate name for Jesus, was born out of Nun: Nun or Nenu being the ancient Egyptian name for the ocean. *Hmt* was also the Egyptian for copper, suggesting that it was the matriarchs who began the Copper Age.

It would be foolish to pretend that we can reconstruct any complete picture of that first religion. Nevertheless, from the findings of archaeology, from ancient mythologies and from the remnants of old beliefs still to be found among certain peoples today, we can deduce enough to give us some idea of what it was like and what it meant to those who followed it.

One thing we can say for certain is that the matriarchal religion spread around the globe. We know that eventually it spread across the Americas. It spread ever wider, as voyagers carried it across the oceans, and it is notable among the Polynesian islands. It is notable that the headstream of the Amazon used to be called the River of the Serpent, for the sacred serpent was one of the most important cult figures of the earth worshippers, its written sign being the coiled snake, generally reduced to a simple spiral. It spread across both Americas retaining the same name *ki*—or variants—as was used in Babylon. It is not hard to understand the symbolism of the serpent, emerging through a dark hole from the inner secrecy of the soil, but there was also a second meaning to it. Each year the snake sloughs off its old skin and comes out seemingly new-made. To the earth worshippers this symbolized the life of man, for they believed that the dead were reborn into the tribe as children. Indeed, it seemed that to them everything proceeded in an endless series of cycles, returning always to its beginning. Time itself was seen as cyclic. The modern mathematical symbol for infinity is supposed to derive from a serpent eating its own tail, and perhaps the same meaning of unendingness attached to the double spiral of the earth worshippers. Blue was the color of the sky and so of the male sky god; red for Mother Earth, hence the origin of our contemporary political symbols, they are as old as that. To the matriarchs death was simply moving from one uterus to another uterus. Left-wing politics has been largely men taking over the women's egalitarian styles and symbols, including the sacredness of the earth, and debauching them.

The bull was another sacred animal, and bull games took place from northern India as far as Spain, the most famous of them being the Cretan bull leaping. The cult of the earth mother continued in Crete right through Minoan times, providing us with a prime source of evidence about it. From Crete we learn that she was often represented between two lions, since she was the goddess of wild animals, and also with doves, since the earth on which all animals live must include the air they breathe. Her religion also included the waters of the earth, which after all cover 70 percent of its surface, and Gaea was thus very much a water goddess as well as goddess of the land. (The name of the Aegean Sea is formed by doubling up her name to make a palindrome.) The eland took the place of the bull on rock carvings in Africa but it probably had the same significance: the Canaanite god El being often addressed as, "Thou bull!"

In general the night was the sacred time and the cult was associated with the darkness of the underworld. Where there were temples they were constructed underground, and some interesting examples have been found in Malta. It seems, though, that some earth-worshipping peoples did not build temples at all. Sir John Marshall reported finding no temples in Mohenjo-Daro, but I think he confusedly called collapsed ziggurats keeps. There appear to have been none in Crete, though in many houses a room was set aside as a shrine to the Earth Mother. When Cortés invaded, the Aztecs of Mexico were using the ziggurats as fighting stations.

The early earth-worshipping societies were matrilineal, with property and status descending not from the father but from the mother. There was a very good reason for this: Paleolithic peoples seem not to know that men played any part in the production of children. In general the standing of women was much higher then than it was later to become. They had a dominating position. These societies were not merely matrilineal but truly matriarchal. Certainly, as priestesses, women played a chief part in the cult of the earth mother. But to them there would seem to have been no notion of Creation or progress, since time was cyclic like the seasons.

Much of this changed when the male-dominated sky-worshipping peoples took over with their cult of a male god in heaven, called by the Greeks Ouranos, by the Egyptians On, and by the Mesopotamians Anu (all names with the same root). Not everything changed, however. The stars were now the first object of worship; the night still retained its own sanctity, because the sky is the home not just of the moon but also of uncountable stars, and it is only at night that the stars are visible. The idea of recurring cycles remained important, since that is how the stars all move, and in the Central and South American religions that were the inheritors of the old sky worship there was an almost obsessional concern with cycles of time. (The same thing is true of all systems of astrology.) Subsequently, however, there grew up a belief in time as directional, a single dimension along which gods and men move toward their vast purposes; this would seem to have begun as part of sun worship and the belief in Divine Creation of the Atlas people, operating through the sovereign, into an almost indefinite, but nevertheless finite, future: quite different from the stars back-packing each night across the sky along identical paths.

As the religion developed, the veneration of the sun took on more than one meaning. There was first of all the visible sun that gave light, warmth and life to the world; but it also came to be seen as the symbol of a cosmic intelligence. When the sun appeared on the first day of Creation, that was the moment when God, in the form of Mind—in Greek *Nous*—entered the universe. The half-Inca historian de la Vega was quite explicit about this duality: "In addition to worshipping the sun as a visible god, to whom they offered sacrifices and dedicated great festivals . . . the Inca kings and their *amautas*, who were the philosophers, perceived by the light of nature the true supreme God our Lord, the maker of heaven and earth," as we shall see from the arguments and phrases some of them applied to the Divine Majesty, whom they called *Pachacamac*. The word is composed of *pacha*, the world, the universe, and *camac*, present participle of the verb *cama*, to animate, derived from the noun *cama*, the soul. *Pachacamac* means "him who gives life to the universe," and in its fullest sense means "him who does to the universe what the soul does to the body." Pachacamac is the Peruvian name for the god the Greeks called Ouranos.

"Inwardly they regarded the Pachacamac with much greater veneration than the Sun, for, as I have mentioned, they did not dare to utter his name, and the Sun they alluded to on every occasion. If asked who was the Pachacamac, they would say: 'He who gave life to the universe and sustained it,' but they did not know him because they had never seen him, so they did not make temples to him or offer him sacrifices, but adored him in their hearts—that is, mentally—and held him to be the unknown god."[2] West Africa has the same principles. "No one has seen God," my friends tell me. The sculptures of the Creator they make are of his lesser manifestations, his hypostases.

The later sun worship was trinitarian, believing that the sun disk was God the father, the king was God the son, while the divinity, who was Pantocrater, ruler of all, and Cosmocrater, ruler of the cosmos, was the Holy Spirit. To the cognoscenti the sun disk was just a symbol for an ignorant peasantry to hold on to: the cosmic intelligence working through the sovereign was what mattered. In Egypt, as widely elsewhere, the divine triad was father, mother and son: e.g. Osiris, Isis and Horus. In the former matriarchal area the Holy Spirit, Santa Sophia, Sacred Wisdom, was female.

By the time sky worship developed, the man's part in the conception of a child was known; indeed, later on, some peoples held that the woman's womb was no more than a passive receptacle, a kind of human seedbed in which the male sperm grew of its own accord into a child. This made inheritance through the male line possible and patrilineal societies became the norm. So too did patriarchy, and from this time on the most dominant positions in society would be held by men. Gynecology was used for political pressure and Apollo, in a Greek play, was made to explain this. There continued to be female deities and priestesses to minister to them, but wherever the pantheon included both gods and goddesses it was always a male god who gradually became the ultimate ruler. The sexual act and the cosmic creation were seen as microscopic and macroscopic versions of the same thing. The making of the universe was the male priapic orgasm on a gigantic scale, and perhaps gave proportionate pleasure in the emission. Hence the religious, not the libidinous, significance of the sacred phallus and the ithyphallic gods. The phallus became a sacred symbol in Europe, in Africa, in America. And, very gradually, the king's power increased and the queen's importance declined. We have portrayed this in Plates 155–158, 160–161, and 163–165. These plates emphasize, perhaps, that sensuousness and mind are not antipathetic but combine in creativity.

Like human mothers, the great earth mother was reduced to a passive substance, animated only by the infusion of the male principle. Male primacy was asserted even at the expense of reversing biology. In Greek myth the Mother Goddess Hera is taken out of the head of Zeus, ignoring the obvious fact that it is always the female out of which the male must come, as the Senufo understood when they made the wooden sculpture in Plate 214, which shows the male symbol, the bird, coming out of the head of the female. In the same topsy-turvy way the woman in Genesis is born out of the man, taken out of his side by the sky father. History was rewritten for the sake of the new, masculine, ruling class. If the goddesses are portrayed as bellicose harridans, Athene or Innana as goddess of war and wisdom, it was surely under male pressure.

Even so, the cult of the sky god did not completely oust that of the earth mother. Understandably, the former was the religion of the patriarchal rulers, but the latter continued among the ordinary mass of people. It was important, therefore, to reconcile the two, if religious conflicts within society were to be avoided. The chief means to this end was the celebration of the hierogamy, the sacred marriage between heaven and earth, and it was for this, among other reasons, that the ziggurats were built, becoming popular in Mesopotamia at the start of the third millennium: post-Flood architecture. Up the sacred stairways of these huge piles the priests ascended from earth level to what must then have seemed the impressive height of seventy feet, and there, in the summit sanctuary, they married the earth, from which they had come, to the sky into which they had climbed, impregnating the virgin found there.

This marriage of earth and sky was embodied in Bronze Age religions. In contemporary mythologies the supreme male god is said to be married to a female consort. For example, the Phoenician El had a wife, Asherat-of-the-Sea, who was clearly the old Mother Goddess. In Africa, too, the ancient religion of the Dogon tribe held that the Creation began when the sky father married earth, while the Egyptians conceived of creation as the union of four male and four female spirits. Later, in the Dogon Creation story, come four bisexual beings, and this too can be seen as a reconciliation of the male and female cults. So also can the curious hybrid animals that started to appear, bulls and lions with wings, or feathered serpents called dragons, each of them a compound of an earth creature with a creature of the sky.

In other ways, too, compromise was found. Though female societies are left-handed, male societies are right-handed, for the right is the side of the stronger arm, the one best used to wield a weapon. One curious upshot of this was the development of boustrophedon writing, which gave an equal place to the right-handed, who most naturally draw the pen from left to right, and the left-handed, who do the opposite. The Amazons, as Fray Carvajal reported, worshipped female idols but also had temples dedicated to the sun, which to them was female, while in Egypt the rule that the pharaoh should marry his sister arose out of the tradition that the property of Egypt passed down through the female side, not the male, and it is said that at marriage Egyptian men promised obedience to their wives. We must suppose that Amazons were not typical matriarchal peoples but a special martial sect—much like the Sikhs to the Hindus—dedicated to opposing the empire building of the men that was exterminating their tribal societies.

Numbers also had special meanings in terms of the earth-sky duality. In general, even numbers were associated with the earth cult and odd numbers with the sky, so that the process of reconciliation is again at work when Plato reports that on Atlantis "the kings were gathered together every fifth and every sixth year alternately, thus giving equal honour to the odd and to the even number."[3] It may be that ideas of sacred numbers influenced even the calculation of the ratio of the circumference of a circle to its diameter. Professor Thom reckoned that the designers of the earliest stone circles in Britain took π as 25/8, though later they adopted the more accurate figure (still used today as a first approximation) of 22/7. The choice of 8 as the basis of the earlier fraction may have been influenced by ritual rather than mathcmatical considerations. Let us emphasize that the English mile divides into eights and is that distance which gives the circumference of the earth as twenty-five thousand miles and the diameter of the earth

PLATE 222
Monuments of the metal purchasers: the Egyptian temple of Medinet Habu, Thebes (restored by Charles Chipiez). Diodorus Siculus writes: "So great was the wealth of Egypt at that period . . . that from the remnants left in the course of sack and after the burning, the treasure which was collected little by little was found to be worth more than three hundred talents of gold and no less than two thousand three hundred talents of silver. There are also in this city . . . remarkable tombs of the early kings and of their successors, which leave to those who aspire to similar magnificence no opportunity to outdo these."[1] The Egyptian name for present-day Thebes was Waset: surely a Set name. Fred Hoyle has supposed that in earlier times the intellectual standard was higher than it is today.[2] The figures given by the demographers compared with standards of creativity would seem to bear him out. The pharaoh was referred to as an incarnation or embodiment of God. His coronation was an epiphany not an apotheosis. He claimed to rule over all lands.[3]

as eight thousand miles: indication of how early the earth was accurately measured.

The symbolic elements of a defeated cult were downgraded or extirpated. An interesting example of this can be seen in the story of the Gadarene swine, in which Jesus transfers the devils from a possessed man into a herd of swine, who promptly plunge down a steep slope into the sea and drown. To Jesus's audience, although twelve hundred years after the event, the memory of the attack by the Peoples of the Sea, the foremost troops led by one Gadeirus, which swept into the Mediterranean to be cut to pieces by the Egyptians, would still be in popular memory. As we have seen, the pig was sacred to the Set people and thus became taboo to Jew and Arab, not, as folk etymology explains, because of a common tapeworm. This parable referred to what was, perhaps, the biggest disaster known to human history, the world war at the end of the Bronze Age, when political power switched, even more radically than in our own day, from sea power to land power.

The ban on the eating of pork among the Arabs and Jews, though it may have had some justification in hygiene, arose from the wish to eliminate the influence of the Set people to whom the pig was sacred: the Set survivors are known to history as the Philistines and Palestine is named after them—much the same story then as now!

The same impulse can be seen at work, long after the end of our period, in the legend of St. Patrick driving all the snakes out of Ireland. A difficult job for a single man one would have thought, and made all the harder by the fact that there were no snakes in Ireland. What happened in reality

The return of Hephaestus to Olympus. From the volute krater of Clitias. The donkey was sacred to the sun god Set, whose name is contained within the name Hephaestus. The ancient Mexicans, like the ancient Greeks, believed in the four ingredients of the world: earth, air, fire and water.[4]

PLATE 223

Interior of the Hypostyle Hall at Karnak. Of the wealth of Thebes at this time the Cambridge Ancient History *writes: "Levantine galleys . . . from these landed sumptuous cargoes of the finest stuffs of Phoenicia, gold and silver vessels of magnificent workmanship from the cunning hand of the Tyrian artificer or the workshops of distant Asia Minor, Cyprus, Crete and the Aegean Islands; exquisite furniture of carved ivory . . . chariots mounted with gold and electrum, and bronze implements of war . . . the annual tribute of gold and silver. . . ."[5] It is worth remembering that with the Egyptians, the origin of everything was in the primeval waters: that their first great god was Osiris, a man god who could save mankind. If he lived in the next world, they lived: if he died, they died. At the birth of Osiris a voice was heard to proclaim that the Lord of all Creation was born. Diodorus Siculus recorded that Osiris was the son of Chronos, Isis was the daughter of Chronos,[6] thus confirming the Middle Eastern contribution to Egyptian culture, which the Semitic words in the Egyptian language confirm.*

I looked around these wonderful temple ruins by moonlight, a lone visitor, having turned the guard into a guide with a small present. Egypt was the source of columned architecture. The temple of Karnak is claimed to be the largest religious shrine in the world. Some or all of Egyptian temples possessed libraries. The Egyptian pharaoh Unas acquired his power in Egypt by god-eating.[7]

was that Christianity overcame the old matriarchal religion of Ireland and eliminated the cult of the serpent, which still remained from the ancient religion of the Earth Goddess. Indeed, the present killings in Ireland may trace back, ultimately, to matriarchal versus patriarchal roots.

Sometimes, however, when several peoples merged into a larger political unit, the gods of all the peoples had to be honored. The Egyptian description of the battle of Megiddo describes how the regiment of Ptah or the regiment of Ammon went into the attack. If you wished to retain their regiments you had to retain their gods. The result of this was a move from monotheism to polytheism: where one small tribe had had a single god, an empire of many tribes had many, and each of them must be found a distinctive place in the pantheon. The old view of religion as progressing from animism to polytheism and from polytheism to monotheism is the opposite of the facts, except insofar as later reformers tried to reverse the process and reintroduce monotheism, as Akhenaton tried unsuccessfully in Egypt and the prophets of Yahweh successfully among the Jews.

The local gods worshipped by particular peoples tended to reflect the ways in which those peoples made their living. For example, the fishermen and merchant sailors at the Mesopotamian port of Eridu had a sea god. Inland, in the cattle country, they worshipped a cattle god, and north of that again a grain god who died each year and was born again like the annual crops they planted. In the same way, beliefs about what happened after death were shaped by the daily experience of the living. It is significant that so many peoples put the abode of the dead beyond the ocean. I believe that they fashioned their heaven as they fashioned their gods, out of the materials of their ordinary working lives, and if the soul crossed the ocean to its ultimate destination in the Paradise Land, "going west," it was because sailing across the ocean was a major fact in the experience of the living. The sun worshippers naturally tended to see the soul as following the daily path of the sun from east to west, so they generally put the afterworld in the west (leading, as we saw, to the association of heaven and hell with America). As a symbol of this, the Valley of the Kings, where some of the pharaohs were buried, was in the desert on the west side of the Nile, and their bodies were carried westward across the river in the funeral barge. However, at an early period, when some voyaging was eastward across the Indian Ocean rather than westward across the Atlantic, the land of the dead was sometimes placed in the east, which can also be seen as the resting place of the sun, where it is before it rises. In fact the sea peoples who exploited both the Pacific and the Atlantic routes referred to the Americas as the land where the sun set and where the sun rose—and little time was wasted between the two! We find Ireland, China, Japan, Egypt, and Mesopotamia agreeing that Paradise lay across a great ocean and that it was somehow associated with the possibility of eternal youth. And in ancient Japan, as in ancient Egypt, was retained the legend of the dragon king of that island, who sank beneath the ocean waves. Marine archaeologists have confirmed the truth of that legend. We merely have to remember that the symbol of Quetzacóatl, the god-king in Mexico at that time, was a dragon; and one of *Quetzalcóatl's* titles was Lord of the Air: the same meaning as *Enlil,* supreme god of the Sumerians.

In our exploration of the great prehistoric system of ocean trading we found traces of the sun worshippers in every continent of the world except Australia. In rituals, in architecture, in myths, pictorial symbols and other ways the sun worshippers left unmistakable evidence of their beliefs. There is no doubt that when the sea peoples emigrated into new lands they took with them—as modern Europeans were to do millennia later—not only their techniques and their political structures but also their gods. Chronos was associated with the moon even more than the sun; Atlas was associated with the sun rather than the moon. Broadly speaking, Christianity embraces the areas of former sun worship, Islam of former moon worship.

One important result of this is still with us today, for those parts of the world that are Christian and Muslim largely coincide with the areas that the early metal traders visited. The spheres of influence of two great religions, seemingly determined by conquest in modern times, have also been defined by the geographical distribution of mining several millennia before the birth of either Christ or Muhammad. When the missionaries of those two religions—respectively with symbols of sun worship and moon worship—set out to spread their doctrines, one reason for their rapid success was that they were not so much bringing a new monotheistic religion as putting their seals on various cultures that the sky worshippers had originally formed. As evidence of this we can take the most prominent symbols of Christianity and Islam, the cross and the crescent moon. Neither was new. As we have seen, both were in common use among the sea peoples and can be found in many different parts of the world in the inscriptions they left behind them. Among other Christian symbols, the halos behind the heads of saints are sun disks, and the Catholic monstrance is clearly modeled on the sun, with its rays shooting out and with the four cardinal points marked. The fish, which was the symbol of the early church, is traditionally explained by using the Greek word *ichthus* as an acronym for "Jesus Christ son of god and saviour," but this seems to me to be a piece of folk etymology. The fish is an ancient religious symbol: in Hinduism, for instance, the symbol of Vishnu and in the West the symbol of Set; and it represents the sea, the sea people, the Anakim, the bronze traders. In some places it also represented the culture heroes from across the ocean, as in the Assyrian carving (Plate 90) of Oannes the Fish Man, one of six who were said to have brought civilization to the Gulf. Notice how similar this figure is to a Christian bishop with a cope and a mitre on his head. For this reason the Gospel was given to fishermen and the pope is known as "the Big Fisherman": the seal he carries on his finger is known as "the Fisherman's Seal." Of course, the Christian gold wedding ring is a solar symbol.

The sacred days of Christianity were also inherited from the religion of the sun, most obviously in the case of the weekly sabbath—not Christday but Sunday. (It is interesting, too, that the Jewish sabbath falls on Saturn's day, Saturn being progenitor of the Jewish god El.) Originally, Christ's birthday was celebrated on January 6, the feast of the Epiphany, but around A.D. 300 the church fathers switched it to December 25, having failed to persuade the Europeans to abandon their traditional celebration of the sun's

PLATE 224

BALTIC ROCK ENGRAVINGS. *Of these Baltic figures of tumblers somersaulting over a boat (a) comes from Scania, (b) from Bohuslan. They resemble the somersaulting over the back of the bull in the bull-grappling games of Crete. The Bronze Age rock engravings of Scandinavia resemble those of the Shang Dynasty of China:*[8] *having a common origin in the Mediterranean, with the metallurgical Telchinese among others. The Bronze Age association of Spain and Italy with the Americas was as fruitful and creative, American tradition suggested, as their Iron Age contact was disastrous.*

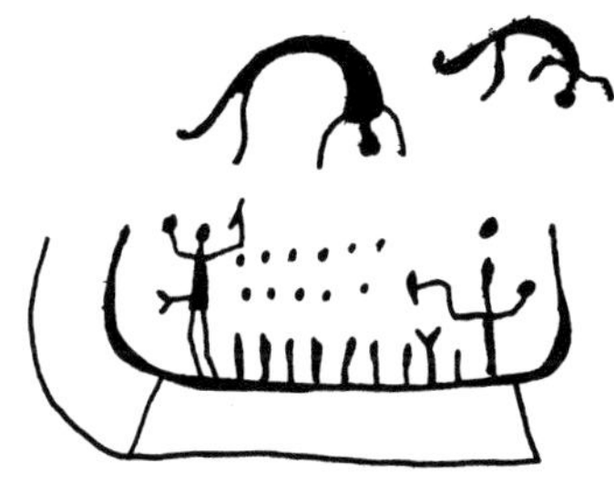

a

b

rebirth on that day, the day when the sun begins to grow in strength and starts his long march back to the north. New dynasties and new faiths destroy the shrines of the old.

It is well known that many Christian churches were built on ancient pagan sites. Canterbury Cathedral on top of a stone circle, for example, St. Paul's on top of a temple to the sun god Ludd, and Notre Dame in Paris on the site of a pagan shrine to that primal lady, the Earth Mother, as its name declares. The churches themselves also betray the origin of their cult, being traditionally oriented with the most holy end to the east. Ask why that is so and you are told that east is the direction of Jerusalem—which is true if you happen to be standing on the north coast of Africa but completely untrue anywhere in Europe or sub-Saharan Africa or Asia. The real reason for the orientation of churches is that the east is where the sun god rises. We must notice again that with one Amerindian tribe the sun god was called *Chise* and with another the sun god was called *Chisis.* This is of fundamental importance and not coincidence. To an illiterate society spelling is optional.

Another misapprehension about Christianity is that it was a development of Judaism. It did indeed originate among the Jewish people of Palestine and some parts of it bear a resemblance to the teaching of the Essene sect. The two fundamental commands of the New Testament, "Thou shalt love the Lord thy God and thy neighbor as thyself," are quotations from the testament of Issacher, a Jewish author who lived a century or two before Christ. Most Christian doctrines, however, belong far more with Philistine beliefs. It is worth noting that, while the Old Testament was written in Hebrew, the New Testament was written in Aramaic, the language of the Persian Empire, who were sun worshippers. An early Christian theologian, the Pseudo-Tertullian, described Christ as "*tantummodo Seth,*" merely Seth, and it is true that the central Christian doctrine of the resurrection of the soul was shared by the Set people, the Osiris people and other Egyptians, along with the Last Judgment and heaven, but not in the same way by the Jews and Mesopotamians generally. And the greatest of Christian historians, Eusebius, said that nothing in Christian doctrine was new, only the church was new, and that Christianity went back to before the time of Moses.[4] Essentially Christianity belongs to a far older tradition than Judaism

Plate 225
Baltic rock engravings of the Bronze Age. These were similar to those of the Mediterranean and of Shang China.

(a comparative newcomer when measured against the antiquity of sun worship). To put it plainly, the Old and New Testaments are records of two different religions and should never have been bound up in the same book: except the believers had been living side by side in Palestine and working the sea routes together for several thousand years even before that. So in the Americas we find among the Amerindians all the trappings of Christianity: penance, confession, baptism, trinitarianism, the virgin birth, mitres, the story of Noah and the Flood, the tower of Babel; in addition to the legends of the white and bearded whiz kids who brought technology from the Old World with them, or so tradition almost everywhere stated.

The New Testament was Philistine, of the Atlas people: the Old Testament was Hebrew, of the Chronos people. Philo of Byblos called them brothers, but of course there was sibling rivalry, too! It was Constantine and other Roman emperors who encouraged this conjunction, to bind the eastern and the western empires together.

The contemporary religion with which Christianity did have much in common was Mithraism, and for some centuries the two cults competed for adherents within the Roman Empire. Mithras was more favored by the legionaries, who called him the Unconquered Sun, *Sol Invictus*. Exactly the same idea is embodied in a mosaic below the high altar of St. Peter's in Rome (Plate 236), which shows Christ as Helios, the sun god, guiding the horses of his triumphant chariot across the sky. The similarity in design between Mithraic temples and Christian churches is also worth noticing.

Where Christianity differed from Mithraism (apart, of course, from its insistence on a divine messiah incarnated as a particular human being) was that Christianity incorporated important elements from the old earth-worshipping religion. The virgin birth is a repetition of the ancient myth, found in various cultures, of the god who conceives a child by a mortal woman; and perhaps we should see the whole doctrine of the trinity as a kind of reconciliation of earth and sky deities, similar to the hierogamy celebrated on Mesopotamian ziggurats. It is argued by some authorities that the Holy Spirit was originally female, and certainly the union of Earth Mother and Sky Father is clear enough in what might be called the unofficial trinity of the Father, the Son and Mary the Mother of God. The name Mary is the same as Mara, meaning in Aramaic "the Lady" and used as the standard term for the Earth Mother. It is also *mare*, the sea, and according to both Greek and Mesopotamian tradition the Gods were born out of Ocean. Furthermore, the navigators' star, the north star, came ultimately to be known as the Star of Mary.

If we accept the importance of the hierogamy we can solve a small puzzle in Christian doctrine: what was Christ doing in hell during the thirty-odd hours he spent there after his death? As the Anglican creed puts it: "He was crucified, dead and buried. He descended into Hell. On the third day he rose again. . . ." Now, quite obviously Christ was not being punished, nor did he go down to liberate the souls of the damned from the devil's power: in the Christian hell they were to remain in torment for all eternity, including Plato and Aristotle, if they had not received Christian baptism. The answer is that "hell" is here being used in a different sense. It is the Netherworld of the Earth Mother, Christ's mother, and he went there to pay his respects to her before ascending to the home of his Sky Father.

Another contradiction in Christian doctrine concerns the resurrection not of Christ himself but of ordinary believers. After death the soul goes up to heaven, to live there forever. But Christianity also teaches the resurrection of the body, which will come alive to enjoy a new dispensation on earth. These incompatible beliefs are simply the legacy of the old religions of sky worship and earth worship. After four thousand years of unresolved rivalry between them, Christianity settled the matter (and made itself acceptable to converts from both sides) by declaring them both to be true.

The marriage of earth and sky cults was never complete in Christianity. In view of its origin it is not surprising that when the conflict could not be reconciled or evaded it was the male sky god who won. In its early days the Christian church looked on women as evil, or at least as sources of temptation, and many would say that it has never been able to escape completely from this perverse view of sexuality. The usual explanation is that this was originally a reaction to the lewdness of the Roman Empire, but my own belief is that it was the association of women with the earth mother that made them unacceptable. The celibacy of the priesthood also derives from the tradition of the sky cult battling with the earth mother across much of the world. Malthus describes this celibacy as a genetic disaster.

The direct worship of the sun was not obliterated by its Christian offshoot for a long time. It had continued under the cult of Jupiter and it continued under Christianity. In the fourth century the Emperor Julian—damned by Christians as "Julian the Apostate"—tried to restore it as the official religion of the Roman Empire, but the attempt failed. By that time the Church had become too powerful to be overthrown by any imperial decree, and no doubt this was in large part due to the attractiveness of its doctrines of immortality. The old religion of the sun gave eternal life only to gods and kings and their royal families and to the men and women sacrificed at royal funerals so that they could accompany their master into the afterlife. As time went by this apotheosis was extended not just to include members of the ruling class but the people in general, but Christianity was the first religion to break all bounds and to offer everyone, even a slave, equally the supreme promise of everlasting life.

Two other aspects of Christianity are worth mentioning as indications of its continuity with older religions. One is the central ritual of the Mass, or Eucharist, for the tradition of god eating that this embodies had no place in Judaism but was part of the Mesopotamian tradition around the Creation. The other is the story that Jesus was the son of a carpenter. The word used in the Greek version of the New Testament, from which modern translations derive, is *tekton*, and while this means carpenter it can also mean master builder or indeed master of any art. It probably has a common root with the second syllable of "Toltec"—the first syllable being Atlas—and the Toltecs of Mexico were always known as the master builders. As we have seen, to this day, if you want a builder in Mexico you ask for a toltec. It is quite likely that the real meaning of the New Testament passage was simply to claim Jesus as the son of the ultimate master craftsman, the world's Creator, and there is, therefore, no contradiction. Perhaps, for democratic reasons, the word has been purposely mistranslated as the carpenter's son. It is also worth noticing that the Egyptian god Ptah, sometimes equated with Hephaestus, was also known as the Master Craftsman. *Ptah* and the Latin *pater* may be related names. The prominent position of Europeans in the earliest civilizations of the world has gone unnoticed.

But the most important connection between Christianity and the religion of the sun lies in its central figure. Christ has often been compared to Adonis or Tammuz, who also died and were reborn, but we can see his truer predecessors in the real young men who, in the old sun religion, offered themselves as willing victims for the salvation of others. Even as kings had once had to die, that is until they invented youthful substitutes for themselves. At the commencement it was the king who had to be humiliated and then to die for the sake of his people. Today it is the people who have to die for the king: the noblest and the best.

Some human sacrifices in ancient America were probably voluntary. At one of the most important feasts in the calendar, for instance, that of the god Tezcatlipoca, a single youth was killed, supposedly, with the youth's consent. The boy was taken to be the earthly image of Tezcatlipoca, and for a year before his death he was made the center of extraordinary reverence, cherished and treated with the greatest respect. He was taught to play the flute, to fetch and carry the reeds and flowers required for offerings. He was taught to hold himself well, to be courteous and gentle of speech. Those who met him kissed the earth and paid him reverential bows. He was free to walk about by day and by night, but he was always accompanied by eight servants dressed like palace lackeys. His vestments were those of a god. (We must ask whether today's regimental officers' mess kit, for many the only chance in this drab world for a young man to wear finery, is psychologically unrelated to this earlier sacrifice?) Is this a psychological foretaste of our present military holocausts?

Twenty days before he was to be sacrificed the keepers changed his clothes for those in which he would end his life. They married him to four virgins who had also received a careful upbringing and who were given the names of four goddesses. Five days before the appointed feast, honor was paid to the youth as to a god, there being much feasting and dancing. Finally the youth was placed in a canoe covered with a canopy. With him went his wives, and they sailed away to a place where there was a low hill. Here the wives were abandoned, and now only the eight servants accompanied the youth to the small and poorly equipped temple. Climbing its steps, on the first of them he broke one of the flutes he had played during his year of prosperity and cherishing; on the second he broke another, on the third another, and so on until he reached the highest part of the temple where the priests were assembled waiting to kill him. They stood in pairs. Binding his hands and his head, they laid him face upward on the block.

A knife of stone was plunged into his breast. It gouged out his heart, which was offered immediately to the Sun.[5]

Here at the heart of Christianity is a clear indication of its true antiquity. As in Buddhism, the historical Gautama is said to have been the twenty-fifth emanation of the Buddha, the other twenty-four having gone unrecorded in prehistoric times, so Jesus of Nazareth was only one of a very, very long line of heroic self-sacrificers. The origins of the line are lost in the profundity of time—if indeed we can speak of an origin in any clear sense. But one thing we do know: this central sacrifice, like so much else in Christianity, was already current as an idea three thousand years before the Crucifixion. It was a part of the religion of the sun god when that religion was spread around the world by the journeying of the god-kings and their emissaries. The Indian god Vishnu had to shed his solar attributes before reincarnating as the savior god, Krishna: so did Set as Christ. It may be chance but it is worth noticing that the mother of the reincarnated Buddha is called Maya and the Buddha himself is called Gautama, not unlike Guatemala.

The theology that came through from certain Greek philosophers was that God, the male Creator, was Mind, *Nous*, working on and shaping the female, cyclic materials of nature. Man partook of Mind, was part of God, and was therefore endowed with free will and responsibility. God, the Creator, worked through the sovereign to create cosmos out of chaos. For Plato, who in his youth had studied in Egypt—as did so many other Greek sages—over many years, God was Goodness whose shape was Beauty, the same Greek word, *kalos*, being used for both Goodness and Beauty, for the two concepts were fundamentally the same. And the world for which the sovereign was responsible was not just the earth but the universe and, coming through the Gnostic Christians, not just our one universe but a universe of universes. So when, with democracy, the people became sovereign, it is not simply a matter of voting once every four or five years, but they have each inherited this incalculable responsibility, the responsibility as part of God to be taking part in His Creation. So our present religions are just fragmentary of this earlier theology, concentrating on bowings and scrapings and the repetition of patter and shibboleths; forgetting the utterly awe-inspiring root from which our contemporary religions originated. The socialist notions of historicism, of Inevitable Human Progress through Science, are unequivocally incompatible with the religious notions of responsibility, the good, creation, guilt, however cheapened and attenuated our present faiths. That earlier religious vision was inconceivably the greater. Religions, like plants, severed from their roots, slowly die.

Each of our major religions is a twig on the great tree of Religion, each twig pretending that the tree does not exist. Nevertheless, in the last lines of his *Prometheus* the poet Shelley would describe the Titans of the Golden Age:

To defy power that seems omnipotent;
To love and bear, to hope till hope creates
From its own wreck the thing it contemplates;
Never to change, nor falter nor repent;
This, like thy glory, Titan, is to be
Good, great and joyous, beautiful and free;
This is alone life, power, empire and victory.

And let us note that the gods of those earlier religions were based on Olympus. Homer describes Olympus: "Where, they say, is the abode of the gods that stands fast forever. Neither is it shaken by wind nor ever wet with rain, nor does snow fall upon it, but the air is outspread clear and cloudless, and over it hovers a radiant whiteness. Therein the blessed gods are glad all their days."[6] This is similar to the ancient description of the Minoan Fields of the Blessed, perhaps California or the river valleys of Peru. Odysseus himself took up with a daughter of Atlas.[7] Olympus and Atlantis were surely variants of the same name after the Greeks finished their long-distance trading and positioned their gods, not in their huge colonies, but back in their homeland, their metropolis, the mother country.

An early Spanish priest remarked that the Aztec god Quetzalcóatl must have been a relative of the devil since he had given the Mexicans a bogus imitation of Christianity: with confession, absolution of sins, baptism, priests practicing fasts, flagellations, with many living in monastic seclusion.

26. God-Kings and Titans

"Ragnarok means, 'the fatal destiny, the end of the gods.' The gods brought down this fatal destiny on their own heads. Had they been able to control their passions the golden age of peace would never have come to an end."

NEW LAROUSSE ENCYCLOPAEDIA

"When we saw so many cities and villages built both in the water and on the land, and this straight level causeway, we couldn't restrain our admiration. It was like the enchantments told about in the book of Amadis [a sixteenth century romance of chivalry] because of the high towers . . . and other buildings all of masonry, which rose from the water. Some of our soldiers asked if what we saw was not a dream."

BERNAL DIAZ DEL CASTILLIO, *The Conquest of New Spain*

At a point in time in the sixth millennium a new phenomenon appeared in the world that was to have a profound effect on all its subsequent history. The first great monuments it left behind were not in what we think of as the centers of ancient civilization, in the Near East or in India, but on the Atlantic coast of Europe. The stone alignments of Brittany, the oldest megalith dated around 5435 B.C., stand as the earliest memorials to this powerful new movement, the triumph of patriarchy and its ultimate embodiment, the god-king. The political hyperbole used to describe this masculine takeover is "the Creation" and the stone alignments of Brittany are there to celebrate it, or so it seems to me: this is their scintillating importance.

It is impossible to give anything like a complete account of how kingship arose and how it spread through the world. What we have is a certain amount of clearly established fact, a good deal of conjecture, and a great need for further open-minded research. As far as we can now make out the story goes like this:

Kingship originated among some of the Aryans, a fair-skinned people, and especially among the blond northerners of Europe whose country is a fatherland rather than a motherland. Sea travel was by this time long developed among the matriarchal societies and it was therefore easy for the new idea to be carried gradually from country to country and from continent to continent. We can see it at its peak in early dynastic Egypt, but the Egyptians did not invent it for themselves. They said that the gods came out of Punt, which we can translate as meaning that kingship came to them through Somalia, the first port of call for ships crossing the Indian Ocean from Mesopotamia or India. Diodorus Siculus says that the god-kings and heroes ruled Egypt for fifteen hundred years before Menes, who was the first king of the First Dynasty and reigned about 3000 B.C. Fair-hairedness was almost everywhere associated with princes, aristocrats and gods—at that very early date.

In Egyptian legend the great culture hero was Osiris, who was said to be a great-grandson of the sun god Ra. It is interesting to look at the list of achievements with which he is credited.[1] First he abolished cannibalism. He taught his still half-savage subjects the art of making agricultural tools, and also taught them how to make bread, wine and beer. Archaeologists have recently found the Sumerians making wine by 3500 B.C. Osiris built the first temples, sculpted the first divine images and laid down the rules governing religious practice. He built towns and gave laws for the townsmen to live by. When he had completed the civilization of Egypt, Osiris set out to conquer Asia, accompanied by Thoth, his grand vizier, and two lieutenants. From there he traveled the world, spreading civilization everywhere and subjecting the different peoples not by force of arms but by gentleness; winning them over with songs and by the playing of various musical instruments. After his death the notion of resurrection was passed on to the world: the voyage after death to another and better world beyond, if you had been approved by the weighing of souls, the Last Judgment, a sort of Parents' Day for parents.

It is easy to dismiss this legend as a pretty story rather than a piece of history. The idea of a whole people yielding to a new ruler on the strength of a song recital is charming but hardly plausible: one suspects the presence of a backing group of heavily armed soldiers. And could one man really have time to visit every country in the world and stay there long enough to civilize it? However, let us once again remember that legends usually embody some element of truth, however much it may have been romanticized over the ages. Underlying the story of Osiris is the fact that around the fourth millennium the techniques of civilization do start to appear in

Plate 226

In 1985, the ruins of an ancient lost city were discovered in a remote forest on the eastern slopes of the Peruvian Andes. Beneath dense vegetation lay a huge metropolis of soaring pyramids and staired terraces, perhaps 24,000 buildings, the center of a civilization that was at its peak 1,000 years ago.

The ruins, estimated to cover at least 120 square miles, included what seemed to be a series of fortresses joined by high walls, inhabited now only by animals of the upper Amazon jungle.

The discovery was reported by Gene Savoy, an American explorer, during preliminary work on a plan to sail a primitive catamaran down the Amazon and across the Atlantic to test his theory of contacts between Mediterranean and pre-Inca Andes cultures.

The ruins were found between 8,000 and 9,000 feet in the mountains overlooking the Maranon River, the main source of the Amazon, about forty miles southwest of the small city of Chachapoyas.

Another report described the customs of this society, which were matriarchal, but one look at the name of the town, Kuelap, identifies it as matriarchal: with different spelling the Great Goddess is called the same almost everywhere.

The metropolis was the home of the powerful and warlike Chachas people, who were conquered by the Incas at the end of the fifteenth century, just a few decades before they in turn were defeated by the Spaniards.

After their own conquest, the Chachas disintegrated and disappeared as a nation. Some of their genetic remnants, however, seem to have lasted in the blond hair and blue eyes of some of the mountain people.

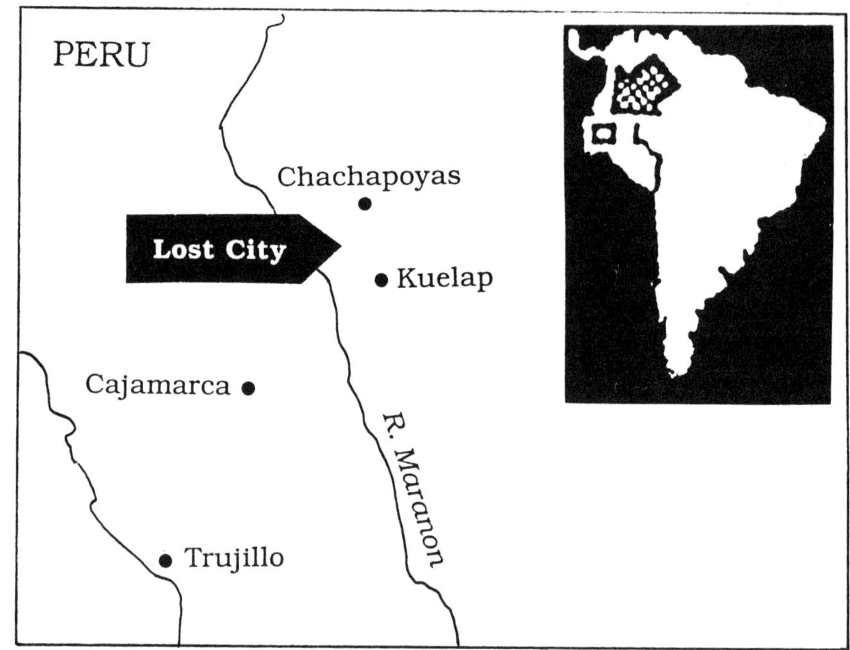

various widely separated places. There is, for example, the first cultivation of cotton in Peru and Mexico, using the hybrid plant from Asian and American stock. It is clear that at this period the new arts of civilized life, including irrigation farming, were being spread around the world along the network of trading routes that had been established millennia earlier by the matriarchal cultures. Pioneers and colonizers from a number of centers probably took part in this movement, and prominent among them may well have been an early Egyptian king named Osiris, or at least people sent out by him. Let us remember that matriarchal groups were small and close-knit: compare this with the military advantage of empires believing in the brotherhood of man under the fatherhood of God, as Isocrates describes it.

The diversity of peoples among the ruling classes is clearly indicated in the Osiris legend. On his return from his travels, Osiris was murdered by his brother Seth, who ruled over the Upper (that is, the southern) Kingdom of Egypt. We can assume that their "brotherhood" was the brotherhood of kingship rather than being meant in the literal sense, for they are described as being racially quite different. Osiris was handsome, dark-skinned and taller than other men, while Seth was red-haired and white-skinned, so it seems likely that Osiris was of Sumerian or Semitic descent and Seth Celtic. Clearly the two kingdoms of Egypt had been taken over by patriarchal rulers of different origins, and both may have reached Egypt

PLATE 227
Mesopotamian splendor. The wealth of the nabobs of Mesopotamia was manifest from even their early days. Woolley, excavating below the present city of Mugayyar, discovered a cemetery from the early dynastic period: the riches from the royal tombs astonished the world: their aptitude of design and rich craftsmanship remain, in Seton Lloyd's words, "one of the marvels of antiquity." Buried with the royal bodies were soldiers and female attendants; in one tomb were seventy-four females killed to accompany the corpse.[1]

Type of open architecture in Assyria (composed by Charles Chipiez). The wealth of the Mesopotamian and European colonies in America is reflected in the English word plutocrat: Pluto being the Roman name for Hades, the ruler of the land beyond the Atlantic where were found the golden apples. Great as was the wealth of Mesopotamia and ancient Egypt, language suggests that, just as today, so in the Bronze Age the heavy money was believed to have been in America. Enormous amounts of tin were used by neo-Assyrian kings.[2] *In Assyria the parasol was the symbol of the most exalted rank, as today in Ghana.*[3] *It is just worth noticing that in Asia Minor as with the San and the Khoikhoi of southern Africa, the hare was associated with the moon.*

by different routes. If they did, then the picture one receives is of a system of patriarchal kingship originating perhaps in Iran, moving to the western seaboard of Europe, spreading as far eastward as the Indus Valley and China, then perhaps flowing to countries such as Egypt that were not yet under its rule. It is important to stress that this was not, like Alexander's empire much later, a matter of conquest by one race or nation over others. It was the prevalence of a system of government in which the kings themselves came from a number of nations and often ruled over peoples of races different from themselves. There were records of Mesopotamian kings addressing these subjects from a ziggurat as "black-headed people,"[2] which must have meant that they, and perhaps the whole ruling class, were not black-haired but blonds, which is, indeed, what another tradition records.[3]

The countries of northwest Europe that have retained the system of monarchy may indeed be where monarchy commenced.

We can conjecture that one way in which kingship was spread was by the younger sons of kings hiving off to found kingdoms for themselves, but it is unlikely that even within one kingdom the crown would always have descended by simple primogeniture. Probably some degree of election was involved and in some countries, such as Egypt, descent through the female line still played a part. The importance of the early matriarchal world has been successfully hidden by the patriarchal societies that came after them.

It is not impossible that, sometimes at least, the takeover of cultures by these early patriarchal kings may have been bloodless, for they brought with them two things that must have been immensely attractive. The first was security of food supply, based on a reliable system of irrigation agriculture wherever that could be practiced. The second was a kind of transcendence. In place of an unchanging cycle of years in which things were sometimes better, sometimes worse, but survival was always enough to aim at, now there was a possibility of splendor, of armies and conquest, of huge labor forces able to undertake the mighty works of irrigation and the building of cities. There were temples and palaces, and in them the priests, the kings and their courts lived, it must have seemed, like gods. It took a long period of successful development before history, which had been looked upon as cyclic like the seasons, came to be seen as the product of a male creator god, through the sovereign creating into an unimaginable future, a vast period ahead, with incalculable potentials, for which the sovereign was but the instrument of God: a process beyond the capacity of the human mind to encompass.

It is not surprising that these rulers became god-kings. At first they did not, it seems, claim to be gods during their own lifetimes. Divinity was a posthumous award from people looking back on their achievements; and it must be said that, if ever mortals did, those first and greatest kings deserved to be deified for their effect on human destiny. They and their descendants provided the governing class at the growing, culturally creative points of five out of the six continents: in the Indus Valley and Persia for Asia, in Egypt for Africa, in Bolivia and Peru for South America, in Mexico for North America and in northern Europe along the Atlantic shores. The male god came to be looked upon as mind giving shape to the female, cyclic nature: nature conceived not only as the earth but as the universe or even a universe of universes: a concept vast beyond belief. This was an alteration in our understanding of time, an alteration of incalculable proportions. Each human mind was a god.

The start of the rule of god-kings in any particular place is recorded in the legends of that culture as "creation." If we believe the god-kings' chroniclers, nothing worth mentioning existed before their arrival; it was all a mere nonexistence. That is why the creation of the world is pretended to occur so late in the history of mankind, after a worldwide, wonderfully successful culture of matriarchal societies had been operating for thousands of years. It also explains why different civilizations give different dates for the Creation. Eusebius, for instance, gives two versions, one a cluster of dates around 5500–5200 B.C. and the other 3900 B.C.[4] The earlier dates apply to Brittany, to northern Europe, to Iran; and the later one to the incorporation of societies from the hills around Mesopotamia into the societies of the god-kings already established on the irrigated fields and their well laid out city-states. Today's interpretation of the word "Creation" is phony—the sort of political nonsense we have grown accustomed to in our day—but for specific peoples this date will be strictly correct. It records the point in time when their tribe was incorporated into the patriarchal world.

One of the difficulties we face in trying to write an account of the god-kings is that their legends attribute to the king himself the deeds of the people over whom he and his successors ruled. This explains how Osiris could be said to have visited and civilized every country in the world, and it is in this sense that we should interpret the story of his death at the hands of Seth: it represents the defeat of the Osiris people by the Seth people. After that defeat, which happened during the fourth millennium, some of the Osiris people crossed the Atlantic to North America. It was the Osiris refugees who ruled in North America under the name of Hades, alias Dionysus. This illustrates another difficulty in disentangling the history of the god-kings: one king or one people could be given different names in different countries. Osiris became Hades in America and he has also been identified with the Greek god Dionysus. The Amerindian religions on the west coast of North America have been described as Dionysiac,[5] and it seems quite possible that this ecstatic cult was spread across both the Atlantic and the Mediterranean by the Osiris people, whose memory was preserved but whose name was changed by the different peoples of different languages whom they civilized. The traditions of emigration from Mesopotamia match the traditions of the arrival of white immigrants into America.

The thing that is clear is the existence of the religio-political system itself. During the second half of the sixth millennium and the first half of the fifth the god-kings—and the people they ruled—spread out over a large part of the earth and began to displace the old matriarchal polities and imposed instead the new way of life based on centralized government, large-scale agriculture and the worship of the sky gods. For several thousand years the god-kings ruled the oceans of the world. Plato may have been exaggerating when he asserted that they divided the whole earth among themselves by lot, but we can believe that they reached a working agreement on spheres of influence, and that perhaps a Golden Age, certainly a broadly peaceable order, prevailed.[6] It seems likely that the seaborne people of this time carried with them enough of a common language to allow them to communicate with one another in any country they visited. The Bible suggests that they were of one language and one speech. When Homer said that the gods were born out of Ocean it was to the maritime age of the earth mother and then the god-kings that he was looking back. Making a decision by lot rather than by war permitted, they thought, God to have a hand in the decision.

There is a curious remark by Diodorus Siculus, made in the course of his discussion of Egyptian kingship. After the union of the Upper and Lower Kingdoms under the First Dynasty, he says, later Egyptian kings were mortals. It is not easy to know exactly what he meant by this, but he seems to be drawing a distinction between the original lines of kings who brought civilization to so many places, including Egypt, and the conquerors who displaced them. Those conquerors, whatever Diodorus might think, styled themselves gods, no doubt using the title to demand unquestioning subservience. They took over the sun as their symbol, so that to the old duality of sun worship—the physical sun and the matriarchal forces—was added a third element, the god-king, to be worshipped as the sun's embodiment on earth. The sun religion was therefore trinitarian, but this religion took a much greater hold on Egypt than on Mesopotamia.

The conquerors of a new breed who took over Egypt came from Sumer, which had been a great power since the middle of the fourth millennium and which has been credited with the invention of bronze. It seems that they provided the first dynasties of Egypt and probably they had been operating in the Nile Valley before that. Sumer can stand as an excellent example of the great powers of this period in history. First, it was both a land and sea power: we know that in the third millennium it controlled the Lebanon and sent ships westward out of the Mediterranean into the Atlantic. Under Lugalzaggisi its empire stretched from Anatolia in the north and Cyprus in the west to the Persian Gulf and Elam. Then around 2400 B.C. the Sumerian empire was conquered by Sargon, the ruler of Akkad, an inland, Semitic state further up the Euphrates, and thereafter Sargon and his heirs, not to mention his brilliant grandson Naram-Sin, governed the combined empire of Sumer and Akkad until around 2100 B.C. It will be remembered that it was Sargon who sent out expeditions to the "tin lands" when tin ran out in Mesopotamia. Then Sumerians resumed control in what is called the Third Dynasty of Ur for a century or so until disaster, probably in the form of earthquake, struck.

The empire fell in 2003 B.C. and power moved away from the seacoast, with the great land empires of Babylon and Assyria dominating the region.

But long before that had happened there had come that strange phenomenon that is at the heart of our story: the Age of the Titans.

Alongside or part of the military and merchant fleets controlled by city-states of Sumer, there existed a number of trading organizations whose activities spanned the globe and which have been commemorated as the fourteen or so Titans of Greek tradition. They flourished in the fourth, third and second millennia, but they were preceded by another group of people. This was the group whose activities were related in Greek legend as the deeds of the hero Heracles: hero because he flourished before the invention of the politicoreligious system of divine kingship, even if various peoples deified him subsequently.

It was the Heracles people who first broke away from the matriarchal societies that had dominated the world until then. They would seem to have got the hell-in with the women. The rivalry between the old and the new powers, and the hatred the newcomers aroused, are symbolized in the legend that tells how the goddess Hera sent two serpents to kill the infant Heracles in his cradle, only for him to strangle them with his bare hands. Translation: one of the matriarchal powers sent soldiers to suppress the newly independent Heracles people, but the soldiers were defeated. The serpents are, of course, the symbols of the earth worshippers.

Another part of the Heracles myth tells how he took agriculture around the world, as Dionysus/Osiris was later said to have taken civilization. This would imply world voyages by the Heracles people as early as 7000 or even 8000 B.C., and this very early date is confirmed by astronomical evidence that we shall be examining later in this chapter. It is also suggested by the curious episode in the myth that has Heracles sailing off in a cooking pot. Presumably this refers to a very primitive form of coracle or a craft in which buoyancy was provided by earthenware floats in the form of sealed jars. Obsidian was being exported from the small Aegean island of Melos by the eleventh millennium B.C.: [7] the obscene arms trade developed as early as that.

Diodorus Siculus, who has quite a lot to say about Heracles, suggests that the club and lion skin with which he was traditionally equipped (see, for example, Plate 233) show that he lived before the age of armor and, therefore, the age of metals.[8] On the other hand one of his subsequent labors seems to put him firmly into the Copper Age. The golden apples of the Hesperides that he was sent to fetch were, I am convinced, the nuggets of pure copper on which the Copper Age was largely built, and that were to be found in economic quantities at only one site in the world—Lake Superior. Heracles was not the first to bring back copper from that source, but the story would lose much of its point if native copper were not still of great importance. This would seem to date it sometime before the smelting of copper ore became generally possible, in the fourth millennium. We must remember that Heracles, Poseidon, etc. were not names for individual people or gods but the totems or divinities of their respective multinationals.

Other exploits seem to belong to other dates. Heracles is credited with clearing the world of wild animals, particularly in India and Crete. Since Crete began to be inhabited, they tell us, around 6000 B.C., that would seem to be the date of this particular labor. Diodorus also says that Heracles was a contemporary of Osiris and makes him responsible for ending the Nile flood. This would put him somewhere around 4000 B.C.

These apparent contradictions resolve themselves if we see Heracles not as one man, nor even as a single culture located in one particular place and period, but as an organization of people probably drawn from several races, based in various ports at various times, and having their rationale in a seagoing tradition that kept their ships moving between countries spread right around the world. It is worth observing that a people of that kind have great flexibility and are proof against many of the disasters that bring down land-based powers. An earthquake or a bloody conquest at one of their bases still leaves their ships free to operate from others, and those who hear about the trouble in time need never return to the disaster area. They can survive periods of upheaval and achieve a surprising longevity.

Legends, as we observed, can never give us an exact history of the events on which they were originally based. Did Osiris or Heracles tame the Nile and so originate the great irrigation culture of Egypt? Quite probably the story was told of their own heroes by the different peoples of Egypt, and with all the movement that went on in the world at that time it is highly likely that the doings of various peoples would have been confused during the centuries when all history was passed on by word of mouth. However, we have enough evidence to be confident that, over a long period of time counted in millennia, there was a seaborne people of great importance who went under the name of Heracles. They seem to have purposely distanced themselves from the prissy women by acts of great heartiness: hunting, wrestling, starting the Olympic Games; compulsive travelers, muscular guys. The name itself is interesting. Hera is represented in the myths as being Heracles' enemy from birth but clearly her name is a part of his. Now, Hera was simply the Greek version of Awa, the Semitic earth mother, and my surmise is that Heracles was the Greek recollection of the Awa-Ak people who left the imprint of their name in so many languages throughout the world. The relationship with Hera immediately becomes clear. In due course the Heracles people took over a part of the copper trade and so achieved a preeminence over the matriarchal peoples who had formerly dominated it. During the long period in which they flourished they left their traces on the Old and New Worlds alike. In Phoenicia, for example, Heracles, renamed Melkarth, was worshipped as a god. The Celts looked on him as their founder and their god. The capital of Crete is Heraklion (Iráklion). Indeed it may well be that the Arawaks of the West Indies were products of the subsequent Golden Age of justice and enlightenment, and so were easy meat for the Carib and Christian, the savages of the Iron Age.

It is not until the second millennium that the Heracles people disappear from the record. Even then their story is not quite over. The Heraclides, that is the Sons of Heracles, were the Dorians who occupied Greece and Crete around 1100 B.C. The very name Dorian may be associated with *uradu*, the Sumerian word for copper, while the English word *copper*, like Cyprus itself, is surely an Ok-Ava name. In the Scottish Highland game "tossing the kaber," which is throwing a tree trunk around, would seem to be a typical Heracles activity, with appropriate appellation.

It was during the time when the Heracles people were still an important power in the world that the age of the Titans began. In Greek myth the Titans were born from the union of Gaea with her son Ouranos, the first of the sky-gods, and in this we can see again the emergence of a new set of people out of the old matriarchal societies under the impact of the new sky cult. The name Titan is thought by some to mean that they were descended from the goddess Titaea: by others that they were just the sons and daughters of Ouranos and Gaea, or sky and earth. Stephanus of Byzantium names the following Titans: Adanus, Ostasus, Andes, Chronos, Rhea, Japetus, Olymbrus. That one Titan is called Andes has not been properly noticed but is highly relevant to our story (for a fuller list see Plate 1).[9]

What, then, was the nature of these literally titanic organizations? At the head of each Titan was a god-king, whereas that was not true of the Heracles people, they were too early for that form of polity. Each Titan society could be made up of people of different races and languages, and what united them was not a common origin but a common culture expressed as a common religion. In that respect we can compare them to the armies of the Crusaders and the Saracens: on each side there were soldiers of many nationalities held together by a shared faith. The Heracles people were at their height before the invention of this religio-political device.

At any one time there were a number of Titans working the trade routes of the world, and there were clashes between these Bronze Age multinationals. Each Titan had particular ports from which it set out, on both sides of the Atlantic and around the Pacific as well, and there might be one port that formed a kind of home base for the organization, as even the most broadly multinational company today is ultimately based in one country. This home port would have to be on the territory of a land power, but the impression one gets is that these places were treated as free ports, rather like Hong Kong or Shanghai under the old Chinese empire: the presence of an alien power was tolerated because of the wealth it brought in through trade. Above all, the Titans were the suppliers of tin and copper, those indispensable metals, as well as of gold and silver, lapis lazuli, incense.

So far as we can make out on present evidence, the more distant trading, not within the Mediterranean but across the Atlantic and Pacific Oceans, was at this time the sphere of the Titans. However, since the Titans were made up from mixtures of peoples, there might be a Cretan or Hittite predominance in one, an alliance of Phoenicians and Amorites heading another, and so on.

When we find evidence of Middle Eastern or European contacts in America and elsewhere, therefore, we have to remember that these contacts were probably made through the medium of one of the Titans. An object of distinctively Egyptian design found in America would not necessarily have been carried there by an Egyptian vessel but on one that belonged to a professional merchant marine working the route between the two countries.

It is clear that the Titans operated on a huge scale, since otherwise they could not have had the effect they did on the peoples of America and West Africa. Still, Amerindian tradition made their numbers small but their skills great. After Zeus's war with the Titans, tradition said, Zeus imprisoned all the Titans in Tartarus: i.e. sent them packing to the New World.

In investigating these fascinating organizations we once again have to use a mixture of legend and archaeological findings. The Greek myths, which are one chief source, give various accounts of the Titans. Interpreting them is not easy, for they give contradictory versions of even such basic facts as the Titans' names and the number of them that existed. In the sense that we are using the word here, I believe that there were fourteen Titans or more, but we have little or no information about most of them and I shall deal here only with the most important, principally Chronos, Poseidon and Atlas, together with Zeus, who, because he was the son of Chronos, was not himself a Titan. Zeus in fact represented a new wave of people who helped to destroy the Titans and who dominated the Mediterranean world after their fall. He represented the patriarchal society and light, by contrast with Ouranos and his night sky and darkness. Zeus was Mind, in Greek *Nous*, and with him came a vast philosophic conception: the concept of limitless Creation. Each human mind was a god: the male god imposing form on the cyclic, female, repetitive forces of nature.

We are again confronted with the inevitable patchiness of the historical and archaeological record. To give just one example, there is a tantalizing reference, as we have seen, in an author known as Stephanus of Byzantium, to a Titan named Andes about whom nothing more is known in historical terms. A further complication is that different peoples gave different names to the same Titan. A great deal more research would be needed before one could even attempt to give a better account of the Titans, and what I hope to do here is simply to show that they did exist, as groups of sea-going peoples, that they dominated three thousand years of the long history of transoceanic trading, and that they were the vitally important multinationals of the Copper and Bronze Ages, imprinting their company logos on the rocks where they traded.

There is one unexpected place in which we can get help in starting to build a chronological framework, and that is in the field of astronomy, the first science of the navigator. To be precise, what we have to look at is the phenomenon known as the precession of the equinoxes.

Spinning around on its axis once a day, the earth acts as a kind of huge gyroscope, so that its axis keeps pointing toward a fixed place in the heavens—nearly, but not exactly. If you could look along that axis, and kept looking century after century, you would see that the position in the sky toward which it points is traveling in a wide, slow circle, so slow that it takes almost twenty-six thousand years to get right around. At the moment it is pointing at what we call the Pole Star, Polaris, and that star therefore gives the direction of north to anyone who can see it—that is, anyone in the Northern Hemisphere. But at earlier periods in history the axis was pointing at different stars, and these stars therefore had to be used in turn as pole stars.

It hardly needs to be said that for any sailor who does not have an accurate chronometer, the pole star is by far the most important star in the sky, the only one whose direction does not vary with the time of day. The constellation in which it stands therefore has a unique status, and during the seafaring ages that constellation was named after the dominant sea people of the time. Plate 229 shows how this worked. From about 10,000 to 5000 B.C. the pole star was in the constellation of Hercules, and from about 4000 to 2000 in that of Draco, the dragon, which was the symbol of the Titans. This matches what we know from other sources. The Heracles people were the thalassocrats for several thousand years from the eighth to the sixth millennium and the Dragon ships then took over. Later, during the first millennium B.C., when the Phoenicians were the dominant sea power, the pole star was dubbed the Phoenician. The constellation of the Great Bear would seem to have been named thus first in North America and passed from there to the Old World, not vice versa.

This interpretation helps to explain one puzzling fact. The constellations notoriously do not resemble the things after which they are named. Hercules looks nothing like a man, Draco nothing like a dragon, and so on. For those constellations that lie around the celestial north pole here at last is a convincing reason for their names.

It would be a mistake, however, to suppose that the Titans followed one after the other in orderly sequence. They existed alongside one another, sometimes competing and fighting, sometimes making arrangements on spheres of activity. As we have already noticed, there was, for example, a conference, recorded by both Homer and Plato and also in a fairly similar Middle Eastern account, at which Zeus, Poseidon and Hades parceled out the world among themselves. At that time Hades was the dominant group in North America, and it was the confusion between America and the Inferno (discussed in Chapter 3) that later gave this name to the land of the dead. Poseidon, identified by the Classical Greeks as the god of the sea, was the Titan chiefly controlling the ocean crossings to Central and South America from the end of the fourth millennium to the middle of the second, while Zeus was becoming dominant in the Mediterranean area. Zeus consigned all his defeated enemies to Tartarus, or America, which may possibly have involved slave labor on the American mines, among other things.

To start at the beginning, it seems that the leader, if the youngest, of the great Titans was the Sumerian-Semitic group known as Chronos. In the myth it is Chronos who, urged on by his mother, Gaea, castrates his father, Ouranos, and again we can see this as a metaphor. Chronos destroys the power of sky-worshipping people. Chronos's name is the Greek word for time. These were indeed a "time people," for it would seem to be chiefly they who erected many of the stone calendar clocks in Britain, whose date can be fixed at 3000–1200 B.C. and that served as both temples and observatories. When the Sumerians were destroyed in Mesopotamia the Poseidon people began to falter in the Americas.

Chronos was not this Titan's only name. In Sumer he was known as Enlil, which means "Lord of the Wind," and many years later, when his power had long been broken, the Romans remembered the god under the name of Saturn and associated him with excellence in agriculture. His emblem, the dragon, suggests another possible identification, for the dragon is conventionally depicted as a winged reptile with the long, coiling body of a snake. It is the dragon symbol of Chronos that we find in the winged serpents of America, Ethiopia and elsewhere. In the succession of Hercules to Draco in the constellations housing the pole star of the period, we find confirmation of the belief that Chronos was the first of the Titans to snatch control of the seas from the sky-worshipping people, although admittedly the dragon might stand for the sea rovers generally. Quetzalcóatl, as we have seen, the god of ancient Mexico, was depicted as a dragon and he also bore the title, "Lord of the Wind." In ancient Mexico, Atl was the name of the Creator God,[9] even as Atlas was the name of the Greek god.

Mediterranean tradition said that the Chronos people were at one time based, among other places, in Italy, Sicily and North Africa, so that it would seem that they then controlled the sea trade by their stranglehold on the central Mediterranean. Semitic power alone did not last very long in the Mediterranean. Somewhere around 1570 B.C. they themselves were overthrown in a great battle called by the Greeks the Titanomachia; they were defeated by the Zeus people, the male sky god of daylight, who defeated the maritime powers that maintained an equal balance between the male and the female. The all-powerful male god, characteristic of the Iron Age, now comes on the scene. The ejection of the Hyksos from Egypt is the start of the Toltecs in Mexico: in Greek tradition Zeus despatches Chronos to Tartarus.

The Poseidon people had been based, among so many other places, in Libya as well as America. They were evidently a dark-haired people, since there is a reference in Homer to "Poseidon of the sable locks." From evidence in West Africa it seems that they traded with that region, using land routes across the Sahara desert, as well as traveling by sea to West Africa in addition to America. A Roman writer, Proclus, quoting an earlier writer, Marcellus, refers to a tradition of a huge continent out in the Atlantic and says that a small island, a thousand stadia long (about 120 miles) was occupied by Poseidon. This sounds like one of the West Indies, perhaps Cuba, which would have been a useful starting point for a move to obtain a position on the mainland. Cuba's full name is Cubagua, and I think that *agua* is the name used for Poseidon's territory. We find it used from Canton in China to Glasgow and Cornwall in Britain.

The event that set the Poseidon people off on their greatest trans-Atlantic adventure is extremely interesting. It was nothing less than the Great Flood, commemorated in the oral traditions of various American cultures and recorded by the Jews in the Bible as Noah's Flood. In the Jewish story God sends the flood to drown the whole world, which had become disobedient to his laws, but as we have already seen there is also a Babylonian version that is more specific in its account of one of the most ruthless episodes in human history. This version is inscribed in cuneiform script on some tablets and it makes clear that what happened was a deliberate act by the very human god-kings.

The year was about 3116 B.C., and the rulers of the Mesopotamian countries who participated in the great irrigation system based on the rivers Tigris and Euphrates had come to feel increasingly threatened by the people over whom they ruled. First, these people had greatly multiplied in numbers, no doubt due to the efficiency of irrigation agriculture in feeding a growing population, and they were becoming unruly—"too noisy" in the words of the Babylonian text. Secondly, the caste system was breaking down. As Genesis puts it, "the sons of God looked on the daughters of men and saw that they were fair," or in other words, the ruling caste was interbreeding with the common people. Thirdly, and dangerously, those common people were beginning to acquire the knowledge of how to make high-technology weapons: they were being taught how to fabricate bronze. This, as the Greek tragedian correctly pointed out, was what was meant by the Promethean theft of fire from the gods. It was not fire itself that was stolen, for that had been widely in use for a million years: it was the technical use of fire. Once the mass of people learned how to use it in the forging of bronze they would become, by sheer numbers, more than a match for their rulers. Those rulers, therefore, meeting secretly, decided on the final solution. They would break the dams, flood the irrigation plain, and drown the whole ungovernable population: that is, after first trying to kill them with disease and, when that failed, by drought, which also failed.

Their first step was to preserve their records by taking them upstream to Nippur, where they were found by excavators in this century. After that they put their plan into action and the whole densely populated land was overwhelmed with water. The work of the Creation was undone in a single, utterly destructive act.

Only one thing did not go according to plan. The god-kings had naturally bound themselves by an oath of secrecy, since their plan would have been unworkable if it once became known. What went wrong was that one of them broke his oath. The king of the port city of Eridu warned his people of what was coming and instructed them to abandon their possessions and take to their ships. The people concerned were those who worshipped Enki or Ea, in other words they were the Poseidon people.[10] The refugees, or a large part of them, made their way across the Atlantic to their island base in the West Indies, and thence controlled much of South and Central America, in fact wherever *agua* is part of the place name.

In the land they left behind an immense labor of reconstruction had to be undertaken, and most of those who had previously done the pick and shovel work were no longer around to do it. No doubt the Bible story is an exaggeration. In a flood of that kind not everyone perishes. Some must have survived, but not enough to relieve the ruling caste of the need to bend their own backs to the work. There is a record that they were loud with their complaint at this indignity. So they co-opted more of the surrounding natives into their society and this is described in a cuneiform text as the Second Creation. However, the land was still not at peace. The history of the revived city-states of Mesopotamia in the third millennium is one of frequent fighting—the warlike Bronze Age at its worst—and one result of that was that when cities were destroyed many of their records were destroyed with them. Paradoxically, though, some of the clay tablets have survived all the better for the destruction, the clay being baked hard when the buildings where they were stored went up in flames.

Meanwhile, the Poseidon people had expanded their influence from their West Indian base and held a dominating position on the mainland of America from Guatemala southward. It is notable that the first Inca is said, in Peruvian tradition, to have arrived at Tiahuanaco after a flood, and still more striking that the Mayan culture bringers, the four Bacabs, arrived from across the Atlantic on August 10, 3113 B.C., according to Las Casas, to escape the Flood, Mayan tradition said. There was a perfect fit with the dating of the Mesopotamian flood of about 3116 and the Babylonian tradition of the broken oath and the sea escape.

In Plato's account, the first historical account of America that exists, the ten sons of Poseidon—that is, the people who followed the Poseidon people in governing America—are said to have been headed by Atlas. Once again we find that the legend, dismissed by historians as fiction, has a substantial truth in it. Atlas was in fact the next Titan to dominate

America, and most particularly the American mines. The fact that both Atlantis and the Atlantic were, as Plato remarks, named after him, clearly points to his preeminence at that time, while the name itself, with its *atl* root, indicates a sea people. In Quechua, a language of Peru, *anta* means, among other things, copper-colored or copper and the name Atlantic may originally have meant Atlas's copper sea, as we have noticed already.

One of the interesting things about Atlas, as he appears in the mythology of the Greeks, is that they did not know where to place him. There are several versions of his story. In Hesiod's *Theogony* he holds up the sky on his shoulders in the way that is generally remembered today; but in Homer[11] he is simply called the Guardian of the Pillars of Heaven. Either way, it is obvious that he must have lived in a mountainous place. The Pillars of Heaven surely have to be mountains, and even if Atlas carries the sky on his own shoulders he has to be somewhere high enough to reach it. The Classical Greeks placed him in the barren mountains of northwest Africa, still known as the Atlas Mountains, but we can discard that idea. The Atlas range is not particularly high, none of its peaks reaching the height of the highest Alps, and the Pillars of Heaven would have to be the tallest of all mountains. Further, the Atlas Mountains are utterly barren, and no powerful ruler could hope to sustain himself, his people and his army in such an inhospitable place. Homer, on the other hand, says that the columns on which Atlas supported the heavens stood far out in the Atlantic Ocean, and Homer is clearly right. We can, I believe, say exactly where they were. They were the huge Andean peaks that soar up around Lake Titicaca, and also the highlands of Mexico.

What has happened here is, once again, the eliding of two ideas, one practical and one metaphorical. The practical one is simply the spectacular height of the mountains, the tallest of them reaching to more than twenty thousand feet. They really do look as if they touched the vault of heaven. The metaphorical one is that Atlas, as a Titan, upheld law and order in an important part of the world, the most important of all in terms of the supply of bronze. In that sense he held up the frame of things. (The same metaphor is used in the old Roman saying "Let justice be done though the sky falls.") And of course this description makes perfect sense of Homer's description of Atlas as "guardian" of the Pillars of Heaven. To sun worshippers fire symbolized dominion over the whole earth.

An important clue to Atlas's origin is in Pliny's *Natural History*[12] where he is called a son of Libya. There is an apparent, but not a real, contradiction here with Plato's statement that Atlas was a son of Poseidon. Plato is pointing to the fact that Atlas succeeded Poseidon in America, while Pliny is making use of a locution that often occurs in the coded language of legends, by which a colony or other breakaway group hived off from an existing state or culture is described as a son or daughter. What Pliny is telling us is that the Atlas people had taken over the Mediterranean coast of Africa. Originally they had been rulers of Mesopotamia, and among them were also the Set people of Egypt, who had been defeated in the battle between Set and Horus. Around the middle of the second millennium they took over from Poseidon as the most powerful group in America, where they became known to the Peruvians as Vira Cocha and to the Mexicans as Huehueteotl, god of fire, or more generally as Toltecs. It cannot be just coincidence that one of the seven daughters of Atlas was known as Maia (in Hesiod's *Theogony* as *Atlantis Maia*). The name tells us about the early beginnings of the Maya of Guatemala as an offshoot of the Atlas people. Again, to sun worshippers, fire symbolized dominion over the whole earth, wherever the sun encircled.

All of this fits in with Homer's observation that Atlas "knew the sea in all its depths," and had perfected astronomy, something that is very hard to reconcile with the conventional picture of Atlas kneeling on a mountaintop with the sky held up on his shoulders. It implies, what I believe is true, that the Atlas people traded in all the main oceans, not only by way of the Atlantic to America but across the Pacific as well.

Our interpretation also fits the description of Atlas, found in various ancient writings, as expert in astronomy. Pliny has Atlas explaining the firmament, and later says that Atlans, son of Libya, was one of those who invented the astrolabe.[13] Pausanias refers to the "Atlantes and those who profess to know the measurements of the earth."[14] Atlas would seem to have been one channel through which the mathematical and astronomical advances of the Babylonians and others reached the Greeks. So far, myth, historical record and my interpretation of what was meant by a Titan all form a coherent account. There is, however, an awkward puzzle that remains to be solved. When Heracles arrives at the Garden of the Hesperides he finds Atlas nearby, holding up the heavens on his shoulders. He persuades Atlas to steal the apples for him by offering to take over his place while he does so, but once Atlas has the apples he is quite happy to leave Heracles to hold up the sky while he makes off. Heracles pleads with him to take over the burden for just a moment while he puts a pad on his head to make the job less painful. Atlas does so and Heracles picks up the apples and walks away with them.

There are some puzzling things about this story, quite apart from the question of how any Titan could be boneheaded enough to fall for such a simple trick. The puzzles concern time and place.

The records we have of the Atlas people in America relate to the second millennium B.C., but by that time the copper nuggets of Lake Superior, which we have identified as the golden apples, were of much less importance—the mines were in fact nearing the end of their importance. Also the great days of the Heracles people, when they were setting out on their worldwide "labors," can be placed several thousand years earlier. In addition, the region of America dominated by the Atlas people was well to the south of Lake Superior, stretching perhaps from Ohio to Peru.

These discrepancies can be explained by one fact that we have to keep constantly in mind. The Classical Greeks were relying on oral traditions that even by their time were very old. The Atlas people's hegemony in America had ended centuries before Hesiod was composing his poetry and the early days of Lake Superior copper were some five millennia in the past. Few Classical Greeks, shut in by the Phoenicians, any longer knew where America (alias Atlantis) was, so it is hardly surprising that they had forgotten the names of the earlier people who had occupied it. The name they did remember was the last one. In the same way that most people today think of all the early inhabitants of Greece as Greeks, forgetting the other races who lived there before them, so the Greeks remembered Atlas because he was the last of his kind. It was the Atlas people who were the dominant sea power when at last the age of the Titans came to an end and the whole transoceanic system of trade began to break up.

The reasons for this final collapse have already been touched on. By far the most important was that the Bronze Age itself came to an end: cheap and plentiful steel replaced the alloy whose ingredients, copper and tin, were the chief articles of the Titans' trade. There was also the gradual increase in land transport that had been going on for some time, greatly helped by the invention first of the wheel as such and later of the light, spoked wheel bound together by an iron rim that replaced the old clumsy solid wheels. As a further step, draft animals were bred for greater efficiency. For some time, aided by these changes, power had been tending to move inland from the sea people to the land people: in Mesopotamia this meant a move up the Tigris and Euphrates. As big empires consolidated their hold over large areas of land, road building and road travel within their boundaries became safer and more feasible. The transition of sea power to land power caused by technical progress has also been the most signal fact in our present century.

Lastly there was the matter of weather. The climatic optimum, which had made North Atlantic ocean travel easier and safer ever since the early voyages of the matriarchal peoples thousands of years before, was in rapid decline. No longer would trees grow on the Shetland Islands: the new cold winds blew too strongly for that.

All the financial factors that had favored the Titans turned against them, but they did not go down without a fight. The battleground was the world, although especially the world of Egypt. Greek tradition correctly reported that the Typhonomachia, the war of Zeus and Athene versus the sea peoples, was literally worldwide.

Earlier the Hyksos had identified their warrior god Sutekh with Set, the old god of Upper Egypt and also the god of the Atlas people. This agrees with the evidence from other sources that the Hyksos alliance contained sea people from Crete and the eastern Mediterranean seaboard, as well as people from further inland. In other words we can see the Hyksos as being, to a large extent, the Old World arm of the Chronos and Atlas people. When they were finally expelled from Egypt in 1575 B.C. it was probably the first major defeat of the Titans as a group by the land powers. With the development of the wheel and roads, power was beginning slowly to shift from the maritime peoples to the land peoples, as it has done again in this century. Paradoxically it was perhaps the sea peoples development of cavalry that had given them the edge over the Egyptians in the first place.

Despite this, the Titans still retained control of the seas, and for a while they may even have extended the range of their influence. Forced out of the eastern Mediterranean, many of those who had been a part of the Hyksos alliance made their way to Mexico and were the driving force behind the new high Toltec culture (otherwise known as Olmec) that sprang into being during the sixteenth century B.C. At least one group of western Semitic sea people followed the Pacific route on its way to America. It is around 1700 B.C. that a high Bronze Age culture appears in the Anyang area of China and there are two striking facts that connect this with a movement of the Titans. First, this period in Chinese art, the Shang period, shares pottery marks with the western Semites of the Mediterranean;[15] second, tradition says that after delaying in China, many of these western Semites went on to Mexico to join forces with the Toltec/Olmecs. Among the Toltec/Olmec figurines there are Oriental faces. Toltec styles stretched from Ohio to Peru. Spinden claimed an earlier culture in Peru: it would, of course, be that of Poseidon.

Secondly there is the salient fact that of the fifty-two potters' marks that have been identified for the Shang period in Kwang Chih Chang's book, forty-nine are of western Semitic origin and three are Aegean. There are also rock engravings in Anyang that are similar to those found in the Baltic of the same period (see Plates 223 and 224): nothing extraordinary about this when we remember that the Mediterranean people were trading around the world.

A little over three centuries after the expulsion of the Hyksos from Egypt the Titans attacked again in a last, desperate attempt to reestablish their position in the Old World. Once again they were headed by the Atlas people, who at this time were known in the Mediterranean as Typhon or as Peleset or Peoples of the Sea, and the force assembled was a mighty one. The American colonies were by this time very powerful political and military units, in some cases more so than the Old World nations whence their colonizers had originally come. The situation was in that way similar to today, when the United States is a far bigger power than Britain, and Brazil than Portugal. The strength of the attackers was increased by the fact that they combined their peoples from all over the world in their alliance. The Baltic forerunners of the Vikings must have been among them, as well as forces from all the American colonies, now acting in concert. To this formidable combination were added various Mediterranean contingents, notably some of the western Semitic sea peoples and also Western European peoples lodged all along the North African coast as far as the frontier of Egypt. The Achaeans were an important part of them, Agamemnon's army of Mycenaeans. In the *Iliad* Homer is describing one small episode in what was a world war, as in this century, fought in two stages and occasioned by the same movement of power from sea people to land people.

The first act of this great alliance of sea peoples was to set about systematically destroying all competing naval powers in the Mediterranean. The siege of Troy was one episode in a far-flung conflict that raged around the world. Troy, controlling the entrance to the Black Sea, fell and was sacked. Ugarit also fell and the Hittite empire was broken up. Greek civilization in Crete was overthrown around 1200 B.C., and at about the same time the Phoenicians pushed into Boeotia, the province next to Attica, and drove out the inhabitants. In Athens a well was dug on the Acropolis to provide water during a siege, which Athens survived: for the earth worshippers and the sky worshippers had joined forces against the sea people. The Mycenaeans as such, part of the attacking force, now disappear from history, although the survivors of the attack are used by the Egyptians as mercenary troops in Palestine and are known to us as Philistines.

The climax of the war was the attempt by the sea peoples to conquer Egypt. Twice they attacked and twice they were defeated, the first time by the Pharaoh Merneptah in 1219 B.C. and the second time by Ramesses III early in the twelfth century, probably about 1182 B.C. It was a disaster for the attackers. The Titans were again driven out of the Mediterranean and this time there was to be no return. Their place was taken by land-based powers with strong trading interests, or else by the Phoenicians, whose colonies were soon spread along the North African coast as far as Cyrenaica and on the south coast of Europe westward from Sardinia. Iron Age transoceanic trading, however, was on a diminished scale and by the time of the Classical Greeks it was restricted, indeed, by the Greeks had been all but forgotten. For one of the results of the devastating war was that the Greeks seem to have lost the art of writing for six hundred years, and the memory of past events was preserved only in the form of legends that grew increasingly corrupt as time passed. All around were graves and monuments and abandoned cities that bore witness to an ancient grandeur, but the history of these things was lost and they were seen as the works not of men but of superhuman beings, of heroes, Titans and gods who had inhabited a world, different from and better than theirs—which of course was true enough.

As we have found elsewhere in this study, these legends cannot be taken as wholly reliable accounts, but they do provide a starting point for investigation and they can help to confirm what we deduce from other sources.

Relating to the last battle of the Titans, Titans collectively called Typhon, there is widespread occurrence of something like the Teutonic legend of *Ragnarok*, made famous by Wagner as the *Götterdämmerung*, or Twilight of the Gods. This is the story of a great conflict around the Baltic after which the old gods have to retreat to a remote fastness and a new race of rulers takes over the world. In Greece there were the two stories of the Titanomachia and the Typhonomachia, the battles of Zeus with the Titans in the sixteenth century B.C. and with Typhon in the thirteenth century B.C. These, I believe, refer to the expulsion of the Hyksos from Egypt and the final defeat of the Peoples of the Sea in 1182 by the Egyptian shipborne archers and the Athenians in alliance, when they attempt a comeback, driven to despair by bankruptcy. Those who were conquered would seem to have been the European part of the American alliance, the western Semites then replacing them in the Americas and subsequently returning to the Mediterranean to fill the power vacuum.

Because the siege of Troy was one small episode in the much larger war we can also use Homer's account. In two ways it provides interesting confirmation. When Odysseus at last returns to his own country, the island of Ithaca, he does so in disguise, as we have seen. To explain his appearance as an impoverished prince he invents a story, saying that a few months after the taking of Troy the fleet had reassembled in Crete, he himself contributing nine ships. They had then attacked Egypt, but the assault was bungled, the invaders were either slaughtered or made prisoner, and Odysseus was one of the few to escape. Now, the point about any cover story is that it has to be convincing: it fails if it does not accord with generally known facts. The people of Ithaca would have known perfectly well if there had or had not been a massive attack on Egypt involving their own people, the Achaeans. It was, after all, the greatest disaster in Achaean history and resulted virtually in their extinction. Homer would never have put this excuse into Odysseus's mouth if the attack on Egypt had not been known to have occurred.

The other way in which the *Odyssey* reinforces our account of the assault by the Peoples of the Sea is in its dating. As Odysseus approaches Ithaca on his return home the sun disappears. This clearly indicates a solar eclipse and the dates on which eclipses have occurred and will occur are known and tabulated with great precision. Dr. Schoch of Munich noticed from the tables that a total solar eclipse was visible from Ithaca at 11:41 on April 10, 1178 B.C., and pointed out that this has never occurred again since then and probably had not occurred for thousands of years before that. This confirms that the date of the fall of Troy matches that of the Peoples of the Sea's war against Egypt, as we know it from Egyptian records. And the quarrel of Typhon with Zeus, Hesiod says, covered the whole earth.[16]

These records tell of an invasion by land and sea. At the time of the first attack, in 1219, we learn that the Pharaoh Merneptah took two weeks

PLATE 228
Naval battle. Egyptian ships engage the Peoples of the Sea in the delta: a relief from the temple of Ramesses III at Medinet Habu, Thebes, c. 1182 B.C. Note the crests of the Philistines and the horned helmet of the Sherdan soldiers, lower right hand corner. This was perhaps the biggest single disaster in human history. Depicted here is one episode in what was a world war, fought in two rounds, like the World Wars of this century. It was the attack launched from Atlantis or the Americas described in Plato's Timaeus.[4] *Posidonius cites Plato and says: "It is possible that the story about the island of Atlantis is not a fiction."*[5] *The pictures of the Egyptian victory show it was no fiction. Proclus tells of stones erected in Egypt that gave the history of Atlantis. Marcellus also tells the story.*[6] *It was this attack by Typhon that finally persuaded the Egyptians to convert Set, the god, into Satan, the devil. America has more or less ruled the world at least once before.*

Detail, monument of Ramesses III at Medinet Habu, twelfth century B.C. The horned helmet was associated with divinity. The Cambridge Ancient History, *using other Egyptian sources, carries a narrative of the same Mediterranean fighting, which was, of course, one part of a world war,*[7] *fought in two waves, currently dated at 1219 and 1182 B.C.*

Various tribes of maritime nations attacked Egypt from the sea during the early decades of the twelfth century before Christ. The Egyptians called them by the collective name "Sea Peoples." To judge by the Egyptian sculptors' depictions on the monument of Ramesses III at Medinet Habu, some of the Sea Peoples appear to have been Nordic, as in the detail (left). Ramesses defeated the invaders. In Libya the Tifinag alphabet survives in use to this day, but in Bronze Age times it was peculiar to the Nordic peoples. The facts suggest that Nordic invaders, during the sixteenth century B.C., rebuffed from Egypt, had settled in Libya and introduced the Tifinag alphabet at that time. In the Bronze Age the North Africans were reputed to have fair or red hair and blue eyes; the Atlantians had correctly decided they would be better placed there to cash in on the carrying trade. It was the collapse of the bronze trade that brought about that last war. In a sense, iron proved to be the democratic metal, but it was associated with disaster. It was Ragnarok, meaning "the fatal destiny, the end of the gods,"[8] *brought about by their own behavior. In the early days they spent their time building palaces, working precious metals and playing checkers. Then they became corrupt.*[9] *Many would seem to have died in fratricidal warfare that led to this disaster.*

to mobilize his troops and that contact was made with the invaders on the western frontier of Egypt. After a six-hour battle the enemy was routed. The defeated Libyan prince, Mauroy, fled alone and was deposed from the chieftaincy.[17]

The Egyptian version of the end of the Titans' predominance has also reached us indirectly through Plato's *Timaeus* and *Critias*, which, it will be remembered, purports to pass on a historical tradition as related by an Egyptian priest. In the course of his description (quoted earlier) of how Poseidon ruled Atlantis, Solon remarks: "Such was the vast power which the god settled in the lost island of Atlantis: and this he afterwards directed against our land."[18] Clearly this is the attack on the Mediterranean powers by the Peoples of the Sea, and in the *Timaeus* there is an even more explicit statement: "The men of Atlantis had subjected the parts of Libya within the columns of Herakles as far as Egypt, and of Europe as far as Tyrrhenia. This vast power, gathered into one, endeavoured to subdue at a blow our country and yours and the whole of the region within the straits. . . ."[19]

One reason Plato's history of the attempted coup by the Peoples of the Sea has not been generally accepted is the dating of it. He reports Solon's informant as putting it nine thousand years before his own time. This is clearly absurd, but it becomes perfectly possible if we remember one simple fact: the early Egyptians counted not by solar years but by lunar cycles (each about twenty-nine days) and the word *year* is here being used in that sense. The Egyptian priest also says that the great conflict took place around the same time as the founding of Athens, which is now reckoned to have been in the thirteenth century B.C. If Solon were living in Egypt about 580 B.C., then his nine thousand "years"—clearly a round number—would be something like seven hundred solar years, and that would put the date of the assault on Egypt quite correctly in the thirteenth century. The dates for this world war, fought in two rounds as in this century, are today given as 1219 and 1182 B.C. The Caribs also used the word "year" of lunar cycles.[20]

There is good reason to suppose that this interpretation of the word *year* is correct. The chief adviser on Egypt to Ptolemy II, an Egyptian named Manetho, native of Sebennytus in Lower Egypt, a priest of Heliopolis, wrote a condensation of history in which he three times stated explicitly in his first chapter that the Egyptians used the word for *year* to mean a lunar cycle. This, he says, accounts for the extravagantly long life spans attributed to pharaohs of the past. (No doubt we can assume the same thing about the great age accorded to Methuselah in the Bible: his 969 years shrink to a credible 78.) Plutarch suggests the same correction and so do others, including Diodorus Siculus and Eusebius. Manetho wrote first in Egyptian hieroglyphs and was subsequently translated into Greek.

Once again, therefore, where we are in a position to check Plato's account we find it to be totally, word for word, correct. I see no reason not to accept

PLATE 229
Teenage Philistine soldiers, some seemingly with their arms smashed, very European-looking, recruited either from North Africa or either side of the Atlantic, portrayed on the walls of Medinet Habu, with the characteristic feather or punk hairstyle.

Below them prisoners of the other members of the Mediterranean sea alliance that took such a thrashing from the Egyptian archers.

Fighting among the allies and widespread earthquakes would seem to have compounded this disaster. In the Baltic the fire god Surt, alias Set, versus Odin and Thor.

Marine archaeology is just commencing using electronic metal detectors and cameras designed to be lowered to great depth. Dr. Robert Menzies of Duke University claimed to have located in 1966 on a flat plain six thousand feet down elaborately carved columns with some sort of inscription upon them and lumps on the otherwise flat plain that he believed to conceal a sunken city off Peru. A great sunken stairway has been located off the coast of Puerto Rico, and numerous structures underwater off Andros and Bimini.[10] In recent years divers have found a sunken Mayan temple off the coast of Yucatán.[11] In the Hebrides the land—tradition said—that sank beneath the waves was called Lochlann.[12] In Greek Atlas and Atlan are synonymous. By Hesiod Atlas is placed near the Hesperides and they are beyond Ocean.[13]

Designs on Mycenaean pottery.

The spiral, Maltese cross, concentric arc motifs on Philistine pottery with the visual pun of the double axe or butterfly, common not only to the Mycenaean and Philistine pottery but also across Africa and America. Mycenaeans and Western Semites were conducting this huge commercial operation across the Americas.

Philistine chief with, to my eyes, a very Scottish face. The Libyans who took part in the attack were recorded by the Egyptians to be white-skinned, red-haired and blue-eyed.[14]

that, through Solon, he was in touch with a genuine historical tradition bearing witness to what we have been exploring in this book. There did exist a worldwide system of trade, largely centered on America, stretching far back. It culminated in the huge organizations that we have identified with the Titans, and when it collapsed, after an all-engulfing war, it carried down with it much of the civilization, not just of the Mediterranean, but of the world. The whole of this has a very contemporary ring! We are discussing the previous occasion when America ruled much of the world. Proclus and Marcellus support Plato's narration. After this defeat the Phoenicians moved out of America back into the Mediterranean. The Baltic tradition of the moral collapse of their ruling class that led to this European war is identical with Plato's explanation. But contemporary with the internecine fighting was earthquake, tidal waves and gigantic fires: much as was occurring both in parts of Greece and the Caribbean of that time with a shifting of the tectonic plates. Ireland was partly swamped by tidal waves. Legend hints that, had the god-kings maintained their integrity, their reign of peace would have continued to the present day. Of the coming of iron, Pliny writes: "Our next subject must be the ores of iron, a metal which is at once the best and the worst servant of humanity, for to bring death more speedily to our fellow man."

When the Spaniards had conquered Mexico and Peru they were more than a little surprized to find so many of their Christian practices part of the Amerindian religions. William Prescott, the great U.S. historian of the Spanish invasion, comments: "One is astonished to find so close a resemblance between the institutions of the American Indian, the ancient Roman and the modern Catholic!"[21] From time to time in his narratives Prescott touches on these resemblances. He points out that *papa* was Mexican for high priest, to be compared with our pope; and *mama* was Peruvian for mother,[22] including the Mother Goddess—as in Sumer and with us today as mother. The Inca calendar held as many sacred days and was as complex as the Christian.[23] The Incas lit their sacred fire with concave mirrors, as did the Romans.[24] Their supreme god had had a virgin birth. Prescott continues: "In the distribution of bread and wine in this high festival, the orthodox Spaniards who first came into the country saw a striking resemblance to the Christian communion; as in the practice of confession, absolution and penance. . . ."[25] They had nuns.[26] In Mexico, the altars on the *teocalli*, or ziggurats, were crowned with perpetual flame, as with Roman temples;[27] the Aztecs, like the Greeks, believed in the Four Ages of the world;[28] like the Hebrews they had a belief in the Deluge and a survivor called Coxcox, while the Mechoacans believed in a Noah called Tezpi, only it was a humming bird, not a dove, sent out from the boat that returned with the twig; the Mexican temple of Cholula was raised by the giants who escaped the Flood, planning to raise the temple to the clouds, but the gods sent fire from heaven to stop them—as in Babylon with the Tower of Babel.

The great Mexican goddess Ciacóatl was known as "our lady and mother"; it was by her "that sin came into the world"; she was associated with a serpent and indeed her name means "serpent goddess." The Mexican god Quetzalcóatl presided over monastic institutions. Pre-Columbian Aztecs believed in the Trinity and the Incarnation, practiced the rites of confession and penance.[29] The cross was a sacred emblem to them and was an object of worship in the temples of Mexico,[30] while Prescott goes on to say of the conquistadors: "Their surprise was heightened when they witnessed a religious rite which reminded them of the Christian communion. On these occasions an image of the tutelary deity of the Aztecs was made of the flour of maize mixed with blood and, after consecration by the priests, was distributed among the people, who, as they ate it, 'showed signs of humiliation and sorrow, declaring it was the flesh of the deity!' How could the Roman Catholic fail to recognise the awful ceremony of the Eucharist?"[31] The Mexicans held to the doctrine of original sin and baptism: like the Hebrews, they believed you could commit adultery with your eyes.[32] And secular education was in the hands of the priests.[33] Quetzalcóatl wore a mitre, symbol of the kings of Upper Egypt and of Set, the onetime god of Upper Egypt, the mitre now worn by Christian bishops, who share most of the above practices. These pre-Columbian Amerindian practices were observed for the Sun god.

William Prescott explains all these parallels away as arising from a chance visit by a Christian, and we have explained already that fundamental cultural changes across two continents cannot be wrought by chance visits but require colonization. Alternatively, Prescott explains it by "the general constitution of man, and the necessities of his moral nature." This, of course, is seen to be ridiculous when we look at societies that were too remote to have had much contact with our earlier trading world: the Aborigines of Australia and Tasmania; the San peoples of southern Africa; the Inuit of the far north. Instead, we found in West Africa that former colonies are marvelously conservative, so that the practices of such people as the Yoruba, the Senufo and the Akan are entirely consistent with their own traditions of origin, and are deeply informative about their former colonial masters. For across America as across West Africa runs the widespread tradition of white women or of white men arriving from the sea—or across the Sahara—bringing the arts of civilization with them to their various associated peoples, who themselves soon came to play an important part in that commercial world of long ago. But we must be totally clear: these practices were all associated in the early Americas with sun worship, not with an early version of Christianity. Quite simply, colonies can give us the best evidence for the mother country. Only Thunapu in Peru seems to represent the early Christian contacts provided by St. Brendan et al.

Eusebius of Caesarea, c. A.D. 265–340, as we have seen, wrote that

Christianity went back to before the time of Moses and that nothing in Christianity was new except the church.[34] For Christianity was trinitarian sun worship purged of its cruel human sacrifice and of the symbolic sun disk itself, hence their sacred day is Sunday, not Christday. The study of Christianity's antecedents in Egypt with the Osiris and Set people, their emigration to the colonies when their position in Egypt became untenable, is essential if Christianity is to be understood today. Hence perhaps the line in the Gospel of St. Matthew: "Out of Egypt have I called my son."[35] And the understanding that Jesus was simply one in a long line of self-sacrificers of the sun religion is suggested when "Caiaphas, who was high priest that year, said to them: You know nothing at all; so you do not understand that it is expedient for you that one man should die for the people, and that the whole nation should not perish."[36] Thus Christianity goes back, the New Testament goes back to the Palestinians, the Philistines, Typhon, the Peoples of the Sea, the Toltecs, the Hyksos, Peru's Vira Cocha, the god Set or Atlas. And the earlier United States of America must have had a fundamental say in Christianity's earlier development. The young man, the noblest and the best, sacrificed each year, was dressed royally because he was in fact a substitute for the king. That is perhaps why Christ was called "King of the Jews" at a time when the Jews did not have kings.

Perhaps it was in order to present the ahistorical, Immaculate Conception of Christianity that the Christians, in the person of Bishop Theophilus, burned down the library of Alexandria in A.D. 389, one of the greatest acts of vandalism in world history.

Chronos and Atlas are said by Philo of Byblos to be brothers: they traded alongside each other across much of the world. Chronos sacrificed his only-begotten son, Iedud. Chronos is associated with or identified with the Jewish El, who sacrificed his only-begotten son, Iesus. In both narratives the Greek for only-begotten is the same word. Chronos and Atlas were held to be the noblest sons of Ouranos.

Hesiod described the dark age that followed the world war thus:

Father will have no common bond with son
Neither will guest with host, nor friend with friend
The brother-love of past days will be gone. . . .
Men will destroy the towns of other men.
The just, the good, the man who keeps his word
Will be despised, but men will praise the bad
And insolent. Might will be right and shame
Will cease to be. Men will do injury
To better men by speaking crooked words
And adding lying oathes, and everywhere
Harsh-voiced and sullen-faced and loving harm,
Envy will walk along with wretched men.

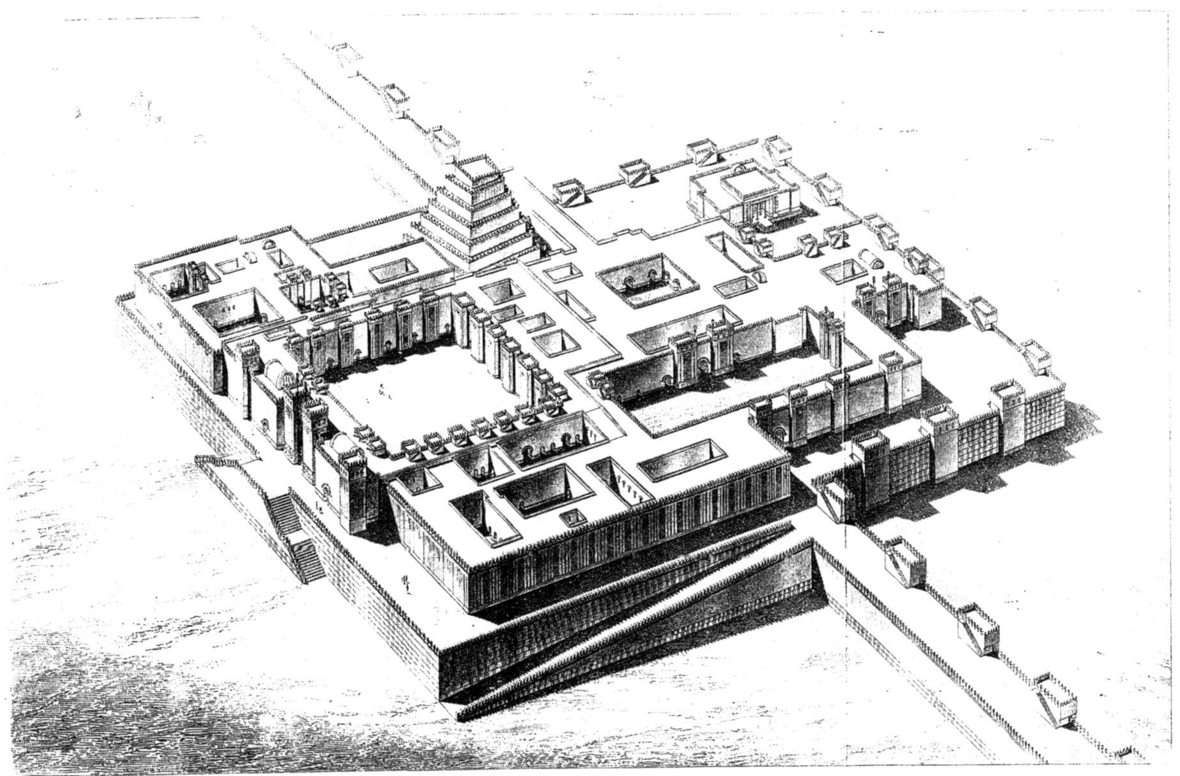

PLATE 230

Reconstruction of the Assyrian palace near Nineveh with the standard ziggurat within the palace grounds. The principal ceremony in the chapel on the top of the ziggurat, we are told, was the symbolic marriage of the earth mother, the virgin, to the sky father. Kind of suggestive! Erishuru, King of Assyria, 1941–1902 B.C., *made Assyria a home for capitalism.*[15] *And the sea peoples had the carrying trade with the same sort of relationship, seemingly, to Assyria as Hong Kong bears to mainland China. Chronos, the Phoenician god, is described as living in "the Isles of the Blest" and living in "the Underworld";*[16] *these are of course the same place—and Chronos being much the same as El we can quote Ezekiel 24:2: "I am El, I sit in the seat of the gods, in the heart of the seas." All this is consistent with the clear and unmistakable Phoenician imprint in Central America, with Phoenician rock inscriptions carved on the rocks of both South and North America, and the tradition of America as being "the Paradise Land." Central American numerology and astronomy were much more similar to those of Mesopotamia than Greece.*[17] *The Mayan calendrical system, however, was similar to that of Egypt and excellent.*[18] *Almost universally, even from very early dates, America was looked upon as "God's own country." For the Syrian goddess Atagartis children were put in sacks and then thrown from the top of the sanctuary; much the same practice went on throughout the Semitic world.*[19] *The city walls of later Nineveh were seven and a half miles in circumference. The Middle Eastern nature of Chronos is shown in our measurements of time, which are functions of six, while so much of European mensuration is in decimals. Assyria fell late seventh century* B.C., *Babylon late sixth century.*[20] *Until then, the famous textiles of Babylonia were an important medium of exchange. The proximity of palace and temple in Assyria, as in Babylon, as in Britain's Westminster, as in Nigeria with the Oba's palace and the chief ju-ju man's shrine, is to make society governable. Expediency.*

This verse describes with prophetic accuracy our contemporary period after the First World War.

Over our period for which there is little or no written record, we have had to depend upon the findings of archaeology; oral tradition that was subsequently recorded; a language grid that holds the history of its peoples like a fly in amber; place names; rock engravings; common scripts and symbols; common architecture; biological evidence; common religions. And the aid in linking all this together is the economic understanding of a period, as to what the critical minerals or materials were, strategic metals, or the equivalent of today's oil trade perhaps.

Once you have lived with, witnessed the profound influence of a colonial period upon the colonized and the conservative nature of the ex-colonies; once you have realized the way histories are written, and continuously rewritten to lie for the benefit of each ruling group, then you can understand the light that former colonies can throw upon the practices and history of the mother country, even though the colonial traditions may have also been cooked to some extent.

In brief, therefore, we have found the name *akawa* associated with the early seafaring matriarchal societies, noticing it in cow, copper, the llama in Quechua called *waka*, the Tibetan yak, coven of witches, the Latin word for water *aqua*, the *kwa* indigenous names for the rivers all down West Africa, Siskiwit Bay and Keweenaw Peninsula with Lake Superior, and so on.

When we find copper is named *anti* in the Aymará language of Bolivia and the Quechua of Peru, we seem to understand the name Anticosti for the island at the mouth of the St. Lawrence, the name Ontario, the name Antilles, the name Andes for the copper mountains and, above all, the Atlantic as Atlas's copper sea.

Then we find gold is called *qori* in Peru and Bolivia and we compare this with the Mycenaean word for gold, *kuruso*.

Then we find *anaku* is the Babylonian-Akkadian name for tin-bronze, a name associated with nearly every alluvial tin deposit or center for the early bronze trade in the world, Canaan included: the Old Testament Tubul-cain meaning smith: not to mention Nigeria's Kano and Nok; Cornwall; Carnac; Coneto; Petseconi; Bangka; Kandy; Cantabrian Mountains; Nok-wane; Wankie; Canary Islands; Non Nok Tha; Sri Lanka and so on: then it all begins to fall into place—perhaps also vicuna and canoe, and Kanak, Larnaca, Knossos, Kanesh, Proconesos and so on, not to mention König, meaning King, and Kahn, meaning conqueror, as in Gerghis Khan.

An indication of the to-ing and fro-ing that went on across the oceans is that the god Hermes was looked upon, not only as herald of Zeus but also of the gods of the lower world or the Americas. He was identified with the Roman god Mercury and the Egyptian Thoth, who brought the arts, including writing, and science, to ancient Egypt. Hermes was also god of unexpected wealth.

The Anunnaki were known to Babylon but were best known as the seven fearsome rulers of the Americas or the lower world. Their name suggests the first great sky god, Anu, exploiting the metals trade.

The name Tartar covered all the tribes of Central Asia. So when the Greeks and Romans called their underworld Tartarus they knew perfectly well that the inhabitants of America were also Mongols. When classical writers recorded that the foundations of Tartarus were of bronze, they were alive to the enormous importance of the former bronze trade of the Americas. It's all so obvious when the evidence is put together as a coherent whole.

27. The End of Atlantis

"Euripides used to say truly that the mountain range of Atlantis rose above the clouds."

EUSEBIUS, *Chronicorum*

"But afterwards there occurred violent earthquakes and floods; and in a single day and night of misfortune . . . the island of Atlantis . . . disappeared in the depths of the sea. For which reason, the sea in those parts is impassable and impenetrable, because there is a shoal of mud in the way; and this was caused by the subsidence of the island."

PLATO, *Timaeus*

That is Plato's account of the end of Atlantis, and it is perhaps the thing most people remember of the legend. It is, after all, a wonderfully romantic story, this huge island with its cities, its farms, its temples and palaces, and all its multitude of people, suddenly within a few hours swallowed up by the water, to disappear forever in the depths of the ocean.

It is unquestionably a memorable legend, but did it happen? In the most literal sense the answer has to be no, but there is nevertheless much truth in it. Under shallow water near the West Indian islands of Andros and Bimini, and five miles deep near Puerto Rico, marine archaeologists have discovered walls and buildings, a pyramid, a circle of pillars and a great stone causeway. The submerged walls off Bimini are built of huge cyclopean stones, like those put up in Mediterranean countries in the Bronze Age, and Bimini is strategically placed to dominate the shipping moving out of the Gulf of Mexico on the main current that then flows eastward across the Atlantic. Here is clear evidence of a New World country linked by trade to the Old World that did sink beneath the waves, whether by slow geological movement or suddenly after an earthquake. And it is worth remembering that Amerindian chiefs on the Caribbean islands described to the conquistadors their islands, more or less correctly, as the entrance to the underworld. Cortés himself initially set up his headquarters on a Caribbean island prior to his advance into Mexico. It would be strategically the best thing for sea people to do.

To this extent the story of the end of Atlantis can be taken literally, but in a larger sense the truth behind it was guessed long ago by Sir Francis Bacon. He surmised that sailors had lost the maritime skills needed to sail to America and, rather than admit it, they said that America was no longer there to find. The disappearance of certain West Indian islands could have provided the starting point for this self-excusing legend.

The reason the skills were lost was that the practice of worldwide navigation gradually petered out. After the last great battle that broke their power, the Titans could perhaps have recovered if conditions had been as favorable as they had been in earlier times and if copper and tin had still commanded high enough prices to pay for the expenses and risks of the journeys. But now the good old times were over forever. The Phoenicians, as we saw, continued the seagoing tradition for a while, moving their bases until they were centered in what was the new city: the city of Carthage; but as Europe slowly recovered from the awful destruction of the twelfth century B.C., "the terrible coming of iron," the Phoenicians found themselves under growing pressure from a land power, and at last Carthage was wiped out by the armies of that greatest of Mediterranean land powers, Rome.

Contact with America was never entirely lost. The Romans, the Jews, the Vikings, the Welsh, the Irish and the Breton fishermen found their way across the Atlantic, while in the Pacific there were voyages and migrations between the mainland and the Americas. But none of this was on the former scale except perhaps for the Vikings from the tideless sea of the Baltic; on the Atlantic side it never amounted to the systematic exploitation of regular trade routes that had been practiced by the Titans and the other sea peoples whose fortunes we have been studying.

The loss to mankind was inestimable. In the Mediterranean world a dark age followed. The high cultures of Mycenae, Crete and elsewhere lay in ruins, and everywhere the civilized empires found their frontiers threatened by barbarians who now had access to the essential substances on which military technology was based, no longer bronze but steel. No wonder people saw the world in pessimistic terms as a steady decline from the Age of Gold, through the Ages of Silver and Bronze to the terrible Age of Iron. This was not just a poetic fancy of writers like Hesiod. The Bronze Age was in truth more violent than the Age of Gold—or perhaps we should say the Age of Copper, the poor man's gold. The Iron Age destroyed the inherited capital of the Bronze Age empires, broke up their elaborate social and intellectual structures, and led to the isolation of what had once been wealthy and leisured colonies in America. This earlier attempt to rule the world from America had ended in total disaster. Perhaps the gentle and kindly Arawaks, whom Columbus encountered, were products—as their *akawa* name suggests—of the early Age of Gold, while Christian and Carib were products of the Age of Iron, the Terrible Coming of Iron, hideous as that was. Professor Whitehead emphasized that "major advances in civilizations are processes that all but wreck the societies in which they occur." We should not forget this.

One inevitable effect of all this destruction was that the records and even the memory of previous ages were obliterated. The loss of knowledge at the end of the Bronze Age was as great as that at the fall of the Roman Empire; indeed it was probably greater, for unlike the twelfth century B.C. Greeks, the Europeans did not lose the art of writing when Rome fell. It is a strange thought, but today, through the findings of archaeology, we know more about the early Mediterranean peoples than the Greeks of Plato's time ever did. After many centuries in which history had to rely on the chance survival of written records, archaeology allows us direct contact with the peoples of the past, if we know how to interpret our findings. Even so, we are still limited. We can only study what happens to have endured and what we have found, and when it comes to marine archaeology that is a severe constraint. Whatever lies sunken in the deep oceans is for the most part lost to us: there can be no systematic exploration of millions of square miles of seabed lying under thousands of feet of water. Perhaps, preserved under deep layers of sediment, there still exist the remains of vessels loaded with tin from the mines of South America or with copper nuggets from Lake Superior. If so, the chances are that they will keep their secrets for quite a long time yet.

The lack of archaeological evidence about the sea peoples is all the more serious in that the land peoples on whose behalf they traded did not record their adventures. At the head of the Persian Gulf and up the Indus River the excavated cities can be seen to have possessed docks and canals: they must have swarmed with sailors. But the scribes who wrote the records of those cities were landsmen and they did not concern themselves with things that had happened, perhaps thousands of miles away, to people who were in any case members of another culture, the culture of the ocean voyagers. In Sumer it is said that life centered around the quays: today it is airports.

So, as the mud of the sea floor sifted slowly down over the wrecks of the traders' ships, time buried the memory of their journeys. As so often in history, time was aided by the malice and jealousy of mankind, for it happens in every age that those who have newly come to power resent the achievements of their predecessors and do their best to obliterate the memory of them. We have seen it in our own century, in Soviet Russia, in the book burnings of Nazi Germany, during the Cultural Revolution in China, in Cambodia under Pol Pot—the dreary list could be prolonged to cover most parts of the world. For the early religion of ancestor worship has today been replaced by ancestor contempt. Each new ruling group "rearranges the truth": so it has been correctly said that history is a narrative of what did not happen written by someone who was not there. However, today's political ethnicity shows that after fifty thousand years little has changed!

The Christian church has, for much of its history, been guilty of this kind of vandalism; in Europe, in Africa and in America it was the practice of Christian conquerors to cleanse the world of the "pagan" relics and records of the conquered. As late as the last century Catholic priests in West Africa set about destroying what was perhaps the richest of all African arts in the Ivory Coast, and in the same way the Spaniards in America annihilated almost all the slender store of written records that the North American Indians possessed (with few exceptions the Indians of South America could not write). One of those who took part in this barbarous destruction of manuscripts, calling them the work of the devil, was Diego de Landa, the second bishop of Yucatán. Later in life he saw his error and, with the help of Indian friends, tried to reconstruct the script the Maya has used.[1] But Bishop Landa would only accept anthropological evidence from Indians under torture!

It is only fair to add that the Incas had systematically destroyed in their subjects all recollection of their former cultures, and that the Aztecs and the earlier god-kings had done just the same. By their arrogant assertion that their coming represented the Creation of the World, they consigned all previous civilizations to the realm of nonexistence, as surely as a Stalinist censor removing a nonperson from the *Soviet Encyclopedia*. In this book we have looked at four ages of history, the earth-worshipping matriarchal societies, the worshippers of the sky god in the form of the stars, the sun-worshipping society of the god-kings, which was the age of the Titans, and the last age of Zeus, or Yahve. It is sadly probable that as the dominant class of each age came to power one of its first endeavors was to wipe out any memory of its predecessors.

The greatest single act of intellectual vandalism was perhaps the burning of the library at Alexandria. This marvelous place contained seven hundred thousand rolls of papyrus, collected by Greek scholars from the huge empire conquered by Alexander, an empire that stretched from India to Carthage. It is impossible to say what light its contents might have shed on the activities of the early sea traders. Did they include records that would have confirmed and amplified the history of Atlantis related to Solon by the Egyptian priest? Part of the library was burned first by Julius Caesar. Rather more than three centuries later the Christians destroyed a reconstructed library at Alexandria, much of it stolen from Pergamum, and a last attempt to keep it in being was defeated when an Arab army under

Amru Ben al Aas was ordered by the caliph to burn all the remaining books. For six months they served to heat the public baths of Alexandria.

Only a few years ago *The New York Times*[2] reported a shameful modern instance of this willful cultivation of ignorance. In 1982 Robert Marx, a diver from Florida, and Dr. Harold E. Edgerton, a professor emeritus at the Massachusetts Institute of Technology, tried to explore an underwater site off the coast of Brazil where Roman amphoras from the second century B.C. had been found. If they could establish that these amphoras were contained within the wreck of a Roman ship it would obviously have made nonsense of the claim that Brazil was first reached by Europeans when Pedro Alvares Cabral, a Portuguese navigator, landed there in A.D. 1500. Using special sonar, Marx and Edgerton searched for the wreck and claimed "we definitely found it." In a hundred hours of diving, Marx said, he found at least two hundred broken amphoras in the mud and "wooden remains underneath where we found all the amphoras." He was not able at that time to do any excavating to bring evidence to the surface but he received permission to do so later. This, however, seems to have created political problems, with some Brazilian newspapers claiming that their own culture hero, Cabral, was being defamed. Three months later, Marx reported, the Brazilian navy not only canceled his permit but sent out a dredger to cover the entire site in mud. It depicts the scholarly dishonesty found almost everywhere that governments influence. The Roman galley off Brazil is consistent with many other Roman remains in the Americas.

It is not only governments that have a vested interest in preserving conventional views of the past. It is a matter of deep regret that many academics, some of them genuinely fine scholars, are prepared to use unworthy methods to suppress opinions that challenge their beliefs in any radical way. Instead of answering the agruments they ridicule those who put them forward and try to create an atmosphere in which it will be impossible for them to be taken seriously. Glyn Daniel stooped to this, as we have seen, when he denounced anyone who believed in Atlantic crossings before Columbus as belonging to the "lunatic fringe of archaeology." Professors are the civil servants of the intellect.

By behaving in this way, historians and archaeologists throw doubt on their own beliefs, for it is generally true that the more scholars are certain of their position, the more politely they argue: they turn to insult when they are unsure of themselves, their cause and their careers. This is understandable enough. An academic can derive no pleasure from admitting that much of what he has spent his life teaching is based on a fallacy. Unfortunately, this kind of approach tends to perpetuate rigidity beyond a single generation of researchers. What young newcomer to the field, with a career to make, wants to earn a reputation for belonging to a lunatic fringe? He would be crossing an intellectual trade-union picket line.

Aside from this kind of academic conservatism there are certain more general biases that are hard to overcome. To anyone living in the modern world it seems common sense that land travel is easier than sea travel, and this is perhaps particularly true of people whose way of life keeps them at a desk. Too many of them show a marked lack of enthusiasm when someone like Thor Heyerdahl ventures out of the study and onto the real ocean. History must be one of the few disciplines with any pretensions to practical method in which there are mutters of "showmanship" when someone puts a received belief to an empirical test.

Then there is the bias, by no means confined to archaeologists, that makes one believe in the superiority of one's own kind. Researchers are working within the modern European tradition, and it is hard for them not to feel that all the really good things in history have been done by people in their tradition. It took a long time for us to get used to the idea that what we call Euclid's geometry[3] was not developed by the recognizably European people whose clean-cut images were carved around the Parthenon, but imported by them from the real originators, whoever they were, men of the Bronze Age. "The Afroasiatic roots of European civilisation"[4] are only slowly being acknowledged, and it will take even longer before it is generally recognized that there may also have been early American inventions. We attribute the invention of bronze to the Sumerians, but it might equally well have been the people living around the tin and copper deposits in the Andes who first tried the momentous experiment of mixing the twin metals. Which way was the knowledge of that technique carried across the Atlantic, westward or eastward? The honest answer must be that we do not know. But certainly in plant breeding we can be confident that America was the superior. Seeds, at least as much as metals, provided the foundation of civilization.

It is worth examining our own feelings about the latter-day conquest of America by the Europeans. Intuitively, most of us see this as an encounter between an advanced, civilized invader and barbarian natives, yet it is not easy to justify this view. By many criteria the highest of the Amerindian cultures were at least as advanced as the contemporary culture of Spain. If those avaricious brutes, the conquistadors, were really more civilized than the Indians they slaughtered it can only be because the test of civilization is the possession of advanced military technology. And if that is so, then the most civilized people in the Europe of 1940 were the Nazis. Every Amerindian city was destroyed in the conquest.

One of the Spanish conquerors of Cuzco, Mancio Serra de Leguicamo, set out his own confession in his will. In a passage addressed to the king, Philip II, he informed him that:

> We found these lands in such a state that there was not even a robber or a vicious or idle man, or adulterous or immoral woman: all such conduct was forbidden. Immoral persons could not exist and everyone had honest and

> profitable occupations. . . . Everything from the most important to the least was ordered and harmonised with great wisdom. The Incas were feared, obeyed, respected, and venerated by their subjects, who considered them to be most capable lords. . . . We were only a small number of Spaniards when we undertook the conquest and I desire his majesty to understand why I have set down this account; it is to unburden my conscience and confess my guilt, for we have transformed the Indians who had such wisdom and committed so few crimes, excesses, or extravagances that the owner of 100,000 pesos of gold or silver would leave his door open placing a broom fixed to a bit of wood across the entrance to show that he was absent: this sign was enough to prevent anyone from entering or taking anything. Thus they scorned us when they saw among us thieves and men who incited their wives and daughters to sin. . . . This kingdom has fallen into such disorder . . . it has passed from one extreme to the other. There was no evil: now there is almost no good.
>
> Christopher Columbus has high praise for the gentleness of the Arawaks and also says that some were as white as Spaniards.

Garcilaso de la Vega was naturally concerned to uphold the reputation of the Incas, but he was generally a reliable reporter and we need not be too skeptical about his assertion that the Incas brought good order, gentleness and technical skills to the savage people in surrounding territories. This was so, de la Vaga tells us, right from the start:

> The first Inca Manco Capac has expressly ordered all the kings who descended from him never to permit bloodshed in any conquest they might make unless it was absolutely necessary and always to attract the Indians with benefits and blandishments, so that they should be loved by the subjects they had conquered with love, and not perpetually hated by those reduced by force of arms.[5]

This is remarkably similar to the behavior attributed to Osiris, and like him the first Inca began by prohibiting cannibalism and human sacrifice. In short, what the Spaniards found in Peru was a living continuation of the great tradition of the early god-kings, with its technical skills in irrigation and agriculture, its orderly bureaucracy, its paternalism and its high ethical standards. With whatever breaks and setbacks, that tradition had lasted six thousand years, since the early days when it first began to flower and gave to mankind the haunting memory of the Golden Age. Later Incas, however, alas, sank deep into human sacrifice.

Fray Bernardino de Sahagún wrote of Mexico: "The Toltecs were the first ones settled here in the land; who were like the inhabitants of Babylon, wise, learned, experienced."[6] Of course, the forebears of some of them had in truth been inhabitants of Babylon—simple as that.

To most people today the idea of a steady decline from the Age of Gold to the Age of Iron is quite alien. We have been brought up to believe in the opposite myth, that of steady and inevitable progress from the squalor and brutality of primitive life to the enlightenment and comfort of the modern academic world. Yet in reality the old myth was no more absurd than the new. The fact that we see ourselves as living at a peak of technical achievement in no way guarantees that the advance will continue, and certainly it is untrue that progress in the past has been either steady or inevitable. Aristotle was closer to the truth with his belief in cycles of knowledge and ignorance in which skills are learned and lost and must be laboriously relearned time and again. The ancient belief was expressed by some of the Greeks, that the world would end in fire, *ecpyrosis*. With the international arms trade as it is today, this is not wide of the mark. The Maya of Guatemala expected the world to end on December 24, A.D. 2011:[7] and with the obscenity of our contemporary arms trade—armaments being the hard drugs of nations—this date may be about correct. No phrase can adequately express the vileness of the arms trade.

This is perhaps the worst of the biases that distort the findings of historians and archaeologists. They cannot bring themselves to believe that people in earlier times possessed any important knowledge of which we are presently ignorant. It seems to them self-evidently ridiculous to suppose that those who lived thousands of years before Aristotle knew more about geography than he did, possessed navigational skills far beyond those of his contemporaries, understood more about some branches of astronomy and the calculation of time, and had measured the earth with an accuracy far surpassing anything achieved before the scientific revolution of the seventeenth century A.D.

If we can rid ourselves of the bias we can see that in many ways—not in all ways, but in many ways—the eighteenth century B.C. could stand comparison with its counterpart A.D. In one form or another the Bronze Age saw the use of underfloor heating, flush lavatories, checks, antibiotics, five-story houses, advanced dentistry, an atomic theory, a postal service and an encyclopedia. It is said that Assyrian metallurgy—and the pharmacopoeia of the Sumerians around 2000 B.C.—were not bettered in Europe until the eighteenth or nineteenth century A.D. One of Thomas Edison's patent applications was refused because something similar had been in use in ancient Egypt in 2000 B.C., and the first Suez Canal was cut around 1230 B.C. To complete our comparison we should perhaps add that in the eighteenth century A.D. the official religion of Europe was a development of the sun worship that was being practiced throughout much of the world three thousand years before the birth of the sun god's latest son in Bethlehem.

Perhaps we find such facts uncomfortable. At any rate they are not widely known, and we too easily call our own ignorance of Bronze Age people their ignorance of the world. We even feel that early men and women must have been less intelligent than we are, though there is not the slightest

Plate 231

The Viking territory (opposite) during four centuries of trade, settlement and piracy extended from the Volga River and the Caspian Sea in Asia, through the Mediterranean and Western Europe to the British Isles, Iceland and North America. The areas in the Old World where the Vikings established permanent colonies are indicated in gray, areas of passing conquest or other brief residence have been omitted. The Norsemen, colonizing America for 350 years, would necessarily be compatriots and sometimes even relations of the Norsemen ruling their European empire; so with all the comings and goings between Vinland, Greenland, Iceland and Scandinavia to within 140 years of Columbus's first voyage, there is no way the existence of North America would not have been widely known, at least across this large area, but obviously very much further afield than that. It should be noted that when the Norsemen first arrived in Greenland they reported finding there "human habitations, both in the eastern and western parts of the country, and fragments of skin boats and stone implements."[1] The Arctic mirage makes Greenland visible from Iceland.[2] When the Vikings first reached Iceland they found Irish monks there seeking solitude. Scandinavian runes have been found carved on the rocks of North America. Rune means "secret wisdom." The English have a phrase for dying, in emulation of the dying sun, "going west." The Ashanti, on the Ashanti gold fields, use "going to Alata," which, with boustrophedon writing, can be rendered as going to Atlas's country, or Atlantis.

evidence that human intelligence has improved since Paleolithic times. In fact, one may need more intelligence, not less, to work with "primitive" techniques. An Australian Aborigine who had never before left the bush and who went for the first time into a supermarket would no doubt be quite at a loss, and the other shoppers might well think him stupid. Yet he could survive on his home ground, in conditions that would kill a sophisticated white man in a few days, by using skills that are infinitely more subtle and demanding than those needed to learn the simple routine of supermarket shopping.

We must recognize that a sailor in a reed boat is not to be written off as a crude savage and a poor navigator. The reed boat is a very intelligent way of using available materials and the navigational techniques of its steersman might well be far beyond the grasp of a modern seaman helplessly dependent on a radar screen and a set of Admiralty charts. We must take our eyes off the roughness of the masonry at Stonehenge and look instead at the refinement of its mathematics. We should probably be very surprised if we could listen in on a conversation between its builders. I suspect that there were wittier men in Bronze Age Britain then than there were when Caesar landed, or in many of the Iron Age centuries that followed.

Wit, like art and science, probably flourishes most where different cultures cross-fertilize each other, as they did when the early sailors passed from continent to continent, carrying with them ideas and techniques as well as goods. We can measure their influence to some extent by looking at the countries they did not visit, those that were hidden away in the interiors of the great land masses and not linked to the sea by navigable rivers. Those places remained backward and uncivilized, as Central Africa did compared with West Africa, as the remoter Indian tribes of Latin

ATLANTIC OCEAN
NORTH SEA
BALTIC SEA
BLACK SEA
MEDITERRANEAN SEA

America did compared with those on or linked to the Atlantic and Pacific shores, as Mongolia did compared with the many civilizations ringing the coast of Eurasia from Western Europe and the Mediterranean to India and China. Furthermore, the backwardness of the continental interiors continued long after the seagoing age came to an end, and it was still clearly evident when the Europeans began to explore and colonize those places in the nineteenth century. Look at the Pacific today, where maritime Japan, Hong Kong, Taiwan, Singapore are incomparably richer than their fellow countrymen on mainland China: and the coastal areas of mainland China in advance of interior China.

In the same way the positive influences of the old trading cultures also persisted. Inevitably they faded as the centuries went by, but in America, and to a lesser extent in Africa and elsewhere, enough remained to show the true source of the civilizations the Europeans encountered and destroyed. If only the conquerors had known more about the origins of the Incas, the Maya and the others, perhaps they might have been less enthusiastic in eradicating their civilizations. After all, it was their own very distant ancestors that had helped initiate the civilizations that they were destroying. It has been stated that there was formerly "in Mexico an intellectual élite comparable to the scholars of Mesopotamia and classical Greece."[8]

If they had understood that the cross did not belong to Christians only but was a symbol shared by all those whose religions grew out of the old worship of the stars and the sky god, and that Montezuma was as much the inheritor of that tradition as the priests in the Spanish caravels; if, above all, the Europeans had been able to acknowledge what all this implied about the origin of their own culture, perhaps it would have mitigated their destructiveness. At least it would have removed a large part of the justification for it and still more for the continuing assault by European administrators and missionaries on native traditions they thought barbarous and ungodly, because they were themselves ignorant of the shared past. Nothing supports intolerance so much as this kind of ignorance. The Christians in America practiced genocide as if they were Communists or Nazis.

History at its best brings us a kind of self-knowledge. That is why it seems to me so important that we should pursue the study of the age of world travel that began so many centuries before our conventional histories begin, went on for so long, and had such a profound influence on everything that followed. Because this great episode of human achievement has gone unrecorded we have been cut off from our own beginnings. When we dig down deep into the past to uncover the traces of the early voyagers and their world, what we find is more than a part of history. It is a part of ourselves. As Thor Heyerdahl points out, history must be studied not just in small sections of time and space—as the universities require—but also as a whole. The history of the world over the last ten thousand years needs

PLATE 232
MESOPOTAMIAN ARCHITECTURE. *Reconstruction of a temple at Eridu, Mesopotamia (top), fourth millennium* B.C. *It is not unlike the headquarters building of a present-day industrial corporation. Religion in modern Europe tends to be a thing somewhat apart that takes place on the Sabbath in churches. In earlier societies the religious and the secular were so continuously interwoven as to be one. By the middle of the fourth millennium* B.C., *the Middle East was making wine and beer and used clepsydras or water clocks, had ivory gaming pieces for their version of chess or checkers, and had given birth to the dream of the Golden Age.*

The ziggurat of Ur (bottom), as it appeared at the time of Abraham (after Woolley). It is about seventy feet high and can be climbed by three converging staircases. The ziggurat was a very specific type of ecclesiastical architecture proliferating in Mesopotamia at the start of the third millennium, seemingly designed for the reconciliation of heaven worship and earth worship. Sumerian influence stretched for thousands of miles in all directions. The top of the ziggurat also supplied a place of refuge in time of flood. The theology of the Mesopotamian cults became the deification of time, exemplified by the sun and moon, whose course so often determines events.[3] Half a million people lived in each of the Sumerian cities of Ur, Lagash, Nippur, Kish, Eridu.[4]

to be considered as a whole, which is the truth of the matter. History should not only be studied in snippets: there has been a planetary coherence in previous millennia and we require to be able to benefit by that experience.

The story of the earlier United States of America in Plato's *Critias* is word for word true except that the translators failed to notice that Egypt, like so many other countries of that time, possessed a lunar calendar not a solar calendar.[9] Had Plato been given the chance to complete the *Critias*, how much we would have benefited! Babylon had a lunar calendar as did early Rome. The Arabs still use one. The Caribs used one.

But scholars have failed to notice that Plato's story of the attack by Atlantis on Egypt is also described in a wholly independent Egyptian record carried by the *Cambridge Ancient History*.[10] They are two independent narratives of the same earth-shaking event: the most important episode in that original world war. The first attack was against the pharaoh Merneptah in 1219 B.C., when the alliance of sea peoples, joined to their relatives the Libyans, were beaten in a six-hour battle in which they suffered heavy losses. The second attack came in 1182 B.C. The alliance of the Thekel, Denyen (possibly Danai), Sherden or Sardinians who fought on both sides, Meshwesh and Shekelesh sea peoples, was cut to pieces by the Egyptian archers and infantry. The *Cambridge Ancient History* quotes the contemporary Egyptian account: "They came with fire, prepared before them, forward to Egypt . . . these were united and they laid their hands upon the land as far as the circle of the earth. . . . The countries, which came from their isles in the midst of the sea, they advanced to Egypt, their hearts relying upon their arms."[11] Fire was the symbol of the sun god and of world domination.

The mistake has been not to appreciate that "the isles in the midst of the sea" were "the isles in the midst of the ocean," or the Americas; that fire went before them because fire was sacred to the Set or Atlas people, that the survivors, known as Philistines, were sent by the Egyptians into Palestine—after whom the country is named—as garrison troops to protect Egypt's Asian frontier. The Philistines used Mycenaean-type pottery because many of them were Mycenaeans, and they also used a script closely similar to Linear A. For the Greek fleet, after destroying Troy and the Troad, had remustered in Crete before attacking Egypt with disastrous effect. The taking of Troy was one small episode in that world war. Toward the end of the *Odyssey*, Odysseus pretends that he and his men joined this ill-fated attack, as we have already seen.

Plato describes how the Atlas kings, the kings of Atlantis, controlled the islands that led up to the Mediterranean, how they controlled the whole of North Africa up to Egypt and the whole of the west Mediterranean up to the Tyrrhenian Sea on their eastern flank, and how they controlled bases across the Pacific on their western flank.

By about 1400 B.C. watchtowers called *talyots* were being constructed in the Balearic Islands, similarly on the island of Sardinia, where they are called Nuraghi, and *talyots* were also built as stone watchtowers in Tunisia. These are Atlas names, with the exception of Sardinia. Watchtowers were also built in the Orkneys, the Shetlands and the northwest tip of Scotland where they are called brochs. They were also built in America and examples can be seen at Horenurep, Utah (Plate 235).[12] The highest mountain peak in Minorca was called Atalayas, again an *atl* name. And of course we have Melitta for Malta, Valetta for its principal harbor, not to mention Atalia and Latin. The strategic power structure for the earlier United States of America was much the same as for the present one: only across the Pacific Atlantis did not depend so much on bases in the Philippines as in

Shang China. Napoleon said that every country has the politics of its geography. The same military structure in the earlier United States as in the contemporary is not therefore without interest. In the Balearics the graves of their notables were shaped like upturned boats and are called *navetas*. At much the same time they were building boat-shaped graves in Sweden[13] and America. And when the Peleset, the Philistines, the Anakim were defeated in the Mediterranean, they were also defeated in the Baltic in the war known as Ragnarok. At the same time the Shang Dynasty came to an end in China. Plato ascribes this defeat to a collapse in self-discipline and morale, which may of course be true, but it was also the invention of steelmaking, and the balance of power beginning to switch from sea people to land people as a result of technological progress. This is Plato's own description of the war that came to him via his uncle Dropides, Solon and the Egyptian priest of Sais: it is one of the first two fragments of American history to survive:

> Let me begin by observing first of all, that nine thousand was the sum of years which had elapsed since the war which was said to have taken place between those who dwelt outside the Pillars of Heracles and those who dwelt within them; this war I am going to describe.
>
> In the days of old, the gods had the whole earth distributed among them by allotment. There was no quarrelling; for you cannot rightly suppose that the gods did not know what was proper for each of them to have, or, knowing this, that they would seek to procure for themselves by contention that which more properly belonged to others. They all of them by just apportionment obtained what they wanted, and peopled their own districts; and when they had peopled them they tended us, their nurselings and possessions, as shepherds tend their flocks, excepting only that they did not use blows or bodily force, as shepherds do, but governed us like pilots from the stern of the vessel, which is an easy way of guiding animals, holding our souls by the rudder of persuasion according to their own pleasure—thus did they guide all mortal creatures.
>
> Now the country was inhabited in those days by various classes of citizens—there were artisans, and there were husbandmen, and there was also a warrior class originally set apart by divine men. The latter dwelt by themselves and had all things suitable for nurture and education; neither had any of them anything of their own, but they regarded all that they had as common property; nor did they claim to receive of the other citizens anything more than their necessary food. And they practised all the pursuits which we yesterday described as those of our imaginary guardians.
>
> And Poseidon, receiving for his lot the island of Atlantis, begat children by a mortal woman and settled them in a part of the island, which I will describe. Looking towards the sea, but in the centre of the whole island, there was a plain which is said to have been the fairest of all plains and

PLATE 233

HERACLES FROM A GREEK CERAMIC. *Wonderfully carved magnetite mirrors were used in early Mexico.*[5] *To the Greeks magnetite was known as the stone of Heracles. With the knowledge that magnetite was in use this early, it seems reasonable to suppose that it was also used as a compass by the Heracles people and other early sailors, hence its name, the stone of Heracles. The Olmecs, 1550* B.C., *had compass-oriented courtyards and earthworks.*

The Olympic Games stemmed from the Games of Heracles. As we have seen, the Heracles people were excessively macho, so in the Highland Games of Scotland, the sport of "tossing the kaber"—tossing a tree trunk around—the name kaber might ultimately stem from akawa, *the name associated with the Great Goddess and thus with Hera-ak as well as Awa-ak.*

Heracles—from a Greek ceramic: his lionskin, bow and arrows prompted Classical Greek writers to suggest that he flourished before the age of metals. He had the reputation of having first cleared Crete, indeed the whole world, of wild animals—the capital of Crete is Heraklion (Iráklion)—and of starting the irrigation agriculture of Egypt, as well as of taking the essentially female arts of agriculture around the world.[6] *In the languages of the Algonquian Indians of North America loan words have been found from Celtic, Egyptian and Semitic, of which the greater number are Semitic. I argue that the golden apples of the Hesperides, which the Heracles people fetched, were the lumps of pure copper from around Lake Superior. Heracles was a god to both Phoenicians and Celts and was named as one of the predynastic rulers of Egypt. When Heracles went for the golden apples of the Hesperides, he found them already guarded by a snake, symbolic of the matriarch's troops, who were clearly copper extracting there first. Alexander the Great lauded Heracles as a fellow adventurer into distant lands, and the Ptolemies of Egypt, and the two royal houses of Sparta, claimed descent from him. Important people in pre-Columbian Peru wore headdresses like his, made from the skin of an animal.*[7] *Gilgamesh, king of Uruk, was also depicted wearing animal skins. Heracles was the benefactor of the whole race of mankind.*[8] *The Heracles myth was known from Mesopotamia to Polynesia millennia ago.*[9] *Dante looked on Heracles as a proto-Christ.*

very fertile. Near the plain again, and also in the centre of the island at a distance of about fifty stadia, there was a mountain not very high on any side. In this mountain there dwelt one of the earth-born primeval men of that country, whose name was Evenor and he had a wife named Leucippe, and they had an only daughter who was called Cleito. The maiden had already reached womanhood, when her father and mother died; Poseidon fell in love with her and had intercourse with her, and breaking the ground, inclosed the hill in which she dwelt all round, making alternate zones of sea and land larger and smaller, encircling one another; there were two of land and three of water, which he turned as with a lathe, each having its circumference equidistant every way from the centre, so that no man could get to the island, for ships and voyages were not as yet.[14] He himself, being a god, found no difficulty in making special arrangements for the centre island, bringing up two springs of water from beneath the earth, one of warm water and the other of cold,[15] and making every variety of food to spring up abundantly from the soil. He also begat and brought up five pairs of twin male children; and dividing the island of Atlantis into ten portions, he gave to the first-born of the eldest pair his mother's dwelling and the surrounding allotment, which was the largest and best, and made him king over the rest; the others he made princes, and gave them rule over many men, and a large territory. And he named them all; the eldest, who was the first king, he named Atlas, and after him the whole island and the ocean were called Atlantic.

Now Atlas had numerous and honourable family, and they retained the kingdom, the eldest son handing it on to his eldest son for many generations; and they had such an amount of wealth as was never before posessed by kings and potentates, and is not ever likely to be again.

Each of the ten kings in his own division and in his own city had the absolute control of the citizens, and, in most cases, of the laws, punishing and slaying whomsoever he would. Now the order of precedence among them and their mutual relations were regulated by the commands of Poseidon which the law had handed down. These were inscribed by the first kings on a pillar of orichalcum, which was situated in the middle of the island, at the temple of Poseidon, whither the kings were gathered together every fifth and every sixth year alternately, thus giving equal honour to the odd and to the even number.

There were many special laws affecting the several kings inscribed about the temples, but the most important was the following: They were not to take up arms against one other, and they were all to come to the rescue if any one in any of their cities attempted to overthrow the royal house; like their ancestors, they were to deliberate in common about war and other matters, giving the supremacy to the descendants of Atlas. And the king was not to have the power of life and death over any of his kinsmen unless he had the assent of the majority of the ten.

Such was the vast power which the god settled in the lost island of Atlantis; and this he afterwards directed against our land for the following reasons, as tradition tells: For many generations, as long as the divine nature lasted in them, they were obedient to the laws, and well-affectioned towards the god, whose seed they were; for they possessed true and in every way great spirits, uniting gentleness with wisdom in the various chances of life, and in their intercourse with one another. They despised everything but virtue, caring little for their present state of life, and thinking lightly of the possession of gold and other property, which seemed only a burden to them; neither were they intoxicated by luxury; nor did wealth deprive them of their self-control; but when the divine portion began to fade away, and became diluted too often and too much with the mortal admixture, and the human nature got the upper hand, they then, being unable to bear their fortune, behaved unseemly.

For these histories tell of a mighty power which unprovoked made an expedition against the whole of Europe and Asia, and to which your city put an end. This power came forth out of the Atlantic Ocean, for in those days the Atlantic was navigable; and there was an island situated in front of the straits which are by you called the pillars of Heracles; the island was larger than Libya and Asia put together, and was the way to other islands, and from these you might pass to the whole of the opposite continent which surrounded the true ocean; for this sea which is within the straits of Heracles is only a harbour, having a narrow entrance, but that other is a real sea, and the surrounding land may be most truly called a boundless continent.

Now in this island of Atlantis there was a great and wonderful empire which had rule over the whole island and several others, and over parts of the continent, and, furthermore, the men of Atlantis had subjected the parts of Libya within the columns of Heracles as far as Egypt, and of Europe as far as Tyrrhenia. This vast power, gathered into one, endeavoured to subdue at a blow our country and yours and the whole of the region within the straits; and then, Solon, your country shone forth, in the excellence of her virtue and strength, among all mankind. She was pre-eminent in courage and military skill and was the leader of the Hellenes. And when the rest fell off from her, being compelled to stand alone, after having undergone the very extremity of danger, she defeated and triumphed over the invaders, and preserved from slavery those who were not yet subjugated, and generously liberated all the rest of us who dwell within the pillars. But afterwards there occurred violent earthquakes and floods; and in a single day and night of misfortune all your warlike men in a body sank into the earth, and the island of Atlantis in like manner disappeared in the depths of the sea. For which reason the sea in those parts is impassable and impenetrable, because there is a shoal of mud in the way; and this was caused by the subsidence of the island.[16]

We have a record here of a huge earthquake in Greece and in the Caribbean at around the same time. Germany suffered similarly from huge earthquakes at the same period as they were fighting the sea people, a period which the Baltic people described as Ragnarok.[17]

In 300 B.C. Crantor, the first editor of the *Timaeus*, believed that every word in Plato's narrative was correct, for he had sent over to Egypt and

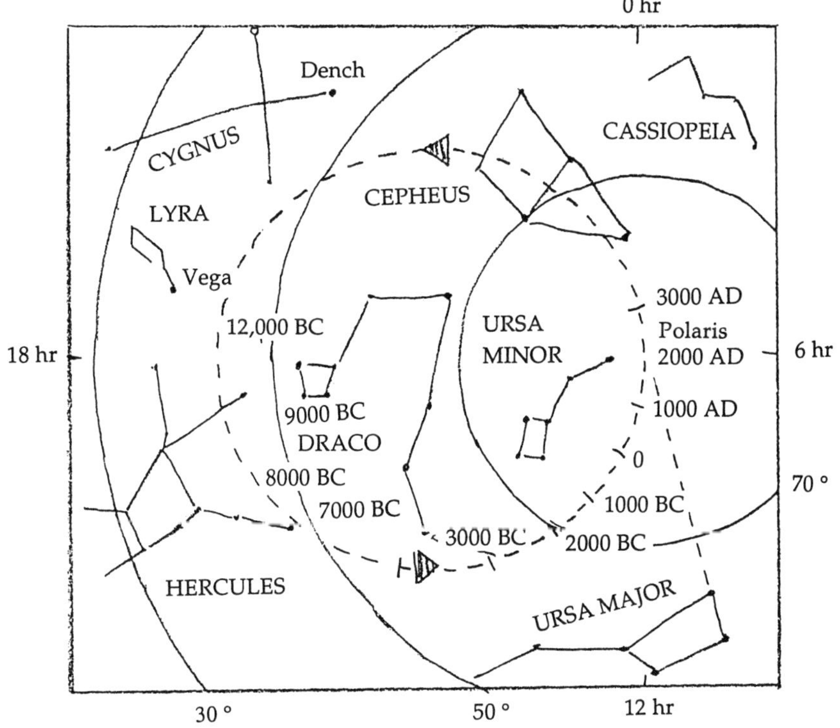

Plate 234

The precession of the equinox. *The wobble of the poles, called the precession of the equinox, takes nearly twenty-six thousand years to complete one revolution. Different stars, therefore, in different millennia, have to supply the Mariner's Star or Pole Star or Star of Mary. The names of the guiding stars or constellations are related to the thalassocrats of the period and can be seen by following the dotted line, with the dates when that point in the circle supplied the pole of the earth, the* axis mundi. *Thus we get the Great Bear symbolizing*[10] *Atlas: the Dragon, Draco, between 2000 and 4000* B.C., *symbolizing Chronos, thus Sumerians and Semites; Hercules between 4000 and 6000* B.C. *to 10,000* B.C.*; then the star Vega, a name presumably for the earth mother, today associated with words like virgin and vagina. Isis, the Egyptian earth mother, was patron of travelers and navigators. The Canadian Delaware Indians called the Great Bear by that name from pre-Columbian times.*[11] *The Canadian Indians believed that every bear on earth was related to one supreme being, the Great Bear in heaven.*[12] *It is a reflection on the then balance of power in the world that this constellation was given a name probably of American, not of Old World, origin: confirming what we have learned from other kinds of evidence where the center of sea power then lay. It is worth noticing that the constellation in the Old World called Scorpio was also called Scorpio by the Maya of Guatemala.*[13] *Heaven was the "starry palace of the gods."*

the priests there had confirmed the story.[18] And, of course, they were right, as we have seen.

In short, once it is understood that the Mesopotamian names Kur[19] and Dilmun both stand for America, the latter not for Bahrain; that the Chinese Fu Sang was the Chinese name for America; that the Japanese Horaisan, the Eternal Land, the Abode of the Blessed, ten years' sailing east of Japan, is the Americas, not Formosa; to the Egyptians Tuat, the Field of Reeds, means the Americas; that Atlantis was the name given to the Americas only when ruled by the Atlas people, the islands as great in size as Africa and Asia and therefore strictly not the little islet of Santorini, seventy-five acres in size, near Crete; that the Hesperides and Tartarus were Greek names referring to the Americas, that Hi Brazil was the old pre-Columbian Portuguese name for the Americas, Irish version Ui Breasail; that it was Armorica to the Bretons, Glas Innes or Avalon to the Welsh, Mag Mel or Tir na Og to the Irish, Vinland to the Scandinavians; then we notice that the stories of emigration from the Old World match and agree with Amerindian—not to mention West African—stories of immigration by white people: it all coheres; it fits together neatly. This is associated in the Americas with an almost identity in ecclesiastical architecture with Mesopotamia; powerful and unmistakable Chinese influence in Central America according to the great sinologist Joseph Needham, Japanese pottery of the third millennium B.C. in Ecuador; similar signs in scripts; the transfer of plants; loan words in languages; pre-Columbian sculpture in America of portraits of Indian, African, Middle Eastern, European faces; identity in astronomical methods between the New World and the Old; similar religious symbols with similar meanings, almost identical religious practices with Christianity in ancient Mexico and Peru; the Mesopotamian names for the earth mother used the length and breadth of the Americas, with in some areas Chissis or Chise as the name of the sun god, spelling optional; blacks and blue-eyed blonds encountered by Columbus and his henchmen among the Amerindians; a multitude of Old World scripts carved on the rocks of America from Scandinavian runes to the Indus Valley script—the coherence of all this makes it indubitable that the Old and the New Worlds were very closely interconnected. My argument goes further: it states that there were periods when the economies of the Old World cannot be understood without reference to the New World, especially, of course, during the Copper and Bronze Ages. And it goes on to suggest that a number of useful inventions presently credited to the foremost nations of the Old World will almost certainly have come from the New World, maybe some, also, from the settlements in Africa. In future, the fatuous phrase "the New World" we must hope will no longer be used. In brief, there has been something of a global village before. Here is Julian the Apostate describing the sun worshippers' trinitarian religion:

> This divine and wholly beautiful universe, from the highest vault of heaven to the lowest limit of the earth, is held together by the continuous providence of the god, has existed from eternity ungenerated, is imperishable for all time to come, and is guarded immediately by nothing else than the Fifth Substance whose culmination is the beams of the sun; and in the second and higher degree, so to speak, by the intelligible world; but in a still loftier sense it is guarded by the King of the whole universe, who is the centre of all things that exist. He, therefore, whether it is right to call him the Supra-Intelligible, or the Idea of Being, and by Being I mean the whole intelligible region, or the One, since the One seems somehow prior to all the rest, or, to use Plato's name for him, the Good; at any rate this uncompounded cause of the whole reveals to all existence beauty, and perfection, and oneness, and irresistible power; and in virtue of the primal creative substance that abides in it, as middle among the middle and intellectual, creative causes, Helios the most mighty god, proceeding from itself and in all things like unto itself. Even so the divine Plato believed, when he writes, 'Therefore (said I) when I spoke of this, understand that I meant the offspring of the Good which the Good begat in his own likeness, and that what the Good is in relation to pure reason and its objects in the intelligible world, such is the sun in the visible world in relation to sight and its objects.' Accordingly his light has the same relation to the visible world as truth has to the

PLATE 235
A grave in Sweden in the form of a ship, such as were also built in the western Mediterranean toward the end of the Bronze Age. The atl *names in the tideless Baltic coincide with the* atl *names in the tideless Mediterranean, indicating the Nordic component among the Peoples of the Sea. Let us look at Catalonia, Atalia, Latin, Melitta, Valetta, Anatolia, etc. and we get an idea of the power of this particular sea people over the Mediterranean at that time. For Lurker says that Seth, alias Atlas, was lord over all non-Egyptian lands. This, almost worldwide rule, is a claim consistent with almost all we know on the subject.*[14]

intelligible world. And he himself as a whole, since he is the son of what is first and greatest, namely, the Idea of Good, and subsists from eternity in the region of its abiding substance, has received also the dominion among the intellectual gods, and himself dispenses to the intellectual gods, those things of which the Good is the cause for the intelligible gods. Now the Good is, I suppose, the cause for the intelligible gods of beauty, existence, perfection and oneness, connecting these and illuminating them with a power that works for good. These accordingly Helios bestows on the intellectual gods also, since he has been appointed by the Good to rule and govern them, even though they came forth and came into being together with him, and that was, I suppose, in order that the cause which resembles the Good may guide the intellectual gods to blessings for them all, and may regulate all things according to pure reason.

A caveat. The picture given us today by archaeologists is that the Indus Valley civilization was destroyed, c. 2003 B.C., not, as was formerly explained, by the salination of the irrigation fields, but by earthquake, and it seems reasonable to deduce that many of the surviving tribes then moved west: the Hittites, who worshipped gods with Indian names, to Anatolia; the Mycenaeans to Greece; the Hebrews to Sumer. At this period the Sumerians themselves had gone under not by military defeat but "by storm," their bodies being described as lying around in the streets: the same earthquakes, the same shifting of the tectonic plates as in the Indus Valley, may well have put paid at the same time to those gifted Sumerian city-states. The Elamites and others who are said to have conquered Sumer were really taking over a power vacuum.

Around 1182 B.C. we have the defeat of the Peoples of the Sea by the Egyptian naval archers rather more than by the Athenians; but, associated with that military defeat, is the tradition of earthquake in the Caribbean where the sea peoples' headquarters were probably situated: the sinking into the earth near Athens "in a day and night of disaster" of the victorious Athenian army—which only earthquake could explain—and the Baltic description of Ragnarok, which is not only of the demoralized members of the sea alliance fighting with each other but, again, of an earthquake disaster in Germany on a horrific scale at the same period.

So when ancient tradition in the Old World as in America tells that the cause of the switch of ruling groups, in the Old World Akawa to Ouranos, Ouranos to Chronos, Chronos to Zeus, was due not only to warfare but to cataclysm, then it is reasonable to suppose that earthquakes were responsible for at least two of the changes. Resultingly, therefore, having happened at least twice before, we should at least be aware that earthquakes might happen again on that most terrifying scale: earthquakes may surely be expected to recur at some time in the future. The Palace of Phaistos in Crete was destroyed three times by earthquake and Greek history generally was believed to have been ruptured by innumerable climatic disasters.

But, specifically, it should be noticed that the blame for this defeat is placed on the moral inadequacy of the attackers: by Plato in his Egyptian narration, by the Baltic people in Ragnarok, even by Homer, who makes clear that the Greeks before the Trojan War were greater, stronger and wiser. And the decline of the Toltecs in America the Amerindians attributed to an identical flaw. The Mycenaeans were finally destroyed by social revolution once their military class had been wiped out, symbolized by Agamemnon being murdered by his wife. Peruvians also carried the similar story of internecine warfare in Peru contemporary with earthquakes on a huge scale. The poet Hesiod says the same thing, describing the same earthquakes and the same war under the poetic guise of Zeus fighting Typhon, synonym for the latter Titans. "So they, with bitter wrath, were fighting continually with one another at that time for full ten years."[20]

Our perspective in time—the belief that the Classical Greeks were ancient, not recent—is as wildly distorted as our present perspective on space—that the New World is indeed a New World. Similarly we shall discover that the Classical Greeks in some things were inferior to the Mycenaean Greeks, as the Classical Greeks themselves stated and correctly believed. For their forebears were the major component of the Atlas people, and the Atlas people claimed, quite correctly, to have carried the whole world on their shoulders, at one time or another. So we find that Set, alias Atlas, was the god of Upper Egypt and, for a limited period, ruled the whole of Egypt; that the blond Seth people, alias Set, ruled Mesopotamia. The language of ancient India is Sanskrit, a sister language to Greek. The port with the dry dock toward the mouth of the Indus is Lothal, as we have seen, a palindrome of Atl; while in Tibet, north of the Indus, we find the Dalai Lama, his Potala palace, his city Minitale, and so on, all seemingly Atlas names. One finds a vague, classical Greek tradition, the ancestors of some of their people having emigrated from Kashmir. Then one finds Atlas names in the Baltic and on the west side of Britain, from Glasgow to Llandaff and the Lleyn Peninsula. And when the Atlas people were eventually pushed out of the Old World in the *Titanomachia*, Mycenaeans and Canaanites crossed the seas and took over the Americas, thus virtually rounding off their world rule. I believe that these brilliant early Greek achievements explain why the Greek dictionary is so rich, subtle and erudite. Our whole perspective must alter. For ease of reading I have used the common expressions in this book, but Classical Greece is not to be called Ancient Greece, Classical Rome is not to be called Ancient Rome, indeed it is not to be described as the Ancient World. It is all too recent, too immediate, too pertinent. Once we set about reconstructing our pasts, of which this book is a first tentative attempt, the word "ancient" should be applied only to events of seven to ten thousand years ago. We can now begin to trace the origins of our principal religions.

28. Summary of the Argument

"Showing a greater fondness for their own opinions than for the truth, they sought to deny and disprove the new things which, if they had cared to look for themselves, their own sense would have demonstrated to them."

GALILEO, *letter to the Grand Duchess Christina*

"Gold is the most exquisite of all things . . . whoever possesses gold can acquire all that he desires in this world. Truly, for gold he can gain entrance for his soul into Paradise."

CHRISTOPHER COLUMBUS

"The real voyage of discovery is not in seeking new landscapes but in having new eyes."

MARCEL PROUST

Recently we have had the five hundredth anniversary of the so-called Discovery of America by Christopher Columbus. This is the summary of the argument, set forth in our pages, that the whole Christopher Columbus exercise is a cheap con trick.

Garcilaso de la Vega, one of the principal sources for Prescott's *Conquest of Peru*, tells the following story. Some seven years before Columbus set out in 1492, a Spanish ship, captained by Alonso Sánchez de Huelva, trading with the Canary Islands was caught in a storm and washed up on a Caribbean island. The crew repaired the vessel and five survivors of the original crew of seventeen returned to Spain. Christopher Columbus, hearing of this, invited them to his house where, in de la Vega's words, he entertained them lavishly: i.e. gave them enough wine to be sure of securing the full story. Then all five of them—who had been fit enough to be entertained lavishly—died after dinner in their host's house and, de la Vega continues, Columbus became heir to all their sufferings and privations.[1] It seems to me to be most probable that they were poisoned. Readers should go back to the source and read it for themselves. There were such huge sums of money and repute involved, perhaps de la Vega would not even hint at murder for fear of meeting the same fate as the unfortunate sailors. Now, the name America is supposedly derived from the name applied to the continent by the German geographer Waldesemuller and is drawn, historians tell us, from the first name of the navigator Vespucci on Columbus's third voyage. But why not the first name of the cabin boy on the second voyage or of the cook on the first voyage? If you examine the map you will find that up till that date newly discovered lands were named after the first name of a monarch or the surname of a commoner, so why Amerigo? At the least why not spell his name correctly? A historian suggests, without giving a source, that Breton fishermen had been fishing for cod off the Newfoundland banks for centuries before Columbus. In the Celtic of Britanny the land in the middle of the sea was called Armorica, a name the Romans had applied to Brittany itself. Waldesemuller had to pretend that the name came from the great Columbus voyages. I would suppose, in contemporary fashion, money may have changed hands. It is just worth noticing that syphilis, an indigenous American disorder, I was told by Italian friends, is known in Italy as the French sickness. It should also be remembered that Columbus's own ship's crew said that they were the first to travel to America since Hanno the Phoenician's time. At least they knew that much, while Columbus himself knew so much more.

As we have seen, America was known to many nations of the Old World by a variety of names. America was looked on then—as now—as the Paradise Land: God's own country. Perhaps the biggest single source of confusion lies in this term, the underworld, which originally meant the Americas—where the sun was at midnight—but was converted by the Christians and others at that time into the inferno: two totally contradictory meanings to the same term, but convenient for raising money for the church.

The Scandinavians, during a warmer 350 years in the North Atlantic, from the beginning of the eleventh century to c. A.D. 1350, had moved from Iceland to first colonizing Greenland and then to colonizing North America. There is not a shadow of a doubt about these colonies in Greenland and North America since their villages have been properly excavated by archaeologists, a Viking boat has been dredged up from the St. Lawrence, and the whole adventure published in sagas, about their American colony which they named Vinland or Wineland. Furthermore, we have one of their priest's description of the North American coastline when his boat inadvertently missed Greenland and coasted along the shores of North America. Before he set off, Columbus went especially to Iceland, Thule, where he must have learned about the colony because the North American colony was not just common knowledge, it was famous, and, as a native Genoese, he could scarcely not have heard what the pope had been up to, for he was single-minded about these matters. That his name in Spanish is spelled Colón is, perhaps, not inappropriate. It is just worth noticing that the anthropologists tell us that the Amerindians along the Pacific coast of North America all have Dionysus-type religions. Columbus's fame has rested upon fraud, murder, and hype—very much in the spirit of our twentieth-century heroes.

Additionally, Columbus's son Ferdinand says that when his father set off he possessed a map with Antillia—the Antilles—already marked on it.[2] While long-distance sailing across the Atlantic had by then diminished due to the deterioration in the climate and the lack of incentive, the memory of the land in the middle of the ocean must have remained lively enough in many coastal areas. In A.D. 1107 King Madoc of Wales sailed away from Wales to found a colony in America and then returned to Wales to recruit additional colonists whom he took back with him. There is an Amerindian language with Welsh words in it. King Madoc was emulating the Scandinavians who now governed Britain. There was also a European article brought up from a Mayan sacred well, a cenote, dated around A.D. 1200. But, of course, the great days of Pacific and Atlantic sailing were far earlier. It had just been agreed that a stone known as the Cherokee stone carries not Cherokee but a Hebrew script on it from between the first and the eighth centuries A.D. Hebrew coins of Bar Kokhba's rebellion, A.D. 150, have been dug up in North America, a Roman pottery head has been found in America, as well as Roman galleys. But this is small beer when compared with the large number of Celtic ogham rock engravings, in addition to numerous Old World scripts, found inscribed on the rocks of New England by Professor Barry Fell and his associates: some of which may be suspect but much would still seem to be genuine. The Irish voyage of St. Brendan to America is dated to A.D. 565–573: there would seem to have been little publicity about that since there was nothing unusual about it. St. Brendan (A.D. 484–578) is said to have been born at Tralee in Kerry. He died as abbot of a Benedictine monastery he had founded at Clonfert in eastern Galway. He is said to have crossed the Atlantic to the "Promised Land of the Saints." The presence of ogham inscriptions across North America would suggest that he was following a living, Irish tradition so that to his trip no particular importance would be attached. Columbus's "discovery of America" is an example, still glaring today, that if you have enough money to spend on PR you can make two and two add up to 174. I believe oghams to be simply a script decoded from tally sticks and their Atlas name suggests that these wooden tally sticks kept the records from very early days indeed.

Julius Caesar in his *De Bello Gallico* records that the druids of Gaul claimed to know the measurements of the different continents and of the planet itself: which everything indicates that the Celts in fact did, and had known them for a very, very long time. And Plutarch, in his narrative "On the Face in the Moon's Orb," seems to describe in one passage the Greek trip from Britain to America. The rocks in Amazonia carry a large number of a great variety of scripts, so totally clear and identifiable that they provide indisputable evidence of the great variety of merchantmen using the river. But of course that was when mariners were literate. Prior to that we have the trademarks of the multinationals, distinguished by their religions, engraved on the rocks: symbols that were universals, not particulars. Down the Amazon came the main supplies of bronze for the Mediterranean during the entire Bronze Age: hence the enormous wealth of Pluto, hence our word plutocrat.

We have pointed out that the American continent tilts from west to east, so the rivers of access to the hinterland flow into the Atlantic, the Andes and the Rockies providing insuperable barriers to shipping on the west side, while the African continent tilts from east to west, with the escarpment providing a substantial barrier against access to the continent on the east side. So while the Pacific contacts with America were important, as were the Indian Ocean contacts with Africa, it was the Atlantic trade that predominated in the Copper and Bronze Ages. We therefore make an in-depth study of West African associations with the Fertile Crescent, showing how close were West African ties with the Mediterranean over a long period of time and thus why African statues appear in second millennium Mexico, and African heads are painted on early Peruvian pottery, and the Navajo god of fire was black and there was a tribe of black men living along the Amazon when Fray Carvajal and Orellana pitched up, part of Pizarro's party. The religions, the living traditions and customs of West Africa, are associated with those of the Fertile Crescent on the one hand and with the Amerindian nations on the other hand, and thus make an important contribution to our story and to our understanding of that early period. We have also pointed out that prior to Columbus, West Africans from Mali had dispatched a fleet of canoes to cross the Atlantic.

We have also pointed out that the only tin that could be used for bronze during the Bronze Age was alluvial tin and that the Akkadian-Babylonian name for tin or tin-bronze, *anaku,* is retained for the tin deposits and the tin/bronze routes of the world: so we have Cornwall in Britain, Nok in the Kano Province of Nigeria, Carnac in Britanny, Non Nok Tha in Thailand, Sri Lanka and Kandy, Canaan where it was imported, Nokwane in Swaziland, Bangka in Indonesia, Coneto in Mexico and Petseconi for the tin hill in Bolivia that, when read boustrophedon, from right to left, simply means tin hill in Akkadian, the Kanaks on the great copper mine of New Caledonia; Tuscany, where there is copper and tin; Larnaca in Cyprus and Knossos in Crete. The island of Marmora was formerly called Proconnesos, or island for tin; tin was to be found in the Cantabrian mountains in Spain; in Cornish the word for tin bearing is *stenak,* perhaps the names Canada and Scandinavia require consideration; Kanesh in Anatolia is next to tin and copper and so is Wankie in Zimbabwe. Kanesh—where, by the first millennium B.C., they had both checks and a women's college.

We point out that while the rock inscriptions provide indisputable evidence as to who the sailors were, the religious trademarks of the earlier Bronze Age multinationals—the sun circle for time or the sun, the spiral for the Earth Mother, the wavy lines of the sea people that appear on all the continents with the exception of Antarctica and Australia—imply just as clearly the cultures that were involved, precisely as the crosses raised by the Portuguese navigators when they sailed around Africa in relatively recent times record their presence and the nature of their religion.

Agriculture started around the same date, 9000 B.C., for Southwest Asia, 7000 B.C. in Southeast Asia, Mexico and Peru.[3] The question can be asked: is this synchronism coincidence? Even for this early date, the answer is probably not, for the following reasons. While primacy in sailing belonged to the matriarchal group, the breakaway group from the martriarchs called Heracles must have dominated the sea routes from 9000–7000 B.C. to have had the constellation carrying the North Star of that period named after it. Classical writers correctly stated that Heracles, normally depicted as armed with a club and clad in a lion skin, is evidence that his floruit preceded the age of metals (c. 6000 B.C.). Tradition reports him to have been a compulsive traveler. He is portrayed traveling in a small round vessel like a coracle, and such vessels in Mesopotamia were called *quffas*, an *akawa* name, it seems, as is probably coracle. Greek tradition reports tales about Heracles: the golden apples of the Hesperides, which had first belonged to the earth mother, were appropriated by Heracles. Now, the Hesperides were in the remote west, across the Atlantic, so when Hyperboreans come into the story, commentators find confusion, not realizing that one standard route to North America was via the northern tip of the Hebrides, or the Orkneys, or Shetland, the land of the Set people, via Iceland and Greenland: indeed the people who lived beyond the North Wind!

Didorus Siculus said Heracles visited all the inhabited world,[4] and elsewhere it is said that he worked in missionary spirit for the benefit of mankind. Across half the world he was famous: father of the Celtic race, producing princes in India, ruling temporarily predynastic Egypt; clearing the entire world of wild beasts, which is of course necessary for agriculture; ceremonial groups in ancient America dressed to resemble him; starting irrigation in Egypt and so on.

We point out that this long-distance sailing was chiefly for metals and that for the 2,500 to 3,000 years of the Copper Age the only large-scale source of copper was around Lake Superior in Canada, first used by the only peoples who were using copper in substantial quantities around the Black Sea. Prior to that the people who worshipped the earth mother, a religion with great depth in time,[5] to whom earth meant the planet earth, which is 70 percent water, along with their breakaway group the Heracles people, took the arts of agriculture around the world around 7000 B.C., which is, in fact, also when copper started to be used. And when the bottle gourd, an Old World plant indigenous to Africa or India, begins to be farmed in America and Thailand.[6] We must allow, however, that small amounts of native copper will have been associated with virtually every copper deposit; each had its quota alongside the oxides and the sulfides.

If we now notice the comment that ancient America at an early period possessed the best domesticators of plants in the world and we back it with the list of American plants that have so greatly benefited mankind—the sweet potato, the potato, maize, the pineapple, tomatoes, more dubiously tobacco, cotton growing in America seemingly preceding cotton growing in India—and we consider the length of time necessary and the persistency necessary to select and breed these plants from their humble origins, then we must consider the quality of the few maritime immigrants who joined with the immigrants from Siberia after their long pilgrimage down the American continent, and what these groups, working together, have contributed to the well-being of the warmer parts of the entire world.

If we now notice that from the earliest times the Americas are referred to as islands, Paradise Islands, one can infer that the speakers knew their entire geography to be able to enter upon that accurate description of them from a very early date indeed. It was in association with immortality and with Paradise that the Americas were described worldwide, as well, of course, as being the place where the sun set and so the place of the dead.

There is considerable disagreement as to the timing for the start of copper extraction from Isle Royale on Lake Superior, depending, it seems, on whether the charcoal carbon dates arose from forest fires or from fire setting to split the rock from which the copper was extracted. But if we add to the fact that for the first two thousand years of the Copper Age virtually the only copper that could be used was in the form of pure or native copper and that Lake Superior possesses the only large-scale deposit of native copper in the world; that the consumption of copper by the industrial countries grew to be on a great scale; the erection of the earliest megaliths in the world began on the northwest coast of Europe, starting in the middle of the sixth millennium B.C., with sophisticated astronomy and mathematics subsequently backing them; the tradition that is consistent is that the system of patriarchal government began in the Atlantic Ocean—"the gods were born out of Ocean"[7]—the type of stone hammers used on Lake Superior for shaping and work-hardening the copper being identical to those used on small copper deposits in Ireland and Cheshire; the name *akawa,* which we have come to associate with matriarchy providing the root for Siskiwit Bay on Isle Royale and Keweenaw of the Keweenaw Peninsula, while allowing for the fact that all the other copper deposits of the world usually carry their quota of pure metal with them; all this to my mind on balance supports the date for copper extraction from Lake Superior as beginning in the early sixth millennium B.C.: and it was the seizure of this trade by the patriarchs from the matriarchs that financed the worldwide export of their religion and their political structures. Subsequently, the all-important bronze trade from the neighborhood of the Andes leads one to support the suggestion that Olympus was simply a corruption of Atlantis. Once the bronze trade had collapsed the seat of the gods was transferred from the Andes to two mountains in Greece. Tradition suggests that the religion of the sky god developed in the Americas, while its worldwide expansion initially was financed out of the metals trade. This is the contribution of the early Americas to the entire world. And the shaft graves running from 4800 B.C. along the Atlantic seaways of Brittany and Britain seem to bear this out. We must begin to inquire which of the major inventions of those early days originated in the so-called New World and were then carried to the Old, not, as is taught, all carried from the Old World to the New.

Resultingly in this book we have been discussing not just the development of early worldwide sailing, but the most important part that the Americas played in early history. Thus in the Mesopotamian tradition that reached us through the Middle Eastern historian Berosus, that the sea people brought all the arts of civilization to Mesopotamia in the fourth millennium and that the sea god was the source of all wisdom—and thereafter the Mesopotamians invented nothing for themselves—we must ask where the various developments were brought from? And being sea people they picked up the tricks from various countries that they were trading with, which, in the last analysis, were countries almost right around the world. We must inquire whether the early history of Christianity, which Eusebius correctly said preceded the time of Moses,[8] was not developed in the New World as much as in the Old.

We argue that all this evidence makes it clear that archaeology on the subject of the age of metals is still in a primitive stage. We point out that there is a useful double check on this carrying trade because the navigators' stars in each period along the precession of the equinox carry the names or the devices of the thalassocrats of the period, from Vega, perhaps the virgin, through to Heracles, through to Draco and the dragon ships, through to the Great Bear or Atlas—the name Great Bear for the constellation more probably emanating from America than the Mediterranean. Compare all the evidence of this book with the comment by Glyn Daniel, editor of the Thames and Hudson series of archaeology books, that anyone who believed that there was contact with America before the Christopher Columbus voyages belonged to the "lunatic fringe of archaeology."

Daniel quotes a remark by the eminent Australian archaeologist Gordon Childe about archaeology in America: "Never been there—peripheral and highly suspect." Professor Stuart Piggott defines his opinion: "We cannot escape the feeling that the Mesoamerican culture, even at its highest, is

Plate 236

Any respectable old-age home will be able to produce seventy septuagenarians. Put their ages vertically, as it were, not horizontally, and we are back to predynastic Egypt. History books brainwash us into believing this is antiquity, a period so remote it is incomprehensible, instead of it being a picture of people dealing with problems not all that different from our own, whose sacrifices and achievements deserve reverence and understanding.

A temple (below) on the island of Lewis, Outer Hebrides—example of the pre-Christian cross. Eusebius taught that Christianity was neither new nor strange, the only new thing was the church.[1] *Julius Caesar said of the Celts of Gaul that they had considerable knowledge of the movements of the heavenly bodies, the size of the earth and of natural philosophy.*[2] *On the island of Lewis tradition says that priests and black men set up the stones.*[3] *In India Kala is connected with time: in Greek, a sister language to Indian Sanskrit,* nisos *means island: so Callanish, the site of the great stone circle on the island of Lewis, may simply mean "time island": which indeed it was. In Greece the mystery rites were called* teletai *and the initiatory shrine the* telesteria, *both Atlas or Set names, who was the sun god. The sacred day to Christians was not, as with Jews, Saturday, the day of Saturn, but Sunday, the day not of Christ but of the sun. They were two different religions, the religion of the Philistines and that of the Jews, squelched together by their exponents to cash in on the act. Most of the impressive megalithic alignments in Britain are lunar,*[4] *which suggests a derivation from the Middle East. The religion of the east Roman Empire was cobbled together with one of the west Roman Empire in order to aid the government of that huge empire.*

Christ as Helios: mosaic below the great altar in St. Peter's, Rome. Helios was the Greek sun god. Christians converted the peoples who were previously sun worshippers. The importance of America to the origins of Christianity still goes unappreciated. The worship of Mithras, the solar and savior deity of the Romans of the first century A.D., *shows many parallels with Christianity. Christian canonization is halfway to apotheosis. Luke (3:38) traces Jesus' descent from the sun god Seth. The Samaritans taught about the chain of purity passing through the Sethians down through the ages.*[5] *The name Ash was used of Seth in Ptolemaic times and ash trees are sacred in some parts of Britain. The sun is sometimes a symbol of Christ in religious art and thought.*

no more than (to adopt a phrase of the seventeenth-century writer, Roger North) '. . . such as an extraordinarily high-spirited judicious Barbarian might be supposed originally to invent'."[9]

The Greeks believed in the four Ages of the World, the four different peoples distinguished by their religions who ruled the Fertile Crescent: Ge, Ouranos, Chronos and Zeus. The Amerindians shared this belief in the Four Ages prior to their own and we must guess—if they were not just repeating the eastern Mediterranean tradition—how they would name them: their earth mother, Ci or Ki; then Hades, alias Sumerian Osiris and Dionysus; then Sumerian Poseidon, alias Ea and Enki, who left the name *agua* across his empire; finally Atlas, alias Set, Typhon, Toltec, Vira Cocha along with the Middle Eastern Chronos people, who took a huge part in the Atlas scene, and thus a huge part in the Americas. Each age was believed, both in the New World and the Old, to have been terminated by climatic disasters, earthquake being included under this heading, and being, indeed, the chief cause. We find at the same time the termination of the Indus Valley civilization by earthquake, of the Sumerian by a storm, and Ireland simultaneously inundated by a tidal wave. Possibly impact from a meteorite brought about the shifting of the tectonic plates.

We can, therefore, reasonably suppose that there were two previous United States of America: the Toltec of Atlantis as described by Marcellus and in Plato's *Critias*, and the equally huge Poseidon empire preceding it. We cannot guess as yet what was the political structure of the Osiris-Hades people but the matriarchy would have consisted, not of federations or empires, but of small, tight-knit communities like African tribes. Yet her name, whether Ki or Ci, Cui or Coya, stretched across much of the length and breadth of both American continents, and would itself provide very persuasive evidence for contact even if the rest of this book did not exist. But that the present United States should be understood to be not the first but the third United States of America is surely beyond doubt, if the loose Titan confederations can be called such. Admittedly the heads of state meeting every fifth and sixth year to sort out their differences stretches the phrase the United States by a trifle; but their capacity to field so large an army in an emergency supports that description. To sum up, during the Copper and Bronze Ages there is no way one will understand the history of the Old World without also considering the history of the New, and its economic importance. In the future there can be no doubt about that. There was a planetary coherence relevant to almost all our forebears in the age of metals.

We have found that cultural borrowings come not from chance contacts between peoples but rather from something more like a colonial relationship. We have found in America this intensive association to have begun with the matriarchal society centred around the Black Sea and their breakaway male associates and rivals, the Heracles people, compulsive

PLATE 237
The U.S. dollar, "the Almighty Dollar," the Oxford English Dictionary *derives from the German* taler *or* thaler *of the German monetary union of 1857. Now,* taler *translates as valley, or downstream, from German into English, and is surely derived from the word* atl, *which we have already found in Atlantic, Baltic, Latvia, Lithuania, Tallin, the Welsh word* llan, *the Mexican and Berber* atl *meaning water, the Greek* thalassa *or* thalatta *meaning sea. So the dollar is necessarily linked with the previous United States of America ruled by the Atlas sea people under the name of Atlantis. "The Almighty Dollar" thus represents a curious, if coincidental, link between these two huge American aggregates so far separate in time—these two United States of America.*

Scuba diver drills (top) into the cyclopean walls on this sea bed off the Caribbean island of Bimini to determine the nature of the rock. Bimini is strategically placed to control ships using the main current out of the Gulf of Mexico. Divers have located submerged pillars, walls, carving around Andros and Bimini.[6] A sunken city has also been located, it is claimed, off the coast of Peru; and other sunken edifices off Guatemala.

Bottom, scuba divers investigate the stone wall. The picture gives the size of the cyclopean stones that were part of the area that sank beneath the waves, leading to one part of the description of Atlantis. Shifting tectonic plates on a major scale would explain this Caribbean subsidence; the loss of the Athenian army by earthquake; and the German earthquakes that seem to be described in their tradition of Ragnarok, and that, in small measure, have been repeated while I write this. American, Greek and German earthquakes would seem to have occurred about the same time at the end of the Bronze Age. Some writers have suggested, without empirical evidence, that the shifting of the tectonic plates was occasioned by the earth being hit by an asteroid.

travelers, bringing the arts of agriculture around 7000 B.C. to Mexico and Peru. We then find them commencing the extraction of pure or native copper from around Isle Royale seemingly in the sixth millennium B.C., despite the reinterpretation of dates, a trade subsequently snatched from the matriarchs by the northern European male-dominated societies, perhaps originally stemming from Iran. Patriarchal fortunes were thereafter founded on the virtual monopoly of the copper trade from North America, the one area in the world where pure copper existed in very substantial quantities, which funded the expansion of the sky religion around the world, in course of time supplying the burgeoning irrigation societies of Mesopotamia, Egypt, America and the Indus Valley: hence, "the Gods were born out of Ocean."

We then find during the fourth millennium B.C. the Osiris people, reported to have taken civilized values around the world, to have been forced out of Egypt by the Set people and to have emigrated to North America where they were known to the Greeks as Hades, to the Romans as Pluto; by repute stone-rich from the American metals trade. Approximately 3116 B.C. the Poseidon people are flooded out of Eridu by Enlil, alias the people known as Chronos, and the Eridu refugees settled a huge area of America, tradition reports by only small numbers in each country. The root of their place names is *agua*, indicating their territories of Guatemala, Cubagua, Nicaragua, Managua, Uruguay, Paraguay, Guanahim and present-day Bolivia: the South American colonies made rich by the metal trade down the rivers, especially copper, gold, silver and bronze. We may eventually appreciate that these associated states must be called the first United States of America. We find the Japanese imprint in Ecuador at the receiving end of the Pacific countercurrent during the first half of the third millennium B.C., and the Indians can be seen to have been trading in Peru, Amazonia, East Africa, Central Africa and Ghana. The Indus civilization collapsed about 2000 B.C. due to earthquakes. Meanwhile, about 2200 B.C. refugees from Babylon at the time of Nimrod quit Babylon, many of them settling in America and some in Nigeria, bringing with them the story of why they emigrated. Perhaps due to the collapse of the Sumerians, the mother country, around 2003 B.C., the Poseidon people in America began to weaken, so when the Hyksos were driven out of Egypt in 1570 B.C., they (the Hyksos), a sea league of Western Semites, Western Europeans, Cretans and Mycenaeans emigrated to Mexico and Peru, the Semitic allies developing the Shang Dynasty of China en route and bringing with them to China the arts of the high Bronze Age, to Anyang and its tin-bearing provinces. The Atlas people then take over power in the Americas from the Poseidon people, their influence stretching from Ohio in the north to Peru in the south, working in America alongside immigrants from China, Japan, Africa and India. The Atlas people thus formed the second United States of America, enriched by the bronze trade and trade in other metals. A position came to be reached that Horus was running Egypt and the Set or Atlas

PLATE 238
A Spanish model of Columbus's flagship, the Santa María, *between eighty and one hundred tons displacement. The exact details of the ship remain unknown.*

The Maltese cross was an important pre-Christian symbol going back to at least the fourth millennium B.C. *in Iran, representing rule over the four quarters of the earth, a symbol that was sacred both in Mexico and Peru, representing some of the earliest white peoples who had brought the arts of civilization to America. The Christians had adopted this ancient symbol: unknown to either party it must have provided one of the chief means of Spanish and Christian deception. The arrival of Cortés was looked on as "the Second Coming." After the Inca Atahuallpu had provided Pizarro as his ransom a room filled from floor to ceiling with gold as Pizarro had demanded, the Christians strangled him. After Montezuma had accepted the lordship of the Spanish king over Mexico, he was accidentally killed by his own people. When the Spaniards conquered the New World, not a single town survived.[7] The Mexican population has been estimated to be 25 million people on the eve of the conquest but only 1,370,000 a century later. What is today called the discovery of America by Columbus is a cover story only for its fearful rediscovery by Spanish Christians. Peru was actually known to its own people as the land of the four quarters, which the cross symbolized. The loot from Montezuma's storehouse alone was so great that a conquistador wrote of it, "I took it for certain that there could not be another such store of wealth in the whole world."[8] The gold looted from one Amerindian town alone, Cuzco, was said to be more than the whole of Europe then possessed.*

people much of the rest of the world, including the Baltic, most of the Mediterranean outside Egypt and also the islands commanding the approaches to the Mediterranean. This was also the time of a powerful Chinese influence on Central America. With the collapse of the bronze trade, from American bases the now bankrupt sea peoples launched desperate attacks against the leading industrial countries of the Old World and were decisively defeated by Egypt and her allies after doing appalling damage. With the rest of the American outposts in the Old World, the Shang Dynasty now terminated in China. The Atlas people were further embarrassed by the submergence of their island headquarters in the Caribbean due to earthquake: earthquakes that had fearful effects elsewhere on our planet, including, it seems, in Greece, Ireland and Germany. The sunken islands of the Caribbean became "the underwater dwelling of the dragon king."

However, many peoples kept up some sort of an American trade subsequent to this, including Celts and many kinds of Indians, partly for the extraction of iron, while trade also continued in some measure across the Pacific. The ogham script in North America evidences a powerful Celtic influence in New England in the Iron Age. As sailors became more literate, so there are more rock engravings that are not now symbolic trademarks but are explicit writing. Deteriorating weather in the Atlantic diminishes the Atlantic trade further but we have clear evidence of Roman and Hebrew contacts with America around the beginning of our era, and records of a small Irish colony planted in America by St. Brendan in the sixth century A.D.—shades of things to come. A temporary improvement in the Atlantic weather permits the Baltic peoples to resume their American colonies so that for some 350 years, from A.D. 1005 to 1350, the Scandinavians were colonizing Vinland, the northeast of the present United States, finally severing their ties when the Atlantic weather had deteriorated once more. While the Scandinavians were colonizing, King Madoc of Wales followed their example and planted a small Welsh colony in North America. Approximately 150 years after the end of the Scandinavian colony, Christopher Columbus goes to Iceland to learn as much about the famous Norse colony as possible and was further inspired by the five survivors of a Spanish ship that had been storm-tossed into the Caribbean—men whom he probably murdered. Columbus followed their track, taking the same middle passage. When the Irish emigrated en masse to America in the nineteenth century A.D. after the potato famine and the Scottish crofters emigrated to America after the Highland clearances, they were simply following this age-old practice.

Even the name America might prove to derive not from a misspelled Amerigo but from the Breton fishermen who had been fishing for cod off the Newfoundland banks, it is said, for centuries before Columbus's trip and called the island in the middle of Ocean Armorica, a name which may itself be ultimately derived from the Sumerian, *amurru*, meaning western, and *Kur*, the Sumerian *Kur*, which stood both for mountain and for the land in the middle of Ocean, the underworld.

This summary of the main periods of Old World sea contact or colonization of the Americas from some nine thousand years prior to the days of Christopher Columbus must also be linked to the Middle East and Mediterranean trade with the Far East on the one side and the British Isles and the Baltic on the other. It restores the maritime dimension to early history with all that that implies in the fields of religion and of historical understanding; for it must be appreciated that almost all peoples had been closely interlinked a rather long time ago: there had been a planetary coherence. Northern Europeans with white hair and Celts with red hair possess an enormously important early history, as both Amerindians and Old World authorities testify. Virtually every sea-bordering country had an all-important early history, which we must now endeavor to recover for them.

Readers can perceive, therefore, that the puzzle before us this year of grace, 1995, is not how America was found but how it was lost. Columbus's Discovery of America was like Livingstone's discovery of the Victoria Falls! Columbus was something of a forerunner to our great twentieth-century heroes: Fraud, Murder, and Hype on a massive scale placed Columbus as a statue in the center of New York.

Readers are asked to assess my array of evidence, judging its truth or falsity by the correctness and coherence of the facts presented. Can any explanation other than long-distance mining and trading be possible for this weight of evidence presented here? We take the inscriptions on the rocks across the Americas that irrefutably define the peoples who carved them. Next to this we put the religious trademarks of the earlier, illiterate sailors, which are found not only in the Americas but worldwide. We take the common signs in scripts that occur both in the Old World and the New, sometimes with identical meaning. We exhibit identical architecture, identical both in form and function. We take the biological evidence, where useful plants had been cultivated half a world away from where they were native. We take the board game of *pachesi* or *patolli*, identical in the Indus Valley civilization and in Peru, for which a mathematician has calculated that the odds are overwhelmingly against their identity being fortuitous. We find the same name for bronze used in the Americas as in the Old World, the same name for the Great Goddess as in the Old World, down the length and breadth of the Americas: related names for gold between the Old World and the New. We note transference of both the cotton seed and the loom that wove it. We take the sculptured portraits of the pre-Columbian New World that are indisputably European, African, Semitic, Indian and perhaps Chinese faces in addition to the indigenous Amerindians. We take a multitude of traditions from almost every coastal part of the Old World describing their forebears voyaging to the Paradise Islands in the middle of Ocean and the stories either match the Amerindian tradition of their arrival or the physical evidence that we possess of their arrivals. There is no sign of their fleets having sunk on the way! And black men and blonds were encountered by the conquistadors still living among the Amerindians when the Spaniards first hit America: doubtless it added to the fun.

The purpose of this ancient long-distance trading becomes steadily clearer: it was chiefly for copper, gold, silver, bronze and subsequently also for a bit of iron. And to the voluptuously endowed mineral wealth of the Andes the Amazon River provided access, with both tin and gold deposits in close proximity to its banks. The Americas provided a refuge, also, for such maritime peoples as were defeated in battle and were mercilessly hounded out of their Old World port cities by their conquerors. America is restored to its proper importance, including for a time worldwide dominion, and the Amazon to being the first river of Paradise, Pishon the gusher, rich in tin and gold; and close to copper and silver in vast abundance.

This book's purpose is to assemble the details of all the to-ing and fro-ing that went on between the so-called Old World and the so-called New World, but it must not for a moment be thought that the native Amerindians or those of mixed blood did not have the preponderant say in events: Amerindian art conclusively proves this, with its own very, very specialized art styles.

It all reads so clear and so simple. However, the consequences of our recognizing these simple facts change our understanding of our own histories and our religions in a way that is devastating. The Americas suddenly become vitally important both to ancient history and to the economies of the Old World in ancient times. We explain all this by economic imperatives, not by the pretentious fatuousness of Jung's collective unconscious. And the religious vision that had been developed by the end of the Bronze Age was incommensurably greater than our own: that is the most important single sentence in this book.

This is why, perhaps, historians have taken to their foxholes and sniped at every suggestion of diffusion they could espy. André Gide wrote: "The new patriotism is to defend the frontiers of the mind."

We know that St. Brendan and his Christian crew sailed to America in the sixth century A.D. But as only a few have a desire or a gift for publicity, there is no reason why there may not have been other Christian voyagers. After all, most of us prefer to live our lives in brackets. So when we encounter so many ingredients of Christianity as part of sun worship in pre-Columbian America we must be sensitive to Eusebius's comment as to Christianity's depth in time.

Yet what we encounter in America is trinitarian sun worship, as indeed we encounter it in Egypt and Palestine four millennia before the days of Christ. Whom the Jews named Joshua, the Greeks named Jesus. Joshua was the son of Nun, meaning Ocean; while Jesus was the son of Mary, otherwise spelled Mare or Sea. Both in Greek and Mesopotamian tradition the gods were all born out of Ocean. As with Osiris, a voice from heaven announced Christ's birth. Jesus was born between a donkey and a bull, respectively symbols for Set and Osiris. His churches face east, for the rising sun; while the halo behind the heads of saints is simply the sun disk. The sacred day of the week is not Christ's day, or the Jewish Saturday, but Sunday, the day of the sun. In America the sun god is called Gisis or Gise, spelling is optional, so the names are the same. In Peru the supreme god also walks on the water. In Paraguay, a virgin gives birth to a marvelous boy who becomes the sun. The principal tenet of the New Testament, "Thou shalt love the Lord thy God and thy neighbor as thyself," is simply a quotation from the testament of Issacher, written 150 years before the birth of Christ. Christmas, celebrating the birth of Christ, December 25, is the day Europeans in pre-Christian times celebrated the birth of the sun. The English word for orientation means, simply, finding the east. In the Gaelic of Scotland to fall on your face is the same as to fall on your east, to fall on your back is the same as to fall on your west. America must become aware of its substantial part in the genesis and development of Christianity. The trident of Poseidon was turned into the three-pronged pitchfork of the devil, for money-raising purposes doubtless.

So when Eusebius, one of the greatest of Christian historians, says that the history of Christianity as a religion goes back to before the time of Moses, only the church is new, he clearly speaks the truth. The churches, however, put across something quite different to their flocks. With the earliest religions out of which Christianity had emerged, time was constant and repetitive, expressed by Christians in the sentence: "As it was in the beginning is now and ever shall be, world without end, Amen." Over thousands of years this had changed to time being directional; to God being Mind; to Creation being a continuing process operating through the sovereign; the Engenderer, developing, not just everywhere the sun circles, but throughout the entire cosmos, creating also through the human Mind, itself God. The vision and the horizons of the religion had formerly been incommensurably greater and inconceivably more demanding. While many good things may have come with the church, a process of miniaturization came with it, trivialization.

In the early days of monarchy, as we have seen, the god-king had to voluntarily sacrifice himself at the end of his fixed and regulated stint, as remained the custom of the Jukun tribe of Nigeria until recently, much as the president of the United States may only serve two terms. Before he was sacrificed, the god-king was compelled, like Christ, first to be scourged and humiliated. This custom surely lies behind Christ being called King of Israel—Israel did not use kings at that time—and being scourged before he was crucified. When the monarch, understandably perhaps, worked a point and persuaded a young man to stand in for him, the young substitute had to be dressed royally in order to enact the part. The German god Odin, like Christ, had perforce to sacrifice himself for all men, and Odin similarly received a spear thrust in his side. Now notice the wholly clear allusion that this self-sacrifice was a well-known custom in Christ's day—with a substantial history behind it—expressed in the Gospel according to St. John: "You know nothing at all, you do not understand that it is expedient for you that one man should die for the people, and that the whole nation should not perish."[10] Add to this the way colonies are conservative and that almost all Christian ritual, including the name Jesus, was apparently observed in the American colonies from centuries or millennia before the time of Christ—as part of sun worship, not as a new belief. In the Greek New Testament Jesus is also the son of Tekton, which can certainly mean carpenter but which, in Greek, can also mean Master of Every Art or Master Builder as it was translated in the American colonies through the name Toltec, so there is in fact no contradiction: Jesus was the Son of the Creator, not the son of a carpenter.

Surely, there is no way all these parallels can be fortuitous. So it is clear that we must take a wholly fresh look at ourselves. There was the wonderfully creative Chalcolithic period of the ocean-spanning matriarchal society flowering around the Black Sea, an area presently in disarray due to corrupt and murderous intellectuals, but formerly the nodal point for the whole world. Following on their heels came the seamen of the eastern Mediterranean, Pelasgians, generally called Heracles; after them the blond northern European seamen providing a ruling class almost worldwide; then the red-haired Celts take over as much in America as in Egypt, North Africa and the Middle East. Egyptian civilization was essentially African, in its day the greatest single source of wealth and power in the world. As Classical Greek is the fundamental study for European scholars, so Egypt provides the fundamental study for African scholarship. This cries out to be noticed. The Sumerians and Semites of the Middle East traded the length and breadth of the world, for a long time running a large part of the Americas, while Indians, Chinese, and Japanese were also sailing far and wide. It became a truly global village until it all crashed at the end of the Bronze Age, due to a collapse in moral standards as much as economic ruin and widespread earthquakes. As the Islamic world restored Greek civilization to modern Europe, so the Classical Greeks themselves had preserved some of the scholarship of the Fertile Crescent for us. But German peoples as well as Africans, Amerindians as well as Indians, Chinese as well as Celts, Semites as well as Sumerians, all made a dazzling contribution at this time to our present world; indeed, every sea-bordering country would seem to have made its contribution.

Creativity was the subject that would seem to have most enthralled the brighter intellects of the later Bronze Age, a subject to which we should now ourselves, many of us, urgently return.

To be able to create our future wisely we must rediscover our past: for Past, Present, and Future are three aspects of One God, Time, known to the ancients as Kronos or Chronos. Until we wake up to the importance of studying all five eras, not just snippets of the last era, we must remain needlessly inexperienced. For we are suffering from amnesia about our own past, substantially occasioned by new religions and new dynasties systematically destroying the records of their predecessors. When the conquistadors arrived the Aztecs were eliminating the records of the peoples whom they had just conquered across Mexico; the Incas were doing the same to the various tribes across their South American empire that they had but recently put together. My labors will be justified not only if I restore the maritime dimension to human history, but if it starts a new movement to learn from and venerate the incredible richness of our different pasts. In Ghana we pour a libation to our ancestors. In some sense this book is my libation.

Appendix I: List of Key Dates

B.C.

40,000 Start of arrival of Siberian Mongols in America across Bering Strait.

9000 Agriculture practiced in Jericho.

8300 End of Ice Age. Slow withdrawal of ice from northern Europe.

8000 Ceramics in Middle East.

7500 Matriarchal society around the Black Sea develops agriculture, with villages, small towns.

Domestication of wheat, barley, etc. Development of long-distance sea travel.

7000 Heracles people take agriculture around the world.

Pottery comes into use.

First use of bottle gourd, *Lagenaria siceraria*, in America. *Lagenaria siceraria* indigenous to Old World. The Francthi cave in southern Greece providing evidence of long-distance sailing, 7500–7000 B.C.

6000 Commencement of copper extraction from Isle Royale in Canada by matriarchal society and then the Heracles and the patriarchal people, using same tools as subsequently used in copper mine in Cheshire, England, and mines in Ireland. Weather in Britain warmer and calmer than it has been since: in fact at an optimum.

5500 The Creation: The patriarchal societies begin their expansion from Brittany, financed out of the copper finds on Isle Royale, Canada; a trade snatched from the women.

First megalith erected c. 5435 B.C. in Brittany, earliest known in the world.

Beginning of irrigation farming in Middle East, with substantial brick houses.

Beginning of Mesopotamian towns.

5000 First writing in Romania on Tartarian tablets.

4800 First shaft graves in Brittany.
Rectangular houses appear in Middle East, also slow wheel for pottery.

4500 Irrigation agriculture started in Egypt, Greek tradition says, by the Heracles people.
First textiles in Peru.

4000 General use of copper smelting. First cotton grown in Mexico.

3900 Eusebius's second date for Creation.

3760 The Jews incorporated into the Creation. Creation meant anthropogeny not cosmogeny.
Start of the Jewish calendar.

3600 First cotton grown in Peru, a hybrid Southeast Asian/native American cotton.

3500 Arrival of the Oannes sea people in Mesopotamia from the Red Sea, bringing the arts of civilization.
The cylinder seal comes into use in Mesopotamia, the principle of the rotary printing press. Highest artistic standards of these seals are at their beginning.

3400 First bronze art in Thailand and Troy.

3200 Proto-Elamite script.

3116 The man-made flood in Mesopotamia: exodus by Poseidon sea people to many parts of the inhabited world but especially to Central and South America.

3113 Arrival of four Bacabs, white and bearded gods, in Guatemala, bringing advanced technology with them, traveling to escape the Flood.

3100 First pharaoh of a united Egypt. Hieroglyph and Hieratic writing.
Battle of Horus and Set. Defeat of Set.

3000 Glass used in Egypt.
Bronze casting.

2800 First building of Stonehenge, focus on lunar eclipses.
The year calculated by the Egyptians by astronomical means as 365¼ days.

2400 Rise of Sargon of Akkad.

2200 Exodus of many Babylonians after collapse of tower of Babel to many countries including Nigeria and America.

2000 Destruction of the Indus Valley civilization by earthquake and of the Sumerians by "a storm."

All the geometry of Euclid available in Babylon; in fact available from Britain to China.

The last crossing by Siberian Mongols into North America.

1800 Antibiotics in Egypt.

Time of Abraham.

1725 Hyksos take over Egypt with use of cavalry.

Shang Dynasty starts in China with sudden arrival of high bronze technology and with pottery marks that are western Semitic.

1600 Use of movable type in Crete.

Use of "Sheffield steel" in Crete.

1570 Hyksos driven out of Egypt.

Toltec culture starts in Mexico.

Possible use of horses and chariots for a limited period in Mexico.

1235–1190 End of Bronze Age.

Widespread fighting: sky worshippers and matriarchal societies allied against the Titans.

Egyptians defeat attacks by Peoples of the Sea. Hittites, Mycenaeans, Phoenicians, Cretans destroyed in the attack, described by Greek tradition as attack by Typhon on Zeus and Athena: fighting literally worldwide.

Dark age in Greece with loss of writing for at least five centuries.

A Suez canal cut: Suez just Zeus, written boustrophedon.

1000 Metallurgy more advanced in Assyria than it will be again until the nineteenth century in Western Europe.

c. 900 Birth of Homer.

429 Birth of Plato.

250 Principle of steam engine shown by Heron of Alexandria: used for producing bogus miracles in temples. Similar sort of whistling bowl in use in America as in Old World.

200 Decimal point used in Guatemala.

Start of imperial house of Japan, claiming descent from Eden, worshipping a sun goddess.

Roman galley off Brazil.

A.D.

200 Camel arrives in Sahara.

500	Bantu arrive in southern Africa. Stirrups invented.
742–814	Charlemagne.
1000–1350	Vikings in America.
1320	Gunpowder in Europe.
1450	Printing in Europe.
1452–1519	Leonardo da Vinci.
1475–1564	Michelangelo.
1492	Columbus's first voyage to America.

Appendix II: Weights and Measures from Berriman's History of Metrology

A. E. Berriman, in 1953, published a book entitled *Historical Metrology* (London-Dent and Sons). He starts by quoting the tenth book of Plato's *Republic:* "Immersion in water makes the straight seem bent; but reason, thus confused by false appearances, is beautifully restored by measuring, numbering and weighing; these drive vague notions of greater or less or more or heavier right out of the minds of the surveyor, the computer, and the clerk of the scales. Surely it is the better part of thought that relies on measurement and calculation?"

After this Berriman proceeds to consider weights and measures used, which he shows are interrelated all the way from Britain to China. I include a few of his details in order to give the required mathematical support to my arguments in this book, which are based on other disciplines. We have discussed the Ashanti, Baoulé, Indus weights above; what is wanting is the details of the Peruvian weights that went with their standard beam scale made out of bone.

1 Greek stade =	600 Greek feet	
1 Roman foot =	$^{24}/_{25}$ Greek feet	
1 Roman foot =	16 Roman digits =	$^{1}/_{54}$ of a meter
100,000 Roman digits =	6000 Greek feet =	a geodetic mile
1 Roman digit =	1 Egyptian digit	
20 Egyptian digits =	1 remen	
1 Egyptian royal cubit =	the diagonal of the square on the remen	
1 royal cubit^2 =	2 remen^2	
1 Roman jugerum =	96 royal cubits^2	
96 royal cubits =	$^{5}/_{8}$ English acre =	100 English square poles if royal cubit is defined as $20^{5}/_{8}$ inches
1 pole =	16.5 English feet =	10 cubits of 19.8 inches
1 Sumerian cubit =	30 Sumerian shushi =	19.8 inches
1 Sumerian cubit =	$^{24}/_{25}$ royal cubit	
12 myriad (100,000) royal square cubits =		$^{+}/-$ 13 jugera

1 Egyptian setat = 1 myriad royal square cubits

1 Palestinian jugon = 8 myriad Palestinian square cubits = 13 jugera

3 Palestinian cubit^2 = 2 royal cubit^2

1 myriad Palestinian cubit^2 = $^{65}/_{64}$ English acre

1 English acre = 1 myriad millionth of terrestrial radius^2

Let us suppose a cubit A = $^{1}/_{10,000,000}$ × terrestrial radius

If the English acre is drawn as a circle it can be inscribed in a square representing the obsolete Scottish acre. If this is expressed as a circle, it can be drawn in a square Irish acre. The Irish acre + 14 square yards = area of a circle of 100 yards diameter, which is the size of the outer earthwork at Stonehenge. A square enclosing this circle = 100 × 100 square yards, probably the size of the Hindu Nirvatana.

Area of swimming pool at Mohenjo-daro = 100 square yards

1 Indus inch (Berriman's name) = 2 Sumerian shushi

25 Indus inches = Akbar's yard = 33 English inches

60 Akbar's yards = 1 jarib

1 jarib^2 1 biga

1 biga = 100 English poles^2 = 1 Roman jugerum

2 jugera = 1 heredium, Roman = 1 arpent, France

The French livre = $^{108}/_{100}$ English pound

A Babylonian stone weight Mina N. (Berriman) = 2 livres

2 livres = 3 librae, Roman

A supposed talent of 60 livres = 1 Greek cubic foot of water at maximum density

The biblical water weight called bath = 60 livres if cubit used is cubit A

1 tun of wine = 252 troy gallons = 36 Roman amphora = 32 Greek cubic feet

The Babylonian talent (Berriman) = 70 Euboic minae

1 Babylonian talent = 70 tower pounds = 50 livres = 54 pounds

1 Euboic talent = 54 tower pounds = mass of 60 cc of gold

1 gold mina (Berriman) = $^{9}/_{10}$ tower pound in mass

The cubic inch of gold used as a standard of mass =

24 English ounces = 25 Roman ounces

Indus weights are related to Roman ounces (Berriman, p 10)

(page 12 he uses mass for weight—for our purposes)

13 setat = 12 jugera

Berriman used the letter k for the sexagesimal number 1.296 or $^{35}/_{27}$

k^2 = 1.68 or $^{42}/_{25}$

k^5 = $^{128}/_{35}$

1 million k sexagesimal second in one circle

The admiralty sea mile is a function of the circumference of the earth—as for deepwater sailors it must be.

The geodetic mile =	length of a sexagesimal minute of arc on any great circle	
∴ The goedetic mile =	$^{1}/_{54}$ of 100,000 meters, or, by calling $^{1}/_{54}$ meter a digit,	
∴ the goedetic mile =	100,000 such digits	
The geodetic digit =	$^{1}/_{54}$ meter = $^{9}/_{16}$ k =	0.729 inches
∴ meter/inch ratio =	39.366	
The geodetic digit =	Roman digit	
16 Roman digits =	1 Roman foot =	$^{3}/_{4}$k = 0.972 English foot
1 Roman digit =	1 Egyptian digit	
1 Egyptian remen =	20 digits	
500 remens =	10 stades, both Greek and Roman	
∴ circumference of earth =	60^3 =	216,000 stades
1 Roman foot =	$^{4}/_{5}$ remen	1 Roman cubit = $^{6}/_{5}$ remen
1 Greek foot =	$^{5}/_{6}$ remen	1 Creek cubit = $^{5}/_{4}$ remen
1 Assyrian foot =	$^{8}/_{9}$ remen	1 Assyrian cubit = $^{4}/_{3}$ remen
1 royal cubit =	$\sqrt{2}$ remen	
1 Talmudist cubit =	$^{3}/_{2}$ remen	
1 Palestinian cubit =	$\sqrt{3}$ remen	

"Recognizing part of this figure sequence in lengths of the royal cubit published in inches, I thought that this cubit might have originated as the radius of a circle having its circumference rated sexagesimally in inches; and that, of course, implied special significance for the inch. This analysis supports the hypothesis that the royal cubit had geometric significance, and that one of its aspects is plausibly expressed by the rating $(50^{k}/\pi)$ = 20.6265 in."

N. B. Sarys says Berriman's calculations are correct. But he asks: are the premises to be relied on?

In particular:

(a) How misleading is the invention of cubit A and the letter k?

(b) As measures are derived from objects, to how many places of decimals were the workmen accurate and is Berriman accurate? He does not mention.

(c) Berriman derives the Greek foot from the Parthenon but does not check it against a multitude of other buildings, objects, etc.; at best it remains a Parthenon foot. And were Dorian, Ionic, Corinthian, Aeolian, etc. feet all the same?

(d) With the relative relationships of numbers to the circumference, radius, hypotenuse of the great circle of the earth, Berriman does not and cannot say how close they came to an accurate measurement and therefore whether his proportions are their proportions.

Berriman *Historical Metrology*

Berriman argues through this book that the accurate meaures are calculated on the distance of the great circle of the earth treated as a sphere, both square measures as well as linear measures.

(This type of thinking is of no consequence to a land people and would be beyond the conceptual powers today for anybody to invent who was not of high intellectual ability: in fact senior wranglers.

(Some of the best brains then from the start of the Copper Age were sea peoples: it was these European sea peoples who began the irrigation societies of the Fertile Crescent and took their system of measuring with them around the world.

(The importance of the stars and their study lay in geodetic measurement once it was known that the earth was a sphere; for astronavigation and for the correct times and dates for religious observances. Hence Ouranos, sky worshippers: the term, "the watchers"—for astronomers: Zoraster [Aristotle] 6000 B.C.: and the early gods Oceanus, Pontus, Phorkys [*ava-ak?*] and Ceto, Themis, etc.: all sea gods and goddesses.

(The intellectual power behind civilization was that of the sea peoples, hence our systems of measures, interrelated across the globe: hence, too, our words governor and government, which go back, through the Latin, to the Greek for helmsman and steering oar, *kibernon.*)

The Ecliptic (OED)

1) The great circle of the celestial sphere which is the apparent orbit of the sun. So called because eclipses can happen only when the moon is on or near this line.
2) The great circle on the terrestrial sphere which at any given moment lies in the plane of the celestial ecliptic.

Node

One of the two points at which the orbit of a planet intersects the ecliptic or in which two great circles of the celestial sphere intersect each other.

Appendix III: Professor Dart on the Prehistoric Mines of Southern Africa

"The Historical Succession of Cultural Impacts upon South Africa" by Professor Raymond A. Dart, University of the Witwatersrand, Johannesburg, South Africa (from *Nature*, March 21, 1925).

Since their discovery by the ivory trader Adam Renders (1868) the famous Zimbabwe ruins in Rhodesia have formed the rallying point around which a fierce and even bitter controversy has raged amongst anthropologists and others. The central point at issue is whether these stately relics owe their existence to an endogenous civilisation, which has since vanished, or to an external and highly advanced culture the impact of which, though powerful, was gradually and ingloriously diminished at a remote historical period. The conflict which has proceeded about this issue has been valuable in causing suggestive data of considerable magnitude to be placed upon record. It has revealed the existence of a stupendous enterprise in mining of gold, copper, tin and pigments which involved virtually the whole territory from the Belgian Congo on the north to the Central Transvaal on the south, and from the Kalahari Desert in the west to the Portuguese East African coast in the east. These undertakings were prosecuted with a finesse which never fails to command the respect of modern engineers. Rhodesia, the centre of the mining area, is found at the present time to be pervaded by excessive monumental remains in the form of monoliths, stone circles and stone buildings, together with vast areas of terraced cultivation. In many instances the buildings reveal a nicety of architecture and a regard for sanitation such as are not characteristic of Southern African natives. Moreover the ornamentation and objects of phallic worship found in numerous sites have betrayed to many the influence of a people with artistic feeling and with a complicated theology and religious ritual, who were probably Phoenician, coming from Sabaca in south-eastern Arabia.

Important as the information at our disposal may be, we are far from an exact knowledge in any of the fields involved in this evidence. There has been as yet no systematic anthropological survey of even a portion of the territory involved. In the absence of detailed and precise data, it has been easy for ill-informed argument to accumulate and the significant issues to be overwhelmed in a sea of conjecture.

It is at this juncture that the painstaking and tireless investigations of a Trappist monk of the Marianhill Monastery in Natal appear to provide decisive information such as has been so long searched for. Equipped with the knowledge of an artist skilled in reproducing and retouching mediaeval works of art in the Cathedrals of Cologne, Bonn and elsewhere, Brother Otto has been copying with infinite patience for some years the Bushman paintings found in the rock shelters of the Kei River Valley, in the eastern portion of the Cape Province. Copies of certain of these he has forwarded to me with notes for the purposes of this article.

Bro. Otto is not the first investigator who has worked in this region. Stow visited a number of the caves here; and another priest, P.M.A. Schweiger, R.M.N., published (*Anthropos*, 1913) certain of the paintings which Bro. Otto has since studied more minutely. It has remained, however, for Bro. Otto to reveal the historical significance of these works of art.

In the first place, Bro. Otto believes he is able to prove that the art of painting was indigenous to this country, and was not introduced from outside. The works which illustrate the beginnings of the art are crude drawings in charcoal, chiefly of animals and later of naked human forms revealing the well-known Bushman characteristics. Apparently, by experimenting with pigments mixed with the juices of the *Euphorbia flora*, works were executed with exceedingly fine brush technique. The pigments, of which a considerable variety was utilised, seem finally to have been rendered impervious to the passage of time and the most rigorous climatic exposures by the discovery of the value of oil as a medium, until latterly the finest works were executed indifferently in the recesses of shelters or on the weather-beaten faces of the rocks outside.

These matters are important enough, but a greater human interest attaches to the discovery that, after their technique had become perfected, the Bushmen found subjects for their artistic exploitation in voyagers who visited their coasts and inland rivers at a period so remote in time that paintings depicting them are sometimes found to be partially covered by an incrustation one sixteenth of an inch in thickness.

From twenty-eight separate sites over an area twenty miles in length along the Kei River, Bro. Otto has collected more than two hundred and fifty copies of painted groups, and has not omitted, to his knowledge, any detail depicted by these primeval artists within this circuit. From this mine of material he is in a position to provide authoritative information concerning the homeland of these visitant voyagers of early times.

A picture from a cave near the confluence of the Ngolosa and Kei Rivers in the Cape Province shows the figures of two naked Bushmen, and of two foreigners—gigantic in Bushmen's estimation, and wearing ancient Asiatic tunics and headgear. The painting depicts a scene in which a piece of clothing is about to be cast over a nude Bush maiden by a bearded man dressed in a Phrygian tunic and cap, and carrying a weapon (sword?). Opposition is expressed in the antagonistic attitude of the naked Bushman, who carries a stick in his hand, while the operations are followed closely by the other massive figure, also clad in a tunic, but wearing a cap of Babylonian design. This figure has no weapon, and is presumably that of a merchant captain. Other pictures of similar alien intruders show them to be usually bearded and armed with bows and arrows, shields and other weapons—swords and javelins—whereas the Bushman in these old pictures is generally unarmed or is armed only with a stone or a stick. It seemed possible from these facts that the Bushman learned the use of the bow from such visitors.

It is amazing to find that the clothing and headgear of the people depicted in this painting have their counterpart upon the bas-reliefs of Babylonia and the ancient painting and sculptures of the Mediterranean area.

It is perhaps equally remarkable that no inferences have been drawn from pictures similar to those in the possession of Bro. Otto. More than twenty years ago there appeared in the *Natal Railway Guide* (1903, page 216) a picture, photographed in Natal by J.E. Middlebrook, which presented the same striking juxtaposition of naked Bushmen and clothed Asiatics of the Babylonic-Phoenician period. This photograph was reproduced for the purposes of an article by D. Waterson in the *Scientific American* (1915, page 191). In the meantime, as mentioned already, Albert Schweiger had published (*Anthropos*, Bd. VIII, 1913) numerous pictures portraying the presence of clothed foreigners which were gathered in the same area as that examined by Bro. Otto. One of these paintings (Tafel XI) shows a Babylonian type of cap.

Pictures of clothed foreigners are also to be found in the classical work of Miss Helen Tongue (*Bushman Paintings*, Oxford 1909). This author has published many plates of paintings copied in the eastern part of the Orange Free State and Cape Province. Plate XV, No. 102, of her work presents a "procession of men and women dressed in cloaks." The faces of the members of the procession are painted white—a feature of no small significance when it is recalled that Bushmen generally represented themselves and other African natives by means of a black or scarlet pigment. Bro. Otto's experience agrees with that of Miss Tongue and of J.E. Middlebrook in finding the features of these alien personages depicted usually by means of a white pigment.

We have seen then, from the independent evidence of at least four people, that foreigners who were clothed in Phoenician and even Babylonian garb were well known to the aboriginal Bushmen of the Eastern Cape

Province, Orange Free State and Natal. But perhaps the most beautiful reproduction of a Phrygian cap was discovered by Father Krauspenhaar a thousand miles north of this region, in Rhodesia, at Rusapi, which is situated on the Beira-Salisbury railway some two hundred miles inland.

In a portion of the same area (Barkly East) as that examined by Miss Tongue are many pictures of clothed and capped Phoenician foreigners, some of which have been reproduced in Dr O. Moszeik's *Malereien der Buschmänner* (Berlin, 1910, pp. 61 and 66). Barkly East is situated on a tributary of the Orange River nearly two hundred miles inland, and consequently we are now in a position to state that the whole of the eastern portion of the African continent for some hundreds of miles inland, which lies between the latitudes of the Zambesi on the north and the Orange and Kei Rivers on the south, was exploited by the *old colonists*, as Bro. Otto terms them, from South-west Asia in remote ancient times. He calls them *old colonists* because he believes he is able to prove conclusively from the paintings that these very ancient voyagers not only visited these territories and carried off their denizens, particularly their women, but also intermarried with them and settled down amongst them, bringing to them novel arts and customs.

The significance of these observations for the unravelling of the Zimbabwe riddle is not far to seek, for they reveal the unsound nature of Randall MacIver's theory of mediaeval and even Bantu origin of the ruins, mines and agricultural terraces south of the Zambesi. The pictorial art of the Bushman has preserved through the lapse of centuries unassailable evidence of the impact of the ancient civilisations of the Eastern Mediterranean and Mesopotamian areas upon a Bushman South Africa which betrayed in their day no evidence of Bantu contamination.

One of the supposedly crucial pieces of evidence produced by MacIver in support of his hypothesis of a mediaeval Rhodesia, the culture of which was of purely Bantu origin, was the constantly recurring discovery of Chinese porcelain in these ruins. The presence of this ware was rather naturally attributed to Portuguese influence. But the Chinese were navigating the Indian and Pacific Oceans in luxurious fashion in the days of Marco Polo, when the Princess Kokachin went by sea from China to Persia. Nearly three centuries before Marco Polo's time, Alberuzi (about A.D. 1030) records that "The reason why in particular Somanath (in China) has become so famous is that it is a harbour for sea-faring people and a station for those who went to and fro between Sufâla in the country of the Zinj and China. E.C. Sachau, (1910, vol. 2, page 104). Indeed, the timid writer of the Periplus found his way south along the African coast so far as Rhapta in the first century of our era, and relates of Arab captains and agents at that period "who are familiar with the natives and intermarry with them, and who know the whole coast." There is every reason for believing that in the early centuries of the Christian era, and perhaps prior thereto, when Chinese arms were pushing far westward upon land, Chinese shipping was contesting with Indian and Arabian vessels the trade of the East African coast, which had already fallen from the hands of Egypt and Mesopotamia and those who brought and carried for these countries.

Miss Helen Tongue states of her Plate XVIII that "the whole appearance of this painting is ancient." The present interest lies in the fact that it portrays a man of light brown complexion, adorned with two necklaces, arrayed in sumptuous apparel, and carrying on his head a peaked Chinese hat. Bro. Otto has also discovered a number of pictures showing this unexpected type of headpiece. In the light of all these facts, it must be realised that MacIver's hastily drawn conclusions are utterly inadequate to explain ethnological problems of the southern end of this continent.

That Rhodesia was brought into direct contact with Arabian and Indian agricultural products is shown by the fact that vines, lemons, figs, and cotton, though not indigenous to South-east Africa, are found on the terraced hills of Inyanga in Rhodesia. "Livingstone, Chapman, Burton, Kirk, and all authorities on Zambesia down to the present day have called attention to the great number of plants, fruits and trees of Indian habitat to be found together on the Rhodesian goldmines area. These are, of course, not indigenous to this country: the now wild *Tonge manga*, a cotton of Indian origin, not the *Tonge cadja*, which is indigenous; also a bean, *Cajanus Indicus*, known in India as the Dhal Plant; the Indian fig, grown wild; and a tree, *Matuvi*, found elsewhere only in India. There is also the *Mahobo-hobo*, which has its habitat only in Southern India and Malaya. In Rhodesia this tree is only found on the area of the prehistoric rock mines, but the vast extent of the country now covered by its forests demonstrates that it arrived in some exceedingly remote time" (*Guide to Rhodesia*, 1924).

Whether Chinese pottery reached Rhodesia by a European or, as is more likely, by a more direct route past India and Arabia, the discovery of it affords us little light upon what was taking place in Southern Africa long before European and even Indian and Chinese contact was possible; and it is precisely here that the evidence accumulated by Bro. Otto is of premier significance, seeing that it demonstrated an extremely ancient cultural impact upon the aboriginal Bushman.

These remarkable pictures also bring into their proper perspective a series of discoveries of a different but allied nature which have been inadequately appreciated hitherto.

About fifty years ago, Mr Thomas Cook, who is still living in Durban, discovered twenty-eight coins in a calabash at a depth of about six feet, on the site of an African hut, near the beach at Fort Grosvenor in Eastern Pondoland. Many of these were so worn that their inscriptions were illegible—illustrating that they had been much handled—but some, which were legible, were described by Mr G.F. Hill, of the British Museum, in the *Classical Review* (of 1897 or 1898). The oldest three coins were of the period of Ptolemy I, II and IV respectively (i.e. 304–204 B.C.) and the other coins examined were Roman coins issued between the dates A.D. 296 and 313, five of them being struck at Alexandria, two at Antioch and one at Cyzicus.

This discovery is not the only one of its kind, for when the monks were building their water reservoir at Marianhill, twenty-six miles from Durban, they found, at a depth of eighteen inches in a recent stratum of sand and humus on the side of a hill, a Hebraic coin of the reign of Simon Maccabaeus (143–136 B.C.) with the inscription "fourth year of the deliverance of Sion" (*Anthropos* Bd. V. 1909, p. 168).

Now it is conceivable that stray Egyptian, Maccabaean, Syrian and other coins might percolate to extreme Southern Africa without any intense cultural movement being afoot; but coins generally signify commerce, and the most cursory examination of any map of Africa south of the Zambesi will show that Palestine and Arabia—those homes of commerce—have left behind very clear evidence of a lengthy contact with this part of the globe. It is by no accident such as might conceivably determine the movement of coins, nor by any philo-Semitic proclivities of the Portuguese, that we find in Portuguese East Africa and the countries adjacent thereto place-names such as Antiocha, Jacobecua, Jacoja, Jacota, Gadsane, Gadzema, Jofane, Gaza, Gizha, Sinoia, Jobo and the like. The two rivers Sabi and Sabie, as well as Lake Sibai, together with Sabia, Sabetsi, Sebaba, Sebakwe, Shebekwe, Shibuto, Shibabara, Chabane, Chiba, Chibi, Chibambala, Chibababa, and so on, owe their names to a people fascinated by the central root Saba, Seba, or Sheba, just as the Dutch have left in South Africa their "fonteins" and "burgs," the English their "Londons" and "Cambridges," and the Scotch their "Dundees" and "Glencoes." So, too, Masibi, Mazibi, Mazibila, Masipe, Mripa, Mriba, and Mareba have an intimate relation with Marib, in the same way as Mocuba, Mokuba, Mkubi, Namoko, Makiki, Muchacha, Machiche, and Machacane recall the Arabian Mocha.

In brief, the themes for the variations provided by hundreds of place-names south of the Zambesi lie in the Asiatic continent, and still await the investigations of specialists in this field. The evidence to be culled from this study will be especially valuable in "dating" and "placing" the different cultural intrusions. Many of the Arabian names are undoubtedly pre-Koranic. In addition to names from Western Asia, there are Indian types such as Ricatla, Mandle, and Kande, and variants of the old name of Japan (Zipangu), namely, Chipanga and Chipinga. I have entered into this matter of place-names in some detail because, rich as the field obviously is, I am not aware of any serious study of this sort made hitherto upon this locality.

We have considered already evidence which indicates that, prior to the coming of the European, not only mediaeval Arabian, but also Indian, Chinese, pre-Koranic Arabian (Himyaritic-Sabaean), Palestinian, Phrygian and even Babylonian influences have played a part in moulding the destinies of the primitive peoples of Southern Africa. There are not lacking evidences that Egypt, too, was in intimate contact with this remote region.

It will be recalled that Dr Karl Peters discovered (Keane's *Gold of Ophir*) in Rhodesia a figurine of an Egyptian courtier—of the period of Thothmes III (Dynasty XVIII)—holding in his hands the scourge of a slave-driver. Further, most authorities concur in believing that the steatopygous Queen of Punt and her daughter portrayed in the spoils of the voyage of the sister of Thothmes III, Queen Hatshepsu's (1501–1479 B.C.) servants to the divine South-land, was a Bushwoman or closely related to one. Thus Sir Flinders Petrie (*History of Egypt*, Vol. 2, 1899) says, "The strange fatness of the queen has been much speculated upon; whether it was a disease such as elephantitis, or was natural fat, has been debated; but as her daughter shows much the same tendency of curve in the back, it is probably the effect of extreme fat, which was considered a beauty, as in South Africa at present." Rawlinson (*Ancient Egypt*, 1893) is still more emphatic when he states, "She belonged, more probably, to one of the dwarfish tribes of which Africa has so many, as Dakos, Bosjesman, and others."

The Land of Punt is generally supposed to have been south-east Arabia or some point along the southern Somali coast: the spices, resins and incense products being in favour of the former; the giraffes, ivory, cynocephalous apes and the like speaking for the latter. Frobenius (*Das Unbekannte Afrika* 1923) has shown on a map the distribution of houses on piles such as were seen by these voyagers to Punt. None such are to be found in Arabia or Somaliland, but they are found on the big rivers of Africa southward from Somaliland. Resins and snuffs have the highest of values amongst the Bush people even in modern times. I do not say that the data are conclusive to prove that God's land, Punt, lay in Africa south of the Zambesi, but the facts are highly suggestive. The products of the country—people, animals, gold, resins, pigments, and the like—were such as this country certainly was producing in plenty at that remote period. At the same time it is a well recognised fact that for centuries, perhaps millennia, prior to Queen Hatshepsu, ships had been navigating the Red Sea, the open ocean and the Persian Gulf between Egypt and Mesopotamia. It is not reasonable then to imagine that the Egyptian queen would render herself a laughing-stock before the civilised world by celebrating the building and decoration of a new temple as extravagant marvels the products of places near by like the coasts of Arabia and Ethiopia. To fit out an expedition for this remote South-land of Punt was always an epochal event, and was carried out only by the greater Pharaohs in times of peace and prosperity and was even then worthy of record. Such expeditions are recounted in the times of Sankh-ka-ra (Dynasty XI) under the nobleman Hannu, of Hatshepsut, of Thothmes III—the Napoleon of Egyptian history—and of Horemheb (all three of Dynasty XVIII), and of Rameses III (Dynasty XX). It is absurd to believe that these proud names in Egyptian history would reckon trips to little beyond the mouth of the Red Sea were worthy of mention when the equipment of voyages three years in duration was commonplace in the chronicles of the pigmy court of Solomon. Even in the humdrum days of Herodotus, the circumnavigation of Africa had not been entirely forgotten, for he relates how King Necho's Phoenician servants had accomplished this hardy feat. His Honour the Administrator of the Transvaal (Prof. Jan H. Hofmeyr) has informed me that the remains of what was presumably an ancient galley were discovered during the laying out of Maitland Cemetery on the Woltemade flats near Cape Town in the 'nineties. At the time the contact of one end of Africa with the other by navigation was undreamt of, and the significance of finding a boat, one hundred and eighty feet in length, buried six feet underground at a distance of three miles from the present coastline, was lost on the workmen, who utilised it for firewood. The event at least indicates that the followers of Prince Henry were not the first to anchor in Table Bay.

The continuity of the Atlantic and Indian Oceans around the southern extremity of Africa was customarily portrayed by the ancient cartographers of Greece (e.g. Globe of Crates), of Arabia (e.g. Idrisi), and of Europe from Venice to Anglo-Saxon England (vide *Encycl. Britt.*). It is difficult to understand how such conceptions could have grown up and persisted in this fashion unless the experiences of ancient voyagers had provided some foundation for them. It is likely that the voyage of Necho's servants was but a repetition of many similar ventures in the storied past. In any case the tale provided by Herodotus is more easily believed when we know that Bushmen from the Zambesi to the south-eastern corner of the continent on the shore coast and for hundreds of miles inland have recorded in portrait the arrivals and the activities of not merely one but untold numbers of invaders at successive historical epochs.

It is not in the contact of any one people but in the endless procession of emissaries from every great navigating power in the Indian Ocean down this coast that one finds an explanation for the prodigious extent of the early mining industry in Southern Africa. Moreover, it is only in terms of this procession that the physical, anthropological, and ethnological problems of this country can be adequately understood. It is impossible here to do more than direct attention to certain aspects of these intricate but highly fascinating studies. It has already been stated that no exhaustive anthropological survey of the region concerned has been made; but if the urgent necessity for such a survey of the paintings, ruins, terraces and mines, and the nature and richness of its prospective fruits, are indicated, these meagre notes will have been justified.

[Professor Dart gave this paper to me himself.]

Notes to Text

Epigraph

1. London: Longman, 1970. p. 2.
2. Quoted in Geoffrey Ashe, *The Quest for America*, London: Pall Mall Press, 1971, p. 12.
3. Leiden: E. J. Brill, 1964. Vol. VIII, p. 5.

Introduction

1. Roy W. Drier and Octave du Temple. *Prehistoric Copper Mining in the Lake Superior Region*, Calumet, Michigan: published privately, 1961, *passim.*
2. Bowman, ed., *Science and the Past*, London: British Museum, 1991, p. 59.

Chapter 1: Economics Underlies History

1. *Odyssey*, Loeb Classical Library, 1919, VII, 81.
2. *Iliad*, Loeb Classical Library, 1919, II, 455–58.
3. 2 Chronicles 4: 2, 4, 5; 1 Kings 7: 15, 23, 25, 26.
4. *Against Apion*, Loeb Classical Library, 1961, I, 70–80.
5. Diodorus Siculus, *History of the World*, London: Giles Calvert, 1653, Book IV, Chapter 2.
6. *Cambridge Ancient History*, 1975, Vol. II, Part 2, p. 214.
7. R. F. Tylecote, *The History of Metallurgy*, London: Institute of Metals, 1992, pp. 1–31.
8. Michael O'Kelly, *Early Ireland*, Cambridge University Press, 1989, p. 152.
9. Forbes, *Studies in Ancient Technology*, Vol. VIII, p. 5.
10. Oxford: Clarendon, 1965, Vol. I, p. 590.
11. *Greek Myths*, London: Cassell, 1965, p. 32.
12. Joseph Alsop, *From the Silent Earth: The Greek Bronze Age*, London: Secker & Warburg, 1964, p. 86.
13. *Copper and Tin*, Hamden, Conn.: Archon, 1973, *passim.*
14. Tylecote, *History of Metallurgy*, p. 5.
15. Singer et al., *History of Technology*, p. 576.
16. Forbes, *Studies in Ancient Technology*, Vol. VII, p. 81.
17. Robert Graves and R. Patai, *Hebrew Myths: The Book of Genesis*, London: Cassell, 1964, p. 79.
18. *Prehistoric Copper Mining in the Lake Superior Region.*
19. Diodorus Siculus, *Complete Works*, Loeb Classical Library, V, 23, 1.
20. Hesiod, *The Homeric Hymns and Homerica*, Loeb Classical Library, 1914, p. xx.
21. *History of the World*, p. 120.

Chapter 2: Tracks on the World Ocean

1. Foreword to James Bailey, *The God-Kings and the Titans*, London: Hodder & Stoughton, 1973, p. 15.
2. F. Folsom and M. E. Folsom, *America's Ancient Treasures*, Albuquerque: University of New Mexico Press, 1983, p. 238.
3. *Histories*, Everyman Library, 1948, Vol. I, p. 194.
4. *Aku-Aku*, London: George Allen & Unwin, 1958, p. 181.
5. T. D. Kendrick, *A History of the Vikings*, London: Methuen, 1930, pp. 370–87.
6. *The Voyaging Stars*, Sydney: Collins, 1978, *passim.*
7. "The Orientation of Mayan Ceremonial Centers," *Annals of the Association of American Geographers*, Vol. 59, No. 5, September 1969.
8. Emile Massoulard, *Préhistoire et Protohistoire d'Égypte*, Paris: Institut D'Ethnologie, 1949, p. 433.
9. *Megalithic Sites in Britain*, Oxford: Clarendon, 1967, Ch. 9 and *passim.* p. 3.
10. W. G. Lambert and A. R. Millard, *Atra-hasis*, Oxford: Clarendon, 1970, p. 12.
11. Glyn Daniel, *The Megalith Builders of Western Europe*, Harmondsworth: Pelican, 1963, p. 105.
12. XIV, 323.
13. *Lives*, Loeb Classical Library, VIII, 8, pp. 20–23.
14. *Moralia*, Loeb Classical Library, 1965–68, XII, p. 185.
15. Plato, *Timaeus*, 26E.
16. *History of the World*, p. 24.

Chapter 3: The Huge Islands in the Middle of Ocean

1. Ruth Whitehouse, ed., *Dictionary of Archaeology*, London: Macmillan, 1983, p. 215.

2. Jacques Soustelle, *The Olmecs*, Norman: University of Oklahoma Press, 1985, p. 147.
3. Carleton Beals, *Nomads and Empire Builders*, Philadelphia: Chilton, 1961, p. 21.
4. A good description of it is given in Verrill and Verrill, *America's Ancient Civilizations*, New York: Putnam, 1953, pp. 199–200.
5. *America's Ancient Civilizations*, p. 297.
6. Trans., Benjamin Jowett, Oxford University Press, p. 442.
7. Ibid., *Critias*, p. 529.
8. Quoted in Felix Jacoby, *Die Fragmente der Griechischen Historiker*, Leiden: E. J. Brill, 1929–30, Vol. II: "A land with cities and where gold and silver are so common that they have less value than iron."
9. *Works*, Vol. V, pp. 19–20.
10. Constance Irwin, *Fair Gods and Stone Faces*, New York: St. Martin's, 1963, p. 219.
11. XII, 941.
12. Irwin, *Fair Gods and Stone Faces*, pp. 11–12.
13. Ibid., pp. 37–38.
14. Thor Heyerdahl, *American Indians in the Pacific*, London: George Allen & Unwin, 1952, p. 281.
15. Lambert and Millard, *Atra-hasis*, p. 133 and *passim.*
16. Victor von Hagen, *The Desert Kingdoms of Peru*, London: Weidenfeld & Nicolson, 1964, p. 79.
17. Hesiod, *Homeric Hymns*. xxxvii.

Chapter 4: The Marks of the Voyagers

1. *Orientalia*, Vol. 37 (1968), Fasc. 1. I discussed these subjects with him personally, in New York.
2. Ibid., p. 212.
3. Marcel Homet, *Sons of the Sun*, London: Neville Spearman, 1963, *passim.*
4. London: Hutchinson, 1963, pp. 36–37.
5. *Sons of the Sun*, pp. 172–73.
6. Verrill and Verrill, *America's Ancient Civilizations*, p. 202.
7. Leo Deuel, *Conquistadors Without Swords*, New York: St. Martin's, 1967, p. 191. Deuel cites the two earliest monumental religious buildings in the Americas at Tlapacoyan and Cuicuilco, without noticing *cui* and *coya* are names for the earth mother.
8. *Peru Before the Incas*, Englewood, N.J.: Prentice Hall, 1967, p. 78.
9. *Studies in Ancient Technology*, Vol. IX, p. 102.
10. Ibid., Vol. VIII, p. 11.
11. George F. Carter, *Man and the Land*, New York: Holt, Rinehart & Winston, 1964, p. 109.
12. Honoré, *In Quest of the White God*, p. 125.
13. Technically, the correction means using a sun declination of +0.5 degrees, the value found by Thom for megalithic calendar clocks. See Elizabeth Chesley Baity, "Mesoamerican Archeoastronomy So Far," in *Archeoastronomy in Pre-Columbian America*, edited by Anthony Aveni, Austin: University of Texas, 1977.
14. *The Exact Sciences in Antiquity*, New York: Harper, 1962, p. 1.
15. Honoré, *In Quest of the White God*, p. 136.
16. Irwin, *Fair Gods and Stone Faces*, pp. 249–50.
17. Ibid., p. 95.
18. Ibid., p. 19.
19. George F. Carter, *Chinese Contacts with America*, College Station: Texas A & M University, p. 15. The author points out that the earliest cultivated grain in China, *setaria*, is also the earliest cultivated grain in Mexico.
20. George F. Carter, *Plants Across the Pacific, Memoirs of the Society for American Archaeology*, N. 9, edited by Jesse D. Jennings, p. 62. I am also indebted to this very interesting and well-argued article for information that follows on cotton, the coconut and the sweet potato.
21. M. D. W. Jeffreys, "Pre-Columbian Negroes in America," *Scientia*, July–August, 1953.
22. Quoted in J. T. Medina, *The Discovery of the Amazon*, New York: American Geographical Society, 1934, p. 214.
23. Quoted in Jeffreys, "*Pre-Columbian Negroes in America.*" Quotations from Gormara and Quatrefages are also from this article.
24. *Sons of the Sun*, pp. 114, 119.
25. Irwin, *Fair Gods and Stone Faces*, pp. 66–71.
26. Verrill and Verrill, *America's Ancient Civilizations*, pp. 105–6.
27. *Fair Gods and Stone Faces*, p. 171.
28. Thomas Joyce, *Central American and West Indian Archaeology*, London: Philip Warner, 1916, p. 198.
29. Ibid., p. 199.
30. Ibid., p. 170.
31. New York: Demeter Press, 1977, *passim.*
32. Carolyne Larrington, *The Feminist Companion to Mythology*, London: Pandora, 1992, p. 342.
34. Bennet Woodcroft, trans., *The Pneumatics of Hero of Alexandria*, London: Taylor Walton & Maberly, 1851, p. 29.

Chapter 5: Birdmen in Africa

1. *Histories*, trans., George Rawlinson, London: Dent, 1910, p. 264.
2. *Peoples, Seas and Ships*, London: Phoenix House, 1966, p. 152. The author also compares the conical stone towers of Zimbabwe with those of Peru.
3. Ibid., p. 16.
4. *Histories*, Vol. V, p. 25.

5. This is the date Professor Dart gave me for the extraction of antimony, *kohl*, for eye shadow. But he obtained his extraordinary date of 40,000 B.C. for the extraction of hematite, iron oxide, from the Ngwenya mine in Swaziland, also for cosmetic purposes.
6. "Ancient Mining of Southern Africa," *South African Geographical Journal*, 7, 1924.
7. K. N. Sastri, *New Light on the Indus Civilisation*, Delhi: Atma Ram, 1957, p. 2.
8. Cicero, *De Natura Deorum*, London: Methuen, xxxvii, 1896, p. 123.
9. J. Gwyn Griffiths, *The Conflict of Horus and Seth*, Liverpool University Press, 1960, pp. 42, 45.
10. 2 Samuel, 21:9.
11. Homer, *Iliad*, XIV, 302.
12. An excellent study has been made of them by Philip Allison of the Department of Antiquities in Lagos, called *Cross River Monoliths*, Lagos: Government Printer, 1968.

Chapter 6: Lands to the East

1. *Mohenjo-Daro, and the Indus Civilisation*, London: Probsthain, 1931, Vol. I, pp. 5, 6, 8.
2. This legend is related by Berossus, the official historian to Antiochus.
3. *New Light on the Indus Civilisation*, pp. 31–35.
4. See *Science*, May 3, 1968.
5. D. P. Agrawal and D. K. Chakrabarti, *Essays in Indian Protohistory*, Delhi: B. R. Publishing, 1979, p. 168. Also the Ionian historian Megasthenes, fl. 300 B.C.
6. Gerald S. Hawkins, *Stonehenge Decoded*, London: Fontana, 1972, p. 50.
7. *New Scientist*, December 21–28, 1991.
8. *Studies in Ancient Technology*, Vol. XI, p. 131.
9. *Penguin Dictionary of Archaeology*, 1972.
10. Reginald Farrer, *In Old Ceylon*, London: Edward Arnold, 1908, p. 18.
11. *An Introduction to the Study of Southwestern Archaeology*, New Haven: Yale University Press, 1962, pp. 477–78.
12. *In Quest of the White God*, p. 168.
13. *America's Ancient Civilizations*, p. 16.
14. Robert Marx, "Who Really Discovered the New World?" *The Explorers Journal*, Winter 1991, p. 112.
15. D. Diringer, *The Alphabet*, London: Hutchinson, 1968, Vol. I, p. 110.
16. Marx, "Who Really Discovered the New World?" *The Explorers Journal*, p. 112.
17. The Phoenician god of the underworld was called Horon (*Penguin Dictionary of Religions*, 1984, p. 253).
18. Gilgamesh, King of Uruk, 2600 B.C., in the Gilgamesh Epic, describes this garden existing across an immense stretch of ocean: "There was the garden of the gods; all round him stood bushes bearing gems. Seeing it he went down at once, for there was fruit of carnelian with the vine hanging from it, beautiful to look at; lapis lazuli leaves hung thick with fruit, sweet to see. For thorns and thistles there were haematite and rare stones, agate, and pearls from out of the sea" Nancy Sandars, trans., Harmondsworth: Penguin, 1960, p. 97.
19. *Encyclopaedia of Religion and Ethics*, Edinburgh: T. and T. Clark, 1971, pp. 700–701.
20. *Journal of Egyptian Archaeology*, London: Egypt Exploration Society, 1939, Vol. 25, p. 184.
21. Ibid., p. 185.
22. Ibid., p. 187.
23. Henriette Mertz, *Pale Ink*, Chicago: published privately, 1953, p. 20.

Chapter 7: Negligible Written Sources for the History of Ancient Africa

1. Lucie Lamy, *Egyptian Mysteries*, London: Thames & Hudson, 1981, p. 77.

Chapter 8: Scientific or Magical Societies

1. Lamy, *Egyptian Mysteries*, p. 14.

Chapter 9: Divine Kingship Worldwide

1. Diodorus Siculus, *Works, III*, p. 56.
2. *Kingship and the Gods*, Chicago University Press, 1948, pp. 84–85.
3. S. H. Hooke, *Babylonian and Assyrian Religion*, Oxford: Blackwell, 1962, p. 60.
4. For various versions of the story: Graves and Patai, *Hebrew Myths*, London: Cassell, 1964, p. 79. Also Hastings, *Encyclopoedia of Religion and Ethics*, II, pp. 700, 701, for the Japanese version of the herb of immortality to be found in Horaisan, reached by a ten-year sail eastward from Japan, an island Paradise carrying all the usual attributes bestowed on ancient America. Chinese tradition of the island in the far reaches of the Pacific is equally associated with perpetual life, as in *Ireland: Tir na Og, land of Eternal Youth.* Michael Astour, in *Hellenosemitica*. Leiden: Brill, 1965. p. 256, tells the identical story around King Minea of Crete and Polyeides.
5. III, 3.
6. Gilgamesh, Tablet XI.
7. R. F. Willetts, *Cretan Cults*, London: Routledge & Kegan Paul, 1962, p. 61.
8. Jan Gonda, *Ancient Indian Kingship from the Religious Point of View*, Leiden: E. J. Brill, 1969, pp. 1, 2, 6, 7, 46, 133.

Chapter 10: The Sea Peoples of the Copper and Bronze Ages

1. *Archaeoastronomy in Pre-Columbian America*, p. 169.
2. Ibid., p. 24. Also notice that the trickster coyotl, the divine cosmic trickster, was associated with the Pleiades.
3. H. Limet, *Toponymie Antique*, Leiden: E. J. Brill, 1975, p. 85.
4. David Anthony, Dmitri Telegin, Dorcas Brown, *Scientific American*, December 1991.

Chapter 11: The Mermaid, a Tradition Across the Atlantic Trade Routes

1. Eusebius, *Chronicorum*, Zurich: Weidmann, 1965, Liber I, pp. 9–13.
2. Hornell, *British Coracles and Irish Curraghs*, London: Quaritch, 1938, p. 76.

Chapter 12: Why the Sea Trade Ended, Bringing Isolation and Backwardness to America and West Africa

1. Homer, *Odyssey*, XIV, 244–72.
2. Dr. Schoch of Munich.

Chapter 13: West African Customs That Are Similar to Those of the Ancient Fertile Crescent

1. William H. Prescott, *The Conquest of Mexico*, London: George Routledge & Sons, n.d., p. 20.
2. Rosalind Hackett, *Religion in Calabar*, Berlin: Mouton de Gruyter, 1989.
3. Loeb Classical Library, LXXIX, 8–10.

Chapter 14: The Philosophy of the Dogon Tribe of Mali; Its Connection with the Fertile Crescent

1. Compare the Dogon name Nummo with the Sumerian and Babylonian Nammu, goddess of the watery deeps. She engendered the other early Mesopotamian gods and in one poem is called the mother of all mortal life (Michael Jordan, *Encyclopaedia of Gods*, London: Kyle Cathie, 1992).
2. M. Griaule, and G. Dieterlen, *Conversations with Ogotemelli*, Oxford University Press, 1965, pp. 84–85.
3. Cf. Plato, *Protagoras* 321.
4. Eric Guerrier, *La Cosmogonie Dogon*, Paris: Robert Laffont, 1975, *passim;* Françoise Michel-Jones, *Retour au Dogon*, Paris: Le Sycomore, 1948, *passim;* Griaule and Dieterlen, *Conversations with Ogotemelli, passim.*
5. Krickeberg et al., *Pre-Columbian American Religions*, London: Weidenfeld & Nicolson, 1968, pp. 306, 309.

Chapter 15: Biblical Creation and the Flood

1. *Works*, III, 56.
2. S. N. Kramer, *Sumerian Mythology*, New York: Harper & Row, 1961, p. 69.
3. The self-styled gods, the royal families, address the plebs, man, as black-headed people. See Lambert and Millard, *Atra-hasis*, p. 141, and van Dijk, *LUGAL UD ME-LAM-bi NIR-GAL*, Leiden: E. J. Brill, 1983, p. 31.
4. Van Dijk, *LUGAL UD*, p. 31.
5. Josephus, *Antiquities of the Jews*, I, 121, 122.
6. See Bailey, *God-Kings and Titans, passim.*
7. *Antiquities of the Jews*, I, 109.
8. Josephus, *Against Apion*, Loeb, 1961, p. 55.
9. De la Vega, *Royal Commentaries of the Incas*, London: University of Texas Press, 1966, Part I, pp. 561–62.

Chapter 16: The Mesopotamian Tradition About Atlas, Alias Seth & Set

1. *Jewish Antiquities*, I, 106.

Chapter 17: Of West Africa and America

1. *Aegyptiaca*, Manetho, Loeb Classical Library, 1948, p. 101.
2. *Florentine Codex*, Book 7, p. 2.
3. Ibid., p. 36.
4. *Oxford Classical Dictionary:* Poseidon.
5. D. J. Wölfel, *Monumenta Linguae Canariae*, Graz: Akademische Druck, Austria, 1965.

Chapter 18: The Sculptor and the Unwritten Tradition

1. Alain Ballabriga, *Le Soleil et le Tartare*, Paris: l'Ecole des Hautes Etudes, 1986, p. 46.

Chapter 19: The Ashanti Gold Weights; Their Connection With the Indus Valley

1. For Sir John Marshall's widespread coverage of the relationship of Mesopotamia and the Indus Valley, see his *Mohenjo-daro and The Indus Civilisation*, London: Probstain, 1931, *passim.*
2. V. N. Misra and Peter Bellwood, eds., *Recent Advances in Indo-Pacific History*, Leiden: E. J. Brill, 1985, p. 286.

Chapter 20: The Biological Evidence for this Early Contact

1. *Hindu States of Sumeria*, Calcutta: K. L. Mukhapadhyay, 1962, p. 27.
2. *American Discovery*, Seattle: Misty Isles Press, 1992, p. 358.

Chapter 21: The Scandal of the Classical Greeks

1. Bertrand Russell described this attitude as follows: "One . . . views the Greeks with almost superstitious reverence, as the inventors of all that is best, and as men of superhuman genius whom the moderns cannot hope to equal."
2. *Life of Plutarch*, London: J. Tonson, 1727, p. 10.
3. *Against Apion*, I, p. 2.
4. *Works*, I, p. 97.
5. *Chronicorum*, pp. 291a, 460a, 461b, 470d-471d.
6. Introduction.
7. *Chronicorum*, p. 472b.
8. *Les Stamates*, trans. P. Voulet, Paris: Edition du Cerf, 1981, I, p. 16.
9. Forbes (Vol. VII, p. 84) gives the following examples among others:

AKKADIAN	GREEK	ENGLISH
hurasu	chrysos	gold
as.mur	smyris	emery
burallu	beryllos	beryl
musu	misy	copper pyrites
sandu	sandyx	red (stone)
pilu, arutu	poros	calcite
gassu	gypsos	gypsum

10. Robert J. Gillings, in his book *Mathematics in the Time of the Pharoahs*, comments as follows on the *Rhind Mathematical Papyrus*, an Egyptian school exercise of around 1900 B.C.: "There we find Egyptian trainee mathematicians dealing with fractions, problems of equitable distribution and accurate measurement, the areas of rectangles, triangles and circles, the volume of a cylinder, geometric and arithmetic progression, the volume of a truncated pyramid, the area of a semi-cylinder and of a hemisphere, weights and measures, squares and square roots." (MIT Press, Cambridge, Massachusetts, p. 16)
11. *Description of Greece*, Loeb Classical Library, 1966, I, 33.

Chapter 22: The Source of the Bronze for the Bronze Age

1. *Goods, Prices and the Organisation of Trade in Ugarit*, Wiesbaden: Dr. Ludwig Reichert Verlag, 1978, p. iii.
2. Copper and Tin.
3. Ibid., pp. 313–315.
4. Ibid., p. 338.
5. Seattle: Misty Isles Press, 1992.

Chapter 24: The First Great Periods of International Trade

1. Eusebius, *Ecclesiastical History*, Loeb Classical Library, 1965, I, pp. xviii, 11.

Chapter 25: Earth Mother: Sky Father

1. S. N. Kramer and J. Maier, *Myths of Enki*, Oxford University Press, 1989, p. 203.
2. *Royal Commentaries of the Incas*, p. 70.
3. *Dialogues*, Jowett, trans., Vol. III, p. 541.
4. *Ecclesiastical History*, pp. xv, xviii, xxxiv, 11.
5. Irene Nicholson, *Mexican and Central American Mythology*, London: Paul Hamlyn, 1969.
6. *Odyssey*, VI, 42–45.
7. Ibid., I, 52.

Chapter 26: God Kings and Titans

1. See, for instance, the *Larousse Encyclopaedia of Mythology*.
2. Kramer and Maier, *Myths of Enki*, 1989 p. 87; also Lambert and Millard, *Atra-hasis*, p. 141.
3. Françoise Bruschweiler, *Inanna*, Leuven: Edition Peeters, 1987, p. 12, "les têtes noires."
4. *Eusebi Chronicorum*, apud Weidmannus, liber prior, pp. 47, 126, 177, 178.
5. Krickeberg et al., *Pre-Columbian American Religions*, p. 220.
6. The Mesopotamian record of this earlier Yalta Conference agrees with the Greek, the world being divided between An, Enlil, Ereshkigal. Bruschweiler, *Inanna*, p. 42; also Lambert and Millard, *Atra-hasis*, pp. 8, 43.
7. Lionel Carson, *The Ancient Mariners*, Princeton University Press, 1991, p. 3.
8. *Works*, 1, 24, 3.
9. Jordan, *Encyclopaedia of Gods*, p. 36.
10. Lambert and Millard, *Atra-hasis*, Clarendon Press, Oxford, 1970 *passim*.
11. *Odyssey*, I, 5.
12. Loeb Classical Library, 1967–72, VII, 203.
13. *Natural History*, III, 31, and VII, 203.
14. *Description of Greece*, I, 33.
15. Kwang-Chih Chang, *Shang Civilization*, New Haven: Yale University Press, 1980, p. 244.
16. *Theogony*, 840–52.
17. *Cambridge Ancient History*, Vol. III, pp. 166–77, 275–92.
18. *Dialogues*, Jowett, trans., Vol. III, p. 542.
19. Ibid., p. 446.
20. Thomas Joyce, *Central American and West Indian Archaeology*, p. 167. Also note the same opinion from

Eusebius, *Chronicorum*, apud Weidmannus, 1967, Vol. I, pp. 18–19.
21. *Conquest of Peru*, London: Richard Bentley, 1847, pp. 102–103.
22. Ibid., p. 8.
23. Ibid., pp. 95–96.
24. Ibid., p. 99.
25. Ibid., p. 100.
26. Ibid., p. 101.
27. Prescott, *Conquest of Mexico*, p. 215.
28. Ibid., pp. 463, 20.
29. Ibid., p. 464.
30. Ibid., p. 465.
31. Ibid., p. 21.
32. Ibid., p. 23.
33. *Ecclesiastical History*, p. xviii.
34. 2:15.
35. John II: 49–50.

Chapter 27: The End of Atlantis

1. It was this reconstruction that was used by Pierre Honoré in his comparison of the Mexican and Cretan scripts (see Plate 33). De Landa's notebooks were found in a library in Europe in the nineteenth century.
2. December 2, 1984.
3. Neugebauer, *The Exact Sciences in Antiquity*, pp. 18–19.
4. The phrase is the subtitle of Martin Bernal's *Black Athena*, but Bernal fails to recognize the very early European inmixture with those very Afroasiatic roots: the history of 1900 B.C. will have been about as complex as that of A.D. 1900.
5. *Royal Commentaries of the Incas*, p. 157.
6. *Florentine Codex*, Book X, p. 165.
7. Michael Coe, *The Maya*, London: Thames & Hudson, 1966, p. 149. This was to be five thousand years after the arrival of their culture heroes.
8. Krickeberg et al., *Pre-Columbian American Religions*, p. 75.
9. Manetho, *Aegyptiaca*, Fr. I, 4; also Fr. 2 and Fr. 3. Also Diodorus Siculus, *History of the World*, p. 13. The Islamic world still uses a lunar calendar. Our English word fortnight derives from the period when time was counted in nights not in days. Plutarch and Strabo agreed with Manetho's thrice-repeated statement in the first chapter of his history of Egypt.
10. 1931, Vol. II, and 1975 Vol. II, Part 2, *passim.*
11. *Cambridge Ancient History*, Vol. II, Chapter 8, p. 174.
12. Folsom and Folsom, *America's Ancient Treasures*, pp. 98–99.
13. *Larousse World Mythology*, London: Paul Hamlyn, 1965, pp. 398–99.
14. Zelia Nuttall, *The Fundamental Principles of Old and New World Civilizations*, New York: Kraus, 1970. p. 293. Nuttall states that in Peru records exist that around the capital the land was divided into alternate zones of land and water.
15. The Incas were found by Pizarro's men to have natural hot and cold water laid on.
16. *Dialogues*, Jowett, trans., pp. 529–43, 445–46.
17. *Larousse World Mythology*, p. 397.
18. J. V. Luce, *The End of Atlantis*, London: Paladin, 1972, p. 13.
19. Kur came to be known in the Old World as a dragon, or Sea-people, the personification of evil for their Viking-type raids. (Jordan, *Encyclopaedia of Gods*, p. 123).
20. *Theogony*, Loeb Classical Library, II. 630 *et seq.* and II. 860 *et seq.*

Chapter 28: Summary of the Argument

1. *Royal Commentaries of the Incas*, Vol. I, p. 13.
2. Ferdinand Columbus, *The Life of the Admiral Christopher Columbus*, trans. B. Keen, New Brunswick, N.J.: Rutgers University Press, 1959, pp. 21, 25.
3. Barbara Bender, *Farming in Prehistory*, London: John Baker, 1975, p. 1, and p. 168, and *passim.* It is now traced back to 9000 B.C. in Jericho. (Ruth Whitehouse, ed., *Dictionary of Archaelogy*, [London: Macmillan, 1983], p. 225.)
4. *Works*, II, 3, 3, 1.
5. A typical earth mother figure has been found in India dating to around 16,000 B.C.
6. George F. Carter, "Why I am No Longer a 'Standard Americanist,' " *Geography*, College Station, Texas, A & M University.
7. See Homer, *Iliad*, XIV, 201.
8. *Ecclesiastical History*, Loeb, Classical Library, 1965, Vol. I, p. xviii.
9. See Bailey, *The God-Kings and the Titans*, p. 275.
10. II:, 49–50.

Notes to Illustrations

Frontispiece

1. Wensinck, *The Ocean in the Literature of the Western Semites*, Sändig Reprint: Verlag, 1968, p. 26.

Introduction

1. Michael Jordan, *Encyclopaedia of Gods*, London: Kyle Cathie, 1992, p. 17.
2. Diodorus Siculus, Book V, 66, 3.
3. Robert J. Forbes, *Studies in Ancient Technology*, Leiden: E. J. Brill, 1965, Vol. III, p. 212.

Chapter 1: Economics Underlies History

1. *Natural History*, Loeb Classical Library, 1967–72, Vol. I, p. 307.
2. William H. Prescott, *The Conquest of Peru*, London: Richard Bentley, 1847, p. 4. Prescott in fact emphasizes that the Amerindians called the Andes "copper mountains" even though, he says, "they might with even more reason have been called mountains of gold."
3. Diodorus Siculus, *Works*, III, 54.
4. *Iliad*, Loeb Classical Library, 1919, XIV, 302.
5. Diodorus Siculus, *Works*, III, 56, 3.
6. Marija Gimbutas, *The Language of the Goddess*, London: Thames & Hudson, 1989, p. xiii.
7. R. F. Willetts, *The Civilization of Ancient Crete*, London: B. T. Batsford, 1976, p. 33.
8. Exodus, 33:31.
9. *Description of Greece*, Loeb Classical Library, 1966, VII, iv, 8.
10. S. G. F. Brandon, *Man and His Destiny*, Manchester University Press, 1962, p. 157.
11. Homer, *Iliad*, Loeb, 1965, II, footnote.
12. Ruth Whitehouse, ed., *Dictionary of Archaeology*, London; Macmillan, 1983, p. 536.
13. Julian the Apostate, quoted in Maarten J. Vermaseren, *Cybele and Attis*, London: Thames & Hudson, 1977, p. 87.
14. D. P. Agrawal, *The Archaeology of India*, London: Curzon Press, 1982, pp. 41, 265.
15. Otta Swire, *The Outer Hebrides and Their Legends*, Edinburgh: Oliver & Boyd, 1966, p. 146.
16. Forbes, *Studies in Ancient Technology*, Vol. IX, p. 3.
17. Christian Zervos, *La Civilisation Hellénique*, Paris: Editions Cahiers d'Art, 1969, p. 41.
18. Gad Rausing, *Prehistoric Boats and Ships of Northwestern Europe*, Malmo: CWK Gleerup, 1984, p. 27.
19. Lionel Casson, *The Ancient Mariners*, Princeton University Press, 1991, p. 3.
20. Herodotus, Loeb Classical Library, 1946, I, 194.

Chapter 2: Tracks on the World Ocean

1. Sir Alan Gardiner, *Egypt of the Pharaohs*, Oxford: Clarendon, 1960, p. 77.
2. Zvi Herman, *Peoples, Seas and Ships*, London: Phoenix House, 1966, pp. 18–19.
3. *Complete Works*, Loeb Classical Library, 1923–32, I, 3, 2.
4. *Cambridge Ancient History*, 1970, Vol I, Part 1, p. 465.
5. Michael David Coogan, *Stories from Ancient Canaan*, Philadelphia: Westminster Press, 1978, *passim*.
6. Paul Johnstone, *The Sea-craft of Prehistory*, London: Routledge & Kegan Paul, 1980, p. 5.
7. Ibid., p. 13.
8. Ibid., p. 216.
9. *Works*, III, 12–13.
10. 1973, Vol. II, Part 1, p. 368.
11. Ibid.
12. Flinders Petrie, *Wisdom of the Egyptians*, Vol. LXIII, London: Quaritch, 1940, p. 146.
13. *Works*, I, 24, 3.
14. Ibid., IV, 8, 5. Also: "He subdued and destroyed all the monsters of the world," which clearly was a necessary accompaniment to agriculture.
15. Ibid., IV, 27, 5 and III, 55, 3.

16. Ibid., I, 2, 4.
17. Diodorus Siculus, *History of the World*, London: Giles Calvert, 1653, p. 265; also Plutarch, *Life of Romulus:* "The Pelasgians had over-run the greater part of the habitable world" (*Lives*, London: J. Tonson, 1727).
18. James Hornell, *British Coracles and Irish Curraghs*, London: Quaritch, 1938, *passim.*
19. *History of the World*, London: Giles Calvert, 1653, Book I, p. 12.
20. Johnstone, *Sea-craft of Prehistory*, p. 186.
21. Constance Irwin, *Fair Gods and Stone Faces*, New York: St. Martin's, 1963, p. 170.
22. Curt Muser, *Facts and Artifacts of Ancient Middle America*, New York: Dutton, 1978.
23. Friedrich Katz, *The Ancient American Civilisations*, London: Weidenfeld & Nicholson, 1972, p. 154.
24. Diego de Landa, *The Maya: Diego de Landa's Account of the Affairs of Yucatan*, trans., A. R. Pagden, Chicago: J. Philip O'Hara, 1975, p. 18.
25. Anthony Aveni, ed., *Archaeoastronomy in Pre-Columbian America*, Austin: University of Texas Press, 1977, p. x.
26. Alain Ballabriga, ed., *Le Soleil et le Tartare*, Paris: L'École des Hautes Études, 1986, p. 91.
27. Pliny, *Natural History*, IV, 104.
28. Marija Gimbutas, *The Gods and Goddesses of Old Europe*, London: Thames & Hudson, 1974, p. 18.
29. John Mercer, *The Canary Islanders*, London: Rex Collings, 1980.
30. *Larousse Encyclopaedia of Archaeology*, London: Hamlyn, 1977, p. 153.
31. Hawkins, *Stonehenge Decoded*, p. 60.
32. XVII, 282–86.
33. Frank Brommer, *Heracles*, New York: Aristide Caratzas, 1986, p. 41. Note that Stesichore, in his *Geronyide*, states that the island of Erythia was "beyond the great oceans."
34. Ballabriga, ed., *Le Soleil et le Tartare*, pp. 10, 49.
35. Ebla Texts, first half of the twenty-fourth century B.C. eds. Cyrus Gordon, Gary Rendsburg, Nathan Winter. Winona Lake, Indiana: Eisenbrauns, 1987.
36. *Oxford Classical Dictionary*, 1949, p. 476.
37. T. P. Cross and C. H. Slover, *Ancient Irish Tales*, Dublin: Allen Figgis, 1969, pp. 3, 12–13.
38. Ballabriga, *Le Soleil et le Tartare*, p. 45.
39. Michael O'Kelly, *Early Ireland*, Cambridge University Press, 1989, p. 152.
40. J. D. Hawkins, ed., *Trade in the Ancient Near East*, London: British School of Archaeology in Iraq, 1977, *passim.*
41. Martin Brennan, *The Stars and the Stones*, London: Thames & Hudson, 1983, p. 17.
42. Donald Lathrap, *The Upper Amazon*, Southampton: Thames & Hudson, 1970, p. 101.
43. F. Folsom and M. E. Folsom, *America's Ancient Treasures*, Albuquerque: University of New Mexico Press, 1983, p. 188.
44. *Handbook of British Archaeology*, London: Papermac, Macmillan, 1987, p. 30.
45. Ruth Whitehouse, ed., 314.
46. Douglas Heggie, *Megalithic Science*, London: Thames & Hudson, 1981, pp. 87, 119, 123, 219.
47. Colin Renfrew, *Before Civilisation*, London: Jonathan Cape, 1973, pp. 239–41.

Chapter 3: The Huge Islands in the Middle of the Ocean

1. Lewis Spence, *The Myths of Mexico and Peru*, London: George Harrap, 1908, pp. 260–61.
2. Arthur Posnansky, *Tiahuanacu: Le Cuna del Hombre Americano*, New York: J. J. Augustin, 1945, Vol. I, pp. 42–43.
3. George Bankes, *Peru Before Pizarro*, Oxford: Phaidon, 1977, p. 165.
4. Muratori, *A Relation of the Missions of Paraguay*, London: J. Marmaduke, 1759, p.34.
5. Pierre Honoré, *In Quest of the White God*, London: Hutchinson, 1963, p. 16.
6. *South American Handbook*, 1975, Bath: Mendip Press, 1975, p. 146.
7. *Indians of the Andes: Aymaras and Quechuas*, New York: Cooper Square Publishers, 1973, p. 143.
8. Margaret Joan Anstee, *Gate of the Sun: A Prospect of Bolivia*, London: Longman, 1970, pp. 96–97.
9. Ibid., p. 121.
10. Robert Anderson, *The Story of the Extinct Civilisations of the West*, London: George Newnes, 1903, p. 181.
11. Bankes, *Peru Before Pizarro*, p. 165.
12. Jacques Soustelle, *The Olmecs*, Norman: University of Oklahoma Press, 1985, p. 147.
13. U. Schmidt et al., *The Conquest of the River Plate*, London: Hakluyt Society, 1891, p. 266.
14. *New Scientist*, December 21–28 1991.
15. Soustelle, *The Olmecs*, p. 147.
16. Stephen Hugh-Jones, *The Palm and the Pleiades*, Cambridge University Press, 1979, p. 18. Elsewhere it is pointed out that the Cabiri were associated with the netherworld.
17. Gaspar de Carvajal, *The Discovery of the Amazon*, New York: American Geographical Society, 1934, p. 183.
18. Thor Heyerdahl, *American Indians in the Pacific*, London: George Allen & Unwin, 1952, p. 274.
19. Marcel Homet, *Sons of the Sun*, London: Neville Spearman, 1963, p. 215.

20. Hernando de Ribera, *Conquest of the River Plate*, London: Hakluyt Society, No. cxxxi, pp. 45, 66, 266.
21. Diodorus Siculus, *History of the World*, pp. 146–47.
22. *Works*, II, 45.
23. Sahagún, *Florentine Codex*, Part 8, p. 36.
24. Ibid., Part 30, p. 165.
25. Richard Diehl, *Tula: The Toltec Capital of Ancient Mexico*, London: Thames and Hudson, 1983, p. 60.
26. Michael Coe, *The Maya*, London: Thames & Hudson, 1966, p. 66.
27. S. G. F. Brandon, *The Saviour God*, Westport, Conn.: Greenwood Press, 1963, p. 118.
28. Sir A. E. Wallis Budge, *The Book of the Dead*, New York: Medici Society, 1913, Vol. 1, p. 266.
29. Irwin, *Fair Gods and Stone Faces*, p. 40.

Chapter 4: The Marks of the Voyagers

1. *The Pneumatics of Hero of Alexandria*, trans., Bennet Woodcroft; London: Taylor, Walton & Maberly, 1851.
2. Frederick Dockstader, *Indian Art of Central America*, London: Cory, Adams & Mackay, 1964, Plate 48.
3. *Works*, XVII, 3, 7.
4. Alfredo Brandão, *A Escrita Prehistória do Brasil*, Rio de Janeiro: Civilizacão Brasiliera, 1937, Estampa III.
5. Manfred Lurker, *The Gods and Symbols of Ancient Egypt*, London: Thames & Hudson, 1980, p. 70.
6. Sahagún, *Florentine Codex*, Book, p. 1.
7. Ibid., Book 9, p. 1.
8. Françoise Bruschweiler, *Inanna*, Leuven: Edition Peeters, 1987, pp. 12, 39, 51, 75.
9. Muser, *Facts and Artifacts of Ancient Middle America*, p. 164.
10. Thor Heyerdahl, *The Ra Expeditions*, London: George Allen & Unwin, 1971, p. 254.
11. II, VI, 31.
12. VII, 203.
13. Gardiner, *Egypt of the Pharaohs*, p. 2.
14. William Prescott, *The Conquest of Mexico*, London: George Routledge & Sons, n.d., p. 167.
15. Ibid., p. 215.
16. Marcel Homet, *On the Trail of the Sun Gods*, London: Neville Spearman, 1965, p. 230.
17. Edward Lanning, *Peru Before the Incas*, Englewood N.J.: Prentice Hall, 1967, p.117.
18. Barrett, *The Egyptian Gods and Goddesses*, London: Aquarian/Thorsans, 1992, p. 127. The Egyptian god Sed, surely a variant spelling, was known as "savior."
19. Ignacio Bernal, *The Olmec World*, Los Angeles: University of California Press, 1973, p. 78.
20. O. Neugebauer, *The Sciences in Antiquity*, New York: Harper, 1962, p. 166.
21. Heyerdahl, *Ra Expeditions*, p. 244.
22. Honoré, *In Quest of the White God*, p. 93.
23. Aveni, ed., *Archaeoastronomy in Pre-Columbian America*, pp. 12, 30.
24. Josephus, *Jewish Antiquities*, Loeb Classical Library, 1967, 120–121.
25. Muntaha Saghieh, *Byblos in the Third Millennium* B.C., Warminster: Aris & Phillips, 1983, p. 124.
26. Garcilaso de la Vega, *Royal Commentaries of the Incas*, London: University of Texas Press, 1966, p. 208.
27. Ibid., p. 236.
28. Clements Markham, *The Rites and Laws of the Incas*, London: Hakluyt Society, 1873, p. 78.
29. De la Vega, *Royal Commentaries of the Incas*, p. 48.
30. Honoré, *In Quest of the White God*, p. 16.
31. Heyerdahl, *American Indians in the Pacific*, pp. 211, 229, 230; see also the Spanish chronicler Cieza de Léon. The white culture hero was a mighty man who taught the people everything to do with law and civilization, to be good to one another and to live without violence.
32. Heyerdahl, *American Indians in the Pacific*, p. 327, the identical description with the Dogon tribe of Mali.
33. Alexander Heidel, *The Gilgamesh Epic and Old Testament Parallels*, Chicago University Press, 1949, p. 58.
34. Parsons and Denevan, *Scientific American*, July 1967, pp. 92–100.
35. David Browman, *Advances in Andian Archaeology*, The Hague: Mouton, 1978, p. 243.
36. J. Eric Thompson, *The Rise and Fall of Maya Civilzation*, Norman: University of Oklahoma Press, 1954, Vol. 1, p. 26.
37. D. Diringer, *The Alphabet*, London: Hutchinson, 1968, p. 85.
38. Samuel Kramer, *The Sumerians*, Chicago: University Press, 1963, p. 75; compare Plato's *Republic*.
39. Ibid., p. 130.
40. *Iliad*, V, 740.
41. *Hesiod's Theogony*, Oxford: Clarendon, 1966, pp. 236, 274, 275.
42. Delia Goetz and S. G. Morley, English translation from the Spanish translation of Adrián Recinos, *Popol Vuh*, London: William Hodge, 1951, p. 81.
43. Katz, *Ancient American Civilizations*, p. 148.
44. S. N. Kramer, *Sumerian Mythology*, London: Harper & Row, 1961, p. 83.
45. Wensinck, *The Ocean in the Literature of the Western Semites*, pp. 2, 4.
46. Ibid., p. 4. The war with Typhon, the Typhonomachia, was on a worldwide scale.
47. H. Te Velde, *Seth, God of Confusion*, Leiden: E. J. Brill, 1977, p. 145.

48. M. L. West, *The Orphic Poems*, Oxford: Clarendon, 1983, p. 162.
49. *The Avebury Cycle*, London: Thames & Hudson, 1977, p. 104.
50. *Popol Vuh*, pp. 194–95.
51. Manetho, *Aegyptiaca*, Loeb Classical Library, 1948, pp. 199, 201.
52. Herodotus, Loeb Classical Library, 1946, II, 119.
53. Arthur Weigall, *Sappho of Lesbos*, Garden City, N.Y.: Garden City Publishing 1932, p. 59.
54. Bianchi, *Greek Mysteries*, Leiden: E. J. Brill, 1976, p. 14.
55. Cyrus Gordon, *Before Columbus*, New York: Crown, 1971, p. 152.
56. Sahagún, *Florentine Codex*, Book 2, p. 1.
57. Aveni, ed., *Archeoastrology in Pre-Columbian America*, p. 24.
58. Katz, *Ancient American Civilizations*, p. 65.
59. Seton Lloyd, *The Archaeology of Mesopotamia*, London: Thames & Hudson, 1978, p. 214.
60. Brandon, *Man and His Destiny*, p. 42.
61. Thompson, *Rise and Fall of Maya Civilization*, p. 152.
62. Landa, *The Maya*, p. 38.
63. *Popul Vuh*, pp. 194–95.
64. Honoré, *In Quest of the White God*, p. 19.
65. Ibid., p. 117.
66. G. W. Conrad and A. A. Demarest, *Religion and Empire*, Cambridge University Press, 1984, p. 31.
67. Katz, *Ancient American Civilzations*, p. 185.
68. E. M. Berens, *Myths and Legends of Ancient Greece and Rome*, London: Blackie & Son, n.d., p. 132.
69. Hesiod, *Theogony*, Loeb, p. 95.
70. Bruschweiler, *Inanna*, p. 51.
71. Ibid., p. 75.
72. Ibid., p. 12.
73. Ibid., p. 46.
74. Kramer, *Sumerian Mythology*, p. 76.
75. S. N. Kramer and J. Maier, *Myths of Enki*, Oxford University Press, 1989, p. 83.
76. Barry Fell, *America B.C.*, New York: Demeter Press, 1977, p. 51.
77. Wauchope, *Handbook of Middle American Indians*, University of Texas Press, Vol. 4, p. 232.
78. *Bronze Age America*, Boston: Little, Brown, 1982, p. 151.
79. Soustelle, *The Olmecs*, p. 158.
80. Irwin, *Fair Gods and Stone Faces*, p. 296.
81. George Jones, *The History of Ancient America*, London: Longman Brown, Green & Longmans, 1843.
82. Honoré, *In Quest of the White God*, p. 25.
83. Diodorus Siculus, *Works*, IV, 5.
84. *Odyssey*, V, 100.
85. Strabo, *Works*, I, 2, 37.
86. Homer, *Odyssey*, V, 160–65.

Chapter 5: Birdmen in Africa

1. Homer, *Iliad*, IX, 381–84.
2. Diodorus Siculus, *Works*, I, 46.
3. Ibid., I, 15, 3–5.
4. Ibid., I, 50, 1–3.
5. Ibid., *History of the World*, London: Giles Calvert, 1653, pp. 36–37.
6. *Dictionary of Gods and Goddesses*, London: Routledge & Kegan Paul, 1987, p. 314.
7. S. R. Rao, *Lothal and the Indus Civilisation*, London: Asia Publishing House, 1973, Figure 22.
8. T. R. Iyengar, *Dravidian India*, New Delhi: Asian Educational Services, 1982, p. 28.
9. D. P. Agrawal, *The Archaeology of India*, London: Curzon Press, 1982, p. 135.
10. Sir John Marhsall, ed., *Mohenjo-daro and the Indus Civilisation*, London: Probsthain, 1931, Vol. II, p. 422.
11. James Pritchard, ed., *Ancient Near Eastern Texts and Pictures*, Princeton University Press, 1969, p. 3.
12. Pedro de Cieza de Léon, *The Incas*, Norman: University of Oklahoma Press, 1959, p. 77.
13. Book I, p. 96.
14. *Cambridge Ancient History*, 1971, Vol. I, Part 2, p. 441.
15. Ibid., Vol. II, Part 2, p. 262.
16. Sharon Heyob, *The Cult of Isis Among the Women in the Graeco-Roman World*, Leiden: E. J. Brill, 1975, p. 41.
17. Émile Massoulard, *Préhistoire et Protohistoire d'Egypte*, Paris: Institut d'Ethnologie, 1949, p. 515.
18. Alessandra Nibbi, *The Sea Peoples and Egypt*, New Jersey: Noyes Press, 1975, p. 126.
19. *History of the World*, p. 12.
20. *Journal of Egyptian Archaeology*, London: Egyptian Exploration Society, 1938, Vol. 24, p. 177.
21. For example, J. van Dijk, *LUGAL UD ME-LAM-bi NIRGAL*, Leiden: E. J. Brill, 1983, p. 31, "les têtes noires." The Sumerian god Enlil was addressed as "Shepherd of the Blackheaded People" (Mark Cohen, *Sumerian Hymnology*, Cincinnati: Ersemma, 1981, p. 146).
22. Heichelheim, *Ancient Economic History*, Leiden: Sijthoff, 1965, pp. 128, 136.
23. *New Larousse Encyclopaedia of Mythology*, London: Hamlyn, 1968, p. 16.
24. Kramer, *Sumerian Mythology*, pp. 18–20.
29. Nibbi, *Sea Peoples and Egypt*, p. 18.
26. Holas, *Les Senoufo*, Paris: Presses Universitaires de France, 1966, p. 143.
27. Steven Sidebotham, *Roman Economic Policy*, Leiden: E. J. Brill, 1986, p. 177.

28. Loeb, VI, XXIV, 88, 82.
29. George F. Carter, "Chinese Contacts with America: Fu Sang Again," *Anthropological Journal of Canada*, Vol. 14, No. 1, 1976, p. 12.
30. Quoted in Diringer, *Alphabet*, Vol. I, pp. 50, 56.
31. A. Ghosh, *Encyclopaedia of Indian Archaeology*, Vol. I, Leiden: E. J. Brill, 1990, p. 19.
32. Katz, *Ancient American Civilizations*, p. 177.
33. Jean Bottéro, *Mésopotamie*, Paris: Gaillimard, 1987, p. 288.
34. Kramer and Maier, *Myths of Enki*, p. 170.
35. *The Land of Shinar*, London: Souvenir Press, 1965, p. 135.
36. Chaim Bemant and Michael Weitzman, *Ebla*, London: Weidenfeld & Nicolson, 1979, p. 153.
37. Kramer and Maier, *Myths of Enki*, pp. 1, 80.
38. Ibid., p. 7.
39. Diringer, *Alphabet*, Vol. I, p. 21.
40. H. Frankfort, *Kingship and the Gods*, Chicago: University Press, 1948, p. 225.
41. *Mohenjo-daro*, Vol. I, p. 58.
42. Herodotus, Loeb, 1946, I, 179.
43. K. D. White, *Greek and Roman Technology*, London: Thames & Hudson, 1984, p. 24.
44. Antonio de Solis, *The History of the Conquest of Mexico by the Spaniards*, London: John Osborn, 1738, p. 298.
45. Marshall, *Mohenjo-daro*, p. 596.
46. Richard Keatinge, ed., *Peruvian Prehistory*, Cambridge University Press, 1988, p. 116.
47. Kramer, *Sumerian Mythology*, p. 66.
48. Kramer, *The Sumerians*, p. 121.
49. Edwin O. James, *Creation and Cosmology*, Leiden: E. J. Brill, 1969, p. 5.
50. Sir Alan Gardiner, *Egyptian Grammar*, Oxford: Clarendon, 1927, p. 552.
51. Coogan, *Stories from Ancient Canaan*, p. 11.
52. Te Velde, *Seth, God of Confusion*, p. 127.

Chapter 6: Lands to the East

1. Solis, *History of the Conquest of Mexico*, p. 298.
2. Agrawal, *Archaeology of India*, p. 135.
3. Swami Sankarananda, *Hindu States of Sumeria*, Calcutta: K. L. Mukhapadhyay, 1962, p. 27.
4. George F. Carter, "Why I Am No Longer a 'Standard Americanist,' " *Geography*, College Station: Texas A&M University, p. 5.
5. Henriette Mertz, *Pale Ink*, Chicago: published privately, 1953, p. 67.
6. Ghosh, *Encyclopaedia of Indian Archaeology*, Vol. II, p. 258.
7. Ibid., p. 260.
8. Whitehouse, ed., *Dictionary of Archaeology*, p. 315.
9. W. Krickeberg, et al., *Pre-Columbian American Religons*, London: Weidenfeld & Nicolson, 1968, p. 1.
10. Homer, *Iliad*, VIII, 478–89.
11. Strabo, *Works*, I, 2, 37 and III, 4.
12. Heyerdahl, *American Indians in the Pacific*, p. 468.
13. Ibid., p. 487.
14. Ibid.
15. *Iliad*, XIV, 201.
16. J. B. Bury, *History of Greece*, London: Macmillan, 1924, p. 89.
17. Ballabriga, *Le Soleil et le Tartare*, pp. 81, 91, 104, 125.
18. *Iliad*, VII, 420. To the Egyptians Nun was the god of the primeval sea from which, the Egyptians correctly appreciated, all life sprang.
19. Whitehouse, ed., *Dictionary of Archaeology*, p. 25.
20. Kwang-Chih Chang, *Shang Civilization*, New Haven: Yale University Press, 1980, 244.
21. David Lewis, *The Voyaging Stars*, Sydney: Collins, 1978, p. 55.
22. Ibid., p. 14.
23. Ibid., p. 159.
24. Ibid., p. 56.
26. Aubrey Burl, *Prehistoric Avebury*, New Haven: Yale University Press, 1979, p. 83.
25. Nors Josephson, *Greek Linguistic Elements in the Polynesia Language*, Heidelberg: Universitäts verlag, 1987, p. 9.
27. Josephson, *Greek Linguistic Elements in the Polynesian Languages, passim.*
28. Ibid. Also the *London Sunday Telegraph*, November 21, 1993.
29. Homet, *On the Trail of the Sun Gods*, p. 208.
30. Heyerdahl, *The Ra Expeditions*, p. 27.
31. R. E. M. Wheeler, *Prehistoric and Roman Wales*, Oxford: Clarendon, 1925, p. 92. He quotes India, Scandinavia, the Caucasus, but fails to include the two Americas.
32. Paul Johnstone, *The Sea-craft of Prehistory*, London: Routledge & Kegan Paul, 1980, p. 217.
33. Campbell, *The Masks of God*, London: Condor Books, 1964, p. 249.
34. *Science and Civilisation in China*, Cambridge University Press, 1965, p. 84.
35. *Larousse Encyclopaedia of Archaeology*, p. 359.
36. Carter, "Why I Am No Longer," p. 2.
37. Mertz, *Pale Ink*, pp. 20–21.
38. Homet, *Sons of the Sun*, Plates 25, 26.
39. Vol. II, p. 89.
40. Krickeberg et al., *Pre-Columbian American Religions*, p. 38.
41. Gimbutas, *The Language of the Goddess*, p. 308.

Chapter 7: Negligible Written Sources for the History of Ancient Africa

1. Michael Dames, *The Silbury Treasure*, London: Thames & Hudson, 1976, p. 53.
2. Katz, *Ancient American Civilisations*, p. 148.
3. Swire, *The Outer Hebrides and Their Legends*, p. 45.
4. Ibid., p. 25.
5. Ibid., p. 218.
6. *New Larousse Encyclopaedia of Mythology*, p. 76.
7. Gimbutas, *The Gods and Goddesses of Old Europe*, p. 18. The Tartarian script goes back to the sixth millennium B.C.
8. Nicholas Guppy, *Wai-Wai*, London: John Murray, 1958, p. 274.
9. Octavio Alvarez, *The Celestial Brides*, Stockbridge, Mass.: Reichner, 1978, p. 241.
10. Pierre Grimal, *The Dictionary of Classical Mythology*, Oxford: Basil Blackwell, 1986, p. 435.
11. P. 164.
12. Ibid., p. 154.
13. Diodorus Siculus, *Works*, III, 2.
14. Honoré, *In Quest of the White God*, p. 164.
15. Zelia Nuttall, *The Fundamental Principals of Old and New World Civilizations*, New York: Kraus, 1970, p. 175.
16. Homet, *Sons of the Sun*, p. 30.
17. Kramer, *The Sumerians*, p. 10.
18. Johnstone, *Sea-craft of Prehistory*, p. 22.
19. Thorkild Jacobsen, *Towards the Image of Tammuz*, Cambridge: Harvard University Press, 1970, p. 4.
20. W. W. Hallo and J. J. A. van Dijk, *The Exaltation of Innana*, New Haven: Yale University Press, 1968, p. 51.
21. P. 27.
22. 28: 2.
23. U. Cassuto, *The Goddess Anath*, Magnes Press, Hebrew University, Jerusalem: 1971, pp. 55–56.
24. W. G. Lambert and A. R. Millard, *Atra-hasis*, Oxford: Clarendon, 1970, p. 89. Professor Lambert most generously gave me several hours of his time to discuss his text.
25. Kramer, *Sumerian Mythology*, pp. 69, 75, 76, 83.
26. De la Vega, *Royal Commentaries of the Incas*, p. 486.
27. Folsom and Folsom, *America's Ancient Treasures*, p. 312.
28. Sir Clements Markham, *The Rites and Laws of the Incas*, London: Hakluyt Society, 1873, p. 82.
29. Thomas Joyce, *Central American and West Indian Archaeology*, London: Philip Warner, 1916, p. 228.
30. "Woe to the land shadowing with wings, which is beyond the rivers of Ethiopia: that sendeth ambassadors by the sea, even in vessels of bullrushes upon the water" (Isaiah 18:1–2).
31. C. J. Bleeker, *Hathor and Thoth*, Leiden: E. J. Brill, 1973, p. 105.

Chapter 8: Scientific or Magical Societies

1. Dames, *The Silbury Treasure*, pp. 152–53.
2. Du Buisson, Robert, *Études sur les Dieux Phéniciens Hérités par l'Empire Romain*, Leiden: E. J. Brill, 1970, p. 137.
3. Brennan, *The Stars and the Stones*, p. 171.
4. Dominique Zahen, *The Bambara*, Leiden: E. J. Brill, 1974, p. 24.
5. Gille, *Les Mécaniciens Grecs*, Paris: Editions du Seuil, 1978, p. 70.

Chapter 9: Divine Kingship Worldwide

1. M. Griaule and Germaine Dieterlen, *Conversations with Ogotemelli*, 1975, p. 210. This is Marcel Griaule writing of the neighboring Dogon.
2. J. Gwyn Griffiths, *The Conflict of Horus and Seth*, Liverpool University Press, 1960, p. 75.
3. A. F. J. Klijn, *Seth in Jewish, Christian and Gnostic Literature*, Leiden: E. J. Brill, 1977, p. 33.
4. Te Velde, *Seth, God of Confusion*, p. 35.
5. Sahagún, *Florentine Codex*, Book 3, p. 12.
6. Sahagún, *Florentine Codex*, Book 8, p. 74.
7. Schmidt et al., *Conquest of the River Plate*, p. 207.
8. Sahagún, *Florentine Codex*, Book 8, p. 74.
9. 36, 200.
10. Hesiod, *Catalogue of Women*, Heinemann, 1914, 2.
11. Herbert J. Spinden, *Maya Art and Civilization*, Indian Hills, Colorado: Falcon's Wing Press, 1957, p. 243.
12. George E. Mylonas, *Mycenae and the Mycenaean Age*, Princeton University Press, 1966, p. 3.
13. Muser, *Facts and Artifacts of Ancient Middle America*, p. 8.
14. *Dialogues of Plato*, Oxford University Press, 1931, Vol. III, p. 536: "They had such an amount of wealth as was never before possessed by Kings and potentates and is not likely ever to be again." "Orichalcum was dug out of the earth . . . being more precious than anything except gold." Orichalcum I take to be tumbago.

Chapter 10: The Sea Peoples of the Copper and Bronze Ages

1. Krickeberg et al., *Pre-Columbian American Religions*, p. 41.
2. S. Brandon, *Saviour God*, p. 118.
3. Bonin, with John Mhiti, *Die Götter Schwarz-Afrikas*, Graz: VS, 1979, p. 379.
4. René Rohr, *Sundials: History, Theory and Practice*, Toronto University Press, 1970, p. 16.
5. Ralph Whitlock, *The Guardian*, October 8, 1986.

6. Donald T. Kauffman, ed., *Baker's Concise Dictionary of Religion*, Grand Rapids, Mich.: Baker Book House, 1985. Lissa was also a goddess in Dahomey, mother of sun and moon.
7. Ibid., p. 291.
8. Coe, *The Maya*, p. 152.
9. Sahagún, *Florentine Codex*, Book 2, p. 1.
10. London: Edward Arnold, 1954, p. 126.
11. West, *Hesiod's Theogony*, p. 218.

Chapter 11: The Mermaid

1. Sahagún, *Florentine Codex*, Book IV, Chapter 9, Figure 31.
2. Quoted in Forbes, *Studies in Ancient Technology*, Vol. VII, p. 228.
3. Heyerdahl, *Ra Expeditions*, p. 252.
4. Griaule, *Conversations with Ogotemelli*, p. 191.
5. Glaze, *Art and Death in a Senufo Village*, Bloomington: Indiana University Press, 1981, p. 74.

Chapter 12: Why the Sea Trade Ended

1. This idea appears through all Gimbutas's work.
2. Griaule, *Conversations with Ogotemelli*, pp. 125–27. Compare with Gerado Reichel-Dolmatoff, *Amazonian Cosmos*, Chicago: University Press, 1971, *passim.*
3. Jan Knappert, *Myths and Legends of the Congo*, Nairobi: Heinemann, 1971, p. 40.
4. Ibid., p. 142.

Chapter 13: West African Customs

1. Nuttall, *Fundamental Principles of Old and New World Civilizations*, p. 253.
2. Mercer, *The Canary Islanders*, p. 161.
3. *The Akan Doctrine of God*, London: Frank Cass, 968, pp. 52, 49.
4. Spinden, *Maya Art and Civilization*, p.347.
5. Krickeberg et al., *Pre-Columbian American Religions*, p. 90.

Chapter 14: The Philosophy of the Dogo Tribe of Mali

1. Kramer and Maier, *Myths of Enki*, p. 121.
2. Ibid., p. 200.
3. C. Kerenyi, *Zeus and Hera*, London: Routledge & Kegan Paul, 1975, p. 127.
4. R. F. Willets, *Cretan Cults and Festivals*, London: Routledge and Kegan Paul, 1962, p. 103.
5. Quoted in Kathleen Freeman, *Ancilla to the Pre-Socratic Philosophers*, Oxford: Basil Blackwell, 1948, p. 2.
6. *History*, Book III, Chapter 98.
7. *Iliad*, XV, 675–80.
8. Coogan, *Stories from Ancient Canaan*, Glossary.
9. Ibid., p. 10.
10. Ibid., p. 119.

Chapter 15: Biblical Creation and the Flood

1. West, *Orphic Hymns*, p. 256.
2. Gimbutas, *Gods and Goddesses of Old Europe*, p. 96.
3. Seton Lloyd, *Archaeology of Mesopotamia*, London: Thames & Hudson, 1978, p. 117.
4. Krickeberg et al., *Pre-Columbian American Religions*, p. 261.
5. Reichel-Dolmatoff, *Amazonian Cosmos*, pp. 130–131.
6. Ibid., p. 246.
7. Ibid., p. 24.

Chapter 16: The Mesopotamian Tradition About Atlas, Alias Seth and Set

1. Folsom and Folsom, *America's Ancient Treasures*, p. 193.
2. Allison, *African Stone Sculptures*, p. 31.
3. Sir A. E. Wallis Budge, *Egyptian Religion*, Arkana, 1897, p. 28.
4. Hart, *Egyptian Myths*, London: British Museum Press, 1990, p. 48.
5. France le Corsu, *Isis, Mythe et Mystères*, Paris: Édition Les Belles Lettres, 1977, p. 7.
6. Barbara Bender, *The Archaeology of Brittany, Normandy and the Channel Islands*, London: Faber & Faber, 1986, p. 129.
7. Ibid., p. 59.
8. Loeb, *Works*, Vol. II, p. 253.
9. Grimal, *Dictionary of Classical Mythology*, p. 463.
10. p. 143.
11. *Description of Greece*, VI, 36, 3.
12. Cyrus Gordon, *Before Columbus*, London: Turnstone Press, 1971, p. 139.

Chapter 18: The Sculptor and the Unwritten Tradition

1. Michael Rice, *Egypt's Making*, London: Routledge, 1990, pp. 98–99.
2. Gimbutas, *Gods and Goddesses of Old Europe*, p. 169.

Chapter 19: The Ashanti Gold Weights

1. *Silbury Treasure*, p. 53.
2. *Works*, I, 27.
3. Diodorus Siculus, *History of the World*, p. 13.
4. Alvarez, *Celestial Brides*, p. 137.
5. Kerenyi, *Zeus and Hera*, pp. 52, 56.
6. Alexander Heidel, *The Babylonian Genesis*, Chicago University Press, 1951, p. 36.
7. Brennan, *The Stars and the Stones*, p. 171.
8. *Journal of Egyptian Archaeology*, London: Egyptian Exploration Society, Vol. XXII, 1936, p. 111.

9. Jean McMann, *Riddles of the Stone Age*, London: Thames & Hudson, 1980, p. 88.
10. *African Stone Sculpture*, London: Lund Humphries, 1968, p. 57.

Chapter 21: The Scandal of the Classical Greeks

1. Gimbutas, *Gods and Goddesses of Old Europe*, p. 169.
2. Jacques Ménard, *Le Feu dans le Proche-Orient Antique*, Leiden: E. J. Brill, 1973, p. 99.
3. Hikkelheber, "Sculptors and Sculptures of the Dan," Proceedings of the First International Congress of Africanists.
4. *New Larousse Encyclopaedia of Mythology*, p. 37.
5. West, *Orphic Poems*, p. 133.
6. El Sayed, *La Déesse Neith de Saïs*, IFAO, 1982, pp. 4, 20.

Chapter 23: Right-handedness and Left-handedness

1. C. Blacker & M. Loewe, *Ancient Cosmologies*, London: George Allen & Unwin, 1975, p. 27.
2. Thompson, *Rise and Fall of Maya Civilization*, p. 244.
3. W. G. Wood-Martin, *Traces of the Elder Faiths of Ireland*, London: Longmans, Green, 1902, pp. 40–46.
4. Du Buisson, *Études sur les Dieux Phéniciens Hérités par l'Empire Romain*, Leiden: E. J. Brill, 1970, p. 2.
5. Kramer & Maier, *Myths of Enki*, p. 138.
6. Ibid., p. 137.
7. Joyce, *Central American and West Indian Archaeology*, Plate III.
8. Irwin, *Fair Gods and Stone Faces*, p. 167. Notice that circumcision, the ritual cutting of a piece of foreskin, was practiced not only by Jews and Muslims, but anciently also by certain peoples of Africa and Peru. (*Baker's Concise Dictionary of Religions*, p. 120.)
9. Robert and Jenifer Marx, *In Quest of the Great White Gods*, New York: Crown, 1992, opposite p. 89.
10. *Moralia*, "On the Face in the Moon's Orb," xxvi.
11. Robert Marx, "Who Really Discovered the New World?," *The Explorers Journal*, Winter 1991, p. 110.
12. Wood-Martin, *Traces of the Elder Faiths of Ireland*, p. 218.
13. Nancy K. Sandars, *The Sea Peoples: Warriors of the Ancient Mediterranean, 1250–1150 B.C.*, London: Thames & Hudson, 1978, p. 146.
14. Chang, *Shang Civilization*, p. 71.
15. Coe, *The Maya*, p. 105.
16. Jesse Jennings, p. 278.
17. Ibid., p. 496.
18. Muser, *Facts and Artifacts of Ancient Middle America*, p. 9.
19. Joyce, *Central American and West Indian Archaeology*, p. 164.
20. Anne Burton, *Diodorus Siculus, Book I: A Commentary*, Leiden: Brill, 1972, p. 62.
21. Muser, *Facts and Artifacts of Ancient Middle America*, p. 78.
22. Rev. Patrick Akoi, *The Sacral Kingship*, Leiden: E. J. Brill, 1959, p. 146.
23. Le Corsu, *Isis, Myth et Mystères.*
24. Burton, *Diodorus Siculus*, pp. 134, 319.
25. Joyce, *Central American and West Indian Archaeology*, p. 164.
26. Muratori, *Relation of the Missions of Paraguay*, pp. 34, 36.
27. Keatinge, ed., *Peruvian Prehistory*, p. 115.
28. Krickeberg et al., *Pre-Columbian American Religions*, p. 133.
29. Gimbutas, *Gods and Goddesses of Old Europe*, p. 201.
30. Patrick Crampton, *Stonehenge of the Kings*, London: John Baker, 1967, p. 64.
31. Leo Frobenius, *The Voice of Africa*, Rudolf Blind, trans., London: Hutchinson, 1913.
32. Ibid., p. 348.
33. Bernal, *Olmec World*, p. 103.
34. Alan W. Shorter, *The Egyptian Gods*, London: Routledge & Kegan Paul, 1978, p. 11.
35. Barrett, *Egyptian Gods and Goddesses*, p. 188.
36. Patrick Boylan, *Thoth, the Hermes of Egypt*, Chicago: Ares, 1979, pp. 115, 117.
37. Marx, "Who Really Discovered the New World?," p. 109.
38. Lurker, *Gods and Symbols of Ancient Egypt*, pp. 42, 66, 67.
39. Burton, *Diodorus Siculus*, I, p. 152.
40. Shorter, *Egyptian Gods*, p. 85.
41. Coogan, *Stories from Ancient Canaan*, p. 119.
42. Vol. II, p. 5.
43. Gimbutas, *Gods and Goddesses of Old Europe, p. 199.*
44. *Works*, III, 2, 3.
45. Edward Taylor, *Anahuac*, London: Longmans Green, 1861, p. 276.
46. Pindar's *Odes of Victory*, Oxford: Basil Blackwell, 1928, p. x.

Chapter 24: The First Great Periods of International Trade

1. Irwin, *Fair Gods and Stone Faces*, p. 171.
2. *The Pyramids of Egypt*, Harmondsworth: Pelican, 1961, p. 294.

Chapter 25: Earth Mother: Sky Father

1. *Works*, I, 46, 5, 6.
2. Quoted in Peter Brown, *Megaliths, Myths and Men*, Poole: Blandford Press, 1976, p. 148.
3. Frankfort, *Kingship and the Gods, passim.*
4. Carolyne Larrington, *The Feminist Companion to Mythology*, Pandora, 1992, p. 369.
5. Vol. 2, 1931, p. 80.
6. *Works*, I, 27, 4.
7. Shorter, *Egyptian Gods*, p. 96.
8. Gad Rausing, *Prehistoric Boats and Ships of Northwestern Europe*, Malmö: CWK Gleerup, 1984, p. 39.

Chapter 26: God-Kings and Titans

1. Jean-Claude Margueron, *Archaeology of Mesopotamia*, Geneva: Nagel, 1965, p. 146.
2. James Muhly, *Copper and Tin*, Hamden, Conn.: Archon, 1973, p. 102.
3. Contenau, *Everyday Life in Babylon and Assyria*, p. 125.
4. Trans., Jowett, 1871, pp. 245–56.
5. Strabo, *Works*, II, 3, 6.
6. Cory, *Ancient Fragments*, Minneapolis: Wizards Bookshelf, 1975, p. 243.
7. *Cambridge Ancient History*, Vol. II, Part 2, 1975, pp. 166–77.
8. *New Larousse Encyclopaedia of Mythology*, p. 275.
9. Ibid., p. 395.
10. Marx and Marx, *In Quest of the Great White Gods, passim.*
11. Ibid., p. 248.
12. Swire, *The Outer Hebrides and Their Legends*, p. 70.
13. *Theogony*, 274, 5.
14. Gardiner, *Egypt of the Pharaohs*, p. 35.
15. *Cambridge Ancient History*, Vol. I, Part 2, 1971, p. 759.
16. Cassuto, *The Goddess Anath*, pp. 53–57.
17. Aveni, ed., *Archeoastronomy in Pre-Columbian America*, p. 30.
18. Ibid., p. 12.
19. Turcan, *Héliogabale*, Paris: Albin Michel, 1985, p. 128.
20. Kramer & Maier, *Myths of Enki*, p. 154.

Chapter 27: The End of Atlantis

1. Quoted in Tim Severin, *The Brendan Voyage*, London: Hutchinson, 1978, p. 203.
2. Ibid., p. 180.
3. Halsberghe, *The Cult of Sol Invictus*, Leiden: E. J. Brill, 1972, p. 43.
4. Cottrell, *Land of Shinar*, p. 135.
5. Bernal, *Olmec World*, p. 78.
6. Diodorus Siculus, *Works*, IV, 8, 5.
7. Bankes, *Peru Before Pizarro*, p. 170.
8. Diodorus Siculus, *Works*, 2, 257.
9. Uhlenbrook, *Heracles*, New York: Bard College, 1986, Foreword.
10. Te Velde, *Seth, God of Confusion*, p. 86. The Canadian Delaware Indians in pre-Columbian times called the Great Bear the Great Bear.
11. Krickeberg, et al., *Pre-Columbian American Religions*, p. 166.
12. K. A. H. Hidding, in *The Sacral Kingship*, Leiden: E. J. Brill, 1959, p. 56.
13. Aveni, ed., *Archaeoastronomy in Pre-Columbian America*, p. 26.
14. *Gods and Symbols of Ancient Egypt*, p. 110.

Chapter 28: Summary of the Argument

1. Eusebius, *Ecclesiastical History*, Loeb Classical Library, 1965, I, p. xv.
2. *De Bello Gallico*, VI, 14, 6.
3. Swire. *The Outer Hebrides and Their Legends*, p. 23.
4. A. Thom, *Megalithic Lunar Observatories*, Oxford: Clarendon, 1973, p. 12.
5. Klijn, *Seth*, p. 116.
6. David Zink, *The Stones of Atlantis*, London: W. H. Allen, 1978, *passim.*
7. Honoré, *In Quest of the White God*, p. 59.
8. Marx and Marx, *In Quest of the Great White Gods*, p. 249.

Bibliography

Adkins, Leley, and Roy Adkins. *Handbook of British Archaeology*. Papermac, 1987.

Agrawal, D. P. *The Archaeology of India*. London: Curzon Press, 1982.

Agrawal, D. P., and D. K. Chakrabarti. *Essays in Indian Protohistory*. Delhi: B. R. Publishing, 1979.

Akoi, Rev. P. *The Sacral Kingship*. Leiden: E. J. Brill, 1959.

Aldred, Cyril. *Akhenaten*. London: Thames & Hudson, 1968.

———. *Egypt to the End of the Old Kingdom*. London: Thames & Hudson, 1965.

Alexander, W. O., and A. C. Street. *Metals in the Service of Man*. Harmondsworth: Pelican, 1965.

Alexiou, S., N. Platon, and H. Guanella. *Ancient Crete*. London: Thames & Hudson, 1968.

Allchin, B., and R. Allchin. *The Birth of Indian Civilisation*. London: Pelican, 1968.

Allison, Philip. *African Stone Sculpture*. London: Lund Humphries.

———. *Cross River Monoliths*. Lagos: Government Printer, 1968.

Alsop, Joseph. *From the Silent Earth: The Greek Bronze Age*. London: Secker & Warburg, 1964.

Alvarez, Octavio. *The Celestial Brides*. Stockbridge, Mass.: Reichner, 1978.

Amiet, Pierre. *Elam*. Auvers-sur-Oise: Archee, 1966.

———. *Les Antiquités du Luristan*. Paris: De Boccard, 1976.

Anati, E. *Camonica Valley*. London: Jonathan Cape, 1964.

Ancient Corinth: A Guide to the Excavations. Athens: Icaros Publishing, 1954.

Anderson, Robert E. *The Story of the Extinct Civilisations of the West*. London: George Newnes, 1903.

Angel, J. Lawrence. *The People of Lerna: Analysis of a Prehistoric Aegean Population*. Washington: Smithsonian Institution Press, 1971.

Anstee, Margaret Joan. *Gate of the Sun: A Prospect of Bolivia*. London: Longman, 1970.

Apollonius Rhodius. *Argonautica*. trans., R. C. Seaton. Loeb Classical Library, London: Heinemann, 1912.

Armour, Robert A. *Gods and Myths of Ancient Egypt*. American University in Cairo Press, 1986.

Arnheim, M. T. W. *Aristocracy in Greek Society*. London: Thames & Hudson, 1977.

Ashe, Geoffrey. *The Quest for America*. London: Pall Mall Press, 1971.

Astour, Michael C. *Hellenosemitica*. Leiden: E. J. Brill, 1967.

Aveni, Anthony, ed. *Archaeoastronomy in Pre-Columbian America*. Austin: University of Texas Press, 1977.

Aveni, A. F., and G. Brotherston. *Calendars in Mesoamerica and Peru*. Oxford: BAR, 1983.

Bacon, Francis. *The New Atlantis*. London, 1617.

Bahti, Tom. *Southwestern Indian Ceremonials*. Las Vegas: KC Publications, 1971.

Baikie, James. *The Sea-Kings of Crete*. London: A & C Black, 1920.

Bailey, James. *The God-Kings and the Titans*. London: Hodder & Stoughton, 1973.

Bakhuizen, S. C. *Chalcis-in-Euboea: Iron and Chalcidians Abroad*. Leiden: E. J. Brill, 1976.

Ballabriga, Alain, ed. *Le Soleil et le Tartare*. Paris: L'École des Hautes Études, 1986.

Ballard, Admiral G. A. *Rulers of the Indian Ocean*. London: Duckworth, 1927.

Bankes, George. *Peru Before Pizarro*. Oxford: Phaidon, 1977.

Barber, R. L. N. *The Cyclades in the Bronze Age*. London: Duckworth, 1987.

Barrau, Jacques, ed. *Plants and the Migrations of Pacific Peoples*. Hawaii: Bishop Museum Press, 1963.

Barrett, Clive. *The Egyptian Gods and Goddesses*. London: Aquarian/Thorsans, 1992.

Bass, George F. "Cape Gelidonya: A Bronze Age Shipwreck—Oldest Known Shipwreck Reveals Splendours of the Bronze Age." *National Geographic Magazine*. December 1987.

Bates, Henry W. *The Naturalist on the River Amazon.* London: John Murray, 1892.

Baudez, Claude F. *Central America.* Geneva: Nagel, 1970.

Baumgarten, Albert I. *The Phoenician History of Philo of Byblos.* Leiden: E. J. Brill, 1981.

Beals, Carleton. *Nomads and Empire Builders.* Philadelphia: Chilton, 1961.

Becher, Capt. A. B. *The Landfall of Columbus on His First Voyage to America.* London: J. D. Potter, 1856.

Bell, Edward. *Early Architecture in Western Asia.* London: G. Bell & Sons, 1924.

———. *Pre-Hellenic Architecture in the Aegean.* London: G. Bell & Sons, 1926.

Bemant, Chaim, and Michael Weitzman. *Ebla.* London: Weidenfeld & Nicolson, 1979.

Bender, Barbara. *The Archaeology of Brittany, Normandy and the Channel Islands.* London: Faber & Faber, 1986.

———. *Farming in Prehistory.* London: John Baker, 1975.

Berens, E. M. *Myths and Legends of Ancient Greece and Rome.* London: Blackie & Son, n.d.

Bergmann, F. G. *Les Amazones dans l'Histoire et dans la Fable.* Colmar, n.d.

Bernal, Ignacio. *A History of Mexican Archaeology.* London: Thames & Hudson, 1980.

———. *The Mexican National Museum of Anthropology.* London: Thames & Hudson, 1968.

———. *The Olmec World.* Los Angeles: University of California Press, 1973.

Bernal, Martin. *Black Athena.* London: Free Association Books, 1987.

Berriman, Algernon E. *Historical Metrology.* London: J. M. Dent & Sons, 1953.

Best, J. G. P., and N. de Vries, eds. *Interaction and Acculturation in the Mediterranean.* Amsterdam: Grüner, 1980.

———. *Thracians and Mycenaeans.* Leiden: E. J. Brill, 1989.

Bianchi, *Greek Mysteries.* Leiden: E. J. Brill, 1976.

Bible. Revised Standard Version. New York: The Bible Societies, 1952.

Blacker, C., and M. Loewe. *Ancient Cosmologies.* London: George Allen & Unwin, 1975.

Bleeker, C. J. *Hathor and Thoth.* Leiden: E. J. Brill, 1973.

Bonin, with John Mhiti. *Die Götter Schwarz-Afrikas,* Graz: VS, 1979.

Bottéro, Jean. *Mésopotamie.* Paris: Gallimard, 1987.

Bowman, ed. *Science and the Past.* London: British Museum, 1991.

Boyd, James W. *Satan and Māra.* Leiden: E. J. Brill, 1975.

Boylan, Patrick. *Thoth, the Hermes of Egypt.* Chicago: Ares, 1979.

Braidwood, Robert J. *The Near East and the Foundations for Civilization.* Eugene: University of Oregon Press, 1962.

Brandão, Alfredo. *A Escrita Prehistória do Brasil.* Rio de Janiero: Civilização Brasiliera, 1937.

Brandon, S. G. F. *Man and His Destiny.* Manchester University Press, 1962.

———. *The Saviour God.* Westport, Conn: Greenwood Press, 1963.

Branigan, Keith. *Pre-Palatial: The Foundations of Palatial Crete.* Amsterdam: Adolf M. Hakkert, 1988.

Braun-Holzinger, E. A. *Figürlichen Bronzen aus Mesopotamien.* Munich: Beck, 1984.

Bray, Warwick. *The Gold of Eldorado.* London: Catalogue of the Royal Academy, 1979.

Breasted, James H. *The Conquest of Civilisation.* London: Harper & Brothers, 1926.

———. *A History of Egypt.* London: Hodder & Stoughton, 1950.

Brennan, Martin. *The Stars and the Stones.* London: Thames & Hudson, 1983.

Brinkman, J. A. *A Political History of Post-Kassite Babylonia.* Rome: Pontificium Institutum Biblicum, 1968.

Briquel, Dominique. *Les Pélasges en Italie.* École Française de Rome, 1984.

Brommer, Frank. *Heracles.* New York: Aristide Caratzas, 1986.

Brøndsted, Johannes. *The Vikings.* Harmondsworth: Pelican, 1965.

Brooks, E., R. Fuerst, J. Hemming, and F. Huxley. *Tribes of the Amazon in Brazil, 1972.* London: Charles Knight, 1973.

Brooks, John. *The South American Handbook.* Bath: Trade and Travel Publications, 1975.

Brotherston, Gordon. *The Key to the Mesoamerican Reckoning of Time.* London: British Museum Occasional Papers, 1982.

Browman, David L. *Advances in Andean Archaeology.* The Hague: Mouton, 1978.

Brown, Dee. *Bury My Heart at Wounded Knee.* London: Barrie & Jenkins, 1970.

Brown, Peter. *Megaliths, Myths and Men.* Poole: Blandford Press, 1976.

Brug, John F. *A Literary and Archaeological Study of the Philistines.* Oxford: BAR, 1985.

Bruschweiler, Françoise. *Inanna.* Leuven: Edition Peeters, 1987.

Buccellati, Giorgio. *The Amorites of the Ur III Period.* Naples: Instituto Orientale di Napoli, 1966.

Budge, Sir A. E. Wallis. *The Book of the Dead.* Vols. I and II, Medici Society, 1913.

———. *Egyptian Language.* London: Routledge & Kegan Paul, 1971.

———. *Osiris and the Egyptian Resurrection.* London: Lee Warner, 1911.

Bureau of American Ethnology. *Thirty-fourth Annual Report.* Washington: Government Printer, 1922.

Burkhart, Louise M. *The Slippery Earth.* Tucson: University of Arizona, 1989.

Burl, Aubrey. *Prehistoric Avebury.* New Haven: Yale University Press, 1979.

Burland, Cottie. *North American Indian Mythology.* London: Paul Hamlyn, 1965.

Burn, A. R. *Minoans, Philistines and Greeks, B. C. 1400–900.* London: Dawsons of Pall Mall, 1968.

Burton, Anne. *Diodorus Siculus Book I—A Commentary.* Leiden: E. J. Brill, 1972.

Bury, J. B. *A History of Greece.* London: Macmillan, 1924.

Bushnell, G. H. S. *Ancient Arts of the Americas.* London: Thames & Hudson, 1965.

———. *The Archaeology of the Santa Elena Peninsula in South West Ecuador.* London: Cambridge University Press, 1951.

———. *Peru.* London: Thames & Hudson, 1956.

Cadogan, Gerald, ed. *The End of the Early Bronze Age in the Aegean.* Leiden: E. J. Brill, 1986.

Calvani, Vittoria. *The World of the Maya.* Geneva: Minerva, 1976.

Cambridge Ancient History. J. B. Bury, S. A. Cook, and F. E. Adcock, eds. Cambridge University Press, Vol. II, 1931. Vol. III, 1965. Vol. IV, 1964.

Cambridge Ancient History. I. E. S. Edwards, C. J. Gadd, N. G. L. Hammond, and E. Sollberger, eds. 1970–75.

Campbell, *The Masks of God.* London: Condor Books, 1964.

Carter, George F. "Chinese Contacts with America: Fu Sang Again." *Anthropological Journal of Canada,* Vol. 14, No. 1, 1976.

———. *Man and the Land.* New York: Holt, Rinehart & Winston, 1964.

———. *Plants Across the Pacific. Memoirs of the Society for American Archaeology,* No. 9. Jesse Jennings, ed.

———. "Why I Am No Longer a 'Standard Americanist.' " *Geography.* College Station: Texas A & M University.

Carvajal, Gaspar de. *The Discovery of the Amazon.* New York: José Toribio Medina for the American Geographic Society, 1934.

Caso, Alfonso. *Los Calendarios Prehispanicos.* Mexico City: Universidad Nacional Autónoma de Mexico, 1967.

Casson, Lionel. *The Ancient Mariners.* Princeton: University Press, 1991.

Cassuto, U. *The Goddess Anath.* Jerusalem: Magnes Press, Hebrew University, 1971.

Castro e Almeida, Virginia de, ed. *Conquests and Discoveries of Henry the Navigator.* London: George Allen & Unwin, 1936.

Ceram, C. W. *Gods, Graves and Scholars.* New York: Knopf, 1951.

Chadwick, John. *The Decipherment of Linear B.* Cambridge University Press, 1990.

———. *The Mycenaean World.* Cambridge University Press, 1976.

Chang, Kwang-Chih. *Shang Civilization.* New Haven: Yale University Press, 1980.

Christopoulos, George A., ed. *Prehistory and Protohistory.* London: Heinemann, 1974.

Cicero. *De Natura Deorum.* London: Methuen, 1896.

Cieza de Léon, Pedro. *The Incas.* Norman: University of Oklahoma Press, 1959.

———. *The Travels of Pedro de Cieza de Léon.* trans. and ed, C. R. Markham. London: Hakluyt Society, 1864.

Clark, Grahame. *World Prehistory in New Perspective.* Cambridge University Press, 1961.

Clark, R. T. Rundle. *Myth and Symbol in Ancient Egypt.* London: Thames & Hudson, 1978.

Clay, Jenny Strauss. *The Politics of Olympus: Form and Meaning in the Major Homeric Hymns.* Princeton University Press, 1989.

Clement of Alexandria. *Les Stomates.* Trans., P. Voulet. Paris: Edition du Cerf, 1981.

Coates, J., and S. McGrail, eds. *The Greek Trireme of the 5th Century B.C.* Greenwich: National Maritime Museum, n.d.

Codex Laud. Oxford University Press, 1966.

Codex Mendoza Aztec Manuscript. Fribourg, Switzerland: Miller Graphics, 1978.

Coe, Michael D. *The Maya.* London: Thames & Hudson, 1966.

Cohane. *The Key.* New York: Crown, 1969.

Cohen. *La Grande Invention de l'Écriture et son Évolution.* Paris: 1958.

Cohen, Mark. *Sumerian Hymnology.* Cincinnati: Ersemma, 1981.

Columbus, Ferdinand. *The Life of Admiral Christopher Columbus.* trans., B. Keen. New Brunswick: Rutgers University Press, 1959.

Conrad, G. W., and A. A. Demarest. *Religion and Empire.* Cambridge University Press, 1988.

Contenau, Georges. *Everyday Life in Babylon and Assyria.* London: Edward Arnold, 1954.

Coogan, Michael D. *Stories from Ancient Canaan.* Philadelphia: Westminster Press, 1978.

Cory. *Ancient Fragments.* Minneapolis: 1975.

Cottrell, Leonard. *The Land of Shinar.* London: Souvenir Press, 1965.

Cowper, H. S. *The Hill of the Graces.* London: Darf, 1983.

Crampton, Patrick. *Stonehenge of the Kings*. London: John Baker, 1967.

Cross, T. P., and C. H. Slover. *Ancient Irish Tales*. Dublin: Allen Figgis, 1969.

Culican, William. *The First Merchant Venturers*. London: Thames & Hudson, 1966.

———. *The Medes and Persians*. London: Thames & Hudson, 1965.

Cummins, Geraldine. *The Fate of Colonel Fawcett*. London: Aquarian Press, 1955.

Dames, Michael. *The Avebury Cycle*. London: Thames & Hudson, 1977.

———. *The Silbury Treasure*. London: Thames & Hudson, 1976.

Daniel, Glyn. *The First Civilizations*. London: Thames & Hudson, 1968.

———. *The Megalith Builders of Western Europe*. Harmondsworth: Pelican, 1963.

Daniel, Glyn, and S. P. O'Riordain. *New Grange*. London: Thames & Hudson, 1964.

Danquah, J. B. *The Akan Doctrine of God*. London: Frank Cass, 1968.

———. In *Ghana Cultural Review*, Vol. 2, No. 2, 1966.

Dart, Raymond A. "Africa's Place in the Emergence of Civilisation." S.A.B.C. *African Arts Magazine*, 1960.

———. "Ancient Mining Industry of Southern Africa." *South African Geographical Journal*, 7, 1924.

———. "The Birth of Symbology." *African Studies*, Vol. 27, No. 1, 1968.

———. "The Earlier Stages of Indian Transoceanic Traffic." *NADA*, 34, 1957.

———. "The Multimillennial Prehistory of Ochre Mining." *NADA*, 1967.

———. "The Recency of Man's Aquatic Past." *New Scientist*, Vol. 7, 1960.

Dart, R. A., and P. Beaumont. "Amazing Antiquity of Mining in Southern Africa." *Nature*, 216, 1967.

Da Silva Ramos, B. *Inscripcões e Traduções da America Prehistórica*. Vols. I and II. Rio de Janiero, 1932–39.

Davies, Nigel. *The Ancient Kingdoms of Mexico*. Harmondsworth: Penguin, 1983.

De Graeve, Marie-Christine. *The Ships of the Ancient Near East*. Leuven: Departement Oriëntalistiek, 1981.

De la Vega, Garcilaso. *Royal Commentaries of the Incas*. London: University of Texas Press, 1966.

Dennison, L. R. *Devil Mountain*. New York: Hastings House, 1942.

Desroches-Noblecourt, C. *Tutenkhamen*. Harmondsworth: Penguin, 1965.

De Terra, Helmut. *Man and Mammoth in Mexico*. London: Hutchinson, 1957.

Deuel, Leo. *Conquistadors Without Swords*. New York: St. Martin's 1967.

Díaz del Castillo, Bernal. *The Conquest of New Spain*. Harmondsworth: Penguin, 1963.

Dickinson, O. T. P. K. *The Origins of Mycenaean Civilisation*. Göteborg: Paul Åströms Förlag, 1977.

Diehl, Richard A. *Tula: The Toltec Capital of Ancient Mexico*. London: Thames & Hudson, 1983.

Diodorus Siculus. *Complete Works*. Trans., Oldfather et al. Loeb Classical Library. London: Heinemann: 1933–67.

———. *History of the World*. London: Giles Calvert, 1653.

Diringer, D. *The Alphabet*. Vols. I and II. London: Hutchinson, 1968.

———. *Writing*. London: Thames & Hudson, 1962.

Dockstader, Frederick J. *Indian Art of Central America*. London: Cory, Adams & Mackay, 1964.

Donnelly, Ignatius. *Atlantis*. London: Sidgwick & Jackson, 1950.

Dothan, Trude. *The Philistines and Their Material Culture*. New Haven: Yale University Press, 1982.

Doumas, Christos. *Early Bronze Age Burial Habits in the Cyclades*. Göteborg: Paul Åströms Förlag, 1977.

Doumas, Christos, ed. *Thera and the Aeagean World*. Vols. I and II. London: published privately, 1978–80.

Drier, R. W., and O. du Temple. *Prehistoric Copper Mining in the Lake Superior Region*. Calumet, Michigan: published privately, 1961.

Du Buisson, Robert. *Études sur les Dieux Phéniciens Hérités par l'Empire Romain*. Leiden: E. J. Brill, 1970.

Dunand, Maurice. *Byblos*. Paris: Librairie Adrien-Maisonneuve, 1963.

Ediger, Donald. *The Well of Sacrifice*. London: Robert Hale, 1973.

Edwards, I. E. S. *The Pyramids of Egypt*. Harmondsworth: Pelican, 1961.

Ekholm, G. F., and G. R. Willey. *Archaeological Frontiers and External Connections*. Austin: University of Texas Press, 1966.

Ekholm-Miller, Susanna. *The Olmec Rock Carving at Xoc, Chiapas, Mexico*. Provo, Utah: Brigham Young University Press, 1973.

Enciso, Jorge. *Designs from Pre-Columbian Mexico*. New York: Dover, 1971.

———. *Design Motifs of Ancient Mexico*. New York: Dover, 1953.

Encyclopaedia of Religion and Ethics. Ed., James Hastings. Edinburgh: T & T Clark, 1971.

Erdoes, Richard. *The Rain Dance People*. New York: Knopf, 1976.

Erman, Adolf. *The Literature of the Ancient Egyptians*. London: Methuen, 1927.

Espinosa, Alfonso de. *The Gaunches of Tenerife*. Trans., C. R. Markham. London: Hakluyt Society, 1907.

Eusebius. *Chronicorum*. Zurich: Weidmann, 1967.

———. *Ecclesiastical History*. Loeb Classical Library, London, 1965.

Evans, J. D. *The Prehistoric Antiquities of the Maltese Islands*. London: Athlone Press, 1971.

Fagan, Brian M., ed. *Avenues to Antiquity: Readings from Scientific American*. San Francisco: W. H. Freeman, 1976.

Fagg, W., and J. Pemberton. *Yoruba Sculpture of West Africa*. London: Collins, 1987.

Fairman, H. W., gen. ed. *Megalithic Enquiries in the West of Britain*. Liverpool University Press, 1969.

Farrell, Robert T., ed. *The Vikings*. London: Phillimore, 1982.

Farrer, Reginald. *In Old Ceylon*. London: Edward Arnold, 1908.

Faulkner, Raymond O. *The Ancient Egyptian Pyramid Texts*. Warminster: Aris & Phillips, 1969.

Fawcett, Lt. Col. P. H. *Exploration Fawcett*. London: Hutchinson, 1953.

Fawns, Sidney. *Tin Deposits of the World*. London: The Mining Journal, n.d.

Feest, Christian F. *Indians of Northeastern North America*. Leiden: E. J. Brill, 1986.

Fell, Barry. *America B. C.* New York: Demeter Press, 1977.

———. *Bronze Age America*. Boston: Little, Brown 1982.

Ferguson, Thomas Stuart. *One Fold and One Shepherd*. Salt Lake City: Olympus, 1962.

Fernández-Armesto, Felipe. *Before Columbus*. London: Macmillan, 1987.

Fleming, Peter. *Brazilian Adventure*. London: Jonathan Cape, 1936.

Folsom, F., and M. E. Folsom. *America's Ancient Treasures*. Albuquerque: University of New Mexico Press, 1983.

Forbes, Robert J. *Studies in Ancient Technology*. Leiden: E. J. Brill, 1964–66.

Frankfort, H. *Cylinder Seals*. Gregg, 1939.

———. *Kingship and the Gods*. Chicago University Press, 1948.

Fraser, John F. *Panama and What It Means*. London: Cassell, 1913.

Frazer, Sir James. *The Golden Bough, Part VI: The Scape Goat*. London: Macmillan, 1933.

Freeman, Kathleen. *Companion to the Pre-Socratic Philosophers*. Oxford: Blackwell, 1946.

———. *God, Man and the State: Greek Concepts*. London: Macdonald, 1952.

French, E. B., and K. A. Wardle. *Problems in Greek Prehistory*. Bristol: Bristol Classical Press, 1988.

Frobenius, Leo. *The Voice of Africa*. Trans., Rudolf Blind. London: Hutchinson, 1913.

Fuson, Robert H. "The Orientation of Mayan Ceremonial Centers." *Annals of the Association of American Geographers*. Vol. 59, No. 3, September 1969.

Gallo, M. G., and R. R. Alvaro. *Oro del Peru: Catalogue of the Oro del Peru Exhibition*. Cape Town: S. A. National Gallery, 1981.

Garcia, L. Pericot. *The Balearic Islands*. London: Thames & Hudson, 1972.

Gardiner, Sir Alan. *Egyptian Grammar*. Oxford: Clarendon, 1927.

———. *Egypt of the Pharaohs*. Oxford: Clarendon, 1960.

Gelfand, Michael. *Shona Ritual*. Johannesburg: Juta, 1959.

Gelling, P., and H. Davidson. *The Chariot of the Sun*. London: Dent, 1969.

Ghosh, A. *Encyclopaedia of Indian Archaeology*. Vols. I and II. Leiden. E. J. Brill, 1990.

Gill, Sam D. *Songs of Life*. Leiden: E. J. Brill, 1979.

Gillings, Robert J. *Mathematics in the Time of the Pharaohs*.

Gimbutas, Marija. *Bronze Age Cultures in Central and Eastern Europe*. The Hague: Mouton, 1965.

———. *The Gods and Goddesses of Old Europe*. London: Thames & Hudson, 1974.

———. *The Language of the Goddess*. London: Thames & Hudson, 1989.

Glaze, Anita. *Art and Death in a Senufe Village*. Bloomington: Indiana University Press, 1981.

Goff, Beatrice L. *Symbols of Ancient Egypt in the Late Period*. The Hague: Mouton, 1979.

———. *Symbols of Mesopotamia*. New Haven: Yale University Press, 1965.

Gonda, Jan. *Ancient Indian Kingship from the Religious Point of View*. Leiden: E. J. Brill, 1969.

Gose, Sri Aurobindo. *Hymns to the Mystic Fire*. Sri Aurobindo Ashram, 1946.

Gordon, Cyrus H. *Before Columbus*. New York: Crown, 1971.

———. *Forgotten Scripts*. London: Thames & Hudson, 1966.

———. *Manuscripts*. Vol. 21, No. 37, 1969.

———. *Orientalia*. Vol. 37, 1968.

———. *Ugarit and Minoan Crete*. New York: Norton, 1966.

———. *Ugaritic Literature*. Roma, 1949.

Graham, J. Walter. *The Palaces of Crete*. Princeton University Press, 1987.

Grant, Campbell. *Rock Art of the North American Indians*. Cambridge University Press, 1983.

———. *The Rock Paintings of the Chumash*. Berkeley: University of California Press, 1965.

Grant, Michael. *The Ancient Mediterranean*. London: Weidenfeld & Nicolson, 1969.

Graves, Robert. *Greek Myths*. London: Cassell, 1965.

Graves, R., and R. Patai. *Hebrew Myths: The Book of Genesis.* London: Cassell, 1964.

Gray, John. *Near-Eastern Mythology.* London: Hamlyn, 1969.

Grayson, A. Kirk *Assyrian Rulers of the Third and Second Millennia B.C.* Toronto University Press, 1987.

Greenhalgh, P. A. L. *Early Greek Warfare: Horsemen and Chariots in the Homeric and Archaic Ages.* London: Cambridge University Press, 1973.

Griaule, M., and G. Dieterlen. *Conversations with Ogotemelli.* Oxford University Press, 1965.

Griffiths, J. Gwyn. *The Conflict of Horus and Seth.* Liverpool University Press, 1960.

———. *The Origins of Osiris and his Cult.* Leiden: E. J. Brill, 1980.

Grimal, Pierre. *The Dictionary of Classical Mythology.* Oxford: Basil Blackwell, 1986.

Grimes, John. *A Concise Dictionary of Indian Philosophy.* State University of New York, 1989

Guerber, Hellene A. *The Myths of Greece and Rome.* London: Harrap, 1908.

Guerra, Francisco. *The Pre-Columbian Mind.* London: Seminar Press, 1971.

Guerrier. *La Cosmogonie Dogon.* Paris: Robert Laffont, 1975.

Guppy, Nicholas. *Wai-Wai.* London: John Murray, 1958.

Hackett, Rosalind. *Religion in Calabar.* Berlin: Mouton de Gruyter, 1989.

Hägg, R., and N. Marinatos, eds. *Sanctuaries and Cults in the Aegean Bronze Age.* Stockholm: Svenska Institutet in Athen, 1981.

Hallo, W. W., and J. J. A. van Dijk. *The Exaltation of Innana.* New Haven: Yale University Press, 1968.

Halsberghe. *The Cult of Sol Invictus.* Leiden: E. J. Brill, 1972.

Hammer, O., and J. D'Andrea, eds. *Treasures of Mexico.* Los Angeles: Armand Hammer Foundation, 1978.

Hanno the Carthaginian. *Periplus or the Circumnavigation (of Africa).* Trans., A. N. Okonomides. Chicago: Ares, 1977.

Harden, Donald. *The Phoenicians.* London: Thames & Hudson, 1962.

Hart. *Egyptian Myths.* London: British Museum Press, 1990.

Hawkes, Jacquetta. *Man and the Sun.* Cresset Press, 1962.

Hawkins, Gerald S. *Stonehenge Decoded.* London: Fontana, 1972.

Hawkins, J. D., ed. *Trade in the Ancient Near East.* London: British School of Archaeology in Iraq, 1977.

Healy, J. F. *Mining and Metallurgy in the Greek and Roman World.* London: Thames & Hudson, 1978.

Heggie, Douglas. *Megalithic Science.* London: Thames & Hudson, 1981.

Heichelheim. *Ancient Economic History.* Leiden: Sijthoff, 1965.

Heidel, Alexander. *The Babylonian Genesis.* Chicago University Press, 1951.

———. *The Gilgamesh Epic and Old Testament Parallels.* Chicago University Press, 1949.

Heltzer, Michael. *Goods, Prices and the Organisation of Trade in Ugarit.* Wiesbaden: Dr. Ludwig Reichert Verlag, 1978.

Henderson, I. *The Picts.* London: Thames & Hudson, 1967.

Herman, Zvi. *Peoples, Seas and Ships.* London: Phoenix House, 1966.

Herodotus. *Histories.* Trans., G. Rawlinson. Everyman Library, London: J. M. Dent & Sons, 1948.

Hesiod. *The Homeric Hymns and Homerica.* Trans., H. Evelyn-White. Loeb Classical Library, London: Heinemann, 1914.

———. *Theogony.* Ed., M. L. West. Oxford University Press, 1966.

———. *Theogony.* Loeb Classical Library, London: Heinemann, 1914.

Heyerdahl, Thor. *Aku-Aku.* London: George Allen & Unwin, 1958.

———. *American Indians in the Pacific.* London: George Allen & Unwin, 1952.

———. *The Ra Expeditions.* London: George Allen & Unwin, 1971.

———. *The Tigris Expedition.* London: George Allen & Unwin, 1980.

Heyob, Sharon Kelly. *The Cult of Isis Among the Women of the Graeco-Roman World.* Leiden: E. J. Brill, 1975.

Hidding, K. A. H. *The Sacral Kingship.* Leiden: Brill, 1959.

Hikkelheber. "Sculptors and Sculptures of the Dan." *Proceedings of the 1st Congress of Africanists.*

Hirth, F., and W. Rockwell. *Chau Ju-Kua on the Chinese and Arab Trade.* Amsterdam: Oriental Press, 1966.

Hogben, Lancelot. *Mathematics for the Millions.* London: George Allen & Unwin, 1951.

Holas. *Les Senoufo.* Paris: Presses Universitaires de France, 1966.

Homer. The *Iliad* and the *Odyssey.* Trans., Murray. Loeb Classical Library, London: Heinemann, 1919.

———. *The Odyssey.* Trans., E. V. Rieu. Harmondsworth: Penguin, 1954.

Homet, Marcel F. *On the Trail of the Sun-Gods.* London: Neville Spearman, 1965.

———. *Sons of the Sun.* London: Neville Spearman, 1963.

Honoré, Pierre. *In Quest of the White God.* London: Hutchinson, 1963.

Hood, Sinclair. *The Home of the Heroes: The Aegean Before the Greeks.* London: Thames & Hudson, 1967.

Hooke, S. H. *Babylonian and Assyrian Religion.* Oxford: Blackwell, 1962.

———. *Middle Eastern Mythology*. London: Pelican, 1963.
Hope, Colin. *The Gold of the Pharaohs*. Melbourne: Museum of Victoria, 1988.
Horn, Aloysius. *The Ivory Coast in the Earlies*. London: Jonathan Cape, 1927.
Hornell, James. *The Archaeology of Gorgona Island, South America*. London: Royal Anthropological Institute, 1926.
———. *The Archaic Sculptured Rocks and Stone Implements of Gorgona Island, South America*. London: Royal Anthropological Institute, 1925.
———. *British Coracles and Irish Curraghs*. London: Quaritch, 1938.
———. *Water Transport*. Cambridge University Press, 1946.
Hudson, W. H. *The Naturalist in La Plata*. London: Chapman & Hall, 1892.
Hugh-Jones, Stephen. *The Palm and the Pleiades*. Cambridge University Press, 1979.
Hultkrantz, Åke. *Prairie and Plains Indians*. Leiden: E. J. Brill, 1973.
Hunt, L. B. "The Long History of Lost Wax Casting." *Gold Bulletin*, Vol. 13, No. 2. International Gold Corporation, April 1980.
Hutchinson, R. W. *Prehistoric Crete*. Harmondsworth: Penguin, 1962.
Hutchinson, Thomas J. *Two Years in Peru*. Volumes I & II. London: Sampson Low, Marston, Low, & Searle, 1873.
Huxley, G. L. *The Early Ionians*. London: Faber & Faber, 1966.
———. *Early Sparta*. London: Faber & Faber, 1962.
Hyginus. *Fabularum Liber*. New York: Garland, 1976.

Irwin, Constance. *Fair Gods and Stone Faces*. New York: St. Martin's, 1963.
Iyengar, T. R. *Dravidian India*. New Delhi: Asian Educational Services, 1982.

Jacobsen, Thorkild. *The Sumerian King List*. Chicago: University Press, 1939.
———. *Towards the Image of Tammuz*. Cambridge: Harvard University Press, 1970.
Jacoby, Felix. *Die Fragmente der Griechischen Historiker*. Vol. II. Leiden: E. J. Brill, 1929–30.
Jairazbhoy, R. A. *Ancient Egyptians and Chinese in America*. London: George Prior, 1974.
———. *Ancient Egyptian Survivals in the Pacific*. London: Karnak House, 1990.
———. *Asians in Pre-Columbian Mexico*. Published privately, 1976.
James, Edwin O. *Creation and Cosmology*. Leiden: E. J. Brill, 1969.
———. *The Tree of Life*. Leiden: E. J. Brill, 1966.
Jane, Cecil, trans. and ed. *The Voyages of Christopher Columbus*. London: Argonaut Press, 1930.
Jeffreys, M. D. W. "Pre-Columbian Negroes in America." *Scientia*, July-August 1953.
Jewell, John H. A. *Dhows at Mombasa*. Nairobi: East Africa Publishing House, 1976.
Jobin, José. *The Mineral Wealth of Brazil*. Rio de Janeiro: José Olympio, c. 1941.
Johnstone, Paul. *The Sea-craft of Prehistory*. London: Routledge & Kegan Paul, 1980.
Jones, Dilwyn. *A Glossary of Ancient Egyptian Nautical Titles and Terms*. London: Routledge & Kegan Paul, 1988.
Jones, George. *The History of Ancient America*. London: Longman Brown, Green & Longmans, 1843.
Jordan, Michael. *Encyclopaedia of Gods*. London: Kyle Cathie, 1992.
Josephson, Nors. *Greek Linguistic Elements in the Polynesian Language*. Heidelberg: Universitätsverlag, 1987.
Josephus, Flavius. *Against Apion*. Loeb Classical Library, London: Heinemann, 1961.
———. *Antiquities of the Jews*. Trans., E. Thompson & W. C. Price. London: Fielding & Walker, 1777.
Journal of Hellenic Studies. Vol. 58, Nos. 1 and 2, 1938. Vol. 74, 1954.
Joyce, Thomas. *Central American and West Indian Archaeology*. London: Philip Warner, 1916.
Julian the Apostate. Ed., Rochefort.
Julius Caesar. *De Bello Gallico*. Trans., Rev. J. Towers. London: Hawes, Clarke & Collins, 1768.

Kampen, M. E. *The Religion of the Maya*. Leiden: E. J. Brill, 1981.
Karageorghis, Vassos. *Kition: Mycenaean and Phoenician Discoveries in Cyprus*. London: Thames & Hudson, 1976.
Katz, Freidrich. *The Ancient American Civilisations*. London: Weidenfeld & Nicolson, 1972.
Kauffman, Donald T., ed. *Baker's Concise Dictionary of Religion*. Grand Rapids, Mich.: Baker Book House, 1985.
Keatinge, Richard W., ed. *Peruvian Prehistory*. Cambridge University Press, 1988.
Keith, A. B., and A. J. Carnoy. *The Mythology of All Races*. Gen. ed., L. H. Gray. Vol. VI, New York: Cooper Square, 1964.
Kelemen, Pál. *Medieval American Art*. Vols. 1 and 2, London: Macmillan, 1944.
Kendrick, T. D. *A History of the Vikings*. London: Methuen, 1930.
Kenyon, Kathleen M. *Amorites and Canaanites*. London: Oxford University Press for the British Academy, 1966.
Kerenyi, L. *Zeus and Hera*. London: Routledge & Kegan Paul, 1975.
Kidder, Alfred V. *An Introduction to the Study of Southwestern*

Archaeology. New Haven: Yale University Press, 1962.

King, Leonard W. *First Steps in Assyrian*. London: Kegan Paul, 1898.

Kinross, Lord. *Between Two Seas*. London: John Murray, 1968.

Kisch, Bruno. *Scales and Weights*. New Haven: Yale University Press, 1977.

Klijn, A. F. J. *Seth in Jewish, Christian and Gnostic Literature*. Leiden: E. J. Brill, 1977.

Knappert, Jan. *Myths and Legends of the Congo*. Nairobi: Heinemann, 1971.

Knauth, Percy. *The Metalsmiths*. Time Life Books, 1982.

Kramer, Samuel N. *Sumerian Mythology*. New York: Harper & Row, 1961.

———. *The Sumerians*. Chicago University Press, 1963.

Kramer, S. N., and J. Maier. *Myths of Enki*. Oxford University Press, 1989.

Krickeberg, W., H. Trimborn, W. Müller, and O. Zerries. *Pre-Columbian American Religions*. London: Weidenfeld & Nicolson, 1968.

Krupp, E. C., ed. *In Search of Ancient Astronomies*. London: Chatto & Windus, 1979.

Krzyszkowska, O., and L. Nixon, eds. *Minoan Society*. Bristol: Bristol Classical Press, 1983.

La Barre, Weston. *The Ghost Dance: Origins of Religions*. London: George Allen & Unwin, 1972.

Lacy, A. D. *Greek Pottery in the Bronze Age*. London: Methuen, 1967.

Lahovary, N. *La Diffusion des Langues Anciennes du Proche-Orient*. Berne: Francke, 1957.

Lambert, WG. *Babylonian Wisdom Literature*. Oxford: Clarendon, 1960.

Lambert, WG., and A. R. Millard. *Atra-hasis*. Oxford: Clarendon, 1970.

Lamy, Lucie. *Egyptian Mysteries*. London: Thames & Hudson, 1981.

Landa, Diego de. *The Maya: Diego de Landa's Account of the Affairs of Yucatan*. Trans., A. R. Pagden. Chicago: J. Philip O'Hara, 1975.

Landström, Björn. *Columbus*. London: George Allen & Unwin, 1967.

Landsverk, O. G. "Runes Dated in Cryptograms: Vikings in North America Before Columbus." *The Explorers Journal*, December 1987.

Landy, Francis. *The Tale of Aqhat*. London: Menard, 1981.

Langdon, S. *The Legend of Etana and the Eagle*. Paris: Geunthner, 1932.

Lange, K., and H. Hirmer. *Egypt*. London: Phaidon, 1968.

Lanning, Edward P. *Peru Before the Incas*. Englewood, N.J.: Prentice Hall, 1967.

Larrington, Carolyne. *The Feminist Companion to Mythology*. London: Pandora, 1992.

Larsen, Mogens Trolle, ed. *Mesopotamia, Power and Propaganda*. Copenhagen: Akademisk Forlag, 1979.

Larousse Encyclopaedia of Archaeology. London: Hamlyn, 1977.

Larousse Encyclopaedia of Mythology. London: Hamlyn, 1959.

Larousse World Mythology. London: Hamlyn, 1965.

Lathrap, Donald W. *The Upper Amazon*. Southampton: Thames & Hudson, 1970.

Lauer, Jean-Philippe. *Saqqara*. London: Thames & Hudson, 1976.

le Corsu, France. *Isis, Mythe et Mystères*. Paris: Édition Les Belles Lettres, 1977.

Léon-Portilla, Miguel. *Pre-Columbian Literatures of Mexico*. Norman: University of Oklahoma Press, 1961.

Levi, Peter. *The Hill of Kronos*. London: Arrow Books, 1987.

Levzinger, Elsy. *Afrique, L'Art des Peuples Noirs*. Paris: Albin Michel, 1962.

Lewis, David. *The Voyaging Stars*. Sydney: Collins, 1978.

Lewis, Jack P. *A Study of the Interpretation of Noah and the Flood in Jewish and Christian Literature*. Leiden: E. J. Brill, 1978.

Limet, H. *Toponymie Antique*. Leiden: E. J. Brill, 1975.

Lister, R. H. "Archaeology for Layman and Scientist at Mesa Verde." *Science*, Vol. 160, No. 3827, May 3, 1968.

Lloyd, Seton. *The Archaeology of Mesopotamia*. London: Thames & Hudson, 1978.

Lothrop, S. K. *Treasures of Ancient America*. Geneva: Skira, 1964.

Lothrop, S. K., and J. Mahler. *Late Nazca Burials in Chaviña, Peru*. Cambridge: Peabody Museum, 1957.

Lucas, Alfred. *Ancient Egyptian Materials and Industries*. London: Edward Arnold, 1934.

Luce, J. V. *The End of Atlantis*. London: Paladin, 1972.

Lurker, Manfred. *The Gods and Symbols of Ancient Egypt*. London: Thames & Hudson, 1980.

Macalister, R. A. Stewart. *The Philistines: Their History and Civilisation*. Oxford University Press, 1914.

Mackenzie, Donald A. *Egyptian Myth and Legend*. London: Gresham, n.d.

———. *Myths of Crete and Pre-Hellenic Europe*. London: Gresham, 1917.

MacKie, Euan. *The Megalith Builders*. Oxford: Phaidon, 1977.

MacNeish, Richard S. *The Prehistory of the Tehuacan Valley*. London: University of Texas Press, 1970.

MacNicol, Nichol, ed. *Hindu Scriptures*. London: Dent, 1938.

Madariaga, Salvador de. *The Rise of the Spanish American Empire*. London: Hollis & Carter, 1947.

Magnusson, M., and H. Pálsson. *The Vinland Sagas*. Harmondsworth: Penguin, 1965.

Mahan, Capt. A. T. *The Interest of America in Sea Power Present and Future*. Boston: Little, Brown, 1903.

Maisels, Charles. *The Emergence of Civilisation*. London: Routledge, 1990.

Manetho. *Aegyptiaca*. Trans., Waddell. Loeb, Classical Library, London: Heinemann, 1948.

Margueron, Jean-Claude. *Mesopotamia*. Geneva: Nagel, 1965.

Markham, Sir Clements. *The Guanches of Tenerife*. London: Hakluyt Society, 1907.

———. *The Rites and Laws of the Incas*. London: Hakluyt Society, 1873.

Marshall, Sir John, ed. *Mohenjo-daro and the Indus Civilisation*. Vols. I, II and III, London: Probsthain, 1931.

Marx, Robert. "Who Really Discovered the New World?" *The Explorers Journal*, Winter 1991.

Marx, Robert, and Jenifer Marx. *In Quest of the Great White Gods*. New York: Crown, 1992.

Mason, Y. Alden. *The Ancient Civilization of Peru*. Harmondsworth: Penguin, 1969.

Maspero, Gaston. *The Dawn of Civilization: Egypt and Chaldaea*. S.P.C.K., London 189.

Masson-Oursel, P., H. Willman-Grabowska, and P. Stern. *Ancient India and Indian Civilisation*. London: Routledge & Kegan Paul, 1967.

Massoulard, Emile. *Préhistoire et Protohistoire d'Égypte*. Paris: Institut d'Ethnologie, 1949.

Matz, Freidrich. *Crete and Early Greece: The Prelude to Greek Art*. London: Methuen, 1962.

Mazar, Amihai. *Excavations at Tell Qasile*. Parts I and II. Institute of Archaeology of the Hebrew University of Jerusalem, 1980, 1985.

McMann, Jean. *Riddles of the Stone Age*. London: Thames & Hudson, 1980.

Medina, J. T. *The Discovery of the Amazon*. New York: American Geographical Society, 1934.

Mee, Christopher. *Rhodes in the Bronze Age*. Warminster: Aris & Phillips, 1982.

Meijer, Fik. *A History of Seafaring in the Classical World*. London: Croom Helm, 1986.

Mellaart, James. *Earliest Civilizations of the Near East*. London: Thames & Hudson, 1965.

Ménard, Jacques. *Le Feu dans le Proche-Orient Antique*. Leiden: E. J. Brill, 1973.

Mera, H. P. *Pueblo Designs*. New York: Dover, 1970.

Mercer, John. *The Canary Islanders*. London: Rex Collings, 1980.

Mercer, Samuel A. B. *A Sumero-Babylonian Sign List*. A.M.S. Press, 1966.

Mertz, Henriette. *Pale Ink*. Chicago: published privately, 1953.

———. *The Wine Dark Sea*. Chicago: published privately, 1964.

Métraux, Alfred. *The Incas*. London: Studio Vista, 1965.

Michel-Jones, Françoise. *Retour au Dogon*. Paris: Le Sycomore, 1948.

Miller, J. Innes. *The Spice Trade of the Roman Empire, 29 B.C.–A.D. 641*. Oxford: Clarendon, 1969.

Misra, V. N., and Peter Bellwood, eds. *Recent Advances in Indo-Pacific Prehistory*. Leiden: E. J. Brill, 1985.

Misra V. N., and M. S. Mate. *Indian Prehistory*. Poona: Deccan College, 1965.

Morelet, Arthur, trans. *Journal du Voyage de Vasco de Gama*. Lyon: Louis Perrin, 1864.

Morris, Ronald. *The Prehistoric Rock Art of Southern Scotland*. London: BAR, 1981

Moscati, Sabatino. *The World of the Phoenicians*. London: Weidenfeld & Nicolson, 1965.

Mosso, Angelo. *The Dawn of Mediterranean Civilization*. London: T. Fisher Unwin, 1910.

Muhly, James. *Copper and Tin*. Hamden, Conn: Archon, 1973.

Muratori. *A Relation of the Missions of Paraguay*. London: J. Marmaduke, 1759.

Muser, Curt. *Facts and Artifacts of Ancient Middle America*. New York: Dutton, 1978.

Mylonas, George E. *Mycenae and the Mycenaean Age*. Princeton University Press, 1966.

Nadvi, A. S. S. *The Arab Navigation*. Lahore: Ashraf, 1966.

Needham, Joseph. *Science and Civilisation in China*. Cambridge University Press, 1965.

Neugebauer, O. *The Exact Sciences in Antiquity*. New York: Harper Torchbook, 1962.

Newby, Percy H. *The Egypt Story*. New York: Chanticleer, 1984.

New Larousse Encyclopaedia of Mythology. London: Hamlyn, 1968.

New Scientist, December 1991, 21–28.

Nibbi, Alessandra. *The Sea Peoples: A Re-examination of the Egyptian Sources*. Oxford: published privately, 1972.

———. *The Sea Peoples and Egypt*. New Jersey: Noyes Press, 1975.

Nicholson, Irene. *Mexican and Central American Mythology*. London: Hamlyn, 1969.

Nilsson, Martin P. *The Mycenaean Origins of Greek Mythology*. University of California Press, 1972.

Nuttall, Zelia. *Archaeological and Ethnological Papers of the Peabody Museum.* New York: Kraus, 1970.
———. *The Fundamental Principles of Old and New World Civilizations.* New York: Kraus, 1970.

Ogden, C. K., ed. *Minoans, Philistines and Greeks.* London: Kegan Paul, Trench, Trubner & Co, 1930.
O'Kelly, Michael. *Early Ireland.* Cambridge University Press, 1989.
Oppenheim, A. Leo. *Letters from Mesopotamia.* Chicago University Press, 1967.
Osborne, Harold. *Indians of the Andes: Aymaras and Quechuas.* New York: Cooper Square Publishers, 1973.
———. *South American Mythology.* London: Hamlyn, 1968.
Oxford Classical Dictionary.

Parish, Sir Woodbine. *Buenos Ayres from the Conquest.* London: John Murray, 1852.
Parrot, André. *Sumer.* London: Thames & Hudson, 1960.
Parrot, A., M. H. Chehab, and S. Mascati. *Les Phéniciens.* Paris: Gallimard, 1975.
Pausanias. *Description of Greece.* Trans., W. H. S. Jones. Loeb Classical Library, London: Heinemann, 1966.
Pearce, Susan M. *The Bronze Age Metalwork of South Western Britain.* Oxford: B.A.R., 1988.
Peet, Rev. Stephen. *Religious Beliefs and Traditions of the Aborigines of North America.* Paper for the Philosophical Society of Great Britain, c. 1887.
Pendlebury, J. D. S. *The Archaeology of Crete.* London: Methuen, 1939.
Penguin Dictionary of Archaeology. Compiled by W. Bray and D. Trump. London: Penguin, 1972.
Penguin Dictionary of Religions. 1984.
Penhallurick, Roger D. *Tin in Antiquity.* London: Institute of Metals, 1986.
Peterson, Frederick. *Ancient Mexico.* London: George Allen & Unwin.
Petrie, Flinders. *Wisdom of the Egyptians.* Vol. 63. London: Quaritch, 1940.
Perrot, G., and C. Chipiez. *Art in Ancient Egypt.* London: Chapman & Hall, 1883.
———. *Art in Chaldea and Assyria.* London: Chapman & Hall, 1884.
Piggott, Stuart. *Prehistoric India.* Harmondsworth: Pelican, 1950.
Piggott, Stuart, ed. *The Dawn of Civilisation.* London: Thames & Hudson.
Pindar. *Odes of Victory.* Oxford: Basil Blackwell, 1928.
Piotrovsky, Boris B. *Urartu.* Geneva: Nagel, 1969.
Pitt-Rivers, George. *The Riddle of the "Labarum" and the Origin of Christian Symbols.* London: George Allen & Unwin, 1966.
Plass, Margaret W. *African Miniatures: The Goldweights of the Ashanti.* London: Lund Humphries, 1967.
Plato. *Dialogues.* Trans., Jowett. Oxford University Press, 1892.
Pliny. *Natural History.* Loeb Classical Library, London: Heinemann, 1967–72.
Plutarch. *Lives.* London: J. Tonson, 1727.
———. *Moralia.* Loeb Classical Library, London: Heinemann, 1965–68.
Poignant, Roslyn. *Oceanic and Australasian Mythology.* Newnes, 1985.
———. *Oceanic Mythology.* London: Hamlyn, 1967.
Popol Vuh: The Sacred Book of the Ancient Quiché Maya. Trans., D. Goetz and S. G. Morley. From Spanish trans. by A. Recinos. London: William Hodge & Co., 1951.
Popper, Sir Karl. *The Open Society and Its Enemies: The Spell of Plato.* London: Routledge, 1945.
Posnansky, Arthur. *Tahuanacu: La Cuna del Hombre Americano.* Vols. I and II: New York: J. J. Augustin, 1945., Vols. III and IV: La Paz: Ministerio de Educación, 1957.
Powell, T. G. E. *The Celts.* London: Thames & Hudson, 1963.
Prescott, William H. *The Conquest of Mexico.* London: George Routledge & Sons, n.d.
———. *The Conquest of Peru.* Vols. I and II. London: Richard Bentley, 1847.
———. *The World of the Incas.* New York: Tudor Publishing, 1970.
Pritchard, James B., ed. *Ancient Near Eastern Texts and Pictures.* Princeton: University Press, 1969.

Radhakrishnan, S. *The Philosophy of the Upanishads.* London: George Allen & Unwin, 1935.
Ramírez Vazquez, Pedro. *The National Museum of Anthropology, Mexico.* New York: Alexis Gregory, 1968.
Randhawa, M. S. *The Cult of Trees and Tree Worship.* New Delhi: All India Fine Arts & Crafts Society, 1964.
Rao, S. R. *Lothal and the Indus Civilisation.* London: Asia Publishing House, 1973.
Rattray, Robert S. *Ashanti.* Oxford: Clarendon, 1923.
Rausing, Gad. *Prehistoric Boats and Ships of Northwestern Europe.* Malmö: C. W. K., Gleerup, 1984.
Rawlinson, George. *History of Phoenicia.* London: Longmans, Green, 1889.
Reichel-Dolmatoff, Gerado. *Amazonian Cosmos.* Chicago & London: University of Chicago Press, 1971.
Renfrew, Colin. *Archaeology and Language.* London: Jonathan Cape, 1987.
———. *Before Civilisation.* London: Jonathan Cape, 1973.
———. *Prehistory of Orkney.* Edinburgh University Press, 1985.
Rice, Michael. *Egypt's Making.* London: Routledge, 1990.

Roes, Anna. *Greek Geometric Art: Its Symbolism and Its Origin.* Oxford University Press, 1933.
Rohr, René R. *Sundials: History, Theory and Practice.* Toronto University Press, 1970.
Roux, Georges. *Ancient Iraq.* London: Pelican, 1966.
Roys, Ralph L. *The Book of Chilam Balam of Chumayel.* Norman: University of Oklahoma Press, 1973.
———. *Ritual of the Bacabs.* Norman: University of Oklahoma Press, 1965.
Ruggles, C. L. N., and A. W. R. Whittle. *Astronomy and Society in Britain, 4000–1500 B.C.* Oxford: B.A.R., 1981.

Saghieh, Muntaha. *Byblos in the Third Millennium B.C.* Warminster: Aris & Phillips, 1983.
Sahagún, Fray Bernardino de. *Florentine Codex: General History of the Things of New Spain.* Trans. C. E. Dibble and A. J. O. Anderson. Santa Fe: The School of American Research, University of Utah, 1951–61.
Sallust. *War Against Jurgurtha.* Loeb Classical Library, London: Heinemann.
Sandars, Nancy K. (Eng. Version) *The Epic of Gilgamesh.* Harmondsworth: Penguin, 1960.
———. *Prehistoric Art in Europe.* Harmondsworth: Penguin, 1968.
———. *The Sea Peoples: Warriors of the Ancient Mediterranean, 1250–1150 B.C.* London: Thames & Hudson, 1978.
Sankarananda, Swami. *Hindu States of Sumeria.* Calcutta: K. L. Mukhapadhyay, 1962.
Sastri, K. N. *New Light on the Indus Civilisation.* Delhi: Atma Ram, 1957.
El Sayed. *La Déesse Neith de Saïs.* IFAO, 1982.
Schefold, K. *Myth and Legend in Early Greek Art.* London: Thames & Hudson, 1966.
Schmidt, U., and A. N. Cabenza de Vaca. Ed., L. L. Dominguez. *The Conquest of the River Plate.* London: Hakluyt Society, 1891.
Schoff, Wilfred, trans. *The Periplus of the Erythraean Sea.* New York & London: Longmans Green, 1912.
Schoolcraft, Henry R. *The Iroquois.* Albany: Erastus H. Pease, 1847.
Schwietzer, Bernhard. *Greek Geometric Art.* London: Phaidon, 1971.
Seneca. *Medea.* Trans., F. J. Miller. Loeb Classical Library, London: Heinemann, 1917.
Severin, Tim. *The Brendan Voyage.* London: Hutchinson, 1978.
———. *The Ulysses Voyage.* London: Hutchinson, 1987.
Sharma. *The Excavation at Kausambi.* University of Allahabad, 1960.
Shorter, Alan W. *The Egyptian Gods,* London: Routledge & Kegan Paul, 1978.
Sidebotham, Steven E. *Roman Economic Policy in the Erythra Thalassa.* Leiden: E. J. Brill, 1986.
Sides, Dorothy Smith. *Decorative Art of the Southwestern Indians.* New York: Dover, 1961.
Silverblatt, Irene. *Moon, Sun and Witches.* Princeton University Press, 1987.
Simkin. *The Traditional Trade of Asia.* Oxford University Press, 1968.
Singer, C. J., E. J. Holmyard, and A. R. Hall. *History of Technology.* Vol. I. Oxford: Clarendon Press, 1965.
Singh, M. M. *Life in North-Eastern India in Pre-Mauryan Times.* Motilal Barnarsidass, 1967.
Skelton, Raleigh A. *History of Cartography.* London: C. A. Watts, 1964.
Smith, Anthony. *Mato Grosso.* London: Michael Joseph, 1971.
Smith, Marian W. *Asia and North America: Trans-Pacific Contacts.* Salt Lake City: The Society for American Archaeology, 1953.
Smith, Sidney. *Babylonian Historical Texts.* Hildesheim: Georg Olms, 1975.
Snodgrass, A. M. *The Dark Age of Greece.* Edinburgh University Press, 1971.
Sokolov, G. *Antique Art on the Northern Black Sea Coast.* Leningrad: Aurora Art Publishers, 1974.
Solis, Antonio de. *The History of the Conquest of Mexico by the Spaniards.* London: John Osborn, 1738.
Sollberger, E. *Texts from Cuneiform Sources.* Vol. I. New York: J. J. Augustin, 1966.
Sophocles. *The Antigone.* Trans., Watling.
Soustelle, Jacques. *The Daily Life of the Aztecs.* Harmondsworth: Pelican, 1955.
———. *The Olmecs.* Norman: University of Oklahoma Press, 1985.
South American Handbook. Bath: Mendip Press, 1975.
Southworth, J. R. *The Mines of Mexico.* Mexico City: published privately, 1905.
Spence, Lewis. *The Myths of Mexico and Peru.* London: George Harrap, 1908.
Spinden, Herbert J. *Maya Art and Civilization.* Indian Hills, Colorado: Falcon's Wing Press, 1957.
Spores, Ronald. *The Mixtec Kings and Their People.* Norman: University of Oklahoma Press, 1967.
Starr, Chester G. *The Origins of Greek Civilisation.* London: Jonathan Cape, 1962.
Stephens, John L. *Incidents of Travel in Central America, Chiapas and Yucatan.* Vols. I and II. London: Arthur Hall, Virtue, 1854.
———. *Incidents of Travel in Yucatan.* Vols. I and II, New York: Harper & Bros., 1843.

Stevenson, Edward L. *Terrestrial and Celestial Globes*. New Haven: Yale University Press, 1921.

Steward, J. H. *Handbook of South American Indians*. Washington: Government Printer, 1946.

Stimson, A. N., and C. St. J. Daniel. *The Cross Staff*. London: Harriet Wynter, 1977.

Stone, Olivia. *Tenerife and Its Six Satellites*. London: Marcus Ward, 1889.

Strabo. *Complete Works*. Loeb Classical Library, London: Heinemann, 1923–32.

Strange, John. *Caphtor/Keftiu: A New Investigation*. Leiden: E. J. Brill, 1980.

Summers, Roger. *Ancient Mining in Rhodesia*. National Museums of Rhodesia, 1969.

Swire, Otta F. *The Outer Hebrides and Their Legends*. Edinburgh: Oliver & Boyd, 1966.

Taylor, E. G. R. *The Haven-Finding Art*. London: Hollis & Carter, 1971.

Taylor, Edward. *Anahuac*. London: Longmans Green, 1861.

Te Velde, H. *Seth, God of Confusion*. Leiden: E. J. Brill, 1977.

Thom, A. *Megalithic Lunar Observatories*. Oxford: Clarendon, 1973.

———. *Megalithic Sites in Britain*. Oxford: Clarendon, 1967.

Thompson, Gunnar. *American Discovery*. Seattle: Misty Isles Press, 1992.

Thompson, J. Eric. *The Rise and Fall of Maya Civilization*. Norman: University of Oklahoma Press, 1954.

Towle, Margaret A. *The Ethnobotany of Pre-Columbian Peru*. Chicago: Aldine, 1961.

Trollope, Anthony. *The West Indies and the Spanish Main*. London: Chapman & Hall, 1860.

Turcan, Robert. *Héliogabale*. Paris: Albin Michel, 1985.

Turner, Frederick W. III, ed. *The Portable North American Indian Reader*. Harmondsworth: Penguin, 1986.

Tylecote, R. F. *The History of Metallurgy*. London: Institute of Metals, 1992.

Tylor, Edward B. *Anahuac*. London: Longmans, Green, Reader & Dyer, 1861.

Uhlenbrook. *Heracles*. New York: Bard College, 1986.

United Arab Republic Antiquities Department. *A Guide to the Egyptian Museum in Cairo*. Cairo: Government Printer, 1968.

Up De Graff, F. W. *Head Hunters of the Amazon*. London: Herbert Jenkins, 1923.

Vaillant, G. C. *The Aztecs of Mexico*. London: Pelican, 1950.

Van Dijk, J. *LUGAL UD ME-LAM-bi NIR-GAL*. Leiden: E. J. Brill, 1983.

Van Heekeren, H. R. *The Bronze-Iron Age of Indonesia*. Gravenhage: Martinus Nijhoff, 1958.

Van Loon, Dr. Hendrik. *Anatolia in the Second Millennium B.C.* Leiden: E. J. Brill, 1985.

Van Selms, Adrianus. *Marriage and Family Life in Ugaritic Literature*. London: Luzac, 1954.

Van Sertima, Ivan. *They Came Before Columbus*. New York: Random House, 1976.

Vasques, M. and G. Vergara. *Costa Rica: 2000 Años de Tesoros*. National Museum of Costa Rica, n.d.

Verrill, A. H. and R. Verrill. *America's Ancient Civilizations*. New York: Putnam, 1953.

Vieyra, Maurice. *Hittite Art 2300–750 B.C.* London: Tiranti, 1955.

Villaret, Bernard. *Le Mexique aux 100 000 Pyramides*. Paris: Berger-Levrault, 1963.

Villas Boas, O., and G. Villas Boas. *Xingu, The Indians, Their Myths*. New York: Farrar, Straus & Giroux, 1970.

Viollet, Roger. *Greece in Photographs*. London: Thames & Hudson, 1955.

Von Hagen, Victor W. *The Ancient Sun Kingdoms*. London: Thames & Hudson, 1962.

———. *The Desert Kingdoms of Peru*. London: Weidenfeld & Nicolson, 1965.

Von Matt, Leonard. *Ancient Crete*. London: Thames & Hudson, 1968.

Von Rosen, Eric. *Archaeological Researches on the Frontier of Argentina and Bolivia in 1901–2*. Smithsonian Report for 1904. Washington, 1905.

Von Wuthenau, Alexander. *Altamerikanische Tonplastiek*. Baden-Baden: Holle Verlag, 1965.

———. *Pre-Columbian Terracottas*. London: Methuen, 1965.

———. *Unexpected Faces in Ancient America*, New York: Crown, 1975.

Voss, Capt. J. C. *Venturesome Voyages*. London: Rupert Hart-Harris, 1949.

Waanders, F. M. J. *The History of* ΤΕΛΟΣ *and* ΤΕΛΕΩ *in Ancient Greek*. Amsterdam: B. R. Grüner, 1983.

Warren, Peter. *The Aegean Civilizations*. Lausanne: Elsevier Phaidon, 1975.

Warmington, E. H. *The Commerce Between the Roman Empire and India*. London: Curzon, 1974.

Wauchope, Robert. *Lost Tribes and Sunken Continents*. Chicago University Press, 1963.

Weigall, Arthur. *Sappho of Lesbos*. Garden City, N.Y.: Garden City Publishing, 1932.

Wensinck, A. J. *The Ocean in the Literature of the Western Semites*. Sändig Reprint Verlag, 1968.

West, M. L. *Hesiod's Theogony*. Oxford: Clarendon, 1966.

———. *The Orphic Poems*. Oxford: Clarendon, 1983.

Westerberg, Karin. *Cypriote Ships from the Bronze Age to c. 500 B.C.* Gothenburg: Paul Åströms Förlag, 1983.

Wheeler, Sir Mortimer. *Civilisation of the Indus Valley.*

Wheeler, R. E. M. *Prehistoric and Roman Wales.* Oxford: Clarendon, 1925.

White, K. D. *Greek and Roman Technology.* London: Thames & Hudson, 1984.

Whitehouse, Ruth, ed. *Dictionary of Archaeology.* London: Macmillan, 1983.

Wilhelm, John. *Guide to Mexico City.* Mexico City: Ediciones Tolteca, 1975.

Willetts, R. F. *The Civilization of Ancient Crete.* London: B. T. Batsford, 1976.

———. *Cretan Cults and Festivals.* London: Routledge & Kegan Paul, 1962.

Willey, Gordon R. *Handbook of Middle American Indians.* Gen. ed., R. Wauchope. Vol II: *Archaeology of Southern Mesoamerica,* London: University of Texas Press, 1965.

Wolf, Eric R. *Sons of the Shaking Earth.* London: University of Chicago Press, 1959.

Wölfel, D. J. *Monumenta Linguae Canariae.* Graz: Akademische Druck, 1965.

Woodcroft, Bennet. *The Pneumatics of Hero of Alexandria.* London: Taylor Walton & Maberly, 1851.

Wood-Martin, W. G. *Traces of the Elder Faiths of Ireland.* London: Longmans, Green, 1902.

Wright, E. V., and D. M. Churchill. *The Boats from North Ferriby, Yorkshire, England.* Proceedings of the Prehistoric Society, Vol. 31, 1965.

Zahen, Dominique. *The Bambara.* Leiden: E. J. Brill, 1974.

Zervos, Christian. *La Civilisation Hellénique.* Paris: Editions Cahiers d'Art, 1969.

Zink, David. *The Stones of Atlantis.* London: W. H. Allen, 1978.

Zubrow, E. B. W., M. C. Fritz, and J. M. Fritz, eds. *New World Archaeology.* San Francisco: W. H. Freeman, 1974.

Index

Illustration Credits

F: map, after Posnansky; 3: map, after Wagner; 5: map, after Penhallurick; 6: writing, from R. E. Willetts, *Ancient Crete;* 7: map, after Lamb; 8: nugget, from R. J. Forbes, *Studies in Ancient Technology*, Leiden: E. J. Brill, 1964–1966; 8: medicine wheel, USDA Forest Service photo; 9: mudhif, from H. and R. Leacroft, *The Buildings of Ancient Mesopotamia;* 10: chronology, courtesy of Professor K. A. Kitchen; 12: ship, 13: ship, after Herman; 13: sea attack, 14: boats, 38: Egyptian seals, 102: falcon, 106: master of animals, 207: Egypt pot, after Massoulard; 14: ship, from Zvi Herman, *Peoples, Seas, and Ships*, J. M. Dent; 16: map, 51: carving, after Irwin; 18: map, from Roger Joussaume, *Les Dolmens pour Les Morts*, Hachette 1985; 18: Boyne stone, from Michael O'Kelly, *Early Ireland*, courtesy of Mrs. Claire O'Kelly; 18: Knockmany, 224: figures, 225: figures, after Gelling and Davidson; 19: Stonehenge, after Thom; 21: ingots, after Fell; 22: Bead, after Evans; 22: Seals, after Ward; 23: megalith, from H. S. Cowper, *The Hill of the Graces;* 24: all, 70: ceramic, 162: all, 169: ceramic, 174: ceramic, 185: ceramic, from Arthur Posnansky, *Tiahuanacu;* 25: tomb, 33: script, 36: obelisk, 43: Gorgons, 49: boy's head, 53: head, 120: axes, 121: script, 207: Inca, from Pierre Honoré, *In Quest of the White God;* 27: map, courtesy of *Mining Journal Limited*, London; 27: Bacabs, from J. Eric S. Thompson., *The Rise and Fall of Maya Civilization*, University of Oklahoma Press, 1954; 28: plate fibula, after Schweitzer; 28: Boat, after Landstrom; 29: hero, from Bennet Woodcroft, *The Pneumatics of Hero of Alexandria;* 41: panpipes, after Ceram; 41: animals, after Heine-Geldern; 42: sarcophagus, Photo William MacQuitty; 49: mask, after Parrot; 49: jade figures, from Victor Von Hagen, *The Ancient Sun Kingdoms;* 50: head, 122: Cuicuilco, 164: Mexican phallus, courtesy of the Instituto Nacional de Antropologia e Historia, Mexico; 56: scripts, 57: scripts, 59: top four, 121: dolmens, from Barry Fell, *America B. C.*, courtesy of Mrs. René Fell; 58: scripts, from Barry Fell, *Bronze Age America*, courtesy of Mrs. René Fell; 60: fresco, Photo Alison Franz; 61: Karnak, 64: palace, 219: both, 222: Thebes, 223: Karnak, from Perrot and Chipiez, *Art in Ancient Egypt;* 62: pot, after Rao; 63: pyramids, Photo Peter Clayton; 69: temple, 227: architecture, 230: Nineveh, from Perrot and Chipiez, *Art in Chaldea and Assyria;* 74: bronze figures, courtesy of The National Museum, New Delhi; 74: Boat, after Johnstone; 75: dock, 76: terracottas, courtesy of the Department of Archaeology and Museums, Pakistan; 76: malwa pot, 79: pottery, courtesy of Grahame Clark, *World Prehistory;* 79: temple, after Emory; 81: map, after Barnard and Sato; 82: knife, from James H. Breased, *History of Egypt*, Hodder & Stoughton; 82: rocks, from Marcel Homet, *Sons of the Sun;* 86: cross-legged goddess, from Marija Gimbutas, *Gods and Goddesses of Old Europe*, courtesy of the author's estate; 86: seated goddess, from James Mellart, *Earliest Civilizations of the Near East;* 88: mermen, from Sir Joseph Needham, *Science and Civilisation in China;* 92: rocks, from Thor Heyerdahl, *Aku Aku;* 94: Tell Asmar, courtesy of the Iraqi Museum, Baghdad; 95: Chinook woman, 131: Canoe, 156: weeping figs, 213: Ohio hand, from F. and M. E. Folsom, *America's Ancient Treasures*, courtesy of Rachel Folsom; 101: misericord, courtesy of the Dean and Chapter of Exeter Cathedral; 103: Easter Island birdman, from Roslyn Poignant, *Oceanic and Australasian Mythology;* 105: arcs and symbol, from Campbell Grant, *Rock Art of the North American Indians;* 108: Tula atlas, 118: altar and Atlantes, from Nigel Davies, *Ancient Kingdoms of Mexico;* 112: god of fire, from the National Museum, Mexico; 115: Toltec pot, after Bernal; 115: Mykenaean, after Mylonas; 121: ziggurat, from C. Blacker and M. Loewe, *Ancient Cosmologies;* 123: seal, 127: Zeus, 193: spinal cord, 210: Asharte, from Du Mesnil du Buisson, *Études sur les dieux phéniciens hérités par l'empire romain;* 125: hieroglyph, 153: hieroglyph, from Sir Alan Gardiner, *Egyptian Grammar;* 126: sacrifice, after Paso y Troncoso; 151: Reseph, after Harden; 154: goddess, after Hutchinson; 155: stones, 156: atl stones, from Philip Allison, *African Stone Sculpture;* 156: phallus, from Bernardo da Silva Ramos, *Inscripcoes e Traducoes da Americ Prehistorica;* 158: Peru phallus, from Harold Osborne, *South American Mythology;* 159: Carnac, from Barbara Bender, *The Archaeology of Brittany, Normandy, and the Channel Islands;* 160: phallus, from Barry Fell, *America B. C.*, photo Peter Garfall; 161: phallus, from Barry Fell, *America B. C.*, photo Joe Germano; 167: map, 168: map, courtesy of Anglovaal Ltd.; 169: vase, 182: lid handle, after Gimbutas; 170: clay figurine, from Michael Dames, *The Silbury Treasure*, courtesy of The National Museum of History, Bucharest; 170: Czech woman, from Nancy Sandars, *Prehistoric Art in Europe*, courtesy of the Moravian Museum, Brno; 170: woman's head, from Musée des Antiquités Nationales, Paris; 171: Asshur, after Andrae; 179: Greenland, photo Joe Germano; 179: Georgia, from F. and M. E. Folsom, *America's Ancient Treasures*, photo Margaret Perryman Smith; 179: Scotland, from Ronald W. B. Morris, *The Prehistoric Rock Art of Argyll;* 190: Tiamat, from J-C Margueron, *Mesopotamia;* 191: head, courtesy of Casa de la Cultura de San Luis Potosi; 191: priestess, from the Museo Nacional de Antropologia, Mexico; 194: Costa Rica stool, from Thomas Joyce, *Central American and West Indian Archaeology;* 194: drum, from Roslyn Poignant, *Oceanic Mythology;* 195: heads, from Alexander Von Wuthenau, *Unexpected Faces in Ancient America*, 1975, reprinted by permission of Crown Publishers, Inc.; 196: sword, Venus, from Robert Marx, *In Quest of the Great White Gods;* 197: boat, courtesy of the Prehistoric Society, London; 198: treasury, from George E. Mylonas, *Mycenae and the Mycenaean Age;* 198: Tiahuanaco, from Victor Von Hagen, *The Ancient Sun Kingdoms;* 207: Xingu stick, after Villas-Boas; 207: tripod jar, photo J. J. Klejman; 209: goddess, from Peter Warren, *The Aegean Civilisations;* 217: script, from D. Diringer, *The Alphabet;* 218: hill, photo Jack Klaff; 222: Hephaestos, after Schefold; 229: kneeling figures, after Wretz; 229: chief, after Ugaritica. While every endeavor has been made to identify and to contact the owner of copyright material that has been used in this book, it may be that inadvertently certain copyright material has not been identified as such, in which case the author and publisher would welcome information that would enable them to set the record straight on reprint.